A POSTMODERN READER

A POSTMODERN READER

Edited by
Joseph Natoli
and
Linda Hutcheon

STATE UNIVERSITY OF NEW YORK PRESS

Production by Ruth Fisher
Marketing by Dana E. Yanulavich

Published by
State University of New York Press, Albany

For information, address the State University of New York Press,
State University Plaza, Albany, NY 12246

Library of Congress Cataloging-in-Publication Data

A Postmodern reader / edited by Joseph Natoli and Linda Hutcheon.
    p.   cm.
  ISBN 0-7914-1638-0 (pbk. : alk. paper). — ISBN 0-7914-1637-2
(hard : alk. paper)
  1. Postmodernism (Literature) 2. College readers. I. Natoli,
Joseph P., 1943– . II. Hutcheon, Linda, 1947– .
PN98.P67P697 1993
808.84'91—dc20   92-39294
                                               CIP

10 9 8 7 6 5 4 3

CONTENTS

INTRODUCTION: Reading *A Postmodern Reader*   vii

I. MODERN/POSTMODERN   1

Preface   1

Zygmunt Bauman, "Postmodernity, or Living with
Ambivalence."   9

Hans Bertens, "The Postmodern *Weltanschauung* and
its Relation to Modernism: an Introductory Survey."   25

Jean-François Lyotard, Excerpts from *The Postmodern
Condition: A Report on Knowledge.*   71

Jürgen Habermas, "Modernity versus Postmodernity."   91

Andreas Huyssen, "Mapping the Postmodern."   105

David J. Herman, "Modernism versus Postmodernism:
Towards an Analytic Distinction."   157

II. REPRESENTING THE POSTMODERN   193

Preface   193

John McGowan, Excerpts from *Postmodernism and
its Critics.*   203

Jacques Derrida, "Structure, Sign, and Play in the
Discourse of the Human Sciences."   223

Linda Hutcheon, "Beginning to Theorize
Postmodernism."   243

Ihab Hassan, "Toward a Concept of Postmodernism."   273

Charles Russell, "The Context of the Concept."   287

III. ENTANGLEMENTS AND COMPLICITIES   299

Preface   299

Fredric Jameson, Excerpts from *Postmodernism,
Or the Cultural Logic of Late Capitalism.*   312

Michel Foucault, Excerpts from *The History of
Sexuality: Volume I: An Introduction.*   333

Jean Baudrillard, "The Precession of Simulacra."   342

Thomas Kuhn, "The Resolution of Revolutions."   376

Cornel West, "Black Culture and Postmodernism."   390

Barbara Creed, "From Here to Modernity: Feminism
and Postmodernism."   398

Jane Flax, Excerpts from *Thinking Fragments.*   419

Stephen Slemon, "Modernism's Last Post."   426

IV. POSTMODERN PRACTICES   441

Preface   441

Henry Giroux, "Postmodernism as Border Pedagogy:
Redefining the Boundaries of Race and Ethnicity."   452

Agnes Heller, "Existentialism, Alienation,
Postmodernism: Cultural Movements as Vehicles
of Change in the Patterns of Everyday Life."   497

bell hooks, "Postmodern Blackness."   510

Paul Maltby, Excerpts from *Dissident Postmodernists.*   519

Houston A. Baker, Jr., "Hybridity, the Rap Race,
and Pedagogy for the 1990s."   538

Catherine Belsey, "Towards Cultural History."   551

Index   569

INTRODUCTION: READING
A POSTMODERN READER

Is a cultural enterprise over, *kaput,* finished when it sits still long enough for you to define it? If it is, then the one we have been calling the "postmodern" is still alive and well and thwarting us daily. This *Reader* attempts to present—however provisionally and temporarily—at least part of its ongoing, lively shape-shifting.

With strong resistance from many quarters, the term "postmodern" has slowly come to be accepted as a general post-1960s period label attached to cultural forms that display certain characteristics such as reflexivity, irony, parody, and often a mixing of the conventions of popular and "high art." As such it has been attached to everything from Madonna's videos to films like *Blue Velvet,* from rap music to a "grand opera" like "The Ghosts of Versailles," from Douglas Adams's *Dirk Gentley's Holistic Detective Agency* to Umberto Eco's *Foucault's Pendulum,* from the "appropriation" art of Barbara Kruger and Hans Haacke to the parodic paintings of Attila Richard Lukacs and Mark Tansey. In short, it has been used to talk about architecture, literature, dance, film, video, theater, television, music, and the visual arts, but also political thought, philosophy, aesthetic criticism and theory, anthropology, geography, historiography, theology, pedagogy, etc.

As any computer search will show, the constantly growing number of books, articles, and special issues of journals addressing postmodern concerns is daunting: a simple bibliographical listing alone might fill this entire volume. Clearly, in Dick Hebdige's words, "the degree of semantic complexity and overload surrounding the term 'postmodernism' at the moment signals that a significant number of people with conflicting interests and opinions feel that there is something sufficiently important at stake here to be worth struggling and arguing over" (1991, 182).

This *Reader* aims to sample some of the skirmishes underway in those struggles and arguments, and to give some sense of what is at stake in them. Its premise is that the postmodern is no more ignorable than is the air we breathe; in a sense, it *is* the social and cultural air we breathe, for it has been linked (as we shall see in the pages to follow) to such vast notions as "the cultural logic of late capitalism" (Jameson), the general condition of knowledge in an age of informational technology (Lyotard), and even a wholesale substitution of the "simulacrum" for the "real" (Baudrillard).

The actual term "postmodern" has been around now for many years, although its meaning has fluctuated dramatically (see, for example, Howe 1959; Hoffmann, Hornung, and Kunow 1977; Kohler 1977; Paterson 1986; Fokkema and Bertens 1986)—but the one thing it usually connotes is change. Stephen Toulmin wrote of a previous, analogous change in these terms: "Evidently, *something* important happened early in the seventeenth century, a result of which—for good or ill, and probably for both—society and culture in Western Europe and North America developed in a different direction from that which they would otherwise have followed" (1990, 12).

This shift from "Scholasticism" to "Modernity" has its echo, many would say, in our present shift from "Modernity" to "Postmodernity." Evidently *something* important is also happening in this last part of the twentieth century, as a result of which—again, probably for both good and ill—society and culture in the same places, Western Europe and North America, are moving along different paths, into different mindsets from those offered us by the Enlightenment and even by later models of modernity.

Unlike other related anthologies, this *Reader* samples and presents some of these general conceptual moves that have made possible the many forms of postmodern*ism* we see around us in the arts and in other discourses. Whatever it is that is happening in this broader thing called postmodern*ity*, it has opened the way for such new counterdisciplinary domains as "cultural studies"—with its deliberate lack of a distinct methodology and its mandate to investigate such broad areas as "the history of cultural studies, gender and sexuality, nationhood and national identity, colonialism and post-colonialism, race and ethnicity, popular culture and its audiences, science and ecology, identity politics, pedagogy, the politics of aesthetics, cultural institutions, the politics of disciplinarity, discourse and textuality, history, and global culture in a postmodern age" (Nelson, Treichler, Grossberg 1992, 1).

To offer only one other of many possible examples, the rise of "Post-Marxism," as seen in the work of Ernesto Laclau and Chantal Mouffe, has also been made possible by a different conceptual "take" on the social and economic order and the role of class analysis in it. Whether we call this shift to postmodernity a change of paradigm or plane or *episteme,* whether we see the postmodern as a moment, a movement, a project, a condition or a period, *something* important is happening. You will see all these different terms used in the various essays that follow, and the accompanying introductory section prefaces have attempted to give voice to the complex overlappings as well as distinctions among them.

As the first readings here suggest, these terms are used to describe a major (and usually a disturbing) shift away from modernity's universalizing and totalizing drive—a drive that was first fueled, in the seventeenth century, by Descartes' foundational ambitions and his faith in reason. Postmodernity's assertion of the value of inclusive "both/and" thinking deliberately contests the exclusive "either/or" binary oppositions of modernity. Postmodern paradox, ambiguity, irony, indeterminacy, and contingency are seen to replace modern closure, unity, order, the absolute, and the rational. These may be very bold and bald categories, but they are ones that essay after essay in this book rearticulates in its own way.

The postmodern valuing of the local and the particular, the provisional and the tentative, is said to contest modernity's privileging of the general and the universal in matters of "Truth, Beauty, Goodness." What disappears with this shift is the comforting security—ethical, ontological, epistemological—that "reason" offered within the modern paradigm: hierarchy and system are put into question, as intellectual grounds and foundations crumble under our feet. Nevertheless, postmodernity's critiques of universalizing modern theories have turned out to be as liberating and empowering as they have been confounding and disturbing (see Harvey 1989)—as shown by the complex responses to typical postmodern positionings, such as those offered by post-structuralism and deconstruction, in various areas of study in the last few years.

As a broad conceptual category, then, postmodernity has been seen to flourish in the predominantly white metropolitan cultures of the Europeanized West; it is critical of, and yet also—inevitably if uncomfortably—implicated within the modern paradigm it contests. That paradigm is actually capacious and heterogeneous enough to include capitalism, patriarchy, and that paradoxical liberal humanism which asserts both the individual subject and something general called "human nature"—often figured as a set of universal and eternal, human and humane values.

Despite its inclusivity (or what some see as its complicity), the critical edge of postmodernity's deconstructing of the modern universalizing tendency comes from its awareness of the value and significance of respecting difference and otherness. This awareness is brought about as much by sustained oppositional social activism of women, gays and lesbians, people of color, and formerly colonized nations as by the more abstract theorizing about power and the mobile field of force relations discussed by philosophers, political theorists, and cultural critics. Cornel West (1990) has defined this as the "new cultural politics of difference."

As we shall see, however, especially in its intersection with identity politics, this postmodern celebration of the different and of cultural "interpermeability" has been accused of running "the risk of effacing real difference" (Chicago Cultural Studies Group 1992, 538). In response to this worry, Henry Giroux argues in an essay in this book that—in the face of the modern neglect of differences of race, ethnicity, and gender in the name of its universalizing formalisms—the postmodern acceptance of a plurality of voices (none of them universal or even grounded in any foundational "truth"), along with its recognition of their partiality, might well lead to a more viable democratic public life.

To move from postmodern*ity* to postmodern*ism* is to shift from this general frame of reference (our primary concern in the *Reader*) into more limited aesthetic and cultural realms. Here, the postmodernist—in various art forms—has been interpreted either as a continuation of the more radical aspects of Euro-American modernism (such as its reflexivity and irony) or else as marking a rupture with such things as the modernist ahistorical bent or its yearning for aesthetic autonomy and closure.

The postmodern interest in issues of subjectivity and representation—who we are and how we "image" ourselves to ourselves—or its concern for ideology and history can be seen in the proliferation of what Linda Hutcheon calls "historiographic metafictions," but those same novels also bear many of the markers of modernist fiction—formal self-consciousness, parody, wordplay, and so on. The fact that there is no agreement on the precise nature of the relation between the modern and the postmodern in many discourses is itself likely an inevitable part of the general condition of postmodernity: an acknowledgment of the impossibility (and, indeed, the undesirability) of reaching any absolute and final "Truth."

If you have followed the reviews in the newspapers or magazines over the last decade, you will know that postmodern art does appear to provoke contradictory (and strong) responses. Both in the media and in scholarly journals, its fiction has been called a literature of replenishment (Barth 1980), on the one hand, and the art of an inflationary economy (Newman 1985), on the other. In short, unlike postmodern*ity* (where there is a general agreement that *something* happened), postmodern*ism* has provoked precious little agreement on anything from the reasons for its existence to its definition, let alone on the evaluation of its effects. As some of the readings in this book suggest, one of the reasons for this disagreement no doubt lies in the paradoxical nature of the beast itself: in its ironic self-undermining critical stance and in its commitment to doubleness—that is, to the juxtaposition and equal weighing of such seeming contraries as the self-reflexive and the historically grounded, the inward-direction of form and the outward-direction of politics.

While some see postmodern art forms as managing to milk the power of traditions and conventions even as they undermine both— at one and the same time purveying and protesting cultural dominants—others see only one half of the doubleness: the complicity or the critique. These radically disparate evaluations and interpretations of postmodernism are in part the result of its own formal paradoxes and particular fence-sitting politics of the "middle ground" (Wilde 1987); the complexity of this strategic doubleness and the resultant political ambidextrousness is what many of the essays sampled in this book seek to explore.

If one of the messages of the postmodern is that cultural values are always local and particular, and not universal and eternal, then we will also have to think about whether—for example—the French figuration of the postmodern should necessarily be the same as the Canadian, or whether the white American need resemble the African-American model. Jean-François Lyotard's defining of the postmodern as marking the death of the grand "metanarratives" that used to make sense of our world for us comes out of a different intellectual and historical frame of reference than does Jurgen Habermas's counterargument that the modernist project of Enlightenment rationality requires completion first. In Germany, it is arguable that modernity was indeed cut short by National Socialism, but Lyotard also develops his definition of the "postmodern condition" out of a particular "report on knowledge" undertaken specifically for the Québec government.

The postmodern revaluing of the "different" over the "same" demands that such distinctions among ways of thinking about the postmodern be both respected and historicized, not disregarded or downplayed.

It is for this reason that this *Reader* attempts to bring together many (often conflicting) points of view on what the postmodern is and how it operates, and that no attempt has been made to offer any single, systematizing, universalizing (in other words, modern) theory of the postmodern. Of course we are aware of the (postmodern) paradox that frames our very act of anthologizing, even when the aim is not to canonize or fix, but instead to sample (amply) and enact what Lévi-Strauss called "intellectual bricolage" (1966, 17).

With no pretence to completion or "coverage," this is necessarily a partial, provisional, strategic, contingent, contestable, and temporary postmodern sampler. We have deliberately called this a *Postmodern Reader,* rather than an anthology of theories of postmodernity, in order to call attention to the level of process—yours—as readers reading a reader. A volume like this may inevitably institutionalize—but perhaps it need not always do so—by granting the reader a place to rest, an Archimedean point outside itself from which to judge.

As readers of the postmodern, you read about it within a constantly changing context, one that no collection can ever fix or stabilize. We too are readers, but also teachers of courses on postmodernism (at all levels). Therefore we have included in this book particular readings that we have found to "work" in the classroom. These include both "user-friendly," accessible texts that have provoked lively discussion, and also those essays that are most frequently cited in the rapidly proliferating literature on the subject.

These samplings (for they can only be that) are organized into four sections. The first series of readings, simply called "Modern/ Postmodern," explores the relation between modernity and postmodernity, and examines exactly what people think is entailed in that *something* important that is busy happening these days. Philosophers, social and political commentators, as well as cultural and literary analysts, present controversial background articles on the complex genealogy of the postmodern as it is traced through such concepts as modernization, modernism, and—especially—modernity. The second section, "Representing The Postmodern," contains readings that debate the possibility—even the desirability—of trying to define the postmodern, especially given its stated agenda of decentering, challenging, and subverting the guiding "metanarratives" of Western culture.

Section III is called "Entanglements And Complicities," and explores the postmodern implication in these very narratives, considering in detail the challenges of feminist, post-colonial, and African-American theory to that complex interrelationship. The fourth and last group of readings moves from theory to "Practices" in order to investigate, in a number of fields, the common denominators of the postmodern condition in action. Given the vast range of postmodern practices and the inevitable restrictions of space in any sampling, the preface to Section IV briefly extends the scope of this discussion into other areas.

As Zygmunt Bauman has put it, "[i]t is not easy to narrate postmodernity" (1992, xxiv). Yet, each of these sections opens with a narrative that introduces the terms of the postmodern debates as enacted within the essays grouped together there. These prefaces are written with Bauman's warning in mind: "The closer they [narratives of postmodernity] come to picturing the postmodern condition as a balanced system, the graver their faults will risk being" (1992, xxiv). And yet, given our common implication in at least the educational narratives of modernity, this is a risk teachers, readers, and *Readers* must take. So, onto the tightrope stretched between modernity's rational order and postmodernity's contingent provisionality step these prefatory acrobats, self-reflexive and multivoiced. There they are joined by every page of this book, and only their audience knows for sure whether there is a safety net below.

Works Cited

Barth, John (1980) "The Literature of Replenishment: Postmodernist Fiction." *The Atlantic.* 245: 65–71.

Bauman, Zygmunt (1992) *Intimations of Postmodernity.* London and New York: Routledge, 1992.

Chicago Cultural Studies Group (1992) "Critical Multiculturalism." *Critical Inquiry.* 18: 530–55.

Fokkema, Douwe and Hans Bertens, ed. (1986) *Approaching Postmodernism.* Amsterdam and Philadelphia: John Benjamins.

Harvey, David (1989) *The Condition of Postmodernity.* Oxford: Blackwell's.

Hebdige, Dick (1991) *Hiding in the Light: Of Images and Things*. New York: Routledge.

Hoffmann, Gerhard, Alfred Hornung, and Rudiger Kunow (1977) " 'Modern,' 'Postmodern,' and 'Contemporary' as Criteria for the Analysis of Twentieth-Century Literature." *Amerikastudien* 22: 19–46.

Howe, Irving (1959) "Mass Society and Postmodern Fiction." *Partisan Review* 26: 420–36.

Kohler, Michael (1977) " 'Postmodernismus': Ein begriffsgeschichtlicher Uberblick." *Amerikastudien* 22: 8–18.

Laclau, Ernesto and Chantal Mouffe (1985) *Hegemony and Socialist Strategy: Towards a Radical Democratic Politics*. London: Verso.

Lévi-Strauss, Claude (1966) *The Savage Mind*. Chicago: U of Chicago P.

Nelson, Cary, Paula A. Treichler, and Laurence Grossberg (1992) "Cultural Studies: An Introduction." In Laurence Grossberg, Cary Nelson, Paula Treichler, eds. *Cultural Studies*. London and New York: Routledge. 1–22.

Newman, Charles (1985) *The Post-Modern Aura: the Act of Fiction in an Age of Inflation*. Evanston, Ill.: Northwestern U P.

Paterson, Janet M. (1986) "Le Roman 'postmoderne': mise au point et perspectives." *Canadian Review of Comparative Literature* 13.2: 238–55.

Toulmin, Stephen (1990) *Cosmopolis: The Hidden Agenda of Modernity*. New York: Free P.

West, Cornel (1990) "The New Cultural Politics of Difference." In Russell Ferguson, Martha Gever, Trinh T. Minh-ha, and Cornel West, eds. *Out There: Marginalization and Contemporary Cultures*. New York: New Museum of Contemporary Art; Cambridge, Mass. and London: MIT P. 19–36.

Wilde, Alan (1987) *Middle Grounds: Studies in Contemporary American Fiction*. Philadelphia: U of Pennsylvania P.

I

Modern/Postmodern

Preface

"Everyone begins the discussion of postmodernism," John McGowan writes in *Postmodernism and Its Critics,* "by asking what the word could possibly mean" (1991, viii). This *Reader* will be no exception, for very few critical terms in recent memory have been as used and abused as "postmodernism." In his detailed survey of this issue included here, Hans Bertens puts the question in terms of "whether there is such a phenomenon as an independent Postmodernism, no matter how many critics have put their lives on the line in its defense." There is no shortage of commentators on the arts today who deny its existence or who claim it is "simply a development within Modernism." Nevertheless, as Andreas Huyssen insists in his "Mapping the Postmodern," a strong argument can be made that— whether or not there has indeed been a "wholesale paradigm shift of the cultural, social, and economic orders"—there is still a "noticeable shift in sensibility, practices, and discourse formations which distinguishes a postmodern set of assumptions, experiences and propositions from that of a preceding period."

In Section II, you will find Ihab Hassan's two-column listing of the differences between these sets of assumptions. While this may be a little too schematic for some people's tastes, Hassan is not alone in seeing more rupture than continuity between the modernist and the postmodernist. Huyssen, however, feels that this "question of historical continuity or discontinuity simply cannot be adequately discussed in terms of such an either/or dichotomy." For instance, he points out that—whichever model you choose—there is little agreement over whether the postmodernist stance vis-à-vis the modernist is critical or affirmative. Part of the reason for the discord is likely the heterogeneity and plurality of the cultural manifestations of what, in the Euro-American context, we have come to call modernism, as well as postmodernism. As we shall see in Section III, there are also political complexities to match these definitional ones.

Nevertheless, even without claiming any fixed dividing line between the two, Bertens finds that he can isolate a couple of "core" concepts from the various postmodernisms he tries to sort out. One is the "ontological uncertainty" that arises from an "awareness of the absence of centers, of privileged languages, higher discourses." This awareness contrasts with the modernist clinging to rationally defined hierarchies and centers and avoiding "the consequences of the radical indeterminacy" that are, on the contrary, accepted by the postmodern. A second "core" notion involves the "postmodern self" as "no longer a coherent entity that has the power to impose (admittedly subjective) order upon its environment. It has become decentered."

Although these differences are presented by Bertens as specifically characterizing two modes of literature, his articulation of them in such broad terms as those of "selfhood" and "centering" suggests a slippage between the description of artistic phenomena and the delineation of a more general philosophical or social condition—that is, a slippage between modernism and modernity, or between postmodernism and postmodernity. But this kind of move is not at all surprising for, as Huyssen points out, we are dealing here with "a new crisis of art's relationship to society." The two are obviously not easily separable, whether (to adopt a term that allows both dimensions to coexist) the "postmodern" be articulated in terms of a universal, diffuse cynicism (Sloterdijk 1987), or a panic sense of the hyperreal and the simulacrum (Kroker and Cook 1986, via Baudrillard; see Section III).

The many, radically different ways critics have found to describe and categorize artistic postmodernism, however, should not obscure the fact that there does appear to be considerable agreement as to what constitutes a definition of modernity, even postmodernity. Because of the fact that, within the particularly modern *episteme* (to use Foucault's term), "postmodern" has become "a loaded and politically volatile word" (Ebert 1991, 8), it is important that we explore what is meant by modernity in these ongoing debates, especially as represented in the essays in this section.

In most accounts, the movement from Renaissance humanism to the start of the "modernist project," as Habermas calls it, begins with Descartes and his famous *cogito ergo sum*. In Toulmin's terms, it entails a shift "to a higher, stratospheric plane, in which nature and ethics conform to abstract, timeless, general, and universal theories" (1990, 35). On this plane, connections among our knowledge of Nature, of ourselves, and of history and society are said to be objectively determined. They provide us with a foundation which systematizes what is seen as an inherently progressive grasp of "truth." Knowledge accrued is, then, not only culture-neutral, but value-free. Thus history itself and any shifts in our ways of seeing ourselves within it can be understood in terms of "a totality of objective facts existing in objective space and time" (Bridges).

This is the plane from which Christopher Norris launches his *What's Wrong with Postmodernism*, in which he attacks the postmodern for effacing "all sense of the difference between truth and falsehood, reality and illusion, serious and non-serious discourse" (1990, 2). From the plane of modernity, the postmodern can only be a demonic form of non-truth and non-certitude that is trying to rob even modernity of its cognitively guaranteed certitude—its bedrock foundation in universal "truth." Stepping off the foundational pedestal, it cavalierly offers to help the entire project of modernity take the same step.

To the postmodern, though, the modern is simply one of the many paths and narratives (or, to use Lyotard's term, *"petites histoires"*) that are always jockeying for position, and begging for our attention and allegiance. Clearly this is a different concept of "truth," as well as of the power of rationality. In thus decentering and deconstructing the modern, the postmodern "does not seek to substitute one truth for another, one standard of beauty for another, one life ideal for another. . . . It braces itself for a life without truths, standards, ideals" (Bauman 1992, ix).

Within the context of modernity, which wants to "pull the rug out from under claims to certainty that lack formal guarantees" (Toulmin 1990, 29), the postmodern is simply lacking in certainty (as rationally established). But the postmodern response would be to claim that this is the entire point, for its shift in "horizon of expectation" cannot be accounted for in terms of the modernist explanatory system—that is, the rationalist, overarching metanarrative. Nevertheless, to complicate matters further, the postmodern mode is itself a complex one that actually inscribes that modern narrative within itself, while resisting being contained by it. It does this through an exposing of modernity's hidden *"hermeneutic filter,* its 'selective will,' which is, at the same time, a *will to distort"* (Couliano 1984/1987, 12). What makes this postmodern reflexive doubleness possible is the presence of other narratives, all acting as filters or lenses on each other, revealing each other's *will to distort*.

From the perspective of modernity, then, there would be no real shift from modern to postmodern; the latter would merely be another challenge to be put in its place by rational means. From the postmodern point of view, too, there might be less a shift here than a momentary standing still within a labyrinth of narratives that are themselves always in motion: the "postmodern"—at the moment we try to narrate its identity, as we are doing here—is merely the temporary node from which we speak. Whether we think of this as a change of *episteme* or period, the modern/postmodern relationship is possibly not unlike that between the Renaissance and modernity. The Renaissance perspective which preceded the modern in fact echoes, in some ways, the postmodern one which followed it— especially in its questioning of the importance of logical analysis and universal meaning. As Toulmin points out: "Renaissance scholars were quite as concerned with circumstantial questions of practice in medicine, law, or morals, as with any timeless, universal matters of philosophical theory. In their eyes, the rhetorical analysis of arguments, which focused on the presentation of cases and the character of audiences, was as worthwhile—indeed, as philosophical—as the formal analysis of their inner logic" (1990, 27).

The Renaissance skepticism Toulmin describes has interesting parallels with Jean-François Lyotard's notion of the postmodern "incredulity toward all metanarratives": "The sixteenth-century followers of classical skepticism never claimed to *refute* rival philosophical positions: such views do not lend themselves to proof or to refutation. Rather, what they had to offer was a new way of understanding human life and motives: like Socrates long ago, and Wittgenstein in our own time, they taught readers to recognize how philosophical theories overreach the limits of human rationality" (Toulmin 1990, 29). So too have Rortian pragmatists and Derridean deconstructivists sought to teach their postmodern readers.

Many theorists have argued in this way that there are obvious links between postmodern thinking and that manifested by Renaissance humanists such as Erasmus, Bacon, Montaigne, Rabelais, Shakespeare, and Giordano Bruno—particularly in their refusal to give up the particular for the sake of the universal, the oral for the written, the local for the general, the timely for the timeless. The response of modernity to both, of course, was to turn on that refusal the power of the ordering, legitimizing, "system-building faculty," the power of reason and method: Bertrand Russell begins the modern section of his *History of Western Philosophy* with the statement that "[t]he first effect of emancipation from the Church was not to make men think rationally, but to open their minds to every sort of antique nonsense" (1945, 502).

In disdaining to privilege or underwrite the productions of the "system-building faculty," the postmodern might also be seen to be open to "every sort of antique nonsense," of course. (In fact, its critics might see that as a not inaccurate description of postmodern architecture.) But not all the attacks on the postmodern have been grounded only in this Cartesian rationalist theory. In fact, the well-known sally of Jurgen Habermas (reprinted in this book) addresses itself specifically to the critics of eighteenth-century Enlightenment thought. Habermas argues that what he calls the "project of modernity" still needs to be completed and that the postmodern is preventing this. Modernity, for him, involves a moral imperative to free humanity from injustices, to extend equality to the oppressed, and to do so not by collapsing the public sphere into an "intermingling of categories such as advertising, politics, entertainment," but by fostering "a formation of opinion in discursive style mediated by reading, reasoning, information" (1985, 97). As he argues in "Modernity versus Postmodernity," this moral imperative has not yet been fulfilled and, as Huyssen notes, Habermas wants to salvage the emancipatory potential of enlightened reason.

Arguing against American neo-conservative thinkers such as Daniel Bell and French poststructuralists like Derrida and Foucault, Habermas is willing to affirm—where, as we have seen, someone like Toulmin would deny—that the Enlightenment had established a "communal grounds of consensus," one that would lead to "the rational organization of everyday social life." Even if, in our century, there has been an unfortunate "splitting off" of science, morality and art (as Habermas shows Max Weber to have argued), that is no reason for giving up the rationalist *"intentions* of the Enlightenment." But Zygmunt Bauman, writing in "Postmodernity, or Living with Ambivalence," counters this with the view that—at a social level, for instance—it is equally a moral necessity *not* to apply those modern totalizing principles to synthesize or resolve ambiguity: "The search for community turns into a major obstacle to its formation. The only consensus likely to stand a chance of success is the acceptance of the heterogeneity of the dissensions."

In opposition to the Habermasian view that the project of modernity put aside its preference for the universal, the general, the timeless over the particular, the local, and the timely, Bauman describes that project as one which simply concealed the parochial basis of its universality. It also transformed any particularity into a "not-yet" universal, thus assuring the freedom from contingency and ambiguity for which Habermas's "communicative rationality" strives. "For most of its history," writes Bauman, "modernity lived in and through self-deception," because of its "obsessively legislating, defining, structuring, segregating, classifying, recording and universalizing state [which] reflected the splendour of universal and absolute standards of truth" (Bauman 1992, xiv). For Habermas, the postmodern is a vague variety of "antimodern"; for Bauman, the distinction rests on the relation of both to ambiguity. While the modern "could dismiss its own uncertainty as a temporary affliction," the postmodern sees "the escape from contingency being as contingent as the condition from which escape is sought."

Andreas Huyssen points out that Habermas's attack on the postmodern is double-edged: it is an indictment both of postmodernism's failure to confront the threat of late capitalism to cultural tradition and its failure to confront the modern—in effect, to work with the modernist project to sort out its successes and failures. The postmodern thus appears not to be engaged at those points where it should be. This perceived lack of resistance and dissidence is usually linked to the "ludic" or playful aspect of postmodernism, and thus to both post-structuralism and, especially, deconstruction. As we shall see in later sections, in the eyes of those seeking a narrative of social intervention in which we "can build a new socially transformative politics of emancipation and freedom from gender, race, and class exploitation" (Ebert 1991, 887), what Lyotard characterizes as the postmodern "anything goes" can amount to a kind of conservativism.

But neo-conservatives also seem to find the postmodern equally undermining and negating in terms of social structure and in what some see as "its repudiation of tradition and the past" (Bell 1980, 302). From this point of view, as Huyssen points out, the postmodern is seen to politicize culture, pulling art out of "the closet of autonomy and high seriousness" and into the arena of clashing narratives—none of which, however, can rest happily on any privileged pedestal or uncontestable foundation. Suddenly the crucial modern distinction between mass culture and high culture, between the popular and the serious, is called into question: the postmodern "anything goes" can now be made to sound more dissident than playful, or—if playful—then only in the undermining way in which Bakhtin's version of the Rabelaisian carnival is.

As Huyssen shows, the rationalist modern enterprise is also employed to hold off the postmodern regress in which no narrative—including the postmodern's—is immune to the demystifying operations of another. That state of on-going, endless critique, of challenge and contest, is what Habermas salvages from the modernist project, however, and makes into the grounds for his "communicative rationality."

In short, as the readings in this section demonstrate, the lines drawn in the modern/postmodern battle are not clear ones; they do not easily break down into the comfortable political binaries of left versus right, radical versus neoconservative. There are many lines, battles, and skirmishes, and this embattled and recursive terrain is full of contradictions and paradoxes. Not only can Lyotard and Habermas not agree with each other on the solution to any of the questions raised, but there are internal impasses as well: Habermas's modernity cannot be communicatively rational and still recognize what Huyssen calls twentieth-century modernism's "nihilistic and anarchic strain," and Lyotard's postmodern incredulity toward all metanarratives must include incredulity toward any means of consensus for grounding that very incredulity.

Here, in "Modernism versus Postmodernism: Towards an Analytic Distinction," David Herman clarifies what is at stake in the opposition between Lyotard and Habermas that has been at the heart of so many of the debates on this subject. Habermas is seen to invest zero value in dissent because his mission is the continual re-questioning of the possibility of consensus in order to reinstate it at a "less coercive level." That reinstatement is hindered precisely by that "nihilistic and anarchic strain" of dissent. Lyotard, instead, is said to place "infinite value upon dissent" because any questioning of the possibility of consensus must lead to dissent, to a "sensitivity to differences" sufficient to destroy a proposed consensus and the coercion it inevitably involves.

Herman argues that the difference between these two thinkers can be understood by tracing them both back to the same Enlightenment attempt to define an emancipatory project. But Lyotard's high valuing of dissent results from a basic structuralist tenet: the *arbitrary* linking of word and world, which leaves us in perpetual need of dissenting from whatever totalizing scheme (or Habermasian rational consensus) might be imposed upon us. On the contrary, Habermas's high valuing of consensus results from the need to bring to the force the *shared* linkage of word and world that will serve to expose "subjective or empty or terroristic" linkages.

For Herman, the debate between Habermas and Lyotard, between seeing either the modern or the postmodern as emancipatory, is in the end undecidable because the two theorists are forming different connections between words and their referents: "We cannot hope to bring to a peaceable end a discussion in which the participants think they share a single vocabulary, but actually do not. We can merely stake out the grounds for conflict." So too can we, in this brief preface to the following introductory essays on the vexed topic of the modern and the postmodern. The "grounds for conflict" are now yours to stake out.

Works Cited

Bauman, Zygmunt (1992) *Intimations of Postmodernity*. New York and London: Routledge.

Bell, Daniel (1980) *The Winding Passage*. Cambridge, Mass.: ABT Books.

Bridges, Tom (1992) "Objectivity, Nihilism and Civic Rationality." PMC-Talk @ NCSUVM; file name BRIDGES ESSAY 3.

Couliano, Ian (1984, 1987) *Eros and Magic in the Renaissance*. Chicago and London: U of Chicago P.

Ebert, Teresa (1991) "The 'Difference' of Postmodern Feminism." *College English* 53.8: 886–904.

Habermas, Jürgen (1985) "A Philosophico-Political Profile." *New Left Review* 151: 75–105.

Kroker, Arthur and David Cook (1986) *The Postmodern Scene: Excremental Culture and Hyper-Aesthetics*. Montreal: New World Perspectives.

McGowan, John (1991) *Postmodernism and Its Critics*. Ithaca, NY: Cornell U P.

Norris, Christopher (1990) *What's Wrong with Postmodernism*. Baltimore: The John Hopkins U P.

Russell, Bertrand (1945) *A History of Western Philosophy*. New York: Simon and Schuster.

Sloterdijk, Peter (1987) *Critique of Cynical Reason*. Trans. Michael Eldred. Minneapolis: U of Minnesota P.

Toulmin, Stephen (1990) *Cosmopolis: The Hidden Agenda of Modernity*. New York: Free P.

Postmodernity, or Living with Ambivalence

Zygmunt Bauman

> We could try to transform our contingency into our destiny.
>
> Agnes Heller

In one respect the social sciences born in the age of Enlightenment have not failed—writes Agnes Heller: "they have provided self-knowledge, and they never ceased providing self-knowledge of *modern* society, of a *contingent* society, of one social among many, *our society.*"[1] And yet, let us observe, this partial success was itself a failure, if judged by the standards of the social sciences' ambition. Whatever modern social sciences did, they did not deliver *on their promise;* instead, with no knowing and even less intending, they delivered something they did not promise; to put it bluntly, they were delivering a reasonable product all along under the false pretences of supplying something else altogether ... Awareness of contingency—of the contingency of the modern self, of the contingency of modern society—was not what they, their prophets, their apostles, their intended converts and aspiring beneficiaries bargained for. If one agrees with Heller that the social sciences, all their self-deception notwithstanding, did supply precious knowledge later to be appreciated as an insight into contingency, one must still insist that they did it while misconceiving the true nature of their business, or that they did it while trying to pass their product for something other than it was (thus remaining—knowingly or unknowingly—in breach of the official trading act . . .): that they informed of *contingency* while believing themselves to narrate *necessity,* of particular *locality* while believing themselves to narrate *universality,* of tradition-bound interpretation while believing themselves to narrate the extraterritorial and extratemporal truth, of undecidability while believing themselves to narrate transparency, of the provisionality of the human condition while believing themselves to narrate the certainty of the world, of the *ambivalence* of man-made design while believing themselves to narrate the *order* of nature.

It was all these beliefs (false beliefs), and not their deliveries (useful deliveries) that made the social sciences, and the mentality from which they arose, and the power structure that contemplated itself in that mentality, *modern.* For most of its history, modernity lived in and through self-deception. Concealment of its own parochiality, conviction that whatever is not universal in its particularity is but not-yet-universal, that the project of universality may be incomplete, but remains most definitely on, was the core of that self-deception. It was perhaps thanks to that self-deception that modernity could deliver both the wondrous and the gruesome things that it did; in this, as in so many other cases, ignorance, so to speak, turned out to be a privilege. The question is: is the fading of self-deception a final fulfillment, emancipation, or the end of modernity?

The distinctive feature of the belief in the truth of one's knowledge is not the conviction that the knowledge in question is satisfying, pleasing, useful, or otherwise worth holding to. Such a conviction does not require the belief in truth for support. More often than not, this conviction can be and is held without worry about authoritative confirmation that the belief in truth is sound. Where one cannot do without the "well grounded concept of truth" is when it comes to tell others that they are in error and hence (1) ought or must change their minds, thus (2) confirming the superiority (read: right to command) of the holder of truth (read: the giver of command). The bid for truth as a claimed quality of knowledge arises therefore solely in the context of hegemony and proselytism; in the context of coexistence of autonomously sustained bodies of knowledge of which at least one refuses to coexist peacefully and respect the existing borders; in the context of plurality that is treated by at least one member as a vexing state to be rectified; in the context of a balance of forces under pressure to turn into asymmetry of power.

Truth is, in other words, a *social relation* (like *power, ownership* or *freedom*): an aspect of a hierarchy built of superiority-inferiority units; more precisely, an aspect of the hegemonic form of domination or of a bid for domination-through-hegemony. Modernity was, from its inception, such a form and such a bid. The part of the world that adopted modern civilization as its structural principle and constitutional value was bent on dominating the rest of the world by dissolving its alterity and assimilating the product of dissolution. The persevering alterity could not but be treated as a temporary nuisance; as an error, sooner or later bound to be supplanted by truth. The battle of order against chaos in worldly affairs was replicated by the war of truth against error on the plane of consciousness. The order bound to be installed and made universal was a *rational* order; the truth bound to be made triumphant was the *universal* (hence apodictic and obligatory) truth. Together, political order and true knowledge blended into a design for *certainty.* The rational-universal world of order and truth would know of no contingency and no ambivalence. The target of certainty and of absolute truth was indistinguishable from the crusading spirit and the project of domination.

While setting itself apart, making itself distinct so that it would be possible to reserve a position of command toward the rest of the *oikoumene,* modernity thought of itself as of the seed of future universality, as of an entity destined to replace all other entities and thus to abolish the very difference between them. It thought of the *differentiation* it perpetrated as of *universalization.* This was modernity's self-deception. This was, however, a self-deception bound to disclose itself even without outside help (there was, anyway, no "outside" left, allowed the legitimacy to disclose anything); a self-deception that could last only as long as it worked toward that disclosure. The self-deception supplied the courage and the confidence to pursue that lonely work of universality that spawned ever more difference; to persevere in such a chase of uniformity as was bound to result in more ambivalence. The self-deception of modernity was pregnant with its self-disclosure.

It is perhaps the fruit of that pregnancy that Agnes Heller dubbed the "death wish" that was to be found at the other end of the long march toward "wish-fulfillment"; that was to be, as we tried to argue here, the latter's inescapable heir and successor. Awareness of contingency, though a prodigal child, was a fully legitimate off-spring of blind self-confidence; it could not but be born of it and it could not be born of any other parent. The residents of the house of modernity had been continuously trained to feel at home under con-ditions of necessity and to feel unhappy at the face of contingency; contingency, they had been told, was that state of discomfort and anxiety from which one needed to escape by making oneself into a binding norm and thus doing away with difference. Present unhap-piness is the realization that this is not to be, that the hope will not come true and hence one needs to learn to live without the hope that supplied the meaning—the only meaning—to life. As Richard Rorty observed: "The vocabularies are, typically, parasitic on the hopes— in the sense that the principal function of the vocabularies is to tell stories about future outcomes which compensate for present sacrifices,"[2]—and, let us add, give name to present sufferings; they narrate the present as *specific* suffering that needs a *concrete* sac-rifice to cease be a suffering *as such*. We are unhappy today, as we have been left with the old vocabulary but without the hope that fed it with life juices. The rustle of desiccated, sapless words reminds us ceaselessly, obtrusively of the void that is where hope once was.

Having been trained to live in necessity, we have found our-selves living in contingency. And yet, being bound to live in contin-gency, we can, as Heller suggests, make "an attempt to transform it into our destiny." One makes something a destiny by embracing the fate: by an act of choice and the will to remain loyal to the choice made. Abandoning the vocabulary parasitic on the hope of (or de-termination for) universality, certainty and transparency is the first choice to be made; the first step on the road to emancipation. We cannot forget contingency any more; were it able to speak, con-tingency would repeat what Nietzsche wrote to his discoverer, friend and prophet Georg Brandes on 4 January 1889 (the day he finally withdrew from the concerns of mundane life): "After you had discovered me, it was no trick to find me: the difficulty now is to lose me . . ."[3] But we can transfer contingency from the vocabulary of dashed hopes into that of the opportunity, from the language of domination into that of emancipation. Heller writes:

> An individual has transformed his or her contingency into his or her destiny if this person has arrived at the consciousness of having made the *best* out of his or her practically infinite pos-sibilities. A society has transformed its contingency into its

destiny if the members of this society arrive at the awareness that they would prefer to live at no other place and at no other time than the here and now.

From Tolerance to Solidarity

But, let us comment, that awareness that ushers into emancipation is not the only thing that happens on the road to contingency as destiny. The emancipation which contingency as destiny makes possible (one of those "practically infinite possibilities") entails the *acceptance* that there are other places and other times that may be with equal justification (or equal absence of good reason) preferred by members of other societies, and that however different they are, the choices cannot be disputed by reference to anything more solid and binding than preference and the determination to stick to the preferred. The preference for one's own, communally shared form of life must therefore be immune to the temptation of cultural crusade. Emancipation means such acceptance of one's own contingency as is grounded in recognition of contingency as the sufficient reason to live and to be allowed to live. It signals the end to the horror of alterity and to the abhorrence of ambivalence. Like truth, emancipation is not a quality of objects, but of the *relation* between them. The relation opened up by the act of emancipation is marked by the end of fear and the beginning of *tolerance*. It is on tolerance that the vocabulary of contingency-as-destiny is bound to be parasitic to allow emancipation to articulate.

As Rorty convincingly explains, the language of necessity, certainty and absolute truth cannot but articulate humiliation—humiliation of the other, of the different, of the not-up-to-the-standard. The language of contingency, on the contrary, creates a chance "of being kind, by avoiding humiliation of others."[4] Let us observe, however, that "being kind" is not the end of the story either—not the final station on the road to emancipation. "Being kind" and the tolerance for which it stands as a locutionary and behavioral symbol may well mean mere indifference and unconcern deriving from resignation (that is, from *fate,* not *destiny*): the Other will not go away and would not become like me, but then I have no means (at the moment, at least, or in the foreseeable future) to force him to go or to change. As we are doomed to share space and time, let us make our coexistence bearable and somewhat less dangerous. By being kind I invite kindness. I hope that my offer of reciprocity will be taken up;

such a hope is my sole weapon. Being kind is but a way to keep the danger at a distance; like the proselytizing urge of yore, it arises out of fear.

To unravel the emancipatory potential of contingency-as-destiny, it would not suffice to avoid humiliating the others. One needs also to *respect* them—and respect them precisely in their otherness, in the preferences they have made, in their right to make preferences. One needs to honour the otherness in the other, the strangeness in the stranger, remembering—with Edmond Jabès—that "the unique is universal," that it is being different that makes us resemble each other and that I cannot respect my own difference but by respecting the difference of the other. "The case of the stranger concerns me not just because I myself am a stranger, but because it raises, for itself, the problems that we confront in principle and in daily applications of liberty, power, duty and fraternity: in the first place, the problem of equality of men; secondly, of our responsibility towards them and towards ourselves."[5] My link with the stranger is revealed as *responsibility,* not just indifferent neutrality or even cognitive acceptance of the similarity of condition (and certainly not through the disdainful version of tolerance: "It serves him well to be like that, and let him be, though I cannot imagine to be such myself"). It is revealed, in other words, as commonality of destiny, not mere resemblance of fate. Shared fate would do with mutual *tolerance;* joint destiny requires *solidarity.*

The right of the Other to his strangerhood is the only way in which my own right may express, establish and defend itself. It is from the right of the Other that my right is put together. The "I am responsible for the Other," and "I am responsible for myself," come to mean the same thing. Having chosen them both, and having them chosen as one thing, one indivisible attitude, not as two correlated, yet separate stances, is the meaning of the reforging contingency from fate into destiny. Call this as you like: fellow-feeling, imaginative identification, empathy; one thing you cannot say about such a choice is that it follows a rule or a command—be it an injunction of reason, a rule empirically demonstrated by truth-seeking knowledge, a command of God or a legal precept.

As a matter of fact, there is not much you can say about the cause of it at all. The new solidarity of the contingent is grounded in silence. Its hopes lie in refraining from asking certain questions and seeking certain answers; it is satisfied with its own contingency and does not wish to be elevated to the status of truth, necessity or certainty, knowing too well (or, rather, feeling intuitively) that it would not survive the promotion. Solidarity comes into its own when the language of necessity—the language of estrangement, discrimination and humiliation, falls out of use. Trying to pinpoint the most decisive mark of the ideal society—in his rendition, the ideal *liberal* society—Richard Rorty settled for people who "would feel no more need to answer the question 'Why are you a liberal'?" In such a society a person "would not need a justification for her sense of human solidarity, for she was not raised to play the language game in which one asks and gets justifications for that sort of belief."[6]

Contingent existence means existence devoid of certainty, and one certainty that is missing at this desolate site of ours, or difficult to be excavated from beneath the debris of modern truths, is the certainty of solidarity. The road from tolerance to solidarity, like any other road, is undetermined; it is itself contingent. And so is the other road, one leading from tolerance to indifference and estrangement; it is equally contingent, and thus equally plausible. The state of tolerance is intrinsically and incurably ambivalent. It lends itself with equal ease, or equal difficulty, to celebratory praise and scornful condemnation; it may give occasion to joy as much as to despair. Living in contingency means living without a guarantee, with just a provisional, pragmatic, Pyrrhonic, until-further-notice certainty, and this includes the emancipatory effect of solidarity.

Modernity could dismiss its own uncertainty as a temporary affliction. Each uncertainty came complete with the recipe for curing it: just one more problem, and problems were defined by their solutions. (Societies, Marx insisted, never put before themselves tasks until means for their execution are available.) The passage from uncertainty to certainty, from ambivalence to transparency seemed to be a matter of time, of resolve, of resources, of *knowledge*. It is an entirely different matter to live with the postmodern awareness of no certain exit from uncertainty; of the escape from contingency being as contingent as the condition from which escape is sought. The discomfort such awareness brings about is the source of specifically postmodern discontents: discontent against the condition fraught with ambivalence, against the contingency that refuses to go away, and against the messengers of the news—those who attempt to spell out and articulate what is new and what is unlikely ever to return to the old: those who, to use again Agnes Heller's terms, call to turn the fate into destiny. What the recipients of the news find difficult to accept is that whatever they resolve to do would lack the comfort of having the truth, or the laws of history, or the umambiguous verdict of reason on its side.

Indeed, anyone seeking practical success would gain little from an insight into the postmodern condition. It cannot be denied that knowledge of this condition fails abominably by the standards set by modern knowledge (or, rather, by the promise that knowledge made and turned into the foundation of its elevated social standing). Awareness of contingency does not "empower": its acquisition does not give the owner advantage over the protagonists in the struggle of wills and purposes, or in the game of cunning and luck. It does not lead to, or sustain, domination. As if to make the score even, it does not aid the struggle against domination either. It is, to put it bluntly, indifferent to the current or prospective structures of domination. Whoever is after domination—current or prospective (or whoever is just prompted to evaluate the quality of knowledge by the power to do things it promises to supply or make respectable) must be infuriated by the blandness of the refusal of that knowledge to validate all claims to superiority. Equally furious must be he who wishes to explode the domination that is.

And yet it is just a matter of perspective whether a trait is seen as an affliction or sign of soundness, a vice or a virtue. Dashing the hope of empowerment-through-knowledge amounts to the emphatic disavowal and rebuttal of the power struggle aimed at ultimate domination. It also amounts to the promotion of coexistence: the only condition whose stability, nay permanence, it allows. The awareness of the postmodern condition discloses tolerance as fate. It also makes possible—just possible—the long road from fate to destiny, from tolerance to solidarity.

The Exorcist and The Omen, or
Modern and Postmodern Limits to Knowledge

Pretences of knowledge can be doubted in two ways. One can point out that there are events for which the kind of knowledge there is (knowledge that has received endorsement from the sites that men of knowledge admit to be sound and credible) does not have a convincing, agreed narrative; events that cannot be made into a story that men of knowledge would recognize as their own. Or one can say that the narrative that knowledge does offer is not the only story that may be told of the events; not even the best story, or at least not the only one able to claim the right to be considered "better tested." The first kind of doubt is modern; the second is postmodern. To say this is not to speak of chronological succession. Both modes of doubt have been around as long as science itself. Their copresence was one of the constitutive features of that modern culture which prodded modernity on its road to post modernity.

The two doubts have been given widely popular (populist?) literary form in the two works of fantasy—both huge box-office successes in their novelistic as well as their cinematic renditions.[7] They may well serve us as parables for the two doubts that silently yet unflaggingly sapped, and in the end toppled modern self-confidence.

Father Damien Karras of William Peter Blatty's novel *The Exorcist* turned exorcist only *after* all his and his professional colleagues' psychiatric routines, based on the most formidable, impeccably scholarly and up-to-date therapeutic skills and scientific knowledge, came to nought. Karras was, one may say, a psychiatrist's psychiatrist. Bearer of the most enviable scientific credentials, an alumnus of the most prestigious professional schools, a universally respected practitioner with a long record of spectacular therapeutic successes, a theorist armed with a truly encyclopedic knowledge of the best scientific psychiatry could offer, a recipient of the most prestigious distinctions the profession could bestow—he was the scientific authority incarnate. Calling him to act on Regan's case was the ultimate resort and last hope of psychiatric science and practice: all his illustrious co-professionals, one by one and all together, tried, did their best and failed; the most up-to-date therapeutic technology proved insufficient. Karras's own actions—much as his accounts of the actions—were kept strictly within the frame of the collectively guarded scientific idiom; they were carefully calculated to restate, reaffirm and reinforce everything the profession believed and wanted its public to believe. Karras was not a witch-doctor or natural healer, that agent of dark and barbaric forces resisting the modern science set to annihilate them; like his learned colleagues who turned to him for help, Karras was a bearer of modern intellect sworn to extinguish the last vestige of superstition.

Up to the last moment—with the ultimate mystery staring in his face—Karras doggedly asserts scientific reason's uncontested right to narrate the evidence, to compose the sole acceptable version of the story—and rebuffs the layperson's temptation to succumb to interpretations that science refused to tolerate. When hapless Regan's mother turns to Karras in utter despair (her "freckled, clasped fingers twitched in her lap")—"I just don't know ... What do *you* think, Father?"—Karras's answer is professionalism itself: "Compulsive behaviour produced by guilt, perhaps, put together with split personality."

"Father, I have *had* all that garbage! Now how can you say that after all you've just seen!"

"If you've seen as many patients in psychiatric wards as I have, you can say it very easily," he assured her . . .

"Then explain all those rappings and things." . . .

"Psychokinesis."

"What?" . . .

"It's not that uncommon, and usually happens around an emotionally disturbed adolescent. Apparently, extreme inner tension of the mind can sometimes trigger some unknown energy that seems to move objects around at a distance. There's nothing supernatural about it. Like Regan's abnormal strength. Again, in pathology it's common. Call it mind over matter, if you will."

"I call it weird." . . .

"The best explanation for any phenomenon," Karras overrode her, "is always the simplest one available that accommodates all the facts." . . .

An so on. Karras would not concede an inch: phenomena are explicable, explanations are available, an energy's being unknown (as yet, of course) is not for that reason inexplicable. One that spent much time in wards where things are seen that a layperson would never set her eyes on, knows that. (You should trust the expert; he *saw* things you would never see.) And—as the final argument, the ultimate reassurance—this is *common* (statistically frequent; it happens to others). And it has its name: a respectable scientific name, like "emotionally disturbed adolescent" or "psychokinesis."

The layperson, particularly one who like Regan's mother has been repeatedly disappointed by learned advice and driven into despair by its practical impotence, may refuse to draw comfort from what now seem empty promises of reason. Indeed, Regan's mother "was staring in unblinking incredulity. 'Father, that's so far out of sight that I think it's almost easier to believe in the *devil!*' . . . For long, troubled seconds, the priest was still. Then he answered softly, 'Well, there's little in this world that I know for a fact.' " Regan's mother suggests another doctrine, another orthodoxy, another explanatory key; Karras responds with *humility*. Prudent modesty, sagacious self-limitation of the scientist, skepticism in the face of the-yet-unknown is his last line of defense against the only real danger: an alternative to science, a legitimate knowledge that does not draw its legitimation from scientific authority. When he finally decides to step into the Unknown (a step made perhaps easier by the fact that, unlike his fellow scientists, but like his patient Regan, he has himself a split personality—he is, after all, a devoted priest must as he is a learned psychiatrist), Karras makes sure that the prerogatives of science are not infringed: "If I go to the Chancery Office, or wherever it is I have to go, to get their permission to perform an exorcism, the first thing I'd have to have is a pretty substantial indication that your daughter's condition isn't a purely psychiatric problem."

David Seltzer's *The Omen* conveys a different message altogether. It speaks out the unspeakable: perhaps science's prerogatives are themselves a sham—nothing but a convenient hideout for the *devil?* Is "the common," by the very fact of being common, reassuringly explicable? Are the explanations that science together with scientifically censored and endorsed common sense have to offer, really the "simplest ones available"? Does not the lauded "simplicity" stand merely for the satisfaction of scientific authority? Do not things, uncommon and common alike, lend themselves to other, alternative, heteronomous descriptions? And if they do, how to choose between the stories? And how are the choices made in practice by those who make them for us?

The Omen contains one series of events, but two narratives. One is the common and the ordinary, and therefore raising no brow: the kind of story told over and over again by the experts and their journalist popularizers, and thus becoming indistinguishable from the world it tells about. The other is a kind of story which the luckless hero of the book, the brilliant and erudite intellectual Thorn, could only suppose—*fear*—to be "his imagination," and (as any other well-informed civilized person certainly would) see as a good reason "to see a psychiatrist." One is the well-known story, repeated *ad nauseam* by the chorus of politicians, journalists and social scientists, of human and state interests, political platforms, not-wholly-eradicated irrational sentiments. The other?

> The coven was made up mostly of working class people, but a few were professional, highly placed men. On the outside they all led respectable lives—this their most valuable weapon against those who worshipped God. It was their mission to create fear and turmoil, to turn men against each other until the time of the Unholy One had come; a small group called Task

Forces would forage out to create chaos wherever possible. The coven in Rome took credit for much of the turmoil in Ireland, using random sabotage to polarize Catholic from Protestant and fan the fires of religious war . . .

[In 1968] Tassone was dispatched by Spiletto to South-East Asia, there organizing a small band of mercenaries in Communist-held Cambodia, to cross into, and disrupt the cease-fire, in South Vietnam. The North blamed it on the South, the South on the North, and within days of Tassone's entrance, the hard-won peace of this land was shattered . . .

Knowing of his knowledge of the country, Spiletto sent Tassone to assist the revolution that eventually brought Idi Amin, the insane African Despot, to power . . .

And so on. Of the second story, "only *they* knew." "No one else had ever had a clue." Once told, their story would make as much sense—no more and no less—of terrorism, senseless killings, hostilities without a cause, civil wars, mass murders, crazy despots, as all the stories that officially guaranteed their rationality. The problem, however, was that this other, apocryphal story has been never told; not in public, that is. Those who saw things told by this story as they happened, all perished; the only surviving witness, Thorn himself, was—naturally—confined to a lunatic asylum. The world found it easier (and more reassuring) to assume that Thorn's unshared beliefs were symptoms of mental disturbance, than to accept the possibility that the world's own truth might have been just one of the many, that to every interpretation, however massively hailed, there might be an alternative. Murder, imprisonment, the verdict of insanity were the worldly truths' last lines of defense. Perhaps the only lines of *effective* defense. ↙

Most of us would easily agree that the explanations Seltzer puts in the mind and on the lips of Thorn are ridiculous or outrageously insane. All the more striking is the point he tries to hammer home—that without recourse to force and suppression, the dominant truth cannot protect itself by the weapons of logic, canons of induction, rules of fact-collecting and all the other devices that, as it claims, suffice to guarantee its superior quality and hence its privileged standing. (Note that it is only Thorn's *story* that sounds unquestionably insane; the supposition that we would not be so sure of its insanity were not the supporting evidence suppressed, does not.) For every sequence of events, there is more than one interpretation that would pass muster. The choice, ultimately, is a political matter . . .

And so there are two doubts. The first kind of doubt does not undermine the authority of science. On the contrary, transforming the ideal of truth into the "imaginary target" of knowledge-producing pursuits, into the horizon of the territory now being travelled through (a horizon always receding and forever elusive, and hence always beyond the reach of practical test)—this doubt effectively *protects* the authority of science from discreditation. In fact, it renders knowledge as such (at the cost of virtually each and any of its specimens) immune to questioning. It sees to it that no hostages are ever given to fate, and that in the game of knowledge the worthiness of the game is never at stake. It guarantees the immortality of knowledge as a truth-gaining enterprise by rendering it independent of the vicissitudes of each specific truth it spawns. It allows the enterprise to go on unabated while being demonstratively abortive: it transforms its very abortiveness into the mainspring—the motive and the legitimation—of its continuing vigour.

Ostensibly, this doubt puts in question the finality of any successive incarnation of the truth ideal. More surreptitiously, yet more importantly, it belittles the significance of any specific case of ignorance. It temporalizes ignorance—and so it disarms the uncertainty and ambiguity that ignorance brings in its wake. Instead of paralyzing action, ignorance prompts more effort and boosts the zeal and determination of actors. Ignorance is a not-yet conquered territory; its very presence is a challenge, and the clinching argument of any pep talk summoning support for the next attack in the interminable, yet always confident of the ultimate victory, offensive of reason. It allows science to declare credibly its determination to work itself out of a job, while constantly staving off the moment when it could be asked to act on its promise: there is always a job to be done, and fighting ignorance is such a job. The first kind of doubt, therefore, harnesses ignorance to the chariot of science. In advance, ignorance is defined as another feather in science's cap. Its resistance is significant solely for the fact that it is about to be broken. Its danger is somewhat less terrifying as it is bound to be chased away—soon. The uncertainty and ambivalence ignorance nurtures is but an occasion to another display of the potency of reason, and so it breeds, ultimately, reassurance.

The second kind of doubt, is anything but innocuous. It hits where it hurts most: it undermines the trust that whatever is being said by science at a given time is the best one can say at that time. It questions the holy of holies—the creed of the superiority of scientific knowledge over any other knowledge. By the same token, it challenges science's right to validate and invalidate, legitimize and delegitimize—to draw the line between knowledge and ignorance, transparency and obscurity, logic and incongruity. Obliquely, it makes thinkable the most heretical of heresies: that instead of being a gallant knight bent on cutting off, one by one, the many heads of the dragon of superstition, science is one story among many, invoking one frail pre-judgment among many.

The second kind of doubt never for a single moment ceased to haunt modern mentality. From the start it was firmly entrenched in the inner recesses of modernity; fear of the "unfoundedness" of certainty was, arguably, the most formidable among modernity's many inner demons. Many times over it put the modern project on the defensive. Even when, for a time, forced into the limbo of the subconscious, it went on poisoning the joy of victorious offensives. Unlike the first kind of doubt, found resonant and useful and therefore rapturously displayed in public, the second kind was treated with unqualified and unremitting hostility: it was marked for total and irrevocable destruction. It stood for everything the transparent and harmonious world that science was to build had to be purified of: unreason, madness, obscurity, undecidability.

Like all doubts, this one was creative as well: it strained human imaginative power to the utmost, giving birth to contraptions so varied as, for instance, Descartes's *cogito*, Husserl's *transcendental reduction*, Popper's principle of *refutation*, Weber's *rational constructs*, or the ever more ingenious research methods that—like the Swiftian wheel at the Academy of Lagado—were hoped to allow any able-bodied man to thresh out the healthy grain of truth from the chaff of error. From Descartes's *malin génie* and up to Husserl's heroic act of *epoché*, the war against uncertainty and ambiguity of evidence went on unabated—the most vivid testimony, if one was needed, to the ubiquitous and perseverant presence of the doubt.

It was the presence of the second kind of doubt—and its presence *as a doubt*, as a belief able to weaken the resolve needed for the success of the project—that was the distinctive mark of modern mentality. It is the disappearance of that doubt *as a doubt* (that is, the retention of the belief, yet the defusion of its past corrosive impact) that marks most vividly the passage of modernity into its postmodern stage. Modernity reaches that new stage (so sharply distinct that one is ever so often tempted to allocate it to an entirely separate era, to describe it in a typically modern style as a negation, pure and simple, of modernity) when it is able to face up to the fact that science, for all one knows and can know, is one story among many. "To face up" means to accept that certainty is not to be, and yet persevere in the pursuit of knowledge born of the determination to smother and week out contingency.

It was the treatment of the first kind of doubt as a temporary nuisance, as an irritant with a limited life-expectancy, sooner or later to be dead and buried, that was another distinctive mark of modern mentality. It was an axiom of that mentality that if there were one thousand potential items of knowledge as yet undisclosed, discovering one of them would leave but nine hundred and ninety-nine in the pool. The abandoning of that axiom marks the passage of modernity into its postmodern stage. Modernity reaches that new stage when it is able to face up to the fact that the growth of knowledge expands the field of ignorance, that with each step towards the horizon new unknown lands appear, and that, to put it most generally, acquisition of knowledge cannot express itself in any other form but awareness of more ignorance. "To face up" to this fact means to know that the journey has no clear destination—and yet persevere in the travel.

There is one more mark of the passage of modernity to its postmodern stage: the two previously separate doubts losing their distinctiveness, becoming semantically indistinguishable, blending into one. The two limits of knowledge appear to be artifacts of modern diffractive vision; their alleged separateness, a projection of the now abandoned design. In place of two limits and two doubts, there is an unworried awareness that there are many stories that need to be told over and over again, each time losing something and adding something to the past versions. There is also a new determination: to guard the conditions in which all stories can be told, and retold, and again told differently. It is in their plurality, and not in the "survival of the fittest" (that is, the extinction of the less fit) that the hope now resides. Richard Rorty gave this new—postmodern—project an epigrammatic precision: "if we take care of political freedom, truth and goodness will take care of themselves."[8] All too often taking care of truth and goodness resulted in the loss of political freedom. Not much truth and goodness has been gained either.

Unlike science and political ideology, freedom promises no certainty and no guarantee of anything. It causes therefore a lot of mental pain. In practice, it means constant exposure to ambivalence: that is, to a situation with no decidable solution, with no foolproof choice, no unreflective knowledge of "how to go on." As Hans Magnus Enzensberger recently remarked, "you can't have a nice democracy . . . Democracy is something which can get very much on your nerves—you are constantly battered by the most obnoxious things. It is like Freudian analysis. All the dirt comes out in democracy."[9] The real problem of the postmodern stage is not to allow things to "get on one's nerves" while hoping that they will not get on one's back. Lacking modernity's iron fist, postmodernity needs nerves of steel.

Notes

1. Agnes Heller, 'From Hermeneutics in Social Science toward a Hermeneutics of Social Science', in *Theory and Society*, vol. 18 (1989), pp. 291–322. Other quotations from Heller that follow come from the same source.

2. Rorty, *Contingency, Irony and Solidarity*, (Cambridge: Cambridge University Press, 1989), p. 86.

3. Quoted after Martin Heidegger, *What is Called Thinking*, trans. F. D. Wieck and J. G. Gray (New York: Harper & Row, 1968), p. 53. Cf. also Shoshana Felman, *Writing and Madness*, trans. Martha Noel Evans and author (Ithaca: Cornell University Press, 1985), p. 62.

4. Rorty, *Contingency, Irony and Solidarity*, p. 91. But remember the inherent dangers of toleration discussed in the introduction. The kindess of the tolerant attitude does not by itself exclude the worst there is in humiliation: the assumption of inherent inferiority of the tolerated object. By itself, toleration may well be just another form in which virtues of the tolerant are re-asserted.

5. Cf. Jabès, *Un Étranger avec, sous le bras, un livre de petit format*, (Paris: Gallimard, 1989), pp. 112–15.

6. Rorty, *Contingency, Irony and Solidarity*, p. 87.

7. Cf. William Peter Blatty, *The Exorcist*—first published by Blond & Briggs in 1972—here quoted from the London Corgi edition of 1974; David Seltzer, *The Omen* (London: Futura Books, 1976).

8. Rorty, *Contingency, Irony and Solidarity*, p. 80.

9. Hans Magnus Enzensberger, "Back in the USSR," *New Statesman and Society* 10 November 1989, p. 29.

The Postmodern *Weltanschauung* and its Relation to Modernism: An Introductory Survey

Hans Bertens

0. Introduction.

Since its cautious beginnings in the late 1950s and early 1960s, critical discussion of the so-called "postmodern" movement has, especially in the last ten years, proliferated in practically all directions. Whereas in its initial phase the debate was limited to a convenient number of critics—convenient from the point of view of writing a survey—such as Irving Howe (1959), Leslie Fiedler and Susan Sontag in the mid-sixties, Ihab Hassan (1969 and ever after), David Antin (1971), William Spanos (1972) and Charles Altieri (1973), since the mid-seventies the debate has turned more and more into a seething turmoil, a free-for-all with no holds barred in which a wide range of critics is participating. Perhaps this view of the matter is slightly exaggerated, but the liveliness, if not vehemence, with which some of them have joined the fray (Klinkowitz 1975; Mellard 1980) does not suggest so.

Hans Bertens, "The Postmodern *Weltaanschauung* and its Relation with Modernism: An Introductory Survey," in *Aproaching Postmodernism* eds. Douwe Fokkema & Hans Bertens (Amsterdam/Philadelphia: John Benjamins Co., 1986), pp. 9–48. Reprinted by permission of publisher and author.

The survey that I am to offer of the postmodern world view as it has emerged in the writings of these critics of Postmodernism, will of course directly confront us with the vexing problem of what is actually constituted by the term Postmodernism, a problem that is still a long way from being solved, as is both suggested by the liveliness of the debate and by a recent statement of Ihab Hassan's, who has more than any other critic contributed to the gradual acceptance of the term. As Hassan points out in a recent article, "the question of Postmodernism remains complex and moot" (Hassan 1983, 25). In fact, nothing much has changed since Köhler published an early survey of the term, seven years ago, and had to conclude that "noch immer keine Übereinstimmung der Autoren darüber herrscht, was als 'postmodern' gelten kann" (Köhler 1977, 16).

In other words, I have no serious hope that this survey will be able to point the way out of the terminological labyrinth into which the term Postmodernism has evolved in the course of the debate. The best I can do is simply tackle the various explicit and implicit definitions or suggestions and see where the effort is going to lead me. My strategy will be based on the assumption—or, if you will, undeniable fact—that Postmodernism is not a monolithic phenomenon. It seems evident to me—and to critics such as Hoffmann *et al.* (1977) and Bradbury (1983), to mention only two of those critics who see variety within terminological unity—that there is more than one Postmodernism. I will attempt to sort out the various postmodernisms, or, rather, the various critical constructs called Postmodernism, that have more or less established themselves at least temporarily over the past twenty-five years. I have in mind such uses of the term as those by, for instance, Irving Howe, William Spanos, Leslie Fiedler and Ihab Hassan, to mention some of the most prominent critics who have written on the question of Postmodernism. That sorting out will initially follow a chronological order, from the earliest still relevant uses of the term up to the early seventies, when Hassan's inclusive concept of Postmodernism changes and, for a time, practically monopolizes the discussion. For the early period, up to 1977, I am indebted to two pioneering articles, to Michael Köhler's " 'Postmodernismus': Ein begriffsgeschichtlicher Überblick" (1977), and to an article by Gerhard Hoffmann, Alfred Hornung, and Rüdiger Kunow, " 'Modern,' 'Postmodern' and Contemporary' as Criteria for the Analysis of 20th Century Literature" (also 1977). Köhler's survey is the best, although, as will appear, not com-

plete history of the term Postmodernism, and the article of Hoffmann *et al.* is a successful effort to systematize and analyse the various uses of the term at the time of writing. Another useful survey
proved to be Wallace Martin's "Postmodernism: Ultima Thule or
Seim Anew?" (1980) although I do not propose to follow Martin's
systematization in the discussion that will follow.

My pluralist approach—to abuse a term that is gaining more
and more importance in descriptions of Postmodernism—will predictably lead to an equally pluralist postmodern *Weltanschauung*. If
the various uses of the term Postmodernism are indeed based upon
sometimes widely different critical constructs, then the world views
identified with these constructs will also show a good deal of variety. Whether it will turn out to be possible to group these world
views under one highly abstracted, encompassing view remains to
be seen. If such an ultimately monolithic construction of Postmodernism as it has been defined by the critics is not possible, if it will
prove impossible to forge unity out of diversity and tension, then the
term Postmodernism will have to be further defined for each of the
competing contenders for the title. Alternatively, one particular use
of the term might be declared "official," in which case the other postmodernisms will need to be relabeled.

The pluralism of my strategy will necessarily extend itself to
the discussion of the relations between Postmodernism and Modernism, including the Avant-garde of the modern period: Dada, Surrealism and other movements. I will of course not be relating the
postmodern views to any single concept of Modernism; Modernism
may not be as unstable a concept as Postmodernism, but it would be
optimistic to say that any characterization of Modernism is widely
accepted. Rather, I will follow the critics that I will be discussing in
their understanding of the concept.

A final word, then, on my choice of material. I have mostly restricted myself to those critical sources that actually made use of
the term postmodern of postmodernist, either with or without a hyphen, with capitals or without capitals (or even with hyphen and
capitals, as in the extreme case of Post-Modern). If it seemed to me
obvious that a writer was referring by another term to what was
generally labeled as postmodern, however, I have not hesitated to
include him. An example would be Federman's discussions of what
he calls "Surfiction," a type of fiction that is subsumed under Postmodernist writing by practically all critics exploring the postmodern fields.

1. A Historical Survey: 1934 to the mid-1970s

1.1. The Term "Postmodern" from 1934 to 1964

The earliest uses of the term are traded by Michael Köhler, in the article already mentioned (Köhler 1977). He discusses Frederico de Oníz' "postmodernismo" (1934), Dudley Fitts's "post-Modern" (1942) and Arnold Toynbee's "Post-Modern" (1947). Köhler's discussion makes clear that these early manifestations of the term are not relevant to my purposes and I will pay no further attention to them. He then goes on to discuss Charles Olson, who repeatedly used the term, without, however, ever arriving at a clear definition: "Als Lyriker und Essayisten scheint es Olson vor allem auf die Suggestivät des Wortes angekommen zu sein. Obwohl es zwischen 1950 und 1958 zu seinem ständigen Wortschatz gehörte, hat er es nie für sich definiert" (Köhler 1977, 11). According to Köhler, Olson's use of the term is similar to that of Toynebee's, and indicates a new episteme—to use Foucault's term—in the history of Western culture, beginning around 1875. If this summed up Olson's position, his use of the term would be of little interest, since it would cast too wide a net for any practical purpose such as distinguishing between Modernism and Postmodernism.

However, Köhler misses an earlier usage term, which may well put Olson's views in a different light. According to Jerome Mazzaro, the American poet Randall Jarrell used "postmodern" in 1946 in his review of Robert Lowell's *Lord Weary's Castle*" "to characterize the movement of which Lowell's verse was a part." Two years later, another American poet, John Berryman, picked up the term, "citing Jarrell as its source." Mazzaro argues that, although there at first sight seems to be a good deal of difference between Olson's and Jarrell's Postmodernism, they may well be in line with each other:

> Joseph N. Riddel's *The Inverted Bell* (1974), which treats the "counterpoetics" of William Carlos Williams in the context of Olson's statement, persuades me that Olson's position as interpreted along the lines of Heidegger as explained by certain French structuralists is not markedly different from what I perceive as Jarrell's meaning. Without the technical language of the structuralists, the formulation of the essential differences between "modernism" and "postmodernism" becomes: in conceiving of language as a fall from unity, modernism seeks to restore the original state often by proposing silence or the de-

struction of language; postmodernism accepts the division and uses language and self-definition . . . as the basis of identity. Modernism tends, as a consequence, to be more mystical in the traditional senses of that word whereas postmodernism, for all its seeming mysticism, is irrevocably worldly and social (Mazzaro 1980, viii).

This interpretation of Olson's Postmodernism is supported by others, for instance Allen and Butterick in their anthology *The Postmoderns: The New American Poetry Revised,* where they honor Olson's pioneering effort and make clear that Olson's Postmodernism rebelled against a formalist Modernism:

> The selections begin with Charles Olson, whose essay "Projective Verse" rallied and focused the energies of the new poetry while forwarding the line of Pound and Williams. He was among the first to see the larger consequences of that poetry, and indeed was the first, in his essays and letters, to use the term "postmodern" in its present significance (Allen and Butterick 1982, 10).

Since in the absence of any attempt at definition on his part Olson's Post-modernism is capable of being interpreted in different ways, I will not, at this point, offer a premature discussion of a Postmodernism that might, I think, be legitimately linked to his poetical practice and to the theoretical writings in which he employs the term. Instead I will refer back to Olson in my discussion of the Postmodernism proposed by such critics as William Spanos and Richard Palmer who, like Mazzaro, envisage a Postmodernism that has strong links with Heidegger's brand of existential philosophy.

Whereas Olson's use of the term "postmodernism"—or at least Mazzaro's and Allen and Butterick's interpretation of that use—is easily identifiable with one of its current "meanings," the views of Irving Howe and Harry Levin on Postmodernism have become decidedly dated; their designation of the term would seem to have survived itself. Still, a closer look at especially Howe's concept of the Postmodern is rewarding, because he gives a detailed description of important social and attitudinal changes, of a new spirit that will later for other critics become an early indication of the shift toward what they conceive to be postmodern views. Even though those later critics fit the new attitudes and the changed social climate of the American 1950s into a different scheme of things, and offer a far more positive evaluation of this shift, they agree on the importance of the large-scale cultural changes that Howe finds in the 1950s.

For Howe and Levin, writing respectively in 1959 and 1960, Postmodernism is essentially a phenomenon of the American 1950s. Both see it as a falling off from Modernism. For Levin the "postmodern" is an "anti-intellectual current" which is resurfacing. For Howe it is that, too, as in the writings of the San Francisco writers, but it is more than that: Howe's Postmodernism includes such writers as Malamud, Mailer and Bellow. For Howe, postwar American society has in the affluence of the fifties become amorphous; he sees an erosion of traditional centers of authority, a neglect or debasement of traditional ceremonies, a widely shared passivity, a loss of strong beliefs, of "causes." As a result, characters in what he terms postmodern novels tend to lack social definition, they too have become amorphous and are basically adrift in a world from which the connections established by tradition and authority have disappeared: "In their distance from fixed social categories and their concern with metaphysical implications of the distance, these novels constitute what I would call 'postmodern' fiction" (Howe 1959, 433). Modernist authors still "tended to assume that the social relations of men in the world of capitalism were established, familiar, knowable" (Howe, 1959, 423), but for Howe's postmodern authors "It was as if our guidelines of both our social thought and literary conventions were being erased" (Howe, 1959, 428). The postmodern writer must do without heroes and without heroic conflicts; he can only fictionalize the "malaise" of the "increasingly shapeless" world he lives in and of his "increasingly fluid" experience.

Although Howe's Postmodernist canon would hardly find any supporters today, his Postmodernism is important in its early recognition of the role that epistemological and ontological doubt would be playing in postwar American literature, especially in the literature called postmodern by other, later critics.

To round off this first section of my survey, in a total contrast to Howe's views, William Van O'Connor developed the opposite view of Postmodernism in his *The New University Wits and the End of Modernism,* published in 1963. O'Connor, who concentrates on British "postmodernism," which includes for him such writers as Philip Larkin, John Wain, Iris Murdoch and Kingsley Amis, claims for his variety of Postmodernism that it moves away from what he sees as Modernist forms of alienation. On the contrary, his Postmodernists are solidly rooted in experience, concerned as they are with "ordinary public life and the affairs of responsible people." O'Connor's Postmodernism has today only historical interest; his implied definition of the term has not survived into the present.

1.2. Postmodernism and the American Counterculture:
      the Mid-Sixties.

Around the mid-sixties the American critic Leslie Fiedler set himself to argue that the apparent breakdown of traditional values that
Irving Howe had described some years earlier should be seen positively rather than negatively. For Fiedler Postmodernism signifies a
total break with the elitism of the Modernist writers. It looks
ahead, is oriented toward the future and is scarcely, if at all, interested in the great Modernist past (Fiedler 1965). As Köhler puts
it, "Man empfand die Gegenwart nun nicht mehr als Antiklimax
eines zu Ende gegangener heroische Zeitalters, sondern als
vielversprechen-den Neubeginn" (Köhler 1977, 12). Fiedler, who
was joined by another American critic, Susan Sontag, found in Postmodernism a "new sensibility" (Sontag's term), a new spontaneity
identified with the American counterculture of the 1960s. In "Cross
the Border—Close the Gap: Postmodernism," published in 1975, but
written much earlier, Fiedler explored further his own brand of
Postmodernism, which tended heavily toward pop art. Bradbury
sees in Fiedler's and Sontag's definition of Postmodernism a "new
post-humanist consciousness" (Bradbury 1983, 323) that rebels
against traditional "humanist" concepts of the nature and function
of art. As Gerald Graff puts it, "Sontag and Fiedler suggest that the
entire artistic tradition of the West has been exposed as a kind of
hyperrational imperialism akin to the aggression and lust for conquest of bourgeois capitalism" (Graff 1979, 31). For Fielder—who
obviously sympathizes with his Postmodernism—the new sensibility derides the pretensions of especially Modernist art; the postmodern novel will draw upon the Western, upon science fiction,
upon pornography, upon other genres considered to be sub-literary,
and it will close the gap between elite and mass culture. It will essentially be a pop-novel, "anti-artistic" and "anti-serious." Furthermore, in its anti-Modernist, anti-intellectual orientation, it will
create new myths—although not the authoritative Modernist
myths—, it will create "a certain rude magic in its authentic context," it will contribute to a magical tribalization in an age dominated by machines, making "a thousand little Wests in the
interstices of a machine civilization" (Fiedler 1975, 365).
    Fiedler's anti-Modernism is shared by Sontag, who is as averse
to "meanings" as he is. As she puts it in "Against Interpretation," "It
doesn't matter whether artists intend, or don't intend, for their

works to be interpreted . . . the merit of these works lies elsewhere than in their 'meanings' " (Sontag 1966, 19). What we have in Sontag is a plea for sensuousness—"In place of a hermeneutics of art we need an erotics of art" (Sontag 1966, 23)—and an extreme formalism: "What matters in *Marienbad* is the pure, untranslatable, sensuous immediacy of some of its images, and its rigorous if narrow solutions to certain problems of cinematic form" (Sontag 1966, 19). For Sontag, then, Postmodernism is characterized by "a flight from interpretation," and that aversion against interpretation gives rise to certain parodic, abstract, or decorative forms, all defying interpretation. Postmodern art may even become "non-art" in order to resist interpretation, and it is this avowed aversion that constitutes a definite break with Modernist art that invited, if not begged interpretation. Postmodern art simply *is* and must be experienced. Modernist art refers to a meaning hidden behind its surface, and must be *understood*. Postmodern art presents itself as surface. Modernist art claims depth behind that surface. We have in Sontag and, although more implicitly, also in Fiedler, a shift toward a far more phenomenal approach of the work of art then the Modernist code, with its insistence on layering and hidden meanings, permitted. The attitude that they identify with Postmodernism is perhaps best described as celebratory—a celebration of immediate, not intellectualized experience. Obviously there are links with the Postmodernism I have tentatively associated with Olson—to whom I will return later—and with later theories on the role that "performance" plays in postmodern art.

Finally, Sontag introduces another characteristic of postmodern art that will later, especially through Ihab Hassan, gain wide acceptance (to be sure, Hassan's approach of that characteristic is slightly different, but similar enough to be mentioned here). In Richard Wasson's words, Sontag claims that "the new art extends its medium and means into the world of science and technology, into the popular, and does away with old distinctions" (Wasson 1974, 1190). He goes on to quote Sontag herself: "From the vantage point of this new sensibility, the beauty of a machine or of the solution to a mathematical problem, of a painting by Jasper Johns, of a film by Jean-Luc Godard, and the personalities and music of the Beatles is equally accessible." This "unitary sensibility," as Sontag calls it, has obvious affinities with what Hassan will later term "immanence." It is totally committed to eclecticism, ranges far and wide across the cultural and scientific landscapes of the twentieth century and recognizes no barriers. As Jürgen Peper puts it in his excellent discussion of Sontag's concept, "Art, science, and 'technology of behavior' merge." Peper's slightly hostile discussion—"at the same time, this unitary sensibility reveals, in a disturbing way, something of Marcuse's 'one-dimensionality' and Pynchon's 'entropy' " (Peper 1977, 65)—is also recommendable for his discussion of the influence of Marshall McLuhan on Sontag's concept.

In his openly hostile analysis of Fiedler, Sontag and the Postmodernism of the American counterculture, Gerald Graff sees not much more than a worshipping of energy at the basis of this particular view of Postmodernism: "a celebration of *energy*—the vitalism of a world that cannot be understood or controlled." Graff finds this same energy in "the poetry of the Beats, the 'Projective' poets, and other poetic continuators of the nativist line of Whitman, Williams and Pound, in the short-lived vogue of the Living Theatre, happenings, and pop art, and in a variety of artistic and also musical experiments with randomness and dissonance" (Graff 1979, 58). Graff's inclusion of the "Projective" poets—whose main spokesman was of course Charles Olson—suggests again the, in my view incontestable link between Fiedler's and Sontag's vitalistic Postmodernism oriented toward an immediacy of experience, and the Postmodernism of Olson and such later critics as William Spanos and Richard Palmer. Graff also suggests the link with the "performative" mode in Postmodernism, a link that I noted above. That "performative" mode—a term not yet current in the mid-sixties—for some critics not only includes as one might suppose, theatrical performances such as those of the Living Theatre, but also that anti-interpretive, playful strain in the fiction of the counterculture that one finds for instance in the novels of Richard Brautigan, and the performing voices one finds in the novels of Raymond Federman and Ronald Sukenick, the so-called "Surfictionists." Again, a fuller discussion will have to wait until later.

According to Graff, this supposedly anti-intellectual and hedonistic Post-modernism refuses "to take art 'seriously' in the old sense," it uses art against its own pretensions, it is boastful of its own vulnerability, it rejects analysis and interpretive criticism—because analysis and interpretation tend to reduce art to abstractions and thereby neutralize its "potentially liberating energies"—and its reflects, finally, "a less soberly rationalistic mode of consciousness, one that is more congenial to myth, tribal ritual, and visionary experience, grounded in a 'protean,' fluid, and undifferentiated concept of the self as opposed to the repressed Western ego" (Graff 1979, 31–32).

Earlier, Richard Wasson had analyzed the Postmodernism of the mid-sixties along the same lines. He sees a number of influences converging toward an ideological justification of the countercultural characteristics summed up by Graff. Important in that justification are Norman O. Brown's and Herbert Marcuse's revisions of Freudian psychology and Northrop Frye's insistence on the erotic function of art. In different ways, Brown and Marcuse both attack what they see as Freud's repressive and finally alienating acceptance of the present reality system as final. For them, an "important counter system is provided by imaginative culture, for these works are closely associated with the wishes and fears of Eros . . . For Marcuse works of art constitute an order of sensuousness that stands against our irrational reality. For Brown, culture, art, is absolutely hostile to the reality principle and to reason which is enslaved to the reality principle." For Brown and Marcuse, "art provides the assurance that Eros, that the pleasure principle, can find its way into the world without terrifying destruction and chaos" (Wasson 1974, 1200). From a completely different angle, Northrop Frye joins this cry for a liberation of Eros: "Eros is the main spokesman for the more abundant life that the social structure fears and resists" (quoted in Wasson 1974, 1198), and for him, too, Eros works in liberating ways primarily through art.

In short, Wasson's analysis attempts to show how the Postmodernism identified by Fiedler and Sontag with the American counterculture was part of a larger context of revolutionary cries for liberation from the constraints—intellectual, social and sexual—of the 1950s.

To return to Graff, his analysis of the development of this Postmodernism complements Wasson's. Graff, following Howe, claims that the "social context of postmodernist fiction" is the alienated middle class of the 1950s. He sees at the basis of Postmodernism a deep cultural crisis, in fact an ontological crisis that undercuts meaning and significance: "The loss of significant external reality, its displacement by myth-making, the domestication and normalization of alienation—these conditions constitute a common point of departure for the writing of our period" (Graff 1979, 62). In spite of this, Graff does not consider Postmodernism to be a radical new departure. On the contrary, he argues that Postmodernism is nothing more than a completion of the Modernist revolt against "traditional realism," a revolt left uncompleted by Modernism itself:

> modern fiction, except in a few instances, did not actually effect the total subjectivization and privatization of human experience called for by modernist theories which defined literature as an expression of inward "consciousness" set over

against the rational discourse of the public, objective world. By contrast, postmodern fiction tends to carry the logic of such modernist theories to their limit . . . (Graff 1979, 208).

In fact, Graff sees Postmodernism—both of the mid-sixties variety and of the self-reflective, metafictional strain that was to develop later in the U.S.—as a logical development out of the premises of Romanticism; he sees an unbroken line from Romantic concepts of art and the artist to Postmodernist views of art and its creators.

To summarize, in the mid-sixties Fiedler and Sontag attempted to define a Postmodernism that had, for them, close ties with the fastest emerging American counterculture and its predecessors, such as the "Projective" and Beat poets. That Postmodernism is anti-interpretive, even anti-intellectual and vitalist; it emphasizes performance and form over meaning and content; it seeks to deflate Modernist pretensions as meaningfulness and seriousness; it seeks to liberate the erotic potential of art and to erase the barriers between high art and low art; it moves toward a total acceptance of the world, including the products of the machine age, and it sometimes moves toward mysticism, a fusion of self and world. Its implicit ideology is reflected in the contemporary writings of Norman O. Brown, Herbert Marcuse, Marshall McLuhan (important for his emphasis on globalization and the role of the media) and in Frye's erotic functioning of art. Other influences are Buckminster Fuller, the ecological and transcendent science fiction of Ursula LeGuin, and the magical world of Carlos Castaneda. It is seen by its practitioners and by its early critics such as Fiedler and Sontag as a radical departure from Modernism, with a value system all its own. However, later critics tend to see continuing links with Modernism (Graff) or with the Avant-garde of the modern period (Hassan and others).

1.3   Postmodernism as an Intellectual Revolt against Modernism

In 1969, Richard Wasson identified a Postmodernism (although he does not use the term) that shares the revolt against Modernism and Modernist assumptions with the Postmodernism of the counterculture, but is far more intellectual and also international, not specifically American.

Wasson traces this type of Postmodernism in four exemplary writers, Iris Murdoch, Alain Robbe-Grillet, John Barth and

Thomas Pynchon. What these writers have in common, despite
their significant differences, is a deep mistrust of Modernist aesthetics. According to Wasson, these writers "are skeptical of modernist notions of metaphor as a species of suprarational truth that
unifies paradoxical opposites and modernist conceptions of myth
which make it a principle of order for art and of discipline for the
subjective self" (Wasson 1969, 460). Consequently, they set out to
subvert metaphor and myth as subjective attempts at ordering, at
transcending the contingency and inaccessibility of the object
world. For them, the world outside the subject (nature, objects,
other people) must be restored in all its object-ness, to its total inaccessibility, and must cease to be part of the subjective consciousness of the writer as was the case in Modernism. The difference and
distance between subject and object must be accepted, not denied
through metaphorical or mythical means; unity of self and world is
an illusion. (It will be clear that Wasson's concept differs here from
the mid-sixties concept, in which such a unity of self and world is
often one of the explicit or implicit aims.) Wasson's article draws the
question of Postmodernism firmly within a philosophical context.
For him, the postmodern is characterized by a radical ontological
doubt, so radical that even Sartre's existentialism is rejected by, for
instance, Robbe-Grillet, who sees in Sartre a hidden complicity between subject and object because in both Sartre's and Camus' fictions the outer world is "always appropriated to the subjectivity of
the hero and the author" (Wasson 1969, 463–64).

Whereas in Fiedler's Postmodernism we find a largely instinc-
tive revolt against the premises of Modernism, in Wasson's concept
we find an intellectual, philosophical revolt. The epistemological basis of Modernist aesthetics is seen as radically unsound, in fact nonexistent, and instead of Modernism's belief in unity, no matter how
hard won, Wasson's Postmodernists believe in a literature that denies unity, that replaces a world that offers ontological anchors, so-
called higher discourses, with "a world of contingency, a world in
which man is free to cope spontaneously with experience" (Wasson
1969, 475–76).

This leaves two qualifying remarks to be made. Firstly, Wasson's man who is "free to cope spontaneously with experience" reminds one of the insistence on spontaneity and immediate
experience of the counterculture. However, within Wasson's scheme
of things a new magic, a new mythology, a transcendence of the gap
between self and world is impossible. Secondly, Wasson, too, sees in
this radical doubt a continuation of Modernist doubts about the self
and about the "meanings" of history: "It would not be difficult to
make a case that the work of these writers really constitutes an-

other manifestation of the modernist rejection of romantic notions of personality and history" (Wasson 1969, 476). Like Graff, Wasson sees in his variety of Postmodernism a radicalization of the doubts that beset Modernism, but were largely kept under control by the Modernist writers.

1.4. Existentialist Postmodernism

Between 1972 and 1976 William Spanos developed a view of Postmodernism that, at least in its claims, differed significantly from earlier postmodernisms. As we will see, however, Spanos' original contribution has affinities with both the concept of Postmodernism related to the counterculture and Wasson's concept of radical epistemological doubt.

Spanos identifies a "variety of 'post-modern' modes of writing"—including Olson's poetry, Fiedler's pop art and Wasson's *nouveau roman*—but goes on to reject them, as "extensions of early iconic modernism," in favor of a truly Postmodernist form of writing:

> I am referring, for example, to the structuralist criticism of Roland Barthes, the phenomenological criticism of Georges Poulet and Jean-Pierre Richard, and the neo-imagism of Marshall McLuhan: the "field poetry" of Charles Olson and the concrete poetry of Pierre Garnier, Ferdinand Kriwet and Franz Mon; the *nouveau roman* of Robbe-Grillet and Michel Butor; the "Happenings" of Allen Kaprow and Claes Oldenburg: and the Pop Art literature advocated by critics such as Leslie Fiedler . . . they are all oriented beyond history or, rather, they all aspire to the spatialization of time. As a result the existential sources of the primary thrust of the postmodern literary imagination have been obscured, thus jeopardizing the . . . post-World War II impulse . . . to engage literature in an ontological dialogue with the world in behalf of the recovery of the authentic historicity of modern man (Spanos 1972, 165–66).

For Spanos, Modernist literature is iconic, indulges in a "religioaesthetic withdrawal from existential time into the eternal simultaneity of essential art" (Spanos 1972, 158), and only *that* literature deserves the name Post-modernist that accepts contingent historicity from an existential point of view. Such a Postmodernist literature refuses "to fulfill causally oriented expectations, to create fictions . . . with beginnings, middles, and ends" (Spanos 1972, 148);

it subverts plot, it disintegrates and atomizes, it attempts "to
dislodge the tranquillized individual from the 'at-home of public-
ness,' from the domesticated, the scientifically charted and organized familiarity of the totalized world . . ." (Spanos 1972, 155). The
"paradigmatic archetype of the postmodern literary imagination is
the anti-detective story" (Spanos 1972, 154), because it violently
frustrates the reader's expectations, refusing to solve the crime and
refusing to offer a totalized world of order and patterning. (The
notion of a postmodern anti-detective story was discussed before
Spanos by Michael Holquist in his "Whodunit and Other Questions"
(Holquist 1971).)

For Spanos, following Wasson's and Hassan's example—more
about Hassan later—Postmodernism is not a strictly American or
British enterprise, but a truly international movement. Its major
formative influence is European existentialism, primarily the existentialism of Heidegger, and a good many of its major practitioners
are Europeans: Sartre, Beckett, Ionesco, Genet, Frisch, Sarraute
and others. Spanos discusses the existential sources of his Postmodernism extensively in a later article, significantly titled "Heidegger,
Kierkegaard, and the Hermeneutic Circle: Towards a Postmodern
Theory of Interpretation as Disclosure" (Spanos 1976). As appears
from the "interpretation as disclosure" in his title, Spanos asserts
that something can be salvaged from the total ontological doubt
that he demands from postmodern literature—a claim that he already formulated in the lengthy passage I quoted from his earlier
article, where he defines as Postmodernist the impulse "to engage
literature in an ontological dialogue with the world in behalf of the
recovery of the authentic historicity of modern man" (Spanos 1972,
166). The postmodern literature that he defines is not playful or
performative, it is not erotically liberating, nor does it offer any new
myths; on the contrary, it is committed to truthfulness, to disclosing
the historicity of man and the contingency of history.

This emphasis on history explains, in my view, why Spanos excludes for instance Roland Barthes and the *nouveau roman* from his
postmodern canon. No doubt, Barthes's structuralism and later
poststructuralism and Robbe-Grillet's insistence on the purely linguistic nature of his fictions strike Spanos as purely formalistic and
aestheticizing evasions of the historical world, evasions of the "historicity of man" that is central in his concept. The self-referentiality
of language espoused by Barthes and Robbe-Grillet must appear to
him as a willful withdrawal from the world of concrete existence.
Even so, his accusation that both Barthes and Robbe-Grillet extend
iconic Modernism is unacceptable since neither would claim an

iconic function for his writings or believe that writing could serve such a function.

The movement toward a Heideggerian ontology is much clearer in another critic with existentialist leanings, Richard Palmer. Palmer attacks Modernism along Spanos' lines, but his view of Postmodernism (or a future Postmodernism) is far less modest than Spanos's. He offers a number of tentative "postmodern modalities of consciousness," of which I will give a few examples, Time may be "round and whole—an essential dimension of being," it may unify past and present, thus adding "depth to a now that always is." Space may become "multiperspectival," "a field with several variables." "Postmodern man may again situate himself in relation to larger forces and meaning," etc. For Palmer, too, an acceptance of contingency, of fragmentation and of historicity is necessary for a postmodern understanding of the world. Yet, more openly than Spanos, Palmer moves in the direction of a new ontology: "Language might become a medium of ontological disclosure in which things take on being through words," and, "In postmodern thinking, truth might transcend the merely pragmatic dimension; it might become the loyal articulation, in language, of what *is*..." (Palmer 1977, 27–29). I emphasize this, because this faith in the ontological possibilities of language is a far cry from other, poststructuralist, views of Postmodernism which declare all attempts to turn any language into an instrument of positive knowledge utterly futile. Palmer might object that his (and Spanos') ontology is not ontology in the traditional sense, but incorporates contingency and historicity. This may be so, but if it isn't, how to explain the utopian hopes he entertains of the interpretive potential of his variety of Postmodernism?

> Perhaps a postmodern hermeneutics of performance will locate the event of interpretive mediation in a place quite different from that it has occupied during the modern epoch. Perhaps it may even restore to the interpreter his ancient shamanic-hermeneutical powers to reveal the hidden, to transform the understanding, even to heal the soul (Palmer 1977, 30–31).

As will already have appeared from my choice of quotations, Palmer sees Postmodernism not as a strictly literary movement. In fact, he claims not to be talking about a movement at all, but about "something closer to an archeological shift in the presuppositions of our thinking ... the issue is the metaphysical basis of our seeing"

(Palmer 1977, 21). Palmer's scope is significantly wider than Spanos's, for he includes in his episteme the American counterculture,
"the growing ecological consciousness and the revival of the mythic,
the occult, the oriental," so that his view of Postmodernism finally
has a good deal in common with that of Leslie Fiedler, in spite of his
existential basis. For Palmer, Postmodernism would seem to signify
a new episteme that has incorporated *and* transcended the total ontological doubt engendered by traditional, rational Western philosophy, and the escape out of the pitfall of Western rationalism—
leading to a totally reductive, essentially nihilistic and exploitative
view of the world—is made possible by Heidegger's existentialism.

To return to William Spanos, in spite of his classification of Olson's "field poetry" as another extension of "iconic modernism," I believe that Wallace Martin is right when he claims a direct link
between Spanos' and Palmer's concepts of Postmodernism and Olson's Postmodernism, however ill-defined: "another postmodernism
emerged from the oral poetry of Olson, Creeley, David Antin, and
Jerome Rothenberg. As represented by William Spanos, it signaled
the end of logocentric metaphysics and the rebirth of the spoken
word as conceived by Heidegger" (Martin 1980, 144).

This position, admittedly more outspoken in Palmer than in
Spanos, who is more cautious with regard to the possibilities of the
spoken word, seems part of a tendency that Charles Russell sees in
contemporary literature: "Much of contemporary literature and
thought expresses this desire for a gnostic state of consciousness, a
mystic union of self and world . . ." (Russell 1974, 356). Such a move
towards a postmodern mysticism is also evident in the Postmodernism of the counterculture, which Spanos classifies as Modernist,
too. The question arises why he would exclude both Olson and the
counterculture from his postmodern gallery, when others see such
obvious similarities between the respective concepts.

If I may venture an answer, it seems to me that Spanos would
argue that Olson's faith in the regenerative possibilities of the spoken word is, in a sense, not earned, and that the same holds for the
counterculture. They have not paid their existential dues: they
move blithely and instinctively toward that union of self and world,
blissfully unaware of the total contingency of life, ignoring, in their
desire for "the rebirth of the spoken word," the historicity of man. It
seems to me that for Spanos Olson and the counterculture are thoroughly a-historical and that they are thereby guilty of existential
mauvaise foi.

Still, in spite of this important difference, which may well boil
down to a difference in approach—intellectual versus intuitive—I

would argue that Spanos' existential Postmodernism may well accommodate that of Olson and, by extension, the concept as it is often used in American poetry criticism. Although not all poets subsumed under the label "postmodern" by, for instance, Charles Altieri, Donald Allen and George Butterick, or Jerome Mazzaro, believe in the powers of the Word, they do broadly share an existentialist bias, suspicious as they are of all higher discourse and of the authority of formalisms. Allen and Butterick define Olson's Postmodernism as "ultimately, an instant-by-instant engagement with reality" (Allen and Butterick 1982, 11) and see the Black Mountain poets, the Beats, and the poets of the New York School as essentially following Olson's example, sometimes with mystical purposes, sometimes not. For them, poetic Postmodernism is "marked by an acceptance of the primordial, of spiritual and sexual necessities, of myth, the latest understandings of science, chance and change, wit and dream" (Allen and Butterick 1982, 12), in short, by an all-embracing acceptance of the here-and-now, an acceptance that is often characterized by a certain reverence, a certain awe that makes some of them even "preliterate, prerational."

Charles Altieri would seem to mediate between Spanos' existential historicity and the mysticism associated with the counterculture: "postmodern poets have been seeking to uncover the ways in which man and nature are unified, so that value can be seen as the result of immanent processes in which man is as much an object as he is agent of creativity . . ." (Altieri 1973, 608). Altieri comes close to the counterculture: "God for the contemporaries manifests itself as energy, as the intense expression of immanent power"; however, his postmodern unification of "man and nature" is not transcendent in the traditional sense of the word, self and object seek unity in the concrete world, not in transcendent metaphysics: "the postmoderns seek to have the universal concretized, they see the particular as numinous, not as representative" (Altieri 1973, 610–611).

Finally, for Mazzaro, postmodern poetry, "for all its seeming mysticism, is irrevocably wordly and social" (Mazzaro 1980, viii), whereas the Modernists tended to be more mythical and impersonal. Mazzaro's Postmodernism includes such poets as Auden, Jarrell, Lowell, Roethke, Berryman and Bishop and apparently excludes those who couple an existentialism with a mystical belief in the "rebirth of the spoken word," such as the Beat poets. Although Mazzaro does not mention Spanos, he brings my discussion back to Spanos' existentialism, stressing how his postmodern poets try to cope with contingent, immediate experience. Yet, although

Mazzaro mentions Heidegger in his introduction, he does not place his Postmodernism in the context of Spanos' attack on Western rationalistic logocentrism. As a result, his postmodern canon is a loose gathering of poets as different as Auden, Berryman and Bishop, who all in their own ways engage the real world in a far more direct, more personal, more committed way than did the Modernist poets.

2.   Toward a Synthesis: from Postmodernisms to Postmodernism

Whereas the concepts of Postmodernism that I have discussed so far tended to isolate certain tendencies and cultural strains in the 1950s and 1960s in order to label them "postmodern," in the 1970s Postmodernism became more and more an inclusive term that gathered to itself all literary and cultural phenomena that could not be classified as either Realist or Modernist. As Köhler could say, in 1977:

> Despite persisting controversies as to what constitutes the characteristic traits of the new area, the term "postmodern" is now generally applied to all cultural phenomena which have emerged since the second World War and are indicative of a change in sensibility and attitude, making the present an age "post the Modern" (Köhler 1977, 8).

Köhler quotes the American art critic John Perreault to the same effect:

> I was forced to use the term post-modern in the Mid-sixties because I wished to discuss art works of all kinds that did not seem to fit within the rules of modernism in art . . . Postmodernism is not a particular style but a cluster of attempts to go beyond modernism. In some cases this means a "revival" of art styles "wiped out" by modernism. In others it means anti-object art or what have you (Köhler 1977, 13).

Although Fiedler's concept of Postmodernism was already fairly inclusive, Postmodernism's real inclusiveness starts with Ihab Hassan's writings on the question of Postmodernism, in particular with his early book *The Dismemberment of Orpheus: Toward a Postmodernist Literature,* in 1971. (Hassan had already published on the emerging phenomenon in 1964 and 1969, but I take his book as my starting-point because with his book Hassan began to permanently influence the debate on Postmodernism.)

I will in this second part of my survey first offer a discussion of Hassan's concept of Postmodernism; then I will briefly mention some other inclusive views, such as those of Matei Calinescu and the French critic Jean-François Lyotard.

2.1. The Postmodernism of Ihab Hassan: the Emerging of a New Episteme

Ihab Hassan is undoubtedly the most prolific of all critics involved in the debate on Postmodernism and it is impossible to trace the development of his concept of Postmodernism—through four books and numerous articles, published over a period of fifteen years—within the scope of this survey. I will, however, try to indicate how Hassan's Postmodernism has become more and more inclusive until it reached the point where it turned into a full-fledged episteme.

In his early writings on the subjects, Hassan sees Postmodernism primarily as an antiformal, anarchic, decreative, antinomian impulse, inspired by a "will to unmaking." This concept is, as Matei Calinescu has pointed out, close to Continental conceptions of the Avant-garde, and Hassan's preliminary postmodern canon supports this view: in *The Dismemberment of Orpheus* he finds the postmodern impulse in the de Sade, in Blake, in 'Pataphysics, in Dada, in Surrealism, in what he calls Aliterature, in Jean Genet, to mention some examples. In his list of examples Dada and Surrealism occupy a central position. (I must say at this point that I see this avant-gardist concept of Postmodernism as more important in his early work than his more existential concept which is also present in *The Dismemberment of Orpheus* and which includes existentialism as a movement and writers such as Hemingway and Beckett.) This postmodern impulse is an impulse in the direction of an art which negates itself (hence the will to unmaking). It signifies a movement toward silence, and manifests itself in "two accents of silence," which together constitute Postmodernism: "a) the negative echo of language, autodestructive, demonic, nihilistic; b) its positive stillness, self-transcendent, sacramental, plenary." As Hoffman *et al.* (1977) point out, Hassan emphasizes "the negative" in his concept at the expense of the "positive stillness," which, as it indicated by Hassan's language—"self-transcendent, sacramental," elsewhere he refers to the "holy refusal" of the Beat poets—may at this point of his career have had definite mystical overtones, the mysticism that Russell called "a gnostic state of consciousness." If not, his "positive stillness" is related to the numinous grace found in immediacy by for instance Charles Altieri.

What is important in Hassan's early concept is that it extends the scope of Postmodernism significantly. With Wasson (1969) he familiarized, if not actually introduced, the notion of an international Postmodernism, thus paving the way for later critics such as Spanos. Even more importantly, he shifted Postmodernism's historic demarcations, thus making it possible to see Postmodernism, or rather, his variety of Postmodernism as the full flowering of what had for a long time been an undercurrent in the history of Western culture. Although he would later retract some of his more ambitious claims and, for instance, focus on James Joyce's *Finnegans Wake* as the first truly postmodern literary work, his historical perspective and his typological approach have decisively influenced later discussions.

As I have already noted, Hassan's later concept of Postmodernism is far more inclusive. As he himself notes, in 1980, "We cannot simply rest—as I sometimes have done—on the assumption that postmodernism is antiformal, anarchic, or decreative; for though it is all of these . . . it also contains the need to discover a 'unitary sensibility' (Sontag), to 'cross the border and close the gap' (Fiedler), and to attain, as I have suggested, a neo-gnostic immediacy of mind" (Hassan 1980b, 121).

However, by 1980 Hassan had incorporated a good deal more into his Postmodernism, turning it to a full-fledged episteme. In the article from which I just quoted he draws for his description of Postmodernism on such contemporary writers and thinkers as Lévi-Strauss, Robbe-Grillet, Lacan, Derrida, Foucault, Deleuze, Barthes, de Man, Brown, Steiner, and others. From the past Nietzsche has begun to loom as a major formative influence—that is, the Nietzsche rediscovered by the French poststructuralists. In other words, Hassan has by 1980 drawn a good deal of structuralist and poststructuralist thinking within his postmodern circle. In the field of literature he has appropriated the non-fiction novel, the American New Journalism, the genres of fantasy and science fiction, and the self-reflexive, metafictional novel to his concept. From France he has added the *nouveau roman* and "the linguistic novel of *Tel Quel*." He has even extended his Postmodernism into the field of criticism, offering his own paracriticsm, a postmodern form of criticism that attempts "to recover the art of multivocation" (Hassan 1975, 25).

This art of multivocation makes it difficult to summarize Hassan's position on Postmodernism. True enough, his work is quite suggestive, as may appear from the following "table that hints at certain characteristics of postmodern," all of which are set off against Modernist characteristics pointing in the opposite direction: "Paraphysics/Dadaism; Antiform (disjunctive, open); Play; Chance; Anarchy; Exhaustion/Silence; Process/Performance; Happening; Participation; Decreation/Deconstruction/Antithesis; Absence; Dispersal; Text/Intertext; Syntagm; Parataxis; Mctonymy; Combination; Rhizome/Surface; Against Interpretation/Misreading; Signifier; *Scriptible* (Writerly); Anti-narrative; The Holy Ghost; Desire; Polymorphous/Androgynous; Schizophrenia; Difference-Differance/Trace; Irony; Indeterminacy; Immanence" (Hassan 1980b, 123). As I said, this list is endlessly suggestive, but it is virtually impossible to point to a stable, well-defined center. As Hoffmann already noted in 1977, Hassan's " 'meanings' of 'silence' and his list of postmodernist writers are almost impossible to reduce to a common denominator" (Hoffmann *et al.* 1977, 34); since then, Hassan's concept has not become any simpler to define.

In a very general way, most of Hassan's postmodern features—and perhaps all of them—are related to Deconstructionism's concept of a decentered world. In other words, they are governed by a radical epistemological and ontological doubt. This is for Hassan Postmodernism's major difference with Modernism: "whereas Modernism—excepting Dada and Surrealism—created its own forms of artistic Authority precisely because the center no longer held. Postmodernism has tended toward artistic Anarchy in deeper complicity with things falling apart—or has tended toward Pop" (Hassan 1975, 59). Whereas the Modernists sought to defend themselves against their own awareness of cosmic chaos, of the impossible fragility of any "center" they might perceive, the Postmodernists have accepted chaos and live in fact in a certain intimacy with it. This Postmodernist recognition of the final demise of all Authority, of all higher discourse, of all centers, leads to an acceptance of chaos and sometimes even to a mystical attunement with a chaotic universe as, for instance, in the cosmic mysticism purveyed by Norman O. Brown, who is included among Hassan's Postmodernists.

This recognition of the final decentering leads to a postmodern world that is characterized by two main tendencies, "indeterminacy" and "immanence." Of these two poles indeterminacy stands primarily for the results of that decentering, of the total disappearance of ontology; immanence stands for the tendency of the human mind to appropriate all of reality to itself (this, too, is of course made possible by decentering). The absolute, irrevocable loss of ontological grounding—which Hassan sees as much in "Heisenberg's Principle of Uncertainty in Physics and Gödel's Proof of Incompleteness (or Indecidability) in all logical systems" as in poststructuralist philosophy, leads for Hassan to a proliferation of postmodern modes. Indeterminacy may lead to magical forms, to mysticism, to transcendentalism, to the cult of apocalyptism (all types of consciousness associated with the counterculture), or to the existential, to the post-existential, to a "dehumanization," to a loss of ego, to ecologism, to fragmentation, to a new futurism, etc., etc. (Hassan 1975, 54–58), provided that these modes of consciousness are not seen as ontologically grounded. This radical indeterminacy may well break down traditional barriers in Western culture: "Religion and science, myth and technology, intuition and reason, popular and high culture, female and male archetypes . . . begin to modify and inform one another . . . lineaments of a new consciousness begin to emerge" (Hassan 1980a, 110). Since no intellectual or moral system, no way of perceiving reality can ultimately be legitimized (Lyotard's term), nothing can *ontologically* claim superiority over anything else and fruitful interchanges have become possible. As Hassan himself points out, indeterminacy is by no means an unequivocal term, it is a tendency towards a total pluralism that may easily accommodate mutually exclusive categories:

> the tendency is really compounded of sub-tendencies which the following words evoke: openness, heterodoxy, pluralism, eclecticism, randomness, revolt, deformation. The latter alone subsumes a dozen current terms of unmaking: decreation, disintegration, deconstruction, decenterment, displacement, difference, discontinuity . . . (Hassan 1983, 27–28).

At the other end of Hassan's Postmodernist spectrum stands the "second major tendency in the postmodern world." This tendency is called "Immanences, a term I employ without religious echo, and by which I mean the capacity of mind to generalize itself in the world, to act upon both self and world, and so become more and more, immediately, its own environment . . ." This tendency, earlier in Hassan's career also called Neo-Gnosticism, and "evoked by such sundry words as dispersal, diffusion, dissemination, diffraction, pulsion, integration, ecumenism, communication, interplay, interdependence, interpenetration, etc.—depends, above all, on the emergence of man as a language animal . . . a creature constituting himself, and increasingly his universe, by symbols of his own making" (Hassan 1983, 29).

In the absence of essences, of ontological centers, man creates himself and his world through a language that is, poststructurally, divorced from the world of objects. It is in the immanence that Hassan discerns a movement towards "the One," towards unification. Whereas indeterminacy leads to fragmentation, tribalization, immanence leads to globalization, through the more and more uniform language of the media—"the immanence of media now effects the dispersal of Logos" (Hassan 1980a, 110)—and through the language of science and technology. Clearly, the ghost of Marshall McLuhan hovers with satisfaction over Hassan's immanence, as does Sontag's unitary sensibility.

Hassan, then, has transformed the initially literary concept of Postmodernism into a cultural concept of vast ramifications— admittedly helped along by Fiedler, Sontag, and others—a concept that depends ultimately on the simultaneous manifestations, even on the interplay, of indeterminacy and immanence, or of "unmaking" and re-making, an unmaking of all authority, a re-making through a decentered language, a "new immanence of language" (Hassan 1980a, 97).

A final word on the origins of Hassan's Postmodernism. Although I have in my account heavily stressed the radical ontological doubt at its center, because that doubt seems to me the most important single constituting element, Hassan has also pointed to Irving Howe's analysis:

> Yet in the end, the epistemic factor proves to be only one of many. The force of the antinomian and indeterminate tendency derives from larger dispositions in society: a rising standard of living in the West, the disruptions of institutional values, freed desires, liberation movements of every kind, schism and secession around the globe, terrorism rampant— in short, the Many asserting their primacy over the One (Hassan 1983, 29).

It is not surprising that Hassan's inclusive postmodern episteme is able to accommodate a host of contemporary literary forms or modes, often kept strictly apart by earlier critics of Postmodernism. Postmodernism includes for Hassan the self-reflexive or metafictional novel, because it reflects the awareness that all language is self-referential, even if it phenomenologically follows its own creation. It includes the novel of linguistic or imagistic generators (the *nouveau roman* and the *Tel Quel* novel) for the same reason. It includes the nonfiction novel because it blurs the distinction between fact and fiction: facts, or at least their various interpretations, are forms of fiction, too. Indeterminacy liberates the imagination from old, outworn categories, and makes a revaluation of such sub-literary genres as fantasy and science-fiction possible. It leads to all sorts of performative modes of self-expression, as in the novels of the Surfictionists, in which reality is a product of the imagination (as it is in fantasy and science fiction.) It may also lead to artistic minimalism, or even towards silence. In other words, the wide range of possible aesthetic reactions to Hassan's indeterminacy leads to a proliferation of literary forms and modes that cannot easily be subsumed under one common denominator. Although Hassan's concept is attractive, because of its inclusiveness, this inclusiveness is, from the point of literary classification, also its major disadvantage. This is the obvious disadvantage of all epistemic concepts. I will therefore, after a short discussion of the other inclusive concepts, return to a more purely literary approach of Postmodernism.

2.2.   The Postmodern Episteme: Other Approaches

Having paid so much attention to Ihab Hassan's postmodern episteme, I will be a good deal briefer about the epistemes of Matei Calinescu and Jean-François Lyotard. This is not to suggest that their concepts of the postmodern episteme are less valuable than Hassan's. However, Hassan seems to me to have laid the foundations for the epistemic view of Postmodernism, and Calinescu's and Lyotard's concepts have a good deal in common with Hassan's.

     To begin with Lyotard, whose *La Condition postmoderne* (1979) is an important contribution to the debate on Postmodernism. (I will, for practical purposes, quote here from a more recent article, "Answering the Question: What Is Postmodernism" (1983), in which he succinctly attempts to answer the question put in the title.) First of all, for Lyotard, the postmodern condition is primarily characterized by a radical epistemological and ontological crisis. As Hassan puts it: "Lyotard's central theme is the desuetude of the 'great narratives' and 'metanarratives,' which organized bourgeois society. The radical crisis, then, is one of 'légitimation'—compare with Habermas's 'legitimation crisis' in *Legitimationsprobleme im Spätkapitalismus*—in every cognitive and social endeavor where a multitude of languages now reign" (Hassan 1983, 26). Let me also quote Hassan's "freely" paraphrased summary of Lyotard's "central theme":

> The postmodern condition is a stranger to disenchantment as to the blind positivity of delegitimation. Where can legitimacy reside after the dissolution of metanarratives? The criterion of functionality is merely technological: it cannot apply to judgments of truth and justice. The consensus obtained by discussion, as Habermas thinks? That criterion violates the heterogeneity of language games. And inventions are always made in dissent. Postmodern knowledge is not only the instrument of power. It refines our sensibilities, awakens them to differences, and strengthens our capacities to bear the incommensurable. It does not find its reason in the agreements or homologies of experts but in the paralogies of inventors.
>
> The open question, then, is this: can a legitimation of social relations, can a just society, be made practical in accordance with a paradox analogous to that of current scientific activity? And of what would such a paradox consist? (Hassan 1983, 26–27)

Before I offer Lyotard's answer to this question, let me point out how this postmodern "theme" differs from Modernist themes. For Lyotard, "modern aesthetics is an aesthetic of the sublime, though a nostalgic one. It allows the unpresentable to be put forward only as the missing contents; but the form, because of its recognizable consistency, continues to offer the reader or viewer matter for solace and pleasure" (Lyotard 1983, 340). I take this to mean that Modernism, although recognizing "the unpresentable," the absence of a center, at the core of things, still ultimately avoided a true confrontation with that absence in what amounted to intellectual cowardice. Postmodernism, which Lyotard sees as a continuation of the Modern, "would be that which, in the modern, puts forward the unpresentable in presentation itself..." (Lyotard 1983, 340). Postmodernist literature is then, for Lyotard, a literature of "unmaking," a literature devoted to exposing the unpresentable in its own *aporias,* and it is also a literature of performance, of "events";

> [the postmodern] puts forward the unpresentable in presentation itself . . . denies itself the solace of good forms, the consensus of a taste which would make it possible to share

collectively the nostalgia for the unattainable . . . searches for
new presentations, not in order to enjoy them but in order to
impart a stronger sense of the unpresentable. A postmodern
writer or artist is in the position of a philosopher: the text he
writes, the work he produces are not in principle governed by
pre-etablished rules, and they cannot be judged according to a
determining judgment, by applying familiar categories to the
text or to the work. Those rules and categories are what the
work of art itself is looking for. The artist and the writer, then,
are working without rules in order to formulate the rules of
what *will have been done*. Hence the fact that work and text
have the character of an *event;* hence also, they always come
too late for their author, or, what amounts to the same thing,
their being put into work, their realization (*mise en oevre*) always begins too soon (Lyotard 1983, 340–41).

Lyotard's insistence on an awareness of the "unpresentable" leads
him to a rejection of those forms of contemporary artistic expression—seen as Postmodernist by, for instance, Fiedler, Sontag, and
the later Hassan—that, like Modernism, avoid the consequences of
the demise of all higher discourse. For him, these so-called Postmodernist forms are no better adapted to our period than anti-modern
forms. Obviously, Lyotard has in mind the products of Sontag's unitary sensibility, of Fiedler's pop art, and of Hassan's tendency towards immanence:

Eclecticism is the degree zero of contemporary general culture: one listens to reggae, watches a western, eats McDon-
ald's food for lunch and local cuisine for dinner, wears Paris
perfume in Tokyo and "retro" clothes in Hong Kong; knowledge
is a matter for TV games. It is easy to find a public for eclectic
works. By becoming kitsch, art panders to the confusion which
reigns in the "taste" of the patrons. Artists, gallery owners,
critics and public wallow together in the "anything goes," and
the epoch is one of slackening. But this realism of the "anything goes" is in fact that of money; in the absence of aesthetic
criteria, it remains possible and useful to assess the value of
works of art according to the profits they yield. Such realism
accomodates all tendencies . . . providing that the tendencies
and needs have purchasing power (Lyotard 1983, 334–35).

The media (*"l'informatique"*) plays an important role in this eclecticism that is intellectually fraudulent, because it does not seek to

present the unpresentable; instead, its attitude is basically hedonistic. To return to the question of a postmodern legitimation, a legitimation in the absence of all previous authority. Lyotard envisages a postmodern era of *"les petites histoires,"* of, as Hassan puts it, "paratactical, paradoxical, paralogical narratives meant to open the structures of knowledge as of politics to language games, to imaginative reconstitutions that permit us either a new breakthrough or a change in the rules of the game itself" (Hassan 1983, 27). This is not a return to a higher discourse, it is an acceptance of a poststructuralist view of language as an instrument for exposing its own decentered character, and for exposing the absence of a center in all narratives. Postmodern legitimation can only be highly provisional, temporary, without ontological grounding. It is local and fragile and incorporates paradox.

If Lyotard is too cautious to claim that a postmodern episteme has already firmly established itself, Matei Calinescu has even more serious reservations about the arrival of a new era: "I must begin by admitting that a pluralist renaissance in contemporary thought, as I see it, is as much a phenomenon-in-the-making as a *desideratum* . . ." (Calinescu 1983, 284). It is this "pluralist renaissance," whatever its status, that is at the center of Calinescu's concept of Postmodernism.

For Calinescu, this "new (postmodern) pluralism" distinguishes itself clearly from Modernism: "With curiously few expectations, modernity's movements of radical skepticism confront us with the striking inconsistency that they were premised on monistic assumptions. Would it then not be the case that even modernity's critique of monism was in fact little more than a search (patient or impatient, darkened by despair or illumined by strange millennial hopes) for a new, all-embracing and all-explaining monism?" (Calinescu 1983, 263–64). But the new pluralism may equally well be placed within a far wider context: ". . . if we abandon the 'logic' of linear time, which characterizes modernity's secularized version of Judeo-Christian eschatology, we immediately realize that the recent trends away from monism belong to the realm of renovation rather than innovation" (Calinescu 1983, 264).

In any case, seen against the background of Modernism's monism or dualism (in those cases where the gap between two heterogeneous kinds of reality was accepted), postmodern pluralism is innovative, accepting the fact that "there are many irreducible principles, and therefore many worlds." Its "dialogic pluralism" leads to "a new interpretation of the category of relation" in a way that is suggestive of Foucault's discursive formations:

Freed from the inescapably linear unfolding of modernity's
concept of time, as well as from the natural attempt to escape
that ineluctable linearity (which took the form of various
philosophical or scientific abstract schemes of *totally reversible*
and ideally controllable concepts of time), historical relativity
tends to appear as a vast network of reciprocal determinations
in which the irreversibility of certain vital choices creates new
patterns of reversibility; it tends to appear as an ongoing process of "creative evolution" without any "objectively" pre-
established *telos* or *eskhaton*. Our consciousness exists in a
multiplicity of (actual and possible) worlds in perpetual "chro-
notopical" change (Calinescu 1983, 284).

For Calinescu, in this pluralist Postmodernism, traditional barriers
may be overcome: "There are, then, postcritical and more broadly
postmodern frames of reference within which, say, mathematics, religion, and the arts, while preserving all their irreducible differences, can be seen as having highly significant common features. We
notice that the recognition of such features . . . renders possible the
resumption of an *intracultural dialogue* that modernity had abandoned" (Calinescu 1983, 275).

Still, Calinescu's pluralism does not lead him into a poststructuralist deconstructionism that has abandoned all attempts at ac-
quiring what might be termed "positive" knowledge. On the
contrary, he sees such a deconstructionism as a "negative monolo-
gism" which can be "translated philosophically as 'negative monism'." What he has in mind is the "monism of absence" of Derrida
and his followers, a monism that he terms a "monism of negation
and of radical agnosticism." In his view, this monism of negation is
used "exclusively for purposes of subversion and disruption of the
One, and never for the *affirmation* of the Many" (Calinescu 1983,
272–273). According to Calinescu, deconstructionism is only *seemingly* pluralistic, but the "multiplicity that is posited by such a pluralism . . . is clearly an empty one: a 'doubling' and 'redoubling' of
absence, an endless repetition, an infinite regress of frames that
frame nothing" (Calinescu 1983, 273). It seems to me that Calinescu's position has much in common with Lyotard's. They see the loss
of higher (monistic) discourse as central in their concepts of Postmodernism, but are reluctant to conclude that such an absence
must necessarily lead to what Lyotard called the "anything goes."
Something may be salvaged out of Deconstructionism's endless repetition of absences; for Lyotard his "petites histoires," for Calinescu
his affirmation of the Many. In the next section of this survey I will

discuss a critic, the American critic, Alan Wilde, who, it seems to me, proposes a concept of Postmodernism that has close affinities with the concepts of both Lyotard and Calinescu, even though Wilde returns to a more strictly literary point of view.

3. Literary Postmodernism Revisited

What emerges from this survey of postmodernisms is that the more recent concepts share at least one central characteristic: a radical epistemological and ontological doubt. Whereas in the early concepts the focus is often elsewhere, beginning with Wasson (1969) and Hassan (1971), this radical doubt moves into the center of Postmodernism and it has occupied that central place ever since. Current disagreements about Postmodernism tend to center on its literary consequences and on the question, whether particular works of literary art are manifestations of that doubt, rather than on this central premise. Even a critic like James Mellard, who rejects the term Postmodernism altogether in favor of "sophisticated Modernism" or "late-phase" Modernism, accepts the centrality of this ontological uncertainty for what he calls sophisticated Modernist writing:

> ... the situation of the late-phase modernist writer has come to this: not only can he not believe in the world "out-there," physical or historical, a belief available to be given up by the early modernists; neither can he believe any longer in most of those modernist authorities posited for the world "in here," the interior world of man's intellect or imagination (Mellard 1980, 140).

In this section of my survey I propose to discuss some 'applied' concepts of Postmodernism, concepts that do not assume epistemic proportions, but that seek to describe more or less successfully defined bodies of Postmodernist literature. My discussion will not be exhaustive, and I am aware that my selection might easily be seen as arbitrary: I will ignore a number of interesting contributions to the debate, such as those of John Barth, Richard Poirier, Philip Stevick, David Lodge, Bruce Morrissette, and others. Their views are either too undefined or too specific for my purposes. To give some examples: Barth, for instance, offers as a "worthy program for postmodernist fiction" the "synthesis or transcension of . . . premodernist and modernist modes of writing," suggesting that the "ideal postmodernist novel will somehow rise above the quarrel between realism and irrealism, formalism and 'contentism,' pure and committed literature, coterie fiction and junk fiction" (Barth 1980, 70). Likewise, Poirier's discussion of the "performing self" is highly interesting and the concept has gained wide currency (although not exclusively through Poirier's good offices), but he too works on a generalized level. Again, Stevick's discussion of what he calls the "new fiction" is extremely informative, especially in his remarks on the techniques it employs, but he casts a very wide net: "New fiction can be differentiated from old on the basis of its fabulation, its willingness to allow the compositional act a self-conscious prominence and to invest that act with love, a sense of game, invention for its own sake, joy" (Stevick 1973, 216).

On the other side of the spectrum, David Lodge is rather precise in his attempts to map postmodern strategies, but he is not much interested in spelling out the postmodern world view, noting that "the general idea of the world resisting the compulsive attempts of the human consciousness to interpret it, of the human predicament being in some sense 'absurd,' does underlie a good deal of postmodern writing . . ." (Lodge 1977, 225). Obviously Lodge rather off-handedly creates homogeneity where others might see diversion. Doesn't Robbe-Grillet—whom he includes in his postmodern canon—refuse to see the world as "absurd?" Where is the postmodern literature that is not informed by the "general idea" that the world resists interpretation? Even more precise than Lodge are, for instance, Bruce Morrissette and Gerhard Hoffmann (Morrissette 1975; Hoffmann 1982), but their contributions, brilliant as they are, fall outside the scope of this survey because of their detailed concentration on the technical aspects of postmodern literature.

I have in the following selection been guided by the golden mean and have chosen to discuss a number of critics who are both interested in the postmodern world view and in the various ways in which this view is given shape in Postmodernist writing. Their concepts are fairly inclusive, yet, at the same time, fairly precise, because they try to distinguish between different modes within the body of postmodern literature, always arguing that these modes have a common source in the disappearance of all centers, of all "privileged languages," to use Russell's term (Russell 1974, 359). Perhaps I have been guided not so much by the golden mean as by my own bias: it seems to me, too, that one will have to distinguish between various modes within Postmodernism in order to bring clarity and to establish the ground rules for a fruitful discussion.

3.1. Graff, Mellard, Wilde and Others

Attempts to describe two or more modes within one larger Postmodernism have been made by Gerald Graff, James M. Mellard, the Surfictionists (Raymond Federman and Ronald Sukenick, notably), Christopher Butler, André le Vot, Alan Wilde, and others. I will briefly review some of the arguments here, and then pay more detailed attention to Alan Wilde's proposal because he includes a subgenre (which he calls "midfiction") usually not included in Postmodernist canons.

Beginning with Graff, we find again the familiar distinction between Modernism and Postmodernism:

> Perceiving that the modernist's seriousness rests on admittedly arbitrary foundations, the postmodern writer treats this seriousness as an object of parody. Whereas modernists turned to art, defined as the imposition of human order upon inhuman chaos . . . postmodernists conclude that, under such conceptions of art and history, art provides no more consolation than any other discredited cultural institution. Postmodernism signifies that the nightmare of history, as modernist esthetic and philosophical traditions have defined history, has overtaken modernism itself (Graff 1979, 55).

As a result, "alienation from significant external reality, from *all* reality, becomes an inescapable condition" (Graff 1979, 55). Graff, who sees Postmodernism as an international movement, sees this alienation as much at work in the novels of Robbe-Grillet (who parodies the Modernists' "respect for truth and significance") as in contemporary American writers such as John Barth and Donald Barthelme who, like Robbe-Grillet, reject the notion of depth: "In postmodern fiction, character, like external reality, is something 'about which nothing is known,' lacking in plausible motive or discoverable depth" (Graff 1979, 53).

This alienation is given fictional substance in two major ways. The first way is exemplified by the work of Borges, in whose stories "techniques of reflexiveness and self-parody suggest a universe in which human consciousness is incapable of transcending its own mythologies" (Graff 1979, 56). This "condition of imprisonment" is "presented from a tragic or tragicomic point of view that forces us to see it *as* a problem" (Graff 1979, 56). This is important for Graff's argument: although Borges' Postmodernism presents "solipsistic distortion as the only possible perspective," it nevertheless presents it as distortion and thereby "implicitly affirms a concept of the normal, if only as a concept which has been tragically lost" (Graff 1979, 56). Borges' Postmodernism is also characterized by its "ability to suggest the historical and social causes for this loss of objective reality" (Graff 1979, 56). In other words, the fiction of Borges may be self-reflexive, it still manages to explain things in recognizable terms; it implicitly offers a " 'realistic' comment" on the reasons for its own existence. Although not all self-reflexive fiction is self-explanatory in the manner of Borges' stories—for Graff, alienation in Barth and Barthelme is "detached from the consciousness of its causes"—still, even in its more radically alienated forms, self-reflexive fiction presents the loss of meaning as a distortion.

A totally different attitude toward alienation is adopted by what Graff calls the "more celebratory forms of postmodernism." In those forms there is no regret over the loss of "an objective order of values," in fact, there is hardly any memory of any previous order. Its disappearance is seen as a liberation. "Dissolution of ego boundaries . . . is viewed as a bracing form of consciousness-expansion and a prelude to growth" (Graff 1979, 57). Graff, who refers here to Susan Sontag's views, has in mind the countercultural Postmodernism on which I have quoted him earlier.

We have then, in Graff, a self-reflexive mode which still has a tenuous intellectual link with reality, and another mode which mindlessly embraces chaos and is, in spite of the dissolution of ego boundaries, thoroughly solipsistic.

This distinction between self-reflexive (or meta-)fiction and a celebratory form of Postmodernism is echoed by some other critics. James Mellard creates within his sophisticated Modernism—his term for Postmodernism—a similar distinction. For him the disappearance of Modernist legitimation strategies leads to the final (postmodern) legitimation: that of the "artistic performance" itself, the work of art as "act, ritual, play." As Mellard puts it: "in the event that myth, archetype, and language are subverted—as they have been by sophisticated modernists—the novelist may then turn for subject and authority or validation to the act of writing itself" (Mellard 1980, 138).

This "performance" is realized in "two antithetical ways: as the process or as the product, as . . . *play* or as *game, act* or *artifact, event* or *icon, context* or *text* . . ." (Mellard 1980, 140). The first way, that stresses "process," and is identified by Mellard with play, act, event, and context, is pragmatic. It stresses "the old values of storytelling, the entertainer's values"; it plays with its audience, with reality, with the conventions of traditional literature. Writers belonging to this category are, for instance, Brautigan, Vonnegut, Barthelme, Sukenick. The second type of Postmodernist performance—identified with game, artifact, icon, and text—takes "an essentially objective stance toward the universe, audience, self and work" (Mellard 1980, 133). It offers self-contained, self-reflexive fictions, such as Nabokov's *Pale Fire* or John Barth's *Lost in the Funhouse*. The "source of authority" here lies not in the performing "voice" of the first category (which Mellard rather confusingly calls the "performative" mode), but "in the object produced—the iconic art object itself"—of course without the 'higher' authority bestowed by Modernism upon iconic art.

Within Postmodernist "performance," then, Mellard distinguishes between two genres, indicated by "the performative term *play* and the artifactive term *game*" (Mellard 1980, 133). Obviously, the two modes have a good deal in common with Graff's self-reflexive fiction and his celebratory forms, except for the fact that Mellard makes no attempt to ground either one of them, no matter how tentatively, in the real world.

Raymond Federman, critic and writer of what he calls "Surfiction," implies the same distinction, although his position is far less clearly articulated. His starting point ("post-existentialist," as he calls it) is the awareness that nothing can be said: the "impossibility of saying the world" (Federman 1978, 127). Following Robbe-Grillet, he claims that the world simply *is* and sees the urge to reveal this state of affairs as characteristic of Postmodernism: "There is . . . behind the new fiction's project an effort of sincerity. A search for a new truth. A genuine effort to reinstate things, the world, and man in their proper places—in a purer state" (Federman 1978, 128). This urge leads postmodern literature in two directions. The first is the direction of meta-fiction. Novels must expose themselves continually as fictions, they must be "an endless denunciation of [their] own fraudulence" (Federman 1978, 122). Knowledge about the world—traditionally claimed by fiction—must be replaced by "the act of searching—researching even—within the fiction itself for the meaning of what it means to write fiction. It is an act of self-reflection . . ." (Federman 1978, 122). Yet, at the same time, a second impulse is at work, a creative impulse fed by the liberating awareness that "everything can be said now." This impulse leads to "long, meandering sentences, delirious verbal articulations, repetitions, lists . . . an entire mechanism of montage and collage," involving not so much self-reflexiveness, but an apparent effort (Federman does not commit himself too openly) "to grab things as they are, to make a reassessment of the world, of its objects, of its people, but without imposing upon them a pre-established signification" (Federman 1978, 127).

On the one hand we have self-reflexivity, inner-directed towards the work of art, on the other hand we have an impulse that is outer-directed and engages the world. This latter impulse is rather vaguely ascribed to a latently present energy in language itself. As Richard Pearce puts it more clearly in his discussion of Surfiction: "the medium asserts itself as an independent source of interest and control" (Pearce 1974, 72). Language would seem to perform itself and to reach out for the world to render the immediacy of experience. Ronald Sukenick, another Surfictionist, makes a similar distinction between a self-conscious and self-enclosed metafiction and a fiction that has other than purely self-reflexive options, and sees the two modes as more or less consecutive:

> That is perhaps the most significant difference between fiction in the sixties and fiction in the seventies. The latter has dropped the sixties' sense of irony about the form, its self-parody and self-consciousness. That self-consciousness has become, in the seventies, a more acute consciousness about the medium and its options (Sukenick 1977, 105).

Charles Russell makes a distinction that may further illuminate the Surfictionist view. For him, contemporary literature (his term for Postmodernist literature) follows two main directions, both of which "engage silence at the base of the artwork" (Russell 1974, 352), denying, in other words, that language can speak truthfully. One direction "emphasizes the epistemological dimension of the artwork. It studies the relationship of the individual to the environment. Properly speaking, it offers not a study of the world, but of how experience is filtered through consciousness" (Russell 1974, 352). Russell's exemplary authors, Pynchon, Kosinski, Brautigan, Sukenick, and Barthelme, offer fictions that center on "imaginative responses to the world." Undercutting Federman's notion that such writing might reassess the world, Russell stresses that responses can indeed be nothing but responses to an essentially inaccessible world. Still, his imaginative responses seems to me identical with Federman's attempts "to grab things as they are." The other direction in postmodern literature is for Russell the self-reflexive one. It "focuses more intently on the presciptive structure of language . . . It is the writer's structural devices, the basis and patterns of meaning, that are of interest" (Russell 1974, 352). As might be expected, writers mentioned here include Borges ("the dominant figure of this group"), Barth, Nabokov and Coover.

Although this subdivision of Postmodernist literature into the two main categories of the metafictional and the performative (to use Mellard's term) is fairly popular, it is by no means the only one. Critics who concentrate somewhat more on form than on vision are apt to come up with different distinctions. Christopher Butler, for instance, sees a dialectic between two major modes: ". . . the dialectic between the huge over-organization of *Finnegans Wake* and the deliberate lack of it in the *Cantos* conditions the whole of the postmodern period; and what mediates between these at all points is the phenomenological concentration upon the mental processes of the artist . . ." (Butler 1980, 5). This interest in the creative process may be combined with either of Butler's major modes and may even become a mode in itself: "The present structuralist insistence upon the play of language, the manipulations of codes by the artist, is in many ways an extension of this interest in the dynamics of the creative process" (Butler 1980, 5). Although it is not his main concern, Butler's discussion also suggests a contrast between a Postmodernist fiction still "embedded in reality" and a Postmodernist fiction that "enforce[s] a peculiarly exclusive attention to its object" and "abjure[s] any mimetic commitments, any correspondence even with the everyday life of the emotions" (Butler 1980, 138). This distinction, not too clearly present in Federman's concept, is central to Alan Wilde's views, to which I will turn in a moment.

Another critic who pays a good deal of attention to form is André Le Vot, who sees "extreme poles of frigid isolation and delirious involvement" in Postmodernist fiction, extremes that leave between them an "empty space . . . that central blank formerly occupied by the traditional novel" (Le Vot 1976, 54). These two poles both presuppose a meaningless, irredeemably fragmented world and an authorial view that is "no longer committed to preserve an order based on an idealistic conception of man and society as was the case with the Modernists" (Le Vot 1976, 46). The frigid pole, associated by Le Vot with a schizoid view of the world, is that of disjunction: "fragmentation and inconsequence are accepted as the rule. The illusions of memory are obliterated, causes and effects considered as reversible, logic and temporality toyed with as period pieces" (Le Vot 1976, 51). The deliriously involved pole, associated with paranoia, is characterized by conjunction, by a consciousness that despite itself becomes involved with the chaos confronting it: "what impresses is the vanishing of the geometrical patterns so prominent in the fracturing [disjunctive] vision. The spectatorial quality, in which sight is the privileged medium gives way to more diffuse sensations verging on synesthesia. Contours and obstacles seem to dissolve in a viscous fluidity, the details are fused into the all-pervading flux and eddies of a unifying ambience" (Le Vot 1976, 53).

Le Vot's modes seem similar to Butler's: paranoid over-organization versus schizoid lack of organization. But that impression may very well be misleading. Le Vot's conjunctive mode, with its emphasis on sensory impressions, reminds one of the narrators of Federman's and Sukenick's Surfictionist novels or of a good many products of the counterculture, where one does not find over-organization—on the contrary—but rather a unifying conscious-ness, unifying in the sense that it accepts unquestioningly. In any case, what Butler and Le Vot illustrate is that distinctions made primarily on the basis of form are problematic; the discussion on Postmodernist techniques and on how these techniques differ sig-nificantly from Modernist techniques is still developing, witness such recent important publications as those of Christine Brooke-Rose (1981) and Gerhard Hoffmann (1982).

To return to the Postmodern *Weltanschauung,* I will conclude this superficial survey of recent critical contributions with a short discussion of Alan Wilde's contribution to the postmodern debate. Wilde is interesting because he expands the concept of Postmodern-ist literature in an unexpected way, including such writers as Max Apple and Stanley Elkin in his postmodern canon—in fact, it is clear that for him such writers have so far created the most com-pelling postmodern fictions.

For Wilde, too, Postmodernism has given up Modernist at-tempts to restore wholeness to a fragmented world and has ac-cepted the contingency of experience:

> If, as I've several times suggested, the defining features of modernism is its ironic vision of disconnection and disjunction, postmodernism, more radical in its perceptions, derives in-stead from a vision of randomness, multiplicity, and contin-gency: in short, a world in need of mending is superseded by one beyond repair. Modernism, spurred by an anxiety to recu-perate a lost wholeness in self-sustaining orders of art or in the unselfconscious depths of the self . . . reaches toward the heroic in the intensity of its desire and of its disillusion. Post-modernism, skeptical of such efforts, presents itself as delib-erately, consciously antiheroic. Confronted with the world's randomness and diversity, in enacts (*urbi et orbi*) that attitude

of suspensiveness which . . . implies the tolerance of a fundamental uncertainty about the meanings and relations of
things in the world and in the universe (Wilde 1981, 131–32).

This postmodern tolerance of uncertainty leads according to Wilde
to a "suspensive irony" that is characteristic for Postmodernist literature. Whereas Modernist irony posited "in opposition to its vision of disjunctiveness a complementary vision of inclusive order,
thereby generating a hope that more often than not outstrips belief," postmodern "suspensive" irony never includes such a complementary vision. Modernist irony is, in the final analysis, "*anironic*,"
postmodern irony never dissolves into absolute vision: "postmodern
ironists, however unlike one another in other respects, are agreed at
least in acknowledging the inevitability of their situation in the
world they describe. Whether or not they are involved with that
world, they are *of* it, their perspective conditioned by a view from
within reality itself" (Wilde 1981, 121).

As appears from this quotation, Wilde's postmodern writers
may either be involved or not involved with their world, and this involvement becomes for Wilde an important distinction. On the one
hand there are the writers who are consciously or unconsciously uninvolved: the metafictionists and Surfictionists. Wilde is bored by
self-reflexive fiction, and thinks it highly over-rated: "the attention
bestowed on it . . . has more to do with the prominence of metacrit-
icism . . . than it does with the intrinsic worth of metafiction itself"
(Wilde 1982, 179). He is irritated by the pretensions of the Surfictionists and claims that they, too, are finally uninvolved in spite of
their protestations to the contrary: "even as they revel in the
world's chaos, these writers deny the world its specificity and provocations . . . What is at work . . . is clearly a process of substitution,
of replacement" (Wilde 1981, 137). Surfiction is for Wilde reductive
and self-enclosed. Its attempts to engage the world are spurious; in
fact, it submits "phenomenal reality to the subjectivizing, idealistic
transformations of consciousness" (Wilde 1981, 141), and is ultimately based upon a reductive aestheticism. Wilde does not even
see Russell's "imaginative responses" in Surfiction, he sees the writer's imagination imposing its own selective patterns upon the
world, and argues that in actual practice the Surfictionists are not
so far removed from Modernism as they would want to be.

For Wilde, then, there is not that much difference between
game and play, between the artifactive and the performative mode:
both have given up the effort to engage the world through language. There is, however, a third Postmodernist mode—called

"midfiction"—which still seeks to be referential and which is even hopeful of establishing (admittedly small) truths. While "accepting the primacy of surface," midfiction finds at least sometimes in that surface "the possibility of genuine if limited affirmation" (Wilde 1981, 123). Midfiction's suspensive irony is at the same time a "generative irony"; it presents an "attempt, inspired by the negotiations of self and world, to create, tentatively and provisionally, anironic enclaves of values in the face of—but not in the place of—a meaningless universe. The world, in short, is accepted as a given and *in its essentials* as beyond change or understanding. But that recognition is not meant to imply either stoic resignation or suicidal despair" (Wilde 1981, 148). Midfiction seeks to affirm in the face of the void, although its "assent" is "local, limited and temporary." In other words, it seeks positive knowledge ("anironic enclaves") without ever losing sight of the fact that knowledge in any absolute sense (a truly "anironic" knowledge) is completely out of reach:

> midfiction describes a narrative form that negotiates the oppositional extremes of realism and reflexivity (both their presuppositions and their technical procedures). Further, it seeks to reveal the extraordinariness of the ordinary, frequently and paradoxically by trafficking in limit situations—thereby subjecting to interrogation the very foundations of the writer's (and the reader's) beliefs. And finally, it invites us not *through* but *in* the relationships and actions of its characters—and by way of some strategic *écart* or swerve in its fabric—to perceive, obliquely and ironically, the moral perplexities of inhabiting a world that is itself, as "text," ontologically ironic, contingent, and problematic (Wilde 1982, 192).

For Wilde, midfiction is the most important mode within Postmodernism (hence perhaps his claim that "postmodernism is essentially an American affair" [Wilde 1981, 12]) and that importance he assigns to it is clearly a consequence of his point of departure: "my position is—although only roughly and in a totally undoctrinaire way—phenomenological" (Wilde 1981, 3). Wilde's position reminds one of those of Lyotard (the "petites histoires") and Calinescu (with his plea for affirmation) and, in spite of all the differences, even of Spanos' existentialist Postmodernism.

In any case, midfiction must be grouped with those concepts of Postmodernism that still see a basis for positive knowledge, no matter how local and provisional, within the framework of an overwhelming ontological doubt. Wilde's concept leads him to provocative interpretations of the fiction of writers such as Donald Barthelme and Robert Coover. More importantly, it offers a place to such writers as Stanley Elkin, who up to now have been clearly an embarrassment to those who attempted to classify them. Elkin's mode is certainly performative, but it is also referential; it is deeply ironic, yet not afraid of meaning. Wilde's midfiction is a welcome new category within the broad spectrum of contemporary writing, no matter how postmodern it will actually turn out to be.

4. Questions and a Few Tentative Conclusions

The first question is of course whether there is such a phenomenon as an independent Postmodernism, no matter how many critics have put their lives on the line in its defense. Others have equally vigorously denied its existence and argued that Postmodernism is simply a development within Modernism (Mellard 1980; Kermode 1968). To complicate this matter further, for a good many of those critics involved in the debate on Postmodernism, criticism itself has become a highly questionable enterprise and has, in fact, become a kind of fiction. Bradbury, for instance, declares: "I see these tactics, methods, and presumptions [concerning periodization] as partaking in some of the fictionality—sometimes the same *kind* of fictionality—that goes into the making of the creative arts themselves" (Bradbury 1983, 311). Poirier even more unhesitatingly sees literary criticism as fiction, as a process of fictionalization comparable to purely literary fictionalization (Poirier 1971, 29). Hassan, too, is very cautious about the epistemological possibilities of criticism and quotes with obvious approval Norman N. Holland's view that "There can be as many readings as there are readers to write them. Can be and should be" (Hassan 1980a, 113). In other words, the radical indeterminacy that is at the heart of recent concepts of Postmodernism forces those critics who accept that indeterminacy to "deconstruct" their own views while offering them. Criticism becomes performance, as in Hassan's "Paracriticisms," and, within the postmodern context, indistinguishable from silence. (The continuing output of such critics does not suggest that they allow their practice to be dictated by theoretical considerations.)

Then there are the obvious problems of canonization and periodization. Is Postmodernism an exclusively American phenomenon (Wilde) or is it international in scope (Wasson, Hassan, Spanos, Lyotard, etc.)? Does it include a subgenre such as the *nouveau roman* (Wasson, Lodge? Hassan, Morrissette, etc.) or does it refuse to include it (Spanos). Does it include the literature and theater of the absurd (Spanos, Durand); does it include Latin American magical realism (Barth); does it include the so-called nonfiction novel (Zavarzadeh)? Does Postmodernism go back to de Sade and other pre-modern anti-establishment, underground figures (Hassan), does it begin with Borges (Graff and others), with Beckett (Lodge), with the existentialism of Heidegger and Sartre (Spanos), with Joyce's *Finnegans Wake* (the later Hassan), or is it strictly a postwar phenomenon (Wilde, Stevick, and others)? The questions proliferate and I will abandon this provisional listing of some of the most pressing ones.

My conclusions do not proliferate, unfortunately. The most important one is obviously that in most concepts, and in practically all recent concepts of Postmodernism the matter of ontological uncertainty is absolutely central. It is the awareness of the absence of centers, of privileged languages, higher discourses, that is seen as the most striking difference with Modernism that, in the view of practically all critics, still clung to certain centers and tried to avoid the consequences of the radical indeterminacy that Postmodernism has accepted. Yet, although there is this decisive difference, most critics also agree that there are, especially in the matter of literary technique, important continuities between Modernism and Postmodernism.

Other important differences that are put forward are the changing role of the reader and the postmodern "loss of self." To begin with the role of the reader, as Hoffmann *et al.* put it: "From a communicational point of view, modernism seems to stress the relationship between the creative sensibility and the work of art, between addresser and message, postmodernism that between message and addressee" (Hoffmann *et al.* 1977, 40). Norman Holland agrees with this: "In general, Postmodern criticism has turned decisively to the relation between reader and text" (Holland 1983, 295). Meaning is the result of interaction; it is not discovered as a given in a text, but it is created in an interactional process between reader and text. Hence the wide-spread notion of criticism as an art form in its own right; it engages the creative faculties of the individual in a way that is seen as not essentially different from other creative processes.

Holland relates this stress on interaction in the reading process to comparable developments in psychoanalysis, where the former notion of a stable identity has given way (at least in what he calls postmodern psychoanalysis) to a new concept of identity, a concept based on interaction: "this theme-and-variations concept of identity decenters the individual in a distinctly Postmodern, metafictional way. You are ficted, and I am ficted, like characters in a Postmodern novel. The most personal, central thing I have, my identity, is not in me but in your interaction with me or in a divided me" (Holland 1983, 304).

Holland's view of identity is widely shared, though often in a more radical form. As we have seen, for Gerald Graff the celebratory mode of Postmodernism is characterized by a "dissolution of ego boundaries;" for Daniel Bell "the various kinds of postmodernism . . . are simply the decomposition of the self in an effort to erase the individual ego" (Bell 1976, 29), and Ihab Hassan notes that "the Self, structuralists and post-structuralists insist, following the intuition of Nietzsche, is really an empty 'place' where many selves come to mingle and depart" (Hassan 1977, 845). For Hoffman this movement in the direction of a less defined, less stable identity is even a shift of epistemic proportions: "The perceivable signs of a tendency toward the disappearance of a subjectivity in modern literature become a fact in postmodern works. Thus a radical gap between modern and postmodern literature is reflected in the opposition of two *épistémès:* subjectively versus loss of subjectivity" (Hoffman *et al.* 1977, 20).

The postmodern self is no longer a coherent entity that has the power to impose (admittedly subjective) order upon its environment. It has become decentered, to repeat Holland's phrase. The radical indeterminacy of Postmodernism has entered the individual ego and has drastically affected its former (supposed) stability. Identity has become as uncertain as everything else.

These seem to me the most general conclusions that can, at this point, be safely drawn. Other, more specific conclusions will for the time being have to wait. My conclusions about the actual practice of Postmodernist literature must be as tentative. It seems to me that we can locate two major modes within Postmodernist literature in the criticism that I have reviewed here: one mode that has given up referentiality and meaning, another one that still seeks to be referential and sometimes even tries to establish local, temporary, and provisional truths.

The nonreferential mode includes self-reflexive or metafictional writing and it also includes performative writing, if that writing does not aim at referentiality and meaning (one might think of the zany playfulness of, for instance, Brautigan). However, performative writing is not necessarily non-referential—it may reflect the phenomenological involvement of a writer with his environment—in which case it would belong in the other mode. The nonreferential mode cannot establish meanings that go beyond the text or beyond the process of writing as it is reflected by the text. A critic who takes exception to this is Gerald Graff, but the "extra-textual" meaning he ascribes to Borges' meta-fiction is not so much "meaning" but a denial of the possibility of meaning. This nonreferential mode is by a good many critics associated with structuralist or poststructuralist views.

The referential mode is broadly associated with a phenomenological approach, in which a subject—far less stable and coherent than in Modernist fiction—actively tries to engage the world. This mode may seek to establish meaning, but not necessarily. It may phenomenologically try to capture the immediacy of experience without imposing meaning upon that experience, or it may—as in the case of some non-fiction novels—merely reflect the surface of what is "out there." On the other hand, it may—as in Wilde's mid-fiction—try to generate provisional meaning. As if this is not confusing enough, any Postmodernist novel may combine these modes within its covers and further blur the picture—after all, eclecticism is widely seen as an important characteristic of Postmodernism. (It is true that some critics, e.g., Butler, see a phenomenological process at work in meta-fiction as well, arguing that the artist phenomenologically observes and reports on the creative process. This is undeniable, I think, but the process is limited to the subject which observes itself; there is no engagement of the outer world.)

These critical distinctions may be helpful, but novels do of course not announce themselves in terms of referentiality or non-referentiality; it is the reader who classifies them as referential, performative, meta-fictional, etc., so that we are ultimately forced into a corner made deeply suspect by Postmodernism itself, the corner of interpretation. The debate on Postmodernism is a long way from being resolved.

References

Allen, Donald and George F. Butterick, 1982. *The Postmoderns: The New American Poetry Revised.* New York: Grove Press.

Altieri, Charles. 1973. "From Symbolist Thought to Immanence: The Ground of Postmodern American Poetics," *Boundary 2,* 1: 605–641.

Antin, David. 1972. "Modernism and Postmodernism: Approaching the Present in American Poetry," *Boundary 2*, 1: 98–133.

Barth, John. 1980. "The Literature of Replenishment: Postmodernist Fiction," *Atlantic Monthly* 245, 1: 65–71.

Bell, Daniel. 1976. *The Cultural Contradictions of Capitalism*. New York: Basic Books.

Benamou, Michel and Charles Caramello, eds. 1977. *Performance in Postmodern Culture*. Madison, Wisconsin: Coda Press.

Bradbury, Malcolm. 1983. "Modernisms/Postmodernisms," in Hassan and Hassan 1983: 311–327.

Brooke-Rose, Christine. 1981. *A Rhetoric of the Unreal: Studies in Narrative and Structure, Especially the Fantastic*. Cambridge: Cambridge University Press.

Butler, Christopher. 1980. *After the Wake: An Essay on the Contemporary Avant-Garde*. Oxford: Oxford University Press.

Calinescu, Matei. 1983. "From the One to the Many: Pluralism in Today's Thought," in Hassan and Hassan 1983: 263–288.

Cunliffe, Marcus, ed. 1975. *American Literature Since 1900*. London: Sphere Books.

Federman, Raymond. 1978. "Fiction Today or the Pursuit of Non-Knowledge," *Humanities in Society* 1, 2:115–131.

Fiedler, Leslie. 1965. "The New Mutants," *Partisan Review* 32: 505–525.

———. 1975. "Cross the Border—Close that Gap: Postmodernism," in Cunliffe 1975: 344–366.

———. 1983. "The Death and Rebirths of the Novel: The View from '82," in Hassan and Hassan 1983: 225–242.

Garvin, Harry R., ed. 1980. *Bucknell Review: Romanticism, Modernism, Postmodernism*. Lewisburg, Pa.: Bucknell University Press.

Graff, Gerald. 1979. *Literature Against Itself: Literary Ideas in Modern Society*. Chicago: University of Chicago Press.

Hassan, Ihab. 1971. *The Dismemberment of Orpheus: Toward a Postmodern Literature*. New York: Oxford University Press.

———. 1975. *Paracriticisms: Seven Speculations of the Times*. Urbana: University of Illinois Press.

———. 1977. "Prometheus as Performer: Toward a Posthumanist Culture," *Georgia Review* 31: 830–850.

————. 1980a. *The Right Promethean Fire: Imagination, Science, and Cultural Change.* Urbana: University of Illinois Press.

————. 1980b. "The Question of Postmodernism" in Garvin 1980: 117–126.

————. 1983. "Ideas of Cultural Change" in Hassan and Hassan 1983: 15–39.

Hassan, Ihab and Sally Hassan, eds. 1983. *Innovation/Renovation: New Perspectives on the Humanities.* Madison: University of Wisconsin Press.

Hoffmann, Gerhard. 1982. "The Fantastic in Fiction: Its 'Reality' Status, its Historical Development and its Transformation in Postmodern Narration," *REAL (Yearbook of Research in English and American Literature)* 1: 267–364.

Hoffmann, Gerhard, Alfred Hornung and Rüdiger Kunow. 1977. " 'Modern', 'Postmodern' and 'Contemporary' as Criteria for the Analysis of 20th Century Literature," *Amerikastudien* 22: 19–46.

Holland, Norman N. 1983. "Postmodern Psychoanalysis," in Hassan and Hassan 1983: 291–309.

Holquist, Michael. 1971. "Whodunit and Other Questions: Metaphysical Detective Stories in Post-War Fiction," *New Literary History* 3: 135–156.

Howe, Irving. 1959. "Mass Society and Post-Modern Fiction," *Partisan Review* 26: 420–436.

Kermode, Frank. 1968. *Continuities.* London: Routledge and Kegan Paul.

Klinkowitz, Jerome. 1975. *Literary Disruptions: The Making of a Post-Contemporary American Fiction.* Urbana: University of Illinois Press.

Köhler, Michael. 1977. " 'Postmodernismus': Ein begriffsgeschichtlicher Überblick," *Amerikastudien* 22: 8–18.

Levin, Harry. 1960. "What Was Modernism," in Levin 1966: 271–295.

————. 1966. *Refractions: Essays in Comparative Literature.* New York: Oxford University Press.

Le Vot, André. 1976. "Disjunctive and Conjunctive Modes in Contemporary American Fiction." *Forum* 14, 1: 44:55.

Lodge, David. 1977. *The Modes of Modern Writing: Metaphor, Metonymy, and the Typology of Modern Literature.* London: Arnold.

Lyotard, Jean-François. 1979. *La Condition postmoderne: Rapport sur le savoir:* Paris: Minuit.

————. 1983. "Answering the Question: What is Postmodernism?" in Hassan and Hassan 1983: 329–341.

Martin, Wallace. 1980. "Postmodernism: Ultima Thule or Seim Anew?" in Garvin 1980: 142–154.

Mazzaro, Jerome. 1980. *Postmodern American Poetry.* Urbana: University of Illinois Press.

Mellard, James M. 1980. *The Exploded Form: The Modernist Novel in America.* Urbana: University of Illinois Press.

Morrissette, Bruce. 1975. "Post-Modern Generative Fiction," *Critical Inquiry* 2: 253–262.

O'Connor, William Van. 1963. *The New University Wits and the End of Modernism.* Carbondale: Southern Illinois University Press.

Palmer, Richard E. 1977. "Towards a Postmodern Hermeneutics of Performance," in Benamou and Caramello 1977: 19–32.

Pearce, Richard. 1974. "Enter the Frame," *TriQuarterly* 30: 71–82.

Peper, Jürgen. 1977. "Postmodernismus: Unitary Sensibility," *Amerikastudien* 22: 65–89.

Poirier, Richard. 1971. *The Performing Self: Compositions and Decompositions in the Language of Contemporary Life.* London: Oxford University Press.

Russell, Charles. 1974. "The Vault of Language: Self-Reflexive Artifice in Contemporary American Fiction," *Modern Fiction Studies* 20: 349–359.

Sontag, Susan. 1966. *Against Interpretation and Other Essays.* New York: Delta.

Spanos, William V. 1972. "The Detective and the Boundary: Some Notes on the Postmodern Literary Imagination," *Boundary 2,* 1: 147–168.

————. 1977. "Breaking the Circle," *Boundary 2,* 5: 421–457.

Stevick, Philip. 1981. *Alternative Pleasures: Postrealist Fiction and the Tradition.* Urbana: University of Illinois Press.

Sukenick, Ronald. 1977. "Fiction in the Seventies: Ten Digressions on Ten Digressions," *Studies in American Fiction 5,* 1: 99–109.

Wasson, Richard. 1969. "Notes on a New Sensibility," *Partisan Review* 36: 460–477.

————. 1974. "From Priest to Prometheus: Culture and Criticism in the Post-Modern Period," *Journal of Modern Literature* 3: 1188–1202.

Wilde, Alan. 1981. *Horizons of Assent: Modernism, Postmodernism, and the Ironic Imagination*. Baltimore: Johns Hopkins University Press.

————. 1982. "Strange Displacements of the Ordinary: Apple, Elkin, Barthelme, and the Problem of the Excluded Middle," *Boundary 2*, 10: 177–201.

Excerpts from *The Postmodern Condition: A Report on Knowledge*

Jean-François Lyotard

Introduction

The object of this study is the condition of knowledge in the most highly developed societies. I have decided to use the word *postmodern* to describe that condition. The word is in current use on the American continent among sociologists and critics; it designates the state of our culture following the transformations which, since the end of the nineteenth century, have altered the game rules for science, literature, and the arts. The present study will place these transformations in the context of the crisis of narratives.

Science has always been in conflict with narratives. Judged by the yardstick of science, the majority of them prove to be fables. But to the extent that science does not restrict itself to stating useful regularities and seeks the truth, it is obliged to legitimate the rules of its own game. It then produces a discourse of legitimation with respect to its own status, a discourse called philosophy. I will use the term *modern* to designate any science that legitimates itself

Jean-François Lyotard, extracts from *The Postmodern Condition: A Report on Knowledge* trans. Geoff Bennington and Brian Massumi, pp. xxiii-xxv, 18–31 Copyright 1979 University of Minnesota Press. Reprinted by permission.

with reference to a metadiscourse of this kind making an explicit appeal to some grand narrative, such as the dialectics of Spirit, the hermeneutics of meaning, the emancipation of the rational or working subject, or the creation of wealth. For example, the rule of consensus between the sender and addressee of a statement with truth-value is deemed acceptable if it is cast in terms of a possible unanimity between rational minds: this is the Enlightenment narrative, in which the hero of knowledge works toward a good ethico-political end—universal peace. As can be seen from this example, if a metanarrative implying a philosophy of history is used to legitimate knowledge, questions are raised concerning the validity of the institutions governing the social bond: these must be legitimated as well. Thus justice is consigned to the grand narrative in the same way as truth.

Simplifying to the extreme, I define *postmodern* as incredulity toward metanarratives. This incredulity is undoubtedly a product of progress in the sciences: but that progress in turn presupposes it. To the obsolescence of the metanarrative apparatus of legitimation corresponds, most notably, the crisis of metaphysical philosophy and of the university institution which in the past relied on it. The narrative function is losing its functors, its great hero, its great dangers, its great voyages, its great goal. It is being dispersed in clouds of narrative language elements—narrative, but also denotative, prescriptive, descriptive, and so on. Conveyed within each cloud are pragmatic valencies specific to its kind. Each of us lives at the intersection of many of these. However, we do not necessarily establish stable language combinations, and the properties of the ones we do establish are not necessarily communicable.

Thus the society of the future falls less within the province of a Newtonian anthropology (such as stucturalism or systems theory) than a pragmatics of language particles. There are many different language games—a heterogeneity of elements. They only give rise to institutions in patches—local determinism.

The decision makers, however, attempt to manage these clouds of sociality according to input/output matrices, following a logic which implies that their elements are commensurable and that the whole is determinable. They allocate our lives for the growth of power. In matters of social justice and of scientific truth alike, the legitimation of that power is based on its optimizing the system's performance—efficiency. The application of this criterion to all of our games necessarily entails a certain level of terror, whether soft or hard: be operational (that is, commensurable) or disappear.

The logic of maximum performance is no doubt inconsistent in many ways, particularly with respect to contradiction in the socio-economic field: it demands both less work (to lower production costs) and more (to lessen the social burden of the idle population). But our incredulity is now such that we no longer expect salvation to rise from these inconsistencies, as did Marx.

Still, the postmodern condition is as much a stranger to dis-enchantment as it is to the blind positivity of delegitimation. Where, after the metanarratives, can legitimacy reside? The operativity criterion is technological; it has no relevance for judging what is true or just. Is legitimacy to be found in consensus obtained through discussion, as Jürgen Habermas thinks? Such consensus does violence to the heterogeneity of language games. And invention is always born of dissension. Postmodern knowledge is not simply a tool of the authorities; it refines our sensitivity to differences and reinforces our ability to tolerate the incommensurable. Its principle is not the expert's homology, but the inventor's paralogy.

Here is the question: is a legitimation of the social bond, a just society, feasible in terms of a paradox analogous to that of scientific activity? What would such a paradox be?

The text that follows is an occasional one. It is a report on knowledge in the most highly developed societies and was presented to the Conseil des Universitiés of the government of Quebec at the request of its president. I would like to thank him for his kindness in allowing its publication.

It remains to be said that the author of the report is a philosopher, not an expert. The latter knows what he knows and what he does not know: the former does not. One concludes, the other questions—two very different language games. I combine them here with the result that neither quite succeeds.

The philosopher at least can console himself with the thought that the formal and pragmatic analysis of certain philosophical and ethico-political discourses of legitimation, which underlies the report, will subsequently see the light of day. The report will have served to introduce that analysis from a somewhat sociologizing slant, one that truncates but at the same time situates it.

Such as it is, I dedicate this report to the Institut Polytechnique de Philosophie of the Université de Paris VIII (Vincennes)—at this very postmodern moment that finds the University nearing what may be its end, while the Institute may just be beginning.

* * *

6. The Pragmatics of Narrative Knowledge

In Section 1, I leveled two objections against the unquestioning acceptance of an instrumental conception of knowledge in the most highly developed societies. Knowledge is not the same as science, especially in its contemporary form; and science, far from successfully obscuring the problem of its legitimacy, cannot avoid raising it with all of its implications, which are no less sociopolitical than epistemological. Let us begin with an analysis of the nature of "narrative" knowledge; by providing a point of comparison, our examination will clarify at least some of the characteristics of the form assumed by scientific knowledge in contemporary society. In addition, it will aid us in understanding how the question of legitimacy is raised or fails to be raised today.

Knowledge [*savoir*] in general cannot be reduced to science, nor even to learning [*connaissance*]. Learning is the set of statements which, to the exclusion of all other statements, denote or describe objects and may be declared true or false. Science is a subset of learning. It is also composed of denotative statements, but imposes two supplementary conditions on their acceptability: the objects to which they refer must be available for repeated access, in other words, they must be accessible in explicit conditions of observation; and it must be possible to decide whether or not a given statement pertains to the language judged relevant by the experts.[1]

But what is meant by the term *knowledge* is not only a set of denotative statements, far from it. It also includes notions of "know-how," "knowing how to live," "how to listen" [*savoir-faire, savoir-vivre, savoir-écouter*], etc. Knowledge, then, is a question of competence that goes beyond the simple determination and application of the criterion of truth, extending to the determination and application of criteria of efficiency (technical qualification), of justice and/or happiness (ethical wisdom), of the beauty of a sound or color (auditory and visual sensibility), etc. Understood in this way, knowledge is what makes someone capable of forming "good" denotative utterances, but also "good" prescriptive and "good" evaluative utterances. . . . It is not a competence relative to a particular class of statements (for example, cognitive ones) to the exclusion of all others. On the contrary, it makes "good" performances in relation to a variety of objects of discourse possible: objects to be known, decided on, evaluated, transformed. . . . From this derives one of the principal features of knowledge: it coincides with an extensive array of competence-building measures and is the only form embodied in a subject constituted by the various areas of competence composing it.

Another characteristic meriting special attention is the relation between this kind of knowledge and custom. What is a "good" prescriptive or evaluative utterance, a "good" performance in denotative or technical matters? They are all judged to be "good" because they conform to the relevant criteria (of justice, beauty, truth, and efficiency respectively) accepted in the social circle of the "knower's" interlocutors. The early philosophers called this mode of legitimating statements opinion.[2] The consensus that permits such knowledge to be circumscribed and makes it possible to distinguish one who knows from one who doesn't (the foreigner, the child) is what constitutes the culture of a people.[3]

This brief reminder of what knowledge can be in the way of training and culture draws on ethnological description for its justification.[4] But anthropological studies and literature that take rapidly developing societies as their object can attest to the survival of this type of knowledge within them, at least in some of their sectors.[5] The very idea of development presupposes a horizon of nondevelopment where, it was assumed, the various areas of competence remain enveloped in the unity of a tradition and are not differentiated according to separate qualifications subject to specific innovations, debates, and inquiries. This opposition does not necessarily imply a difference in nature between "primitive" and "civilized" man,[6] but is compatible with the premise of a formal identity between "the savage mind" and scientific thought;[7] it is even compatible with the (apparently contrary) premise of the superiority of customary knowledge over the contemporary dispersion of competence.[8]

It is fair to say that there is one point on which all of the investigations agree, regardless of which scenario they propose to dramatize and understand the distance separating the customary state of knowledge from its state in the scientific age: the preeminence of the narrative form in the formulation of traditional knowledge. Some study this form for its own sake;[9] others see it as the diachronic costume of the structural operators that, according to them, properly constitute the knowledge in question;[10] still others bring to it an "economic" interpretation in the Freudian sense of the term.[11] All that is important here is the fact that its form is narrative. Narration is the quintessential form of customary knowledge, in more ways than one.

First, the popular stories themselves recount what could be called positive or negative apprenticeships (*Bildungen*): in other

words, the successes or failures greeting the hero's undertakings.
These successes or failures either bestow legitimacy upon social
institutions (the function of myths), or represent positive or negative models (the successful or unsuccessful hero) of integration
into established institutions (legends and tales). Thus the narratives allow the society in which they are told, on the one hand, to
define its criteria of competence and, on the other, to evaluate according to those criteria what is performed or can be performed
within it.

Second, the narrative form, unlike the developed forms of the
discourse of knowledge, lends itself to a great variety of language
games. Denotative statements concerning, for example, the state of
the sky and the flora and fauna easily slip in; so do deontic statements prescribing what should be done with respect to these same
referents, or with respect to kinship, the difference between the
sexes, children, neighbors, foreigners, etc. Interrogative statements
are implied, for example, in episodes involving challenges (respond
to a question, choose one from a number of things); evaluative statements also enter in, etc. The areas of competence whose criteria the
narrative supplies or applies are thus tightly woven together in the
web it forms, ordered by the unified viewpoint characteristic of this
kind of knowledge.

We shall examine in somewhat more detail a third property,
which relates to the transmission of narratives. Their narration
usually obeys rules that define the pragmatics of their transmission. I do not mean to say that a given society institutionally assigns the role of narrator to certain categories on the basis of age,
sex, or family or professional group. What I am getting at is a pragmatics of popular narratives that is, so to speak, intrinsic to them.
For example, a Cashinahua[12] storyteller always begins his narration with a fixed formula: "Here is the story of——— , as I've always
heard it told. I will tell it to you in my turn. Listen." And he brings
it to a close with another, also invariable, formula: "Here ends the
story of ——— . The man who has told it to you is ——— (Cashinahua name), or to the Whites——— (Spanish or Portuguese
name)."[13]

A quick analysis of this double pragmatic instruction reveals
the following: the narrator's only claim to competence for telling the
story is the fact that he has heard it himself. The current narratee
gains potential access to the same authority simply by listening. It
is claimed that the narrative is a faithful transmission (even if the
narrative performance is highly inventive) and that it has been told
"forever": therefore the hero, a Cashinahuan, was himself once a

narratee, and perhaps a narrator, of the very same story. This similarity of condition allows for the possibility that the current narrator could be the hero of a narrative, just as the Ancestor was. In fact, he is necessarily such a hero because he bears a name, declined at the end of his narration, and that name was given to him in conformity with the canonic narrative legitimating the assignment of patronyms among the Cashinahua.

The pragmatic rule illustrated by this example cannot, of course, be universalized.[14] But it gives insight into what is a generally recognized property of traditional knowledge. The narrative "posts" (sender, addressee, hero) are so organized that the right to occupy the post of sender receives the following double grounding: it is based upon the fact of having occupied the post of addressee, and of having been recounted oneself, by virtue of the name one bears, by a previous narrative—in other words, having been positioned as the diegetic reference of other narrative events.[15] The knowledge transmitted by these narrations is in no way limited to the functions of enunciation; it determines in a single stroke what one must say in order to be heard, what one must listen to in order to speak, and what role one must play (on the scene of diegetic reality) to be the object of a narrative.

Thus the speech acts[16] relevant to this form of knowledge are performed not only by the speaker, but also by the listener, as well as by the third party referred to. The knowledge arising from such an apparatus may seem "condensed" in comparison with what I call "developed" knowledge. Our example clearly illustrates that a narrative tradition is also the tradition of the criteria defining a threefold competence—"know-how," "knowing how to speak," and "knowing how to hear" [savoir-faire, savoir-dire, savoir-entendre]— through which the community's relationship to itself and its environment is played out. What is transmitted through these narratives is the set of pragmatic rules that constitutes the social bond.

A fourth aspect of narrative knowledge meriting careful examination is its effect on time. Narrative form follows a rhythm; it is the synthesis of a meter beating time in regular periods and of accent modifying the length or amplitude of certain of those periods.[17] This vibratory, musical property of narrative is clearly revealed in the ritual performance of certain Cashinahua tales: they are handed down in initiation ceremonies, in absolutely fixed form, in a language whose meaning is obscured by lexical and syntactic anomalies, and they are sung as interminable, monotonous chants.[18] It is a strange brand of knowledge, you may say, that does not even make itself understood to the young men to whom it is addressed!

And yet this kind of knowledge is quite common; nursery rhymes are of this type, and repetitive forms of contemporary music have tried to recapture or at least approximate it. It exhibits a surprising feature: as meter takes precedence over accent in the production of sound (spoken or not), time ceases to be a support for memory to become an immemorial beating that, in the absence of a noticeable separation between periods, prevents their being numbered and consigns them to oblivion.[19] Consider the form of popular sayings, proverbs, and maxims: they are like splinters of potential narratives, or molds of old ones, which have continued to circulate on certain levels of the contemporary social edifice. In their prosody can be recognized the mark of that strange temporalization that jars the golden rule of our knowledge: "never forget."

Now there must be a congruence between this lethal function of narrative knowledge and the functions, cited earlier, of criteria formation, the unification of areas of competence, and social regulation. By way of a simplifying fiction, we can hypothesize that, against all expectations, a collectivity that takes narrative as its key form of competence has no need to remember its past. It finds the raw material for its social bond not only in the meaning of the narratives it recounts, but also in the act of reciting them. The narratives' reference may seem to belong to the past, but in reality it is always contemporaneous with the act of recitation. It is the present act that on each of its occurrences marshals in the ephemeral temporality inhabiting the space between the "I have heard" and the "you will hear."

The important thing about the pragmatic protocol of this kind of narration is that it betokens a theoretical identity between each of the narrative's occurrences. This may not in fact be the case, and often is not, and we should not blind ourselves to the element of humor or anxiety noticeable in the respect this etiquette inspires. The fact remains that what is emphasized is the metrical beat of the narrative occurrences, not each performance's differences in accent. It is in this sense that this mode of temporality can be said to be simultaneously evanescent and immemorial.[20]

Finally, a culture that gives precedence to the narrative form doubtless has no more of a need for special procedures to authorize its narratives than it has to remember its past. It is hard to imagine such a culture first isolating the post of narrator from the others in order to give it a privileged status in narrative pragmatics, then inquiring into what right the narrator (who is thus disconnected

from the narratee and diegesis) might have to recount what he recounts, and finally undertaking the analysis or anamnesis of its
own legitimacy. It is even harder to imagine it handing over the authority for its narratives to some incomprehensible subject of narration. The narratives themselves have this authority. In a sense,
the people are only that which actualizes the narratives: once
again, they do this not only by recounting them, but also by listening to them and recounting themselves through them; in other
words, by putting them into "play" in their institutions—thus by assigning themselves the posts of narratee and diegesis as well as the
post of narrator.

There is, then, an incommensurability between popular narrative pragmatics, which provides immediate legitimation, and the
language game known to the West as the question of legitimacy—or
rather, legitimacy as a referent in the game of inquiry. Narratives,
as we have seen, determine criteria of competence and/or illustrate
how they are to be applied. They thus define what has the right to
be said and done in the culture in question, and since they are
themselves a part of that culture, they are legitimated by the simple fact that they do what they do.

7. The Pragmatics of Scientific Knowledge

Let us attempt to characterize, if only in summary fashion, the classical conception of the pragmatics of scientific knowledge. In the
process, we will distinguish between the research game and the
teaching game.

Copernicus states that the path of the planets is circular.[21]
Whether this proposition is true or false, it carries within it a set of
tensions, all of which affect each of the pragmatic posts it brings
into play: sender, addressee, and referent. These "tensions" are
classes of prescriptions which regulate the admissibility of the
statement as "scientific."

First, the sender should speak the truth about the referent,
the path of the planets. What does this mean? That on the one hand
he is supposed to be able to provide proof of what he says, and on the
other hand he is supposed to be able to refute any opposing or contradictory statements concerning the same referent.

Second, it should be possible for the addressee validly to give
(or refuse) his assent to the statement he hears. This implies that

he is himself a potential sender, since when he formulates his agreement or disagreement he will be subject to the same double requirement (or proof or refutation) that Copernicus was. He is therefore supposed to have, potentially, the same qualities as Copernicus: he is his equal. But this will only before known when he speaks and under the above conditions. Before that, it will be impossible to say whether or not he is a scientific scholar.

Third, the referent (the path of the planets) of which Copernicus speaks is supposed to be "expressed" by his statement in conformity with what it actually is. But since what it is can only be known through statements of the same order as that of Copernicus, the rule of adequation becomes problematical. What I say is true because I prove that it is—but what proof is there that my proof is true?

The scientific solution of this difficulty consists in the observance of two rules. The first of these is dialectical or even rhetorical in the forensic sense:[22] a referent is that which is susceptible to proof and can be used as evidence in a debate. Not: I can prove something because reality is the way I say it is. But: as long as I can produce proof, it is permissible to think that reality is the way I say it is.[23] The second rule is metaphysical; the same referent cannot supply a plurality of contradictory or inconsistent proofs. Or stated differently: "God" is not deceptive.[24]

These two rules underlie what nineteenth-century science calls verification and twentieth-century science, falsification.[25] They allow a horizon of consensus to be brought to the debate between partners (the sender and the addressee). Not every consensus is a sign of truth; but it is presumed that the truth of a statement necessarily draws a consensus.

That covers research. It should be evident that research appeals to teaching as its necessary complement: the scientists needs an addressee who can in turn become the sender; he needs a partner. Otherwise, the verification of his statements would be impossible, since the nonrenewal of the requisite skills would eventually bring an end to the necessary, contradictory debate. Not only the truth of a scientist's statement, but also his competence, is at stake in that debate. One's competence is never an accomplished fact. It depends on whether or not the statement proposed is considered by one's peers to be worth discussion in a sequence of argumentation and refutation. The truth of the statement and the competence of its sender are thus subject to the collective approval of a group of persons who are competent on an equal basis. Equals are needed and must be created.

Didactics is what ensures that this reproduction takes place. It is different from the dialectical game of research. Briefly, its first presupposition is that the addressee, the student, does not know what the sender knows: obviously, that is why he has something to learn. Its second presupposition is that the student can learn what the sender knows and become an expert whose competence is equal to that of his master.[26] This double requirement supposes a third: that there are statements for which the exchange of arguments and the production of proof constituting the pragmatics of research are considered to have been sufficient, and which can therefore be transmitted through teaching as they stand, in the guise of indisputable truths.

In other words, you teach what you know: such is the expert. But as the student (the addressee of the didactic process) improves his skills, the expert can confide to him what he does not know but is trying to learn (at least if the expert is also involved in research). In this way, the student is introduced to the dialectics of research, or the game of producing scientific knowledge.

If we compare the pragmatics of science to that of narrative knowledge, we know the following properties:

1. Scientific knowledge requires that one language game, denotation, be retained and all others excluded. A statement's truth-value is the criterion determining its acceptability. Of course, we find other classes of statements, such as interrogatives ("How can we explain that . . . ?") and prescriptives ("Take a finite series of elements . . ."). But they are only present as turning points in the dialectical argumentation, which must end in a denotative statement.[27] In this context, then, one is "learned" if one can produce a true statement about a referent, and one is a scientist if one can produce verifiable or falsifiable statements about referents accessible to the experts.

2. Scientific knowledge is in this way set apart from the language games that combine to form the social bond. Unlike narrative knowledge, it is no longer a direct and shared component of the bond. But it is indirectly a component of it, because it develops into a profession and gives rise to institutions, and in modern societies language games consolidate themselves in the form of institutions run by qualified partners (the professional class). The relation between knowledge and society (that is, the sum total of partners in

the general agonistics, excluding scientists in their professional capacity) becomes one of mutual exteriority. A new
problem appears—that of the relationship between the scientific institution and society. Can this problem be solved
by didactics, for example, by the premise that any social
atom can acquire scientific competence?

3. Within the bounds of the game of research, the competence
required concerns the post of sender alone. There is no particular competence required of the addressee (it is required
only in didactics—the student must be intelligent). And
there is no competence required of the referent. Even in the
case of the human sciences, where it is an aspect of human
conduct, the referent is in principle external to the partners
engaged in scientific dialectics. Here, in contrast to the narrative game, a person does not have to know how to be what
knowledge says he is.

4. A statement of science gains no validity from the fact of being reported. Even in the case of pedagogy, it is taught only
if it is still verifiable in the present through argumentation
and proof. In itself, it is never secure from "falsification."[28]
The knowledge that has accumulated in the form of already
accepted statements can always be challenged. But conversely, any new statement that contradicts a previously
approved statement regarding the same referent can be accepted as valid only if it refutes the previous statement by
producing arguments and proofs.

5. The game of science thus implies a diachronic temporality,
that is, a memory and a project. The current sender of a scientific statement is supposed to be acquainted with previous statements concerning its referent (bibliography) and
only proposes a new statement on the subject if it differs
from the previous ones. Here, what I have called the "accent" of each performance, and by that token the polemical
function of the game, takes precedence over the "meter."
This diachrony, which assumes memory and a search for
the new, represents in principle a cumulative process. Its
"rhythm," or the relationship between accent and meter, is
variable.[29]

These properties are well known. But they are worth recalling
for two reasons. First, drawing a parallel between science and non-

scientific (narrative) knowledge helps us understand, or at least sense, that the former's existence is no more—and no less—necessary than the latter's. Both are composed of sets of statements; the statements are "moves" made by the players within the framework of generally applicable rules; these rules are specific to each particular kind of knowledge, and the "moves" judged to be "good" in one cannot be of the same type as those judged "good" in another, unless it happens that way by chance.

It is therefore impossible to judge the existence or validity of narrative knowledge on the basis of scientific knowledge and vice versa: the relevant criteria are different. All we can do is gaze in wonderment at the diversity of discursive species, just as we do at the diversity of plant or animal species. Lamenting the "loss of meaning" in postmodernity boils down to mourning the fact that knowledge is no longer principally narrative. Such a reaction does not necessarily follow. Neither does an attempt to derive or engender (using operators like development) scientific knowledge from narrative knowledge, as if the former contained the latter in an embryonic state.

Nevertheless, language species, like living species, are interrelated, and their relations are far from harmonious. The second point justifying this quick reminder on the properties of the language game of science concerns, precisely, its relation to narrative knowledge. I have said that narrative knowledge does not give priority to the question of its own legitimation and that it certifies itself in the pragmatics of its own transmission without having recourse to argumentation and proof. This is why its incomprehension of the problems of scientific discourse is accompanied by a certain tolerance: it approaches such discourse primarily as a variant in the family of narrative cultures.[30] The opposite is not true. The scientist questions the validity of narrative statements and concludes that they are never subject to argumentation or proof.[31] He classifies them as belonging to a different mentality: savage, primitive, underdeveloped, backward, alienated, composed of opinions, customs, authority, prejudice, ignorance, ideology. Narratives are fables, myths, legends, fit only for women and children. At best, attempts are made to throw some rays of light into this obscurantism, to civilize, educate, develop.

This unequal relationship is an intrinsic effect of the rules specific to each game. We all know its symptoms. It is the entire history of cultural imperialism from the dawn of Western civilization. It is important to recognize its special tenor, which sets it apart from all other forms of imperialism: it is governed by the demand for legitimation.

8. The Narrative Function and the Legitimation of Knowledge

Today the problem of legitimation is no longer considered a failing of the language game of science. It would be more accurate to say that it has itself been legitimated as a problem, that is, as a heuristic driving force. But this way of dealing with it by reversing the situation of a recent date. Before it came to this point (what some call positivism), scientific knowledge sought other solutions. It is remarkable that for a long time it could not help resorting for its solutions to procedures that, overtly or not, belong to narrative knowledge.

This return of the narrative in the non-narrative, in one form or another, should not be thought of as having been superseded once and for all. A crude proof of this: what do scientists do when they appear on television or are interviewed in the newspaper after making a "discovery"? They recount an epic of knowledge that is in fact wholly unepic. They play by the rules of the narrative game; its influence remains considerable not only on the users of the media, but also on the scientist's sentiments. This fact is neither trivial nor accessory: it concerns the relationship of scientific knowledge to "popular" knowledge, or what is left of it. The state spends large amounts of money to enable science to pass itself off as an epic: the State's own credibility is based on that epic, which it uses to obtain the public consent its decision makers need.[32]

It is not inconceivable that the recourse to narrative is inevitable, at least to the extent that the language game of science desires its statements to be true but does not have the resources to legitimate their truth on its own. If this is the case, it is necessary to admit an irreducible need for history understood, as outlined above—not as a need to remember or to project (a need for historicity, for accent), but on the contrary as a need to forget (a need for *metrum*).

We are anticipating ourselves. But as we proceed we should keep in mind that the apparently obsolete solutions that have been found for the problem of legitimation are not obsolete in principle, but only in their expression; we should not be surprised if we find that they have persisted to this day in other forms. Do not we ourselves, at this moment, feel obliged to mount a narrative of scientific knowledge in the West in order to clarify its status?

The new language game of science posed the problem of its own legitimation at the very beginning—in Plato. This is not the proper place for an exegesis of the passages in the *Dialogues* in which the pragmatics of science is set in motion, either explicitly as a theme or implicitly as a presupposition. The game of dialogue, with its specific requirements, encapsulates that pragmatics, enveloping within itself its two functions of research and teaching. We encounter some of the same rules previously enumerated: argumentation with a view only to consensus (*homologia*); the unicity of the referent as a guarantee for the possibility of agreement; parity between partners; and even an indirect recognition that it is a question of a game and not a destiny, since those who refuse to accept the rules, out of weakness or crudeness, are excluded.[33]

There remains the fact that, given the scientific nature of the game, the question of its own legitimacy must be among those raised in the dialogues. A well-known example of this, which is all the more important since it links this question to that of sociopolitical authority from the start, is to be found in books 6 and 7 of *The Republic*. As we know, the answer, at least part of it, comes in the form of a narrative—the allegory of the cave, which recounts how and why men yearn for narratives and fail to recognize knowledge. Knowledge is thus founded on the narrative of its own martyrdom.

There is more. The legitimation effort, the *Dialogues* of Plato, gives ammunition to narrative by virtue of its own form: each of the dialogues takes the form of a narrative of a scientific discussion. It is of little consequence here that the story of the debate is shown rather than reported, staged rather than narrated,[34] and is therefore more closely related to tragedy than epic. The fact is that the Platonic discourse that inaugurates science is not scientific, precisely to the extent that it attempts to legitimate science. Scientific knowledge cannot know and make known that it is the true knowledge without resorting to the other, narrative, kind of knowledge, which from its point of view is no knowledge at all. Without such recourse it would be in the position of presupposing its own validity and would be stooping to what it condemns: begging the question, proceeding on prejudice. But does it not fall into the same trap by using narrative as its authority?

This is not the place to chart the recurrence of the narrative in the scientific by way of the latter's discourses of legitimation, which include but are not limited to the great ancient, medieval, and classical philosophies. Endless torment. As resolute a philosophy as that of Descartes can only demonstrate the legitimacy of science through what Valéry called the story of a mind,[35] or else in a *Bildungsroman,* which is what the *Discourse on Method* amounts to. Aristotle was doubtless one of the most modern of all in separating the rules to which statements declared scientific must conform (the *Organon*) from the search for their legitimacy in a discourse on Being (the *Metaphysics*). Even more modern was his suggestion that scientific knowledge, including its pretension to express the being of the referent, is composed only of arguments and proofs—in other words, of dialectics.[36]

With modern science, two new features appear in the problematic of legitimation. To begin with, it leaves behind the metaphysical search for a first proof or transcendental authority as a response to the question: "How do you prove the proof?" or, more generally, "Who decides the conditions of truth?" It is recognized that the conditions of truth, in other words, the rules of the game of science, are immanent in that game, that they can only be established within the bonds of a debate that is already scientific in nature, and that there is no other proof that the rules are good than the consensus extended to them by the experts.

Accompanying the modern proclivity to define the conditions of a discourse in a discourse on those conditions is a renewed dignity for narrative (popular) cultures, already noticeable in Renaissance Humanism and variously present in the Enlightenment, the *Sturm und Drang,* German idealist philosophy, and the historical school in France. Narration is no longer an involuntary lapse in the legitimation process. The explicit appeal to narrative in the problematic of knowledge is concomitant with the liberation of the bourgeois classes from the traditional authorities. Narrative knowledge makes a resurgence in the West as a way of solving the problem of legitimating the new authorities. It is natural in a narrative problematic for such a question to solicit the name of a hero as its response: *Who* has the right to decide for society? Who is the subject whose prescriptions are norms for those they obligate?

This way of inquiring into sociopolitical legitimacy combines with the new scientific attitude: the nature of the hero is the people, the sign of legitimacy is the people's consensus, and their mode of creating norms in deliberation. The notion of progress is a necessary outgrowth of this. It represents nothing other than the movement by which knowledge is presumed to accumulate—but this movement is extended to the new sociopolitical subject. The people debate among themselves about what is just or unjust in the same way that the scientific community debates about what is true or false; they accumulate civil laws just as scientists accumulate scientific laws; they perfect their rules of consensus just as the scientists produce new "paradigms" to revise their rules in light of what they have learned.[37]

It is clear that what is meant here by "the people" is entirely different from what is implied by traditional narrative knowledge, which, as we have seen, requires to instituting deliberation, no cumulative progression, no pretension to universality; these are the operators of scientific knowledge. It is therefore not at all surprising that the representatives of the new process of legitimation by "the people" should be at the same time actively involved in destroying the traditional knowledge of peoples, perceived from the point forward as minorities or potential separatist movements destined only to spread obscurantism.[38]

We can see too that the real existence of this necessarily abstract subject (it is abstract because it is uniquely modeled on the paradigm of the subject of knowledge—that is, one who sends-receives denotative statements with truth-value to the exclusion of other language games) depends on the institutions within which that subject is supposed to deliberate and decide, and which comprise all or part of the State. The question of the State becomes intimately entwined with that of scientific knowledge.

But it is also clear that this interlocking is many sided. The "people" (the nation, or even humanity), and especially their political institutions, are not content to know—they legislate. That is, they formulate prescriptions that have the status of norms.[39] They therefore exercise their competence not only with respect to denotative utterances concerning what is true, but also prescriptive utterances with pretentions to justice. As already said, what characterizes narrative knowledge, what forms the basis of our conception of it, precisely that it combines both of these kinds of competence, not to mention all the others.

The mode of legitimation we are discussing, which reintroduces narrative as the validity of knowledge, can thus take two routes, depending on whether it represents the subject of the narrative as cognitive or practical, as a hero of knowledge or a hero of liberty. Because of this alternative, not only does the meaning of legitimation vary, but it is already apparent that narrative itself is incapable of describing that meaning adequately.

Notes

1. See Karl Popper, *Logik der Forschung* (Wien: Springer, 1935) [Eng. trans. Popper et al., *The Logic of Scientific Discovery* (New York: Basic

Books, 1949)], and "Normal Science and its Dangers," in Imre Lakatos and Alan Musgrave, eds., *Criticism and the Growth of Knowledge* (Cambridge: Cambridge University Press, 1970).

2. See Jean Beaufret, *Le Poème de Parménide* (Paris: Presses Universitaires de France, 1955).

3. Again in the sense of *Bildung* (or, in English, "culture"), as accredited by culturalism. The term is preromantic and romantic; cf. Hegel's *Volksgeist*.

4. See the American culturalist school: Cora DuBois, Abram Kardiner, Ralph Linton, Margaret Mead.

5. See studies of the institution of European folklore traditions from the end of the eighteenth century in their relation to romanticism, for example, the brothers Grimm and Vuk Karadic (Serbian folktales).

6. This was, briefly stated, Lucien Lévy Bruhl's thesis in *La Mentalité primitive* (Paris: Alcan, 1922) [Eng. trans. Lillian Clare, *Primitive Mentality* (New York: Macmillan, 1923)].

7. Claude Lévi-Strauss, *La Pensée sauvage* (Paris: Plon, 1962) [Eng. trans. *The Savage Mind* (Chicago, University of Chicago, 1966)].

8. Robert Jaulin, *La paix blanche* (Paris: Seuil, 1970).

9. Vladimir Propp, *Morphology of the Folktale,* trans. Laurence Scott with intro. by Suatana Pirkora-Jakobson [Publications of the American Folklore Society, Bibliographical and Special Series, no. 9 (Bloomington, Ind., 1958); 2d ed. rev. (Austin, Tex. University of Texas Press, 1968).

10. Claude Lévi-Strauss, "La Structure des Mythes" (1955), in *Anthropologie Structurale* (Paris: Plon, 1958) [Eng. trans. Claire Jacobson and Brooke Grundfest Schoepf, *Structural Anthropology* (New York: Basic Books, 1963)], and "La Structure et la forme: Réflexions sur un ouvrage de Vladimir Propp, *Cahiers de l'Institut de science èconomique appliquèe,* 99, series M, 7 (1960) [in Claude Lévi-Strauss, *Structural Anthropology II,* trans. Monique Layton (New York: Basic Books, 1976). The essay will also be included in Vladimir Propp, *Theory and History of Folklore,* trans. Ariadna and Richard Martin, intro. by Anatoly Liberman, Theory and History of Literature, vol. 5 (Minneapolis: University of Minnesota Press, 1984].

11. Geza Róheim, *Psychoanalysis and Anthropology* (New York: International Universities Press, 1959).

12. André M. d'Ans, *Le Dit des vrais hommes* (Paris: Union Générale d'Edition, 1978).

13. Ibid., p. 7.

14. I have made use of it here because of the pragmatic "etiquette" surrounding the transmission of the narratives; the anthropologist details it with great care. See Pierre Clastres, *Le grand Parler: Mythes et chants sacrés des Indiens Guarani* (Paris: Seuil, 1972).

15. For a narratology that treats the pragmatic dimension, see Gérard Genette, *Figures III* (Paris: Seuil, 1972) [Eng. trans. Jane E. Lewin, *Narrative Discourse* (New York: Cornell University Press, 1980).

16. John Searle, *Speech Acts* (Cambridge: Cambridge University Press, 1969).

17. The relationship between meter and accent, which constitutes and dissolves rhythm, is at the center of Hegel's reflection on speculation. See sec. 4 of the preface to the *Phenomenology of Spirit*.

18. I would like to thank André M. d'Ans for kindly providing this information.

19. See Daniel Charles's analyses in *Le Temps de la voix* (Paris: Delarge, 1978) and those of Dominique Avron in *L'Appareil musical* (Paris: Union Générale d'Edition, 1978).

20. See Mircea Eliade, *Le Mythe de l'eternel retour: Archétypes et répétitions* (Paris: Gallimard, 1949) [Eng. trans. Willard R. Trask, *The Myth of the Eternal Return* (New York: Pantheon Books, 1954)].

21. The example is borrowed from Frege, "Über Sinn und Bedeutung" (1892) [Eng. trans. Max Black and Peter Geach, "On Sense and Reference," in *Translations from the Philosophical Writings of Gottlob Frege* (Oxford: Blackwell, 1960)].

22. Bruno Latour and Paolo Fabbri, "Rhétorique de la science," *Actes de la recherche en sciences sociales 13* (1977): 81–95.

23. Gaston Bachelard, *Le Nouvel Esprit scientifique* (Paris: Presses Universitaires de France, 1934).

24. Descartes, *Méditations métaphysiques* (1641), Méditation 4.

25. See for example Karl G. Hempel, *Philosophy of Natural Science* (Englewood Cliffs, N.J.: Prentice-Hall, 1966).

26. There is no space here to discuss the difficulties raised by this double presupposition. See Vincent Descombes, *L'Inconscient malgré lui* (Paris: Editions de Minuit, 1977).

27. This remark avoids a major difficulty, one that would also arise in the examination of narration: the distinction between language games and discursive games. I will not discuss it here.

28. In the sense indicated in note 25.

29. Thomas Kuhn, *The Structure of Scientific Revolutions* (Chicago: University of Chicago Press, 1962).

30. Cf. children's attitude toward their first science lessons, or the way natives interpret the ethnologist's explanations (see Lévi-Strauss, *The Savage Mind* [note 7], chap. 1).

31. That is why Métraux commented to Clastres, "To be able to study a primitive society, it already has to be a little decayed." In effect, the native informant must be able to see his own society through the eyes of the ethnologist; he must be able to question the functioning of its institutions and therefore their legitimacy. Reflecting on his failure with the Achè tribe, Clastres concludes, "And so the Aché accepted presents they had not asked for while at the same time refusing attempts at a dialogue, because they were strong enough not to need it: we would start talking when they were sick" [quoted by M. Cartry in "Pierre Clastres," *Libre 4* (1978)].

32. On scientistic ideology, see *Survivre* 9 (1971), reprinted in Jaubert and Lévy-Leblond, *(Auto)critique* (note 26), pp. 51ff. At the end of their collection there is a biobliography listing periodicals and groups fighting against the various forms of subordination of science to the system.

33. Victor Goldschmidt, *Les Dialogues de Platon* (Paris: Presses Universitaires de France, 1947).

34. These terms are borrowed from Genette, *Figures 111.*

35. Paul Valéry, *Introduction à la méthode de Léonard de Vinci* (1894) [(Paris: Gallimard, 1957): this volume also contains "Marginalia" (1930), "Note et digression" (1919), "Léonard et les philosophes" (1929); Eng. trans. in *The Collected Works of Paul Valéry,* ed. Jackson Matthews (Princeton: Princeton University Press, 1956–75), vol. 8].

36. Pierre Aubenque, *Le Problème de l'Etre chez Aristote* (Paris: Presses Universitaires de France, 1962).

37. Pierre Duhem, *Essai sur la notion de théorie physique de Platon à Galilée* (Paris: Hermann, 1908) [Eng. trans. Edmund Doland and Chaninah Maschler, *To Save the Phenomena: An Essay in the Idea of Physical Theory from Plato to Galileo* (Chicago: University of Chicago Press, 1969)]; Alexandre Koyré, *Etudes Galiléennes* (1940; Paris: Hermann, 1966 [Eng. trans. John Mephan, *Galileo Studies* (Hassocks, Eng.: Harvester Press, 1978)]; Thomas Kuhn, *Structure of Scientific Revolutions.*

38. Michel de Certeau, Dominique Julia, Jacques Revel, *Une Politique de la langue: La Rèvolution Française et les patois* (Paris: Gallimard, 1975).

39. On the distinction between prescriptions and norms, see G. Kalinowski, "Du Métalanguage en logique. Réflexions sur la logique déontique et son rapport avec la logique des normes," *Documents de travail* 48 (Università di Urbino, 1975).

Modernity versus Postmodernity*

Jürgen Habermas

Last year, architects were admitted to the Biennial in Venice, following painters and filmmakers. The note sounded at this first Architecture Biennial .was one of disappointment. I would describe it by saying that those who exhibited in Venice formed an avant-garde of reversed fronts. I mean that they sacrificed the tradition of modernity in order to make room for a new historicism. Upon this occasion, a critic of the German newspaper, *Frankfurter Allgemeine Zeitung,* advanced a thesis whose significance reaches beyond this particular event; it is a diagnosis of our times: "Postmodernity definitely presents itself as Antimodernity." This statement describes an emotional current of our times which has penetrated all spheres of intellectual life. It has placed on the agenda theories of postenlightenment, postmodernity, even of posthistory.

From history we know the phrase:

---

* This essay was delivered as a James Lecture of The New York Institute for the Humanities at New York University on March 5, 1981. It had been delivered first in German in September 1980 when Habermas was awarded the Theodor W. Adorno prize by the city of Frankfurt. It was first published in *New German Critique* 22 (Winter 1981).

"The Ancients and the Moderns"

Let me begin by defining these concepts. The term "modern" has a long history, one which has been investigated by Hans Robert Jauss. The word "modern" in its Latin form "modernus" was used for the first time in the late 5th century in order to distinguish the present, which had become officially Christian, from the Roman and pagan past. With varying content, the term "modern" again and again expresses the consciousness of an epoch that relates itself to the past of antiquity, in order to view itself as the result of a transition from the old to the new.

Some writers restrict this concept of "modernity" to the Renaissance, but this is historically too narrow. People considered themselves modern during the period of Charles the Great, in the 12th century, as well as in France in the late 17th century, at the time of the famous "Querelle des Anciens et des Modernes." This is to say, the term "modern" appeared and reappeared exactly during those periods in Europe when the consciousness of a new epoch formed itself through a renewed relationship to the ancients—whenever, moreover, antiquity was considered a model to be recovered through some kind of imitation.

The spell which the classics of the ancient world cast upon the spirit of later times was first dissolved with the ideals of the French Enlightenment. Specifically, the idea of being "modern" by looking back to the ancients changed with the belief, inspired by modern science, in the infinite progress of knowledge and in the infinite advance towards social and moral betterment. Another form of modernist consciousness was formed in the wake of this change. The romantic modernist sought to oppose the antique ideals of the classicists; he looked for a new historical epoch, and found it in the idealized Middle Ages. However, this new ideal age, established early in the 19th century, did not remain a fixed ideal. In the course of the 19th century, there emerged out of this romantic spirit that radicalized consciousness of modernity which freed itself from all specific historical ties. This most recent modernism simply makes an abstract opposition between tradition and the present; and we are, in a way, still the contemporaries of that kind of aesthetic modernity which first appeared in the midst of the 19th century. Since then, the distinguishing mark of works, which count as modern, is the "new." The characteristic of such works is "the new" which will be overcome and made obsolete through the novelty of the next style. But, while that which is merely "stylish" will soon become outmoded, that which is modern preserves a secret tie to the classical. Of course, whatever can survive time has always been considered to be a classic. But the emphatically modern document no longer borrows this power of being a classic from the authority of a past epoch; instead, a modern work becomes a classic because it has once been authentically modern. Our sense of modernity creates its own self-enclosed canons of being classic. In this sense we speak, e.g., in view of the history of modern art, of classical modernity. The relation between "modern" and "classical" has definitely lost a fixed historical reference.

The Discipline of Aesthetic Modernity

The spirit and discipline of aesthetic modernity assumed clear contours in the work of Baudelaire. Modernity then unfolded in various avant-garde movements, and finally reached its climax in the Café Voltaire of the Dadaists, and in Surrealism. Aesthetic modernity is characterized by attitudes which find a common focus in a changed consciousness of time. This time consciousness expresses itself through metaphors of the vanguard and the avant-garde. The avant-garde understands itself as invading unknown territory, exposing itself to the dangers of sudden, of shocking encounters, conquering an as yet unoccupied future. The avant-garde must find a direction in a landscape into which no one seems to have yet ventured.

But these forward gropings, this anticipation of an undefined future and the cult of the new, mean in fact the exaltation of the present. The new time consciousness, which enters philosophy in the writings of Bergson, does more than express the experience of mobility in society, acceleration in history, of discontinuity in everyday life. The new value placed on the transitory, the elusive, and the ephemeral, the very celebration of dynamism, discloses the longing for an undefiled, an immaculate and stable present.

This explains the rather abstract language in which the modernist temper has spoken of the "past." Individual epochs lose their distinct forces. Historical memory is replaced by the heroic affinity of the present with the extremes of history: a sense of time wherein decadence immediately recognizes itself in the barbaric, the wild and the primitive. We observe the anarchistic intention of blowing up the continuum of history, and we can account for it in terms of the subversive force of this new aesthetic consciousness. Modernity revolts against the normalizing functions of tradition; modernity lives on the experience of rebelling against all that is normative. This revolt is one way to neutralize the standards of both, morality and utility. This aesthetic consciousness continuously stages a dialectical play between secrecy and public scandal; it is addicted to the fascination of that horror which accompanies the act of profaning, and is yet always in flight from the trivial results of profanation.

On the other hand, the time consciousness articulated in avant-garde art is not simply ahistorical; it is directed against what might be called a false normativity in history. The modern, avant-garde spirit has sought, instead, to use the past in a different way; it disposes over those pasts which have been made available by the objectifying scholarship of historicism, but it opposes at the same time a neutralized history, which is locked up in the museum of historicism.

Drawing upon the spirit of surrealism, Walter Benjamin constructs the relationship of modernity to history, in what I would call a post-historicist attitude. He reminds us of the self-understanding of the French Revolution: "The Revolution cited ancient Rome, just as fashion cites an antiquated dress. Fashion has a scent for what is current, whenever this moves within the thicket of what was once." This is Benjamin's concept of the *Jetztzeit,* of the present as a moment of revelation; a time, in which splinters of a messianic presence are enmeshed. In this sense, for Robespierre, the antique Rome was a past laden with momentary revelations.

Now, this spirit of aesthetic modernity has recently begun to age. It has been recited once more in the 1960s; after the 1970s, however, we must admit to ourselves that this modernism arouses a much fainter response today than it did fifteen years ago. Octavio Paz, a fellow traveller of modernity, noted already in the middle of the 1960s that "the avant-garde of 1967 repeats the deeds and gestures of those of 1917. We are experiencing the end of the idea of modern art." The work of Peter Bürger has since taught us to speak of "post-avant-garde" art; this term is chosen to indicate the failure of the surrealist rebellion. But, what is the meaning of this failure? Does it signal a farewell to modernity? Thinking more generally, does the existence of a post-avant-garde mean there is a transition to that broader phenomenon called postmodernity?

This is in fact how Daniel Bell, the most brilliant of the American neoconservatives, interprets matters. In his book, *The Cultural Contradictions of Capitalism,* Bell argues that the crises of the developed societies of the West are to be traced back to a split between culture and society. Modernist culture has come to penetrate the values of everyday life; the life-world is infected by modernism. Because of the forces of modernism, the principle of unlimited self-realization, the demand for authentic self-experience and the subjectivism of a hyperstimulated sensitivity have come to be dominant. This temperament unleashes hedonistic motives irreconcilable with the discipline of professional life in society, Bell says. Moreover, modernist culture is altogether incompatible with the moral basis of a purposive rational conduct of life. In this manner, Bell places the burden of responsibility for the dissolution of the Protestant ethic (a phenomenon which has already disturbed Max Weber), on the "adversary culture." Culture, in its modern form, stirs up hatred against the conventions and virtues of an everyday life, which has become rationalized under the pressures of economic and administrative imperatives.

I would call your attention to a complex wrinkle in this view. The impulse of modernity, we are told on the other hand, is exhausted; anyone who considers himself avant-garde can read his own death warrant. Although the avant-garde is still considered to be expanding, it is supposedly no longer creative. Modernism is dominant but dead. For the neoconservative, the question then arises: how can norms arise in society which will limit liberalism, reestablish the ethic of discipline and work? What new norms will put a brake on the levelling caused by the social welfare state, so that the virtues of individual competition for achievement can again dominate? Bell sees a religious revival to be the only solution. Religious faith tied to a faith in tradition will provide individuals with clearly defined identities, and with existential security.

Cultural Modernity and Societal Modernization

One can certainly not conjure up by magic the compelling beliefs which command authority. Analyses like Bell's, therefore, only result in an attitude which is spreading in Germany no less than here in the States: an intellectual and political confrontation with the carriers of cultural modernity. I cite Peter Steinfells, an observer of the new style which the neoconservatives have imposed upon the intellectual scene in the 1970s.

The struggles takes the form of exposing every manifestation of what could be considered an oppositionist mentality and tracing its "logic" so as to link it to various forms of extremism: drawing the connection between modernism and nihilism . . . between government regulation and totalitarianism, between criticism of arms expenditures and subservience to communism, between Women's liberation or homosexual rights and the destruction of the family . . . between the Left generally and terrorism, anti-semitism, and fascism. . . . (Steinfells, *The Neoconservatives,* 65)

The *ad hominem* approach and the bitterness of these intellectual accusations have also been trumpeted loudly in Germany. They should not be explained so much in terms of the psychology of neoconservative writers; rather, they are rooted in the analytical weaknesses of neoconservative doctrine itself.

Neoconservatism shifts onto cultural modernism the uncomfortable burdens of a more or less successful capitalist modernization of the economy and society. The neoconservative doctrine blurs the relationship between the welcomed process of societal modernization on the one hand, and the lamented cultural development on the other. The neoconservative does not uncover the economic and social causes for the altered attitudes towards work, consumption, achievement, and leisure. Consequently, he attributes all of the following—hedonism, the lack of social identification, the lack of obedience, narcissism, the withdrawal from status and achievement competition—to the domain of "culture." In fact, however, culture is intervening in the creation of all these problems in only a very indirect and mediated fashion.

In the neoconservative view, those intellectuals who still feel themselves committed to the project of modernity are then presented as taking the place of those unanalyzed causes. The mood which feeds neoconservatism today in no way originates from the discontents about the antinomian consequences of a culture breaking from the museums into the stream of ordinary life. These discontents have not been called into life by modernist intellectuals. They are rooted in deep seated reactions against the process of *societal* modernization. Under the pressures of the dynamics of economic growth and the organizational accomplishments of the state, this social modernization penetrates deeper and deeper into previous forms of human existence. I would describe this subordination of the life-worlds under system's imperatives as a matter of disturbing the communicative infrastructure of everyday life.

Thus, for example, neo-populist protests only bring to expression in pointed fashion a widespread fear regarding the destruction of the urban and natural environment, and of forms of human sociability. There is a certain irony about these protests in terms of neoconservatism. The task of passing on a cultural tradition, of social integration, and of socialization require the adherence to a criterion of communicative rationalization occasions for protest and discontent originate exactly when communicative action, centered on the reproduction and transmission of values and norms, are penetrated by a form of modernization guided by standards of economic and administrative rationality; however, those very spheres are dependent on quite different standards of rationalization—on the standards of what I would call communicative rationality. But, neoconservative doctrines turn our attention precisely away from such societal processes: they project the causes, which they do not bring to light, onto the plane of a subversive culture and its advocates.

To be sure, cultural modernity generates its own aporias as well. Independently from the consequences of *societal* modernization, and from *within the perspective* of *cultural* development itself, there originate motives for doubting the project of modernity. Having dealt with a feeble kind of criticism of modernity—that of neoconservatism—let me now move our discussion of modernity and its discontents into a different domain that touches on these aporias of cultural modernity, issues which often serve only as a pretense for those positions (which either call for a postmodernity, or recommend a return to some form of premodernity or which throw modernity radically overboard).

The Project of Enlightenment

The idea of modernity is intimately tied to the development of European art; but what I call "the project of modernity" comes only into focus when we dispense with the usual concentration upon art. Let me start a different analysis by recalling an idea from Max Weber. He characterized cultural modernity as the separation of the substantive reason expressed in religion and metaphysics into three autonomous spheres. They are: science, morality and art. These came to be differentiated because the unified world conceptions of religion and metaphysics fell apart. Since the 18th century, the problems inherited from these older world-views could be rearranged so as to fall under specific aspects of validity: truth, normative rightness, authenticity and beauty. They could then be handled as questions of knowledge, or of justice and morality, or of taste.

Scientific discourse, theories of morality, jurisprudence, the production and criticism of art, could in turn be institutionalized. Each domain of culture could be made to correspond to cultural professions, in which problems could be dealt with as the concern of special experts. This professionalized treatment of the cultural tradition brings to the fore the intrinsic structures of each of the three dimensions of culture. There appear the structures of cognitive-instrumental, moral-practical, and of aesthetic-expressive rationality, each of these under the control of specialists who seem more adept at being logical in these particular ways than other people are. As a result, the distance has grown between the culture of the experts and that of the larger public. What accrues to culture through specialized treatment and reflexion does not immediately and necessarily become the property of everyday praxis. With cultural rationalization of this sort, the threat increases that the life-world, whose traditional substance has already been devalued, will become more and more impoverished.

The project of modernity formulated in the 18th century by the philosophers of the Enlightenment consisted in their efforts to develop objective science, universal morality and law, and autonomous art, according to their inner logic. At the same time, this project intended to release the cognitive potentials of each of these domains to set them free from their esoteric forms. The Enlightenment philosophers wanted to utilize this accumulation of specialized culture for the enrichment of everyday life, that is to say, for the rational organization of everyday social life.

Enlightenment thinkers of the cast of mind of Condorcet still had the extravagant expectation that the arts and the sciences would promote not only the control of natural forces, but would also further understanding of the world and of the self, would promote moral progress, the justice of institutions, and even the happiness of human beings. The 20th century has shattered this optimism. The differentiation of science, morality, and art has come to mean the autonomy of the segments treated by the specialist and at the same time letting them split off from the hermeneutics of everyday communication. This splitting off is the problem that has given rise to those efforts to "negate" the culture of expertise. But the problem won't go away: should we try to hold on to the *intentions* of the Enlightenment, feeble as they may be, or should we declare the entire project of modernity a lost cause? I now want to return to the problem of artistic culture, having explained why, historically, that aesthetic modernity is a part only of cultural modernity in general.

The False Programs of the Negation of Culture

Greatly oversimplifying, I would say in the history of modern art one can detect a trend toward ever greater autonomy in the definition and practice of art. The category of "beauty" and the domain of beautiful objects were first constituted in the Renaissance. In the course of the 18th century, literature, the fine arts and music were institutionalized as activities independent from sacred and courtly life. Finally, around the middle of the 19th century an aestheticist conception of art emerged, which encouraged the artist to produce his work according to the distinct consciousness of art for art's sake. The autonomy of the aesthetic sphere could then become a deliberate project: the talented artist could lend authentic expression to those experiences he had in encountering his own de-centered subjectivity, detached from the constraints of routinized cognition and everyday action.

In the mid-19th century, in painting and literature, a movement begin which Octavio Paz finds epitomized already in the art criticism of Baudelaire. Color, lines, sounds and movement ceased to serve primarily the cause of representation; the media of expression and the techniques of production themselves became the aesthetic object. Theodor W. Adorno could therefore begin his *Aesthetic Theory* with the following sentence: "It is now taken for granted that nothing which concerns art can be taken for granted any more: neither art itself, nor art in its relationship to the whole, nor even the right of art to exist." And this is what surrealism then denied: *das Existenzrecht der Kunst als Kunst*. To be sure, surrealism would not have challenged the right of art to exist, if modern art no longer had advanced a promise of happiness concerning its own relationship "to the whole" of life. For Schiller, such a promise was delivered by aesthetic intuition, but not fulfilled by it. Schiller's *Letters on the Aesthetic Education of Man* speak to us of a utopia reaching beyond art itself. But by the time of Baudelaire, who repeated this *promesse de bonheur*, via art, the utopia of reconciliation with society had gone sour. A relation of opposites had come into being; art had become a critical mirror, showing the irreconcilable nature of the aesthetic and the social world. This modernist transformation was all the more painfully realized, the more art alienated itself from life and withdrew into the untouchableness of complete autonomy. Out of such emotional currents finally gathered those explosive energies which unloaded themselves in the surrealist attempt to blow up the autarkical sphere of art and to force a reconciliation of art and life.

But all those attempts to level art and life, fiction and praxis, appearance and reality to one plane; the attempts to remove the distinction between artifact and object of use, between conscious staging and spontaneous excitement; the attempts to declare everything to be art and everyone to be artist, to retract all criteria and to equate aesthetic judgment with the expression of subjective experiences—all these undertakings have proved themselves to be sort of nonsense experiments. These experiments have served to bring back to life, and to illuminate all the more glaringly, exactly those structures of art which they were meant to dissolve. They gave a new legitimacy, as an end in itself, to appearance as the medium of fiction, to the transcendence of the art work over society, to be concentrated and planned character of artistic production as well as to the special cognitive status of judgments of taste. The radical attempt to negate art has ended up ironically by giving due exactly to these categories through which Enlightenment aesthetics had circumscribed its object domain. The surrealists waged the most extreme warfare, but two mistakes in particular destroyed their revolt. First, when the containers of an autonomously developed cultural sphere are shattered, the contents get dispersed. Nothing remains from a desublimated meaning or a destructured form; an emancipatory effect does not follow.

Their second mistake has more important consequences. In everyday communication, cognitive meanings, moral expectations, subjective expressions and evaluations must relate to one another. Communication processes need a cultural tradition covering all spheres—cognitive, moral-practical and expressive. A rationalized everyday life, therefore, could hardly be saved from cultural impoverishment through breaking open a single cultural sphere—art— and so providing access to just one of the specialized knowledge complexes. The surrealist revolt would have replaced only one abstraction.

In the sphere of theoretical knowledge and morality as well, there are parallels to this failed attempt of what we might call the false negation of culture. Only they are less pronounced. Since the days of the Young Hegelians, there has been talk about the negation of philosophy. Since Marx, the question of the relationship of theory and practice has been posed. However, Marxist intellectuals joined a social movement; and only at its peripheries were there sectarian attempts to carry out a program of the negation of philosophy similar to the surrealist program to negate art. A parallel to the surrealist mistakes becomes visible in these programs when one observes the consequences of dogmatism and of moral rigorism.

A reified everyday praxis can be cured only by creating uncon-strained interaction of the cognitive with the moral-practical and the aesthetic-expressive elements. Reification cannot be overcome by forcing just one of those highly stylized cultural spheres to open up and become more accessible. Instead, we see under certain cir-cumstances a relationship emerge between terroristic activities and the overextension of any one of these spheres into other domains: examples would be tendencies to aestheticize politics, or to replace politics by moral rigorism or to submit it to the dogmatism of a doc-trine. These phenomena should not lead us, however, into denounc-ing the intentions of the surviving Enlightenment tradition as intentions rooted in a "terroristic reason." Those who lump together the very project of modernity with the state of consciousness and the spectacular action of the individual terrorist are no less short-sighted than those who would claim that the incomparably more persistent and extensive bureaucratic terror practiced in the dark, in the cellars of the military and secret police, and in camps and institutions, is the *raison d'être* of the modern state, only because this kind of administrative terror makes use of the coercive means of modern bureaucracies.

Alternatives

I think that instead of giving up modernity and its project as a lost cause, we should learn from the mistakes of those extravagant pro-grams which have tried to negate modernity. Perhaps the types of reception of art may offer an example which at least indicates the direction of a way out.

Bourgeois art had two expectations at once from its audiences. On the one hand, the layman who enjoyed art should educate him-self to become an expert. On the other hand, he should also behave as a competent consumer who uses art and relates aesthetic expe-riences to his own life problems. This second, and seemingly harm-less, manner of experiencing art has lost its radical implications, exactly because it had a confused relation to the attitude of being expert and professional.

To be sure, artistic production would dry up, if it were not car-ried out in the form of a specialized treatment of autonomous prob-lems, and if it were to cease to be the concern of experts who do not pay so much attention to exoteric questions. Both artists and critics accept thereby the fact that such problems fall under the spell of what I earlier called the "inner logic" of a cultural domain. But this sharp delineation, this exclusive concentration on one aspect of validity alone, and the exclusion of aspects of truth and justice, breaks down as soon as aesthetic experience is drawn into an individual life history and is absorbed into ordinary life. The reception of art by the layman, or by the "everyday expert," goes in a rather different direction than the reception of art by the professional critic.

Albrecht Wellmer has drawn my attention to one way that an aesthetic experience which is not framed around the experts' critical judgments of taste can have its significance altered: as soon as such an experience is used to illuminate a life-historical situation and is related to life problems, it enters into a language game which is no longer that of the aesthetic critic. The aesthetic experience then not only renews the intepretation of our needs in whose light we perceive the world. It permeates as well our cognitive significations and our normative expectations and changes the manner in which all these moments refer to one another. Let me give an example of this process.

This manner of receiving and relating to art is suggested in the first volume of the work *The Aesthetics of Resistance* by the German-Swedish writer Peter Weiss. Weiss describes the process of reappropriating art by presenting a group of politically motivated, knowledge-hungry workers in 1937 in Berlin. These were young people, who, through an evening high school education, acquired the intellectual means to fathom the general and the social history of European art. Out of the resilient edifice of the objective mind, embodied in works of art which they saw again and again in the museums in Berlin, they started removing their own chips of stone, which they gathered together and reassembled in the context of their own milieu. This milieu was far removed from that of traditional education as well as from the then existing regime. These young workers went back and forth between the edifice of European art and their own milieu until they were able to illuminate both.

In examples like this which illustrate the reappropriation of the expert's culture from the standpoint of the life-world, we can discern an element which does justice to the intentions of the hopeless surrealist revolts, perhaps even more to Brecht's and Benjamin's interests in how art works, which lost their aura, could yet be received in illuminating ways. In sum, the project of modernity has not yet been fulfilled. And the reception of art is only one of at least three of its aspects. The project aims at a differentiated relinking of modern culture with an everyday praxis that still depends on vital heritages, but would be impoverished through mere traditionalism. This new connection, however, can only be established under the condition that societal modernization will also be steered in a different direction. The life-world has to become able to develop institutions out of itself which sets limits to the internal dynamics and to the imperatives of an almost autonomous economic system and its administrative complements.

If I am not mistaken, the chances for this today are not very good. More or less in the entire Western world, a climate has developed that furthers capitalist modernization processes as well as trends critical of cultural modernism. The disillusionment with the very failures of those programs that called for the negation of art and philosophy has come to serve as a pretense for conservative positions. Let me briefly distinguish the antimodernism of the young conservatives from the premodernism of the old conservatives and from the postmodernism of the neoconservatives.

The *Young Conservatives* recapitulate the basic experience of aesthetic modernity. They claim as their own the revelations of a decentered subjectivity, emancipated from the imperatives of work and usefulness, and with this experience they step outside the modern world. On the basis of modernistic attitudes, they justify an irreconcilable anti-modernism. They remove into the sphere of the far away and the archaic the spontaneous powers of imagination, of self-experience and of emotionality. To instrumental reason, they juxtapose in manichean fashion a principle only accessible through evocation, be it the will to power or sovereignty, Being or the dionysiac force of the poetical. In France this line leads from Bataille via Foucault to Derrida.

The *Old Conservatives* do not allow themselves to be contaminated by cultural modernism. They observe the decline of substantive reason, the differentiation of science, morality and art, the modern world view and its merely procedural rationality, with sadness and recommend a withdrawal to a position *anterior* to modernity.

Neo-Aristotelianism, in particular, enjoys a certain success today. In view of the problematic of ecology, it allows itself to call for a cosmological ethic. As belonging to this school, which originates with Leo Strauss, one can count for example the interesting works of Hans Jonas and Robert Spaemann.

Finally, the *Neoconservatives* welcome the development of modern science, as long as this only goes beyond its sphere to carry forward technical progress, capitalist growth and rational administration. Moreover, they recommend a politics of defusing the explosive content of cultural modernity. According to one thesis, science, when properly understood, has become irrevocably meaningless for the orientation of the life-world. A further thesis is that politics must be kept as far aloof as possible from the demands of moral-practical justification. And a third thesis asserts the pure immanence of art, disputes that it has a utopian content, and points to its illusory character in order to limit the aesthetic experience to privacy. One could name here the early Wittgenstein, Carl Schmitt of the middle period, and Gottfried Benn of the late period. But with the decisive confinement of science, morality and art to autonomous spheres separated from the life-world and administered by experts, what remains from the project of cultural modernity is only what we would have if we were to give up the project of modernity altogether. As a replacement one points to traditions, which, however, are held to be immune to demands of (normative) justification and validation.

This typology is like any other, of course, a simplification; but it may not prove totally useless for the analysis of contemporary intellectual and political confrontations. I fear that the ideas of antimodernity, together with an additional touch of premodernity, are becoming popular in the circles of alternative culture. When one observes the transformations of consciousness within political parties in Germany, a new ideological shift (*Tendenzwende*) becomes visible. And this is the alliance of postmodernists with premodernists. It seems to me that there is no party in particular that monopolizes the abuse of intellectuals and the position of neoconservatism. I therefore have good reason to be thankful for the liberal spirit in which the city of Frankfurt offers me a prize bearing the name of Theodor Adorno. Adorno, a most significant son of this city, who as philosopher and writer has stamped the image of the intellectual in our country in incomparable fashion; even more, who has become the very image of emulation for the intellectual.

Translated by Seyla Ben-Habib

Mapping the Postmodern

Andreas Huyssen

A Story

In the summer of 1982 I visited the Seventh Documenta in Kassel, Germany, a periodic exhibition which documents the latest trends in contemporary art every four or five years. My then five-year-old son Daniel was with me, and he succeeded, unintentionally, in making the latest in postmodernism quite palpable to me. Approaching the Fridericianum, the museum housing the exhibit, we saw a huge and extended wall of rocks, seemingly heaped haphazardly alongside the museum. It was a work by Joseph Beuys, one of the key figures of the postmodern scene for at least a decade. Coming close we realized that thousands of huge basalt blocks were arranged in a triangle formation the smallest angle of which pointed at a newly planted tree—all of it part of what Beuys calls a social sculpture and what in a more traditional terminology would have been called a form of applied art. Beuys had issued an appeal to the citizens of

This essay was first published in *New German Critique* 33 (Fall 1984), 5–52.

Kassel, a dismal provincial city rebuilt in concrete after the heavy
bombings of the last great war, to plant a tree with each of his 7000
"planting stones." The appeal—at least initially—had been enthu-
siastically received by a populace usually not interested in the latest blessings of the art world. Daniel, for his part, loved the rocks.
I watched him climb up and down, across and back again. "Is this
art?" he asked matter-of-factly. I talked to him about Beuys's ecological politics and about the slow death of the German forests
(*Waldsterben*) due to acid rain. As he kept moving around on the
rocks, listening distractedly, I gave him a few simple concepts about
art in the making, sculpture as monument or anti-monument, art
for climbing on, and ultimately, art for vanishing—the rocks after
all would disappear from the museum site as people would begin to
plant the trees.

Later in the museum, however, things turned out quite differently. In the first halls we filed past a golden pillar, actually a metal
cylinder entirely covered with golden leaves (by James Lee Byars),
and an extended golden wall by Kounellis, with a clothes stand including hat and coat placed before it. Had the artist, as a latter day
Wu Tao-Tse, vanished into the wall, into his work, leaving only his
hat and coat? No matter how suggestive we might find the juxtaposition of the banal clothes stand and the preciosity of the doorless
shining wall, one thing seemed clear: "Am Golde hängt, zum Golde
drängt die Postmoderne."

Several rooms further on we encountered Mario Merz's spiral
table made out of glass, steel, wood, and plates of sandstone, with
bushlike twigs sticking out of the external parameter of the spiral
formation—again, it seemed, an attempt to overlay the typical hard
materials of the modernist era, steel and glass, with softer, more
"natural" ones, in this case sandstone and wood. There were connotations of Stonehenge and ritual, domesticated and brought down to
living-room size, to be sure. I was trying to hold together in my mind
the eclecticism of materials used by Merz with the nostalgic eclecticism of postmodern architecture or the pastiche of expressionism
in the painting of the *neuen Wilden,* prominently exhibited in another building of this Documenta show. I was trying, in other words,
to spin a red thread through the labyrinth of the postmodern. Then,
in a flash, the pattern became clear. As Daniel tried to feel the surfaces and crevices of Merz's work, as he ran his fingers alongside the
stone plates and over the glass, a guard rushed over shouting:
"Nicht berühren! Das ist Kunst!" (Don't touch! This is art!) And a
while later, tired from so much art, he sat down on Carl André's

solid cedar blocks only to be chased away with the admonition that art was not for sitting on.

Here it was again, that old notion of art: no touching, no trespassing. The museum as temple, the artist as prophet, the work as relic and cult object, the halo restored. Suddenly the privileging of gold in this exhibit made a lot of sense. The guards, of course, only performed what Rudi Fuchs, organizer of this Documenta and in touch with current trends, had in mind all along: "To disentangle art from the diverse pressures and social perversions it has to bear."[1] The debates of the last fifteen to twenty years about ways of seeing and experiencing contemporary art, about imaging and image making, about the entanglements between avantgarde art, media iconography, and advertising seemed to have been wiped out, the slate cleaned for a new romanticism. But then it fits in all too well with, say, the celebrations of the prophetic word in the more recent writings of Peter Handke, with the aura of the "postmodern" in the New York art scene, with the self-stylization of the filmmaker as *auteur* in *Burden of Dreams,* a recent documentary about the making of Werner Herzog's *Fitzcarraldo.* Think of *Fitzcarraldo's* closing images—opera on a ship on the Amazon. *Bâteau Ivre* was briefly considered by the Documenta organizers as the title for the exhibit. But while Herzog's worn-out steam boat was indeed a *bâteau ivre*—opera in the jungle, a ship moved across a mountain— the *bâteau ivre* of Kassel was only sobering in its pretentiousness. Consider this, taken from Fuchs's catalogue introduction: "After all the artist is one of the last practitioners of distinct individuality." Or, again *Originalton* Fuchs: "Here, then, begins our exhibition; here is the euphoria of Hölderlin, the quiet logic of T. S. Eliot, the unfinished dream of Coleridge. When the French traveller who discovered the Niagara Falls returned to New York, one of his sophisticated friends believed his fantastic story. What is your proof, they asked. My proof, he said, is that I have seen it."[2]

Niagara Falls and Documenta 7—indeed we have seen it all before. Art as nature, nature as art. The halo Baudelaire once lost on a crowded Paris boulevard is back, the aura restored, Baudelaire, Marx, and Benjamin forgotten. The gesture in all of this is patently anti-modern and anti-avantgarde. Sure, one could argue that in his recourse to Hölderlin, Coleridge, and Eliot, Fuchs tries to revive the modernist dogma itself—yet another postmodern nostalgia, another sentimental return to a time when art was still art. But what distinguishes this nostalgia from the "real thing," and what ultimately makes it anti-modernist, is its loss of

irony, reflexiveness and self-doubt, its cheerful abandonment of a
critical consciousness, its ostentatious self-confidence and the *mise
en scène* of its conviction (visible even in the spatial arrangements
inside the Fridericianum) that there must be a realm of purity for
art, a space beyond those unfortunate "diverse pressures and social
perversions" art has had to bear.[3]

This latest trend within the trajectory of postmodernism, embodied for me in the Documenta 7, rests on an all but total confusion
of codes: it is anti-modern and highly eclectic, but dresses up as a
return to the modernist tradition; it is anti-avantgarde in that it
simply chooses to drop the avantgarde's crucial concern for a new
art in an alternative society, but it pretends to be avantgarde in its
presentation of current trends; and, in a certain sense, it is even
anti-postmodern in that it abandons any reflection of the problems
which the exhaustion of high modernism originally brought about,
problems which postmodern art in its better moments, has attempted to address aesthetically and sometimes even politically.
Documenta 7 can stand as the perfect aesthetic simulacrum: facile
eclecticism combined with aesthetic amnesia and delusions of gran-
deur. It represents the kind of postmodern restoration of a domesticated modernism which seems to be gaining ground in the age of
Kohl-Thatcher-Reagan and it parallels the conservative political attacks on the culture of the 1960s which have increased in volume
and viciousness in these past years.

The Problem

If this were all that could be said about postmodernism it would not
be worth the trouble of taking up the subject at all. I might just as
well stop right here and join the formidable chorus of those who lament the loss of quality and proclaim the decline of the arts since
the 1960s. My argument, however, will be a different one. While the
recent media hype about postmodernism in architecture and the
arts has propelled the phenomenon into the limelight, it has also
tended to obscure its long and complex history. Much of my ensuing
argument will be based on the premise that what appears on one
level as the latest fad, advertising pitch, and hollow spectacle is
part of a slowly emerging cultural transformation in Western societies, a change in sensibility for which the term 'postmodernism' is
actually, at least for now, wholly adequate. The nature and depth of
that transformation are debatable, but transformation it is. I don't

want to be misunderstood as claiming that there is a wholesale paradigm shift of the cultural, social, and economic orders;[4] any such claim clearly would be overblown. But in an important sector of our culture there is a noticeable shift in sensibility, practices, and discourse formations which distinguishes a postmodern set of assumptions, experiences, and propositions from that of a preceding period. What needs further exploration is whether this transformation has generated genuinely new aesthetic forms in the various arts or whether it mainly recycles techniques and strategies of modernism itself, reinscribing them into an altered cultural context.

Of course, there are good reasons why any attempt to take the postmodern seriously on its own terms meets with so much resistance. It is indeed tempting to dismiss many of the current manifestations of postmodernism as a fraud perpetrated on a gullible public by the New York art market in which reputations are built and gobbled up faster than painters can paint: witness the frenzied brushwork of the new expressionists. It is also easy to argue that much of the contemporary inter-arts, mixed-media and performance culture, which once seemed as it were, the eternal recurrence of the *déjà vu*. With good reason we may remain skeptical toward the revival of the Wagnerian *Gesamtkunstwerk* as postmodern spectacle in Syberberg or Robert Wilson. The current Wagner cult may indeed be a symptom of a happy collusion between the megalomania of the postmodern and that of the premodern on the edge of modernism. The search for the grail, it seems, is on.

But it is almost too easy to ridicule the postmodernism of the current New York art scene or of Documenta 7. Such total rejection will blind us to postmodernism's critical potential which, I believe, also exists, even though it may be difficult to identify.[5] The notion of the art work as critique actually informs some of the more thoughtful condemnations of postmodernism, which is accused of having abandoned the critical stance that once characterized modernism. However, the familiar ideas of what constitutes a critical art (*Parteilichkeit* and vanguardism, *l'art engagé,* critical realism, or the aesthetic of negativity, the refusal of representation, abstraction, reflexiveness) have lost much of their explanatory and normative powers in recent decades. This is precisely the dilemma of art in a postmodern age. Nevertheless, I see no reason to jettison the notion of a critical art altogether. The pressures to do so are not new; they have been formidable in capitalist culture ever since romanticism, and if our postmodernity makes it exceedingly difficult to hold on to an older notion of art as critique, then the task is to redefine the possibilities of critique in postmodern terms rather than relegating it to oblivion. If the postmodern is discussed as a historical condition rather than only as style it becomes possible and indeed important to unlock the critical moment in postmodernism itself and to sharpen its cutting edge, however blunt it may seem at first sight. What will no longer do is either to eulogize or to ridicule postmodernism *en bloc*. The postmodern must be salvaged from its champions and from its detractors. This essay is meant to contribute to that project.

In much of the postmodernism debate, a very conventional thought pattern has asserted itself. Either it is said that postmodernism is continuous with modernism, in which case the whole debate opposing the two is specious; or, it is claimed that there is a radical rupture, a break with modernism, which is then evaluated in either positive or negative terms. But the question of historical continuity or discontinuity simply cannot be adequately discussed in terms of such an either/or dichotomy. To have questioned the validity of such dichotomous thought patterns is of course one of the major achievements of Derridean deconstruction. But the poststructuralist notion of endless textuality ultimately cripples any meaningful historical reflection on temporal units shorter than, say, the long wave of metaphysics from Plato to Heidegger or the spread of *modernité* from the mid-19th century to the present. The problem with such historical macro-schemes, in relation to postmodernism, is that they prevent the phenomenon from even coming into focus.

I will therefore take a different route. I will not attempt here to define what postmodernism *is*. The term "*post*modernism" itself should guard us against such an approach as it positions the phenomenon as relational. Modernism as that from which postmodernism is breaking away remains inscribed into the very word with which we describe our distance from modernism. Thus keeping in mind postmodernism's relational nature, I will simply start from the *Selbstverständnis* of the postmodern as it has shaped various discourses since the 1960s. What I hope to provide in this essay is something like a large-scale map of the postmodern which surveys several territories and on which the various postmodern artistic and critical practices could find their aesthetic and political place. Within the trajectory of the postmodern in the United States I will distinguish several phases and directions. My primary aim is to emphasize some of the historical contingencies and pressures that have shaped recent aesthetic and cultural debates but have either been ignored or systematically blocked out in critical theory *à l'américaine*. While drawing on developments in architecture, literature, and the visual arts, my focus will be primarily on the critical discourse about the postmodern: postmodernism in relation to, respectively, modernism, the avantgarde, neo-conservatism, and poststructuralism. Each of these constellations represents a somewhat separate layer of the postmodern and will be presented as such. And, finally, central elements of the *Begriffsgeschichte* of the term will be discussed in relation to a broader set of questions that have arisen in recent debates about modernism, modernity, and the historical avantgarde.[6] A crucial question for me concerns the extent to which modernism and the avantgarde as forms of an adversary culture were nevertheless conceptually and practically bound up with capitalist modernization and/or with communist vanguardism, that modernization's twin brother. As I hope this essay will show, postmodernism's critical dimension lies precisely in its radical questioning of those presuppositions which linked modernism and the avantgarde to the mindset of modernization.

The Exhaustion of the Modernist Movement

Let me begin, then, with some brief remarks about the trajectory and migrations of the term "postmodernism." In literary criticism it goes back as far as the late 1950s when it was used by Irving Howe and Harry Levin to lament the levelling off of the modernist movement. Howe and Levin were looking back nostalgically to what already seemed like a richer past. "Postmodernism" was first used emphatically in the 1960s by literary critics such as Leslie Fiedler and Ihab Hassan who held widely divergent views of what a postmodern literature was. It was only during the early and mid-1970s that the term gained a much wider currency, encompassing first architecture, then dance, theater, painting, film, and music. While the postmodern break with classical modernism was fairly visible in architecture and the visual arts, the notion of a postmodern rupture in literature has been much harder to ascertain. At some point in the late 1970s, "postmodernism," not without American prodding, migrated to Europe via Paris and Frankfurt. Kristeva and Lyotard took it up in France, Habermas in Germany. In the United States, meanwhile, critics had begun to discuss the interface of postmodernism with French poststructuralism in its peculiar American adaptation, often simply on the assumption that the avantgarde in theory somehow had to be homologous to the avantgarde in literature and the arts. While skepticism about the feasibility of an artistic avantgarde was on the rise in the 1970s, the vitality of theory, despite its many enemies, never seemed in serious doubt. To some, indeed, it appeared as if the cultural energies that had fueled the art movements of the 1960s were flowing during the 1970s into the body of theory, leaving the artistic enterprise high and dry. While such an observation is at best of impressionistic value and also not quite fair to the arts, it does seem reasonable to say that, with post-modernism's big-bang logic of expansion irreversible, the maze of the postmodern became ever more impenetrable. By the early 1980s the modernism/postmodernism constellation in the arts and the modernity/postmodernity constellation in social theory had become one of the most contested terrains in the intellectual life of Western societies. And the terrain is contested precisely because there is so much more at stake than the existence or non-existence of a new artistic style, so much more also than just the "correct" theoretical line.

Nowhere does the break with modernism seem more obvious than in recent American architecture. Nothing could be further from Mies van der Rohe's functionalist glass curtain walls than the gesture of random historical citation which prevails on so many postmodern façades. Take, for example, Philip Johnson's AT&T highrise, which is appropriately broken up into a neoclassical mid-section, Roman colonnades at the street level, and a Chippendale pediment at the top. Indeed, a growing nostalgia for various life forms of the past seems to be a strong undercurrent in the culture of the 1970s and 1980s. And it is tempting to dismiss this historical eclecticism, found not only in architecture, but in the arts, in film, in literature, and in the mass culture of recent years, as the cultural equivalent of the neoconservative nostalgia for the good old days and as a manifest sign of the declining rate of creativity in late cap-italism. But is this nostalgia for the past, the often frenzied and ex-ploitative search for usable traditions, and the growing fascination with pre-modern and primitive cultures—is all of this rooted only in the cultural institutions' perpetual need for spectacle and frill, and thus perfectly compatible with the status quo? Or does it per-haps also express some genuine and legitimate dissatisfaction with modernity and the unquestioned belief in the perpetual moderniza-tion of art? If the latter is the case, which I believe it is, then how can the search for alternative traditions, whether emergent or re-sidual, be made culturally productive without yielding to the pres-sures of conservatism which, with a vise-like grip, lays claim to the very concept of tradition? I am not arguing here that all manifes-tations of the postmodern recuperation of the past are to be wel-

comed because somehow they are in tune with the Zeitgeist. I also
don't want to be misunderstood as arguing that postmodernism's
fashionable repudiation of the high modernist aesthetic and its
boredom with the propositions of Marx and Freud, Picasso and
Brecht, Kafka and Joyce, Schönberg and Stravinsky are somehow
marks a major cultural advance. Where postmodernism simply jet-
tisons modernism it just yields to the cultural apparatus' demands
that it legitimize itself as radically new, and it revives the philistine
prejudices modernism faced in its own time.

But even if postmodernism's own propositions don't seem convincing—as embodied, for example, in the buildings by Philip
Johnson, Michael Graves and others—that does not mean that continued adherence to an older set of modernist propositions would
guarantee the emergence of more convincing buildings or works of
art. The recent neoconservative attempt to reinstate a domesticated version of modernism as the only worthwhile truth of 20th-
century culture—manifest for instance in the 1984 Beckmann
exhibit in Berlin and in many articles in Hilton Kramer's *New Criterion*—is a strategy aimed at burying the political and aesthetic
critiques of certain forms of modernism which have gained ground
since the 1960s. But the problem with modernism is not just the fact
that it can be integrated into a conservative ideology of art. After
all, that already happened once on a major scale in the 1950s.[7] The
larger problem we recognize today, it seems to me, is the closeness
of various forms of modernism in its own time to the mindset of
modernization, whether in its capitalist or communist version. Of
course, modernism was never a monolithic phenomenon, and it contained *both* the modernization euphoria of futurism, constructivism, and Neue Sachlichkeit and some of the starkest critiques of
modernization in the various modern forms of "romantic anti-
capitalism."[8] The problem I address in this essay is not what modernism *really was,* but rather how it was perceived retrospectively,
what dominant values and knowledge it carried, and how it functioned ideologically and culturally after World War II. It is a specific image of modernism that had become the bone of contention for
the postmoderns, and that image has to be reconstructed if we want
to understand postmodernism's problematic relationship to the
modernist tradition and its claims to difference.

Architecture gives us the most palpable example of the issues
at stake. The modernist utopia embodied in the building programs
of the Bauhaus, of Mies, Gropius, and Le Corbusier, was part of a
heroic attempt after the Great War and the Russian Revolution to

rebuild a war-ravaged Europe in the image of the new, and to make building a vital part of the envisioned renewal of society. A new Enlightenment demanded rational design for a rational society, but the new rationality was overlaid with a utopian fervor which ultimately made it veer back into myth—the myth of modernization. Ruthless denial of the past was as much an essential component of the modern movement as its call for modernization through standardization and rationalization. It is well-known how the modernist utopia shipwrecked on its own internal contradictions and, more importantly, on politics and history.[9] Gropius, Mies and others were forced into exile, Albert Speer took their place in Germany. After 1945, modernist architecture was largely deprived of its social vision and became increasingly an architecture of power and representation. Rather than standing as harbingers and promises of the new life, modernist housing projects became symbols of alienation and dehumanization, a fate they shared with the assembly line, that other agent of the new which had been greeted with exuberant enthusiasm in the 1920s by Leninists and Fordists alike.

Charles Jencks, one of the most well-known popularizing chroniclers of the agony of the modern movement and spokesman for a postmodern architecture, dates modern architecture's symbolic demise July 15, 1972, at 3:32 p.m. At that time several slab blocks of St. Louis' Pruitt-Igoe Housing (built by Minoru Yamasaki in the 1950s) were dynamited, and the collapse was dramatically displayed on the evening news. The modern machine for living, as Le Corbusier had called it with the technological euphoria so typical of the 1920s, had become unlivable, the modernist experiment, so it seemed, obsolete. Jencks takes pains to distinguish the initial vision of the modern movement from the sins committed in its name later on. And yet, on balance he agrees with those who, since the 1960s, have argued against modernism's hidden dependence on the machine metaphor and the production paradigm, and against its taking the factory as the primary model for all buildings. It has become commonplace in postmodernist circles to favor a reintroduction of multivalent symbolic dimensions into architecture, a mixing of codes, an appropriation of local vernaculars and regional traditions.[10] Thus Jencks suggests that architects look two ways simultaneously, "towards the traditional slow-changing codes and particular ethnic meanings of a neighborhood, and towards the fast-changing codes of architectural fashion and professionalism."[11] Such schizophrenia, Jencks holds, is symptomatic of the postmodern moment in architecture; and one might well ask whether it does not apply to contemporary culture at large, which increasingly seems to privilege what Bloch called *Ungleichzeitigkeiten* (nonsynchronisms),[12] rather than favoring only what Adorno, the theorist of modernism par excellence, described as *der fortgeschrittenste Materialstand der Kunst* (the most advanced state of artistic material). Where such postmodern schizophrenia is creative tension resulting in ambitious and successful buildings, and where conversely, it veers off into an incoherent and arbitrary shuffling of styles, will remain a matter of debate. We should also not forget that the mixing of codes, the appropriation of regional traditions, and the uses of symbolic dimensions other than the machine were never entirely unknown to the architects of the International Style. In order to arrive at his postmodernism, Jencks ironically had to exacerbate the very view of modernist architecture which he persistently attacks.

One of the most telling documents of the break of postmodernism with the modernist dogma is a book coauthored by Robert Venturi, Denise Scott-Brown, and Steven Izenour and entitled *Learning from Las Vegas*. Rereading this book and earlier writings by Venturi from the 1960s today,[13] one is struck by the proximity of Venturi's strategies and solutions to the pop sensibility of those years. Time and again the authors use pop art's break with the austere canon of high modernist painting and pop's uncritical espousal of the commercial vernacular of consumer culture as an inspiration for their work. What Madison Avenue was for Andy Warhol, what the comics and the Western were for Leslie Fiedler, the landscape of Las Vegas was for Venturi and his group. The rhetoric of *Learning from Las Vegas* is predicated on the glorification of the billboard strip and of the ruthless shlock of casino culture. In Kenneth Frampton's ironic words, it offers a reading of Las Vegas as "an authentic outburst of popular phantasy."[14] I think it would be gratuitous to ridicule such odd notions of cultural populism today. While there is something patently absurd about such propositions, we have to acknowledge the power they mustered to explode the reified dogmas of modernism and to reopen a set of questions which the modernism gospel of the 1940s and 1950s had largely blocked from view: questions of ornament and metaphor in architecture, of figuration and realism in painting, of story and representation in literature, of the body in music and theater. Pop in the broadest sense was the context in which a notion of the postmodern first took shape, and from the beginning until today, the most significant trends within postmodernism have challenged modernism's relentless hostility to mass culture.

Postmodernism in the 1960s: An American Avantgarde?

I will now suggest a historical distinction between the postmodernism of the 1960s and that of the 1970s and early 1980s. My argument will roughly be this: 1960s' and 1970s' postmodernism both rejected or criticized a certain version of modernism. Against the codified high modernism of the preceding decades, the postmodernism of the 1960s tried to revitalize the heritage of the European avantgarde and to give it an American form along what one could call in short-hand the Duchamp-Cage-Warhol axis. By the 1970s, that avantgardist postmodernism of the 1960s had in turn exhausted its potential, even though some of its manifestations continued well into the new decade. What was new in the 1970s was, on the one hand, the emergence of a culture of eclecticism, a largely affirmative postmodernism which had abandoned any claim to critique, transgression or negation; and, on the other hand, an alternative postmodernism in which resistance, critique, and negation of the status quo were redefined in non-modernist and non-avantgardist terms, terms which match the political developments in contemporary culture more effectively than the older theories of modernism. Let me elaborate.

What were the connotations of the term postmodernism in the 1960s? Roughly since the mid-1950s literature and the arts witnessed a rebellion of a new generation of artists such as Rauschenberg and Jasper Johns, Kerouac, Ginsberg and the Beats, Burroughs and Barthelme against the dominance of abstract expressionism, serial music, and classical literary modernism.[15] The rebellion of the artists was soon joined by critics such as Susan Sontag, Leslie Fiedler, and Ihab Hassan who all vigorously though in very different ways and to a different degree, argued for the postmodern. Sontag advocated camp and a new sensibility, Fiedler sang the praise of popular literature and genital enlightenment, and Hassan—closer than the others to the moderns—advocated a literature of silence, trying to mediate between the "tradition of the new" and post-war literary developments. By that time, modernism had of course been safely established as the canon in the academy, the museums and the gallery network. In that canon the New York School of abstract expressionism represented the epitome of that long trajectory of the modern which had begun in Paris in the 1850s and 1860s and which had inexorably led to New York—the American victory in culture following on the heels of the victory on the battlefields of World War II. By the 1960s artists and critics alike shared a sense of a fundamentally new situation. The assumed postmodern rupture with the past was felt as a loss: art and literature's claims to truth and human value seemed exhausted, the belief in the constitutive power of the modern imagination just another delusion. Or it was felt as a breakthrough toward an ultimate liberation of instinct and consciousness, into the global village of McLuhanacy, the new Eden of polymorphous perversity, Paradise Now, as the Living Theater proclaimed it on stage. Thus critics of postmodernism such as Gerald Graff have correctly identified two strains of the postmodern culture of the 1960s: the apocalyptic desperate strain and the visionary celebratory strain, both of which, Graff claims, already existed within modernism.[16] While this is certainly true, it misses an important point. The ire of the postmodernists was directed not so much against modernism as such, but rather against a certain austere image of "high modernism," as advanced by the New Critics and other custodians of modernist culture. Such a view, which avoids the false dichotomy of choosing either continuity or discontinuity, is supported by a retrospective essay by John Barth. In a 1980 piece in *The Atlantic,* entitled "The Literature of Replenishment," Barth criticizes his own 1968 essay "The Literature of Exhaustion," which seemed at the time to offer an adequate summary of the apocalyptic strain. Barth now suggests that what his earlier piece was really about "was the effective 'exhaustion' not of language or of literature but of the aesthetic of high modernism."[17] And he goes on to describe Beckett's *Stories and Texts for Nothing* and Nabokov's *Pale Fire* as late modernist marvels, distinct from such postmodernist writers as Italo Calvino and Gabriel Marquez. Cultural critics like Daniel Bell, on the other hand, would simply claim that the postmodernism of the 1960s was the "logical culmination of modernist intentions,"[18] a view which rephrases Lionel Trilling's despairing observation that the demonstrators of the 1960s were practicing modernism in the streets. But my point here is precisely that high modernism had never seen fit to be in the streets in the first place, that its earlier undeniably adversary role was superseded in the 1960s by a very different culture of confrontation in the streets *and* in art works, and that this culture of confrontation transformed inherited ideological notions of style, form and creativity, artistic autonomy and the imagination to which modernism had by then succumbed. Critics like Bell and Graff saw the rebellion of the late 1950s and the 1960s as continuous with modernism's earlier nihilistic and anarchic strain; rather than seeing it as a postmodernist revolt against classical modernism, they interpreted it as a profusion of modernist impulses into everyday life. And in some sense they were absolutely right, except that this "success" of modernism fundamentally altered the terms of how modernist culture was to be perceived. Again, my argument here is that the revolt of the 1960s was never a rejection of modernism *per se,* but rather a revolt against that version of modernism which had been domesticated in the 1950s, become part of the liberal-conservative consensus of the times, and which had even been turned into a propaganda weapon in the cultural-political arsenal of Cold War anticommunism. The modernism against which artists rebelled was no longer felt to be an adversary culture. It no longer opposed a dominant class and its world view, nor had it maintained its programmatic purity from contamination by the culture industry. In other words, the revolt sprang precisely from the success of modernism, from the fact that in the United States, as in West Germany and France, for that matter, modernism had been perverted into a form of affirmative culture.

I would go on to argue that the global view which sees the 1960s as part of the modern movement extending from Manet and Baudelaire, if not from romanticism, to the present is not able to account for the specifically American character of postmodernism. After all, the term accrued its emphatic connotations in the United States, not in Europe. I would even claim that it could not have been invented in Europe at the time. For a variety of reasons, it would not have made any sense there. West Germany was still busy rediscovering its own moderns who had been burnt and banned during the Third Reich. If anything, the 1960s in West Germany produced a major shift in evaluation and interest from one set of moderns to another: from Benn, Kafka, and Thomas Mann to Brecht, the left expressionists and the political writers of the 1920s, from Heidegger and Jaspers to Adorno and Benjamin, from Schöneberg and Webern to Eisler, from Kirchner and Beckmann to Grosz and Heartfield. It was a search for alternative cultural traditions within modernity and as such directed against the politics of a depoliticized version of modernism that had come to provide much needed cultural legitimation for the Adenauer restoration. During the 1950s, the myths of "the golden twenties," the "conservative revolution," and universal existentialist *Angst,* all helped block out and suppress the realities of the fascist past. From the depths of barbarism and the rubble of its cities, West Germany was trying to reclaim a civilized modernity and to find a cultural identity tuned to international modernism which would make others forget Germany's past as predator and pariah of the modern world. Given this context, neither the variations on modernism of the 1950s nor the struggle of the 1960s for alternative democratic and socialist cultural traditions could have possibly been construed as *post-modern*. The very notion of postmodernism has emerged in Germany only since the late 1970s and then not in relation to the culture of the 1960s, but narrowly in relation to recent architectural developments and, perhaps more importantly, in the context of the new social movements and their radical critique of modernity.[19]

In France, too, the 1960s witnessed a return to modernism rather than a step beyond it, even though for different reasons than in Germany, some of which I will discuss in the later section on poststructuralism. In the context of French intellectual life, the term "postmodernism" was simply not around in the 1960s, and even today it does not seem to imply a major break with modernism as it does in the U.S.

I would now like to sketch four major characteristics of the early phase of postmodernism which all point to postmodernism's continuity with the international tradition of the modern, yes, but which—and this is my point—also establish American postmodernism as a movement *sui generis*.[20]

First, the postmodernism of the 1960s was characterized by a temporal imagination which displayed a powerful sense of the future and of new frontiers, of rupture and discontinuity, of crisis and generational conflict, an imagination reminiscent of earlier continental avantgarde movements such as Dada and surrealism rather than of high modernism. Thus the revival of Marcel Duchamp as godfather of 1960s postmodernism is no historical accident. And yet, the historical constellation in which the postmodernism of the 1960s played itself out (from the Bay of Pigs and the civil rights movement to the campus revolts, the anti-war movement and the counterculture) makes this avantgarde specifically American, even where its vocabulary of aesthetic forms and techniques was not radically new.

Secondly, the early phase of postmodernism included an iconoclastic attack on what Peter Bürger has tried to capture theoretically as the "institution art." By that term Bürger refers first and foremost to the ways in which art's role in society is perceived and defined, and, secondly, to ways in which art is produced, marketed, distributed, and consumed. In his book *Theory of the Avantgarde* Bürger has argued that the major goal of the historical European avantgarde (Dada, early surrealism, the postrevolutionary Russian avantgarde[21]) was to undermine, attack and transform the bourgeois institution art and its ideology of autonomy rather than only changing artistic and literary modes of representation. Bürger's

approach to the question of art as institution in bourgeois society
goes a long way toward suggesting useful distinctions between modernism and the avantgarde, distinctions which in turn can help us
place the American avantgarde of the 1960s. In Bürger's account the
European avantgarde was primarily an attack on the highness of
high art and on art's separateness from everyday life as it had
evolved in 19-century aestheticism and its repudiation of realism.
Bürger argues that the avantgarde attempted to reintegrate art
and life or, to use his Hegelian-Marxist formula, to sublate art into
life, and he sees this reintegration attempt, I think correctly, as a
major break with the aestheticist tradition of the later 19th century. The value of Bürger's account for contemporary American debates is that it permits us to distinguish different stages and
different projects within the trajectory of the modern. The usual
equation of the avantgarde with modernism can indeed no longer be
maintained. Contrary to the avantgarde's intention to merge art
and life, modernism always remained bound up with the more traditional notion of the autonomous art work, with the construction of
form and meaning (however estranged or ambiguous, displaced or
undecidable such meaning might be), and with the specialized status of the aesthetic.[22] The politically important point of Bürger's account for my argument about the 1960s is this: The historical
avantgarde's iconoclastic attack on cultural institutions and on traditional modes of representation presupposed a society in which
high art played an essential role in legitimizing hegemony, or, to put
it in more neutral terms, to support a cultural establishment and
its claims to aesthetic knowledge. It had been the achievement of
the historical avantgarde to demystify and to undermine the legitimizing discourse of high art in European society. The various modernisms of this century, on the other hand, have either maintained
or restored versions of high culture, a task which was certainly facilitated by the ultimate and perhaps unavoidable failure of the historical avantgarde to reintegrate art and life. And yet, I would
suggest that it was this specific radicalism of the avantgarde, directed against the institutionalization of high art as a discourse of
hegemony and a machinery of meaning, that recommended itself as
a source of energy and inspiration to the American postmodernists
of the 1960s. Perhaps for the first time in American culture an
avantgardist revolt against a tradition of high art and what was
perceived as its hegemonic role made political sense. High art had
indeed become institutionalized in the burgeoning museum, gallery,
concert, record, and paperback culture of the 1950s. Modernism itself had entered the mainstream via mass reproduction and the cul-

ture industry. And, during the Kennedy years, high culture even began to take on functions of political representation with Robert Frost and Pablo Casals, Malraux and Stravinsky at the White House. The irony in all of this is that the first time the U.S. had something resembling an "institution art" in the emphatic European sense, it was modernism itself, the kind of art whose purpose had always been to resist institutionalization. In the form of happenings, pop vernacular, psychedelic art, acid rock, alternative and street theater, the postmodernism of the 1960s was groping to recapture the adversary ethos which had nourished modern art in its earlier stages, but which it seemed no longer able to sustain. Of course, the "success" of the pop avantgarde, which itself had sprung full-blown from advertising in the first place, immediately made it profitable and thus sucked it into a more highly developed culture industry than the earlier European avantgarde ever had to contend with. But despite such cooption through commodification the pop avantgarde retained a certain cutting edge in its proximity to the 1960s culture of confrontation.[23] No matter how deluded about its potential effectiveness, the attack on the institution art was always also an attack on hegemonic social institutions, and the raging battles of the 1960s over whether or not pop was legitimate art prove the point.

Thirdly, many of the early advocates of postmodernism shared the technological optimism of segments of the 1920s avantgarde. What photography and film had been to Vertov and Tretyakov, Brecht, Heartfield, and Benjamin in that period, television, video, and the computer were for the prophets of a technological aesthetic in the 1960s. McLuhan's cybernetic and technocratic media eschatology and Hassan's praise for "runaway technology," the "boundless dispersal by media," "the computer as substitute consciousness"— all of this combined easily with euphoric visions of a postindustrial society. Even if compared to the equally exuberant technological optimism of the 1920s, it is striking to see in retrospect how uncritically media technology and the cybernetic paradigm were espoused in the 1960s by conservatives, liberals, and leftists alike.[24]

The enthusiasm for the new media leads me to the fourth trend within early postmodernism. There emerged a vigorous, though again largely uncritical attempt to validate popular culture as a challenge to the canon of high art, modernist or traditional. This "populist" trend of the 1960s with its celebration of rock 'n' roll and folk music, of the imagery of everyday life and of the multiple forms of popular literature gained much of its energy in the context of the counter-culture and by a next to total abandonment of an earlier American tradition of a critique of modern mass culture. Leslie Fiedler's incantation of the prefix "post" in his essay "The New Mutants" had an exhilarating effect at the time.[25] The postmodern harbored the promise of a "post-white," "post-male," "post-humanist," "post-Puritan" world. It is easy to see how all of Fiedler's adjectives aim at the modernist dogma and at the cultural establishment's notion of what Western Civilization was all about. Susan Sontag's camp aesthetic did much the same. Even though it was less populist, it certainly was as hostile to high modernism. There is a curious contradiction in all this. Fiedler's populism reiterates precisely that adversarial relationship between high art and mass culture which, in the accounts of Clement Greenberg and Theodor W. Adorno, was one of the pillars of the modernist dogma Fiedler had set out to undermine. Fiedler just takes his position on the other shore, opposite Greenberg and Adorno, as it were, validating the popular and pounding away at "elitism." And yet, Fiedler's call to cross the border and close the gap between high art and mass culture as well as his implied political critique of what later came to be called "eurocentrism" and "logocentrism" can serve as an important marker for subsequent developments within postmodernism. A new creative relationship between high art and certain forms of mass culture is, to my mind, indeed one of the major marks of difference between high modernism and the art and literature which followed it in the 1970s and 1980s both in Europe and the United States. And it is precisely the recent self-assertion of minority cultures and their emergence into public consciousness which has undermined the modernist belief that high and low culture have to be categorically kept apart; such rigorous segregation simply does not make much sense *within* a given minority culture which has always existed outside in the shadow of the dominant high culture.

In conclusion, I would say that from an American perspective the postmodernism of the 1960s had some of the makings of a genuine avantgarde movement, even if the overall political situation of 1960s' America was in no way comparable to that of Berlin or Moscow in the early 1920s when the tenuous and short-lived alliance between avantgardism and vanguard politics was forged. For a number of historical reasons the ethos of artistic avantgardism as iconoclasm, as probing reflection upon the ontological status of art in modern society, as an attempt to forge another life was culturally not yet as exhausted in the U.S. of the 1960s as it was in Europe at the same time. From a European perspective, therefore, it all looked like the endgame of the historical avantgarde rather than like the breakthrough to new frontiers it claimed to be. My point here is that

American postmodernism of the 1960s was both: an American avantgarde *and* the endgame of international avantgardism. And I would go on to argue that it is indeed important for the cultural historian to analyze such *Ungleichzeitigkeiten* within modernity and to relate them to the very specific constellations and contexts of national and regional cultures and histories. The view that the culture of modernity is essentially internationalist—with its cutting edge moving in space and time from Paris in the later 19th and early 20th centuries to Moscow and Berlin in the 1920s and to New York in the 1940s—is a view tied to a teleology of modern art whose unspoken subtext is the ideology of modernization. It is precisely this teleology and ideology of modernization which has become increasingly problematic in our postmodern age, problematic not so much perhaps in its descriptive powers relating to past events, but certainly in its normative claims.

Postmodernism in the 1970s and 1980s

In some sense, I might argue that what I have mapped so far is really the prehistory of the postmodern. After all, the term postmodernism only gained wide currency in the 1970s while much of the language used to describe the art, architecture, and literature of the 1960s was still derived—and plausibly so—from the rhetoric of avantgardism and from what I have called the ideology of modernization. The cultural developments of the 1970s, however, are sufficiently different to warrant a separate description. One of the major differences, indeed, seems to be that the rhetoric of avantgardism has faded fast in the 1970s so that one can speak perhaps only now of a genuinely postmodern and post-avantgarde culture. Even if, with the benefit of hindsight, future historians of culture were to opt for such a usage of the term, I would still argue that the adversary and critical elements in the notion of postmodernism can only be fully grasped if one takes the late 1950s as the starting point of a mapping of the postmodern. If we were to focus only on the 1970s, the adversary moment of the postmodern would be much harder to work out precisely because of the shift within the intrajectory of postmodernism that lies somewhere in the fault lines between "the '60s" and "the '70s."

By the mid-1970s, certain basic assumptions of the preceding decade had either vanished or been transformed. The sense of a "futurist revolt" (Fiedler) was gone. The iconoclastic gestures of the

pop, rock, and sex avantgardes seemed exhausted since their increasingly commercialized circulation had deprived them of their
avantgardist status. The earlier optimism about technology, media
and popular culture had given way to more sober and critical assessments: television as pollution rather than panacea. In the years
of Watergate and the drawn-out agony of the Vietnam war, of the
oil-shock and the dire predictions of the Club of Rome, it was indeed
difficult to maintain the confidence and exuberance of the 1960s.
Counter-culture, New Left and anti-war movement were ever more
frequently denounced as infantile aberrations of American history.
It was easy to see that the 1960s were over. But it is more difficult
to describe the emerging cultural scene which seemed much more
amorphous and scattered than that of the 1960s. One might begin
by saying that the battle against the normative pressures of high
modernism waged during the 1960s had been successful—too
successful, some would argue. While the 1960s could still be discussed in terms of a logical sequence of styles (Pop, Op, Kinetic,
Minimal, Concept) or in equally modernist terms of art versus anti-
art and non-art, such distinctions have increasingly lost ground in
the 1970s.

The situation in the 1970s seems to be characterized rather by
an ever wider dispersal and dissemination of artistic practices all
working out of the ruins of the modernist edifice, raiding it for
ideas, plundering its vocabulary and supplementing it with randomly chosen images and motifs from pre-modern and non-modern
cultures as well as from contemporary mass culture. Modernist
styles have actually not been abolished, but, as one art critic recently observed, continue "to enjoy a kind of half-life in mass
culture,"[26] for instance in advertising, record cover design, furni-
ture and household items, science fiction illustration, window displays, etc. Yet another way of putting it would be to say that all
modernist and avantgardist techniques, forms and images are now
stored for instant recall in the computerized memory banks of our
culture. But the same memory also stores all of pre-modernist art
as well as the genres, codes, and image worlds of popular cultures
and modern mass culture. How precisely these enormously expanded capacities for information storage, processing, and recall
have affected artists and their work remains to be analyzed. But
one thing seems clear: the great divide that separated high modernism from mass culture and that was codified in the various
classical accounts of modernism no longer seems relevant to postmodern artistic or critical sensibilities.

Since the categorical demand for the uncompromising segregation of high and low has lost much of its persuasive power, we may be in a better position now to understand the political pressures and historical contingencies which shaped such accounts in the first place. I would suggest that the primary place of what I am calling the great divide was the age of Stalin and Hitler when the threat of totalitarian control over all culture forged a variety of defensive strategies meant to protect high culture in general, not just modernism. Thus conservative culture critics such as Ortega y Gasset argued that high culture needed to be protected from the "revolt of the masses." Left critics like Adorno insisted that genuine art resist its incorporation into the capitalist culture industry which he defined as the total administration of culture from above. And even Lukács, the left critic of modernism *par excellence,* developed his theory of high bourgeois realism not in unison with but in antagonism to the Zhdanovist dogma of socialist realism and its deadly practice of censorship.

It is surely no coincidence that the Western codification of modernism as canon of the 20th century took place during the 1940s and 1950s, preceding and during the Cold War. I am not reducing the great modernist works, by way of a simple ideology critique of their function to a ploy in the cultural strategies of the Cold War. What I am suggesting, however, is that the age of Hitler, Stalin, and the Cold War produced specific accounts of modernism, such as those of Clement Greenberg and Adorno,[27] whose aesthetic categories cannot be totally divorced from the pressures of that era. And it is in this sense, I would argue, that the logic of modernism advocated by those critics has become an aesthetic dead end to the extent that it has been upheld as rigid guideline for further artistic production and critical evaluation. As against such dogma, the postmodern has indeed opened up new directions and new visions. As the confrontation between "bad" socialist realism and the "good" art of the free world began to lose its ideological momentum in an age of *détente,* the whole relationship between modernism and mass culture as well as the problem of realism could be reassessed in less reified terms. While the issue was already raised in the 1960s, e.g., in pop art and various forms of documentary literature, it was only in the 1970s that artists increasingly drew on popular or mass cultural forms and genres, overlaying them with modernist and/or avantgardist strategies. A major body of work representing this tendency is the New German Cinema, and here especially the films of Rainer Werner Fassbinder, whose success in the United States can

be explained precisely in those terms. It is also no coincidence that
the diversity of mass culture was now recognized and analyzed by
critics who increasingly began to work themselves out from under
the modernist dogma that all mass culture is monolithic Kitsch,
psychologically regressive and mind-destroying. The possibilities
for experimental meshing and mixing of mass culture and modernism seemed promising and produced some of the most successful
and ambitious art and literature of the 1970s. Needless to say, it
also produced aesthetic failures and fiascos, but then modernism itself did not only produce masterworks.

It was especially the art, writing, film-making and criticism of
women and minority artists with their recuperation of buried and
mutilated traditions, their emphasis on exploring forms of gender-
and race-based subjectivity in aesthetic productions and experiences, and their refusal to be limited to standard canonizations,
which added a whole new dimension to the critique of high modernism and to the emergence of alternative forms of culture. Thus, we
have come to see modernism's imaginary relationship to African
and Oriental art as deeply problematic, and will not approach, say,
contemporary Latin American writers other than by praising them
for being good modernists, who, naturally, learned their craft in
Paris. Women's criticism has shed some new light on the modernist
canon itself from a variety of different feminist perspectives. Without succumbing to the kind of feminine essentialism which is one of
the more problematic sides of the feminist enterprise, it just seems
obvious that were it not for the critical gaze of feminist criticism,
the male determinations and obsessions of Italian futurism, Vorti-
cism, Russian constructivism, Neue Sachlichkeit or surrealism
would probably still be blocked from our view; and the writings of
Marie Luise Fleisser and Ingeborg Bachmann, the paintings of Fr-
ida Kahlo would still be known only to a handful of specialists. Of
course such new insights can be interpreted in multiple ways, and
the debate about gender and sexuality, male and female authorship
and reader/spectatorship in literature and the arts is far from over,
its implications for a new image of modernism not yet fully
elaborated.

In light of these developments it is somewhat baffling that
feminist criticism has so far largely stayed away from the postmodernism debate which is considered not to be pertinent to feminist
concerns. The fact that to date only male critics have addressed the
problem of modernity/postmodernity, however, does not mean that it
does not concern women. I would argue—and here I am in full
agreement with Craig Owens[28]—that women's art, literature, and

criticism are an important part of the postmodern culture of the 1970s and 1980s and indeed a measure of the vitality and energy of that culture. Actually, the suspicion is in order that the conservative turn of these past years has indeed something to do with the sociologically significant emergence of various forms of "otherness" in the cultural sphere, all of which are perceived as a threat to the stability and sanctity of canon and tradition. Current attempts to restore a 1950s version of high modernism for the 1980s certainly point in that direction. And it is in this context that the question of neo-conservatism becomes politically central to the debate about the postmodern.

Habermas and the Question of Neo-Conservatism

Both in Europe and the U.S., the waning of the 1960s was accompanied by the rise of neo-conservatism, and soon enough there emerged a new constellation characterized by the terms "postmodernism" and "neo-conservatism." Even though their relationship was never fully elaborated, the left took them to be compatible with each other or even identical, arguing that postmodernism was the kind of affirmative art that could happily coexist with political and cultural neo-conservatism. Until very recently, the question of the postmodern was simply not taken seriously on the left,[29] not to speak of those traditionalists in the academy or the museum for whom there is still nothing new and worthwhile under the sun since the advent of modernism. The left's ridiculing of postmodernism was of a piece with its often haughty and dogmatic critique of the countercultural impulses of the 1960s. During much of the 1970s, after all, the thrashing of the 1960s was as much a pastime of the left as it was the gospel according to Daniel Bell.

Now, there is no doubt that much of what went under the label of postmodernism in the 1970s is indeed affirmative, not critical, in nature, and often, especially in literature, remarkably similar to tendencies of modernism which it so vocally repudiates. But not all of it is simply affirmative, and the wholesale writing off of postmodernism as a symptom of capitalist culture in decline is reductive, unhistorical and all too reminiscent of Lukács's attacks on modernism in the 1930s. Can one really make such clear-cut distinctions as to uphold modernism, today, as the only valid form of 20th-century "realism,"[30] an art that is adequate to the *condition moderne,* while simultaneously reserving all the old epitheta—inferior, decadent, pathological—to postmodernism? And isn't it ironic that many of the same critics who will insist on this distinction are the first ones to declare emphatically that modernism already had it all and that there is really nothing new in postmodernism. . . .

I would instead argue that in order not to become the Lukács of the postmodern by opposing, today, a "good" modernism to a "bad" postmodernism, we try to salvage the postmodern from its assumed total collusion with neo-conservatism wherever possible; and that we explore the question whether postmodernism might not harbor productive contradictions, perhaps even a critical and oppositional potential. If the postmodern is indeed a historical and cultural condition (however transitional or incipient), then oppositional cultural practices and strategies must be located *within* postmodernism, not necessarily in its gleaming façades, to be sure, but neither in some outside ghetto of a properly "progressive" or a correctly "aesthetic" art. Just as Marx analyzed the culture of modernity dialectically as bringing both progress and destruction,[31] the culture of postmodernity, too, must be grasped in its gains as well as in its losses, in its promises as well as in its depravations; and yet, it may be precisely one of the characteristics of the postmodern that the relationship between progress and destruction of cultural forms, between tradition and modernity can no longer be understood today the same way Marx understood it at the dawn of modernist culture.

It was, of course, Jürgen Habermas's intervention which, for the first time, raised the question of postmodernism's relationship to neoconservatism in a theoretically and historically complex way. Ironically, however, the effect of Habermas's argument, which identified the postmodern with various forms of conservatism, was to reinforce leftist cultural stereotypes rather than challenge them. In his 1980 Adorno-prize lecture,[32] which has become a focal point for the debate, Habermas criticized both conservatism (old, neo, and young) and postmodernism for not coming to terms either with the exigencies of culture in late capitalism or with the successes and failures of modernism itself. Significantly, Habermas's notion of modernity—the modernity he wishes to see continued and completed—is purged of modernism's nihilistic and anarchic strain just as his opponents', e.g., Lyotard's,[33] notion of an aesthetic (post)modernism is determined to liquidate any trace of the enlightened modernity inherited from the 18th century which provides the basis for Habermas's notion of modern culture. Rather than rehearsing the theoretical differences between Habermas and Lyotard one more time—a task which Martin Jay has performed admirably in a recent article on "Habermas and Modernism"[34]—I want to point to the German context of Habermas's reflections which is too readily forgotten in American debates, since Habermas himself refers to it only marginally.

Habermas's attack on postmodern conservatisms took place on the heels of the political *Tendenzwende* of the mid-1970s, the conservative backlash which has affected several Western countries. He could cite an analysis of American neo-conservatism without even having to belabor the point that the neo-conservative strategies to regain cultural hegemony and to wipe out the effect of the 1960s in political and cultural life are very similar in the FRG. But the national contingencies of Habermas's arguments are at least as important. He was writing at the tail lend of a major thrust of modernization of German cultural and political life which seemed to have gone awry sometime during the 1970s, producing high levels of disillusionment both with the utopian hopes and the pragmatic promises of 1968/69. Against the growing cynicism, which has since then been brilliantly diagnosed and criticized in Peter Sloterdijk's *Kritik der zynischen Vernunft* as a form of "enlightened false consciousness,"[35] Habermas tries to salvage the emancipatory potential of enlightened reason which to him is the *sine qua non* of political democracy. habermas defends a substantive notion of communicative rationality, especially against those who will collapse reason with domination, believing that by abandoning reason they free themselves from domination. Of course Habermas's whole project of a critical social theory revolves around a defense of enlightened modernity, which is *not* identical with the aesthetic modernism of literary critics and art historians. It is directed simultaneously against political conservatism (neo or old) and against what he perceives, not unlike Adorno, as the cultural irrationality of a post-Nietzschean aestheticism embodied in surrealism and subsequently in much of contemporary French theory. The defense of enlightenment in Germany is and remains an attempt to fend off the reaction from the right.

During the 1970s, Habermas could observe how German art and literature abandoned the explicit political commitments of the 1960s, a decade often described in Germany as a "second enlightenment"; how autobiography and *Erfahrungstexte* replaced the documentary experiments in prose and drama of the preceding decade; how political poetry and art made way for a new subjectivity, a new romanticism, a new mythology; how a new generation of students and young intellectuals became increasingly weary of theory, left politics and social science, preferring instead to flock toward the revelations of ethnology and myth. Even though

Habermas does not address the art and literature of the 1970s directly—with the exception of the late work of Peter Weiss, which is itself an exception—it seems not too much to assume that he interpreted this cultural shift in light of the political *Tendenzwende*. Perhaps his labelling of Foucault and Derrida as young conservatives is as much a response to German cultural developments as it is to the French theorists themselves. Such a speculation may draw plausibility from the fact that since the late 1970s certain forms of French theory have been quite influential, especially in the subcultures of Berlin and Frankfurt, among those of the younger generation who have turned away from critical theory made in Germany.

It would be only a small step, then, for Habermas to conclude that a post-modern, post-avantgarde art indeed fits in all too smoothly with various forms of conservatism, and is predicated on abandoning the emancipatory project of modernity. But to me, there remains the question of whether these aspects of the 1970s—despite their occasionally high levels of self-indulgence, narcissism, and false immediacy—do not also represent a deepening and a constructive displacement of the emancipatory impulses of the 1960s. But one does not have to share Habermas's positions on modernity and modernism to see that he did indeed raise the most important issues at stake in a form that avoided the usual apologies and facile polemics about modernity and postmodernity.

His questions were these: How does postmodernism relate to modernism? How are political conservatism, cultural eclecticism or pluralism, tradition, modernity, and anti-modernity interrelated in contemporary Western culture? To what extent can the cultural and social formation of the 1970s be characterized as postmodern? And further, to what extent is postmodernism a revolt against reason and enlightenment, and at what point do such revolts become reactionary—a question heavily loaded with the weight of recent German history? In comparison, the standard American accounts of postmodernism too often remain entirely tied to questions of aesthetic style or strategy; the occasional nod toward theories of a postindustrial society is usually intended as a reminder that any form of Marxist or neo-Marxist thought is simply obsolete. In the American debate, three positions can be schematically outlined. Postmodernism is dismissed outright as a fraud and modernism held up as the universal truth, a view which reflects the thinking of the 1950s. Or modernism is condemned as elitist and postmodernism praised as populist, a view which reflects the thinking of the 1960s. Or there is the truly 1970s proposition that "anything goes," which is consumer capitalism's cynical version of "nothing works," but which at least recognizes that the older dichotomies have lost much of their meaning. Needless to say, none of these positions ever reached the level of Habermas's interrogation.

However, there were problems not so much with the questions Habermas raised, as with some of the answers he suggested. Thus his attack on Foucault and Derrida as young conservatives drew immediate fire from poststructuralist quarters, where the reproach was turned around and Habermas himself was labelled a conservative. At this point, the debate was quickly reduced to the silly question: "Mirror, mirror on the wall, who is the least conservative of us all?" And yet, the battle between "Frankfurters and French fries," as Rainer Nägele once referred to it, is instructive because it highlights two fundamentally different visions of modernity. The French vision of modernity begins with Nietzsche and Mallarmé and is thus quite close to what literary criticism describes as modernism. Modernity for the French is primarily—though by no means exclusively—an aesthetic question relating to the energies released by the deliberate destruction of language and other forms of representation. For Habermas, on the other hand, modernity goes back to the best traditions of the Enlightenment, which he tries to salvage and to reinscribe into the present philosophical discourse in a new form. In this, Habermas differs radically from an earlier generation of Frankfurt School critics, Adorno and Horkheimer who, in *The Dialectic of Enlightenment,* developed a view of modernity which seems to be much closer in sensibility to current French theory than to Habermas. But even though Adorno and Horkheimer's assessment of the enlightenment was so much more pessimistic than Habermas's,[36] they also held on to a substantive notion of reason and subjectivity which much of French theory has abandoned. It seems that in the context of the French discourse, enlightenment is simply identified with a history of terror and incarceration that reaches from the Jacobins via the *métarécits* of Hegel and Marx to the Soviet Gulag. I think Habermas is right in rejecting that view as too limited and as politically dangerous. Auschwitz, after all, did *not* result from too much enlightened reason—even though it was organized as a perfectly rationalized death factory—but from a violent anti-enlightenment and anti-modernity affect, which exploited modernity ruthlessly for its own purposes. At the same time, Habermas's turn against the French post-Nietzschean vision of *modernité* as simply anti-modern or, as it were, postmodern, itself implies too limited an account of modernity, at least as far as aesthetic modernity is concerned.

In the uproar over Habermas's attack on the French poststructuralists, the American and European neo-conservatives were all
but forgotten, but I think we should at least take cognizance of what
cultural neo-conservatives actually say about postmodernism. The
answer is fairly simple and straightforward: they reject it and they
think it is dangerous. Two examples: Daniel Bell, whose book on the
postindustrial society has been quoted time and again as supporting sociological evidence by advocates of postmodernism, actually
rejects postmodernism as a dangerous popularization of the modernist aesthetic. Bell's modernism only aims at aesthetic pleasure,
immediate gratification and intensity of experience, all of which, to
him, promote hedonism and anarchy. It is easy to see how such a
jaundiced view of modernism is quite under the spell of those "terrible" 1960s and cannot at all be reconciled with the austere high
modernism of a Kafka, a Schönberg or a T. S. Eliot. At any rate, Bell
sees modernism as something like an earlier society's chemical
waste deposit which, during the 1960s, began to spill over, not unlike Love Canal, into the mainstream of culture, polluting it to the
core. Ultimately, Bell argues in *The Cultural Contradictions of Capitalism,* modernism and postmodernism together are responsible for
the crisis of contemporary capitalism.[37] Bell—a postmodernist?
Certainly not in the aesthetic sense, for Bell actually shares Habermas's rejection of the nihilistic and aestheticist trend within mod-
ernist/postmodernist culture. But Habermas may have been right
in the broader political sense. For Bell's critique of contemporary
capitalist culture is energized by a vision of a society in which the
values and norms of everyday life would no longer be infected by
aesthetic modernism, a society which, within Bell's framework, one
might have to call post-modern. But any such reflection on neo-
conservatism as a form of anti-liberal, anti-progressive postmodernity remains beside the point. Given the aesthetic force-field of the
term postmodernism, no neo-conservative today, would dream of
identifying the neo-conservative project as postmodern.

On the contrary, cultural neo-conservatives often appear as
the last-ditch defenders and champions of modernism. Thus in the
editorial to the first issue of *The New Criterion* and in an accompanying essay entitled "Postmodern: Art and Culture in the 1980s,"[38]
Hilton Kramer rejects the postmodern and counters it with a nostalgic call for the restoration of modernist standards of quality. Differences between Bell's and Kramer's accounts of modernism
notwithstanding, their assessments of postmodernism are identical. In the culture of the 1970s, they will only see loss of quality, dissolution of the imagination, decline of standards and values, and

the triumph of nihilism. But their agenda is not art history. Their agenda is political. Bell argues that postmodernism "undermines the social structure itself by striking at the motivational and psychic-reward system which has sustained it."[39] Kramer attacks the politicization of culture which, in his view, the 1970s have inherited from the 1960s, that "insidious assault on the mind." And like Rudi Fuchs and the 1982 Documenta, he goes on to shove art back into the closet of autonomy and high seriousness where it is supposed to uphold the new criterion of truth. Hilton Kramer—a postmodernist? No, Habermas was simply wrong, it seems, in his linkage of the postmodern with neo-conservatism. But again the situation is more complex than it seems. For Habermas, modernity means critique, enlightenment, and human emancipation, and he is not willing to jettison this political impulse because doing so would terminate left politics once and for all. Contrary to Habermas, the neo-conservative resorts to an established tradition of standards and values which are immune to criticism and change. To Habermas, even Hilton Kramer's neo-conservative defense of a modernism deprived of its adversary cutting edge would have to appear as postmodern, postmodern in the sense of anti-modern. The question in all of this is absolutely not whether the classics of modernism are or are not great works of art. Only a fool could deny that they are. But a problem does surface when their greatness is used as unsurpassable model and appealed to in order to stifle contemporary artistic production. Where that happens, modernism itself is pressed into the service of anti-modern resentment, a figure of discourse which has a long history in the multiple *querelles des anciens et des modernes*.

The only place where Habermas could rest assured of neo-conservative applause is in his attack on Foucault and Derrida. Any such applause, however, would carry the proviso that neither Foucault or Derrida be associated with conservatism. And yet, Habermas was right, in a sense, to connect the postmodernism problematic with poststructuralism. Roughly since the late 1970s, debates about aesthetic postmodernism and poststructuralist criticism have intersected in the United States. The relentless hostility of neo-conservatives to both poststructuralism and postmodernism may not prove the point, but it is certainly suggestive. Thus the February 1984 issue of *The New Criterion* contains a report by Hilton Kramer on the Modern Language Association's centennial convention in New York, and the report is polemically entitled "The MLA Centennial Follies." The major target of the polemic is precisely French poststructuralism and its American appropriation. But the point is not the quality or the lack thereof in certain presentations at the convention. Again, the real issue is a political one. Deconstruction, feminist criticism, Marxist criticism, all lumped together as undesirable aliens, are said to have subverted American intellectual life via the academy. Reading Kramer, the cultural apocalypse seems near, and there would be no reason for surprise if *The New Criterion* were soon to call for an import quota on foreign theory.

What, then, can one conclude from these ideological skirmishes for a mapping of postmodernism in the 1970s and 1980s? First, Habermas was both right and wrong about the collusion of conservatism and postmodernism, depending on whether the issue is the neo-conservative political vision of a post-modern society freed from all aesthetic, i.e., hedonistic, modernist and postmodernist subversions, or whether the issue is aesthetic postmodernism. Secondly, Habermas and the neo-conservatives are right in insisting that postmodernism is not so much a question of style as it is a question of politics and culture at large. The neo-conservative lament about the politicization of culture since the 1960s is only ironic in this context since they themselves have a thoroughly political notion of culture. Thirdly, the neo-conservatives are also right in suggesting that there are continuities between the oppositional culture of the 1960s and that of the 1970s. But their obsessive fixation on the 1960s, which they try to purge from the history books, blinds them to what is different and new in the cultural developments of the 1970s. And, fourthly, the attack on poststructuralism by Habermas and the American neo-conservatives raises the question of what to make of that fascinating interweaving and intersecting of poststructuralism with postmodernism, a phenomenon that is much more relevant in the U.S. than in France. It is to this question that I will now turn in my discussion of the critical discourse of American postmodernism in the 1970s and 1980s.

Poststructuralism: Modern or Postmodern?

The neo-conservative hostility toward both is not really enough to establish a substantive link between postmodernism and poststructuralism; and it may indeed be more difficult to establish such a link than it would seem at first. Certainly, since the late 1970s we have seen a consensus emerge in the U.S. that if postmodernism represents the contemporary "avantgarde" in the arts, poststruc-

turalism must be its equivalent in "critical theory."[40] Such a paral-
lelization is itself favored by theories and practices of textuality and
intertextuality which blur the boundaries between the literary and
the critical text, and thus it is not surprising that the names of the
French *maîtres penseurs* of our time occur with striking regularity
in the discourse on the postmodern.[41] On a superficial level, the
parallels seem indeed obvious. Just as postmodern art and literature have taken the place of an earlier modernism as the major
trend of our times, poststructuralist criticism has decisively passed
beyond the tenets of its major predecessor, the New Criticism. And
just as the New Critics championed modernism, so the story goes,
poststructuralism—as one of the most vital forces of the intellectual life of the 1970s—must somehow be allied with the art and literature of its own time, i.e., with postmodernism.[42] Actually, such
thinking, which is quite prevalent if not always made explicit, gives
us a first indication of how American postmodernism still lives in
the shadow of the moderns. For there is no theoretical or historical
reason to elevate the synchronism of the New Criticism with high
modernism into norm or dogma. Mere simultaneity of critical and
artistic discourse formations does not *per se* mean that they have to
overlap, unless, of course, the boundaries between them are inten-
tionally dismantled, as they are in modernist and postmodernist literature as well as in poststructuralist discourse.

And yet, however much postmodernism and poststructuralism
in the U.S. may overlap and mesh, they are far from identical or
even homologous. I do not question that the theoretical discourse of
the 1970s has had a profound impact on the work of a considerable
number of artists both in Europe and in the U.S. What I do question, however, is the way in which this impact is automatically evaluated in the U.S. as postmodern and thus sucked into the orbit of
the kind of critical discourse that emphasizes radical rupture and
discontinuity. Actually, both in France and in the U.S. poststructuralism is much closer to modernism than is usually assumed by the
advocates of postmodernism. The distance that does exist between
the critical discourses of the New Criticism and poststructuralism
(a constellation which is only pertinent in the U.S., not in France) is
not identical with the differences between modernism and postmodernism. I will argue that poststructuralism is primarily a discourse
of and about modernism,[43] and that if we are to locate the postmodern in poststructuralism it will have to be found in the ways various
forms of poststructuralism have opened up new problematics in
modernism and have reinscribed modernism into the discourse formations of our own time.

Let me elaborate my view that poststructuralism can be perceived, to a significant degree, as a theory of modernism. I will limit myself here to certain points that relate back to my discussion of the modernism/postmodernism constellation in the 1960s and 1970s: the questions of aestheticsm and mass culture, subjectivity and gender.

If it is true that postmodernity is a historical condition making it sufficiently unique and different from modernity, then it is striking to see how deeply the poststructuralist critical discourse—in its obsession with *écriture* and writing, allegory and rhetoric, and in its displacement of revolution and politics to the aesthetic—is embedded in that very modernist tradition which, at least in American eyes, it presumably transcends. What we find time and again is that American poststructuralist writers and critics emphatically privilege aesthetic innovation and experiment; that they call for self-reflexiveness, not, to be sure, of the author-subject, but of the text; that they purge life, reality, history, society from the work of art and its reception, and construct a new autonomy, based on a pristine notion of textuality, a new art for art's sake which is presumably the only kind possible after the failure of all and any commitment. The insight that the subject is constituted in language and the notion that there is nothing outside the text have led to the privileging of the aesthetic and the linguistic which aestheticism has always promoted to justify its imperial claims. The list of 'no longer possibles' (realism, representation, subjectivity, history, etc., etc.) is as long in poststructuralism as it used to be in modernism, and it is very similar indeed.

Much recent writing has challenged the American domestication of French poststructuralism.[44] But it is not enough to claim that in the transfer to the U.S. French theory lost the political edge it has in France. The fact is that even in France the political implications of certain forms of poststructuralism are hotly debated and in doubt.[45] It is not just the institutional pressures of American literary criticism which have depoliticized French theory; the aestheticist trend *within* poststructuralism itself has facilitated the peculiar American reception. Thus it is no coincidence that the politically weakest body of French writing (Derrida and the late Barthes) has been privileged in American literature departments over the more politically intended projects of Foucault and Baudrillard, Kristeva and Lyotard. But even in the more politically conscious and self-conscious theoretical writing in France, the tradition of modernist aestheticism—mediated through an extremely selective reading of Nietzsche—is so powerful a presence that the notion of a radical rupture between the modern and the postmodern cannot possibly make much sense. It is furthermore striking that despite the considerable differences between the various poststructuralist projects, none of them seems informed in any substantial way by postmodernist works of art. Rarely, if ever, do they even address postmodernist works. In itself, this does not vitiate the power of the theory. But it does make for a kind of dubbing where the poststructuralist language is not in sync with the lips and movements of the postmodern body. There is no doubt that center stage in critical theory is held by the classical modernists: Flaubert, Proust and Bataille in Barthes; Nietzsche and Heidegger, Mallarmé and Artaud in Derrida; Nietzsche, Magritte and Bataille in Foucault; Mallarmé and Lautréamont, Joyce and Artaud in Kristeva; Freud in Lacan; Brecht in Althusser and Macherey, and so on *ad infinitum*. The enemies still are realism and representation, mass culture and standardization, grammar, communication, and the presumably all-powerful homogenizing pressures of the modern State.

I think we must begin to entertain the notion that rather than offering a *theory of postmodernity* and developing an analysis of contemporary culture, French theory provides us primarily with an *archeology of modernity,* a theory of modernism at the stage of its exhaustion. It is as if the creative powers of modernism had migrated into theory and come to full self-consciousness in the poststructuralist text—the owl of Minerva spreading its wings at the fall of dusk. Poststructuralism offers a theory of modernism characterized by *Nachträglichkeit,* both in the psychoanalytic and the historical senses. Despite its ties to the tradition of modernist aestheticism, it offers a reading of modernism which differs substantially from those offered by the New Critics, by Adorno or by Greenberg. It is no longer the modernism of "the age of anxiety," the ascetic and tortured modernism of a Kafka, a modernism of negativity and alienation, ambiguity and abstraction, the modernism of the closed and finished work of art. Rather, it is a modernism of playful transgression, of an unlimited weaving of textuality, a modernism all confident in its rejection of representation and reality, in its denial of the subject, of history, and of the subject of history: a modernism quite dogmatic in its rejection of presence and in its unending praise of lacks and absences, deferrals and traces which produce, presumably, not anxiety but, in Roland Barthes' terms, *jouissance,* bliss.[46]

But if poststructuralism can be seen as the *revenant* of modernism in the guise of theory, then that would also be precisely what makes it postmodern. It is a postmodernism that works itself out

not as a rejection of modernism, but rather as a retrospective reading which, in some cases, is fully aware of modernism's limitations
and failed political ambitions. The dilemma of modernism had been
its inability, despite the best intentions, to mount an effective critique of bourgeois modernity and modernization. The fate of the historical avantgarde especially had proven how modern art, even
where it ventured beyond art for art's sake, was ultimately forced
back into the aesthetic realm. Thus the gesture of poststructuralism, to the extent that it abandons all pretense to a critique that
would go beyond language games, beyond epistemology and the aesthetic, seems at least plausible and logical. It certain frees art and
literature from that overload of responsibilities—to change life,
change society, change the world—on which the historical avant-
garde shipwrecked, and which lived on in France through the 1950s
and 1960s embodied in the figure of Jean Paul Sartre. Seen in this
light, poststructuralism seems to seal the fate of the modernist
project which, even where it limited itself to the aesthetic sphere,
always upheld a vision of a redemption of modern life through culture. That such visions are no longer possible to sustain may be at
the heart of the postmodern condition, and it may ultimately vitiate
the poststructuralist attempt to salvage aesthetic modernism for
the late 20th century. At any rate, it all begins to ring false when
poststructuralism presents itself, as it frequently does in American
writings, as the latest "avantgarde" in criticism, thus ironically assuming, in its institutional *Selbstverständnis,* the kind of teleological posturing which poststructuralism itself has done so much to
criticize.

But even where such pretense to academic avantgardism is not
the issue, one may well ask whether the theoretically sustained
self-limitation to language and textuality has not been too high a
price to pay; and whether it is not this self-limitation (with all it
entails) which makes this poststructuralist modernism look like the
atrophy of an earlier aestheticism rather than its innovative transformation. I say atrophy because the turn-of-the-century European
aestheticism could still hope to establish a realm of beauty in opposition to what it perceived as the vulgarities of everyday bourgeois life, an artificial paradise thoroughly hostile to official politics
and the kind of jingoism known in Germany as *Hurrapatriotismus.*
Such an adversary function of aestheticism, however, can hardly be
maintained at a time when capital itself has taken the aesthetic
straight into the commodity in the form of styling, advertising, and
packaging. In an age of commodity aesthetics, aestheticism itself
has become questionable either as an adversary or as a hibernating

strategy. To insist on the adversary function of *écriture* and of breaking linguistic codes when every second ad bristles with domesticated avantgardist and modernist strategies strikes me as caught precisely in that very overestimation of art's transformative *function* for society which is the signature of an earlier, modernist, age. Unless, of course, *écriture* is merely practiced as a glass bead game in happy, resigned, or cynical isolation from the realm the uninitiated keep calling reality.

Take the later Roland Barthes.[47] His *The Pleasure of the Text* has become a major, almost canonical formulation of the postmodern for many American literary critics who may not want to remember that already twenty years ago Susan Sontag had called for an erotics of art intended to replace the stuffy and stifling project of academic interpretation. Whatever the differences between Barthes' *jouissance* and Sontag's erotics (the rigors of New Criticism and structuralism being the respective *Feindbilder*), Sontag's gesture, at the time, was a relatively radical one precisely in that it insisted on presence, on a sensual experience of cultural artifacts; in that it attacked rather than legitimized a socially sanctioned canon whose prime values were objectivity and distance, coolness and irony; and in that it licensed the flight from the lofty horizons of high culture into the netherlands of pop and camp.

Barthes, on the other hand, positions himself safely within high culture and the modernist canon, maintaining equal distance from the reactionary right which champions anti-intellectual pleasures and the pleasure of anti-intellectualism, and the boring left which favors knowledge, commitment, combat, and disdains hedonism. The left may indeed have forgotten, as Barthes claims, the cigars of Marx and Brecht.[48] But however convincing cigars may or may not be as signifiers of hedonism, Barthes himself certainly forgets Brecht's constant and purposeful immersion in popular and mass culture. Barthes' very un-Brechtian distinction between *plaisir* and *jouissance*—which he simultaneously makes and unmakes[49]—reiterates one of the most tired topoi of the modernist aesthetic and of bourgeois culture at large: there are the lower pleasures for the rabble, i.e., mass culture, and then there is the *nouvelle cuisine* of the pleasure of the text, of *jouissance*. Barthes himself describes *jouissance* as a "mandarin praxis,"[50] as a conscious retreat, and he describes modern mass culture in the most simplistic terms as petit-bourgeois. Thus his appraisal of *jouissance* depends on the adoption of that traditional view of mass culture that the right and the left, both of which he so emphatically rejects, have shared over the decades.

This becomes even more explicit in *The Pleasure of the Text* where we read: "The bastard form of mass culture is humiliated repetition: content, ideological schema, the blurring of contradictions—these are repeated, but the superficial forms are varied: always new books, new programs, new films, new items, but always the same meaning."[51] Word for word, such sentences could have been written by Adorno in the 1940s. But, then, everybody knows that Adorno's was a theory of modernism, not of postmodernism. Or was it? Given the ravenous eclecticism of postmodernism, it has recently become fashionable to include even Adorno and Benjamin in the canon of postmodernists *avant la lettre*—truly a case of the critical text writing itself without the interference of any historical consciousness whatsoever. Yet the closeness of some of Barthes's basic propositions to the modernist aesthetic could make such a rapprochement plausible. But then one might want to stop talking of postmodernism altogether, and take Barthes's writing for what it is: a theory of modernism which manages to turn the dung of post-68 political disillusionment into the gold of aesthetic bliss. The melancholy science of Critical Theory has been transformed miraculously into a new "gay science," but it still is, essentially, a theory of modernist literature.

Barthes and his American fans ostensibly reject the modernist notion of negativity replacing it with play, bliss, *jouissance,* i.e., with a presumably critical form of affirmation. But the very distinction between the *jouissance* provided by the modernist, "writerly" text and the mere pleasure (*plaisir*) provided by "the text that contents, fills, grants euphoria,"[52] reintroduces, through the back door, the same high culture/low culture divide and the same type of evaluations that were constitutive of classical modernism. The negativity of Adorno's aesthetic was predicated on the consciousness of the mental and sensual depravations of modern mass culture and on his relentless hostility to a society which needs such depravation to reproduce itself. The euphoric American appropriation of Barthes's *jouissance* is predicated on ignoring such problems and on enjoying, not unlike the 1984 yuppies, the pleasures of writerly connoisseurism and textual gentrification. That, indeed, may be a reason why Barthes has hit a nerve in the American academy of the Reagan years, making him the favorite son who has finally abandoned his earlier radicalism and come to embrace the finer pleasures of life, pardon, the text.[53] But the problems with the older theories of a modernism of negativity are not solved by somersaulting from anxiety and alienation into the bliss of *jouissance.* Such a leap diminishes the wrenching experiences of modernity articulated in modernist art and literature; it remains bound to the modernist paradigm by way of simple reversal; and it does very little to elucidate the problem of the postmodern.

Just as Barthes's theoretical distinctions between *plaisir* and *jouissance,* the readerly and the writerly text, remain within the orbit of modernist aesthetics, so the predominant poststructuralist notions about authorship and subjectivity reiterate propositions known from modernism itself. A few brief comments will have to suffice.

In a discussion of Flaubert and the writerly, i.e., modernist, text Barthes writes: "He [Flaubert] does not stop the play of codes (or stops it only partially), so that (and this is indubitably the proof of writing) *one never knows if he is responsible for what he writes* (if there is a subject *behind* his language); for the very being of writing (the meaning of the labor that constitutes it) is to keep the question *Who is speaking?* from ever being answered."[54] A similarly prescriptive denial of authorial subjectivity underlies Foucault's discourse analysis. Thus Foucault ends his influential essay "What Is an Author?" by asking rehtorically "What matter who's speaking?" Faoucault's "murmur of indifference"[55] affects both the writing and the speaking subject, and the argument assumes its full polemical force with the much broader anti-humanist proposition, inherited from structuralism, of the "death of the subject." But none of this is more than a further elaboration of the modernist critique of traditional idealist and romantic notions of authorship and authenticity, originality and intentionality, self-centered subjectivity and personal identity. More importantly, it seems to me that as a postmodern, having gone through the modernist purgatory, I would ask different questions. Isn't the "death of the subject/author" position tied by mere reversal to the very ideology that invariably glorifies the artist as genius, whether for marketing purposes or out of conviction and habit? Hasn't capitalist modernization itself fragmented and dissolved bourgeois subjectivity and authorship, thus making attacks on such notions somewhat quixotic? And, finally, doesn't poststructuralism, where it simply denies the subject altogether, jettison the chance of challenging the *ideology of the subject* (as male, white, and middle-class) by developing alternative and different notions of subjectivity?

To reject the validity of the question "Who is writing?" or "Who is speaking?" is simply no longer a radical position in 1984. It merely duplicates on the level of aesthetics and theory what capitalism as a system of exchange relations produces tendentially in everyday life: the denial of subjectivity in the very process of its

construction. Poststructuralism thus attacks the appearance of capitalist culture—individualism writ large—but misses its essence;
like modernism, it is always also in sync with rather than opposed
to the real processes of modernization.

The postmoderns have recognized this dilemma. They counter
the modernist litany of the death of the subject by working toward
new theories and practices of speaking, writing and acting
subjects.[56] The question of how codes, texts, images, and other cultural artifacts constitute subjectivity is increasingly being raised as
an always already historical question. And to raise the question of
subjectivity at all no longer carries the stigma of being caught in
the trap of bourgeois or petit-bourgeois ideology; the discourse of
subjectivity has been cut loose from its moorings in bourgeois individualism. It is certainly no accident that questions of subjectivity
and authorship have resurfaced with a vengeance in the postmodern text. After all, it *does* matter who is speaking or writing.

Summing up, then, we face the paradox that a body of theories
of modernism and modernity, developed in France since the 1960s,
has come to be viewed, in the U.S., as the embodiment of the postmodern in theory. In a certain sense, this development is perfectly
logical. Poststructuralism's readings of modernism are new and exciting enough to be considered somehow beyond modernism as it
has been perceived before; in this way poststructuralist criticism in
the U.S. yields to the very real reassures of the postmodern. But
against any facile conflation of poststructuralism with the postmodern, we must insist on the fundamental non-identity of the two phenomena. In America, too, poststructuralism offers a theory of
modernism, not a theory of the postmodern.

As to the French theorists themselves, they rarely speak of the
postmodern. Lyotard's *La Condition Postmoderne,* we must remember, is the exception, to the rule.[57] What French intellectuals explicitly analyze and reflect upon is *le texte moderne* and *la modernité.*
Where they talk about the postmodern at all, as in the cases of Lyotard and Kristeva,[58] the question seems to have been prompted by
American friends, and the discussion almost immediately and invariably turns back to problems of the modernist aesthetic. For
Kristeva, the question of postmodernism is the question of how anything can be written in the 20th century and how we can talk about
this writing. She goes on to say that postmodernism is "that literature which writes itself with the more or less conscious intention
of expanding the signifiable and thus the human realm."[59] With the
Bataillean formulation of writing-as-experience of limits, she sees
the major writing since Mallarmé and Joyce, Artaud and Bur-

roughs as the "exploration of the typical imaginary relationship, that to the mother, through the most radical and problematic aspect of this relationship, language."[60] Kristeva's is a fascinating and novel approach to the question of modernist literature, and one that understands itself as a political intervention. But it does not yield much for an exploration of the differences between modernity and postmodernity. Thus it cannot surprise that Kristeva still shares with Barthes and the classical theorists of modernism an aversion to the media whose function, she claims, is to collectivize all systems of signs thus enforcing contemporary society's general tendency toward uniformity.

Lyotard, who like Kristeva and unlike the deconstructionists is a political thinker, defines the postmodern, in his essay "Answering the Question: What is Postmodernism?," as a recurring stage within the modern itself. He turns to the Kantian sublime for a theory of the nonrepresentable essential to modern art and literature. Paramount are his interest in rejecting representation, which is linked to terror and totalitarianism, and his demand for radical experimentation in the arts. At first sight, the turn to Kant seems plausible in the sense that Kant's autonomy aesthetic and notion of "disinterested pleasure" stands at the threshold of a modernist aesthetic, at a crucial juncture of that differentiation of spheres which has been so important in social thought from Weber to Habermas. And yet, the turn to Kant's sublime forgets that the 18th-century fascination with the sublime of the universe, the cosmos, expresses precisely that very desire of totality and representation which Lyotard so abhors and persistently criticizes in Habermas' work.[61] Perhaps Lyotard's text says more here than it means to. If historically the notion of the sublime harbors a secret desire for totality, then perhaps Lyotard's sublime can be read as an attempt to totalize the aesthetic realm by fusing it with all other spheres of life, thus wiping out the differentiations between the aesthetic realm and the life-world on which Kant did after all insist. At any rate, it is no coincidence that the first moderns in Germany, the Jena romantics, built their aesthetic strategies of the fragment precisely on a rejection of the sublime which to them had become a sign of the falseness of bourgeois accommodation to absolutist culture. Even today the sublime has not lost its link to terror which, in Lyotard's reading, it opposes. For what would be more sublime and unrepresentable than the nuclear holocaust, the bomb being the signifier of an ultimate sublime? But apart from the question whether or not the sublime is an adequate aesthetic category to theorize contemporary art and literature, it is clear that in Lyotard's essay the postmodern as aesthetic phenomenon is not seen as distinct from modernism. The crucial historical distinction which Lyotard offers in *La Condition Postmoderne* is that between the *métarécits* of liberation (the French tradition of enlightened modernity) and of totality (the German Hegelian/Marxist tradition) on the one hand, and the modernist experimental discourse of language games on the other. Enlightened modernity and its presumable consequences are pitted against aesthetic modernism. The irony in all of this, as Fred Jameson has remarked,[62] is that Lyotard's commitment to radical experimentation is politically "very closely related to the conception of the revolutionary nature of high modernism that Habermas faithfully inherited from the Frankfurt School."

No doubt, there are historically and intellectually specific reasons for the French resistance to acknowledging the problem of the postmodern as a historical problem of the late 20th century. At the same time, the force of the French rereading of modernism proper is itself shaped by the pressures of the 1960s and 1970s, and it has thus raised many of the key questions pertinent to the culture of our own time. But it still has done very little toward illuminating an emerging postmodern culture, and it has largely remained blind to or uninterested in many of the most promising artistic endeavors today. French theory of the 1960s and 1970s has offered us exhilarating fireworks which illuminate a crucial segment of the trajectory of modernism, but, as appropriate with fireworks, after dusk has fallen. This view is borne out by none less than Michel Foucault who, in the late 1970s, criticized his own earlier fascination with language and epistemology as a limited project of an earlier decade: "The whole relentless theorization of writing which we saw in the 1960s was doubtless only a swansong."[63] Swansong of modernism, indeed; but as such already a moment of the postmodern. Foucault's view of the intellectual movement of the 1960s as a swansong, it seems to me, is closer to the truth than its American rewriting, during the 1970s, as the latest avantgarde.

Whither Postmodernism?

The cultural history of the 1970s still has to be written, and the various postmodernisms in art, literature, dance, theater, architecture, film, video, and music will have to be discussed separately and in detail. All I want to do now is to offer a framework for relating some recent cultural and political changes to postmodernism, changes which already lie outside the conceptual network of "modernism/ avantgardism" and have so far rarely been included in the postmodernism debate.[64]

I would argue that the contemporary arts—in the widest possible sense, whether they call themselves postmodernist or reject that label—can no longer be regarded as just another phase in the sequence of modernist and avantgardist movements which began in Paris in the 1850s and 1860s and which maintained an ethos of cultural progress and vanguardism through the 1960s. On this level, postmodernism cannot be regarded simply as a sequel to modernism, as the latest step in the never-ending revolt of modernism against itself. The postmodern sensibility of our time is different from both modernism *and* avantgardism precisely in that it raises the question of cultural tradition and conservation in the most fundamental way as an aesthetic and a political issue. It doesn't always do it successfully, and often does it exploitatively. And yet, my main point about contemporary postmodernism is that it operates in a field of tension between tradition and innovation, conservation and renewal, mass culture and high art, in which the second terms are no longer automatically privileged over the first; a field of tension which can no longer be grasped in categories such as progress vs. reaction, left vs. right, present vs. past, modernism vs. realism, abstraction vs. representation, avantgarde vs. Kitsch. The fact that such dichotomies, which after all are central to the classical accounts of modernism, have broken down is part of the shift I have been trying to describe. I could also state the shift in the following terms: Modernism and the avantgarde were always closely related to social and industrial modernization. They were related to it as an adversary culture, yes, but they drew their energies, not unlike Poe's *Man of the Crowd,* from their proximity to the crises brought about by modernization and progress. Modernization—such was the widely held belief, even when the word was not around—had to be traversed. There was a vision of emerging on the other side. The modern was a world-scale drama played out on the European and American stage, with mythic modern man as its hero and with modern art as a driving force, just as Saint-Simon had envisioned it already in 1825. Such heroic visions of modernity and of art as a force of social change (or, for that matter, resistance to undesired change) are a thing of the past, admirable for sure, but no longer in tune with current sensibilities, except perhaps with an emerging apocalyptic sensibility as the flip side of modernist heroism.

Seen in this light, postmodernism at its deepest level represents not just another crisis within the perpetual cycle of boom and

bust, exhaustion and renewal, which has characterized the trajectory of modernist culture. It rather represents a new type of crisis *of*
that modernist culture itself. Of course, this claim has been made
before, and fascism indeed was a formidable crisis *of* modernist culture. But fascism was never the alternative to modernity it pre-
tended to be, and our situation today is very different from that of
the Weimar Republic in its agony. It was only in the 1970s that the
historical limits of modernism, modernity, and modernization came
into sharp focus. The growing sense that we are not bound to *complete* the project of modernity (Habermas' phrase) and still do not
necessarily have to lapse into irrationality or into apocalyptic
frenzy, the sense that art is not exclusively pursuing some telos of
abstraction, non-representation, and sublimity—all of this has
opened up a host of possibilities for creative endeavors today. And in
certain ways it has altered our views of modernism itself. Rather
than being bound to a one-way history of modernism which interprets it as a logical unfolding toward some imaginary goal, and
which thus is based on a whole series of exclusions, we are beginning to explore its contradictions and contingencies, its tensions
and internal resistances to its own "forward" movement. Postmodernism is far from making modernism obsolete. On the contrary, it
casts a new light on it and appropriates many of its aesthetic strategies and techniques inserting them and making them work in
new constellations. What has become obsolete, however, are those
codifications of modernism in critical discourse which, however
subliminally, are based on a teleological view of progress and modernization. Ironically, these normative and often reductive codifications have actually prepared the ground for the repudiation of
modernism which goes by the name of the postmodern. Confronted
with the critic who argues that this or that novel is not up to the
latest in narrative technique, that it is regressive, behind the times
and thus uninteresting, the postmodernist is right in rejecting modernism. But such rejection affects only that trend within modernism which has been codified into a narrow dogma, not modernism as
such. In some ways, the story of modernism and postmodernism is
like the story of the hedgehog and the hare: the hare could not win
because there always was more than just one hedgehog. But the
hare was still the better runner. . . .

The crisis of modernism is more than just a crisis of those
trends within it which tie it to the ideology of modernization. In the
age of late capitalism, it is also a new crisis of art's relationship to
society. At their most emphatic, modernism and avantgardism attributed to art a privileged status in the processes of social change.

Even the aestheticist withdrawal from the concern of social change is still bound to it by virtue of its denial of the status quo and the construction of an artificial paradise of exquisite beauty. When social change seemed beyond grasp or took an undesired turn, art was still privileged as the only authentic voice of critique and protest, even when it seemed to withdraw into itself. The classical accounts of high modernism attest to that fact. To admit that these were heroic illusions—perhaps even necessary illusions in art's struggle to survive in dignity in a capitalist society—is not to deny the importance of art in social life.

But modernism's running feud with mass society and mass culture as well as the avantgarde's attack on high art as a support system of cultural hegemony always took place on the pedestal of high art itself. And certainly that is where the avantgarde has been installed after its failure, in the 1920s, to create a more encompassing space for art in social life. To continue to demand today that high art leave the pedestal and relocate elsewhere (wherever that might be) is to pose the problem in obsolete terms. The pedestal of high art and high culture no longer occupies the privileged space it used to, just as the cohesion of the class which erected its monuments on that pedestal is a thing of the past; recent conservative attempts in a number of Western countries to restore dignity of the classics of Western Civilization, from Plato via Adam Smith to the high modernists, and to send students back to the basics, prove the point. I am not saying here that the pedestal of high art does not exist any more. Of course it does, but it is not what it used to be. Since the 1960s, artistic activities have become much more diffuse and harder to contain in safe categories or stable institutions such as the academy, the museum or even the established gallery network. To some, this dispersal of cultural and artistic practices and activities will involve a sense of loss and disorientation; others will experience it as a new freedom, a cultural liberation. Neither may be entirely wrong, but we should recognize that it was not only recent theory or criticism that deprived the univalent, exclusive and totalizing accounts of modernism of their hegemonic role. It was the activities of artists, writers, film makers, architects, and performers that have propelled us beyond a narrow vision of modernism and given us a new lease on modernism itself.

In political terms, the erosion of the triple dogma modernism/modernity/avantgardism can be contextually related to the emergence of the problematic of "otherness," which has asserted itself in the sociopolitical sphere as much as in the cultural sphere. I cannot discuss here the various and multiple forms of otherness as they emerge from differences in subjectivity, gender and sexuality, race and class, temporal *Ungleichzeitigkeiten* and spatial geographic locations and dislocations. But I want to mention at least four recent phenomena which, in my mind, are and will remain constitutive of postmodern culture for some time to come.

Despite all its noble aspirations and achievements, we have come to recognize that the culture of enlightened modernity has also always (though by no means exclusively) been a culture of inner and outer imperialism, a reading already offered by Adorno and Horkheimer in the 1940s and an insight not unfamiliar to those of our ancestors involved in the multitude of struggles against rampant modernization. Such imperialism, which works inside and outside, on the micro and macro levels, no longer goes unchallenged either politically, economically, or culturally. Whether these challenges will usher in a more habitable, less violent and more democratic world remains to be seen, and it is easy to be skeptical. But enlightened cynicism is as insufficient an answer as blue-eyed enthusiasm for peace and nature.

The women's movement has led to some significant changes in social structure and cultural attitudes which must be sustained even in the face of the recent grotesque revival of American machismo. Directly and indirectly, the women's movement has nourished the emergence of women as a self-confident and creative force in the arts, in literature, film, and criticism. The ways in which we now raise questions of gender and sexuality, reading and writing, subjectivity and enunciation, voice and performance are unthinkable without the impact of feminism, even though many of these activities may take place on the margin or even outside the movement proper. Feminist critics have also contributed substantially to revisions of the history of modernism, not just by unearthing forgotten artists, but also by approaching the male modernists in novel ways. This is true also of the "new French feminists" and their theorization of the feminine in modernist writing, even though they often insist on maintaining a polemical distance from an American-type feminism.[65]

During the 1970s, questions of ecology and environment have deepened from single-issue politics to a broad critique of modernity and modernization, a trend which is politically and culturally much stronger in West Germany than in the U.S. A new ecological sensibility manifests itself not only in political and regional subcultures, in alternative life-styles, and the new social movements in Europe, but it also affects art and literature in a variety of ways: the work of Joseph Beuys, certain land art projects, Christo's California running fence, the new nature poetry, the return to local traditions, dialects, and so on. It was especially due to the growing ecological sensibility that the link between certain forms of modernism and technological modernization has come under critical scrutiny.

There is a growing awareness that other cultures, non-European, non-Western cultures must be met by means other than conquest or domination, as Paul Ricoeur put it more than twenty years ago, and that the erotic and aesthetic fascination with "the Orient" and "the primitive"—so prominent in Western culture, including modernism—is deeply problematic. This awareness will have to translate into a type of intellectual work different from that of the modernist intellectual who typically spoke with the confidence of standing at the cutting edge of time and of being able to speak for others. Foucault's notion of the local and specific intellectual as opposed to the "universal" intellectual of modernity may provide a way out of the dilemma of being locked into our own culture and traditions while simultaneously recognizing their limitations.

In conclusion, it is easy to see that a postmodernist culture emerging from these political, social, and cultural constellations will have to be a postmodernism of resistance, including resistance to that easy postmodernism of the "anything goes" variety. Resistance will always have to be specific and contingent upon the cultural field within which it operates. It cannot be defined simply in terms of negativity or nonidentity à la Adorno, nor will the litanies of a totalizing, collective project suffice. At the same time, the very notion of resistance may itself be problematic in its simple opposition to affirmation. After all, there are affirmative forms of resistance and resisting forms of affirmation. But this may be more a semantic problem than a problem of practice. And it should not keep us from making judgments. How such resistance can be articulated in art works in ways that would satisfy the needs of the political *and* those of the aesthetic, of the producers and of the recipients, cannot be prescribed, and it will remain open to trial, error and debate. But it is time to abandon that dead-end dichotomy of politics and aesthetics which for too long has dominated accounts of modernism, including the aestheticist trend within poststructuralism. The point is not to eliminate the productive tension between the political and the aesthetic, between history and the text, between engagement and the mission of art. The point is to heighten that tension, even to rediscover it and to bring it back into focus in the arts as well as in criticism. No matter how troubling it may be, the landscape of the postmodern surrounds us. It simultaneously delimits and opens our horizons. It's our problem and our hope.

Notes

1. Catalogue, *Documenta 7* (Kassel: Paul Dierichs, n.d. [1982]), xv.

2. Ibid.

3. Of course, this is not meant as a "fair" evaluation of the show or of all the works exhibited in it. It should be clear that what I am concerned with here is the dramaturgy of the show, the way it was conceptualized and presented to the public. For a more comprehensive discussion of Documenta 7, see Benjamin H. D. Buchloh, "Documenta 7: A Dictionary of Received Ideas," *October,* 22 (Fall 1982), 105–126.

4. On this question see Fredric Jameson, "Postmodernism or the Cultural Logic of Capitalism," *New Left Review,* 146 (July–August 1984), 53–92, whose attempt to identify postmodernism with a new stage in the developmental logic of capital, I feel, overstates the case.

5. For a distinction between a critical and an affirmative postmodernism, see Hal Foster's introduction to *The Anti-Aesthetic* (Port Townsend, Washington: Bay Press, 1984). Foster's later essay in *New German Critique,* 33 (Fall 1984), however, indicates a change of mind with regard to the critical potential of postmodernism.

6. For an earlier attempt to give a *Begriffsgeschichte* of postmodernism in literature, see the various essays in *Amerikastudien,* 22:1 (1977), 9–46 (includes a valuable bibliography). Cf. also Ihab Hassan, *The Dismemberment of Orpheus,* second edition (Madison: University of Wisconsin Press, 1982), especially the new "Postface 1982: Toward a Concept of Postmodernism," 259–271.—The debate about modernity and modernization in history and the social sciences is too broad to document here; for an excellent survey of the pertinent literature, see Hans-Ulrich Wehler, *Modernisierungstheorie und Geschichte* (Göttingen: Vandenhoeck & Ruprecht, 1975).—On the question of modernity and the arts, see Matei Calinescu, *Faces of Modernity* (Bloomington: Indiana University Press, 1977); Marshall Berman, *All That Is Solid Melts Into Air: The Experience of Modernity* (New York: Simon & Schuster, 1982); Eugene Lunn, *Marxism and Modernism* (Berkeley and Los Angeles: University of California Press, 1982); Peter Bürger, *Theory of the Avantgarde* (Minneapolis: University of Minnesota Press, 1984). Also important for this debate is the recent work by cultural historians on specific cities and their culture, e.g., Carl Schorske's and Robert Waissenberger's work on fin-de-siècle Vienna, Peter Gay's and John Willett's work on the Weimar Republic, and, for a discussion of American anti-modernism at the turn of the century, T. J. Jackson Lear's *No Place of Grace* (New York: Pantheon, 1981).

7. On the ideological and political function of modernism in the 1950s cf. Jost Hermand, "Modernism Restored: West German Painting in the 1950s," *New German Critique,* 32 (Spring/Summer 1984), 23–41; and Serge

Guilbaut, *How New York Stole the Idea of Modern Art* (Chicago: Chicago University Press, 1983).

8. For a thorough discussion of this concept see Robert Sayre and Michel Löwry, "Figures of Romantic Anti-Capitalism," *New German Critique,* 32 (Spring/Summer 1984), 42–92.

9. For an excellent discussion of the politics of architecture in the Weimar Republic see the exhibition catalogue *Wem gehört die Welt: Kunst und Gesellschaft in der Weimarer Republik* (Berlin: Neue Gesellschaft für die bildende Kunst, 1977), 38–157. Cf. also Robert Hughes, "Trouble in Utopia," in *The Shock of the New* (New York: Alfred A. Knopf, 1981), 164–211.

10. The fact that such strategies can cut different ways politically is shown by Kenneth Frampton in his essay "Towards a Critical Regionalism," in *The Anti-Aesthetic,* 23–38.

11. Charles A. Jencks, *The Language of Postmodern Architecture* (New York: Rizzoli, 1977), 97.

12. For Bloch's concept of *Ungleichzeitigkeit,* see Ernst Bloch, "Non-Synchronism and the Obligation to its Dialectics," and Anson Rabinbach's "Ernst Bloch's *Heritage of our Times* and Fascism," in *New German Critique,* 11 (Spring 1977), 5–38.

13. Robert Venturi, Denise Scott Brown, Stephen Izenour, *Learning from Las Vegas* (Cambridge: MIT Press, 1972). Cf. also the earlier study by Venturi, *Complexity and Contradiction in Architecture* (New York: Museum of Modern Art, 1966).

14. Kenneth Frampton, *Modern Architecture: A Critical History* (New York and Toronto: Oxford University Press, 1980), 290.

15. I am mainly concerned here with the *Selbstverständnis* of the artists, and not with the question of whether their work really went beyond modernism or whether it was in all cases politically "progressive." On the politics of the Beat rebellion see Barbara Ehrenreich, *The Hearts of Men* (New York: Doubleday, 1984), esp. 52–67.

16. Gerald Graff, "The Myth of the Postmodern Breakthrough," in *Literature Against Itself* (Chicago: University of Chicago Press, 1979), 31–62.

17. John Barth, "The Literature of Replenishment: Postmodernist Fiction," *Atlantic Monthly,* 245:1 (January 1980), 65–71.

18. Daniel Bell, *The Cultural Contradictions of Capitalism* (New York: Basic Books, 1976), 51.

19. The specific connotations the notion of postmodernity has taken on in the German peace and anti-nuke movements as well as within the

Green Party will not be discussed here, as this article is primarily concerned with the American debate.—In German intellectual life, the work of Peter Sloterdijk is eminently relevant for these issues, although Sloterdijk does not use the word "postmodern"; Peter Sloterdijk, *Kritik der zynischen Vernunft*, 2 vols. (Frankfurt am Main: Suhrkamp, 1983), American translation forthcoming from University of Minnesota Press. Equally pertinent is the peculiar German reception of French theory, especially of Foucault, Baudrillard, and Lyotard; see for example *Der Tod der Moderne. Eine Diskussion* (Tübingen: Konkursbuchverlag, 1983). On the apocalyptic shading of the postmodern in Germany see Ulrich Horstmann, *Das Untier. Konturen einer Philosophie der Menschenflucht* (Wien-Berlin: Medusa, 1983).

20. The following section will draw on arguments developed less fully in the preceding article entitled "The Search for Tradition: Avantgarde and Post-modernism in the 1970s."

21. Peter Bürger, *Theory of the Avant-Garde* (Minneapolis: University of Minnesota Press, 1984). The fact that Bürger reserves the term avantgarde for mainly these three movements may strike the American reader as idiosyncratic or as unnecessarily limited unless the place of the argument within the tradition of 20th-century German aesthetic thought from Brecht and Benjamin to Adorno is understood.

22. This difference between modernism and the avantgarde was one of the pivotal points of disagreement between Benjamin and Adorno in the late 1930s, a debate to which Bürger owes a lot. Confronted with the successful fusion of aesthetics, politics, and everyday life in fascist Germany, Adorno condemned the avantgarde's intention to merge art with life and continued to insist, in best modernist fashion, on the autonomy of art; Benjamin, on the other hand, looking backward to the radical experiments in Paris, Moscow, and Berlin in the 1920s, found a messianic promise in the avantgarde, especially in surrealism, a fact which may help explain Benjamin's strange (and, I think, mistaken) appropriation in the U.S. as a postmodern critic *avant la lettre*.

23. Cf. my essay, "The Cultural Politics of Pop." From a different perspective, Dick Hebdige developed a similar argument about British pop culture at a talk he gave last year at the Center for Twentieth Century Studies at the University of Wisconsin-Milwaukee.

24. The Left's fascination with the media was perhaps more pronounced in Germany than it was in the United States. Those were the years when Brecht's radio theory and Benjamin's "The Work of Art in the Age of Mechanical Reproduction" almost became cult texts. See, for example, Hans Magnus Enzensberger, "Baukasten zu einer Theorie der Medien," *Kursbuch*, 20 (March 1970), 159–186. Reprinted in H. M. E., *Palaver* (Frankfurt am Main: Suhrkamp, 1974). The old belief in the democratizing potential of

the media is also intimated on the last pages of Lyotard's *The Postmodern Condition,* not in relation to radio, film or television, but in relation to computers.

25. Leslie Fiedler, "The New Mutants" (1965), *A Fiedler Reader* (New York: Stein and Day, 1977), 189–210.

26. Edward Lucie-Smith, *Art in the Seventies* (Ithaca: Cornell University Press, 1980), 11.

27. For a lucid discussion of Greenberg's theory of modern art in its historical context see T. J. Clark, "Clement Greenberg's Theory of Art," *Critical Inquiry,* 9:1 (September 1982), 139–156. For a different view of Greenberg see Ingeborg Hoesterey, "Die Moderne am Ende? Zu den ästhetischen Positionen von Jürgen Habermas und Clement Greenberg," *Zeitschrift für Ästhetik und allgemeine Kunstwissenschaft,* 29:2 (1984). On Adorno's theory of modernism see Eugene Lunn, *Marxism and Modernism* (Berkeley and Los Angeles: University of California Press, 1982); Peter Bürger, *Vermittlung-Rezeption-Funktion* (Frankfurt am Main: Suhrkamp, 1979), esp. 79–92; Burkhardt Lindner and W. Martin Lüdke, eds., *Materialien zur ästhetischen Theorie: Th. W. Adornos Konstruktion der Moderne* (Frankfurt am Main: Suhrkamp, 1980).

28. See Craig Owens, "The Discourse of Others," in Hal Foster, ed., *The Anti-Aesthetic,* 65–90.

29. It is with the recent publications of Fred Jameson and of Hal Foster's *The Anti-Aesthetic* that things have begun to change.

30. Of course, those who hold this view will not utter the word "realism" as it is tarnished by its traditionally close association with the notions of "reflection," "representation," and a transparent reality; but the persuasive power of the modernist doctrine owes much to the underlying idea that only modernist art and literature are somehow adequate to our time.

31. For a work that remains very much in the orbit of Marx's notion of modernity and tied to the political and cultural impulses of the American 1960s see Marshall Berman, *All That Is Solid Melts Into Air: The Experience of Modernity* (New York: Simon and Schuster, 1982). For a critique of Berman see David Bathrick, "Marxism and Modernism," *New German Critique,* 33 (Fall 1984), 207–218.

32. Jürgen Habermas, "Modernity versus Postmodernity," *New German Critique,* 22 (Winter 1981), 3–14. (Reprinted in Foster, ed., *The Anti-Aesthetic.*)

33. Jean-François Lyotard, "Answering the Question: What is Postmodernism?," in *The Postmodern Condition* (Minneapolis: University of Minnesota Press, 1984), 71–82.

34. Martin Jay, "Habermas and Modernism," *Praxis International,* 4:1 (April 1984), 1–14. Cf. in the same issue Richard Rorty, "Habermas and Lyotard on Postmodernity," 32–44.

35. Peter Sloterdijk, *Kritik der zynischen Vernunft.* The first two chapters of Sloterdijk's essay appeared in English in *New German Critique,* 33 (Fall 1984), 190–206. Sloterdijk himself tries to salvage the emancipatory potential of reason in ways fundamentally different from Habermas', ways which could indeed be called postmodern. For a brief, but incisive discussion in English of Sloterdijk's work see Leslie A. Adelson, "Against the Enlightenment: A Theory with Teeth for the 1980s," *German Quarterly,* 57:4 (Fall 1984), 625–631.

36. Cf. Jürgen Habermas, "The Entwinement of Myth and Enlightenment: Re-reading *Dialectic of Enlightenment,*" *New German Critique,* 26 (Spring–Summer 1982), 13–30.

37. Of course there is another line of argument in the book which *does* link the crisis of capitalist culture to economic developments. But I think that as a rendering of Bell's polemical stance my description is valid.

38. The editors, "A Note on *The New Criterion,*" *The New Criterion,* 1:1 (September 1982), 1–5. Hilton Kramer, "Postmodern: Art and Culture in the 1980s," ibid., 36–42.

39. Bell, *The Cultural Contradictions of Capitalism,* 54.

40. I follow the current usage in which the term "critical theory" refers to a multitude of recent theoretical and interdisciplinary endeavors in the humanities. Originally, Critical Theory was a much more focused term that referred to the theory developed by the Frankfurt School since the 1930s. Today, however, the critical theory of the Frankfurt School is itself only a part of an expanded field of critical theories, and this may ultimately benefit its reinscription in contemporary critical discourse.

41. The same is not always true the other way round, however. Thus American practitioners of deconstruction usually are not very eager to address the problem of the postmodern. Actually, American deconstruction, such as practiced by the late Paul de Man, seems altogether unwilling to grant a distinction between the modern and the postmodern at all. Where de Man addresses the problem of modernity directly, as in his seminal essay "Literary History and Literary Modernity" in *Blindness and Insight,* he projects characteristics and insights of modernism back into the past so that ultimately all literature becomes, in a sense, essentially modernist.

42. A cautionary note may be in order here. The term poststructuralism is by now about as amorphous as 'postmodernism,' and it encompasses a variety of quite different theoretical endeavors. For the purposes of my discussion, however, the differences can be bracketed temporarily in order to approach certain similarities between different poststructuralist projects.

43. This part of the argument draws on the work about Foucault by John Rajchman, "Foucault, or the Ends of Modernism," *October,* 24 (Spring 1983), 37–62, and on the discussion of Derrida as a theorist of modernism in Jochen Schulte-Sasse's introduction to Peter Bürger, *Theory of the Avant-garde,* vii–xlvii.

44. Jonathan Arac, Wlad Godzich, Wallace Martin, eds., *The Yale Critics: Deconstruction in America* (Minneapolis: University of Minnesota Press, 1983).

45. See Nancy Fraser, "The French Derrideans: Politicizing Deconstruction or Deconstructing Politics," *New German Critique,* 33 (Fall 1984), 127–154.

46. 'Bliss' is an inadequate rendering of *jouissance* as the English term lacks the crucial bodily and hedonistic connotations of the French word.

47. My intention is not to reduce Barthes to the positions taken in his later work. The American success of this work, however, makes it permissible to treat it as a symptom, or, if you will, as a *"mythologie."*

48. Roland Barthes, *The Pleasure of the Text* (New York: Hill and Wang, 1975), 22.

49. See Tania Modleski, "The Terror of Pleasure: The Contemporary Horror Film and Postmodern Theory," paper given at a conference on mass culture, Center of Twentieth Century Studies, University of Wisconsin-Milwaukee, April 1984.

50. Barthes, *The Pleasure of the Text,* 38.

51. Ibid., 41 f.

52. Ibid., 14.

53. Thus the fate of pleasure according to Barthes was extensively discussed at a forum of the 1983 MLA Convention while, in a session on the future of literary criticism, various speakers extolled the emergence of a new historical criticism. This, it seems to me, marks an important line of conflict and tension in the current litcrit scene in the U.S.

54. Roland Barthes, S/Z (New York: Hill and Wang, 1974), 140.

55. Michel Foucault, "What Is an Author?" in *Language, Countermemory, Practice* (Ithaca: Cornell University Press, 1977), 138.

56. This shift in interest back to questions of subjectivity is actually also present in some of the later poststructuralist writings, for instance in Kristeva's work on the symbolic and the semiotic and in Foucault's work on sexuality. On Foucault see Biddy Martin, "Feminism, Criticism, and

Foucault," *New German Critique,* 27 (Fall 1982), 3–30. On the relevance of Kristeva's work for the American context see Alice Jardine, "Theories of the Feminine," *Enclitic,* 4:2 (Fall 1980), 5–15; and "Pre-Texts for the Transatlantic Feminist," *Yale French Studies,* 62 (1981), 220–236. Cf. also Teresa de Lauretis, *Alice Doesn't: Feminism, Semiotics, Cinema* (Bloomington: Indiana University Press, 1984), especially ch. 6 "Semiotics and Experience."

57. Jean François Lyotard, *La Condition Postmoderne* (Paris: Minuit, 1979). English translation *The Postmodern Condition* (Minneapolis: University of Minnesota Press, 1984).

58. The English translation of *La Condition Postmoderne* includes the essay, important for the aesthetic debate, "Answering the Question: What is Postmodernism?" For Kristeva's statement on the postmodern see "Postmodernism?" *Bucknell Review,* 25:11 (1980), 136–141.

59. Kristeva, "Postmodernism?" 137.

60. Ibid., 139 f.

61. In fact, *The Postmodern Condition* is a sustained attack on the intellectual and political traditions of the Enlightenment embodied for Lyotard in the work of Jürgen Habermas.

62. Fredric Jameson, "Foreword" to Lyotard, *The Postmodern Condition* p. xvi.

63. Michel Foucault, "Truth and Power," in *Power/Knowledge* (New York: Pantheon, 1980), 127.

64. The major exception is Craig Owens, "The Discourse of Others," in Hal Foster, ed., *The Anti-Aesthetic,* 65–98.

65. Cf. Elaine Marks and Isabelle de Courtivron, eds., *New French Feminisms* (Amherst: University of Massachusetts Press, 1980). For a critical view of French theories of the feminine cf. the work by Alice Jardine cited in note 56 and her essay "Gynesis," *diacritics,* 12:2 (Summer 1982), 54–65.

Modernism versus Postmodernism:
Towards an Analytic Distinction

David J. Herman

In recent theoretical and critical debate, efforts to pose a distinction between "modernism" and "postmodernism" have become both overwhelmingly voluminous and forbiddingly complex. Amid the welter of dispute, however, two broad lines of argumentation can be discerned. Each line of argument begins from ostensibly the same constellation of values and commitments, a constellation at whose core lies what I shall for the moment characterize as a commitment to the progressive, emancipatory, and *eo ipso* utopian energies of cultural production in general. But each side of the debate finds this constellation of values realized most fully in the opposite sociocultural, quasi-historical category—either the modern or the postmodern, as the case may be. Thus one and the same set of evaluative criteria allows commentators to specify in two contradictory ways the relation that modernism bears to postmodernism. On the basis of these criteria modernism can be seen, under different conditions of observation, either as (1) the genuinely emancipatory cultural movement to which postmodernism is but a parasitical and reactionary successor, or as (2) a germ of liberation whose outworn husk it took the radical energies of postmodernism to strip away at last.

David J. Herman, "Modernism versus Postmodernism; Towards an Analytic Distinction," *Poetics Today* 12:1 pp. 55–86 Copyright 1991, Duke University Press, Durham, NC. Reprinted by permission.

Although my language here may imply otherwise, I do not mean to invoke the spectre of Heisenberg so as to suggest that we subsume the modernism/postmodernism relation under the more general problem of interpretive relativism. Nor shall I sketch the perils of explaining modernism and postmodernism by means of the developmental or teleological model presupposed by both alternatives (1) and (2). Instead, I shall conduct my argument at a level of analysis that, it seems to me, allows me to forestall both the relativistic and teleological difficulties to which other explorations of this issue may be prone. I mean to attack the problem at hand by examining the criteria developed in attempts to identify the emancipatory project of modern or, mutatis mutandis, postmodern culture.

My suggestion is that we subject to a form of genealogical analysis the criteria that stipulate one or the other of these projects as emancipatory in the first place. Such an analysis, I submit, leads us back to the Enlightenment. But because the Enlightenment functions not only as a wellspring but also as a metonymy for progressive ideals in our particular era, my own exploration will take me outside the realm of Nietzschean or Foucauldian genealogy proper. I mean to factor into the modernism/postmodernism debate the way the *concept* of Enlightenment has been used in that debate. The Enlightenment will thus function here more as a point of philosophical triangulation than as a historical entity, although it remains a sort of force field in which we can identify what Foucault (1984b [1971]) would call the *Herkunft* (descent) or *Entstehung* (emergence) of modernist or postmodernist characteristics. My contention is that the way we think about the Enlightenment also suggests a way, not to circumvent, but to rethink the debate between modernism and postmodernism.

As it has been conceived, the Enlightenment in fact marks an unstable conjuncture of two phenomena: on the one hand, the elaboration of a highly progressivist ethos; on the other hand, an increased sensitivity to epistemological problems bound up with the notion of representation. I would contend, further, that the unstable energies of this conjuncture are absorbed and redistributed, in different ways, by the movements or categories we designate "modernism" and "postmodernism." Indeed, my own chief concern is to trace the modern and postmodern vicissitudes of a belief in progress that also, quintessentially, disbelieves its own representations of the world.

Accordingly, my sense is that the shift connoted by the "post" in postmodernism should neither be minimized through a vicious relativism nor aggrandized through a naively teleological schema. The shift is neither one that changes with the critic, nor one that drags the theorist willy-nilly in its supracultural wake. Rather, the shift from modern to postmodern suggests a kind of lateral movement—not so much an advancement as a realignment— within the somewhat implosive conceptual matrix whose emergence we associate with the Enlightenment. By moving back toward what I take to be the conceptual preconditions of both these sociocultural categories, I hope to avoid what Brian McHale has termed the "apocalyptic metanarrative of the postmodernist breakthrough" (1988, 550). But at the same time, I believe that a genealogical account will provide grounds for making, not an absolute or pseudo-ontological, but an analytic distinction between modernism and postmodernism.[1]

First, by examining recent analyses of modernism and its relation to postmodernism, I shall substantiate my claim that two broad lines of argument encompass discussion of the issue. In the process I shall focus attention on what I have described as a general theoretical commitment to the emancipatory or utopian energies of cultural production. I shall then attempt to measure this commitment against the construct of Enlightenment—an imaginative horizon of progressivism as such.

In order to lend greater specificity and concreteness to my discussion, finally, I shall apply to two works—predictably, one typically characterized as modernist and the other as postmodernist— the explanatory model that I develop in confrontation with other theoretical and critical discourse. The two works are Virginia Woolf's *Orlando* (1928) and Michael Herr's *Dispatches* (1978), the agonizing testimony of a war correspondent on assignment in Vietnam. I have isolated these two works because each has as major emphases both the idea of progress and the problem of representation. In tracing the trajectory of these paired concerns as they appear in Woolf and then in Herr, I shall also be measuring and assessing what I have termed the lateral—if at times vertiginous—drift that warrants the "post" in postmodernism.

I
-

In *Decline of the New*, Irving Howe conjectures that "we have reached the end of one of those recurrent periods of cultural unrest, innovation, and excitement that we call the 'modern'" (1970, 192).

Howe traces this "Decline of the New" to a situation in which "certain assumptions concerning modern society, which have long provided novelists with symbolic economies and dramatic conveniences, are no longer quite so available as they were a few decades ago" (ibid., 196). In fact, Howe suggests that the various deficiencies of postmodern fiction can be reduced to this central problem: "How can one represent malaise, which by its nature is vague and without shape?" (ibid., 200). And even though Howe, as if to protect himself from charges of unmitigated pessimism, is careful to describe these "new difficulties" as presenting also "new possibilities" for postmodernist writers, one senses that Howe's hopeful afterthought remains just that.

Howe's indictment of postmodern culture at least has, as Benjamin said of the stridencies and vociferations of the war-crazed Futurists, the virtue of clarity (Benjamin 1969a [1936], 242). For throughout Howe's analysis sounds the melancholic death knell for what Howe takes to be a mordant modernism. The reasons for Howe's nostalgic tone are of crucial importance here. Why is it, exactly, that for Howe postmodern fiction—that is to say, fiction premised on a "distance from fixed social categories and [a] concern for the metaphysical implications of that distance" (ibid., 203)—corresponds, not to an expansion, alteration, or reassessment, but to a *decline* of the new?

A glance at Howe's nine-point list of the "traits or symptoms" of postmodern culture reveals that, for Howe, the debasement of modernist "symbolic economies" has as its precise correlate a postmodernist sense of hopelessness, passivity, and indeed impotence.[2] The postmodernist problem, you will remember, is how to *represent* malaise. Just to the extent that "traditional ceremonies" are "debased into mere occasions for public display," it seems, "passivity becomes a widespread social attitude" (ibid., 197). And just insofar as "opinion is manufactured systematically and 'scientifically,' . . . reflection upon the nature of society is replaced by observation of its mechanics" (ibid.). Interestingly, Howe's view, at least on one level, anticipates that of Habermas, who, in *Legitimation Crisis* (1975), identifies as an element of advanced-capitalist social crisis a dichotomy between the symbolic and procedural techniques of what he calls "administrative rationality"—a split between what administrations portray themselves as capable of doing and what they actually can do and need to do in order to preserve the status quo (Habermas 1975, 61–94). For both Habermas and Howe, the deterioration of liberal, progressivist ideals[3] bears a positive correlation—if not a causal or feedback-loop relation—to the breakup of representational schemes, taken in the broadest sense.

From mention of Habermas in this context one passes naturally to Lyotard's polemic against Habermas in *The Postmodern Condition* (1984 [1979]). Jameson, in his well-known "Foreword" to that book, pinpoints as its thematic core

> the so-called crisis of representation, in which an essentially realistic epistemology, which conceives of representation as the reproduction, for subjectivity, of an objectivity that lies outside it—projects a mirror theory of knowledge and art, whose fundamental evaluative categories are those of adequacy, accuracy and Truth itself. (Jameson 1984a, viii)

In suggesting how Lyotard's model calls into question representational realism, however, Jameson tells only half the story. Jameson fails to make explicit the mechanism by which what counts as an epistemological and social "crisis" for Habermas and, as we shall see, for Jameson himself also counts, for Lyotard and others, as the condition of possibility for knowledge itself—as well as for the rational amelioration of society.[4]

We can perhaps best approach this paradox through Habermas's seminal essay on "Modernity versus Postmodernity" (1981a), which in large part catalyzed the very debate Habermas there describes. Discussing an earlier crisis of representation, the one concomitant with Surrealism, Habermas contends that "nothing remains from a desublimated meaning or a destructured form; an emancipatory effect does not follow. . . . A reified everyday praxis can be cured only by creating unconstrained interaction of the cognitive with the moral-practical and the aesthetic-expressive elements" into which "cultural modernity" has been differentiated (Habermas 1981a, 10–11). In other words, for Habermas any "emancipatory effect" follows, not from a crisis in representation, but from defusing that crisis through what Habermas elsewhere terms "communicative competence"[5]—the ability to negotiate and deploy not just "aesthetic-expressive" but also "purposive-rational" and "moral-practical" language games. In turn, this sort of competence is a precondition for any highly generalized form of consensus, a form of consensus in which we could reconcile the "language game . . . of the aesthetic critic" with those by means of which we designate and enact "our cognitive significations and our normative expectations" (ibid., 12).

On Habermas's view, modernism, if coeval with the fragmentation of these three language games, can also initiate an effort to reunite our fractured symbolic or rather pragmatic economies. As Habermas puts it, "The [unfulfilled] project [of modernity] aims at a differentiated relinking of modern culture with an everyday praxis that still depends on vital heritages, but would be impoverished through mere traditionalism" (ibid., 13). By contrast, postmodernism, with its "decisive confinement of science, morality and art to autonomous spheres separated from the life-world and administered by experts" (ibid., 14), actively resists the sort of interpenetration of discourse whose impetus Habermas detects in modernism proper.

At most, then, the crisis of representation marked by Surrealism or, more generally, modernism is for Habermas epiphenomenal in nature; it registers the subordination of the *Lebenswelt* under advanced-capitalist, systemic "imperatives," a subordination that Habermas redescribes as "a matter of disturbing the communicative infrastructure of everyday life" (ibid., 7). Modernism indicates where that infrastructure must be buttressed by more far-reaching communicative competence, thus enabling informed consensus and ipso facto the defusion of any crisis in legitimation or, by extension, representation. In contrast, postmodernism by its very nature defeats any attempt to broaden such consensus, and thus prolongs and exacerbates crisis.

For Lyotard, conversely, prolonging and exacerbating dissent over our representational schemes is the only means for averting what he calls "terror"—the coercive application of those same systemic imperatives that Habermas ranges against the Lebenswelt. In effect, Lyotard worries about the ease with which Habermas's communicative consensus might be transformed into an anticommunicative reign of terror. As Lyotard puts it: "By terror I mean the efficiency gained by eliminating, or threatening to eliminate, a player from the language game one shares with him. He is silenced or consents, not because he has been refuted, but because his ability to participate has been threatened" (1984 [1979], 63–64). For this reason, consensus vis-à-vis interpretive or representational norms remains, ideally, "a horizon that is never reached" (ibid., 61). For this reason, too, in order to articulate the basis for a heterogeneous, dissent-ridden, and thus optimized "scientific pragmatics," it is "necessary to posit the existence of a power that destabilizes the capacity for explanation, manifested in the promulgation of new norms for understanding" (ibid.).

Lyotard goes on to generalize thus:

The problems of internal communication experienced by the scientific community in the course of its work of dismantling and remounting its languages are comparable in nature to the problems experienced by the social collectivity when, deprived of its narrative culture, it must reexamine its own internal communication and in the process question the nature of the legitimacy of the decisions made in its name. (Ibid., 62)

Insofar as Lyotard poses such "reexamination" against the dynamic of terror, however, we see here the deeply inconsistent nature of Lyotard's entire enterprise. For although he suggests that "consensus has become an outmoded and suspect value" (ibid., 66), to the extent that for him "justice as a value is neither outmoded nor suspect" (ibid.). Lyotard's own account nonetheless remains indebted to what he identifies as—in order to distance himself from—the Enlightenment metanarrative of knowledge as emancipatory. It is just that Lyotard alters the basis for any rational emancipation of humanity. Social justice comes to depend, not on the ever-increasing refinement of representational schemes, but on an ever greater awareness of the contingent and localized—the unstable—nature of all norms for representing the world. In Lyotard's parlance, this emancipatory awareness amounts to a paralogic "orientation [that] favors a multiplicity of finite meta-arguments, by which I mean argumentation that concerns metaprescriptives and is limited in space and time" (ibid.).

I have taken such pains to set forth Habermas's and Lyotard's views because, together, those views provide the parameters of my own discussion. More precisely, their views present an ostensibly irresolvable paradox that I shall attempt here to resolve. The nature of that paradox should by now be evident. For both Lyotard and Habermas, the "post" in postmodernism serves as a kind of index of the degree or intensity of dissent if modernism questions the possibility of consensus, but only so as to reinstate it at some more all-encompassing yet less coercive level, postmodernism questions the possibility of consensus in order to destroy it and thus the possibility of coercion that consensus brings in its wake. Of course, what is paradoxical about all this is that Habermas and Lyotard, working with what appears to be the same set of assumptions, arrive at opposite conclusions.

On the one hand, Habermas sets up an inverse relation between what I have termed the index of dissent and what might be termed the index of emancipatory potential: total consensus about ways of representing the world corresponds to maximal emancipation from oppressive social hierarchies—and by extension from oppressive disequilibria in the sphere of scientific and technological development. On the other hand, Lyotard sets up a proportional relation between the index of dissent and the index of emancipatory potential. Paralogy, the proliferation of destabilizing "moves" within a given language game, the diversity of now merely local metaprescriptives—in short, the simultaneous elaboration of conflicting representational schemes: all this replaces reasoned consensus as the basis of change for the better. Thus, one and the same set of progressivist criteria—criteria that make primary the utopian or transformative energies of cultural production—confers both zero and infinite value upon dissent; the irresolvable conflict of representational schemes now helps, now impedes, the perfection of the world.

But Habermas's and Lyotard's own disagreement over the value and function of disagreement must be ascribed to something more than the mere vagaries of temperament. At stake here, rather, is what Foucault would term an *episteme:* a "general system of thought whose network, in its positivity, renders an interplay of simultaneous and apparently contradictory opinions possible" (1970 [1966], 75). As a step toward analyzing this episteme in greater detail, I wish to bring more squarely within its basic parameters the modernism/postmodernism debate at large. In this way, I hope to confirm the generality and pervasiveness of the conceptual structure or, more loosely, the "paradox" that I have isolated. That in turn should underscore the importance of a genealogical analysis of this structure or paradox.

Let me begin with participants in the debate whose contributions may be grouped around the parameter that I have used Habermas to define. In the first place, Jameson, in "Postmodernism, or the Cultural Logic of Late Capitalism," makes the claim that because "postmodernism is a historical phenomenon, . . . the attempt to conceptualize it in terms of moral or moralizing judgements must finally be identified as a category-mistake" (1984b, 85). If "the complacent (yet delirious) camp-following celebration of this aesthetic new world . . . is surely unacceptable, . . . it is also logical to reject moralizing condemnations of the postmodern and of its essential triviality, when juxtaposed against the Utopian 'high seriousness' of the great modernisms" (ibid.).

But then what are we to do with the Jameson of *Marxism and Form* (1971), in which, while explicating Marcuse via Schiller's emphasis on the practical (and progressive) implications of aesthetic play, Jameson arguably uses Marcuse to speak for himself:

For where in the older society (as in Marx's classic analysis) Utopian thought represented a diversion of revolutionary energy into idle wish-fulfillments and imaginary satisfactions, in our own time the very nature of the Utopian concept has undergone a dialectical reversal. Now it is practical thinking which everywhere represents a capitulation to the system itself. . . . The Utopian idea, on the contrary, keeps alive the possibility of a world qualitatively distinct from this one and takes the form of a stubborn negation of all that is. (1971, 110–11)

In his own later analysis of postmodernism, precisely to the extent that Jameson correlates with the shift from modernism to postmodernism a marked narrowing or rather elimination of this sort of utopian vision,[6] Jameson falls short of the difficult task that, he there claims, Marx has set for us: "To think [one and the same development] positively *and* negatively all at once; to achieve, in other words, a type of thinking that would be capable of grasping the demonstrably baleful features of [that development] along with its extraordinary and liberating dynamism simultaneously, within a single thought" (Jameson 1984b, 86).

In his characterization of postmodernism as such, I would contend, Jameson goes out of his way to minimize the "liberating dynamism" of postmodernist art. Jameson waits until the end of his essay before formulating Marx's "austere dialectic," and only then does he voice a kind of extended afterthought, characterizing the "difficulties" of postmodernism as "possibilities" as well. Even then, like Howe and for the same reasons, Jameson does not so much qualify and supplement his analysis as attempt to forestall or seconod-guess criticisms of what might be construed as an excessively pessimistic view of postmodern culture.[7]

More important, however, is the specific symptom that determines Jameson's negative diagnosis of postmodernism. For on Jameson's model, as on Habermas's, it is the breakdown of representational consensus—the decline of our ability to articulate and agree upon the minimal conditions for a successful representation—that enables us to detect, in the movement from modernism to postmodernism, an ominous lapse in the progressive energies of cultural production. Witness Jameson's diagnosis of what he calls the "nostalgia mode" in postmodern art:

The approach to the present by way of the art language of the simulacrum, or of the pastiche of the stereotypical past, endows present reality and the openness of present history with the spell and distance of a glossy mirage. But this mesmerizing new aesthetic mode itself emerged as an elaborated symptom of the waning of our historicity, of our lived possibility of experiencing history in some active way: . . . [the new aesthetic demonstrates], through these inner contradictions, the enormity of a situation in which we seem increasingly incapable of fashioning representations of our own current experience. (ibid., 68)

As on Howe's, postmodern culture on Jameson's view suggests a decline not only of traditional, but also of genuinely "new" (that is, cumulatively more effective or informative) representational schemes. This decline, which Jameson broadly associates with the degeneration of parody into pastiche, both corresponds and contributes to widespread cultural passivity and impotence. Despite Jameson's explicit claims to the contrary, therefore, we are implicitly asked to arrive at the "moralizing judgement" that postmodernism, at least on one level, means a powerlessness to act positively and constructively within the present historical moment.

In general, using the problem of representation as an analytic tool, we can unpack the "moral" content of each of Jameson's theoretical moves. It is this problem that determines, for instance, the difference between "modernist styles," in which "hegemonic" linguistic norms can at least be satirized and parodied, versus "postmodernist codes," which betoken "a linguistic fragmentation of social life itself to the point where the norm itself is eclipsed [or] reduced to a neutral and reified media speech, . . . a field of stylistic and discursive heterogeneity without a norm" (ibid., 65). How can we *not* feel opprobrium for a situation in which the enemy ("faceless masters"), no longer clearly differentiated from ourselves, hides within a virtual jungle of representational codes?

The problem of representation also motivates Jameson's discussion of postmodern culture as a "schizophrenic" breakdown of the signifying chain. In such cultural schizophrenia, indeed, Jameson discerns the utter distinction of the idea of Utopia:

If . . . the subject has lost its capacity actively to extend its protensions [sic] and re-tensions across the temporal manifold, and to organize its past and future into coherent experience, it becomes difficult enough to see how the cultural productions of such a subject could result in anything but "heaps of fragments" and in a practice of the randomly heterogeneous and fragmentary. (Ibid., 71)

And in his extended analysis of John Portman's Bonaventure Hotel, finally, Jameson arrives at the disconcerting notion of a "postmodern hyperspace," in which a vertiginous disorientation a fortiori deprives us of the ability to improve our circumstances: "[Portman's building] has . . . succeeded in transcending the capacities of the individual human body to locate itself, to organize its immediate surroundings perceptually, and cognitively to map its position in a mappable external world" (ibid., 83). The first step toward regaining our utopian aspirations, Jameson will go on to argue, is for us to come to an agreement upon a "map" that represents just where our culture stands today.

But it is not just Jameson who follows Habermas in basing the possibility of social amelioration upon a consensus of representations. Consider, for instance, Terry Eagleton's "Capitalism, Modernism and Postmodernism" (1985), whose opening, and whose publication in the *New Left Review,* suggests that it is meant to be a sort of follow-up to Jameson's article. In formulating his position, Eagleton focuses on that questioning of representation with which, as I have suggested, both modernism and postmodernism begin. Like Habermas and Jameson, further, Eagleton differentiates between modernism and postmodernism by the intensity or degree or extent of the antirepresentational energies of modernist versus postmodernist art:

> The productivist aesthetics of the early twentieth-century avant garde spurned the notion of artistic "representation" for an art which would be less "reflection" than material intervention and organizing force. The aesthetics of postmodernism is a dark parody of such anti-representationalism: if art no longer reflects it is not because it seeks to change the world rather than mimic it, but because there is in truth nothing to be reflected, no reality which is not itself already image, spectacle, simulacrum, gratuitous fiction. (Eagleton 1985, 62)

As this passage indicates, differences in degrees of dissents are easily transmuted into differences in kinds of aesthetics. For Eagleton, on the one hand, modernism is an aesthetic category in which antirepresentationalism is ultimately recuperated into that consensus of representational norms—that Utopia—toward which art's "material intervention" in fact aims. On the other hand, Eagleton sees postmodernism as the aesthetic category in which this process is inverted: art's material intervention gets subsumed under the incessant antirepresentational machinery of aesthetic production itself. On this model, the utopian energies of cultural production depend for their existence and effectiveness on our learning when and where to reinscribe mimesis—that is to say, (consensus of representational schemes)—witin the antimimetic, contestatory dynamic of interventionist art. For Eagleton, modernism still allows us to enact this reinscription; postmodernism does not.

Thus, when Eagleton makes the claim that "there is a difference . . . between the "meaninglessness" fostered by some postmodernism, and the "meaninglessness" deliberately injected by some trends of avantgarde culture into bourgeois normality" (ibid., 70), we return to what bothered Howe and Jameson about antirepresentationalism: once no longer "deliberately injected," and instead merely "fostered" by forces beyond our control, crises in representation are crises just to the extent that they rob us of the power to act deliberately and effectively upon our surroundings. Such crises, indeed, eventually rob us of our capacity to imagine better things.

As Eagleton would have it, "postmodernism . . . commits the apocalyptic error of believing that the discrediting of this particular representational epistemology is the death of truth itself" (ibid.). With modernism, conversely, Eagleton associates "the Marxist habit of extracting the progressive moment from an otherwise unpalatable or ambivalent reality" (ibid., 68). Further, in language that harks back to Ernst Bloch's notion of art as an "anticipatory illumination" of Utopia (Bloch 1988 [1959]), and to Benjamin's notion of the *Jetztzeit* that unites past, present, and future within a single messianic or revolutionary temporality (Benjamin 1969b [1940]), Eagleton suggests that modernist antirepresentationalism is progressive because it negates the "brute objectivity of random subjectivity" (Eagleton 1985, 70) that is the hallmark of postmodernism, and instead represents always nascent utopian possibilities, the incipient actuality of a different and better world:

> If modernism lives its history as peculiarly, insistently *present,* it also experiences a sense that this present moment is somehow of the *future,* to which the present is nothing more than an orientation; so that the idea of the Now, of the present as full presence eclipsing the past, is itself intermittently eclipsed by an awareness of the present as deferment, as an empty excited openness to a future which is in one sense already here, in another sense yet to come. (Ibid., 66–67)

Like Habermas and Jameson, Eagleton in effect relegates antirepresentationalism—dissent for the sake of dissent—to the status and function of a triggering mechanism. At most, it serves as the emancipatory harbinger of a future in which there will be no cause for disagreement.

But what if we turn to the other parameter of this debate and look at commentators who *define* emancipation as disagreement? In "Postmodernism: A Preface," Hal Foster prefaces *The Anti-Aesthetic* (1983) by making a distinction between "a postmodernism which seeks to deconstruct modernism and resist the status quo and a postmodernism which repudiates the former to celebrate the latter: a postmodernism of resistance and a postmodernism of reaction" (1983, xi–xii). Foster sketches the postmodernist "deconstruction" of modernism thus:

> The rubric "anti-aesthetic" . . . is *not* intended as one more assertion of the negation of art or of representation as such. It was modernism that was marked by such "negations," espoused in the anarchic hope of an "emancipatory effect" or in the utopian dream of a time of pure presence, a space beyond representation. This is not the case here: [we may] take for granted that we are never outside representation—or rather, never outside its politics. Here then, "anti-aesthetic" is the sign not of a modern nihilism—which so often transgressed the law only to confirm it—but rather a critique which destructures the order of representations in order to reinscribe them. (Ibid., xv)

But reinscribe this untranscendable play of representations how? And where?

—Precisely in the "new strategy of interference" (ibid., xvi) that Foster, pace Gramsci, proposes for postmodern art. To this extent, Foster's account of postmodernism smacks of the same "anarchic hope for an 'emancipatory effect' " by which he stigmatizes modernism proper. It is just that, in postmodernism, this effect follows, not from the desire for "a space beyond representation," but from the mechanisms by which that desire and that space may be deferred. As Craig Owens puts it in one of the essays included in Foster's collection: "Postmodernism [in contrast to modernism] neither brackets nor suspends the referent but works instead to problematize the activity of reference" (ibid., 95).[8] For Foster, it seems, Owens's problematization of the act of referring corresponds to "interference" with the thing referred to.

It is in Linda Hutcheon's *Poetics of Postmodernism* (1988), however, that this dynamic takes on fuller substance. More clearly than
in the essays Foster himself collects, we see in Hutcheon's text the
utopian connotations of what, on Foster's view, amounts to a postmodernism that resists by representing—or rather by problematizing what it means to represent.

In her preface to the book, Hutcheon remarks that she has
chosen to use the "-ize" form of a number of terms (theorize, contextualize, etc.) in order "to underline the concept of *process* that is
at the heart of the postmodern" (1988, xi). Hutcheon asserts that, in
postmodern artifacts, "it is the process of negotiating the postmodern contradictions that is brought to the fore, not any satisfactorily
completed and closed production that results from their resolution"
(ibid.). If this emphasis on process over resolution sets Hutcheon
apart from Habermas, it also determines Hutcheon's isolation of
"historiographic metafiction" as *the* postmodern literary form—a
form in which the teleological patterning or process of historiography itself becomes the stuff of fiction (ibid., 87ff.). Hutcheon's contention is that, both formally and thematically, a sense of the
provisional and localized nature of our representations of the past is
what shapes postmodern fiction.

This emphasis on the process and provisionality of representation also explains why Hutcheon accords parody or intertextuality a central role in postmodern culture. What both Jameson and
Eagleton decry as postmodernism's debilitating proliferation of
simulacra, which replace any agreed-upon reality that might be
grasped and improved. Hutcheon hails as a healthy refusal to close
off or totalize interpretive and representational schemes—a refusal
that is a precondition for progressive change. Discussing postmodern fiction in particular, Hutcheon asserts:

> Historiographic metafictions . . . use parody not only to restore
> history and memory in the face of the distortions of the "his-
> tory of forgetting" . . . but also, at the same time, to put into
> question the authority of any act of writing by locating the dis-
> courses of both history and fiction within an ever-expanding
> intertextual network that mocks any notion of either single or-
> igin or simple causality. (Ibid., 129)

Because Hutcheon defines parody, not as "the ridiculing imitation
[in terms of which parody is conceived by] the standard theories and
definitions . . . rooted in eighteenth-century theories of wit," but
rather as "repetition with critical difference that allows ironic sig-

nalling of difference at the heart of similarity" (ibid., 26), Hutcheon, unlike Jameson, can acknowledge the postmodern intensification of moral uncertainty while still preserving a distinction between parody and pastiche.[9] What Hutcheon's discussion implies, ultimately, is that parody, in order to function, need not proceed from a stable center or closed system of values; in fact, parody marks the threshold at which art invests pastiche with broadly emancipatory energies.

For Hutcheon, the defining gesture of postmodernism is precisely the parodic dissolution and reconstitution of tradition—its constructive misrepresentation, as it were. As Hutcheon puts it in her *Theory of Parody:* "The kind of parody upon which I wish to focus is an integrated structural modeling process of revisiting, replaying, inverting, and 'trans-contextualizing' previous works of art. Perhaps the archetypal manifestation of this process is what is now called Post-Modern [sic] architecture" (1980, 11). Despite Hutcheon's own explicit claim that "the postmodern marks neither a radical Utopian change nor [to echo Baudrillard] a lamentable decline to hyperreal simulacra" (1988, xiii), however, I would argue that postmodernism's quintessentially parodistic gesture, as Hutcheon construes it, is also fundamentally utopian.

Consider Hutcheon's distinction between the "autotelic self-reflexion" of late-modernist "surfiction" and the more heteroreferential, and properly postmodern, project of historiographic metafiction (ibid., 40ff.). If postmodern fiction eludes the Scylla of what Hutcheon calls "analytico-referential discourse" (ibid., 74–75), which stresses and aims for maximal transparency between reference and referent, representation and thing represented, it also avoids the Charybdis of metafictional solipsism, which treats discourse itself as the sole object of all representation. For Hutcheon, postmodern fiction takes as its referent *both* the endless imbrications of discourse itself *and* the "historical world" (ibid., 141). By implication, postmodernism, through self-consciousness about representation, contests and defers the given in order to remodel it, not to abandon it in favor of some modernist abyss of auto-referentiality.

In this way Hutcheon, giving substance to Foster's view, by the same token inverts Eagleton's: it is the postmodern, not the modern, that allows us to put antirepresentationalism to good use. The postmodern does this by healing what on Eagleton's model remains a rift between, on the one hand, the antirepresentational dynamic of modernist art as such and, on the other hand, the possibilities for that art's "material intervention," its "interference" in the world at large. Or, I should say, whereas Eagleton must ultimately resort to something like Habermassian consensus—in order to legitimate decisions as to when and where art should materially intervene or interfere—Hutcheon's view is that postmodern art gets anchored to the material or "historical" world through the very heterogeneity and profusion of its own representations. In this sense, Hutcheon's view of postmodernism encapsulates the paradox that Foucault uncovers within Baudelairean modernity: "The high value of the present is indissociable from a desperate eagerness to imagine it, to imagine it otherwise than it is, and to transform it not by destroying it but by grasping it in what it is" (Foucault 1984a, 41).

Precisely by subverting "analytico-referential discourse," postmodernism reinscribes the material referent—now seen as inherently unstable and contestable—in the very process of representation itself Vis-à-vis postmodernist art, it seems, the world can be grasped and improved precisely because we cannot and should not attempt to say just what it is. Undecidability serves as the fulcrum of change, the Archimedean lever by which to pry Utopia from the grip of facticity.

If mine were a "dialectical" line of inquiry, such as Adorno's, I might now make the following theoretical move: The modernism/postmodernism debate suggests the extent to which neither consensus nor dissent, in and of themselves, can lay claim to genuinely emancipatory energies. The vehemence and prolongation of this debate, in fact, confirm the one-sidedness of views that posit as a necessary feature of progress *either* the conflict *or* the harmony of representational schemes. We can only conclude that consensus and dissent are merely oscillating moments in a fluid process by means of which alone things in general can be altered for the better.

However, I find this dialectical move neither compelling nor illuminating—in part because the utopian thrust of the dialectical synthesis or *Aufhebung* is itself implicated in the very problem under consideration. This problem, as I have indicated and now wish to substantiate, can be rethought through the way we conceive of the Enlightenment: on the one hand, as a belief in the perfectibility of the world; on the other hand, as a sense of the irreducibly imperfect nature of our representations of that world. My contention is that we cannot arbitrate the modernism/postmodernism debate without recourse to at least a kind of genealogy of the concerns that inform its main premises. Alternatively, by attaching these premises to a larger interpretive framework, we can undercut the grounds upon which this debate has set itself up as irresolvable and interminable. But I do not mean simply to terminate the debate; I mean to resolve its often paradoxical nature into the broader cultural contradictions—the episteme—from which it arises.

II

As Hellmut O. Pappe remarks, in his article in *The Dictionary of the History of Ideas,* the Enlightenment "in general terms . . . was characterized by a turning away from dogma and traditional conventions, a critical reappraisal of established authority in the fields of religion, politics, philosophy, and the arts" (Pappe 1973, 90). "While the old metaphysics, Hobbes' 'Aristotelity,' was relegated to the background," continues Pappe, thinkers stressed a new "individualism and [a] conception of knowledge as being merely provisional" (ibid.). Thus Locke, as Pappe notes, "dwells [more] on the *limits* of reason" than did Bacon, who in the previous century stressed the mind's power of discovery—its *ars inveniendi* (ibid., 95). If, for instance, Locke's critique of innate ideas highlights the importance of the perceiving subject, at the same time it places certainty on a continuum with delusion, or at least deception, since the sole source of knowledge—the subject's representations of the world—is also the occasion of what Kant would later call (correctable but inevitable) empirical illusion.

On the same model, according to which the burden of epistemological responsibility gets shifted to the shoulders of the individual, it is not surprising that Descartes, at the advent of "modern" philosophy, should make certainty itself depend on the indubitability—the clarity and distinctness—of the solitary mind's self-doubt. Nor is it surprising that, some years later, Berkeley should found existence upon representation, *esse* upon *percipi,* and suggest that, but for God, the only ontological insurance policy available would be that of unblinking vigilance. For Berkeley, of course, as soon as we stop representing things to ourselves, they disappear into the vacuum of our now-cosmic inattention. The cost of freeing ourselves from the authority of past masters thus appears enormous. As appeal to tradition gave way to empiricism, it seems, the critique of earlier inaccuracies became inextricably intertwined with a kind of paralyzing, self-absorbed fear of present ones. For as Ernst Cassirer notes, the transition from pre-Enlightenment reliance on authority to Enlightenment self-doubt suggests how "thought cannot turn toward the world of external objects without at the same time reverting to itself; in the same act it attempts to ascertain the truth of nature and its own truth" (1955 [1932], 93). As a result of this Enlightenment "act," which Horkheimer situates in the breakup of synthesizing *Vernunft* into merely analytic or instrumental *Verstand,* critique becomes synonymous with doubt, reason with skepticism (Jay 1984, 72–73).

But this is not all. As Horkheimer and Adorno argue in *Dialectic of Enlightenment* (1988 [1944]), the process of demythologization, the critique of tradition, itself breeds the myth of the given, the cult of facts. Such facts our representations can, by definition, merely re-present or approximate. Here again we see commentators make a connection between difficulties in representation and powerlessness to act, since the authors connect the advance of positivism with the process of reification. Not only do we leap from the frying pan of myth to the fire of remythologized positivism, but crises of representation are both the cause and effect of this dynamic. As the authors put it, "Mythology itself set off the unending process of enlightenment in which ever and again, with the inevitability of necessity, every specific theoretic view succumbs to the destructive criticism that it is only a belief" (ibid., 11). Thus, Horkheimer and Adorno remark that "the capacity of representation is the vehicle of progress and regression at one and the same time" (ibid., 35). Representation functions as a hinge on which pivot both critique and resignation, both analysis and bewilderment, both production and impotence.

Foucault accounts for this double life of representation by suggesting that the Enlightenment or "Classical Age" marks a point of rupture with the Renaissance episteme of resemblance—a rupture as a result of which, as James Creech asserts, the problem of representation "attained unquestioned generality" (Creech 1986, 7). Foucault, to this extent, follows the line Heidegger sets out in "The Age of the World Picture": "The fact that whatever is comes into being in and through representatedness transforms the age in which this occurs into a new age in contrast with the preceding one. . . . The world picture does not change from an earlier medieval one into a modern one, but rather the fact that the world becomes picture at all is what distinguishes the essence of the modern age" (Heidegger 1977 [1938], 130). Foucault himself focuses on what is at stake in this transition from the "essence" of the premodern, prerepresentational era to that of the modern, representational era—although he probably would not traffic in these Heideggerian categories.

As Foucault puts it, in the Enlightenment, "the simultaneously endless and closed, full and tautological world of resemblance . . . finds itself dissociated and, as it were, split down the middle" (1970 [1966], 58). More specifically,

> on the one side, we shall find the signs that have become tools of analysis, marks of identity and difference, principles whereby things can be reduced to order, keys for a taxonomy; and, on the other, the empirical and murmuring resemblance of things, that unreacting similitude that lies beneath thought and furnishes the infinite raw material for divisions and distributions. (Ibid.)

At this point I can begin to indicate the functions and effects of what I have isolated as the second element necessary for rethinking the modernism/postmodernism debate.

This second element—the belief in the perfectibility of the world—exactly bisects the problem of representation. Or, to put it another way, the idea of Utopia occupies the space between what Foucault terms the "principles whereby things can be reduced to order," on the one hand, and "the infinite raw material" of the brutely "empirical," on the other. Utopia becomes visible, paradoxically, at just that point where representation hesitates in self-doubt. The idea of progress in general (just like, on Lyotard's model, the idea of aesthetic innovation in particular [1984 [1979], "Appendix"] depends on a dialectic of the presentable and the unpresentable. And I submit that what we call modernism and postmodernism are attempts to keep in place and to shrink together, respectively, the parameters within which we, via the Enlightenment, conceptualize progess itself.

Let me back up a bit, however, and define these parameters more clearly, articulate more sharply the limit-cases of what we can and cannot present. In *The Heavenly City of the Eighteenth-Century Philosophers,* Carl Becker discusses how the "Heavenly City" envisioned by medieval thinkers such as Augustine was, during the Enlightenment, "shifted to earthly foundations, and the business of justification transferred from divine to human hands" (1932, 49). As Becker puts it, "To be enlightened was to understand . . . that it was not in the Holy Writ, but in the great book of nature, open for all mankind to read, that the laws of God had been recorded" (ibid., 51). But the reason why, for the eighteenth-century philosophers, "the new heaven had to be located somewhere within the confines of the earthly life"—the reason why "the celestial heaven was to be dismantled in order to be rebuilt on earth"—was that "it was an article of philosophical faith that the end of life is life itself, the perfected temporal life of man" (ibid., 129). Thus, as Pappe (citing Buffon) remarks, in Enlightenment thought, "what distinguishes mankind particularly from the animal world . . . is the perfectibility of the species and the institutions of society" (1973, 92–93).

But then just why is it that, as Becker notes, "the age of reason had scarcely run half its course before the Philosophers were admitting the feebleness of reason, putting the ban on flippancy, and turning to the study of useful, that is to say, factual, subjects" (1932, 84)? Becker suggests that this was because the effort on the part of abstract reason to reconcile custom and nature could not accommodate the ethical categories of "good" and "bad," in terms of which bad or destructive customs could be isolated and eliminated (ibid., 86ff.). On this account, one effort to realize Utopia (collapsing custom into *N*ature) in effect undercuts another (critiquing customs that hinder the improvement of *n*ature). But I believe we can derive a more powerful explanation for the internal problems of the utopian project. This explanation stems from the way in which the idea of Utopia depends on an interplay between "abstract reason" and "factual subjects"—between what Foucault terms the order of representation and the empirical world that limits and to some extent negates that order.

On this explanation, implicit in Heidegger, the uncanny of eighteenth-century utopian ideals is a sort of uncompromising facticity. As Heidegger says in "The Age of the World Picture," "To represent means to bring what is present at hand before oneself as something standing over against, to relate it to oneself, to the one representing it, and to force it back into this relationship with oneself as the normative realm" (1977 [1938], 131). To this extent, conceiving of the world as a "picture" or representation coincides exactly with the advent of human "subjectivity," which accordingly takes on a double sense. Thus Heidegger suggests that

> only where man is essentially already subject does there exist the possibility of his slipping into the aberration of subjectivism in the sense of individualism. But also, only where man *remains* subject does the positive struggle against individualism and for the community as the sphere of those goals that govern all achievement and usefulness have any meaning. (Ibid., 133)

Although we may not wish to retain Heidegger's rather unwieldy categories of subject and object, we can still use his formulation to rethink modernism and postmodernism.

More specifically, Heidegger's treatment of representation and subjectivity shows how, in order for the idea of Utopia to make sense, there must paradoxically be insuperable resistance to it in the world at large. This, after all, is one of the major points of Adorno's essay on "Subject and Object" (1987 [1969]). There, by showing how what is subjective is also always objective and how what is objective is also always subjective, Adorno locates the possibility of Utopia between the two bugbears of Idealism and Nominalism. For utopian thought to be possible in the first place, by implication, there must be aspects of the world irreducible to any given representational scheme or set of schemes currently in use or in conflict. Only where there is always already a world unamenable to a subject's utopian hope does that hope escape what Heidegger calls "the aberration of subjectivism in the sense of individualism."

This conceptual formation, I submit, is precisely the vehicle by which the notion of Enlightenment enters the debate on modernism and postmodernism. Or, I should say, this formation determines how we wage that debate. Whereas modernism recuperates and accentuates the basic outline of this formation, postmodernism in effect compresses and deforms it. Postmodernism, I suggest, marks an attempt to transmute the order of representation into the finite raw material of nature itself; modernism thrives on the irresolvable tension between abstract reason and factual subjects, representation and reality—the latter two terms now taking on a specifically modernist charge. Put otherwise, the trend leading from symbolism to modernism was to confer upon highly particularized signifiers ever more limited access to transcendental signifieds; modernism, in parallel with something like Benjamin's notion of allegory, turns into a thematic difficulty that very access to latent meanings which symbolism took for granted. But postmodernism deranges the entire symbolist-modernist economy. In complicity with a work like Derrida's *Of Grammatology,* postmodernism ascribes a sort of transcendental energy to the play of signifiers themselves. And if, for modernism, utopian hopes are spawned by the conflict between word and thing, postmodernism bases the idea of Utopia on a strange new materiality resident in words themselves.

The foregoing may seem to contradict my own earlier remarks relating modernism to Habermassian (noncoercive) consensus and postmodernism to Lyotardian (antiterroristic) dissent. But I believe this objection to be superficial. If the modernist project, in order to avoid an empty or "subjective" idea of Utopia, preserves an Enlightenment separation between words and things, this does not diminish but rather increases the importance of consensus. Consensus, after all, provides a corrective to empty or, worse, terroristic ideas: the larger the community of language users that agrees on a certain way of relating representations to the world, the more likely, at least for that particular community, that other relations between words and things will prove subjective or empty or terroristic. The gap between reference and referent, in fact, drives the dynamic by which consensus forms, then breaks apart, then forms again *in seriatim,* as evidence against a given representational scheme (local representations it cannot account for) begins to outweigh evidence for that scheme (local representations it can account for).

Likewise, if postmodernism, as opposed to modernism, abolishes the gap between reference and referent, and instead invests representation itself with a sort of material density that is the stuff of Utopia, this in no way implies that dissent is impossible or unimportant. To the contrary, dissent becomes at once present reality and anticipation of the future. Since the postmodernist can no longer appeal to material referents in arbitrating competing representations, such arbitration of competing views itself provides the only grounds for knowledge and for hope. The alternative to dissent is in fact inertia, and death. The materiality that postmodernism confers upon our views themselves suggests that, unless we continually examine and reshape those views, hope will be dissipated in that same hall of mirrors in which reality as such gives way to an infinite montage of simulacra.

In the space remaining, I cannot hope to confirm this general model for understanding modernism and postmodernism. This would require nothing less than an extended survey of a significant percentage of the literature grouped under both these categories. Such an undertaking clearly would amount to a book-length study, at the least. However, I believe that I have succeeded in adumbrating broader cultural or conceptual linkages and connections that help account for the undecidability of the modernism/postmodernism debate—as it is currently waged. This debate is undecidable precisely because, despite the deceptive appearance of common assumptions, the debaters define in different ways such crucial terms as "representation" and "progress." Supporters of cultural modernism, given their presuppositions about words and things, cannot help but base their utopian aspirations on consensus. Conversely, supporters of postmodernism, given their assumptions about the materiality of representations, cannot help but invest sheer disagreement with a sort of exhilarating, even transcendental, energy. We cannot hope to bring to a peaceable end a discussion in which the participants think they share a single vocabulary, but actually do not. We can merely stake out the grounds for conflict.

In what follows, I shall focus on Woolf's *Orlando* (1928) and Herr's *Dispatches* (1978) in order to make, in the context of literature itself, some first, rough indications of the subtle shifts in vocabulary that I have described in the context of theory. I do not mean to suggest that these indications amount to proof for my overall argument; I offer them merely to make that argument seem perhaps slightly less abstract.

III

As an extended parody of biography, as well as a critique of prevalent attitudes toward gender, Woolf's *Orlando* is at one level premised on the conventional nature of our modes of representation. More precisely, it satirizes views that pose themselves as "natural," instead of admitting to their own conventional, agreed-upon (or disagreed-upon) character.

From the start of the novel we must, by a formal mechanism, see things not as they are but from a distance, ironically. We are forced to look through the eyes of a nameless and quasi-objective narrator, a benighted "biographer" who, working with grossly insufficient documentation and yet overestimating the certainty of historical explanation in general, is at many points the butt of our humor. This priggish biographer is always at great pains to distinguish his or her own historical and factual methods from the more unsavory ones of the novelist. At the opening, for instance, the narrator remarks with unself-conscious absurdity that "directly we glance at [Orlando's] eyes and forehead, we have to admit a thousand disagreeables which it is the aim of every good biographer to ignore" (Woolf 1928, 15). At another point, the narrator vows to "put it [all] in a nutshell, leaving the novelist to smooth out the crumpled silk and all its implications" (ibid., 73). But even apart from asking us to laugh at its ludicrous narrator, who so rigidly and ineptly differentiates between history and fantasy, *Orlando* concerns itself with the way our views of things necessarily depend on a sort of tense equilibrium of fact and fiction. Thus, when the young Orlando attempts to describe nature in a poem, and "in order to match the shade of green precisely [looks] at the thing itself," he is suddenly unable to write any more (ibid., 16–17). For, as the narrator puts it, "nature and letters seem to have a natural antipathy; bring them together and they tear each other to pieces" (ibid., 17).

Woolf's novel as a whole, however, does just that: it brings together "nature" and "letters," life and art, fact and fiction, thing and representation, and lets them "tear each other to pieces." In this conflict neither nature nor letters wins out. And this fight to the draw between representation and reality—"thought and life are as the poles asunder" (ibid., 267)—is precisely what sustains Woolf's utopian project in the novel.

Consider, for instance, the way Woolf, through the narrator, parodies the biographer's attention to archival detail:[10]

> The revolution which broke out during [Orlando's] period of office [as ambassador to Turkey], and the fire which followed, have so damaged or destroyed all those papers from which any trustworthy record could be drawn, that what we can give is lamentably incomplete. Often the paper was scorched a deep brown in the middle of the most important sentence. Just when we thought to elucidate a secret that has puzzled historians for a hundred years, there was a hole in the manuscript big enough to put your finger through. We have done our best to piece out a meagre summary from the charred fragments that remain: but often it has been necessary to speculate, to surmise, and even to make use of the imagination. (Ibid., 119)

The holes the narrator refers to here Woolf later figures by means of fragmentary sentences separated by ellipses (ibid.: 126ff.). To the extent that we are forced to construe these incomplete sentences into a coherent, quasi-historical narrative, Woolf highlights the guesswork that necessarily compromises, and yet also initiates, any effort to provide a transparent representation of the facts of the matter.[11]

Indeed, in the relation between the burned manuscript and what we must actively construe from it, we find a replica of the relation that, for Woolf, convention in general bears to nature. It is a relation not of congruence but of partiality, of incompleteness, of difference. The utopian thrust of *Orlando* consists precisely in Woolf's effort to make explicit this difference, particularly the difference between the way we compartmentalize gender through convention and the way gender is "naturally" ambiguous. Woolf's chief concern, that is to say, is with the constant adjustment of representation to nature, required by the irreducible or structural difference between conventions and things. This perpetual readjustment in turn requires shifting the grounds of consensus. In *Orlando,* specifically, it is through humor and parody that Woolf attempts to destroy an outmoded form of consensus. Woolf shocks us into a laughter that seems to mark a sudden access of Utopia, in which, in the face of inhibiting conventions, men are naturally women too and vice versa. Here, Woolf's unspoken premise is that things by their very nature will not and should not always be thought of the way they have been viewed up to now. Orlando's transformation into a woman midway through the novel is the objective correlative of this premise.

But by the same token, Utopia, in the final analysis, depends not on achieving correspondence but on perpetuating difference between representations and reality. The moment representations calcify into the way things are, the flicker of utopian hope gets snuffed out altogether. For this reason, *Orlando* ultimately locates the idea of Utopia, not in the recognition of androgyny, but in a sort of celebration of our ignorance of the world as it really is. As Woolf finally allows her narrator to say: "Did we not pray once in a way to wrap up in a book something so hard, so rare, one could swear it was life's meaning? . . . Back we must go and say straight out to the reader who waits a tiptoe to hear what life is—Alas, we don't know" (ibid., 271). The narrator enjoys a similar revelation a few pages later: "Life? Literature? One to be made into the other? But how monstrously difficult!" (ibid., 285). This difficulty, to resort to Howe's terms, is also the condition of possibility not only for Woolf's novel but for the progressiveness of its vision as well.

Consider how the novel's complex system of imagery—imagery that figures an androgynous world—is at last recuperated into a kind of utopian indeterminacy. At one level, to be sure, Woolf's imagery provides the syntax of a counter-narrative, an alternative account set against culturally repressive master narratives of sexuality and gender. Thus, we have, on the one hand, hard, linear images: the frozen Thames; the spine-like roots of Orlando's oak tree; the spires of buildings; and pens and quills, important in their own right for Woolf's indictment of phallocentric conventions that attempt to make the *nature* of writing masculine. And we have, on the other hand, fluid, curvilinear imagery: Orlando's flowing skirts; the melting, coursing Thames; the curvaceous sweep of birds wheeling across the sky. These two chains of imagery intersect at a number of places, as when, during a Proustian moment in the novel's opening, we first meet Orlando in a room where "bars of darkness," or shadows, frame "pools of light" as sunlight passes through a coat of arms in the window (ibid., 14). Similarly, Orlando at one point looks out over London and sees "the spires and domes of the city churches, the smooth bulk of its banks, the opulent and ample curves of its halls and meeting-places" (ibid., 223). Even more significantly, perhaps, the overall structure of the novel also mirrors the deconstruction of gender that is its subject: the hard "spine" or mock-teleological framework of the novel is crossed and recrossed by recurring, cyclical digressions on the difficulty of constructing any such framework.

But these imagistic or structural approximations of androgyny are an effect of utopian hope, not its cause. Its cause is the failure, the strangely liberating failure, of our representational schemes to tell us, at any given moment, how things really are. This failure of representation, after all, is what eventually allows us to make the transition, to progress, from views of gender as monolithic and single to views of gender as androgynous and double.

Woolf, for this reason, makes the breakdown of representation central to Orlando's experience. At the end of the book, Orlando comes to the realization that "everything was partly something else, and each gained an odd moving power from this union of itself and something not itself so that with this mixture of truth and falsehood her mind became like a forest in which things moved; lights and shadows changed, and one thing became another" (ibid., 323). The recognition of gender as androgynous, arguably, is but a special case of recognizing the extent to which what we think of as discrete, self-sufficient representations of the world are always implicated in a host of other representations, such that we never enjoy a transparent relation to things as they are. This more general problem of representation, of course, is precisely the nerve of Hegel's discussion of sense-data in the *Phenomenology*. Orlando himself faces the problem again when, in his attempts to escape metaphor so as to describe what love in itself really is, he continually falls upon "another metaphor, by Jupiter!" (ibid., 101). That is to say:

> Every single thing, once he tried to dislodge it from its place in his mind, he found thus cumbered with another matter like the lump of glass which, after a year at the bottom of the sea, is grown about with bones and dragon-flies, and coins and the tresses of drowned women. (Ibid.)

On this model, the very systematicity or coherence, the nexus of our representations is what makes it impossible for us to grasp the nature of things. It is also what makes possible the hope that we can systematically alter, for the better, our too-rigid beliefs about the nature of gender. Utopia is not the asymptote at which the gap between representation and reality finally gets closed; utopian hope names the mechanism by which this gap allows us to envision, realize, and then re-envision—ad infinitum—a better world.

In Herr's *Dispatches,* however, there is no question of perpetually adjusting representations to reality. There is merely the interminable analysis of representation itself. This paradoxically confers an oddly compelling density upon views and practices that, in and of themselves, lay no claim to the substance of what is. Accordingly, taking responsibility for our representations becomes the first precondition for progress.

The opening section of *Dispatches,* "Breathing In," begins with a description of an old map of Vietnam. Ironically, "the paper [of the map] had buckled in its frame after years in the wet Saigon heat, laying a kind of veil over the countries it depicted" (Herr 1978, 1). But even though the old, wrinkled map veils what it is supposed to represent, Herr, inverting the criteria for representational fidelity, suggests that the old map is better than current ones. As Herr puts it, "Even the most detailed maps didn't reveal much anymore; reading them was like trying to read the faces of the Vietnamese, and that was like trying to read the wind" (ibid.). In short,

> we knew that the uses of most information were flexible, different pieces of ground told different stories to different people. We also knew that for years now there had been no country here but the war. (Ibid.)[12]

We must therefore set Herr's account against Jameson's dictum that postmodern art be transmuted into a sort of cognitive mapping. For Herr, we must always judge a map by the purposes for which it was made since every map, no matter what the adjustments in scale, by its very nature proves incommensurable with what it figures. Herr thus shifts emphasis from the adequacy of mapping to its motives, from the mechanics to the politics, the ethics of representation.

Consider Herr's treatment of the specifically linguistic mapping of Vietnam. Throughout the book, the disjunction between words and things, like the incommensurability of maps and terrain, remains a given. In contrast to Woolf's emphasis in *Orlando,* it no longer makes sense, no longer is interesting, really, to talk about linguistic conventions versus natural conditions. It only makes sense to talk about the effects of the different vocabularies flourishing at any given time. For this reason, Herr brings our attention to bear on the destructive effects of the military's vocabulary, in terms of which "small, isolated firefights [are] afterwards described as strategy" (ibid., 24); in terms of which "killing a man was nothing more than depriving him of his vigor" (ibid., 43); in terms of which, in short, "the jargon of Progress got blown into your head like bullets" (ibid., 231). This sort of jargon can be traced back to "the cheer-crazed language of the MACV Information Office, [a language full of] things like 'discreet burst' (one of those tore an old grandfather and two children to bits as they ran along a paddy wall one day . . .), 'friendly casualties' (not warm, not fun), 'meeting engagement' (ambush), concluding usually with 17 or 117 or 317 enemy dead and American losses 'described as light' " (ibid., 239–40).

But it is not just a matter of critiquing the special vocabulary designed by the military to garner support for its doomed war effort. Conceptually, if not morally, Herr places on a continuum with the military's pernicious system of representation the soldiers' substitution of magical for empirical causality in their daily existences. In the jungle Herr witnesses everything from "guys dressed up in Batman fetishes," to soldiers carrying around "five-pound Bibles from home, crosses, St. Christophers, mezuzahs, locks of hair, girlfriends' underwear, snaps of their families, their wives, their dogs, their cows, their cars, pictures of John Kennedy, Lyndon Johnson, Martin Luther King, Huey Newton, the Pope, Che Guevara, the Beatles, Jimi Hendrix, wiggier than cargo cultists" (ibid., 59). Another standard good-luck charm is a fellow soldier who has narrowly escaped death (ibid., 60, 135). But the point to remember here is that, in effect, the army's doublespeak and the soldiers' talismans both serve the same apotropaic function: the high command frames "the jargon of Progress" in the face of complete tactical breakdown; the infantrymen and marines develop totemic logic in the face of experience too terrible to comprehend by any other means. In neither case is the adequacy or inadequacy of representation to reality the primary focus. Rather, Herr isolates the systematic effects of modes of representing. For the evil that the "grunts" try to avert through totems and charms is brought down upon their heads precisely by the high command's charmed representations of war. Since Herr looks chiefly at the pragmatics of representation in general, instead of the "adequacy" or "inadequacy" of this or that particular view, the real culprit in *Dispatches* is not the military itself but the military's form of representational practice.

Indeed, by adopting a consistently antivoyeuristic standpoint, by avoiding throughout "the mistake of thinking that all you needed

to perform a witness act were your eyes" (ibid., 69), Herr suggests
how accountability is inseparable from the "witness act" of representation. This is another way of saying that Herr ascribes a kind of
materiality to our views themselves. Herr begins his account by describing how he "went to cover the war and the war covered me,"
just to the extent that "it took the war to teach [me] that you were
as responsible for everything you saw as you were for everything
you did" (ibid.: 20). In fact, it took Herr only "a month to lose that
feeling of being a spectator to something that was part game, part
show" (ibid.: 180). After that, things began to look "like images
caught in a flash with all the hard shadows left in" (ibid., 276).

The "hard shadows" of war, as Herr notes, are exactly what
gets taken out by the war-movie industry—an industry whose basic
mechanism is voyeuristic, separating the "witness act" from any
sense of personal accountability or complicity:

> You don't know what a media freak is until you've seen the way
> a few of those grunts would run around during a fight when
> they knew that there was a television crew nearby; they were
> actually making war movies in their heads, doing little guts-
> and-glory Leatherneck tap dances under fire, getting their
> pimples shot off for the networks. . . . We'd all seen too many
> movies, stayed too long in Television City, years of media glut
> had made certain connections difficult. The first few times I
> got fired at or saw combat deaths, nothing really happened, all
> the responses got locked in my head. It was some familiar vi-
> olence, only moved over to another medium. (Ibid., 225)

Herr has to unlearn this essentially passive, voyeuristic response to
war by relearning how representation is an inherently active, constructive process. Thus Herr remarks at one point that "finding
[one's place in the war] was like listening to esoteric music, you
didn't hear it in any essential way through all the repetitions until
your own breath had entered it and become another instrument,
and by then it wasn't just music anymore, it was experience" (ibid.,
68). It is just such a recognition of the *instrumentality* of our views
that keeps alive in Herr's account the small flame of utopian hope.

In Woolf, too, views are instrumental. But they are instrumental only to the extent that their modes of distribution determine
what counts as consensus or convention at any given moment. In
turn, what counts as convention determines, to all extents and purposes, what counts as real. Representation thus enjoys a mediated
relationship with reality: consensus is the lever by means of which

Woolf's quasi-anarchic representations can exert their utopian force on the order of the Real. In Herr, however, I would argue that representation enjoys an unmediated relationship with reality—to use terms put into question by the nature of Herr's account. More precisely, in *Dispatches* views are instrumental not because they reflect conformity to or departure from a system of conventions, and thus indirectly remodel the Real; views are instrumental because the "witness act" is, after all, a real act, performed in a specific context, and followed by specific effects. Utopian hope thus stems not from attempts to break apart and reform broad reaches of consensus, but from local acts of responsible representation, as it were. For Herr, implicitly, not taking the world to be as others say it is initiates the process by which we, one by one, make the world other than it is. And what this isolated and somewhat forlorn gesture loses in the way of modernist scope, it gains in the way of postmodernist intensity.

Notes

1. In *Postmodernist Fiction,* McHale sets up one version of this sort of analytic distinction: "Postmodern fiction differs from modernist fiction just as a poetics dominated by ontological issues differs from one dominated by epistemological ones" (1987, xii). For McHale the shift from modernist to postmodernist fiction therefore signifies a change in dominant, in the specifically Jakobsonian sense of that term. As McHale puts it, "Although it would be perfectly possible to interrogate a postmodernist text about its epistemological implications, it is more *urgent* to interrogate it about its ontological implications. In postmodernist texts, in other words, epistemology is *backgrounded,* as the price for foregrounding ontology" (ibid., 11).

But in my own account, as we shall see, I wish to argue that the demarcation of epistemology and ontology is from the start an essentially *modernist* gesture—a vestigial trace of the concept of Enlightenment, a trace that gets differently inscribed in postmodernism. Thus, despite his caveat that "intractable epistemological uncertainty becomes at a certain point ontological plurality or instability" and vice versa (ibid.), McHale's model remains, in my view, an important symptom of what it purports to diagnose. In articulating grounds for an analytic distinction between modernism and postmodernism, McHale's analysis is circularly implicated in one of the categories he means to analyze. For this reason my own analysis will focus on the related but separate issue of representation, which functions as what Adorno might call a "force field" where both epistemological issues (how we know or represent) and ontological issues (what there is to be known or represented) are locked in irresolvable conflict. I submit that in accounting for the shift from modernism to postmodernism, we should not prematurely defuse this conflict by speaking of a change in dominant, but instead isolate through genealogy the devious means by which the conflict perpetuates itself in altered form.

2. Despite efforts to shift the accent from value judgments to a descriptive taxonomy, Alan Wilde, in *Horizons of Assent* (1981), a much more theoretically sophisticated text than Howe's, retains and transmogrifies Howe's dislike of postmodernism's passivity. Opposing modernism's disjunctive to postmodernism's "suspensive" irony, Wilde suggests that "acceptance is the key word here. Modernist irony, absolute and equivocal, expresses a resolute consciousness of different and equal possibilities so ranged as to defy solution," although modernism still "reaches through order toward stability." In "postmodern irony, by contrast, . . . an indecision about the meanings or relations of things is matched by a willingness to live with uncertainty, to tolerate and, in some cases, welcome a world seen as random and multiple, even, at times, absurd" (1981, 44). If this passage does not make clear the extent to which Wilde comes down on the side of an actively struggling modernism versus a passively bewildered postmodernism, consider Wilde's language on the next page: "As the large, imposing structures that embody the modernist crisis become, from the thirties onward, increasingly modest and various, crisis itself, redefined as an almost continuous response to a decentered or uncentered world turns, quite simply, into anxiety, that uneasy burden of contingent existence" (ibid., 45). For other places where Wilde attempts to characterize modernism and postmodernism by an ostensibly neutral taxonomy of ironies, and instead ends up inscribing that taxonomy within an overarching devaluation of passivity and powerlessness, see, e.g., pages 131, 165.

3. Compare in this connection Harry Levin's language in *Refractions: Essays in Comparative Literature* (1966). Citing Edwin Muir's and H. L. Mencken's programmatic writings about modernism, Levin himself writes: "Modernity, they argued, does not necessarily mean the very latest thing; rather it is a program of cultural emancipation, 'a principle of life itself' which can only be maintained by 'constantly struggling' " (1966, 277).

4. Necessarily, I am oversimplifying matters: in both Jameson's and Habermas's accounts of modernism and postmodernism (at least implicitly) crises of representation or, correlatively, of legitimation act as triggering mechanisms for long-term emancipatory effects. For my present purposes, however, it is helpful to identify, according to their explicit valuation of crisis, two basic types of accounts of modernism and postmodernism. And I do not believe it wide of the mark to assert that for Habermas emancipation stems from the eventual resolution of crises built into the advanced-capitalist system, whereas for Lyotard emancipation depends precisely on those crises' perpetuation.

5. In *Theorie des kommunikativen Handelus* (Habermas 1981b). See also *Legitimation Crisis* (1975), in which Habermas discusses the distinction between particular and "generalizable interests": this distinction presupposes, most fundamentally, Habermas's notion of communicative competence. As Habermas puts it, "The discursively formed will may be called 'rational' because the formal properties of discourse and of the deliberative situation sufficiently guarantee that a consensus can arise only through appropriately interpreted, *generalizable* interests, by which I mean needs *that can be communicatively shared.* The limits of a decisionistic treatment of practical questions are overcome as soon as argumentation is expected to test the generaliz*ability* of interests, instead of being resigned to an impenetrable pluralism of apparently ultimate value orientations" (1975, 108). Or, more briefly, "insofar as norms express generalizable interests, they are based on *rational consensus.* . . . Insofar as norms do not regulate generalizable interests, they are based on force" (ibid., 111). Compare, in this connection too, Habermas's (chronologically earlier) "Introduction" to *Theory and Practice* (1974 [1971]).

For my overall sense of Habermas's project, I am indebted to Albrecht Wellmer's discussion of Habermas vis-à-vis Weber, and of Horkheimer and Adorno, in "Reason, Utopia and the *Dialectic of Enlightenment"* (Wellmer 1985).

6. Look closely, for instance, at the language Jameson uses in analyzing Van Gogh's (modernist) "Peasant Shoes" versus Andy Warhol's (postmodernist) "Diamond Dust Shoes" (1984b, 58–60). In Van Gogh's work, "the willed and violent transformation of a drab peasant object world into the most glorious materialization of pure colour in oil paint is to be seen as a Utopian gesture: as an act of compensation which ends up producing a whole new Utopian realm of the senses" (ibid., 58–59). In Warhol's work, by contrast, there is "no way to complete the hermeneutic gesture, and to restore to these oddments that whole larger lived context of the dance hall or ball"; there is only a "new kind of flatness or depthlessness, a new kind of superficiality in the most literal sense" (ibid., 60).

7. It is debatable how successful Jameson actually is at countering such criticisms, however. Against his final six pages, we must weigh, for example, the unrelievedly pessimistic tone of most of his subheadings: "The Waning of Affect," "Euphoria and Self-Annihilation," " 'Historicism' Effaces History," "The Hysterical Sublime," etc. For an instance where Jameson's position comes remarkably close to Howe's, moreover, see Jameson's list of the "constitutive features of the postmodern" (1984b, 58), one of which is the same "bewildering new world space" to which Howe attributes our current passivity and powerlessness.

8. Owens's remark is quoted by Gregory Ulmer in "The Object of Post-Criticism" (Ulmer 1983, 83–110).

9. In her earlier book, *A Theory of Parody,* Hutcheon asserts that "ironic 'trans-contextualization' is what distinguishes parody from pastiche or imitation" (1980, 12). To the extent that such "trans-contextualization"

avoids the "nostalgic imitation of past models," and instead marks a "stylistic confrontation, a modern recoding which establishes difference at the heart of similarity" (ibid., 8), parody, for Hutcheon, takes on utopian connotations. It repeats segments of tradition in order to attach them (although always incompletely) to a larger chain of such segments, much as Benjamin's *Jetztzeit* fuses analytically separable temporal moments into a messianic *nunc stans* (1969b [1940]). As Hutcheon puts it, "Parody [offers] a workable and effective stance toward the past in its paradoxical strategy of repetition as a source of freedom" (Hutcheon 1980, 10).

10. See also, in the same chapter, Woolf's parody of the biographer's or historian's careful documentation of sources generally. Our "information" about Orlando's doings at this juncture comes, first, from the diary of one John Fenner Brigge, who eventually falls out of a tree and thus loses his vantage point on a crucial social gathering (1928, 126–27). Then we are told that our source is the rather breathy and excitable (thus manifestly untrustworthy) correspondence of a certain Penelope Hartopp (ibid.: 128). Next, Woolf names a newspaper account as her source (ibid., 129), and, after that, the eyewitness account of a "washerwoman" provides us with another link in the absurdly overstretched chain of information about Orlando (ibid., 131).

11. To my mind, therefore, Woolf's novel is already an example of the "historiographic metafiction" that Hutcheon makes into *the* postmodern fictional genre.

12. In the first sentence of this passage, and in some of my other quotations from *Dispatches,* notice Herr's refusal to write hypotactically: Herr often uses commas to string together clauses that would normally be placed in hierarchical order, logically speaking, through connectives or conjunctions or particles of some sort. Herr thus achieves a style highly similar to that of Walter Faber, Frisch's narrator in *Homo Faber.* Faber employs the somewhat awkward style of a report because he is largely unable to process or order his experiences. Herr uses the same style for the same reason and for another as well: to encourage precisely that active participation from the reader, that "witness act," which Herr sets over passive, voyeuristic forms of witnessing or representation.

References and Related Works

Adorno, Theodor
  1987 [1969] "Subject and Object," in *The Essential Frankfurt School Reader,* edited by Andrew Arato and Eike Gebhardt, 497–511 (New York: Continuum).

Anderson, Perry
1984 "Modernity and Revolution," *New Left Review* 144 (March-April): 96–113.

Becker, Carl L.
1932 *The Heavenly City of the Eighteenth-Century Philosophers* (New Haven: Yale University Press).

Benjamin, Walter
1969a [1936] "The Work of Art in the Age of Mechanical Reproduction," in *Illuminations,* edited by Hannah Arendt, translated by Harry Zohn (New York: Schocken Books).
1969b [1940] "Theses on the Philosophy of History," in *Illuminations,* edited by Hannah Arendt, translated by Harry Zohn (New York: Schocken Books).

Bloch, Ernst
1988 [1959] "The Artistic Illusion as the Visible Anticipatory Illumination," in *The Utopian Function of Art and Literature: Selected Essays,* translated by Jack Zipes and Frank Mecklenburg (Cambridge, MA: MIT Press).

Cassirer, Ernst
1955 [1932] *The Philosophy of Enlightenment,* translated by Fritz C. A. Roelin and James P. Pettegrove (Boston: Beacon Press).

Creech, James
1986 *Diderot: Thresholds of Representation* (Columbus: Ohio State University Press).

Derrida, Jacques
1982 "Sending: On Representation," *Social Research* 49(2): 295–326.

Eagleton, Terry
1985 "Capitalism, Modernism and Postmodernism," *New Left Review* 152 (July-August): 60–73.

Foster, Hal, ed.
1983 *The Anti-Aesthetic: Essays on Postmodern Culture* (Seattle: Bay Press).

Foucault, Michel
1970 [1966] *The Order of Things* (New York: Vintage Books).
1984a "What Is Enlightenment?" in *The Foucault Reader,* edited by Paul Rabinow, 32–50 (New York: Pantheon Books).
1984b [1971] "Nietzsche, Genealogy, History," in *The Foucault Reader,* edited by Paul Rabinow, 76–100 (New York: Pantheon Books).

Habermas, Jürgen
1974 [1971] "Introduction: Some Difficulties in the Attempt to Link

Theory and Praxis," in *Theory and Practice,* translated by John Viertel (Boston: Beacon Press).

1975 *Legitimation Crisis,* translated by Thomas McCarthy (Boston: Beacon Press).

1981a "Modernity versus Postmodernity," *New German Critique* 22 (Winter): 3–14.

1981b *Theorie des kommunikativen Handelns* (Frankfurt am Main: Suhrkamp Verlag).

Heidegger, Martin

1977 [1938] "The Age of the World Picture," in *The Question Concerning Technology and Other Essays,* translated by William Lovitt, 115–54 (New York: Harper Torchbooks).

Herr, Michael

1978 *Dispatches* (New York: Avon Books).

Horkheimer, Max, and Theodor Adorno

1988 [1944] *Dialectic of Enlightenment,* translated by John Cumming (New York: Continuum).

Howe, Irving

1970 *Decline of the New* (New York: Harcourt, Brace and World).

Hutcheon, Linda

1980 *A Theory of Parody: The Teachings of Twentieth-Century Art Forms* (New York: Methuen).

1988 *A Poetics of Postmodernism* (New York: Routledge).

Jameson, Fredric

1971 *Marxism and Form: Twentieth-Century Dialectical Theories of Literature* (Princeton: Princeton University Press).

1984a "Foreword" to Lyotard 1984 [1979]: vii–xxi.

1984b "Postmodernism, or the Cultural Logic of Late Capitalism," *New Left Review* 146 (July-August): 53–92.

Jay, Martin

1984 *Adorno* (Cambridge, MA: Harvard University Press).

Levin, Harry

1966 *Refractions: Essays in Comparative Literature* (New York: Oxford University Press).

Lyotard, Jean-François

1984 [1979] *The Postmodern Condition: A Report on Knowledge,* translated by Geoff Bennington and Brian Massumi (Minneapolis: University of Minnesota Press).

McHale, Brian

1987 *Postmodernist Fiction* (New York: Methuen).

1988 "Telling Postmodernist Stories," *Poetics Today* 9(3): 545–71.

Pappe, Hellmut O.
1973 "Enlightenment," in *The Dictionary of the History of Ideas,* Philip P. Wiener, Editor in Chief, 89–100 (New York: Scribner's).

Rorty, Richard
1985 "Habermas and Lyotard on Postmodernity," in *Habermas and Modernity,* edited by Richard J. Bernstein, 161–75 (Cambridge, MA: MIT Press).

Ulmer, Gregory
1983 "The Object of Post-Criticism," in Foster 1983: 83–110.

Wellmer, Albrecht
1985 "Reason, Utopia and the *Dialectic of Enlightenment,*" in *Habermas and Modernity,* edited by Richard J. Bernstein, 35–66 (Cambridge, MA: MIT Press).

Wernick, Andrew
1984 "Structuralism and the Dislocation of the French Rationalist Project," in *The Structural Allegory: Reconstructive Encounters with New French Thought,* edited by John Fekete, 130–49 (Minneapolis: University of Minnesota Press).

Wilde, Alan
1981 *Horizons of Assent: Modernism, Postmodernism and the Ironic Imagination* (Baltimore: Johns Hopkins University Press).

Woolf, Virginia
1928 *Orlando* (New York: Harcourt Brace Jovanovich).

II

REPRESENTING THE POSTMODERN

Preface

"So you hear me read me see me begin.

I begin . . . don't both of us begin? Yet as your eye sweeps over these lines—not like a wind, because not a limb bends or a letter trembles, but rather more simply—as you read do you find me here in your lap like a robe?"

So writes William Gass in a postmodern essay entitled "Emerson and the Essay" (1985, 9). Postmodern Provisional Truism (the only kind there is) Number One: the postmodern is awash with (awkward and self-conscious) paradoxes. How, for instance, can we introduce a discussion about the way in which postmodernism is represented, when it is the postmodern itself that has problematized the very notion of representation? By revealing and critically deconstructing the ideological presuppositions that always "go without saying" in a culture, it has managed to render all the images and stories we use to explain ourselves to ourselves anything but innocent and neutral.

Without the foundational security of modernity, as we have been seeing, the postmodern inevitably looks to the conditions and contexts of the *construction* both of those particular (self-) representations and of the entire process itself. Therefore, the representation of postmodernism in this section—like the one in this entire *Reader,* of course—can only be a partial, provisional, and "loaded" one. Within those limitations, then (and very self-consciously), we offer you a range of voices—often disagreeing with one another—arguing about just how the postmodern might be represented and how it might work.

As the readings in the last section suggest, it is probably impossible to begin to define the postmodern without coming to terms with the modern (see also Calinescu 1977, 120–44; Silliman 1987; Laffey 1987). This is only fitting, for one of the teachings of the postmodern is that history and context can never be ignored. As John McGowan explains in this book, the postmodern definitely has its precursors: traces of its ideological and conceptual apparatus can be found in the writings of Kant, Hegel, Marx, and Nietzsche. To this list, Jacques Derrida adds the names of Freud and Heidegger. While some also look to the role of the emancipatory political movements of the 1960s—civil rights, the women's movement, and so on—in forming postmodern views of the importance of difference and otherness (in this book, both Huyssen and Hutcheon), it is most often those major philosophical challenges to the modern bases of Western metaphysics that most people see as making the postmodern possible.

As we have seen, for many commentators today, the shift from a modern to a postmodern paradigm is as radical in its cognitive, perceptual, and affective implications as was the move from the Renaissance to the modern one. Derrida's early, influential essay, "Structure, Sign and Play in the Discourse of the Human Sciences" (reprinted in this book, but dating back to 1967), articulates the theory of this latest moment of rupture. This recent break occurred, argues Derrida, when accepted philosophical notions of such things as teleological origin and center, being as presence, and other "givens" (such as coherence, structure, totality, and ground) gave way to a decentered concept of signification as play—the moment when, "in the absence of a center or origin, everything became discourse."

In Section I, this moment of rupture was seen to mark the birth of postmodernity, in opposition to what Habermas calls the "project of modernity." In Derrida's terms, the modern "seeks to decipher, dreams of deciphering a truth or an origin which escapes play and the order of the sign"; however, the postmodern "is no longer turned toward the origin, affirms play and tries to pass beyond man and humanism, the name of man being the name of that being who . . . has dreamed of full presence, the reassuring foundation, the origin and the end of play." Derrida is not alone in his confronting and contesting of the definition of the human (or of what we once unproblematically referred to as "man").

Edward Said points to the unsettling effect of the work of Michel Foucault in similar terms: "If we are inclined to think of man as an entity resisting the flux of experience, then because of Foucault and what he says of linguistics, ethnology, and psychoanalysis, man is dissolved in the overarching waves, in the quanta, the striations of language itself, turning finally into little more than a constituted subject, a speaking pronoun, fixed indecisively in the eternal, ongoing rush of discourse" (Said 1975, 287). Neither Foucault nor Derrida specifically labels this shift in the notion of subjectivity "postmodern," though Derrida does describe it as the birth of a "terrifying form of monstrosity."

This postpartem representation is both playful and prophetic; it certainly implies a radical break between the modern and the postmodern. As we have seen, there is still considerable debate over whether the more appropriate model for their interrelationship might be one of continuity, as the very incorporating nature of the name post*modern* suggests. Yet, as Charles Russell argues here in "The Context of the Concept," "occasionally, a work, an artist, or a movement will introduce a new stylistic element, raise a particular aesthetic question, or propose an interpretation of art and experience that may at first appear to be merely the next logical step in accepted art history, but which subsequently must be seen as revealing the fatal limitations of current patterns of seeing or reading, and as having, in fact, effected a fundamental transformation of the practices of art or literature."

In this article and in his book, *Poets, Prophets, and Revolutionaries: The Literary Avant-garde from Rimbaud through Postmodernism* (1985), Russell investigates—on the level of the aesthetic—the connections and distinctions to be made among modernism, the avant-garde, and the postmodern. He argues that modernists "found in art a feasible, self-sustaining activity the more self-conscious and abstract it became"; the avant-garde, however, "engaged in formal experimentation in the belief that a radically individualistic or vangard perspective and language would in some way transform the manner in which society saw itself, and consequently the way people behaved." In its own way the postmodern combined the two, bringing to them Derrida's insight into the discursive nature of "everything": in Russell's terms, it applied "the model of art as a self-contained discourse to social discourse as well," and recognized that "as a language, art cannot be considered separately from cultural languages in general."

To put it in still another way, "[u]nlike modernism, where the work of art was a closed entity whose meanings were fixed and central and which accordingly encouraged explication or decipherment, postmodernism is dispersed. It invites collaboration" (Trachtenberg 1985, xii). What does this move toward a collaborative aesthetic model do to the privileged position of the author—as the romantic creator, or even as the controlling artist figure of modernism? As William Spanos has explained, the modern author as prime authority is replaced by a demystified postmodern one, aware of the culturally constituted status of his/her authorship, an agent *in* history, speaking to historical readers inscribed by a historical occasion (1987, 246).

This is why, as explored in the first section, the move from postmoder*nity* to postmoder*nism* is an easy, and even necessary, one to make. Such an overt implication of the aesthetic in the social and historical is, in fact, one of the major concerns of postmodern narrative. Perhaps for this reason, the novel has often been the privileged genre of postmodern literary critical studies (see, for instance, Hutcheon 1988 and 1989; McHale 1987; Varsava 1990; Carroll 1982; Thiher 1984; Newman 1985; McCaffery 1982 and 1986; Klinkowitz 1980, 1984, and 1985; Wilde 1981 and 1987).

But the relevance of this particular representation of the postmodern for other fields as well can be seen in Ihab Hassan's long list of philosophers, psychoanalysts, literary theorists, choreographers, artists, composers, writers, and directors in his "Toward a Concept of Postmodernism," and Linda Hutcheon's use of examples from architecture, film, photography, painting, autobiography, journalism, theory, music, and fiction, in her "Beginning to Theorize Postmodernism." What Hutcheon also points to here is the postmodern refusal to invest with any representational power the traditional modernist hierarchies of judgment about what constitutes "art."

Andreas Huyssen argues at length, in his *After the Great Divide: Modernism, Mass Culture, Postmodernism* (1986), that the breakdown of the divide between "high" and "popular" art is one of the most characteristic and contested things about the postmodern—something Leslie Fiedler had noted as early as 1965 in his essay "The New Mutants." The resulting heterogeneity of discourse has always upset those operating within a purist, modern paradigm—be it in architecture or music. Of course, other things upset them too—and perhaps one way of trying to represent the postmodern would be to look at precisely those irritants.

As this text you are reading now illustrates, the self-reflexivity of postmodern discourses often provokes those writing about them to be equally self-conscious. This is usually cited as the First Irritant: reflexivity is seen as coy, arch, "cute," or narcissistic and solipsistic—be it in artistic or critical discourses. Yet the counterargument would be that such a mode of address seems to be the only possible one that could remain faithful to its subject. Derrida notes that Claude Lévi-Strauss recognized that his work on myth had to be reflexive; it had to "have the form of that of which it speaks." If it was to "avoid the violence that consists in centering a language which describes an acentric structure," it had to avoid going "back to the source, to the center, to the founding basis, to the principle"— in other words, back to what constitutes legitimation within the project of modernity. Sometimes, however, that move back might not be avoidable: McGowan discusses in this book the difficulty of trying to describe the postmodern "conditions that allow for difference and novelties" without relying on universalizing or transcendental—that is, modern—claims about "this or that being *the* way that humans interact in the world." He then goes on to make his own "transcendental claim about a necessary condition of theoretical thought"—but does so in full awareness of his step onto the different plane of modernity.

What Russell calls this "emphatic self-reflexiveness" is indeed characteristic of postmodernist discourses of all kinds; within an aesthetic frame of reference, its precursor can be found in modernist notions of formal autonomy. But whereas modernist art turned its meaning back upon itself, exploring itself as "a mode of meaning, of cognition, of perception and expression," as Russell notes, it did so in the name of order, structure, form—i.e., in the name of everything modern which the postmodern may invoke, but simultaneously seeks to ironize and challenge, by moving outward to other contexts, to social and cultural discourses.

Similarly, within a theoretical frame, Derrida sees Lévi-Strauss's "critical search for a new status of discourse" as involving "the stated abandonment of all reference to a *center,* a *subject,* a privileged *reference,* an origin, or an absolute *archia.*" This decentering challenge to scientific positivism finds its parallel in postmodern "interrogations of humanist certainties" (Hutcheon) regarding what modernity offered as definitions of Truth, Beauty, and Goodness. Within the paradigm of postmodernity, the question is: how can either a humanist or a positivist position offer something as universal and eternal when postmodern memory—reversing modern amnesia—can show it to be rooted in very particular times and places, genders and classes? What value can "origin" have in a parodic culture where, as Derrida notes, "every discourse is *bricoleur*—in Lévi-Strauss's sense of the word—using the intertextual "means at hand" around itself to construct meaning?

Suddenly everything is questioned and questionable, nothing stable and sure; irony reigns. Italian philosopher Gianni Vattimo (1988) has coined the term "weak thought" (*pensiero debole*) to describe his attempt to work with, rather than be paralyzed by, this loss of the certainty and stability of the Cartesian order. Fundamentally contradictory and provisional, this is philosophy which knows it cannot dismiss what it calls "reason-domination" (or what we are here calling the Cartesian paradigm of modernity) because it is implicated in it; but neither does it seek to avoid the challenge to that Enlightenment project, as we have seen some accusing Habermas of doing.

What all the readings in this section should provide is a sense that, whatever representation of the postmodern we might choose, it too is going to be subject to this same self-questioning reflexivity. Does this mean that it is impossible to find any terms in which to discuss the postmodern, or that it is futile even to try to do so? A typical postmodern response is likely in order: yes and no. As long as we accept that our act of representing is itself open to a postmodern critical reading, however, we might continue in our provisional attempt to locate at least a few main sites of overlapping concern across a variety of discourses. Letting ourselves once again be guided by the Irritant Model: if reflexivity—and, with it, parody—provokes the greatest ire on the part of anti-postmodernists, then those ironic paradoxes, not to say contradictions, with which we began this preface must run a close second. McGowan notes the "prevalence of the logic of contradiction in postmodern thought": "Marxism, structuralism, poststructuralism, and other derivatives of Hegelianism (including psychoanalysis) all render visible contradictions that are somehow both immanent and hard to discern."

The postmodern tendency to celebrate the different and the resistant comes from this "logic of contradiction" that implies, not a monolithic and homogeneous (modern) concept of culture, but a notion that incorporates and validates multiplicity, heterogeneity, and diversity. In Lyotard's terms: "Postmodern knowledge . . . refines our sensitivity to differences and reinforces our ability to tolerate the incommensurable" (1984, xxv). The impact of such a postmodern shift can be seen, as Derrida notes, in things like the structuralist challenge to the unexamined ethnocentricity of the discipline of ethnology. McGowan explains that "[p]ostmodernism finds in difference that principle of multiplicity, or irreducibility, that allows it to escape the totalizing visions it associates with necessity and unfreedom."

The "ex-centric" (Hutcheon)—those marginalized by their not fitting into such totalizing visions—are also contributing greatly to the redefining of subjectivity in terms of a paradoxical "decentralized community," where the local and the regional replace the supposedly universal and permanent values in whose name modernity could exclude and marginalize. This is the territory for which Hassan coins the name "indetermanence"—the melding of indeterminacies ("ambiguity, discontinuity, heterodoxy, pluralism, randomness, revolt, perversion, deformation") and immanences ("diffusion, dissemination, pulsion, interplay, communication, interdependence").

Our list of irritants is rapidly getting longer, for each of the above descriptive terms easily translates into a term of abuse in some critics' minds. For them, it all translates into "cultural relativisim" and a decline of "standards" of judgment. Modernity's overarching, totalizing frame of reference aimed to wipe out earlier frames. As Lyotard puts it, the modern legitimated itself by reference to a metadiscourse structured on a *"grand récit"*: "the rule of consensus between the sender and addressee of a statement with truth-value is deemed acceptable if it is cast in terms of a possible unanimity between rational minds" (1984, xxiii).

Postmodernism, on the contrary, has no real means by which it could discard any narrative—past, present or future. Its refusal of origin and ground makes it seem—at least from a modern perspective—utterly indecisive. Nevertheless, increasingly these days, there would still seem to be conceptual space available for "a hard, rigorous relativism that regards knowledge as a social product, a matter of dialogue between different versions of the world, including different languages, ideologies, and modes of representations" (Mitchell 1986, 38). As part of that dialogue, the postmodern also bears within itself the narrative of modernity, deploying it reflexively and parodically, even in its most refractory provocations to it.

As our (perhaps perverse) urge to attempt to write prefatory introductions to these various sections reveals, nothing can escape being caught up in and responding to that modern explanatory frame. Yet, in this (for many, irritating) terrain of "incompleteness" (Russell), "supplementarity" (Derrida), and "provisionality" (Hutcheon), the tentative is perhaps a more appropriate mode of address than the definite, and so we find titles like *"Toward* a Concept of Postmodernism" or *"Beginning* to Theory Postmodernism."

But does this provisional caution not risk being (or being considered) a cop-out? For those working with a distinct political agenda, it would appear so: "It is critical choice that determines whether a single perspective becomes absolutist; it is fear of this critical choice that motivates postmodernism to keep on the move" (Birch 1991, 5). What Hutcheon calls the complicitous critique of aesthetic postmodernism, its tendency at one and the same time to install and subvert that which it contests, has become a major point of contention in the postmodern debates in general, we we shall see in the next section.

Is there any way out of this, out of what, in a modern context, looks like a real impasse? Derrida admits that even his challenges to the history of metaphysics are also inevitably compromised: "We have no language—no syntax and no lexicon—which is foreign to this history; we can pronounce not a single destructive proposition which has not already had to slip into the form, the logic, and the implicit postulations of precisely what it seeks to contest." The paradox he sees as Lévi-Strauss's "double intention"—"to preserve as an instrument something whose truth-value he criticizes"—is repeated in McGowan's conclusion that "like Nietzsche, postmodern theory often finds itself in the position of affirming (and desiring) something that it also declares impossible to attain." Hassan may offer a neat two-column table of the differences between modernism and postmodernism—but he then asserts that this is really a "provisional scheme" and that its "dichotomies . . . remain insecure, equivocal." In other words, like this preface itself, all attempts to represent the postmodern can only knowingly fall into typically postmodern paradoxes, and the political implication of these ironic contradictions form the focus of Section III, "Entanglements and Complicities."

Works Cited

Birch, David
    (1991) "Postmodernist Chutneys." *Textual Practice.* 5.1: 1–7.

Calinescu, Matei
    (1977) *Faces of Modernity.* Bloomington: Indiana University Press.

Carroll, David
    (1982) *The Subject in Question: The Languages of Theory and the Strategies of Fiction.* Chicago: University of Chicago Press.

Fiedler, Leslie
    (1965) "The New Mutants." *Partisan Review.* 32.4: 505–25.

Gass, William H.
    (1985) *Habitations of the Word: Essays.* New York: Simon and Schuster.

Hutcheon, Linda
(1988) *A Poetics of Postmodernism: History, Theory, Fiction.* New York and London: Routledge.

―――.

(1989) *The Politics of Postmodernism.* New York and London: Routledge.

Huyssen, Andreas
(1986) *After the Great Divide: Modernism, Mass Culture, Postmodernism.* Bloomington: Indiana University Press.

Klinkowitz, Jerome
(1980) *Literary Disruptions: The Making of a Post-Contemporary American Fiction.* 2nd ed. Urbana: University of Illinois Press.

―――.

(1984) *The Self-Apparent Word: Fiction as Language/Language as Fiction.* Carbondale: Southern Illinois University Press.

―――.

(1985) *Literary Subversions: New American Fiction and the Practice of Criticism.* Carbondale and Edwardsville: Southern Illinois University Press.

Laffey, John
(1987) "Cacophonic Rites: Modernism and Postmodernism." *Historical Reflections/Réflexions Historiques.* 14.1: 1–32.

Lyotard, Jean-François
(1984) *The Postmodern Condition: A Report on Knowledge.* Trans. Geoff Bennington and Brian Massumi. Minneapolis: University of Minnesota Press.

McCaffery, Larry
(1982) *The Metafictional Muse.* Pittsburgh, Pa: University of Pittsburgh Press.

―――.

(1986) *Postmodern Fiction: A Bio-bibliographical Guide.* New York: Greenwood Press.

McHale, Brian
(1987) *Postmodernist Fiction.* London and New York: Methuen.

Mitchell, W. J. T.
(1986) *Iconology: Image, Text, Ideology.* Chicago: University of Chicago Press.

Newman, Charles
(1985) *The Post-Modern Aura: The Art of Fiction in an Age of Inflation.* Evanston, Ill.: Northwestern University Press.

Russell, Charles
(1985) *Poets, Prophets and Revolutionaries: The Literary Avant-garde from Rimbaud through Postmodernism*. New York and Oxford: Oxford University Press.

Said, Edward
(1975) *Beginnings: Intention and Method*. New York: Basic.

Silliman, Ron
(1987) " 'Postmodernism': Sign for a Struggle, the Struggle for the Sign." *Poetics Journal* 7: 18–39.

Spanos, William V.
(1987) *Repetitions: The Postmodern Occasion in Literature and Culture*. Baton Rouge: Louisiana State University Press.

Thiher, Allen
(1984) *Words in Reflection: Modern Language Theory and Postmodern Fiction*. Chicago: University of Chicago Press.

Trachtenberg, Stanley, ed.
(1985) *The Postmodern Moment: A Handbook of Contemporary Innovation in the Arts*. Westport, Conn: Greenwood Press.

Varsava, Jerry
(1990) *Contingent Meanings: Postmodern Fiction, Mimesis, and the Reader*. Tallahassee: Florida State University Press.

Vattimo, Gianni
(1988) *The End of Modernity: Nihilism and Hermeneutics in Postmodern Culture*. Trans. Jon R. Snyder. Baltimore: Johns Hopkins University Press.

Wilde, Alan
(1981) *Horizons of Assent: Modernism, Postmodernism, and the Ironic Imagination*. Baltimore: Johns Hopkins University Press.

————.

(1987) *Middle Grounds: Studies in Contemporary American Fiction*. Philadelphia: University of Pennsylvania Press.

Excerpts from *Postmodernism and Its Critics*

John McGowan

Postmodern writers inevitably find themselves continually at odds with Kant. Ironist theory wants to repudiate the bias toward the universal that Kant built into theory and wishes to argue that, whatever Kant's good intentions toward difference, the effect of designating universal conditions of rationality that define the essentially human is to exclude various differences as, by definition, nonhuman. In addition, postmodern theory has at times questioned the serene Kantian confidence in the powers of reflection by adopting the more troubling view that we are least likely to understand our own motives and conditions of existence.[1] Finally, postmodernism with its suspicion of autonomy, has questioned the barriers that Kant erects between the different spheres of the public and the private, and of pure reason, practical reason, and aesthetic judgment.[2] At its most extreme, postmodernism would like to move away from the certainties that Kant's transcendental deduction provides, abandoning the claim to uncover necessities in favor of projecting us into the differential play of practices, meanings, and options that it portrays as the terrain of human endeavor.

To scuttle the Kantian version of theory, however, has proved none too easy. For one thing, ironist theory retains Kant's bias toward the human, his exclusive interest in the world humans make and inhabit. For another, the description of our condition as one of insertion within networks (or systems) of differential play is hard put to avoid transcendental claims in the process of arguing that such *is* our condition. The play itself might not require any transcendental knowledge, but to describe the play usually does. (And Kant, of course, never claims that apprehension of objects requires knowledge of the categories; theory for Kant reveals necessities that operate whether we know of them or not.) Postmodern theory is suspicious of all identifications of necessary conditions, worrying that these discovered necessities are merely used to close down certain possibilities, to attempt to control from above the proliferation of differences, of oppositions, and of unforeseen novelties. But it is very difficult to describe the conditions that allow for differences and novelties themselves without relying on transcendental claims about this or that being *the* way that humans interact in the world. In fact, to make my own transcendental claim about a necessary condition of theoretical thought, I believe that once the processes of meaning formation or social interaction are discussed, the identification of enabling conditions for certain types of human behavior cannot be avoided, no matter how hard the writer tries.

Most troubling for me is Kant's resolute ahistoricism. While it may turn out that we want to identify some transcendental conditions as everywhere applicable, I think that we would do better to begin by trying to describe the conditions that foster the experiences of humans in particular cultures and at particular times. Whether a historicist transcendentalism is a complete contradiction in terms, so utterly foreign to Kant's thought as to be inconceivable, is of course a matter of debate. Hegel's work suggests that a historicist theory can still aspire to identify fundamental conditions within a circumscribed time and place, while also suggesting that such an outlook radically questions Kantian assumptions about reason's autonomy from the empirical and the individual's autonomy from the social.

* * *

Those postmodern philosophers who follow the Hegelian as opposed to the Kantian path reject Hegel's ontological and/or teleological visions of an eventual reconciliation of Spirit with the objective order and with man in his rational essence. Instead, postmodern Hegelianism adopts a covert ontology that posits meaning as constituted by a relational totality, while stressing the internal divisions (contradictions) within that totality. Contradiction is adopted as the inevitable, necessary status of thought and of being-in-the-(social)-world. Thus postmodern theory pictures us as permanently immersed in the intermediate stages of Hegel's historical narrative, a position that brings Hegel's latent antihumanism and assertions of agents' ignorance to the forefront.

The prevalence of the logic of contradiction in postmodern thought is perhaps so obvious as to escape notice. Certainly, the continental propensity to accept contradictions explains much of the oft-commented-upon failure for a dialogue to develop between continental and Anglo-American philosophy. Marxism, structuralism, poststructuralism, and other derivatives of Hegelianism (including psychoanalysis) all render visible contradictions that are somehow both immanent and hard to discern. Marx and Freud still retain (in the notions of a communist society and in the cure) some hope for eventual overcoming of contradiction, but structuralism and poststructuralism find in contradiction (binary oppositions or the antinomies revealed by a deconstructive reading) both beginning and end. The contradiction generates texts and actions and the interpreter's revelation of contradiction brings his task to an end. These theorists believe contradiction is inevitable because they adopt the Hegelian notion that thought necessarily expands until it meets it negation. We might say that thought, like Napoleon or Hitler, will annex all territories to itself until it meets a resistance it cannot overcome, its definitive negation. Hegel's Spirit finally annexes everything, but contemporary theory retains a hope that no thought or totality has Spirit's power. (In its darkest moments, postmodernism accords such power to capitalism, which has led Stuart Hall to characterize postmodern politics as the desperate search to see if there is discernible somewhere some faint kick against the machine.) Somewhere out there a contradiction can be found that suggests capitalism's limits, that can serve as the starting point for resistance, for the reestablishment of distance, difference, dialogue, of the two-dimensional as opposed to the one-dimensional. The insistence that all thought will meet an other that it cannot completely subdue is at once covert ontology and political hope.

Postmodernism's ontology rests on its claims that the contradictions uncovered by its interpretations *really* exist, although hidden to the agent/author, who always want to present his text as the successful achievement of unified, coherent thinking. The interpreter can reveal the inevitable limits to unity and success, embodied in contradictions the author cannot face consciously. We can see that the kind of necessity recovered in this location of contra-diction at the foundation of all thought comes very close to a Kan-tian revelation of the necessary conditions of thought itself. But apart from sharing an ultimate transcendent claim, the differences between neo-Kantian and neo-Hegelian thought are far more im-portant than the similarities. Kantian philosophy aims to recon-struct what makes thought (and experience) coherent; Hegelianism shorn of eventual reconciliation demonstrates thought's continual incoherence. Ironist theory understands thought as nontransparent to itself (although neo-Kantians continually point out that this in-sistence contradicts the postmodern theorists' own clarity about the nature of thought and its nontransparency), inevitably entangled in contradiction, and situated within a systematic whole that estab-lishes thought's possibility but also generates the divisions and con-tradictions characteristic of thought.

When we turn to Hegel's politics we begin to see why ironist theory must reject Hegel's explicit ontology of reconciliation to the rationality of the real as embodied in Spirit. In keeping with his emphasis on the way that totalities confer meaning on particulars. Hegel's vision of society is directed against all forms of liberal indi-vidualism and of negative liberty. For Hegel, the individual can have no identity and no purpose apart from the social order within which he exists, and thus a freedom that is defined as autonomy from the social order would be completely vacuous. An individual thus freed would have no self that could act on this freedom. The liberal belief in sovereign individuals who preexist society, which is only formed at a later date through a "contract" among the individ-uals, reverses the actual causal sequence. The individual is always born into a social order (is situated within a family) and only devel-ops a sense of self in relation to others who define his or her limits and, crucially, who extend their acknowledgement or "recognition" of the individual's selfhood. If every particular gains its identity through its confrontation with and/or relation to another, then the Hegelian notion of 'recognition' " indicates that for conscious selves the crucial confrontation is with another conscious self. "Self-consciousness," the awareness of one's self as a bounded, defined en-tity, "exists in itself and for itself, in that, and by the fact that it exists for another self-consciousness; that is to say, it *is* only by be-ing acknowledged or "recognized" (1967b, 229). I take the concept of recognition to imply not only that identity is conferred upon the self by others, but also that this conferral cannot be evaded. Action is by selves because selves are the social form that consciousness takes. Freedom cannot entail an escape from society, for even if such an escape were possible it would hardly be desirable because it would obliterate the very agent who was to gain freedom.

Which is not to say that gaining a self is an unmixed blessing. Hegel presents a "positive" form of freedom, in which the individual discovers and fulfills her complete potential within the framework offered by the social order. In its most chilling form, this freedom consists in the perfect reconciliation of self with society, where the self wills for itself what society asks of it. Of course, Hegel's ontology ensures that such a reconciliation is not a forced subjection of self to society, since both are essentially the same. Self and society alike find their true essence when they conform to the fundamental reality of Spirit. "Freedom is nothing but the recognition and adoption of such universal substantial objects as Right and Law, and the production of a reality that is accordant with them—the State" (1956, 59). The perfectly rational self and the perfectly rational state would never come into conflict, and the state's laws would provide the environment in which the self would be liberated into the fullest realization of its essence.

This prior definition of purpose is what troubles most subsequent readers of Hegel. (The other troubling point is his willingness so easily to identify the State with embodied Reason and his seeming lack of criteria for determining in what instances the State is corrupt, does not truly represent Spirit.) If, as so often seems to be the case, individuals manifest a great variety of purposes and experience themselves as in conflict with social forms and other individuals, what justifies the identification of a universal and pre-existing standard to which all must conform? Hegel's answer that the standard of rationality already exists and is immanent in humans appears a newer version of Plato's vision of a forgotten knowledge that all possess and that once recalled will foster political unity; Hegel's version of this Platonic notion appears to generate a political vision every bit as tyrannical as Plato's. Conflict will only exist during the time when the principle of rationality is imperfectly understood.

Once again, Hegel's vision is technically humanist (since the rationality he aims to uncover is all our own), but practically anti-humanist insofar as a standard not available to humans (at a given moment in history) defines society's and individuals' proper goals. Contemporary political visions almost all reject Hegel's notion of a predetermined purpose, insisting instead that freedom must involve the human creation of purposes not yet forged. Where that freedom rests with each individual, we have deontological, liberal negative liberty. Where, following Rousseau, that freedom rests

with society as a collective body, we have a version of "positive freedom" that insists on the openness of the future, on the boundless
possibilities of human creativity.

Postmodern thought runs into what I consider its deepest
problems at just this point—and I devote the next chapter to a full
discussion of this issue. But let me anticipate the argument by suggesting postmodernism's troubled relation to Hegelian politics.
With the exception of Richard Rorty, the writers I discuss are prepared to accept the Hegelian denial of negative liberty on the
ground that it makes no sense to accord the individual an autonomous existence. Individuals cannot have purposes apart from the
social relations that constitute them; thus negative liberty must be
an illusion and devoid of content. Postmodernism's stress on contradiction as opposed to reconciliation, however, leads it to look for
something that exists in resistance to society and the state. Furthermore, postmodernism's implicit or explicit political commitment to changing the existing order of capitalist society also makes
a search for resistant entities necessary. Thus postmodern theory
has a built-in tendency to celebrate the resistant, while at the same
time holding to a relational view of how entities are constituted
that fails to explain how the resistant can even exist. In addition,
postmodernism's hostility to self (which it associates with bourgeois
humanism) means that it must locate resistance somewhere other
than in individuals. The prevalent reverence for resistance (or opposition) indicates a hope for some kind of (even if limited) distance
from society, and the political ideal of distance has always found its
expression in notions of negative liberty. The end result is an uneasy combination of a Hegelian (holistic) analysis of present conditions with an anarchistic politics that is very close to the liberalism
postmodern writers claim to despise.

The version of positive freedom that can be derived from Hegel
is found on the holistic premise that the individual is not self-
sufficient and can only be understood in relation to the social.
Albrecht Wellmer provides a good overview of this position. His
summary is explicitly derived from the work of Hegel and Charles
Taylor:

> If ... human individuals are essentially *social* individuals, if,
> in their very individuality, they are constituted and, as it were,
> permeated by the culture, traditions, and institutions of the
> society to which they belong, then their freedom as well must
> have a social character. Even as *individual* freedom this free-

dom must have a *communal* character, or at least an essentially communal aspect, expressing and manifesting itself in
the way in which the individual participates in and contributes to the communal practices of his society. The originary locus of freedom, then, would not be the isolated individual, but
a society that is the medium of individuation through socialization; freedom would have to be thought of as ultimately re-
siding in the structures, institutions, practices, and traditions
of a larger social whole. But since this larger social whole is
what it is only through being kept alive, "reproduced," and interpreted by the individuals who are part of it, individual and
"public" freedom now become inextricably intertwined. (1989,
228–29)

My contention is that postmodern thought accepts the premises of
the social production of individuals that Wellmer outlines here, but
it cannot find a way to describe social "structures, institutions,
practices, and traditions" as anything but oppressive, as never productive of freedom. Postmodernism remains stuck on its identification of communities with tyranny.[3] The terms of individual life
within the whole provides one central issue in Hegel's *Philosophy of
Right,* a book that I attempt to recast in contemporary terms in my
closing chapter. At stake is describing the minimal terms of connection between selves and social groups that allows them to "recognize" others' claims to participation in the society's political and
material life.

*   *   *

[P]ostmodern Marxists often try to abandon Marx's teleological vision and its concomitant notion of legitimacy. Instead, these
postmodern writers simply affirm the right of each social group to
its own interests, an affirmation based partly on the epistemological grounds that disinterested behavior or knowledge is impossible
and partly on the political grounds that groups can only preserve
their differences and resist oppression if they aggressively promote
their interests. Abandoning Marxist teleology, then, means accepting that social conflict is perpetual, just as abandoning Hegelian teleology entails accepting the ubiquity of contradiction. This position
involves the complete repudiation of any notion of legitimate social
authority or political agenda. All power and all goals are the products of interest, with no claims on others who do not share those
interests.

One further variant of Marx's thoughts on power—the notion of ideology—has been particularly influential in postmodern thought. Although Marx himself rarely uses the word *ideology* or discusses the concept after the early text of *The German Ideology* (written by Marx and Engels in 1845–46 but not published during either man's lifetime), the notion has become central to many twentieth-century versions of Marxism. Very simply, *ideology* can be defined in two ways, with each definition highlighting one of the two factors in Marx's confusing and contradictory use of the term. Definition 1 takes ideology as the ideas or beliefs possessed by any group of virtue of its social position. This definition simply posits the determination of consciousness by one's place in the relations of material production; since everyone has such a determinate place, everyone would possess or produce an ideology. Definition 2 takes ideology as the conscious (or superstructural or idealistic or cultural) legitimation of the prevailing social arrangements, a legitimation whose most salient feature is its denial of the facts of social conflict that reveal those arrangements' partiality. For Marx and Engels, the "German ideology" is work that denies partiality by denying that material production and its relations are the core of social arrangements; rather, the ideologists locate unity elsewhere, in a national spirit or culture or patriotism, because a good, hard look at material conditions would make the lack of unity obvious. Any and every claim to have achieved social unity does well to take this Marxist skepticism into account.

These two definitions of ideology would not conflict if ideology in the second sense was limited to the dominant class. But Marx waffles on the question of what ideas (or ideological vision) we might expect a given individual, as a member of a class, to hold. He sometimes take the straightforward position that one's class position determines one's ideas; we can predict that the bourgeoisie and the proletariat will conflict on the ideological as well as the economic plane. At other times, however, Marx proposes what has been called "the dominant ideology thesis," which holds that the ruling class is able to impose its own ideolological views on society as a whole.[4] "The ideas of the ruling class are in every epoch the ruling ideas, i.e., the class which is the ruling *material* force of society, is at the same time its ruling *intellectual* force. The class which has the means of material production at its disposal, has control at the same time over the means of mental production, so that thereby, generally speaking, the ideas of those who lack the means of production are subject to it" (1970, 64). This statement greatly extends the range of the ruling class's power: Not only do the other classes live within social arrangements formed by the dominant class, but their very apprehension of those arrangements, the ways they think about themselves and their social position, are seen as given to them by the dominant class.

Steven Lukes has usefully distinguished three "dimensions" of power. In the first, "to exercise power is to prevail over the contrary preferences of others" (1986, 9); in the second power also includes "controlling the agenda," that is, determining what issues will ever get staged as matters to be contested or decided. The third dimension "incorporates power of the first two kinds, but also allows that power may operate to shape and modify desires and beliefs in a manner contrary to people's interests" (1986a, 10). Marx shows little interest in Lukes's second dimension, but his notion of "ruling ideas" involves a jump from the first dimension to the third. This notion of an imposed ideology, which explains the "false consciousness" of a nonrevolutionary working class, has proved a useful way for twentieth-century Marxism to explain the proletariat's lack of enthusiasm for socialism. Of course, the existence of a dominant ideology also introduces a formidable obstacle to achieving any socialist future, since it makes power that more impregnable. One response to the notion of a dominant ideology has been Western Marxism's shift in interest to the cultural (rhetorical) terrain of combatting the dominant's culture representation of itself. I do not believe that such a shift has proved very useful, especially when combined with a belief that the masses' "false consciousness" must be corrected.

* * *

The classic epistemological problem raised by Marx's theory of ideology is how he can account for his own immunity. If all ideas are motivated by economic interest or if all ideas carry the stamp of the ruling class's views, then how can Marx explain his own privileged access to real causes? This objection, (sometimes referred to as "Mannheim's paradox," since it was first formulated by Karl Mannheim) has troubled Marxists, especially those who are already uneasy with Marx's foundational claims. Alvin Gouldner, examining the concrete interests that Marxism serves, comes to the conclusion that Marxism is the ideology of the intellectuals, not of the proletariat. Gouldner sees Marxism as afflicted by a peculiar false consciousness of its own—the belief that a socialist society would benefit workers rather than the intellectuals who most follow Marx.[5] Postmodern Marxists have been less overtly hostile to the proponents of Marxism than Gouldner has, but they generally have adopted a similar claim that no privileged position can exist and that Marxism's own ideas should thus be fully acknowledged as "interested" and hence ideological in their own right.

* * *

For now I want only to suggest how close this postmodern Marxism can find itself to the Nietzschean notion of the will to power. Marx's teleology (his goal of the one-class society in which everyone's interests are the same and thus relations of domination no longer exist) and his ontology (his ability to reveal the real material conditions that explain—allow for a correct interpretation of—a group's ideology) provide him with concepts and ethical norms (goals) that are outside the play of power. Postmodern Marxism looks with suspicion upon these escape valves, with the result that contemporary Marxism is both more and less holistic than Marx himself. More holistic insofar as the rule of power is everywhere; we are always *within* power relations, whereas Marx envisioned a place of knowledge apart from power and an eventual society in which power did not figure. Less holistic insofar as the whole of power is always characterized by conflict, and the very idea of a nonconflicted whole where everyone has the same interest is given up as both impossible and undesirable.

The alignment of postmodern Marxism with Nietzsche would be complete if the postmoderns simply affirmed the fact of perpetual conflict. Postmodern thought, however, while often adopting Nietzsche's enshrinement of power in the place of disinterested knowledge or of any action not motivated by the wish to dominate, usually retains the Marxist hope of diminishing (at least) the sway of power over social groups and social selves. For Nietzsche, freedom and power are joined, either with freedom understood as the utmost exercise of one's own will to power or (as I discuss below) with freedom connected to the affirmation of being dominated. But for Marx and most postmodern writers, freedom is still something that is contrasted to power and imagined as a release from power's constraints, not an exercise, or an acceptance, of power. And it is in asserting the primacy of the social that the Marxist finds a way to counter the Nietzschean portrait of endless conflict. Since power constructs and is subsequently embedded in the social relations that establish the terms of individual life in any given society, there remains the hope that certain social relations will afford greater freedom, will minimize domination. In other words, to return to Luke's definition of power, certain social arrangements will reduce the chances that one social group will *consistently* "prevail over the contrary preferences of others," always be in the position to set the agenda, and be situated in a position that allows it "to modify" the desires and beliefs of others. The goal is not necessarily the cessation of all social conflict but the prevention of predetermined outcomes of premature resolutions. Nietzsche has little to say about how social conditions shape the play of power; Marxists are obsessed with social determinants, and they associate freedom with social arrangements that either prevent the play of power altogether (the traditional vision of communism) or with social arrangements that make the play as equal as possible for all participants. Thus while Marxists practice the Nietzschean hermeneutic of suspicion that reveals the fact of power behind practices pretending to something else, they also practice a second hermeneutic of suspicion meant to reveal the institutionalization of inequities that give certain groups an often irresistible advantage in social conflicts.

Because Marx believes that the individual's location within a set of social relations is inescapable, he is fully committed to a version of positive freedom. To live where power does not predetermine the outcome of conflicts or one's own determinate position in social relations is not to live outside society but to live within a society that is set up in such a way as to ensure the possibility of freedom. Social arrangements are certainly *the* primary locus of domination for Marx, but they are also the only possible place for the establishment of the conditions of freedom. The movement from necessity to freedom is completely within the social, is a movement of social transformation. "Only in community with others," Marx and Engels write, "has each individual the means of cultivating his gifts in all directions; only in community, therefore, is personal freedom possible" (1970, 83). A Marxist politics must, at the least, consider the form community should take in order to promote the kinds of freedom we desire. The abrogation of that necessary act of imagination, the pursuit of freedom apart from a vision of the social context that underwrites its possibility, belongs to anarchist or liberal versions of a negative freedom that the individual enjoys prior to, apart from, or after the abolition of the social order. Nietzsche offers a particularly influential version of such negative freedom, and postmodern Marxism will never drift entirely into Nietzsche's camp so long as it keeps its sights on the primacy of the social.

The Marxist desire for freedom from domination is everywhere present in postmodern thought, even if only as an implicit norm that intellectuals find hard to justify and even harder to imagine achieving. Marx himself unfortunately proves little help in trying to consider how freedom might emerge from situations of dominance.

In his most extremely deterministic moments, Marx portrays freedom's emergence as an inevitable future development of capitalism.
Obviously, given capitalism's endurance, this Marxist version of history's movement toward socialism offers no hope. More useful, perhaps, is the notion that different groups within a society, by virtue
of the different positions they occupy in the social whole, will have
different aspirations and visions. If we emphasize this aspect of
Marx, the hold of the dominant ideology will be mitigated, the opportunities for conflict and for alternative visions multiplied, the
notion that a dominant social order also generates internal resistance introduced, and a theoretical explanation of novelty and change
offered. Marx, read this way, appears close to presenting a view that
is now associated with Foucault, namely that power itself produces
the possibility of freedom and the terms within which freedom is
enacted. The classic Marxist formulation of this relationship of
power to freedom is the claim that the bourgeoisie creates the proletariat who will bring the realm of freedom. In other words, power
inevitably creates social relations and social situations that afford
certain strategic possibilities to the agents within those situations
and relations. The options for these agents are certainly finite and
context-dependent, but power can neither predict nor fix the limits
of that range of options in advance. The space of freedom becomes
what power has made possible (inadvertently or not) and cannot
control. Each new social configuration (constructed by the ruling
class) makes new actions possible, and the playing out of these possibilities by different agents in different positions leads to results
that power could not have determined in advance and that, in some
cases prove inimical to power's, to the dominant group's, interest.

This more optimistic view of power's relation to freedom articulated, it remains necessary to supplement this interpretation of
Marx through Foucault with the Marx who is concerned with the
concrete resolution of conflicts within particular societies. The trouble with the play of resistance at particular sites of confrontation
with power is that Foucault often seems to locate freedom in the
play and write as if we have achieved our goal when we have theoretically satisfied ourselves that "practices of freedom" are possible.
What such an account misses is that something is usually at stake
in confrontations and that we designate a dominant and a dominated partner in such relations on the basis of how the confrontation's resolution leaves one party relatively better off or more
satisfied than the other. The portrait of productive power ignores
how specific social arrangements bias possible outcomes from the
start and what arrangements might work to mitigate such bias.

Foucault focuses too exclusively on activity (the freedom to engage in confrontation) rather than on *what* agents hope to gain from such confrontations. From the standpoint of productive power, all social arrangements, apart from the limit case of total domination, are pretty much the same, affording various possibilities for freedom. Not much can be said about the relative superiority of any particular social configuration over any other.[6] But the Marxist notion of positive freedom rests on the conviction that different social contexts can make all the difference between a condition of freedom and a condition of unfreedom. I think we need to hold on to that conviction. And as I argued in the preceding chapter, Marx's own refusal to consider the possible legitimacy of any social forms prior to the completely socialist society stands in the way of his taking full advantage of his sensitivity toward the difference that social contexts can make.

In sum, Marx is crucial because he shifts the creation of the world from Spirit to power and because he locates freedom in opposition to power. (Even if we see freedom as produced by power in Marx, that freedom is used to overthrow the power that produced it.) The postmodern refusal of Marx's teleological vision of a society without power can push Marxism toward Nietzsche, but the differentiation of freedom from power and the emphasis on social conditions prevents a full slide into a Nietzschean affirmation of the will to power. Postmodernism noticeably retains the Marxist desire to find a way to mitigate power's sway and the Marxist reliance on transformed social arrangements to achieve that mitigation. But Marx makes power so strong—especially in the dominant ideology thesis—that freedom's chances often appear dim. Marx has a tendency to see social conditions not as a dialectical product of conflicting forces but rather as the pure produce of one force: the economic base or the ruling class. In this tendency to see a part as governing the structure of the whole, we find the origins of the stagnant, evil monolith that replaces both Hegel's benign totality and Marx's hopeful vision of communist society in so many postmodern texts.

* * *

Poststructuralism's enchantment with Nietzsche takes a rather peculiar direction. The acceptance of Nietzsche's extreme skepticism about traditional philosophical concepts such as substance, truth, and reason grounds ironist theory's robust assertions about the collapse of epistemology. That such assertions reintroduce a totalizing view suggests that poststructuralism wants to use Nietzsche's skeptical views but exhibits a strong ambivalence toward the extreme atomism that underlies those views. Nietzsche's atomism conflicts with the postmodern habit of linking all particulars to determinant contexts, or, more strongly stated, from poststructuralism's adherence to the Hegelian insistence (found in structuralism as well) that particulars have no significance in and of themselves but are constituted by their relationships within a whole. Nietzsche's atomism reenters postmodern theory, however, in its understanding of the politically desirable. Postmodernism inherits from Nietzsche an extreme version of negative freedom, the association of freedom with detachment from determinate wholes. As a result, contemporary critics are torn between their interpretive bias toward holistic, Hegelian explanations and their desire for an anarchistic, negative freedom. This conflict makes the freedom they desire appear impossible to achieve, a position that Nietzsche already foreshadows in his own insistence on the tragic character of life and the necessity of suffering.

Nietzsche's skepticism embraces both the externalist and the internalist perspectives that Hilary Putnam differentiates. His rejection of metaphysical realism is most succinctly stated in the assertion, "There are no facts, only interpretations,"[7] a phrase that has echoed throughout the work of the poststructuralists. If truth and knowledge depend on the exact correspondence of our representations (either mental images of words) with some actually existing state of affairs, then Nietzsche insists that truth and knowledge are impossible to achieve. "The world . . . has no meaning behind it, but countless meanings.—'Perspectivism.' It is our needs that interpret the world; our drives and their For and Against. Every drive is a kind of lust to rule; each one has its perspective that it would like to compel all the other drives to accept as a norm" (1968, 267). No single state of affairs emerges as the true object of knowledge; instead, there are as many worlds as there are perspectives. Nietzsche makes it clear that his "perspectivism" does not amount to subjective relativism, because the self is never a single perspective but composed of the multiplicity of its "drives." (Of course, Nietzsche's denial of the self's reality is not consistently maintained throughout his work; in several crucial instances, he writes as if the self is the most fundamental unit in his ontology.) The very notion of the "self" as referring meaningfully to some identifiable entity is an interpretation made from a certain perspective.

*   *   *

Gilles Deleuze condemns the notion that power is its own end in Nietzsche, expressing scorn from those who read Nietzsche "as if power were the ultimate aim of the will and also its essential motive" (1983, 80). Both Deleuze's interpretation of the will to power and that interpretation's consequences provide a good indication of the poststructuralist use of Nietzsche. (Cornel West calls Deleuze's *Nietzsche and Philosophy,* with "its provocative and often persuasive attack on Hegel and dialectics from a Nietzschean viewpoint," the "originary text of poststructuralism" [1988, 28].) For Deleuze, the will to power cannot be seeking for power, because such a search implies the situation presented in Hegel as the dialectic of the master and slave. Power necessarily involves a relation to others in which the master's power is *recognized* by those over whom he has that power; recognition necessarily requires representation, a capturing of power within a code that allows it to be signified and hence recognized. And, for Deleuze, trying the will to power to an established code for representing power necessarily domesticates it. "When we make power an object of representation we necessarily make it dependent upon the factor according to which a thing is represented or not, recognized or not. Now, only values which are already current, only accepted values, give criteria of recognition this way" (1983, 81). The will to power aims for the *"creation* of new values" (1983, 82), not for dominance over others or over the material world.

What is crucial in Deleuze's reading of the will to power is the emphasis that such creation can only occur outside of any established social order or any preexisting representational system; new values can only be created in solitude. Thus the will to power can be understood only within a celebration of difference. "The question which Nietzsche constantly repeats, 'what does a will want, what does this one or that one want?,' must not be understood as the search for a goal, a motive or an object for this will. What a will wants is to affirm its difference. In its essential relation with the 'other' a will makes its difference an object of affirmation. 'The pleasure of knowing oneself different,' the enjoyment of difference; this is the new, aggressive and elevated conceptual element that [Nietzsche] substitutes for the heavy notion of the dialectic" (1983, 9).[8] Where Hegel reconciles differences in the moment of *Aufhebung,* Nietzsche wills and affirms difference. And "Nietzsche announces that willing *liberates"* (1983, 84).

What Deleuze finds in Nietzsche, then, is an affirmation of difference that is connected to a distancing of self from social and representational systems. (Note that Deleuze here accepts without question the identification of the willing agent with the self, ignoring in this early text [published in France in 1962] Nietzsche's own intermittent deconstruction of the self. Later on, of course, Deleuze [in *Anti-Oedipus* most crucially] will deny the self's unity as an entity or agent, locating difference *within* as well as between the self and others.) The establishment of difference is associated with freedom and is contrasted to the oppressive consequences of the Hegelian dialectic's final revelation of identity. Where dialectic leads to unity, the will to power as affirmation of difference produces multiplicity. "The monism of the will to power is inseparable from a pluralist typology" (1983, 86), by which Deleuze means that Nietzsche's reduction of everything to the will to power (hence the theory's "monism") has the effect of generating a multiplicity of types, since each will to power will realize itself differently.[9]

* * *

The neat notion that postmodernism undercuts the Nietzschean move out of society also breaks down when we consider the essentialist uses to which poststructuralism has put Nietzsche. Deleuze's work provides a good example. He does not present difference and multiplicity as socially created, and he affirms difference as liberating in and of itself, no matter what the circumstances. Difference is an ontological fact in Deleuze's work, which can be recognized in this case as an acceptance of Nietzsche's ontological atomism. (An adoption of difference as the fundamental nature of the real does not of course commit one to an individualism of a modernist or existentialist sort. In *Anti-Oedipus,* Deleuze and Guattari insist on the differential nature of the self itself. But we should recognize that they take the multitudinous self as originary; the self only achieves a spurious and oppressive unity later on. And they understand the reaffirmation of the self's multiplicity as a key move toward freedom). Difference can only appear such a potent and desirable concept within a perspective that understands freedom negatively. And difference itself can only be understood negatively when some kind of step outside the Hegelian whole is imagined, because differences within the Hegelian whole are positive differences, recognized as positional articulations of the whole. In most postmodern interpretations, differences are only effects within a whole, effects that are recuperated when we explain how they were generated by that whole. Hence the atomistic emphasis on difference is only momentary, since interpretation leads back from the particulars to the systematic conditions of their production and significance. Even while adopting the Hegelian denial of atomism as its model of interpretation, poststructuralism adopts Nietzsche's atomism as its model for freedom.

Postmodernism finds in difference that principle of multiplicity, or irreducibility, that allows it to escape the totalizing visions it associates with necessity and unfreedom. What I want to emphasize is that this commitment to difference stems from a negative image of freedom. The need for the concept of difference often leads postmodern writers to abandon their usual reliance on historical contexts to declare difference a universal fact. Furthermore, postmodernism only half believes in the fact and efficacy of difference; it remains torn between its Hegelian and Nietzschean convictions, a fact dramatized by Deleuze's need to interpret Nietzsche entirely in terms of his rejection of Hegel. "There is no possible compromise between Hegel and Nietzsche" (1983, 195).

Postmodernism can never entirely embrace the chaos of difference. It continually oscillates between its identification of the necessities to which that play is answerable and more pleasant visions of liberation. In Nietzsche's case that oscillation is revealed in his continual undermining of the possibility of autonomy as he reinscribes the will within the dynamics of a will to power to which all are instinctively bound; or as he genealogically explains the generation of the circumstances within which the will must operate; or as he describes the fated confrontation of will with a world that always frustrates it and causes suffering; or as he denies the very notion of self and of "free will" that would allow the will to power to be associated with freedom. Postmodernism's anarchistic moment gains its very intensity from its coexistence with continued holistic theorizing about necessary conditions of human action and thought. Its particular oscillation between the monolithic and the pluralistic appears determined by its susceptibility to the logic of totalizing, Hegelian explanations, even while it yearns for a multiplicity that it associates with freedom. Politically, this combination yields a desire for a pluralistic society within a social order that can universally guarantee certain rights, freedoms, and economic goods. The conjunction of these seemingly contradictory (or at least problematically reconcilable) perspectives is best explained by postmodernism's complete adherence to a vision of negative freedom (even if it often believes such freedom to be unattainable). Nietzsche's work discredits for twentieth-century humanistic intellectuals the versions of positive liberty found in Hegel and Marx. Of course, Nietzsche did not achieve this feat alone, but he offers a version of negative liberty radical enough to release the concept from its guilt of association with bourgeois liberalism and thus to allow its becoming an orthodoxy precisely among those intellectuals who understand themselves as engaged in a battle to the death with liberal capitalism. As is by now clear, I believe that only a recommitment to positive freedom can actually provide an effective platform for the kinds of political transformation that humanistic intellectuals profess to seek.

Nietzsche's legacy to postmodernist theory, then, is his deeply ambiguous atomism, which embodies a radical desire for freedom (understood negatively) and provides a powerfully skeptical ontology in his battle against the truth value of human representational schemes, discourses of knowledge, and moral systems. Atomism's ambiguity resides in the fact that, pursued to its logical end, it must also undermine Nietzsche's own truth claims and his own image of freedom. In the chaotic world of atomistic impulses, percepts, and experiences, all explanatory schemes must fail because random chaos is the only reality, and all freedom must be impossible because there can be no agent who directs or chooses the movements of will. Postmodern Nietzscheans, no more than Nietzsche himself, cannot hope to adhere to such an extreme atomism consistently; rather, they will repeat in their own way Nietzsche's movement between truth claims and the deconstruction of truth, between the aspiration toward negative freedom and the deconstruction of negative freedom's possibility. As a result, like Nietzsche, postmodern theory often finds itself in the position of affirming (and desiring) something that it also declares impossible to attain.

Notes

1. Foucault's assertion, in *The Archaeology of Knowledge,* (New York: Pantheon, 1972) that "it is not possible for us to describe our own archive, since it is from within these rules that we speak" (130) offers but one instance of the widespread notion that it is easier to decipher the determinants of others' behavior than the determinants of one's own.

2. Deleuze's lack of patience with Kant is shared by many postmodern writers, although not by Lyotard. For Deleuze, Kant "seems to have confused the positivity of critique with a humble recognition of the rights of the criticised. There has never been a more conciliatory or respectful total critique. The opposition between project and results . . . is easily explained. Kant merely pushed a very old conception of critique to the limit, a conception which saw critique as a force which should be brought to bear on all claims to knowledge and truth, but not on knowledge and truth themselves; a force which should be brought to bear on all claims to morality, but not on

morality itself. Thus total critique turns into the politics of compromise: even before the battle the spheres of influence have already been shared out"—Gilles Deleuze and Felix Gwattari. *Anti-Oedipus* (Minneapolis: University of Minnesota Press, 1983), 89.

3. See Iris Marion Young. "The Ideal of Community and the Politics of Difference." In Linda J. Nicholson, ed. *Feminism/Postmodernism* (New York: Routledge, 1990) for a typical postmodernism insistence that ideals of community "generate exclusions" that conflict with the desirable "openness to unassimilated otherness" which characterizes "a politics of difference" (301). Yet when she turns to describing the "norm for the unoppressive city" (301) that could underwrite the politics of difference, Young unwittingly, but I think inevitably, begins from the fact that even large, anonymous modern cities retain "a continuing sense of national or ethnic identity with millions of other people" (317).

4. Nicholas Abercrombie *et. al., The Dominant Ideology Thesis.* (London: George Allen & Unwin, 1980) offer what I think is an absolutely correct and devastating attack on "the dominant ideology thesis," arguing that the constraints of the economic and social facts of life keep people going about their daily business, not some intellectual consent that has been manufactured by the ideological forces of the ruling class.

5. I am summarizing here the complex, and compelling, argument made in Alvin W. Gouldner. *The Future of Intellectuals and The Rise of the New Class* (New York: Oxford, 1982), a work that fully justifies Gouldner's description of himself as an "outlaw Marxist."

6. I discuss Foucault's notion of productive power more fully in the next chapter. His lack of interest in the specific institutional frameworks in which power confrontations take place is illustrated in the interview titled "Space, Knowledge, and Power" in *The Foucault Reader* (New York: Pantheon, 1984), 239–56: "I do not think that it is possible to say that one thing is of the order of 'liberation' and another is of the order of 'oppression.' . . . I do not think that there is anything that is functionally—by its very nature—absolutely liberating. Liberty is a *practice*. So there may, in fact, always be a certain number of projects whose aim is to modify some constraints, to loosen, or even to break them, but none of these projects can, simply by its nature, assure that people will have liberty automatically, that it will be established by the project itself. The liberty of men is never assured by the institutions and laws that are intended to guarantee them. This is why almost all of these laws and institutions are quite capable of being turned around. Not because they are ambiguous, but simply because 'liberty' is what must be exercised" (245). My point is not that liberty can be guaranteed, or that liberty is not something that must be exercised, but that there is still a lot to be said about the differing possibilities for liberty being exercised in different social conditions. To claim that "almost all" laws and institutions leave some space for abuse does not necessarily mean we

cannot distinguish between laws that provide wider opportunities for inequity than others. The Marxist, I am arguing, will place more emphasis than Foucault does on the effect that different social arrangements can make on the possibility of *practicing* liberty.

7. See Arthur Danto, *Nietzsche as Philosopher* (New York: Columbia University Press, 1980), 76 and Friedrich Nietzsche, *The Will to Power* (New York: Vintage Books, 1968), 267.

8. The passages from Nietzsche that Deleuze quotes here can be found in *Beyond Good and Evil* (Hammondsworth, Eng.: Penguin Books, 1973), 260.

9. The connection of Nietzsche's version of negative freedom to what I have been calling Kierkegaardian irony, as well as its connection to the fantasy of a private language, is made absolutely clear in Charles Altieri's excellent essay on *Ecce Homo*. ("*Ecce Homo*: Narcissism, Power, Pathos, and the Status of Autobiographical Representations," in *Why Nietzsche Now?* Bloomington: Indiana University Press, 1985). Altieri is interested in how the very desire for self-creation and the subsequent need to stage that self-creation for others undermine the claims of the self-creator to be utterly independent of social norms and social usages.

Structure, Sign, and Play in the Discourse of the Human Sciences[1]

Jacques Derrida

Perhaps something has occurred in the history of the concept of structure that could be called an "event," if this loaded word did not entail a meaning which it is precisely the function of structural—or structuralist—thought to reduce or to suspect. But let me use the term "event" anyway, employing it with caution and as if in quotation marks. In this sense, this event will have the exterior form of a *rupture* and a *redoubling*.

It would be easy enough to show that the concept of structure and even the word "structure" itself are as old as the *epistème*—that is to say, as old as western science and western philosophy—and that their roots thrust deep into the soil of ordinary language, into whose deepest recesses the *epistème* plunges to gather them together once more, making them part of itself in a metaphorical displacement. Nevertheless, up until the event which I wish to mark out and define, structure—or rather the structurality of struc-

Jacques Derrida, "Structure, Sign and Play in the Discourse of the Human Sciences," in *The Languages of Criticism and the Sciences of Man: The Structuralist Controversy* eds. Richard Macksey and Eugenio Donato. pp. 247–265 Copyright 1970 The Johns Hopkins University Press. Reprinted by permission.

ture—although it has always been involved, has always been neutralized or reduced, and this by a process of giving it a center or
referring it to a point of presence, a fixed origin. The function of this
center was not only to orient, balance, and organize the structure—
one cannot in fact conceive of an unorganized structure—but above
all to make sure that the organizing principle of the structure would
limit what we might call the *freeplay* of the structure. No doubt that
by orienting and organizing the coherence of the system, the center
of a structure permits the freeplay of its elements inside the total
form. And even today the notion of a structure lacking any center
represents the unthinkable itself.

Nevertheless, the center also closes off the freeplay it opens up
and makes possible. *Qua* center, it is the point at which the substitution of contents, elements, or terms is no longer possible. At the
center, the permutation or the transformation of elements (which
may of course be structures enclosed within a structure) is forbidden. At least this permutation has always remained *interdicted*[2] (I
use this word deliberately). Thus it has always been thought that
the center, which is by definition unique, constituted that very
thing within a structure which governs the structure, while escaping structurality. This is why classical thought concerning structure
could say that the center is, paradoxically, *within* the structure and
outside it. The center is at the center of the totality, and yet, since
the center does not belong to the totality (is not part of the totality),
the totality *has its center elsewhere*. The center is not the center. The
concept of centered structure—although it represents coherence itself, the condition of the *epistème* as philosophy or science—is contradictorily coherent. And, as always, coherence in contradiction
expresses the force of a desire. The concept of centered structure is
in fact the concept of a freeplay based on a fundamental ground, a
freeplay which is constituted upon a fundamental immobility and a
reassuring certitude, which is itself beyond the reach of the
freeplay. With this certitude anxiety can be mastered, for anxiety is
invariably the result of a certain mode of being implicated in the
game, of being caught by the game, of being as it were from the very
beginning at stake in the game.[3] From the basis of what we therefore call the center (and which, because it can be either inside or
outside, is as readily called the origin as the end, as readily *archè* as
telos), the repetitions, the substitutions, the transformations, and
the permutations are always *taken* from a history of meaning
[*sens*]—that is, a history, period—whose origin may always be
revealed or whose end may always be anticipated in the form of
presence. This is why one could perhaps say that the movement

of any archeology, like that of any eschatology, is an accomplice of this reduction of the structurality of structure and always attempts to conceive of structure from the basis of a full presence which is out of play.

If this is so, the whole history of the concept of structure, before the rupture I spoke of, must be thought of as a series of substitutions of center for center, as a linked chain of determinations of the center. Successively, and in a regulated fashion, the center receives different forms or names. The history of metaphysics, like the history of the West, is the history of these metaphors and metonymies. Its matrix— if you will pardon me for demonstrating so little and for being so elliptical in order to bring me more quickly to my principal theme—is the determination of being as *presence* in all the senses of this word. It would be possible to show that all the names related to fundamentals, to principles, or to the center have always designated the constant of a presence—*eidos, archè, telos, energeia, ousia* (essence, existence, substance, subject) *aletheia,* transcendentality, consciousness, or conscience, God, man, and so forth.

The event I called a rupture, the disruption I alluded to at the beginning of this paper, would presumably have come about when the structurality of structure had to begin to be thought, that is to say, repeated, and this is why I said that this disruption was repetition in all of the senses of this word. From then on it became necessary to think the law which governed, as it were, the desire for the center in the constitution of structure and the process of signification prescribing its displacements and its substitutions for this law of the central presence—but a central presence which was never itself, which has always already been transported outside itself in its surrogate. The surrogate does not substitute itself for anything which has somehow pre-existed it. From then on it was probably necessary to begin to think that there was no center, that the center would not be thought in the form of a being-present, that the center had no natural locus, that it was not a fixed locus but a function, a sort of non-locus in which an infinite number of sign-substitutions came into play. This moment was that in which language invaded the universal problematic; that in which, in the absence of a center or origin, everything became discourse—provided we can agree on this word—that is to say, when everything became a system where the central signified, the original or transcendental signified, is never absolutely present outside a system of differences. The absence of the transcendental signified extends the domain and the interplay of signification *ad infinitum.*

Where and how does this decentering, this notion of the structurality of structure, occur? It would be somewhat naïve to refer to an event, a doctrine, or an author in order to designate this occurrence. It is no doubt part of the totality of an era, our own, but still it has already begun to proclaim itself and begun to *work*. Nevertheless, if I wished to give some sort of indication by choosing one or two "names," and by recalling those authors in whose discourses this occurrence has most nearly maintained its most radical formulation, I would probably cite the Nietschean critique of metaphysics, the critique of the concepts of being and truth, for which were substituted the concepts of play, interpretation, and sign (sign without truth present); the Freudian critique or self-presence, that is, the critique of consciousness, of the subject, of self-identity and of self-proximity or self-possession; and, more radically, the Heideggerean destruction of metaphysics, of onto-theology, of the determination of being as presence. But all these destructive discourses and all their analogues are trapped in a sort of circle. This circle is unique. It describes the form of the relationship between the history of metaphysics and the destruction of the history of metaphysics. *There is no sense* in doing without the concepts of metaphysics in order to attack metaphysics. We have no language—no syntax and no lexicon—which is alien to this history; we cannot utter a single destructive proposition which has not already slipped into the form, the logic, and the implicit postulations of precisely what it seeks to contest. To pick out one example from many: the metaphysics of presence is attacked with the help of the concept of the *sign*. But from the moment anyone wishes this to show, as I suggested a moment ago, that there is no transcendental or privileged signified and that the domain or the interplay of signification has, henceforth, no limit, he ought to extend his refusal to the concept and to the word sign itself—which is precisely what cannot be done. For the signification "sign" has always been comprehended and determined, in its sense, as sign-of, signifier referring to a signified, signifier different from its signified. If one erases the radical difference between signifier and signified, it is the word signifier itself which ought to be abandoned as a metaphysical concept. When Lèvi-Strauss says in the preface to *The Raw and the Cooked*[4] that he has "sought to transcend the opposition between the sensible and the intelligible by placing [himself] from the very beginning at the level of signs," the necessity, the force, and the legitimacy of his act cannot make us forget that the concept of the sign cannot in itself surpass or bypass this opposition between the sensible and the intelligible. The concept of the sign is determined by this opposition:

through and throughout the totality of its history and by its system. But we cannot do without the concept of the sign, we cannot give up this metaphysical complicity without also giving up the critique we are directing against this complicity, without the risk of erasing difference [altogether] in the self-identity of a signified reducing into itself its signifier, or, what amounts to the same thing, simply expelling it outside itself. For there are two heterogenous ways of erasing the difference between the signifier and the signified: one, the classic way, consists in reducing or deriving the signifier, that is to say, ultimately in *submitting* the sign to thought; the other, the one we are using here against the first one, consists in putting into question the system in which the preceding reduction functioned: first and foremost, the opposition between the sensible and the intelligible. The *paradox* is that the metaphysical reduction of the sign needed the opposition it was reducing. The opposition is part of the system, along with the reduction. And what I am saying here about the sign can be extended to all the concepts and all the sentences of metaphysics, in particular to the discourse on "structure." But there are many ways of being caught in this circle. They are all more or less naïve, more or less empirical, more or less systematic, more or less close to the formulation or even to the formalization of this circle. It is these differences which explain the multiplicity of destructive discourses and the disagreement between those who make them. It was within concepts inherited from metaphysics that Nietzsche, Freud, and Heidegger worked, for example. Since these concepts are not elements or atoms and since they are taken from a syntax and a system, every particular borrowing drags along with it the whole of metaphysics. This is what allows these destroyers to destroy each other reciprocally—for example, Heidegger considering Nietzsche, with as much lucidity and rigor as bad faith and misconstruction, as the last metaphysician, the last "Platonist." One could do the same for Heidegger himself, for Freud, or for a number of others. And today no exercise is more widespread.

What is the relevance of this formal schéma when we turn to what are called the "human sciences"? One of them perhaps occupies a privileged place—ethnology. One can in fact assume that ethnology could have been born as a science only at the moment when a de-centering had come about: at the moment when European culture—and, in consequence, the history of metaphysics and of its concepts—had been *dislocated,* driven from its locus, and forced to stop considering itself as the culture of reference. This moment is not first and foremost a moment of philosophical or scientific discourse, it is also a moment which is political, economic, technical, and so forth. One can say in total assurance that there is nothing fortuitous about the fact that the critique of ethnocentrism—the very condition of ethnology—should be systematically and historically contemporaneous with the destruction of the history of metaphysics. Both belong to a single and same era.

Ethnology—like any science—comes about within the element of discourse. And it is primarily a European science employing traditional concepts, however much of it may struggle against them. Consequently, whether he wants to or not—and this does not depend on a decision on his part—the ethnologist accepts into his discourse the premises of ethnocentrism at the very moment when he is employed in denouncing them. This necessity is irreducible; it is not a historical contingency. We ought to consider very carefully all its implications. But if nobody can escape this necessity, and if no one is therefore responsible for giving in to it, however little, this does not mean that all the ways of giving in to it are of an equal pertinence. The quality and the fecundity of a discourse are perhaps measured by the critical rigor with which this relationship to the history of metaphysics and to inherited concepts is thought. Here it is a question of a critical relationship to the language of the human sciences and a question of a critical responsibility of the discourse. It is a question of putting expressly and systematically the problem of the status of a discourse which borrows from a heritage the resources necessary for the deconstruction of that heritage itself. A problem of *economy* and *strategy*.

If I now go on to employ an examination of the texts of Lévi-Strauss as an example, it is not only because of the privilege accorded to ethnology among the human sciences, nor yet because the thought of Lévi-Strauss weighs heavily on the contemporary theoretical situation. It is above all because a certain choice has made itself evident in the work of Lévi-Strauss and because a certain doctrine has been elaborated there, and precisely in a *more or less explicit manner,* in relation to this critique of language and to this critical language in the human sciences.

In order to follow this movement in the text of Lévi-Strauss, let me choose as one guiding thread among others the opposition between nature and culture. In spite of all its rejuvenations and its disguises, this opposition is congenital to philosophy. It is even older than Plato. It is at least as old as the Sophists. Since the statement of the opposition—*physis/nomos, physis/technè*—it has been passed on to us by a whole historical chain which opposes "nature" to the law, to education, to art, to technics—and also to liberty, to the arbitrary, to history, to society, to the mind, and so on. From the beginnings of his quest and from his first book, *The Elementary Structures of Kinship,*[5] Lévi-Strauss has felt at one and the same time the necessity of utilizing this opposition and the impossibility of making it acceptable. In the *Elementary Structures,* he begins from this axiom or definition: that belongs to nature which is *universal* and spontaneous, not depending on any particular culture or on any determinate norm. That belongs to culture, on the other hand, which depends on a system of *norms* regulating society and is therefore capable of *varying* from one social structure to another. These two definitions are of the traditional type. But, in the very first pages of the *Elementary Structures,* Lévi-Strauss, who has begun to give these concepts an acceptable standing, encounters what he calls a *scandal,* that is to say, something which no longer tolerates the nature/culture opposition he has accepted and which seems to require *at one and the same time* the predicates of nature and those of culture. This scandal is the *incest-prohibition.* The incest-prohibition is universal; in this sense one could call it natural. But it is also a prohibition, a system of norms and interdicts; in this sense one could call it cultural.

> Let us assume therefore that everything universal in man derives from the order of nature and is characterized by spontaneity, that everything which is subject to a norm belongs to culture and presents the attributes of the relative and the particular. We then find ourselves confronted by a fact, or rather an ensemble of facts, which, in the light of the preceding definitions, is not far from appearing as a scandal: the prohibition of incest presents without the least equivocation, and indissolubly linked together, the two characteristics in which we recognized the contradictory attributes of two exclusive orders. The prohibition of incest constitutes a rule, but a rule, alone of all the social rules, which possesses at the same time a universal character (9).

Obviously there is no scandal except in the *interior* of a system of concepts sanctioning the difference between nature and culture. In beginning his work with the *factum* of the incest-prohibition, Lévi-Strauss thus puts himself in a position entailing that this difference, which has always been assumed to be self-evident, becomes obliterated or disputed. For, from the moment that the incest-prohibition can no longer be conceived within the nature/culture opposition, it can no longer be said that it is a scandalous fact, a nucleus of opacity within a network of transparent significations.

The incest-prohibition is no longer scandal one meets with or comes up against in the domain of traditional concepts; it is something which escapes these concepts and certainly precedes them—probably as the condition of their possibility. It could perhaps be said that the whole of philosophical conceptualization, systematically relating itself to the nature/culture opposition, is designed to leave in the domain of the unthinkable the very thing that makes this conceptualization possible: the origin of the prohibition of incest.

I have dealt too cursorily with this example, only one among so many others, but the example nevertheless reveals that language bears within itself the necessity of its own critique. This critique may be undertaken along two tracks, in two "manners." Once the limit of nature/culture opposition makes itself felt, one might want to question systematically and rigorously the history of these concepts. This is a first action. Such a systematic and historic questioning would be neither a philological nor a philosophical action in the classic sense of these words. Concerning oneself with the founding concepts of the whole history of philosophy, de-constituting them, is not to undertake the task of the philologist or of the classic historian of philosophy. In spite of appearances, it is probably the most daring way of making the beginnings of a step outside of philosophy. The step "outside philosophy" is much more difficult to conceive than is generally imagined by those who think they made it long ago with cavalier ease, and who are in general swallowed up in metaphysics by the whole body of the discourse that they claim to have disengaged from it.

In order to avoid the possibly sterilizing effect of the first way, the other choice—which I feel corresponds more nearly to the way chosen by Lévi-Strauss—consists in conserving in the field of empirical discovery all these old concepts, while at the same time exposing here and there their limits, treating them as tools which can still be of use. No longer is any truth-value attributed to them; there is a readiness to abandon them if necessary if other instruments should appear more useful. In the meantime, their relative efficacy is exploited, and they are employed to destroy the old machinery to which they belong and of which they themselves are pieces. Thus it is that the language of the human sciences criticizes *itself*. Lévi-Strauss thinks that in this way he can separate *method* from *truth,* the instruments of the method and the objective significations aimed at by it. One could almost say that this is the primary affirmation of Lévi-Strauss; in any event, the first words of the *Elementary Structures* are: "One begins to understand that the distinction between state of nature and state of society (we would be more apt to say today: state of nature and state of culture), while lacking any acceptable historical signification, presents a value which fully justifies its use by modern sociology: its value as a methodological instrument."

Lévi-Strauss will always remain faithful to this double intention: to preserve as an instrument that whose truth-value he criticizes.

On the one hand, he will continue in effect to contest the value of the nature/culture opposition. More than thirteen years after the *Elementary Structures, The Savage Mind*[8] faithfully echoes the text I have just quoted: "The opposition between nature and culture which I have previously insisted on seems today to offer value which is above all methodological." And this methodological value is not affected by its "ontological" non-value (as could be said, if this notion were not suspect here): "It would not be enough to have absorbed particular humanities into a genera humanity; this first enterprise prepares the way for others . . . which belong to the natural and exact sciences: to reintegrate culture into nature, and finally, to reintegrate life into the totality of its physiochemical conditions" (327).

On the other hand, still in *The Savage Mind,* he presents as what he calls *bricolage*[7] which might be called the discourse of this method. The *bricoleur,* says Lévi-Strauss, is someone who uses "the means at hand," that is, the instruments he finds at his disposition around him, those which are already there, which had not been especially conceived with an eye to the operation for which they are to be used and to which one tries by trial and error to adapt them, not hesitating to change them whenever it appears necessary, or to try several of them at once, even if their form and their origin are heterogenous—and so forth. There is therefore a critique of language in the form of *bricolage,* and it has even been possible to say that *bricolage* is the critical language itself. I am thinking in particular of the article by G. Genette, "Structuralisme et Critique littéraire," published in homage to Lévi-Strauss in a special issue of *L'Arc* (no. 26, 1965), where it is stated that the analysis of *bricolage* could "be applied almost word for word" to criticism, and especially to "literary criticism."[8]

If one calls *bricolage* the necessity of borrowing one's concepts from the text of a heritage which is more or less coherent or ruined, it must be said that every discourse is *bricoleur.* The engineer, whom Lévi-Strauss opposes to the *bricoleur,* should be the one to construct the totality of his language, syntax, and lexicon. In this sense the engineer is a myth. A subject who would supposedly be the absolute origin of his own discourse and would supposedly construct it "out of nothing," "out of whole cloth," would be the creator of the *verbe*, the *verbe* itself. The notion of the engineer who had supposedly broken with all forms of *bricolage* is therefore a theological idea; and since Lévi-Strauss tells us elsewhere that *bricolage* is mythopoetic, the odds are that the engineer is a myth produced by the *bricoleur*. From the moment that we cease to believe in such an engineer and in a discourse breaking with the received historical discourse, as soon as it is admitted that every finite discourse is bound by a certain *bricolage*, and that the engineer and the scientist are also species of *bricoleurs* then the very idea of *bricolage* is menaced and the difference in which it took on its meaning decomposes.

This brings out the second thread which might guide us in what is being unraveled here.

Lévi-Strauss describes *bricolage* not only as an intellectual activity but also as a mythopoetical activity. One reads in *The Savage Mind*, "Like *bricolage* on the technical level, mythical reflection can attain brilliant and unforeseen results on the intellectual level. Reciprocally, the mythopoetical character of *bricolage* has often been noted" (26).

But the remarkable endeavor of Lévi-Strauss is not simply to put forward, notably in the most recent of his investigations, a structural science or knowledge of myths and of mythological activity. His endeavor also appears—I would say almost from the first— in the status which he accords to his own discourse, on myths, to what he calls his "mythologicals." It is here that his discourse on the myth reflects on itself and criticizes itself. And this moment, this critical period, is evidently of concern to all the languages which share the field of the human sciences. What does Lévi-Strauss say of his "mythologicals"? It is here that we rediscover the mythopoetical virtue (power) of *bricolage*. In effect, what appears most fascinating in this critical search for a new status of the discourse is the stated abandonment of all reference to a *center*, to a *subject*, to a privileged *reference*, to an origin, or to an absolute *archè*. The theme of this decentering could be followed throughout the "Overture" to his last book, *The Raw and the Cooked*. I shall simply remark on a few key points.

1) From the very start, Lévi-Strauss recognizes that the Bororo myth which he employs in the book as the "reference-myth" does not merit this name and this treatment. The name is specious and the use of the myth improper. This myth deserves no more than any other its referential privilege:

In fact the Bororo myth which will from now on be designated by the name *reference-myth* is, as I shall try to show, nothing other than a more or less forced transformation of other myths originating either in the same society or in societies more or less far removed. It would therefore have been legitimate to choose as my point of departure any representative of the group whatsoever. From this point of view, the interest of the reference-myth does not depend on its typical character, but rather on its irregular position in the midst of a group (10).

2) There is no unity or absolute source of the myth. The focus or the source of the myth are always shadows and virtualities which are elusive, unactualizable, and nonexistent in the first place. Everything begins with the structure, the configuration, the relationship. The discourse on this acentric structure, the myth, that is, cannot itself have an absolute subject or an absolute center. In order not to short change the form and the movement of the myth, that violence which consists in centering a language which is describing an acentric structure must be avoided. In this context, therefore it is necessary to forego scientific or philosophical discourse, to renounce the *epistèmè* which absolutely requires, which is the absolute requirement that we go back to the source, to the center, to the founding basis, to the principle, and so on. In opposition to *epistèmic* discourse, structural discourse on myths—*mythological* discourse— must itself be mythomorphic. It must have the form of that of which it speaks. This is what Lévi-Strauss says in *The Raw and the Cooked,* from which I would now like to quote a long and remarkable passage:

In effect the study of myths poses a methodological problem by the fact that it cannot conform to the Cartesian principle of dividing the difficulty into as many parts as are necessary to resolve. There exists no veritable end or term to mythical analysis, no secret unity which could be grasped at the end of the work of decomposition. The themes duplicate themselves to infinity. When we think we have disentangled them from each other and can hold them separate, it is only to realize that they are joining together again, in response to the attraction of unforeseen affinities. In consequence, the unity of the myth is only tendential and projective; it never reflects a state or a moment of the myth. An imaginary phenomenon implied by the endeavor to interpret, its role is to give a synthetic form to the myth and to impede its dissolution into the confusion of contraries. It could therefore be said that the science or knowledge of myths is an *anaclastic,* taking this ancient term in the widest sense authorized by its etymology, a science which admits into its definition the study of the reflected rays along with that of the broken ones. But, unlike philosophical reflection, which claims to go all the way back to its source, the reflections in question here concern rays without any other than a virtual focus.... In wanting to imitate the spontaneous movement of mythical thought, my enterprise, itself too brief and too long, has had to yield to its demands and respect its rhythm. Thus is this book, on myths itself and in its own way, a myth.

This statement is repeated a little farther on (20): "Since myths themselves rest on second-order codes (the first-order codes being those in which language consists), this book thus offers the rough draft of a third-order code, destined to insure the reciprocal possibility of translation of several myths. This is why it would not be wrong to consider it a myth: the myth of mythology, as it were." It is by this absence of any real and fixed center of the mythical or mythological discourse that the musical model chosen by Lévi-Strauss for the composition of his book is apparently justified. The absence of a center is here the absence of a subject and the absence of an author: "The myth and the musical work thus appear as orchestra conductors whose listeners are the silent performers. If it be asked where the real focus of the work is to be found, it must be replied that its determination is impossible. Music and mythology bring man face to face with virtual objects whose shadow alone is actual.... Myths have no authors" (25).

Thus it is at this point that ethnographic *bricolage* deliberately assumes its mythopoetic function. But by the same token, this function makes the philosophical or epistemological requirement of a center appear as mythological, that is to say, as a historical illusion.

Nevertheless, even if one yields to the necessity of what Lévi-Strauss has done, one cannot ignore its risks. If the mythological is mythomorphic, are all discourses on myths equivalent? Shall we have to abandon any epistemological requirement which permits us to distinguish between several qualities of discourse on the myth? A classic question, but inevitable. We cannot reply—and I do not believe Lévi-Strauss replies to it—as long as the problem of the relationships between the philosopheme or the theorem, on the one hand, and the mytheme or the mythopoem (e), on the other, has not been expressly posed. This is no small problem. For lack of expressly posing this problem, we condemn ourselves to transforming the claimed transgression of philosophy into an unperceived fault in the interior of the philosophical field. Empiricism would be the genus of which these faults would always be the species. Trans-philosophical concepts would be transformed into philosophical naïvetés. One could give many examples to demonstrate this risk: the concepts of sign, history, truth, and so forth. What I want to emphasize is simply that the passage beyond philosophy does not consist in turning the page of philosophy (which usually comes down to philosophizing badly), but in continuing to read philosophers *in a certain way.* The risk I am speaking of is always assumed by Lévi-Strauss and it is the very price of his endeavor. I have said that empiricism is the matrix of all the faults menacing a discourse which continues, as with Lévi-Strauss in particular, to elect to be scientific. If we wanted to pose the problem of empiricism and *bricolage* in depth, we would probably end up very quickly with a number of propositions absolutely contradictory in relation to the status of discourse in structural ethnography. On the one hand, structuralism justly claims to be the critique of empiricism. But at the same time there is not a single book or study by Lévi-Strauss which does not offer itself as an empirical essay which can always be completed or invalidated by new information. The structural schemata are always proposed as hypotheses resulting from a finite quantity of information and which are subjected to the proof of experience. Numerous texts could be used to demonstrate this double postulation. Let us turn once again to the "Overture" of *The Raw and the Cooked,* where it seems clear that if this postulation is double, it is because it is a question here of a language on language:

> Critics who might take me to task for not having begun by making an exhaustive inventory of South American myths before analyzing them would be making a serious mistake about the nature and the role of these documents. The totality of the myths of a people is of the order of the discourse. Provided that this people does not become physically or morally extinct, this totality is never closed. Such a criticism would therefore be equivalent to reproaching a linguist with writing the grammar of a language without having recorded the totality of the words which have been uttered since that language came into existence and without knowing the verbal exchanges which will take place as long as the language continues to exist.

Experience proves that an absurdly small number of sentences . . . allows the linguist to elaborate a grammar of the language he is studying. And even a partial grammar or an outline of a grammar represents valuable acquisitions in the case of unknown languages. Syntax does not wait until it has been possible to enumerate a theoretically unlimited series of events before becoming manifest, because syntax consists in the body of rules which presides over the generation of these events. And it is precisely a syntax of South American mythology that I wanted to outline. Should new texts appear to enrich the mythical discourse, then this will provide an opportunity to check or modify the way in which certain grammatical laws have been formulated, an opportunity to discard certain of them and an opportunity to discover new ones. But in no instance can the requirement of a total mythical discourse be raised as an objection. For we have just seen that such a requirement has no meaning (15–16).

Totalization is therefore defined at one time as *useless,* at another time as *impossible.* This is no doubt the result of the fact that there are two ways of conceiving the limit of totalization. And I assert once again that these two determinations coexist implicitly in the discourses of Lévi-Strauss. Totalization can be judged impossible in the classical style: one then refers to the empirical endeavor of a subject or of a finite discourse in a vain and breathless quest of an infinite richness which it can never master. There is too much, more than one can say. But nontotalization can also be determined in another way: not from the standpoint of the concept of finitude as assigning us to an empirical view, but from the standpoint of the concept of *freeplay.* If totalization no longer has any meaning, it is not because the infinity of a field cannot be covered by a finite glance or a finite discourse, but because the nature of the field— that is, language and a finite language—excludes totalization. This field is in fact that of *freeplay,* that is to say, a field of infinite substitutions in the closure of a finite ensemble. This field permits these infinite substitutions only because it is finite, that is to say, because instead of being an inexhaustible field, as in the classical hypothesis, instead of being too large, there is something missing from it: a center which arrests and founds the freeplay of substitutions. One could say—rigorously using that word whose scandalous signification is always obliterated in French—that this movement of the freeplay, permitted by the lack, the absence of a center or origin, is the movement of *supplementarity.* One cannot determine the center, the sign which *supplements*[9] it, which takes its place in its absence—because this sign adds itself, occurs in addition, over and above, comes as a *supplement*.[10] The movement of signification adds something, which results in the fact that there is always more, but this addition is a floating one because it comes to perform a vicarious function, to supplement a lack on the part of the signified. Although Lévi-Strauss in his use of the word "supplementary" never emphasizes as I am doing here the two directions of meaning which are so strangely compounded within it, it is not by chance that he uses this word twice in his "Introduction to the Work of Marcel Mauss,"[11] at the point where he is speaking of the "superabundance of signifier, in relation to the signifieds to which this superabundance can refer":

> In his endeavor to understand the world, man therefore always has at his disposition a surplus of signification (which he portions out amongst things according to the laws of symbolic thought—which it is the task of ethnologists and linguists to study). This distribution of a *supplementary* allowance [*ration supplémentaire*]—if it is permissible to put it that way—is absolutely necessary in order that on the whole the available signifier and the signified it aims at may remain in the relationship of complementarity which is the very condition of the use of symbolic thought (xlix).

(It could no doubt be demonstrated that this *ration supplémentaire* of signification is the origin of the *ratio* itself.) The word reappears a little farther on, after Lévi-Strauss has mentioned "this floating signifier, which is the servitude of all finite thought":

> In other words—and taking as our guide Mauss's precept that all social phenomena can be assimilated to language—we see in *mana, Wakau, oranda* and other notions of the same type, the conscious expression of a semantic function, whose role it is to permit symbolic thought to operate in spite of the contradiction which is proper to it. In this way are explained the apparently insoluble antinomies attached to this notion. . . . At one and the same time force and action, quality and state, substantive and verb; abstract and concrete, omnipresent and localized—*mana* is in effect all these things. But it is not precisely because it is none of these things that *mana* is a simple form, or more exactly, a symbol in the pure state, and therefore capable of becoming charged with any sort of symbolic content whatever? In the system of symbols constituted by all cosmologies, *mana* would simply be a *valeur symbolique*

zéro, that is to say, a sign marking the necessity of a symbolic content *supplementary* [my italics] to that with which the signified is already loaded, but which can take on any value required, provided only that this value still remains part of the available reserve and is not, as phonologists put it, a group-term.

Lévi-Strauss adds the note:

> Linguists have already been led to formulate hypotheses of this type. For example: "A zero phoneme is opposed to all the other phonemes in French in that it entails no differential characters and no constant phonetic value. On the contrary, the proper function of the zero phoneme is to be opposed to phoneme absence." (R. Jakobson and J. Lutz, "Notes on the French Phonemic Pattern," *Word,* vol. 5, no. 2 [August 1949], p. 155). Similarly, if we schematize the conception I am proposing here, it could almost be said that the function of notions like *mana* is to be opposed to the absence of signification, without entailing by itself any particular signification (1 and note).

The *superabundance* of the signifier, its *supplementary* character, is thus the result of a finitude, that is to say, the result of a lack which must be *supplemented.*

It can now be understood why the concept of freeplay is important in Lévi-Strauss. His references to all sorts of games, notably to roulette, are very frequent, especially in his *Conversations,*[12] in *Race and History,*[13] and in *The Savage Mind.* This reference to the game or freeplay is always caught up in a tension.

It is in tension with history, first of all. This is a classical problem, objections to which are now well worn or used up. I shall simply indicate what seems to me the formality of the problem: by reducing history, Lévi-Strauss has treated as it deserves a concept which has always been in complicity with a teleological and eschatological metaphysics, in other words, paradoxically, in complicity with that philosophy of presence to which it was believed history could be opposed. The thematic of historicity, although it seems to be a somewhat late arrival in philosophy, has always been required by the determination of being as presence. With or without etymology, and in spite of the classic antagonism which opposes these significations throughout all of classical thought, it could be shown that the concept of *epistèmè* has always called forth that of *historia,* if history is always the unity of a becoming, as tradition of truth or development of science or knowledge oriented toward the appropriation of truth in presence and self-presence, toward knowledge in consciousness-of-self.[14] History has always been conceived as the movement of a resumption of history, a diversion between two presences. But if it is legitimate to suspect this concept of history, there is a risk, if it is reduced without an express statement of the problem I am indicating here, of falling back into an anhistoricism of a classical type, that is to say, in a determinate moment of the history of metaphysics. Such is the algebraic formality of the problem as I see it. More concretely, in the work of Lévi-Strauss it must be recognized that the respect for structurality, for the internal originality of the structure, compels a neutralization of time and history. For example, the appearance of a new structure, of an original system, always comes about—and this is the very condition of its structural specificity—by a rupture with its past, its origin, and its cause. One can therefore describe what is peculiar to the structural organization only by not taking into account, in the very moment of this description, its past conditions: by failing to pose the problem of the passage from one structure to another, by putting history into parentheses. In this "structuralist" moment, the concepts of chance and discontinuity are indispensable. And Lévi-Strauss does in fact often appeal to them as he does, for instance, for that structure of structures, language, of which he says in the "Introduction to the Work of Marcel Mauss" that it "could only have been born in one fell swoop":

> Whatever may have been the moment and the circumstances of its appearance in the scale of animal life, language could only have been born in one fell swoop. Things could not have set about signifying progressively. Following a transformation the study of which is not the concern of the social sciences, but rather of biology and psychology, a crossing over came about from a stage where nothing had a meaning to another where everything possessed it (xlvi).

This standpoint does not prevent Lévi-Strauss from recognizing the slowness, the process of maturing, the continuous toil of factual transformations, history (for example, in *Race and History*). But, in accordance with an act which was also Rousseau's and Husserl's, he must "brush aside all the facts" at the moment when he wishes to recapture the specificity of a structure. Like Rousseau, he must always conceive of the origin of a new structure on the model of

catastrophe—an overturning of nature in nature, a natural inter-
ruption of the natural sequence, a brushing aside *of* nature.

Besides the tension of freeplay with history, there is also tension of freeplay with presence. Freeplay is the disruption of presence. The presence of an element is always a signifying and
substitutive reference inscribed in a system of differences and the
movement of a chain. Freeplay is always an interplay of absence and
presence, but if it is to be radically conceived, freeplay must be conceived of before the alternative of presence and absence; being must
be conceived of as presence or absence beginning with the possibility
of freeplay and not the other way around. If Lévi-Strauss, better
than any other, has brought to light the freeplay of repetition and
the repetition of freeplay, one no less perceives in his work a sort of
ethic of presence, an ethic of nostalgia for origins, an ethic of archaic
and natural innocence, of a purity of presence and self-presence in
speech[15]—an ethic, nostalgia, and even remorse which he often presents as the motivation of the ethnological project when he moves
toward archaic societies—exemplary societies in his eyes. These
texts are well known.

As a turning toward the presence, lost or impossible, of the absent origin, this structuralist thematic of broken immediateness is
thus the sad, *negative,* nostalgic, guilty, Rousseauist facet of the
thinking of freeplay of which the Nietzschean *affirmation*—the joyous affirmation of the freeplay of the world and without truth, without origin, offered to an active interpretation—would be the other
side. *This affirmation then determines the non-center otherwise than
as loss of the center.* And it plays the game without security. For
there is a *sure* freeplay: that which is limited to the *substitution* of
given and existing, present, pieces. In absolute chance, affirmation
also surrenders itself to *genetic* indetermination, to the *seminal* adventure of the trace.[16]

There are thus two interpretations of interpretation, of structure, of sign, of freeplay. The one seeks to decipher, dreams of deciphering, a truth or an origin which is free from freeplay and from
the order of the sign, and lives like an exile the necessity of interpretation. The other, which is no longer turned toward the origin,
affirms freeplay and tries to pass beyond man and humanism, the
name man being the name of that being who, throughout the history of metaphysics or of ontotheology—in other words, through the
history of all of his history—has dreamed of full presence, the reassuring foundation, the origin and the end of the game. The second
interpretation of interpretation, to which Nietzsche showed us the
way, does not seek in ethnography, as Lévi-Strauss wished, the "in-

spiration of a new humanism" (again from the "Introduction to the Work of Marcel Mauss").

There are more than enough indications today to suggest we might perceive that these two interpretations of interpretation—which are absolutely irreconcilable even if we live them simultaneously and reconcile them in an obscure economy—together share the field which we call, in such a problematic fashion, the human sciences.

For my part, although these two interpretations must acknowledge and accentuate their difference and define their irreducibility, I do not believe that today there is any question of *choosing*—in the first place because here we are in a region (let's say, provisionally, a region of historicity) where the category of choice seems particularly trivial; and in the second, because we must first try to conceive of the common ground, and the *différence* of this irreducible difference.[17] Here there is a sort of question, call it historical, of which we are only glimpsing today the *conception, the formation, the gestation, the labor*. I employ these words, I admit, with a glance toward the business of childbearing—but also with a glance toward those who, in a company from which I do not exclude myself, turn their eyes away in the face of the as yet unnameable which is proclaiming itself and which can do so, as is necessary whenever a birth is in the offing, only under the species of the non-species, in the formless, mute, infant, and terrifying form of monstrosity.

Notes

1. "La Structure, le signe et le jeu dans le discours des sciences humaines." The text which follows is a translation of the revised version of M. Derrida's communication. The word "jeu" is variously translated here as "play," "interplay," game," and "stake," besides the normative translation "freeplay." All footnotes to this article are additions by the translator.

2. *Interdite:* "forbidden," "disconcerted," "confounded," "speechless."

3. ". . . qui naît toujours d'une certaine manière d'être impliqué dans le jeu, d'être pris au jeu, d'être comme être d'entrée de jeu dans le jeu."

4. *Le cru et le cuit* (Paris: Plon, 1964).

5. *Les structures élémentaires de la parenté* (Paris: Presses Universitaires de France, 1949).

6. *La pensée sauvage* (Paris: Plon, 1962).

7. A *bricoleur* is a jack-of-all-trades, someone who potters about with odds-and-ends, who puts things together out of bits and pieces.

8. Reprinted in: G. Genette, *Figures* (Paris: Editions du Seuil, 1966), p. 145.

9. The point being that the word, both in English and French, means "to supply a deficiency," on the one hand, and "to supply something additional," on the other.

10. "... ce signe s'ajoute, vient en sus, en *supplément.*"

11. "Introduction à l'oeuvre de Marcel Mauss," in: Marcel Mauss, *Sociologie et anthropologie* (Paris: Presses Universitaires de France, 1950).

12. Presumably: G. Charbonnier, *Entretiens avec Claude Lévi-Strauss* (Paris: Plon-Julliard, 1961).

13. *Race and History* (Paris: UNESCO Publications, 1958).

14. "... l'unité d'un devenir, comme tradition de la vérité dans la présence et la présence à soi, vers le savoir dans la conscience de soi."

15. "... de la présence à soi dans la parole."

16. Tournée vers la présence, perdue ou impossible, de l'origine absente, cette thématique structuraliste de l'immédiateté rompue est donc la face triste, *négative,* nostalgique, coupable, rousseauiste, de la pensé du jeu dont *l'affirmation* nietzschéenne, l'affirmation joyeuse du jeu du monde et de l'innocence du devenir, l'affirmation d'un monde de signes sans faute, sans vérité, sans origine, offert à une interprétation active, serait l'autre face. *Cette affirmation détermine alors le* non-centre *autrement que comme perte du centre.* Et elle joue sans sécurité. Car il y a un jeu *sûr:* celui qui se limite à la *substitution* de pièces *données et existantes, présentes.* Dans le hasard absolu, l'affirmation se livre aussi à l'indétermination *génétique,* a l'aventure *séminale* de la trace."

17. From *différer,* in the sense of "to postpone," "put off," "defer." Elsewhere Derrida uses the word as a synonym for the German *Aufschub:* "postponement," and relates it to the central Freudian concepts of *Verspätung, Nachträglichkeit,* and to the "*détours* to death" of *Beyond the Pleasure Principle* by Sigmund Freud (Standard Edition, ed. James Strachey, vol. XIX, London, 1961), Chap. V.

Beginning to Theorize Postmodernism

Linda Hutcheon

Clearly, then, the time has come to theorize the term [post-modernism], if not to define it, before it fades from awkward neologism to derelict cliché without ever attaining to the dignity of a cultural concept.

(Ihab Hassan)

Of all the terms bandied about in both current cultural theory and contemporary writing on the arts, postmodernism must be the most over- and under-defined. It is usually accompanied by a grand flourish of negativized rhetoric: we hear of discontinuity, disruption, dislocation, decentering, indeterminacy and anti-totalization. What all of these words literally do (by their disavowing prefixes, *dis-*, *de-*, *in*, *anti-*) is incorporate that which they aim to contest—as does, arguably, the term *post*modernism itself. I point to this simple verbal fact in order to begin my "theorizing" of the cultural enterprise to which we seem to have given such a provocative label. First and foremost, I should like to argue, postmodernism is a contradictory phenomenon that uses and abuses, installs and then subverts, the very concepts it challenges—be it in literature, painting, sculpture,

Linda Hutcheon, "Beginning to Theorize Postmodernism," *Textual Practice* 1:1, p. 10–31 Copyright 1987 Methuen & Co. Reprinted by permission.

film, video, dance, television, music, philosophy, aesthetic theory, psychoanalysis, linguistics of historiography. These are some of the realms from which my "theorizing" will proceed, and my examples will always be specific, because what I want to avoid are those polemical generalizations (often by those inimical to postmodernism—Jameson 1984a; Eagleton 1985; Newman 1985) that leave us guessing about just what it is that is being called postmodernist, though they are never in doubt as to its undesirability. Some assume a generally accepted "tacit definition" (Carmello 1983); others locate the beast by temporal (after 1945? 1968? 1970? 1980?) or economic signposting (late capitalism). But, in as pluralist and fragmented a culture as that of the Western world today, such designations are not terribly useful if they intend to generalize about all the vagaries of culture. After all, what does television's *Dallas* have in common with the architecture of Ricardo Bofill? What does John Cage's music share with a play (or film) like *Amadeus*?

In other words, postmodernism cannot simply be used as a synonym for the contemporary. And it does not really describe an international cultural phenomenon, for it is primarily European and American (North and South). Although the concept of *modernism* is largely an Anglo-American one (Suleiman 1986), this should not limit the poetics of *postmodernism* to that culture, especially since those who would argue that very stand are usually the ones to find room to sneak in the French *nouveau roman* (Wilde 1981; Brooke-Rose 1981; Lodge 1977). And almost everyone (e.g. Barth 1980) wants to be sure to include what Severo Sarduy (1974) has labelled not postmodernist but "neo-baroque" in a Spanish culture where "modernism" has a rather different meaning.

I offer instead, then, a specific, if polemical start from which to operate as a cultural activity that can be discerned in most art forms and many currents of thought today, what I want to call postmodernism is fundamentally contradictory, resolutely historical and inescapably political. Its contradictions may well be those of late capitalist society but, whatever the cause, these contradictions are certainly manifest in the important postmodern concept of 'the presence of the past'. This was the title given to the 1980 Venice Biennale which marked the institutional recognition of postmodernism in architecture. Italian architect Paolo Portoghesi's (1983) analysis of the twenty façades of the "Strada Novissima"—whose very newness lay paradoxically in its historical parody—shows how architecture has been rethinking modernism's purist break with history. This is not a nostalgic return; it is a critical revisiting, an ironic dialogue with the past of both art and society, a recalling of a critically shared vocabulary of architectural forms. 'The past whose presence we claim is not a golden age to be recuperated,' argues Portoghesi (1983, 26). Its aesthetic forms and its social formations are problematized by critical reflection. The same is true of the postmodernist rethinking of figurative painting in art and historical narrative in fiction and poetry: it is always a critical reworking, never a nostalgic "return." Herein lies the governing role of irony in postmodernism. Stanley Tigerman's dialogue with history in his projects for family houses modelled on Raphael's Villa Madama is an ironic one: his miniaturization of the monumental forces is a rethinking of the social function of architecture—both then and now.

Because it is contradictory and works within the very systems it attempts to subvert, postmodernism can probably not be considered a new paradigm (even in some extension of the Kuhnian sense of the term). It has not replaced liberal humanism, even if it has seriously challenged it. It may mark, however, the site of the struggle of the emergence of something new. The manifestations in art of this struggle may be those undefinable, bizarre works like Terry Gilliam's film, *Brazil*. The postmodern ironic rethinking of history is here textualized in the many general parodic references to other movies: *A Clockwork Orange, 1984*, Gilliam's own *Time Bandits* and Monty Python sketches, and Japanese epics, to name but a few. The more specific parodic recalls range from *Star Wars'* Darth Vadar to the Odessa Steps sequence in Eisenstein's *Battleship Potemkin*. In *Brazil*, however, the baby carriage on the steps is replaced by a vacuum cleaner, and the result is to reduce epic tragedy to the bathos of the mechanical and debased (also achieved, of course, through the symbolic verbal suggestion of emptiness: "vacuum" in that sense). Along with this ironic reworking of the history of film comes a temporal historical warp: the film is set, we are told, at 8.49 A.M. some time in the twentieth century. The décor does not help us identify the time more precisely. The fashions mix the absurdly futuristic with 1930s styling; an oddly old-fashioned and dingy setting belies the omnipresence of computers—though even they are not the sleekly designed creatures of today. Among the other typically postmodern contradictions in this movie is the coexistence of heterogeneous filmic genres: fantasy utopia and grim dystopia; absurd slapstick comedy and tragedy (the Tuttle/Buttle mix-up); the romantic adventure tale and the political documentary.

While all forms of contemporary art and thought have examples of this kind of postmodernist contradiction, here I (like most writers on the subject) shall be privileging the genre of novel, and one form in particular, a form that I want to label "historiographic metafiction." By this I mean those well-known and popular novels which are both intensely self-reflexive and yet lay claim to historical events and personages: *The French Lieutenant's Woman, Midnight's Children, Ragtime, Legs, G., Famous Last Words.* In most of the critical work on postmodernism, it is narrative—in fiction, history and theory—that has been the major focus of attention. Historiographic metafiction incorporates all three areas of concern: its theoretical self-awareness of history and fiction as human constructs (*historiographic meta*fiction) is made the grounds for its rethinking and reworking of the forms and contents of the past. This kind of fiction has often been noticed, but its paradigmatic quality has been passed by: it is commonly labelled in terms of something else—for example, as 'midfiction' (Wilde 1981) or 'paramodernist' (Malmgren 1985). Such labelling is another mark of the inherent contradictoriness of historiographic metafiction, for it always works *within* conventions in order to subvert them. It is not pure metafiction, nor is it the same as the historical novel or the non-fictional novel. Gabriel García Márquez's *One Hundred Years of Solitude* has often been discussed in exactly the contradictory terms that I think define postmodernism. For example, Larry McCaffery sees it as both metafictionally self-reflexive and yet speaking to us powerfully about real political and historical realities: 'It has thus become a kind of model for the contemporary writer, being self-conscious about its literary heritage and about the limits of mimesis . . . but yet managing to reconnect its readers to the world outside the page' (1982, 264). What McCaffery here adds as almost an afterthought at the end of his book, *The Metafictional Muse,* is my starting point.

Most theorists of postmodernism who see it as a 'cultural dominant' (Jameson 1984a, 56) agree that it is characterized by the results of late capitalist dissolution of bourgeois hegemony and the development of mass culture (see Jameson 1984a (via Lefebvre 1968); Russell 1980; Egbert 1970; Calinescu 1977). I would agree and, in fact, argue that the increasing tendency towards uniformity in mass culture is one of the totalizing forces that postmodernism exists to challenge—challenge, but not deny. It does seek to assert difference, not homogeneous identity, but the very concept of difference could be said to entail a typically postmodernist contradiction: "difference" unlike "otherness," has no exact opposite against which to define itself. Thomas Pynchon allegorizes otherness in *Gravity's Rainbow* (1973) through the single, if anarchic, "we-system" that exists as the counterforce of the totalizing "They-system" (though it is also implicated in it). Postmodernist difference—or rather differences, in the plural—is always multiple and provisional.

Postmodernist culture, then, has a contradictory relationship to what we usually label the dominant or liberal humanist culture.

It does not deny it, as some have asserted (Newman 1985, 42; Palmer 1977, 364). Instead, it contests it from within its own assumptions. Modernists like Eliot and Joyce have usually been seen as profoundly humanistic (Stern 1971, 26) in their paradoxical desire for stable aesthetic and moral values, even in the face of their realization of the inevitable absence of such universals. Postmodernism differs from this not in its humanistic contradictions but in the provisionality of its response to them: it refuses to posit any structure, or what Lyotard (1984a) calls master narrative—such as art or myth—which, for such modernists, would have been consolatory. It argues that such systems are indeed attractive, perhaps even necessary; but this does not make them any the less illusory. For Lyotard, postmodernism is characterized by exactly this kind of incredulity towards master and meta-narratives. Those who lament the "loss of meaning" in the world or in art are really mourning the fact that knowledge is no longer primarily narrative knowledge of this kind (1984a, 26)). This does not mean that knowledge somehow disappears. There is no radically new paradigm here, even if there is change.

It is no longer big news that the master narratives of bourgeois liberalism are under attack. There is a long history of many such skeptical sieges to positivism and humanism, and today's foot-soldiers of theory—Foucault, Derrida, Habermas, Rorty, Baudrillard—follow in the footsteps of Nietzsche, Heidegger, Marx and Freud, to name but a few, in their challenges to the empiricist, rationalist, humanist assumptions of our cultural systems, including those of science (Graham 1982, 148; Toulmin 1972). Foucault's early rethinking of the history of ideas in terms of an "archaeology" (*The Order of Things,* 1970; *The Archaeology of Knowledge,* 1972) that might stand outside the universalizing assumptions of humanism is one such attempt, whatever its obvious weaknesses. So is Derrida's more radical contesting of Cartesian and Platonic views of the mind as a system of closed meanings (see Harrison 1985, 6). In these terms, Habermas's work appears perhaps somewhat less radical in his desire to work from within the system of "Enlightenment" rationality and yet manage to critique it at the same time. This is what Lyotard has attacked as just another totalizing narrative (1984b). And Jameson (1984b) has argued that both Lyotard and Habermas are resting their arguments on different but equally strong legitimizing 'narrative archetypes'.

This game of meta-narrative one-upmanship could go on and on, since arguably Jameson's Marxism leaves him vulnerable too. But this is not the point. What is important in all these internalized

challenges to humanism is the interrogation of the notion of consensus. Whatever narratives or systems that once allowed us to
think we could unproblematically define public agreement have
now been questioned by the acknowledgement of differences—in
theory and in artistic practice. In its most extreme formulation,
the result is that consensus becomes the illusion of consensus,
whether it be defined in terms of minority (educated, sensitive, élitist) or mass (commercial, popular, conventional) culture, for *both*
are manifestations of late capitalist, bourgeois, informational, postindustrial society in which social reality is structured by discourses
(in the plural)—or so postmodernism endeavours to teach.

What this means is that the familiar humanist separation of
art and life (or human imagination and order versus chaos and disorder) no longer holds. Postmodernist contradictory art still installs
that order, but it then uses it to demystify our everyday processes of
structuring chaos, of imparting or assigning meaning (D'haen 1986,
225). For example, within a positivistic frame of reference, photographs could be accepted as neutral representations, as windows on
the world. In the postmodernist photos of Heribert Berkert or Ger
Dekkers, they still represent (for they cannot avoid reference), but
what they represent is self-consciously shown to be highly filtered
by the discursive and aesthetic assumptions of the camera holder
(Davis 1977). While not wanting to go as far as Morse Peckham
(1965) and argue that the arts are somehow "biologically" necessary
for social change, I would like to suggest that, in its very contradictions, postmodernist art might be able to dramatize and even provoke change from within. It is not that the modernist world was "a
world in need of mending" and the postmodernist one "beyond re-
pair" (Wilde 1981, 131). Postmodernism works to show that all repairs are human constructs, but that from that very fact they derive
their value as well as their limitations. All repairs are both comforting and illusory. Postmodernist interrogations of humanist certainties live within this kind of contradiction.

Perhaps it is another inheritance from the sixties to believe
that challenging and questioning are positive values (even if solutions to problems are not offered), for the knowledge derived from
such enquiry may be the only possible condition of change. In the
late 1950s, in *Mythologies,* Roland Barthes had prefigured this kind
of thinking in his Brechtian challenges to all that is "natural" or
"goes without saying" in our culture—that is, all that is considered
universal and eternal, and therefore unchangeable. He suggested
the need to question and demystify first, and then work for change.
The sixties were the time of ideological formation for many of the

postmodernist thinkers and artists of the eighties, and it is now that we can see the results of that formation.

Perhaps, as some have argued, the sixties themselves (i.e., at the time) produced no enduring innovation in aesthetics, but I would argue that they did provide the background, though not the definition, of postmodernism (cf. Bertens 1986, 17). They were crucial in developing a different concept of the possible function of art, one that would contest the "Arnoldian" or humanist moral view with its élitist class bias (see Williams 1960, xiii). One of the functions of art in mass culture, argued Susan Sontag, would be to "modify consciousness" (1967, 304). And many cultural commentators since have argued that the energies of the sixties have changed the framework and structure of how we consider art (e.g. Wasson 1974). The conservatism of the late seventies and eighties may have its impact when the thinkers and artists being formed now begin to produce their work (cf. McCaffery 1982), but to call Foucault or Lyotard a neo-conservative—as did Habermas (1983, 14)—is historically and ideologically inaccurate (see Calinescu 1986, 246; Giddens 1981, 17).

The political, social and intellectual experiences of the sixties helped make it possible for postmodernism to be seen as what Kristeva calls "writing-as-experience-of-limits" (1980, 137): limits of language, of subjectivity, of sexual identity and, we might also add, of systematization and uniformization. This interrogating (and even pushing) of limits has contributed to the "crisis in legitimation" that Lyotard and Habermas see (differently) as part of the postmodern condition. It has certainly meant a rethinking and putting into question of the bases of our Western modes of thinking that we usually label, rather generally, liberal humanism.

What precisely, though, is being challenged? First of all, institutions have come under scrutiny: from the media to the university, from museums to theatres. The important contemporary debate about the margins and the boundaries of social and artistic conventions (see Culler 1983–4) is the result of a typically postmodernist transgressing of previously accepted limits: those of particular arts, of genres, of art itself. Rauschenberg's narrative (or discursive) work, *Rebus,* or Cy Twombly's series of Spenserian texts are indicative of the fruitful straddling of the borderline between the literary and visual arts. As early as 1969, Theodore Ziolkowski had noted that the "new arts are so closely related that we cannot hide complacently behind the arbitrary walls of self-contained disciplines: poetics inevitably gives way to general aesthetics, considerations of the novel move easily to the film, while the new poetry often has more in common with contemporary music and art than with the poetry of the past" (1969, 113). The years since have only verified and intensified this perception. The borders between literary genres have become fluid: who can tell any more what the limits are between the novel and the short-story collection (Alice Munro's *Lives of Girls and Women*), the novel and the long poem (Michael Ondaatje's *Coming Through Slaughter*), the novel and autobiography (Maxine Hong Kingston's *China Men*), the novel and history (Salman Rushdie's *Shame*), the novel and biography (John Banville's *Kepler*)? But, in any of these examples, the conventions of the two genres are played off against each other; there is no simple, unproblematic merging. In Carlos Fuentes's *The Death of Artemio Cruz,* the title already points to the ironic inversion of biographical conventions: it is the death, not the life, that will be the focus. The subsequent narrative complications of three voices (first, second and third person) and three tenses (present, future, past) disseminate but also reassert (in a typically postmodernist way) the enunciative situation or discursive context of the work. The traditional verifying third-person, past-tense voice of History and realism is both installed and undercut by the others.

Clearly the most important boundaries crossed have been those between fiction and non-fiction and—by extension—between art and life. In the March 1986 issue of *Esquire* magazine, Jerzy Kosinski published a piece in the "Documentary" section called "Death in Cannes," a narrative of the last days and subsequent death of the French biologist Jacques Monod. Typically postmodernist, the text refuses the omniscience and omnipresence of the third person and engages instead in a dialogue between a narrative voice (which both is and is not Kosinski's) and a projected reader. Its viewpoint is avowedly limited, provisional, personal. However, it also works and plays with the conventions of both literary realism and journalistic facticity: the text is accompanied by photographs of the author and the subject. The commentary uses these photos to make us, as readers, aware of our expectations of both narrative and pictorial interpretation, including our naïve but common trust in the representational veracity of photography. One set of photos is introduced with the words "I bet the smiling picture was taken last. I always bet on a happy ending" (1986, 82), but the subsequent prose section ends: "look at the pictures if you must but . . . don't bet on them. Bet on the worth of a word" (82). But we come to learn later that there are events—like Monod's death—that are beyond both words and pictures.

Kosinski calls this postmodernist form of writing "autofiction": "fiction" because all memory is fictionalizing; "auto" because it is, for him, "a literary genre, generous enough to let the author adopt the nature of his fictional protagonist—not the other way around" (82). When he "quotes" Monod, he tells the fictive and questioning reader that it is in his own "*autolingua*—the inner language of the storyteller" (86). In his earlier novel, *Blind Date* (1977), Kosinski had used Monod's death and the text of his *Chance and Necessity* (1971) as structuring concepts in the novel: from both, he learned of our need to rid ourselves of illusions of totalizing explanations and systems of ethics. But it is not just this kind of historiographic metafiction that challenges the borders between life and art, that plays on the margins of genre. Painting and sculpture, for instance, come together with similar impact in some of the three-dimensional canvases of Robert Rauschenberg and Tom Wesselman (see D'haen 1986 and Owens 1980). And, of course, much has been made of the blurring of the distinctions between the discourses of theory and literature in the works of Jacques Derrida and Roland Barthes—or somewhat less fashionably, if no less provocatively, in some of the writing of Ihab Hassan (1975, 1980a) and Zulfikar Ghose (1983).

In addition to being "borderline" enquiries, most of these postmodernist texts are also specifically parodic in their intertextual relation to the traditions and conventions of the genres involved. When Eliot recalled Dante or Virgil in *The Waste Land,* one sensed a kind of wishful call to continuity beneath the fragmented echoing. It is precisely this that is contested in postmodernist parody, where it is often ironic discontinuity that is revealed at the heart of continuity, difference at the heart of similarity (Hutcheon 1985). Parody is a perfect postmodernist form in some senses, for it paradoxically both incorporates and challenges that which it parodies. It also forces a reconsideration of the idea of origin or originality that is compatible with other postmodernist interrogations of liberal humanist assumptions. While Jameson (1983, 114–19) sees this loss of the modernist unique, individual style as negative, as an imprisoning of the text in the past through pastiche, it has been seen by postmodernist *artists* as a liberating challenge to a definition of subjectivity and creativity that has ignored the role of history in art and thought. On Rauschenberg's use of reproduction and parody in his work, Douglas Crimp writes: 'The fiction of the creating subject gives way to the frank confiscation, quotation, excerptation, accumulation and repetition of already existing images. Notions of originality, authenticity and presence . . . are undermined' (1983, 53).

The same is true of the fiction of John Fowles or the music of George Rochberg. As Foucault noted, the concepts of subjective consciousness and continuity that are now being questioned are tied up with an entire set of ideas that have been dominant in our culture until now: "the point of creation, the unity of a work, of a period, of a theme . . . the mark of originality and the infinite wealth of hidden meanings" (1972, 230).

Another consequence of this far-reaching postmodernist enquiry into the nature of subjectivity (or of the self) is the frequent challenge to traditional notions of perspective, especially in narrative and painting. The perceiving subject is no longer assumed to be a coherent, meaning-generating entity. Narrators in fiction become either disconcertingly multiple and hard to locate (as in D. M. Thomas's *The White Hotel*) or resolutely provisional and limited— often undermining their own seeming omniscience (as in Salman Rushdie's *Midnight Children*). In Charles Russell's terms, with postmodernism we start to encounter and are challenged by "an art of shifting perspective, of double self-consciousness of local and extended meaning" (1980, 192).

As Foucault and others have suggested, linked to this contesting of the unified and coherent self is a more general questioning of *any* totalizing or homogenizing system. Provisionality and heterogeneity contaminate any neat attempts at unifying coherence—formal or thematic. Historical and narrative continuity and closure are contested, but again from within. The teleology of art forms— from fiction to music—is both suggested and transformed. The center no longer completely holds; from the decentered perspective, the "marginal" and the ex-centric (be it in race, gender or ethnicity) take on new significance in the light of the implied recognition that our culture is not really the homogeneous monolith (i.e. male, white, Western) we might have assumed. The concept of alienated otherness (based on binary oppositions that conceal hierarchies) gives way, as I have argued, to that of differences: to the assertion not of centralized sameness but of decentralized community— another postmodernist paradox. The local and the regional are stressed in the face of mass culture and a kind of vast global informational village that McLuhan could only have dreamed of. Culture (with a capital C and in the singular) has become cultures (uncapitalized and plural), as documented at length by our social scientists. And this appears to be happening in spite of—and, I would argue, maybe even because of—the homogenizing impulse of the consumer society of late capitalism—yet another postmodernist contradiction. In attempting to define what he called the "trans-avant-garde," the Italian art critic Achille Bonito Oliva found he had to talk of differences as much as similarities from country to country (1984, 71–3): it would seem that the "presence of the past" depends on the local and culture-specific nature of each past.

In this sort of context, different kinds of texts will take on value—the ones that operate what Derrida calls "breaches or infractions"—for it is they that can lead us to suspect the very concept of 'art' (1981, 69). In Derrida's words, such artistic practices seem "to mark and to organize a structure of resistance to the philosophical conceptuality that allegedly dominated and comprehended them, whether directly, or whether through categories derived from this philosophical fund, the categories of esthetics, rhetoric, or traditional criticism" (69). Of course, Derrida's own texts belong solely to neither philosophical nor literary discourse, though they partake of both in a deliberately self-reflexive and contradictory (postmodern) manner.

Derrida's constant self-consciousness about the status of his own discourse raises another question that must be faced by anyone—like myself—writing on postmodernism. From what position does one "theorize" (even self-consciously) a disparate, contradictory, multivalent, current cultural phenomenon? Stanley Fish (1986) has wittily pointed out the "anti-foundationalist" paradox that I too find myself in when I comment on the importance of Derrida's critical self-consciousness. In Fish's ironic terms: "Ye shall know that truth is not what it seems and *that* truth shall set you free." Barthes, of course, had seen the same danger earlier as he watched demystification become part of the *doxa* (1977, 166). Similarly Christopher Norris has noted that, in textualizing all forms of knowledge, deconstruction theory often, in its very unmasking of rhetorical strategies, still itself lays claim to the status of "theoretical knowledge" (1985, 22). Most postmodernist theory, however, realizes this paradox or contradiction. Rorty, Baudrillard, Foucault, Lyotard and others seem to imply that any knowledge cannot escape complicity with meta-narratives, with the fictions that render possible any claim to "truth," however provisional. What they add, however, is that *no* narrative can be a natural "master" narrative; there are no natural hierarchies, only those we construct. It is this kind of self-implicating questioning that should allow postmodernist theory to challenge narratives that do presume to "master" status, without necessarily assuming that status for itself.

Postmodernist art similarly asserts and then deliberately undermines such principles as value, order, meaning, control and identity (Russell 1985, 247) that have been the basic premises of

bourgeois liberalism. Those humanistic principles are still operative in our culture, but for many they are no longer seen as eternal
and unchallengeable. The contradictions of both postmodernist theory and practice are positioned within the system and yet work to
allow its premises to be seen as fictions or as ideological structures.
This does not necessarily destroy their "truth" value, but it does define the conditions of that "truth." Such a process reveals rather
than conceals the tracks of the signifying systems that constitute
our world—that is, systems constructed by us in answer to our
needs. However important these systems are, they are not natural,
given or universal. The very limitations imposed by the postmodern
view are also perhaps ways of opening new doors: perhaps now we
can better study the interrelations of social, aesthetic, philosophical
and ideological constructs. In order to do so, postmodernist critique
must acknowledge its own position as an ideological one (Newman
1985, 60). I think the formal and thematic contradictions of postmodernist art and theory work to do just that: to call attention both
to what is being contested and what is being offered as a critical response to that, and to do so in a self-aware way that admits its own
provisionality.

In writing about these postmodernist contradictions, then, I
clearly would not want to fall into the trap of suggesting any "transcendental identity" (Radhakrishnan 1983, 33) or essence for postmodernism. I see it as an ongoing cultural process or activity, and I
think that what we need, more than a fixed and fixing definition, is
a "poetics," an open, ever-changing theoretical structure by which to
order both our cultural knowledge and our critical procedures. This
would not be a poetics in the structuralist sense of the word, but
would go beyond the study of literary discourse to the study of
cultural practice and theory. As Tzvetan Todorov realized in a later
expanding and translating of his 1968 *Introduction to Poetics:* "Literature is inconceivable outside a typology of discourses" (1981, 71).
Art and theory about art (and culture) should both be part of a poetics of postmodernism. Richard Rorty has posited the existence of
"poetic" moments "as occurring periodically in many different areas
of culture—science, philosophy, painting and politics, as well as the
lyric and the drama" (1984, 4). But this is no coincidental moment;
it is made, not found. As Rorty explains:

> it is a mistake to think that Derrida, or anybody else, "recog-
> nized" problems about the nature of textuality or writing
> which had been ignored by the tradition. What he did was to

think up ways of speaking which made old ways of speaking optional, and thus more or less dubious. (Rorty 1984, 23n.)

It is both a way of speaking—a discourse—and a cultural process that a poetics would seek to articulate.

A poetics of postmodernism would not posit any relation of causality or identity among the arts or between art and theory. It would merely offer, as provisional hypothesis, perceived overlappings of concern, here specifically with regard to the contradictions of postmodernism. It would not be a matter of reading literature as continuous with theory, nor seeing literary theory as an imperialistic intellectual practice (White 1978, 261). The interaction of theory and practice in postmodernism is a complex one of shared responses and common provocations. There are also, of course, many postmodernist artists who double as theorists—Eco, Lodge, Bradbury, Barth—though they have rarely become the major theorists or apologists of their own work as the *nouveaux romanciers* (from Robbe-Grillet to Ricardou) and surfictionists (Federman and Sukenick especially) have tended to do. What a poetics of postmodernism would articulate is less the theories of Eco in relation to *The Name of the Rose* than the overlappings of concern between, for instance, the contradictory form of the writing of theory in Lyotard's *Le Différend* (1983) and that of a novel like Peter Ackroyd's *Hawksmoor* (1985). Their sequentially ordered sections are equally disrupted by a particularly dense network of interconnections and intertexts, and each enacts or performs, as well as theorizes, the paradoxes of continuity and disconnection, of totalizing interpretation and the impossibility of final meaning. In Lyotard's own words:

> A postmodern artist or writer is in the position of a philosopher: the text he writes, the work he produces are not in principle governed by preestablished rules, and they cannot be judged according to a determining judgment, by applying familiar categories to the text or to the work. Those rules and categories are what the work of art itself is looking for. (1984b, 81).

Jameson has listed "theoretical discourse" among the manifestations of postmodernism (1983, 112), and this would include not just the obvious post-structuralist philosophical and literary theory but also analytic philosophy, psychoanalysis, linguistics, historiography, sociology and other areas. Recently critics have begun to notice the similarities of concern between various kinds of theory and current literary discourse, sometimes to condemn (Newman 1985, 118), sometimes merely to describe (Hassan 1986). With novels like Ian Watson's *The Embedding* around, it is not surprising that the link would be made. I do not at all think, however, that this has contributed to any "inflation of discourse" at the expense of historical contextualization (Newman 1985, 10), primarily because historiography is itself taking part in what LaCapra has called a "reconceptualization of culture in terms of collective discourses" (1985, 46). By this he does not mean to imply that historians no longer concern themselves with "archivally based documentary realism," but only that, within the discipline of history, there is also a growing concern with redefining intellectual history as "the study of social meaning as historically constituted" (46; see too White 1973, 1980, 1981, 1984). This is exactly what historiographic metafiction is doing: Graham Swift's *Waterland,* Rudy Wiebe's *The Temptations of Big Bear,* Ian Watson's *Chekhov's Journey.*

In the past, history has often been used in criticism of the novel as a kind of model of the realistic pole of representation. Postmodernist fiction problematizes this model to query the relation of both history to reality and reality to language. In Lionel Gossman's terms:

> Modern history and modern literature [I would say *post*modern in both cases] have both rejected the ideal of representation that dominated them for so long. Both now conceive of their work as exploration, testing, creation of new meanings, rather than as disclosure or revelation of meanings already in some sense 'there', but not immediately perceptible. (1978, 38–39)

The view that postmodernism relegates history to "the dustbin of an obsolete episteme, arguing gleefully that history does not exist except as text" (Huyssen 1981, 35), is simply wrong. History is not made obsolete; it is, however, being rethought—as a human construct. And, in arguing that *history* does not exist except as text, it does not stupidly and 'gleefully' deny that the *past* existed, but only that its accessibility to us now is entirely conditioned by textuality. We cannot know the past except through its texts: its documents, its evidence, even its eye-witness accounts are *texts.* And postmodernist novels—*The Scorched-Wood People, Flaubert's Parrot, Antichthon, The White Hotel*—teach us about both this fact and its consequences.

Along with the obvious and much publicized case of post-modern architecture (Jencks 1977, 1980a, 1980b), it has been (American) black and (general) feminist theory and practice that have been particularly important in this postmodernist refocusing on historicity, both formally (largely through parodic intertextuality) and thematically. Works like Ishmael Reed's *Mumbo Jumbo,* Maxine Hong Kingston's *China Men* and Gayl Jones's *Corregidora* have gone far to expose—very self-reflexively—the myth- or illusion-making tendencies of historiography. They have also linked racial and/or gender differences to questions of discourse and of authority and power that are at the heart of the postmodernist enterprise in general and, in particular, of both black theory and feminism. All are theoretical discourses that have their roots in a reflection on actual praxis and continue to derive their critical force from their conjunction with that social and aesthetic practice (on feminism, see de Lauretis 1984, 184). It is true that, as Susan Suleiman (1986, 268, n. 12) acutely noted, literary discussions of postmodernism often appear to exclude the work of women (and, one might add, often of blacks as well), even though female (and black) explorations of narrative and linguistic form have been among the most contesting and radical. Certainly women and American black artists' use of parody to challenge the male white tradition from within, their use of irony to implicate and yet to critique, is distinctly paradoxical and postmodernist. Both black and feminist thought have shown how it is possible to move theory out of the ivory tower and into the larger world of social praxis, as theorists like Said (1983) have been advocating. Arguably, women have helped develop the post-modern valuing of the margins and the ex-centric as a way out of the power problematic of centres and of male/female oppositions (Kamuf 1982). Certainly Susan Swan's *The Biggest Modern Woman of the World,* a biographical metafiction about a real (and, by definition, ex-centric) giantess, would suggest precisely this in its opposition to what the protagonist sees as "emblem fatigue": "an affliction peculiar to giants [or women or blacks of ethnic minorities] who are always having to shoulder giant expectations from normal folk" (Swan 1983, 139).

There are other works which have come close to articulating the kind of poetics I think we need, though all offer a somewhat more limited version. But they too have investigated the overlappings of concern between current philosophical and literary theory and practice. Evan Watkins's *The Critical Act: Criticism and Community* (1978) aims to derive a theory of literature that can "elicit from recent poetry in particular the means of talking about and

talking back to developments in theory" (x). His model, however, is
one of "dialectical reciprocity," which often implies a causal relationship (12) that the sort of poetics I envisage would avoid.

David Carroll's fine study, *The Subject in Question: The Languages of Theory and the Strategies of Fiction* (1982), is somewhat
more limited than a general poetics of postmodernism would be, for
it focuses on aporias and contradictions specifically in the work of
Jacques Derrida and Claude Simon in order to study the limitations
of both theory and fiction in examining the problem of history—limitations that are made evident by the confrontation of theory with
practice. As I see it, however, a poetics would not seek to place itself
in a position *between* theory and practice (Carroll 1982, 2) on the
question of history, so much as in a position *within* both. A work like
Peter Uwe Hohendahl's *The Institution of Criticism* (1982), while
limited to the German context, is useful here in showing the kind of
question that a poetics placed within both theory and practice must
ask, especially regarding the norms and standards of *criticism:* the
autonomous institution that mediates theory and practice in the
field of literary studies.

Allen Thiher's *Words in Reflection: Modern Language Theory
and Postmodern Fiction* (1984) comes closest to defining a general
poetics, in that it studies some current theories, together with
contemporary literary practice, in order to show what he feels to
be a major "displacement in the way we think and, perhaps more
important, write the past" (189). However, this lucid and thorough
study limits itself to modern language theory and linguistically
self-reflexive metafiction and posits a kind of influence model (of
theory over fiction) that a poetics of postmodernism would not be
willing to do. Rather than separate theory from practice, it would
seek to integrate them and would organize itself around issues (representation, textuality, subjectivity, ideology, and so on) which both
theory and art problematize and continually reformulate in para-
doxial terms.

First, however, any poetics of postmodernism should come to
terms with the immense amount of material that has already been
written on the subject of postmodernism in all fields. The debate invariably begins over the meaning of the prefix, "post-"—a four-letter
word if ever there was one. Does it have as negative a ring of supersession and rejection as many contend (Barth 1980)? I would argue that, as is most clear perhaps in postmodern architecture, the
"Post Position" (Culler 1982, 81) signals its contradictory dependence on and independence from that which temporally preceded it
and which literally made it possible. Postmodernism's relation to

modernism is, therefore, typically contradictory. It marks neither a simple and radical break from it nor a straightforward continuity with it: it is both and neither. And this would be the case in aesthetic, philosophical or ideological terms.

Of the many arguments mounted on either side of the modernist/postmodernist debate, let me here consider only one in detail, a recent and influential one: that of Terry Eagleton in his 1985 article, "Capitalism, modernism and postmodernism." In fact, much of what is offered here is repeated in other theorizing on postmodernism. Like many before him (both defenders like Lyotard and detractors like Jameson), Eagleton separates practice and theory, choosing to argue only in abstract theoretical terms and seeming almost deliberately to avoid mention of exactly what kind of aesthetic practice is actually being talked about. This strategy, however clever and certainly convenient, leads only to endless confusion. My first response to this article, for instance, was that from the descriptive theorizing alone, Eagleton, like Jameson, must mean something quite different from what I do by postmodernism in art. Yet they both make passing references to architecture, and so I suppose I must presume, though I cannot prove it from their texts, that we are all indeed talking of the same kind of artistic manifestation. And so I shall proceed on that assumption. (I should also note that I find it ironic that, like Jameson, Eagleton finds himself in the same hostile position *vis-à-vis* postmodernism as Lukács had been *vis-à-vis* modernism, but that Eagleton looks to precisely what Lukács had denigrated for his set of valid norms and values: postmodernism becomes a 'sick joke' or parody of modernism (Eagleton 1985, 60).

I want to look at each of Eagleton's eight major points in the light of the postmodernist artistic practice I have been discussing, for I think that his absolutist binary thinking—which makes postmodernism into the negative and opposite of modernism—denies much of the complexity of that art. His theory is neat, but maybe too neat. For example, can the historical and discursive contextualizing of Doctorow's *Ragtime* really be considered to be dehistoricized and devoid of historical memory? It may alter received historical opinion, but it does not evade the notions of historicity or historical determination. Is the highly individualized and problematic voice of Saleem Sinai in *Midnight's Children* really to be dubbed "depthless" and without style? Is that novel (or are Coover's *The Public Burning* or Doctorow's *The Book of Daniel*) seriously to be labelled as empty of political content? Yet Eagleton asserts all of this—minus the examples—as defining what he calls postmodernism (61).

I would again ask: in Findley's *Famous Last Words,* does the obvious "performativity" of the text really "replace truth" (63), or does it, rather, question *whose* notion of truth gains power and authority over others' and then examine the process of how it does so? The Brechtian involvement of the reader—both textualized (Quinn) and extratextual (us)—is something Eagleton appears to approve of in the modernist "revolutionary" avant-garde. But it is also a very postmodernist strategy, and here leads to the acknowledgement, not of truth, but of truths in the plural—truths that are socially, ideologically and historically conditioned. Eagleton sees that postmodernism dissolves modernist boundaries, but regards this as negative, an act of becoming "coextensive with commodified life itself" (68). However, historiographic metafiction like Puig's *Kiss of the Spider Woman* works precisely to combat any aestheticist fetishing of art by *refusing* to bracket exactly what Eagleton wants to see put *back* into art: "the referent or real historical world" (67). What such fiction also does, though, is problematize both the nature of the referent and its relation to the real, historical world by its paradoxical combination of metafictional self-reflexivity with historical subject matter. How, then, could Cortázar's *A Manual for Manuel* be reduced to a celebration of "kitsch" (68) Is all art that introduces non-high forms (journalism or the spy story) by definition kitsch? What Eagleton (like Jameson (1984a) before him) seems to ignore is the subversive potential of irony, parody and humour in contesting the universalizing pretensions of "serious" art.

Eagleton broadens the scope of his attack on postmodernism by describing it as "confidently post-metaphysical" (70). The one thing which the provisional, contradictory postmodernism enterprise is *not* is "confidently" anything. A novel like Banville's *Doctor Copernicus* does not confidently accept that things are things, as Eagleton asserts. Its entire formal and thematic energy is founded in its philosophical problematizing of the nature of reference, of the relation of word to thing, of discourse to experience. Postmodernist texts like *The White Hotel* or *Kepler* do not confidently disintegrate and banish the humanist subject either, though Eagleton says that postmodernism (in his theoretical term) does. They *do* disturb humanist certainties about the nature of the self and of the role of consciousness and Cartesian reason (or positivistic science), but they do so by inscribing that subjectivity and only then contesting it.

I have deliberately discussed each of Eagleton's eight points in terms of specific examples in order to illustrate the dangers of separating neat theory from messy practice. A poetics of postmodernism must deal with *both* and can theorize only on the basis of all the forms of postmodernist discourse available to it. The constant complaint either that postmodernism is ahistorical or, if it uses history, that it does so in a naïve and nostalgic way, just will not stand up in the light of actual novels such as those listed above or films like *Crossroads* or *Zelig*. What starts to look naïve, by contrast, is the reductive belief that any recall of the past must, by definition, be sentimental nostalgia or antiquarianism. What postmodernism does, as its very name suggests, is confront and contest any modernist discarding *or* recuperating of the past in the name of the future. It suggests no search for transcendent, timeless meaning but rather a re-evaluation of, and a dialogue with the past in the light of the present. We could call this, once again, "the presence of the past" or perhaps its "present-ification" (Hassan 1983). It does not deny the *existence* of the past; it does question whether we can ever *know* that past other than through its textualized remains.

These constant binary oppositions set up in the writing on postmodernism—between past and present, modern and postmodern, and so on—should probably be called into question, if only because, like the rhetoric of rupture (*dis*continuity, *de*centering, etc), *post*modernism literally constitutes its own paradoxical identity, and does so in an uneasy, contradictory relationship of constant slippage. So much that has been written on this subject has physically taken the form of opposing columns, usually labelled "modernist versus postmodernist" (see Hassan 1975, 1980b; cf. Lethen 1986, 235–36)—a structure that denies the mixed, plural and contradictory nature of the postmodernist enterprise.

Whether this complexity is a result of our particularly contradictory age, caught between "myths of totality" and "ideologies of fracture" (Hassan 1980a, 191), is another question. Surely many ages could be so described. Whatever the cause, a poetics of postmodernism should try to come to grips with some of the obvious paradoxes in both theory and practice. Let me offer a few more examples: one would be the contradiction of a (textual) self-referentiality that is constantly confronted with (textual) discursive contextualizing, especially when it is done in such a way that the self-reflexivity inevitably moves toward surrounding discourses, as in the case of historiographic metafiction. Another major contradiction to be faced would be the irony of Lyotard's (1984a) obviously meta-narrative theory of postmodernism's incredulity to meta-narrative (see Lacoue-Labarthe 1984) or of Foucault's early anti-totalizing epistemic totalizations. These are typically paradoxical: they are the masterful denials of mastery, the cohesive attacks on cohesion, that characterize postmodernist theory. Similarly, historiographic metafiction—like postmodernist painting, sculpture and photography—inscribes and then subverts its mimetic engagement with the world. It does not reject it (Graff 1979); nor does it merely accept it (Butler 1980, 93; Wilde 1981, 170). But it does irrevocably change any simple notions of realism of reference, by confronting the discourse of art with the discourse of history.

A further postmodernist paradox that this particular kind of fiction enacts is to be found in its bridging of the gap between élite and popular art, a gap which mass culture has perhaps broadened. Many have noted postmodernism's attraction to popular art forms (Fiedler 1975) such as the dective story (Fowles's *A Maggot*) or the western (*Doctorow's Welcome to Hard Times* or Berger's *Little Big Man*). But what has not been dealt with is the paradox that novels like *The French Lieutenant's Woman* or *The Name of the Rose* themselves are both popular bestsellers and objects of intense academic study. I would argue that, as typically postmodernist contradictory texts, novels like these parodically use and abuse the conventions of both popular and élite literature, and do so in a such a way that they can actually *use* the invasive culture industry to challenge its own commodification processes from within. If élitist culture has indeed been fragmented into specialist disciplines, as many have argued, then hybrid novels like these work both to address and to subvert that fragmentation through their pluralizing recourse to the discourses of history, sociology, theology, political science, economics, philosophy, semiotics, literature, literary criticism, and so on. Historiographic metafiction clearly acknowledges that postmodernism operates in a complex institutional and discursive network of élite, official, mass and popular cultures. Postmodernism may not offer any final answers, but perhaps it can begin to ask questions that may eventually lead to answers of some kind.

Unresolved paradoxes may be unsatisfying to those in need of absolute and final answers, but to postmodernist thinkers and artists they have been the source of intellectual energy which has provoked new articulations of the postmodern condition. Despite the obvious danger, they do not appear to have brought on what LaCapra has called a "lemming-like fascination for discursive impasses" (1985, 141) which might threaten to undermine *any* working concept of 'theorizing'. The model of contradictions offered here—while admittedly only another model—would hope to open up any poetics of postmodernism to plural, contestatory elements without necessarily reducing or recuperating them. In order to try to avoid the tempting trap of co-option, it is necessary to acknowledge the fact that such a position is itself an ideology, one that is profoundly implicated in that which it seeks to theorize. We cannot exempt our own "discriminating scholarly discourse," as Douwe

Fokkema would like (1986, 2), for it too is as institutionalized as the fiction or the painting or the philosophy or the history it would pretend to scrutinize. Within such a 'postmodernist' ideology, a poetics of postmodernism would only self-consciously enact the metalinguistic contradiction of being inside and outside, complicitous and distanced, inscribing and contesting its own provisional formulations. Such an enterprise would obviously not yield any universal truths, but then that would not be what it sought to do. To move from the desire and expectation of sure and single meaning to a recognition of the value of differences and even contradictions might be a tentative first step towards accepting responsibility for both art and theory *as signifying processes*. In other words, maybe we could begin to study the implications of both our *making* and our *making sense* of our culture.

References

Ackroyd, Peter
(1985) *Hawksmoor.* London: Hamish Hamilton.

Banville, John
(1976) *Doctor Copernicus.* New York: Norton.

Banville, John
(1981) *Kepler.* London: Secker & Warburg.

Barnes, Julian
(1984) *Flaubert's Parrot.* London: Cape.

Barth, John
(1980) "The literature of replenishment: postmodern fiction," *The Atlantic* (January), 65–71.

Barthes, Roland
(1973) *Mythologies.* Trans. Annette Lavers. London: Granada.

Barthes, Roland
(1977) *Image—Music—Text.* Trans. Stephen Heath. New York: Hill & Wang.

Berger, John
(1972) *G.* New York: Pantheon.

Berger, Thomas
(1964) *Little Big Man.* New York: Dial.

Bertens, Hans
(1986) "The postmodern *Weltanschauung* and its relation with modernism: an introductory survey." In Fokkema and Bertens 1986, 9–51.

Brooke-Rose, Christine
(1981) *A Rhetoric of the Unreal: Studies in Narrative and Structure, Especially of the Fantastic.* Cambridge: Cambridge University Press.

Butler, Christopher
(1980) *After the Wake: An Essay on the Contemporary Avant-Garde.* Oxford: Oxford University Press.

Calinescu, Matei
(1977) *Faces of Modernity.* Bloomington: Indiana University Press.

Calinescu, Matei
(1986) "Postmodernism and some paradoxes of periodization." In Fokkema and Bertens 1986, 239–54.

Canary, Robert H. and Kozicki, Henry (eds)
(1978) *The Writing of History: Literary Form and Historical Understanding.* Madison: University of Wisconsin Press.

Carmello, Charles
(1983) *Silverless Mirrors: Book, Self and Postmodern American Fiction.* Tallahassee: University Presses of Florida.

Carroll, David
(1982) *The Subject in Question: The Languages of Theory and the Strategies of Fiction.* Chicago: University of Chicago Press.

Coover, Robert
(1977) *The Public Burning.* New York: Viking.

Cortázar, Julio
(1978) *A Manual for Manuel.* Trans. Gregory Rabassa. New York: Pantheon.

Crimp, Douglas
(1983) "On the museum's ruins." In Foster 1983, 43–56.

Culler, Jonathan
(1982) *On Deconstruction: Theory and Criticism after Structuralism.* Ithaca, NY: Cornell University Press.

Culler, Jonathan
(1983–84) "At the boundaries: Barthes and Derrida." In Sussman 1983–4, 23–41.

Cunliffe, Marcus (ed.)
(1975) *American Literature Since 1900.* London: Barrie & Jenkins.

Davis, Douglas
(1977) *Artculture: Essays on the Post-Modern*. New York: Harper & Row.

de Lauretis, Teresa
(1984) *Alice Doesn't: Feminism, Semiotics, Cinema*. Bloomington: Indiana University Press.

Derrida, Jacques
(1981) *Positions*. Trans. Alan Bass. Chicago: University of Chicago Press.

D'haen, Theo
(1986) "Postmodernism in American fiction and art." In Fokkema and Bertens 1986, 211–31.

Doctorow, E. L.
(1960) *Welcome to Hard Times*. New York: Simon & Schuster.

Doctorow, E. L.
(1971) *The Book of Daniel*. New York: Bantam.

Doctorow, E. L.
(1975) *Ragtime*. New York: Random House.

Eagleton, Terry
(1985) "Capitalism, modernism and postmodernism," *New Left Review*, 152, 60–73.

Eco, Umberto
(1983) *The Name of the Rose*. Trans. William Weaver. New York: Harcourt, Brace, Jovanovich.

Egbert, Donald D.
(1970) *Social Radicalism in the Arts*. New York: Knopf.

Fiedler, Leslie
(1975) "Cross the border—close that gap: postmodernism." In Cunliffe 1975, 344–66.

Findley, Timothy
(1981) *Famous Last Words*. Toronto and Vancouver: Clarke, Irwin.

Fish, Stanley
(1986) "Critical self-consciousness or can we know what we are doing?" Lecture at McMaster University, 4 April 1986.

Fokkema, Douwe
(1986) "Preliminary remarks." In Fokkema and Bertens 1986, 1–8.

Fokkema, Douwe and Bertens, Hans (eds)
(1986) *Approaching Postmodernism*. Amsterdam and Philadelphia: John Benjamins.

Foster, Hal (ed.)
(1983) *The Anti-Aesthetic: Essays on Postmodern Culture.* Port
Townsend, Washington: Bay Press.

Foucault, Michel
(1970) *The Order of Things: An Archaeology of the Human Sciences.*
New York: Pantheon.

Foucault, Michel
(1972) *The Archaeology of Knowledge and the Discourse on Language.*
Trans. A. M. Sheridan Smith. New York: Pantheon.

Fowles, John
(1969) *The French Lieutenant's Woman.* Boston and Toronto: Little,
Brown.

Fowles, John
(1985) *A Maggot.* Toronto: Collins.

Fuentes, Carlos
(1964) *The Death of Artemio Cruz.* Trans. Sam Hileman. New York:
Farrar, Straus & Giroux.

Garciá Márquez, Gabriel
(1971) *One Hundred Years of Solitude.* Trans. Gregory Rabassa. New
York: Avon.

Garvin, Harry R. (ed.)
(1980) *Romanticism, Modernism, Postmodernism.* Lewisberg: Bucknell
University Press. London: Associated University Press.

Ghose, Zulfikar
(1983) *The Fiction of Reality.* London: Macmillan.

Giddens, Anthony
(1981) "Modernism and post-modernism," *New German Critique,* 22
(Winter), 15–18.

Gossman, Lionel
(1978) "History and literature: reproduction or signification." In Canary and Kosicki 1978, 3–39.

Graff, Gerald
(1979) *Literature Against Itself.* Chicago: University of Chicago Press.

Graham, Joseph F.
(1982) "Critical persuasion: in response to Stanley Fish." In Spanos,
Bové and O'Hara 1982, 147–58.

Habermas, Jürgen
(1983) "Modernity—an incomplete project." Trans. Seyla Ben-Habib. In
Foster 1983, 3–15.

Harrison, Bernard
(1985) "Deconstructing Derrida." *Comparative Criticism,* 7, 3–24.

Hassan, Ihab (ed.)
(1971) *Liberations: New Essays on the Humanities in Revolution.* Middletown, Conn.: Wesleyan University Press.

Hassan, Ihab
(1975) *Paracriticisms: Seven Speculations of the Times.* Urbana: University of Illinois Press.

Hassan, Ihab
(1980a) *The Right Promethean Fire: Imagination, Science, and Cultural Change.* Urbana: University of Illinois Press.

Hassan, Ihab
(1980b) "The question of postmodernism." In Garvin 1980, 117–26.

Hassan, Ihab
(1983) "Postmodernism: a vanishing horizon." In MLA session, 'Toward a postmodern theory of genre: the new new novel'.

Hassan, Ihab
(1986) "Pluralism in postmodern perspective," *Critical Inquiry,* 12, 3, 503–20.

Hohendahl, Peter Uwe
(1982) *The Institution of Criticism.* Ithaca, NY: Cornell University Press.

Hutcheon, Linda
(1985) *A Theory of Parody: The Teachings of Twentieth-Century Art Forms.* London and New York: Methuen.

Huyssen, Andreas
(1981) "The search for tradition: avant-garde and postmodernism in the 1970s," *New German Critique,* 22 (Winter), 23–40.

Jameson, Fredric
(1983) "Postmodernism and consumer society." In Foster 1983, 111–25.

Jameson, Fredric
(1984a) "Postmodernism, or the cultural logic of late capitalism," *New Left Review,* 146 (July-August), 53–92.

Jameson, Fredric
(1984b) "Foreword" to Lyotard 1984a, vii–xxi.

Jencks, Charles
(1977) *The Language of Post-Modern Architecture.* London: Academy.

Jencks, Charles
(1980a) *Post-Modern Classicism: The New Synthesis.* London: Academy.

Jencks, Charles
(1980b) *Late-Modern Architecture and Other Essays*. London: Academy.

Jones, Gayl
(1975) *Corregidora*. New York: Random House.

Kamuf, Peggy
(1982) "Replacing feminist criticism," *Diacritics*, 12, 42–7.

Kennedy, William
(1978) *Legs*. Harmondsworth: Penguin.

Kingston, Maxine Hong
(1981) *China Men*. New York: Ballantine.

Kosinski, Jerzy
(1977) *Blind Date*. Boston, Mass.: Houghton Mifflin.

Kosinski, Jerzy
(1986) "Death in Cannes," *Esquire* (March), 81–9.

Kristeva, Julia
(1980) "Postmodernism?" In Garvin 1980, 136–41.

LaCapra, Dominick
(1985) *History and Criticism*, Ithaca, NY: Cornell University Press.

Lacoue-Labarthe, Philippe
(1984) "Talks," trans. Christopher Fynsk, *Diacritics*, 14, 3, 24–37.

Lefebvre, Henri
(1968) *La Vie quotidienne dans le monde moderne*. Paris: Gallimard.

Lethen, Helmut
(1986) "Modernism cut in half: the exclusion of the avant-garde and the debate on postmodernism." In Fokkema and Bertens 1986, 233–8.

Lodge, David
(1977) *The Modes of Modern Writing: Metaphor, Metonymy, and the Typology of Modern Literature*. London: Edward Arnold.

Lyotard, Jean-François
(1983) *Le Différend*. Paris: Minuit.

Lyotard, Jean-François
(1984a) *The Postmodern Condition: A Report on Knowledge*. Trans. Geoff Bennington and Brian Massumi. Minneapolis: University of Minnesota Press.

Lyotard, Jean-François
(1984b) 'Answering the question: what is postmodernism?' Trans. Régis Durand. In Lyotard 1984a, 71–82.

McCaffery, Larry
(1982) *The Metafictional Muse*. Pittsburg: University of Pittsburg
Press.

Malmgren, Carl Darryl
(1985) *Fictional Space in the Modernist and Postmodernist American
Novel*. Lewisburg: Bucknell University Press.

Monod, Jacques
(1971) *Chance and Necessity*. New York: Knopf.

Moreno, César Fernández (ed.)
(1974) *America Latina en su literatura*. 2nd edn. Buenos Aires:
Siglo XXI.

Munro, Alice
(1972) *Lives of Girls and Women: A Novel*. New York: McGraw-Hill.

Newman, Charles
(1985) *The Post-Modern Aura: The Act of Fiction in an Age of Inflation*.
Evanston, Ill.: Northwestern University Press.

Norris, Christopher
(1985) *The Contest of Faculties: Philosophy and Theory after Deconstruction*. London and New York: Methuen.

Oliva, Achille Bonito
(1984) "La trans-avanguardia," *Il Verri*, 1–2, 7th series (Marzo-
Giugno), 56–79.

Ondaatje, Michael
(1976) *Coming Through Slaughter*. Toronto: House of Anansi.

Owens, Craig
(1980) 'The allegorical impulse: toward a theory of postmodernism',
pt 2, *October*, 13, 59–80.

Palmer, Richard E.
(1977) "Postmodernity and hermeneutics," *Boundary*, 2, 5, 2, 363–93.

Peckham, Morse
(1965) *Man's Rage for Chaos: Biology, Behavior, and the Arts*. Philadelphia: Chilton Books.

Portoghesi, Paolo
(1983) *Postmodern: The Architecture of the Postindustrial Society*. New
York: Rizzoli.

Puig, Manuel
(1978–9) *Kiss of the Spider Woman*. New York: Random House.

Pynchon, Thomas
(1973) *Gravity's Rainbow*. New York: Viking.

Radhakrishnan, Rajagoplan
(1983) "The post-modern event and the end of logocentrism," *Boundary*, 2, 12, 1, 33–60.

Reed, Ishmael
(1972) *Mumbo Jumbo*, Garden City, NY: Doubleday.

Rorty, Richard
(1984) "Deconstruction and circumvention," *Critical Inquiry*, 11, 1, 1–23.

Rushdie, Salman
(1982) *Midnight's Children*. London: Picador.

Rushdie, Salman
(1983) *Shame*. London: Picador.

Russell, Charles
(1980) "The context of the concept." In Garvin 1980, 181–93.

Russell, Charles
(1985) *Poets, Prophets, and Revolutionaries: The Literary Avant-garde from Rimbaud through Postmodernism*. New York and Oxford: Oxford University Press.

Said, Edward W.
(1983) *The World, the Text, and the Critic*. Cambridge, Mass.: Harvard University Press.

Sarduy, Severo
(1974) "El barroco y el neobarroco." In Moreno 1974, 167–84.

Scott, Chris
(1982) *Antichthon*. Montreal: Quadrant.

Sontag, Susan
(1967) *Against Interpretation and Other Essays*. New York: Dell.

Spanos, William V., Bové, Paul A. and O'Hara, Daniel (eds)
(1982) *The Question of Textuality: Strategies of Reading in Contemporary American Criticism*. Bloomington: Indiana University Press.

Stern, Daniel
(1971) "The mysterious new novel." In Hassan 1971, 22–37.

Suleiman, Susan Rubin
(1986) "Naming and difference: reflections on 'modernism *versus* postmodernism' in literature." In Fokkema and Bertens 1986, 255–70.

Sussman, Herbert L. (ed.)
(1983–4) *At the Boundaries*. Boston, Mass.: Northeastern University Press.

Swan, Susan
(1983) *The Biggest Modern Woman of the World*. Toronto: Lester and
Orpen Dennys.

Swift, Graham
(1983) *Waterland*. London: Heinemann.

Thiher, Allen
(1984) *Words in Reflection: Modern Language Theory and Postmodern
Fiction*. Chicago: University of Chicago Press.

Thomas, D. M.
(1981) *The White Hotel*. Harmondsworth: Penguin.

Todorov, Tzvetan
(1981) *Introduction to Poetics*. Trans. Richard Howard. Minneapolis:
University of Minnesota Press.

Toulmin, Stephen
(1972) *Human Understanding*. 2 vols. Princeton, NJ: Princeton University Press.

Wasson, Richard
(1974) "From priest to Prometheus: culture and criticism in the postmodern period," *Journal of Modern Literature*, 3, 5, 1188–1202.

Watkins, Evan
(1978) *The Critical Act: Criticism and Community*. New Haven, Conn.,
and London: Yale University Press.

Watson, Ian
(1975) *The Embedding*. London: Quartet.

Watson, Ian
(1983) *Chekov's Journey*. London: Gollancz.

White, Hayden
(1973) *Metahistory: The Historical Imagination in Nineteenth-Century
Europe*. Baltimore: Johns Hopkins University Press.

White, Hayden
(1978) *Tropics of Discourse: Essays in Cultural Criticism*. Baltimore
and London: Johns Hopkins University Press.

White, Hayden
(1980) "The value of narrativity in the representation of reality," *Critical Inquiry*, 7, 1, 5–27.

White, Hayden
(1981) "The narrativization of real events," *Critical Inquiry*, 7, 4,
793–8.

White, Hayden
(1984) "The question of narrative in contemporary historical theory,"
History and Theory, 23, 1–33.

Wiebe, Rudy
(1973) *The Temptations of Big Bear.* Toronto: McClelland & Stewart.

Wiebe, Rudy
(1977) *The Scorched-Wood People.* Toronto: McClelland & Stewart.

Wilde, Alan
(1981) *Horizons of Assent: Modernism, Postmodernism, and the Ironic
Imagination.* Baltimore: Johns Hopkins University Press.

Williams, Raymond
(1960) *Culture and Society 1780–1950.* Garden City, NY: Doubleday.

Ziolkowski, Theodore
(1969) "Toward a post-modern aesthetics?," *Mosaic,* 2, 4, 112–19.

Toward a Concept of Postmodernism

Ihab Hassan

The strains of silence in literature, from Sade to Beckett, convey complexities of language, culture, and consciousness as these contest themselves and one another. Such eerie music may yield an experience, an intuition, of postmodernism but no concept or definition of it. Perhaps I can move here toward such a concept by putting forth certain queries. I begin with the most obvious: can we really perceive a phenomenon, in Western societies generally and in their literatures particularly, that needs to be distinguished from modernism, needs to be named? If so, will the provisional rubric "postmodernism" serve? Can we then—or even should we at this time—construct of this phenomenon some probative scheme, both chronological and typological, that may account for its various trends and counter-trends, its artistic, epistemic, and social character? And how would this phenomenon—let us call it postmodernism—relate itself to such earlier modes of change as turn-of-the-century avant-gardes or the high modernism of the twenties? Finally, what difficulties would inhere in any such act of definition, such a tentative heuristic scheme?

I am not certain that I can wholly satisfy my own questions, though I can assay some answers that may help to focus the larger problem. History, I take it, moves in measures both continuous and discontinuous. Thus the prevalence of postmodernism today, if indeed it prevails, does not suggest that ideas of institutions of the past cease to shape the present. Rather, traditions develop, and even types suffer a seachange. Certainly, the powerful cultural assumptions generated by, say, Darwin, Marx, Bauldelaire, Nietzsche, Cézanne, Debussy, Freud, and Einstein still pervade the Western mind. Certainly those assumptions have been reconceived, not once but many times—else history would repeat itself, forever the same. In this perspective postmodernism may appear as a significant revision, if not an original *èpistèmé,* of twentieth-century Western societies.

Some names, piled here pell-mell, may serve to adumbrate postmodernism, or at least suggest its range of assumptions: Jacques Derrida, Jean-François Lyotard (philosophy), Michel Foucault, Hayden White (history), Jacques Lacan, Gilles Deleuze, R. D. Laing, Norman O. Brown (psychoanalysis), Herbert Marcuse, Jean Baudrillard, Jürgen Habermas (political philosophy), Thomas Kuhn, Paul Feyerabend (philosophy of science), Roland Barthes, Julia Kristeva, Wolfgang Iser, the "Yale Critics" (literary theory), Merce Cunningham, Alwin Nikolais, Meredith Monk (dance), John Cage, Karlheinz Stockhausen, Pierre Boulez (music), Robert Rauschenberg, Jean Tinguely, Joseph Beuys (art), Robert Venturi, Charles Jencks, Brent Bolin (architecture), and various authors from Samuel Beckett, Eugène Ionesco, Jorge Luis Borges, Max Bense, and Vladimir Nabokov to Harold Pinter, B. S. Johnson, Rayner Heppenstall, Christine Brooke-Rose, Helmut Heissenbüttel, Jürgen Becker, Peter Handke, Thomas Bernhardt, Ernest Jandl, Gabriel García Márquez, Julio Cortázar, Alain Robbe-Grillet, Michel Butor, Maurice Roche, Philippe Sollers, and, in America, John Barth, William Burroughs, Thomas Pynchon, Donald Barthelme, Walter Abish, John Ashbery, David Antin, Sam Shepard, and Robert Wilson. Indubitably, these names are far too heterogenous to form a movement, paradigm, or school. Still, they may evoke a number of related cultural tendencies, a constellation of values, a repertoire of procedures and attitudes. These we call *postmodernism.*

Whence this term? Its origin remains uncertain, though we know that Federico de Onís used the word *postmodernismo* in his *Antología de la poesía española e hispanoamericana* (1882–1932), published in Madrid in 1934; and Dudley Fitts picked it up again in his *Anthology of Contemporary Latin-American Poetry* of 1942.[1] Both meant thus to indicate a minor reaction to modernism already latent within it, reverting to the early twentieth century. The term also appeared in Arnold Toynbee's *A Study of History* as early as D. C. Somervell's first-volume abridgement in 1947. For Toynbee, Post-Modernism designated a new historical cycle in Western civilization, starting around 1875, which we now scarcely begin to discern. Somewhat later, during the fifties, Charles Olson often spoke of postmodernism with more sweep than lapidary definition.

But prophets and poets enjoy an ample sense of time, which few literary scholars seem to afford. In 1959 and 1960, Irving Howe and Harry Levin wrote of postmodernism rather disconsolately as a falling off from the great modernist movement.[2] It remained for Leslie Fiedler and myself, among others, to employ the term during the sixties with premature approbation, and even with a touch of bravado.[3] Fiedler had it in mind to challenge the elitism of the high modernist tradition in the name of popular culture. I wanted to explore the impulse of self-unmaking which is part of the literary tradition of silence. Pop and silence, or mass culture and deconstruction, or Superman and Godot—or as I shall later argue, immanence and indeterminacy—may all be aspects of the postmodern universe. But all this must wait upon more patient analysis, longer history.

Yet the history of literary terms serves only to confirm the irrational genius of language. We come closer to the question of postmodernism itself by acknowledging the psychopolitics, if not the psychopathology, of academic life. Let us admit it: there is a will to power in nomenclature, as well as in people or texts. A new term opens for its proponents a space in language. A critical concept or system is a "poor" poem of the intellectual imagination. The battle of the books is also an ontic battle against death. That may be why Max Planck believed that one never manages to convince one's opponents—not even in theoretical physics!—one simply tries to outlive them. William James described the process in less morbid terms: novelties are first repudiated as nonsense, then declared obvious, then appropriated by former adversaries as their own discoveries.

I do not mean to take my stand with the postmoderns against the (ancient) moderns. In an age of frantic intellectual fashions, values can be too recklessly voided, and tomorrow can quickly preempt today or yesteryear. Nor is it merely a matter of fashions; for the sense of supervention may express some cultural urgency that partakes less of hope than fear. This much we recall: Lionel Trilling entitled one of his most thoughtful works *Beyond Culture* (1965); Kenneth Boulding argued that "postcivilization" is an essential part of *The Meaning of the 20th Century* (1964); and George Steiner could have subtitled his essay, *In Bluebeard's Castle* (1971); "Notes Toward the Definition of Postculture." Before them, Roderick Seidenberg published his *Post-Historic Man* exactly in mid-century; and most recently, I have myself speculated, in *The Right Promethean Fire* (1980), about the advent of a posthumanist era. As Daniel Bell put it: "It used to be that the great literary modifier was the word *beyond*. . . . But we seem to have exhausted the beyond, and today the sociological modifier is *post*."[4]

My point here is double: in the question of postmodernism, there is a will and counter-will to intellectual power, an imperial desire of the mind, but this will and desire are themselves caught in a historical moment of supervention, if not exactly of obsolescence. The reception or denial of postmodernism thus remains contingent on the psychopolitics of academic life—including the various dispositions of people and power in our universities, of critical factions and personal frictions, of boundaries that arbitrarily include or exclude—no less than on the imperatives of the culture at large. This much, reflexivity seems to demand from us at the start.

But reflection demands also that we address a number of conceptual problems that both conceal and constitute postmodernism itself. I shall try to isolate ten of these, commencing with the simpler, moving toward the more intractable.

1. The word postmodernism sounds not only awkward, uncouth; it evokes what it wishes to surpass or suppress, modernism itself. The term thus contains its enemy within, as the terms romanticism and classicism, baroque and rococo, do not. Moreover, it denotes temporal linearity and connotes belatedness, even decadence, to which no post-modernist would admit. But what better name have we to give this curious age? The Atomic, or Space, or Television, Age? These technological tags lack theoretical definition. Or shall we call it the Age of Indetermanence (indeterminacy + immanence) as I have half-antically proposed?[5] Or better still, shall we simply live and let others live to call us what they may?

2. Like other categorical terms—say poststructuralism, or modernism, or romanticism for that matter—postmodernism suffers from a certain *semantic* instability: that is, no clear consensus about its meaning exists among scholars. The general difficulty is compounded in this case by two factors: (a) the relative youth, indeed brash adolescence, of

the term postmodernism, and (b) its semantic kinship to more current terms, themselves equally unstable. Thus some critics mean by postmodernism what others call avant-gardism or even neo-avant-gardism, while still others would call the same phenomenon simply modernism. This can make for inspired debates.[6]

3. A related difficulty concerns the *historical* instability of many literary concepts, their openness to change. Who, in this epoch of fierce misprisions, would dare to claim that romanticism is apprehended by Coleridge, Pater, Lovejoy, Abrams, Peckham, and Bloom in quite the same way? There is already some evidence that postmodernism, and modernism even more, are beginning to slip and slide in time, threatening to make any diacritical distinction between them desperate.[7] But perhaps the phenomenon, akin to Hubble's "red shift" in astronomy, may someday serve to measure the historical velocity of literary concepts.

4. Modernism and postmodernism are not separated by an Iron Curtain or Chinese Wall; for history is a palimpsest, and culture is permeable to time past, time present, and time future. We are all, I suspect, a little Victorian, Modern, and Postmodern, at once. And an author may, in his or her own lifetime, easily write both a modernist and postmodernist work. (Contrast Joyce's *Portrait of the Artist as a Young Man* with his *Finnegans Wake*.) More generally, on a certain level of narrative abstraction, modernism itself may be rightly assimilated to romanticism, romanticism related to the enlightenment, the latter to the renaissance, and so back, if not to the Olduvai Gorge, then certainly to ancient Greece.

5. This means that a "period," as I have already intimated, must be perceived in terms *both* of continuity *and* discontinuity, the two perspectives being complementary and partial. The Apollonian view, rangy and abstract, discerns only historical conjunctions; the Dionysian feeling, sensuous though nearly purblind, touches only the disjunctive moment. Thus postmodernism, by invoking two divinities at once, engages a double view. Sameness and difference, unity and rupture, filiation and revolt, all must be honored if we are to attend to history, apprehend (perceive, understand) change, both as a spatial, mental structure

and as a temporal, physical process, both as pattern and unique event.

6. Thus a "period" is generally not a period at all; it is rather both a diachronic and synchronic construct. Postmodernism, again, like modernism or romanticism, is no exception; it requires *both* historical *and* theoretical definition. We would not seriously claim an inaugural "date" for it as Virginia Woolf pertly did for modernism, though we may sometimes woefully imagine that postmodernism began "in or about September, 1939." Thus we continually discover "antecedents" of postmodernism— in Sterne, Sade, Blake, Lautréamont, Rimbaud, Jarry, Tzara, Hofmannsthal, Gertrude Stein, the later Joyce, the later Pound, Duchamp, Artaud, Roussel, Bataille, Broch, Queneau, and Kafka. What this really indicates is that we have created in our mind a model of postmodernism, a particular typology of culture and imagination, and have proceeded to "rediscover" the affinities of various authors and different moments with that model. We have, that is, reinvented our ancestors—and always shall. Consequently, "older" authors can be postmodern—Kafka, Beckett, Borges, Nabokov, Gombrowicz—while "younger" authors needs not be so—Styron, Updike, Capote, Irving, Doctorow, Gardner.

7. As we have seen, any definition of postmodernism calls upon a four-fold vision of complementarities, embracing continuity and discontinuity, diachrony and synchrony. But a definition of the concept also requires a dialectical vision; for defining traits are often antithetical, and to ignore this tendency of historical reality is to lapse into single vision and Newton's sleep. Defining traits are dialectical and also plural; to elect a single trait as an absolute criterion of postmodern grace is to make of all other writers preterites.[8] Thus we can not simply rest—as I have sometimes done—on the assumption that postmodernism is antiformal, anarchic, or decreative; for though it is indeed all these, and despite its fanatic will to unmaking, it also contains the need to discover a "unitary sensibility" (Sontag), to "cross the border and close the gap" (Fiedler), and to attain, as I have suggested, an immanence of discourse, an expanded noetic intervention, a "neo-gnostic im-mediacy of mind."[9]

8. All this leads to the prior problem of periodization itself, which is also that of literary history conceived as a particular apprehension of change. Indeed, the concept of postmodernism applies some theory of innovation, renovation, novation, or simply change. But which one? Heraclitean? Viconian? Darwinian? Marxist? Freudian? Kuhnian? Derridean? Eclectic?[10] Or is a "theory of change" itself an oxymoron best suited to ideologues intolerant of the ambiguities of time? Should postmodernism, then, be left—at least for the moment—unconceptualized, a kind of literary-historical "difference" or "trace"?[11]

9. Postmodernism can expand into a still large problem: is it only an artistic tendency or also a social phenomenon, perhaps even a mutation in Western humanism? If so, how are the various aspects of this phenomenon—psychological, philosophical, economic, political—joined or disjoined? In short, can we understand postmodernism in literature without some attempt to perceive the lineaments of a postmodern society, a Toynbeean postmodernity, or future Foucauldian *épistémè*, of which the literary tendency I have been discussing is but a single, elitist strain?[12]

10. Finally, though not least vexing, is postmodernism an honorific term, used insidiously to valorize writers, however disparate, whom we otherwise esteem, to hail trends, however discordant, which we somehow approve? Or is it, on the contrary, a term of opprobrium and objurgation? In short, is postmodernism a descriptive as well as evaluative or normative category of literary thought? Or does it belong, as Charles Altieri notes, to that category of "essentially contested concepts" in philosophy that never wholly exhaust their constitutive confusions?[13]

No doubt, other conceptual problems lurk in the matter of postmodernism. Such problems, however, can not finally inhibit the intellectual imagination, the desire to apprehend our historical presence in noetic constructs that reveal our being to ourselves. I move, therefore, to propose a provisional scheme that the literature of silence, from Sade to Beckett, seems to envisage, and do so by distinguishing, tentatively, between three modes of artistic change in the last hundred years. I call these avant-garde, modern, and postmodern, though I realize that all three have conspired together to create that "tradition of the new" that, since Baudelaire, brought "into being an art whose history regardless of the credos of its practitioners, has consisted of leaps from vanguard to vanguard, and political mass movements whose aim has been the total renovation not only of social institutions but of man himself."[14]

By avant-garde, I means those movements that agitated the earlier part of our century, including 'Pataphysics, Cubism, Futurism, Dadaism, Surrealism, Suprematism, Constructivism, Merzism, de Stijl—some of which I have already discussed in this work. Anarchic, these assaulted the bourgeoisie with their art, their manifestoes, their antics. But their activism could also turn inward, becoming suicidal—as happened later to some postmodernists like Rudolf Schwartzkogler. Once full of brio and bravura, these movements have all but vanished now, leaving only their story, at once fugacious and exemplary. Modernism, however, proved more stable, aloof, hieratic, like the French Symbolism from which it derived; even its experiments now seem olympian. Enacted by such "individual talents" as Valéry, Proust, and Gide, the early Joyce, Yeats, and Lawrence, Rilke, Mann, and Musil, the early Pound, Eliot, and Faulkner, it commanded high authority, leading Delmore Schwartz to chant in *Shenandoah:* "Let us consider where the great men are/ Who will obsess the child when he can read . . . " But if much of modernism appears hieratic, hypotactical, and formalist, postmodernism strikes us by contrast as playful, paratactical, and deconstructionist. In this it recalls the irreverent spirit of the avantgarde, and so carries sometimes the label of neo-avant-garde. Yet postmodernism remains "cooler," in McLuhan's sense, than older vanguards—cooler, less cliquish, and far less aversive to the pop, electronic society of which it is a part, and so hospitable to kitsch.

Can we distinguish postmodernism further? Perhaps certain schematic differences from modernism will provide a start:

Modernism	Postmodernism
Romanticism/Symbolism	'Pataphysics/Dadaism
Form (conjunctive, closed)	Antiform (disjunctive, open)
Purpose	Play
Design	Chance
Hierarchy	Anarchy
Mastery/Logos	Exhaustion/Silence
Art Object/Finished Work	Process/Performance/Happening
Distance	Participation
Creation/Totalization	Decreation/Deconstruction

Synthesis	Antithesis
Presence	Absence
Centering	Dispersal
Genre/Boundary	Text/Intertext
Semantics	Rhetoric
Paradigm	Syntagm
Hypotaxis	Parataxis
Metaphor	Metonymy
Selection	Combination
Root/Depth	Rhizome/Surface
Interpretation/Reading	Against Interpretation/Misreading
Signified	Signifier
Lisible (Readerly)	*Scriptible* (Writerly)
Narrative/*Grande Histoire*	Anti-narrative/*Petite Histoire*
Master Code	Idiolect
Symptom	Desire
Type	Mutant
Genital/Phallic	Polymorphous/Androgynous
Paranoia	Schizophrenia
Origin/Cause	Difference-Differance/Trace
God the Father	The Holy Ghost
Metaphysics	Irony
Determinancy	Indeterminancy
Transcendence	Immanence

The preceding table draws on ideas in many fields—rhetoric, linguistics, literary theory, philosophy, anthropology, psychoanalysis, political science, even theology—and draws on many authors—European and American—aligned with diverse movements, groups, and views. Yet the dichotomies this table represents remain insecure, equivocal. For differences shift, defer, even collapse; concepts in any one vertical column are not all equivalent; and inversions and exceptions, in both modernism and postmodernism, abound. Still, I would submit that rubrics in the right column point to the postmodern tendency, the tendency of indetermanence, and so may bring us closer to its historical and theoretical definition.

The time has come, however, to explain a little that neologism: "indetermanence." I have used that term to designate two central, constitutive tendencies in postmodernism: one of indeterminancy, the other of immanence. The two tendencies are not dialectical; for they are not exactly antithetical; nor do they lead to a synthesis. Each contains its own contradictions, and alludes to elements of the other. Their interplay suggests the action of a "polylectic," pervading postmodernism. Since I have discussed this topic at some length earlier, I can avert to it here briefly.[15]

By indeterminacy, or better still, *indeterminacies,* I mean a complex referent that these diverse concepts help to delineate: ambiguity, discontinuity, heterodoxy, pluralism, randomness, revolt, perversion, deformation. The latter alone subsumes a dozen current terms of unmaking: decreation, disintegration, deconstruction, decenterment, displacement, difference, discontinuity, disjunction, disappearance, decomposition, de-definition, demystification, detotalization, delegitimization—let alone more technical terms referring to the rhetoric of irony, rupture, silence. Through all these signs moves a vast will to unmaking, affecting the body politic, the body cognitive, the erotic body, the individual psyche—the entire realm of discourse in the West. In literature alone our ideas of author, audience, reading, writing, book, genre, critical theory, and of literature itself, have all suddenly become questionable. And in criticism? Roland Barthes speaks of literature as "loss," "perversion," "dissolution"; Wolfgang Iser formulates a theory of reading based on textual "blanks"; Paul de Man conceives rhetoric—that is, literature—as a force that "radically suspends logic and opens up vertiginous possibilities of referential aberration"; and Geoffrey Hartman affirms that "contemporary criticism aims at the hermeneutics of indeterminacy."[16]

Such uncertain diffractions make for vast dispersals. Thus I call the second major tendency of postmodernism *immanences,* a term that I employ without religious echo to designate the capacity of mind to generalize itself in symbols, intervene more and more into nature, act upon itself through its own abstractions and so become, increasingly, im-mediately, by its own environment. This noetic tendency may be evoked further by such sundry concepts as diffusion, dissemination, pulsion, interplay, communication, interdependence, which all derive from the emergence of human beings as language animals, *homo pictor* or *homo significans,* gnostic creatures constituting themselves, and determinedly their universe, by symbols of their own making. Is "this not the sign that the whole of this configuration is about to topple, and that man is in the process of perishing as the being of language continues to shine ever brighter upon our horizon?" Foucault famously asks.[17] Meanwhile, the public world dissolves as fact and fiction blend, history becomes derealized by media into a happening, science takes its own models as the only accessible reality, cybernetics confronts us with the enigma of artificial intelligence, and technologies project our perceptions to the edge of the receding universe or into the ghostly interstices of matter.[18] Everywhere—even deep in Lacan's "lettered unconscious," more dense than a black hole in space—everywhere we encounter that immanence called Language, with all its literary ambiguities, epistemic conundrums, and political distractions.[19]

No doubt these tendencies may seem less rife in England, say, than in America or France where the term postmodernism, reversing the recent direction of poststructuralist flow, has now come into use.[20] But the fact in most developed societies remains: as an artistic, philosophical, and social phenomenon, postmodernism veers toward open, playful, optative, provisional (open in time as well as in structure or space), disjunctive, or indeterminate forms, a discourse of ironies and fragments, a "white ideology" of absences and fractures, a desire of diffractions, an invocation of complex, articulate silences. Postmodernism veers towards all these yet implies a different, if not antithetical, movement toward pervasive procedures, ubiquitous interactions, immanent codes, media, languages. Thus our earth seems caught in the process of planetization, transhumanization, even as it breaks up into sects, tribes, factions of every kind. Thus, too, terrorism and totalitarianism, schism and ecumenism, summon one another, and authorities decreate themselves even as societies search for new grounds of authority. One may well wonder: is some decisive historical mutation—involving art and science, high and low culture, the male and female principles, parts and wholes, involving the One and the Many as pre-Socratics used to say—active in our midst? Or does the dismemberment of Orpheus prove no more than the mind's need to make but one more construction of life's mutabilities and human mortality?

And what construction lies beyond, behind, within, that construction?

Notes

1. For the best history of the term *postmodernism* see Michael Köhler, " 'Postmodernismus': Ein begriffsgeschichtlicher Überblick," *Amerikastudien,* vol. 22, no. 1 (1977). That same issue contains other excellent discussions and bibliographies on the term; see particularly Gerhard Hoffmann, Alfred Hornung, and Rüdiger Kunow, " 'Modern,' 'Postmodern,' and 'Contemporary' as Criteria for the Analysis of 20th Century Literature."

2. Irving Howe, "Mass Society and Postmodern Fiction," *Partisan Review,* vol. 26, no. 3 (Summer 1959), reprinted in his *Decline of the New* (New

York, 1970), 190–207; and Harry Levin, "What Was Modernism?", Massachusetts Review, vol. 1, no. 4 (August 1960), reprinted in *Refractions* (New York, 1966), 271–295.

3. Leslie Fiedler, "The New Mutants," *Partisan Review*, vol. 32, no. 4 (Fall 1965), reprinted in his *Collected Essays*, vol. 2 (New York, 1971), 379–400; and Ihab Hassan, "Frontiers of Criticism: Metaphors of Silence," *Virginia Quarterly*, vol. 46, no. 1 (Winter 1970). In earlier essays I had also used the term "Anti-literature" and "the literature of silence" in a proximate sense; see, for instance Ihab Hassan, "The Literature of Silence," *Encounter*, vol. 28, no. 1 (January 1967), and pp. 3–22 above.

4. Daniel Bell, *The Coming of Post-Industrial Society* (New York, 1973), 53.

5. See pp. 46–83 [in *The Postmodern Turn.*]

6. Matei Calinescu, for instance, tends to assimilate "postmodern" to "neo-avant-garde" and sometimes to "avant-garde," in *Faces of Modernity: Avant-Garde, Decadence, Kitsch* (Bloomington, 1977), though later he discriminates between these terms thoughtfully, in "Avant-Garde, Neo-Avant-Garde, and Postmodernism," unpublished manuscript. Miklos Szabolcsi would identify "modern" with "avant-garde" and call "postmodern" the "neo-avant-garde," in "Avant-Garde, Neo-Avant-Garde, Modernism: Questions and Suggestions," *New Literary History*, vol. 3, no 1 (Autumn 1971); while Paul de Man would call "modern" the innovative element, the perpetual "moment of crisis" in the literature of every period, in "Literary History and Literary Modernity," in *Blindness and Insight* (New York, 1971), chapter 8; in a similar vein, William V. Spanos employs the term "postmodernism" to indicate "not fundamentally a chronological event, but rather a permanent mode of human understanding," in "De-Struction and the Question of Postmodern Literature: Towards a Definition," *Par Rapport*, vol. 2, no. 2 (Summer 1979), 107. And even John Barth, as inward as any writer with postmodernism, now argues that postmodernism is a synthesis yet to come, and what we had assumed to be postmodernism all along was only late modernism, in "The Literature of Replenishment: Post modernist Fiction," *Atlantic Monthly* 245, no. 1 (January 1980).

7. In my own earlier and later essays on the subject, I can discern such a slight shift. See "POSTmodernISM," pp. 25–45 above, "Joyce, Beckett, and the Postmodern Imagination," *TriQuarterly* 34 (Fall 1975), and "Culture, Indeterminacy, and Immanence," pp. 46–83 above.

8. Though some critics have argued that postmodernism is primarily "temporal" and others that it is mainly "spatial," it is in the particular relation between these single categories that postmodernism probably reveals itself. See the two seemingly contradictory views of William V. Spanos, "The Detective at the Boundary," in *Existentialism* 2, ed. William V. Spanos (New York, 1976), 163–89; and Jürgen Peper, "Postmodernismus: Unitary Sensibility," *Amerikastudien*, vol. 22, no. 1 (1977).

9. Susan Sontag, "One Culture and the New Sensibility," in *Against Interpretation* (New York, 1967), 293–304; Leslie Fiedler, "Cross the Border—Close the Gap," in *Collected Essays,* vol. 2 (New York, 1971), 461–85; and Ihab Hassan, "The New Gnosticism," *Paracriticism: Seven Speculations of the Times* (Urbana, 1975), chapter 6.

10. For some views of this, see Ihab Hassan and Sally Hassan, eds. *Innovation/Renovation: Recent Trends and Reconceptions in Western Culture* (Madison, Wis., 1983).

11. At stake here is the idea of literary periodicity, challenged by current French thought. For other views of literary and historical change, including "hierarchic organization" of time, see Leonard Meyer, *Music, the Arts and Ideas* (Chicago, 1967), 93, 102; Calinescu, *Faces of Modernity,* 147ff; Ralph Cohen, "Innovation and Variation: Literary Change and Georgic Poetry," in Ralph Cohen and Murray Krieger, *Literature and History* (Los Angeles, 1974); and my *Paracriticisms,* chapter 7. A harder question is one Geoffrey Hartman asks: "With so much historical knowledge, how can we avoid historicism, or the staging of history as a drama in which epiphanic raptures are replaced by epistemic ruptures?" Or, again, how can we "formulate a theory of reading that would be historical rather than historicist"? *Saving the Text: Literature/Derrida/Philosophy* (Baltimore, 1981), xx.

12. Writers as different as Marshall McLuhan and Leslie Fiedler have explored the media and pop aspects of postmodernism for two decades, thought their efforts are now out of fashion in some circles. The difference between postmodernism, as a contemporary artistic tendency, and postmodernity, as a cultural phenomenon, perhaps even an era of history, is discussed by Richard E. Palmer 5in "Postmodernity and Hermeneutics," *Boundary* 2, vol. 5, no. 2 (Winter 1977).

13. Charles Altieri, "Postmodernism: A Question of Definition," *Par Rapport,* vol. 2, no. 2 (Summer 1979), 90. This leads Altieri to conclude: "The best one can do who believes himself post-modern . . . is to articulate spaces of mind in which the confusions can not paralyze because one enjoys the energies and glimpses of our condition which they produce," p. 99.

14. Harold Rosenberg, *The Tradition of the New* (New York, 1961), 9.

15. See pp. 65–72 [in *The Postmodern Turn*]. Also, my "Innovation/Renovation: Toward a Cultural Theory of Change," *Innovation/Renovation,* chapter 1.

16. See, for instance, Roland Barthes and Maurice Nadeau, *Sur la littérature* (Paris, 1980), 7, 16, 19f, 41; Wolfgang Iser, *The Act of Reading* (Baltimore, 1978), *passim;* Paul de Man, *Allegories of Reading* (New Haven, Conn., 1979), 10; and Geoffrey H. Hartman, *Criticism in the Wilderness* (New Haven, 1980), 41.

17. Michel Foucault, *The Order of Things* (New York, 1970), 386.

18. "Just as Pascal sought to throw the dice with God . . . so do the decisions theorists, and the new intellectual technology, seek their own *tableau entier*—the compass of rationality itself," Daniel Bell remarks in "Technology, Nature, and Society," in *Technology and the Frontiers of Knowledge* (Garden City, 1975), 53. See also the more acute analysis of *"l'informatique"* by Jean-François Lyotard, *La Condition postmoderne* (Paris, 1979, *passim.*

19. This tendency also makes the abstract, conceptual, and irrealist character of so much postmodern art. See Suzi Gablik, *Progress in Art* (New York, 1977), whose argument was prefigured by Ortega y Gasset, *The Dehumanization of Art* (Princeton, 1968). Note also that Ortega presaged the gnostic or noetic tendency to which I refer here in 1925: "Man humanizes the world, injects it, impregnates it with his own ideal substance and is finally entitled to imagine that one day or another, in the far depths of time, this terrible outer world will become so saturated with man that our descendants will be able to travel through it as today we mentally travel through our own most inmost selves—he finally imagines that the world, without ceasing to be like the world, will one day be changed into something like a materialized soul, and, as in Shakespeare's *Tempest,* the winds will blow at the bidding of Ariel, the spirit of ideas," p. 184.

20. Though postmodernism and poststructuralism can not be identified, they clearly reveal many affinities. Thus in the course of one brief essay, Julia Kristeva comments on both immanence and indeterminacy in terms of her own: "postmodernism is that literature which writes itself with the more or less conscious intention of expanding the signifiable, and thus human, realm"; and again: "At this degree of singularity, we are faced with idiolects, proliferating uncontrollably." Julia Kristeva, "Postmodernism?" in *Romanticism, Modernism, Postmodernism,* ed. Harry R. Garvin (Lewisberg, Pa. 1980), 137, 141.

The Context of the Concept

Charles Russell

Preface

Prior to Joseph Kosuth's show in Eindhoven, three posters were placed on billboards throughout the city. There were no identifying markings that would link them to Kosuth or an art exhibit. They were placed amidst groups of posters all of which were part of a local election campaign that was in progress the month before the museum show. When the show opened, Kosuth's posters were prominently displayed, now in the *art* context of a ten-year retrospective of his artwork. Here are the three texts:

> *Re-read this text. This text, which is only part of a larger discourse (stop for a moment and look around you) wants you to re-read it. At this point, right now, its meaning is provided by you; perhaps if you re-read it (even starting here in the middle of the fourth line) you might locate the subject of this text and that discourse (look around again) which includes you and the object of this text. This sign, these words, as you can see from their location, have a specific meaning. Without this horizon of*

Charles Russell, "The Context of the Concept," *Bucknell Review's Romanticism, Modernism, Postmodernism*, ed. Harry R. Garvin, pp. 181–93. Copyright 1980 Associated University Presses. Reprinted by permission.

*meaning your sense of freedom (the one that understands that
this text is addressing you) might read all this as being empty.*

*This discourse around you takes certain things for granted, like
this. Perhaps this sign you are reading is wrong, but it seems to
it that parts or things of this conversation change constantly,
yet what doesn't change is how they mean. In other words, our
relationship with these 'things.' What's said here doesn't really
seem to matter, as long as this structure (this thing you are looking at that's part of organized culture) as a form maintains and
extends the frame of its own system. Here you have it. Yet, what
it's saying is only part of what it's saying.*

*Is this local? Is this text, this discourse, 'out there' as part of
the real world or is its meaning trapped here? This text is
Dutch, perhaps this sign is Dutch, we (this sign and you) are in
Eindhoven. The discourse around us is speaking locally, but
where is it located? If this discourse, this text, could 'see itself'
it would be capable of defining its structure (kinds of relationships) and describing its context (as politics, as culture, as a
text, as a blank).*

New works of art and literature generally appear to follow recognizable patterns of historical development. Even within that period
of frequent and strident declarations of ever-new aesthetic movements—the age of modernism and the avant-garde—each work or
movement that announced itself was an evident manifestation of
the underlying conceptual patterns that defined the modern aesthetic experience.

But occasionally, a work, an artist, or a movement will introduce a new stylistic element, raise a particular aesthetic question,
or propose an interpretation of art and experience that may at
first appear to be merely the next logical step in accepted art history, but which subsequently must be seen as revealing the fatal
limitations of current patterns of seeing or reading, and as having,
in fact, effected a fundamental transformation of the practices of
art or literature. Such is the case with the recently emergent art
and literature known under the somewhat provisional name of the
"postmodern." At once the legitimate, the logical—even the necessary—outgrowth of modernism, the postmodern presages a radical
alteration of art, of its means of describing the world, its relationship to its audience, and, ultimately, its social function. And while
similar claims for the uniqueness or historical significance of nu-

merous avant-garde movements have characterized modern art history, it is important to see that postmodernism is not tied solely to a single artist or movement, but defines a broad cultural phenomenon evident in the visual arts, literature, music, and dance of Europe and the United States, as well as in their philosophy, criticism, linguistics, communication theory, anthropology, and the social sciences—these all generally under the particular influence of structuralism.

Postmodern literature and art share with structuralism a commitment to the investigation of the nature, the determinants, the limits and the possibilities of language, seen either in its most immediate terms as the particular practice of writing or creating artworks, or, by necessary extension, in the relationship of specific works of meaning to language in a broader sense—as aesthetic or cultural discourse, society's semiotic systems, or ultimately, ideology.

This focus on the "language" of art and on cultural codes of signification is discernible in the work of artists such as Joseph Kosuth, the conceptual art movement in general, and to a lesser extent in minimal, narrative and performance art, as well as in the literary work of the French new novelists, Robbe-Grillet, Sollers, Roche, and Ricardou in particular, and in the Americas, the fiction of Borges, Nabokov, Barth, Pynchon, Coover, Federman, Gass, and Cortazar. The work of these postmoderns is characterized by an emphatic self-reflexiveness. It presents itself as a direct manifestation of aesthetic language investigating itself *as language;* that is, the text or artwork points to itself as a particular expression of a specific meaning system, as a construct that explicitly says something about the process of creating meaning. Instead of presuming and attempting to speak about or illustrate the phenomenal world, the artwork regards itself as the primary reality. There is little effort to (re)present the world, so the artwork devalues the referential dimension of language. Rather, meaning is turned back upon itself as the artwork explores itself as a mode of meaning, of cognition, of perception and expression. Insofar as it seeks a world of significance external to itself, the world is described as a network of socially established meaning systems, the discourse of our culture.

This is, consequently, an art of extreme abstraction. Specific messages are secondary to the process of creating those messages. At most, there is only a glimpse of a shared experiential reality. There is little effort to (re)present the world, so the viewer or reader is challenged instead to focus on how that reality is dependent upon the conventions of aesthetic and social discourse to be understood.

Clearly, this is a formalist art in its most extreme sense, for it does little more than investigate, and make an art out of, the formal elements of the art experience. In doing so, postmodern art betrays its ties to modernism. For what essentially defined modernism was its self-conscious formal experimentation, an experimentation devoted to discovering the special validity of art and literature in a culture apparently indifferent to anything but a material and socially validating conception of art.

It is a commonplace that modernist art was an expression of artists' rejection of the dominant values of bourgeois culture and represented a search for an aesthetic dimension of significance, meaning, and value as an alternative to the material concerns of capitalist society. Modernist literature and art, established simultaneously by the work of Flaubert and Manet, consequently expressed its felt alienation both by consciously devaluing the referential dimension of the artwork—its subject matter—and by explicitly emphasizing its formal conventions—the idiosyncratic, personal style of the artist. The work of succeeding artists was characterized by formal innovations designed either to describe experience so as to lay bare realms of spiritual or aesthetic significance latent in a debased social domain, or to establish a mode and context of value independent of secular society.

It is helpful to distinguish between two tendencies within modern art—that of modernism, per se, and that of the avant-garde. Both recognized the general alienation of the artist from capitalist culture and saw in art a means to assert some kind of alternative value system. In general, the modernists—Flaubert, Mallarmé, Yeats, Eliot, Joyce, Rilke, or the impressionists, cubists, or action painters, for example—placed primary emphasis on either some ahistorical value system in culture (religion, myth, individual perception or psychological depth) or on the rewards of the self-contained aesthetic realm as it eventually became the socially accepted province of art. In effect, the modernists found in art a feasible, self-sustaining activity the more self-conscious and abstract it became. The avant-garde, on the other hand—Rimbaud, Mayakovsky, the expressionists, dada, the surrealists, among others—engaged in formal experimentation in the belief that a radically individualistic or vanguard perspective and language would in some way transform the manner in which society saw itself, and consequently in the way people behaved. As an art of social antagonism, the avant-garde demanded that the artist and audience maintain a critical distance from their culture in order to analyze and act upon it.

Both tendencies were caught in the paradox, however, that increased attention to formal experimentation necessarily led to an increased sense of separation of art and the artist from the social context. The self-consciousness that characterized modern art by defining itself in opposition of culture could never lead, as a result, beyond a hermeticism that was felt to be alternatively a trap and a privilege.

Modernism's fate, consequently, was to disintegrate into an extreme form of defensive individualism. Individual or coterie self-consciousness, individual or coterie experimentation, perspective, or style led not to a resolution of art's antagonistic relationship to society, but to creative individualism's and art's descent into the absurd. In Camus's theory of the absurd, in existentialism and its correlative, abstract expressionism, one encounters the last gasps of the diminishing individualism of modernism. The heroic, if melodramatic, image of the artist, writer, or philosopher struggling to create a realm of personal or collective significance in the face of a world perceived as essentially meaningless both sums up the modernist ethic and aesthetic and, ironically, self-consciously declares that ethic to be absurd. What is revealed here are the inability of individual action, private language, or artistic style to alter society and its institutions, and modernism's failure to create significant meaning in its presumed isolation from that society. Hermeticism and the self-consciousness it allows are finally seen to be forms of self-mystification. The dynamics of modernist art move from an awareness of alienation to a justification of self-consciousness, but that self-consciousness leads to the necessity of radically questioning the fundamental premises of its constitution and social rule. It has finally to become self-reflexive.

The emergence of self-reflexive art during the 1960s was the seeming development of the hermetic tradition of modernist art. Indeed, the revival of interest in Duchamp signaled its ties to one of the major, if at the time underrated, theoreticians of modernism. For what had been taken by his contemporaries as ironic games now were seen as ideas and works that revealed the basic premises and limits of modernism. What the artists of the sixties, especially Kosuth and the conceptual artists (but also John Cage, Merce Cunningham, and their compatriots) learned from Duchamp was that hermetic art mecessarily tended toward tautology, and that art which self-consciously established itself in opposition to cultural meaning systems could ultimately end by only referring to itself. As is well known, when Duchamp placed an industrial object in an art context (a gallery or a museum), he effectively deracinated the object from its functional and referential relationship to the world and made it an art object. In doing so, he was only carrying the modernist devaluation of subject matter to its logical extreme. The result was less to say something about the external world—of urinals or bottleracks—than to force a self-reflexive awareness of the art context—either the tradition of romantic imagery (the ironic "fountain"), or the meaning system that constitutes art and the art context. At the same time, he demystified the modernist idealization of art as some inherently superior and meaningful activity.

The legacy of Duchamp, as Kosuth suggests in "Art after Philosophy," is an art that is less interested in speaking about the world (within either traditional or innovative styles or languages) than about the fact that as art it is *speaking* about something.[1] For if modernist art needed to speak *differently,* even to speak in total abstraction, nonetheless it assumed it was communicating something, that in personal and collective terms it had a function. A recurring problem of modernism was that the audience constantly needed to learn the conventions of the new aesthetic styles and languages as well as interpret their particular messages. But what self-reflexive, postmodernist art demands first of all is that the justifying premises and structural bases of that speaking—no matter what the convention or style—be investigated in order to see what permits, shapes, and generates what is said.

The tautological view of art concerns itself with the fact that art is a product of the dependent relationship between an artwork and the art context (the idea of art). As Duchamp showed, any object becomes an artwork merely by being placed within the framework of art (when viewed aesthetically), and, concurrently, that framework is constituted solely as a pattern of organizing and giving aesthetic meaning to individual works. To approach the art process, then, as a system of self-generating meaning is to introduce the analogy of language—here, specifically, the structural analysis of language. Art is seen as a form of discourse having its own grammatical and syntactical relationships (the conventions of art in general, and any specific movement in particular) and its own signifiers (words, texts, artworks) that are governed by the conventions and which permit something to be "said." Artworks, like words, may signify the external world, but to analyze them structurally, or self-reflexively, is to unveil the nature and configuration of the conventions (grammar) or the art context (language), without speaking directly of their referential dimension.

Any study of the literature of the sixties and seventies must therefore confront art's primary concern with the language of art, with what constitutes art as a mode of discourse, a system of meaning. It must ask, with the artist, how meaning emerges from the artwork and the art context or from the literary text and language.

The self-reflexive artwork's subject, then, is its own unfolding as a construct of meaning. The writings of Borges, Barth, Sollers, Robbe-Grillet, Heissenbüttel, Duras, Coover, Pynchon, and Blanchot, among many others, continually turn back from their referential possibilities toward the linguistic domain in order to force the audience to observe and critique the processes of creation, questioning, and eventual deconstruction of the literary text. Similarly, the silences of minimal art point backward toward the formalism of modernist abstraction, but demand, in the perspective of the sixties, that the audience be aware of the "phenomenology of making"[2] and viewing that is latent in the audience's interaction with the inert object in the gallery space (the art context). But it is even more clear in the work of the conceptual artists—whether it be that of Kosuth, Buren, Haacke, the Bechers, Art and Language, Weiner, or any other—that the subject of the artwork is primarily, if not totally, the theoretical justification of the art practice as a mode of meaning. Any single work, while "significant" in itself, when seen in linguistic terms only "signifies" in the context of a semiotic system; it only has meaning as an intermediary term in the field of aesthetic discourse that it makes "visible."

The revelation of the tautological structure of the discourse of art is the link between the postmodern and modern sensibilities. Here, postmodernism is merely basing itself upon the logical conclusions of modernist practices. But the significant contribution of postmodernism is to apply the model of art as a self-contained discourse to social discourse as well, and to recognize that as a language, art cannot be considered separately from cultural languages in general. It is to recognize that no matter how hermetic it may declare itself to be, any particular meaning system in society takes its place amongst—and receives social validation from—the total pattern of semiotic systems that structure society. So, ironically, while modernism's self-conscious formalism led it to isolate the formal concerns of art from the social referent, postmodernism's self-reflexive formalism sees that language *as form* is intimately entwined with social discourse.

If tautological art declares art to be a function of the art context, it also asks what the art context is a function of. What is the nature of one's personal experience of art and what are the connections between that and the culture's values and belief systems? Why, for instance, does a public or private museum go to the expense of mounting exhibits, particularly of modern—here "conceptual"—art? What meaning does an artwork have that would also make it a prime investment commodity? What is the relationship between the valuation of art by the collector and the curator? What is it about art that would make intellectuals want to write about it, and what is their connection to the institutions of cultural recuperation? How is the art context contained in, parallel to, or separate from other forms of social discourse: a political campaign, an economic system, the dynamics of "repressive desublimation" (Marcuse)? And furthermore, what is it about an artwork that makes people want to view it, to experience it and think about it?

Postmodern art, consequently, entails an important shift of perspective. For rather than a particular artwork representing an individualistic attempt to alter the language of art in culture, and by extension culture itself, the self-reflexive artwork sees itself already defined by existent discourse that it can lay bare before the artist and viewer. Rather than continuing the bathos of modernist alienation, the postmodern work willfully accepts the complexities of its relationship to culture and its systems of discourse. Rather than the drama of the vulnerable, self-conscious artwork confronting meaningless existence, recent art presents us with the fact that the world, if anything, is too meaningful, that the work is unavoidably *connected* to the world.

Now this does not mean that the work necessarily accepts the nature of its ties to social discourse, but it does suggest that the artwork's first responsibility is to understand the conditions that allow it to exist *as art*. The primary structuralist lesson is that there is no "natural" naive world that is the innocent subject of the creator's vision. Whatever is perceived, known, described, or presented in art or experience is already charged with meaning by the conceptual patterns governing the artist's orientation and cultural recognition. Thus, paradoxically, hermetic self-reflexiveness leads to an expanded vision, a vision of interconnectedness in society, of "intertextuality" or even "inter-contextuality."

As self-conscious explorations of their respective meaning systems, art and literature do not presume to be privileged languages—languages more valid than, or the bases of, other languages. In fact, they tend to deny the priority of any single language or privileged infrastructure. But because the means of their self-reflexive investigations are the very subjects of those investigations, the languages of art assert their singular position within cultural discourse. Illuminating itself, the artwork simultaneously casts light on the workings of aesthetic conceptualization and on art's sociological situation. Self-reflexive art establishes a principle of homologous perspectives: the text or artwork is to the art context as the art context is to the social context (also called by some the "social text").

This shifting focus from the hermetic text to extended discourse is apparent in all the arts of the past two decades. The careers of several writers and artists, in fact, recapitulate the movement from modernist self-consciousness to self-reflexiveness, to postmodern contextualism. The works of Beckett, Barth, Robbe-Grillet, Sollers, and Coover, for example, display an early concern with the limits of existential positioning and the difficulty of describing the phenomenal world, but then focus on the problems of presenting their subjects within, and as problems of, the literary context, and some finally move toward a questioning of the purely literary in terms of larger, even political, contexts. Joseph Kosuth's own work originally accented the ambiguities of linguistic and artistic referentiality ("One and Three Chairs"), then studied art and meaning systems as tautological structures ("Art as Idea as Idea"), and now insists on the social and political context of art as system ("The Artist as Anthropologist").

Each of these texts and artworks is to be seen as only a fragment of something larger—of art and the social text. What is necessary to observe is how a particular text is structured and determined by the concerns of the artist, by the determinants of art at its specific historical moment, and by the social placement of art in its culture. Thus, in the work of Kosuth, for example, we are presented with a text directly addressing us, a text with a message, but one which insists that the content of the message (even as instructions about how to read it) is less important than the system of discourse it is part of: *what it's saying is only part of what it's saying.*

This announcement of the text's incompleteness is a basic strategy of postmodern literature and art. For no matter how unidimensional and seemingly complete in itself tautological art may try to be as it attempts to make its language its subject, that language must invariably point to its limits (silence) or its entwinement with other forms of social discourse. As a result, postmodern art is often an art of distrust and disruption. It demands that the reader and audience participate in the process of demystifying the seeming neutrality, the seductive functionalism, of language. It is a concern common among recent writers. Sollers, for example, in his novel *Lois* struggles to make the reader aware of the "immediacy of the apparent non-being of language." For it is the structure of any particular discourse, be it artistic, literary, or ideological, that determines the meaning of any specific message, since, as the structuralists have demonstrated, meaning only exists within its meaning system as a product of the interaction of semantic elements. Meaning does not reside in the words themselves: *it seems to it that parts or things of this conversation change constantly, yet what doesn't change is how they mean.* . . . *What's said* here *doesn't really seem to matter, as long as this structure (this thing you are looking at that's part of organized culture) as a* form *maintains and extends the frame of its own system.*

Meaning is always a question of relationships: of words within sentences; of sentences within texts; of texts within discourse and its contexts. But since meaning usually points away from its own constitutive elements, we rarely perceive the process that determines what is said. To make discourse evident is the main goal of postmodern literature and art. To reveal the absolute and intimate connection between ourselves as speakers and listeners and our socially determined patterns of perceiving, thinking, expressing, and acting is the function of self-reflexive artworks. Meaning as a system, culture as a web of discourses, individual identity as a product of social codes of behavior—these are the themes of our art.

The discourse around you takes certain things for granted. We, as writers, artists, or users of language, normally take language and its usage for granted. But postmodern art would teach us not only to accept discourse naively, but to recognize that it takes *us* for granted. For just as each statement is a product of its linguistic positioning within a preestablished code of signification, our ways of articulating ourselves, our desires, our fears and our actions originate not solely in our individual sense of self, but in the social ideologies by which we speak and live. Our unconscious participation in such discourse *maintains and extends the frame of its* [the discourse's] *own system.* As Sollers has commented: "In the last analysis, we are only our system of reading/writing, in a concrete and practical way. . . . To write, to make writing appear, is not to dispose of privileged knowledge: it is to discover what everyone knows but no one can say. It is to try, *just once,* to raise the veil which maintains us in an obscurity we have not chosen."[3]

We have not chosen the discourses that we use, any more than we have chosen our culture. Nor can we create new discourses out of our mere desire, as the modernists and avant-garde wished. And neither can we withdraw from the discourses that we use and that surround us. All that is possible, it seems, is to make what is transparent opaque and visible, and in the process discover the complex nature of our use and enclosure in the languages of our society. *At this point, right now, its meaning is provided by you; perhaps if you re-read it ... you might locate the subject of this text and that discourse (look around again) which includes you and the object of this text.*

This recognition of the loss of individualist self-creation and freedom is far removed from the anguished alienation of the modernist sensibility. (But it may identify the origin of that sensed "loss of self" that so plagued the modernists.) Rather, it is the first step in realizing the nature of our position within culture so that we might not be mystified by appeals to the ideal of a self-protective, elitist hermeticism. In fact, to be aware of the ideological import of all cultural discourse allows us to ask what were the ideological assumptions of an art that assumed the world was essentially meaningless and which, at the same time, asserted that an individual could only find true value within increasingly tentative self-justifying meaning systems.

Moving beyond the hermeticism and alienation of modernism, postmodern art engages the reader and audience in the *processes* of signification that shape the experience of art. Sollers states: "The essential question today is no longer the *writer* and the *work* (still less the "work of art") but instead *writing* and *reading*. Consequently, we must define a new space including these two phenomena as reciprocal and simultaneous: a curved space, a *milieu* of exchanges and reversibility in which we would finally be on the same side as our language."[4]

We are enveloped by the discourses that surround us and that we use. But insofar as we become conscious of how meaning is both prefigured by the structure of discourse and how it is articulated solely by our participation within language, we potentially become critics and shapers of discourse. Instead of modernist transcendence of the social milieu, we are offered active participation in its being and potential transformation. The implied activism of postmodern art links it to the tradition of the avant-garde. For what is at stake here are the social possibilities of art. Rather than as a "work" of art, postmodern art offers itself as a process of *working*— a dynamic of speaker and context struggling to situate themselves in a historical continuity.

The function of this self-conscious art of fragments, disruption, and demystification is to teach its audience to envision language as a "transformational milieu" (Sollers). If self-reflexive art studies the synchonic structure of discourse that determines what can be said at any particular cultural moment, the awareness of the active role that self-conscious individuals (and groups) have within that discourse opens up the diachronic dimension of the possibility of its and the culture's transformation. This is not, however, the avant-garde faith in the artist's visionary role as creator of new languages or as seer of our potential futures. In fact, there is little projection of the shape of future transformation in postmodern art. But it is an appeal to collective self-consciousness within language and within the web of discourses that each single language invokes.

Henceforth, the artist and audience will seek to make explicit their existence within language and cultural discourse. Each statement, written and read, need assert its particular message and reflect on its context. The dialectics of speaker and language, of text and context, of personal belief and social ideology, will shape the aesthetic experience. We encounter and are challenged by an art of shifting perspective, of double self-consciousness, of local and extended meaning. *"The discourse around us is speaking locally, but where is it located? If this discourse, this text, could 'see itself' it would be capable of defining its structure (kinds of relationships) and describing its context (as politics, as culture, as a text, as a blank)."*

Notes

1. Joseph Kosuth, "Art after Philosophy," in Ursula Meyer, *Conceptual Art* (New York: Dutton, 1972), p. 162.

2. Robert Morris's term. See Robert Morris, "Some Notes on the Phenomenology of Making," *Artforum,* March 1970.

3. Philippe Sollers, "The Novel and the Experience of Limits," in Raymond Federman, ed., *Surfiction* (Chicago: Swallow Press, 1975), pp. 72–73.

4. Ibid., pp. 68–69.

III

Entanglements and Complicities

Preface

A postmodern question, postmodernly put: if word and world are only arbitrarily connected, if what we say and sign is grounded only upon a foundation that we construct (and thus have constructed variously in different places and at different times), then are all our representations, all our chains of world-and-word, "always already" forged within a kind of construct-in-sway? This awkward, but real, question is usually posed in terms of whether postmodernism is "compelled to say" or repeat what power has already legislated, in the very act of linking word with world. Can postmodernism offer a critique of the imposed repetitions of power, "while never pretending to be able to operate outside them" (Hutcheon 1989, 25)?

The contest seems clear. On the one hand, there is the view that what we are here going to call the "entanglements" of competing representations—none of which can assert a "foundationalist" argument for its claims which itself does not engender an opposing "foundationalist" counter-argument—can in fact "de-doxify" what Roland Barthes calls the "doxa," or the official and unacknowledged systems of meaning (and representation), by which we know our culture and ourselves. On the other hand, to use Frederic Jameson's terms from the essay reprinted in this book, we have instead the degeneration of "a genuinely dialectical attempt to think our present of time in History" into a postmodern "logic of the simulacrum," which exposes postmodernism's complicity with the "whole new wave of American military and economic domination throughout the world." While that is put rather strongly (and perhaps in rather too Amero-centric terms), it does give you a sense of what is seen to be at stake here.

Yet, the contest only seems clear if a single version of what a critical or "de-doxifying" postmodernism is (and how it is achieved) can be agreed upon. Any view of a complicitous or co-opted postmodernism reopens a whole Pandora's box of rival pronouncements regarding what Barthes called the "sciences of ideology." From a postmodern perspective, how could we argue that the Marxist dialectic, for instance, rises to the level of what Jameson calls "genuine" ideological critique, while the postmodern falls into pernicious "co-optation"?

E. Ann Kaplan claims that even Hal Foster's "postmodernism of resistance" (which "seeks to question rather than exploit cultural codes, to explore rather than conceal social and political affiliations," [Foster 1983, xii]) does not manage to rise above the modern metanarrative dependence upon binary oppositions. For any real change to occur, she implies, we would need to move "beyond/away from the various positionings (not only aesthetic, but those dealing with class, race, and gender) of previous totalizing theories" (Kaplan 1988, 5). While Kaplan sees the possibility of such a moving away from the dominant cultural oppositions as still "nebulous and distant," the purveyors of a view of an even more negative view of the postmodern as utterly co-opted see the loss of oppositions (and thus dialectic) as a succumbing to the singleness of monism of that "logic of the simulacrum."

Many critics today—Jameson, Terry Eagleton, Christopher Norris, among them—confine that monism and logic to the postmodern, and thus see it as dominated totally by late capitalism. It is therefore made amenable to a Marxist analysis, whose "very nature requires a superior, transcendental space outside of the totality it describes" (Montag 1988, 95). For some, however, this stand *outside* is precisely the problem, not the solution; it is the sign of working within a modern perspective that is precisely what is being called into question by the postmodern.

The workings of that "project of modernity" can be seen in the very terminology used by Terry Eagleton in his response to Jameson in the essay, "Capitalism, Modernism and Postmodernism," where he affirms the existence and value of such things as "the referent or real historical world" (1985, 67), "the ruling social order" (67), "a rational discourse of ethical or political value," (70) and "transformed rationality"—all things that the postmodern has problematized precisely through its entangling of the many narrative linkages among referents, histories, discourses, rationalities. But these modern terms of reference (based, as Kaplan noted, on binary oppositions) are still strong ones among opponents of the postmodern:

some present postmodernity or postmodernism as collapsing vital distinctions between "concept and metaphor, speech and writing, *logos* and *mimesis,* reason and rhetoric, art which remains 'inside' the frame of aesthetic representation and art which exceeds or transgresses the limits laid down by that framing discourse" (Norris and Benjamin 1989, 30).

Instead of thinking in terms of a possible wholesale change in perspective, and thus seeing the postmodern as challenging precisely that kind of binary thinking (and its implicit hierarchies), such critics see the postmodern as evading, or refusing to resolve, these pressing contradictions of the "cultural logic of late capitalism," and thus failing to enter the "tradition of enlightened *Ideologiekritik.*" By definition, then, the postmodern is complicitous with that logic: "the 'post' in post-modernism would indicate not so much a movement *beyond* as a form of regressive or disabling historical amnesia, one that simply plays along with the styles, fashions, and consumer demands of a thoroughly commodified culture" (Norris and Benjamin 30).

The debate here concerns whether the postmodern's many entangled and deliberately non-prioritized narratives can not only inscribe, but at the same time also challenge, whatever "doxa" needs challenging—whether that be articulated in terms of the logic of capital or the simulacrum, totalizing theories, or cultural binary oppositions. In short, can the postmodern ever be outside the domain of power and the dominant ideology? If not, from what position can its critique be launched? The general problem exposed, however, is that of defining the position from which any of us can speak— ever (Kaplan 1988, 2). Recently there have been a number of spirited attempts to find a way out of this seeming impasse, such as Stephen R. Yarbrough's "postmodern humanism," intended to help us "in good conscience to make decisions again" (1992, 22). But if the postmodern does challenge the modern project and put into question what that project would consider "all truth-claims, all standards of valid argumentation or efforts to separate a notational 'real' from the various forms of superinduced fantasy or mass-media stimulation" (Norris 1991, 30), then how would one frame or articulate a position even within this debate itself?

For Marxist critics, the postmodern (at least, as so described) has absolutely no tools with which to interrogate or demystify that within which it is hopelessly enmeshed—that is, the dominant late capitalist nightmare of high-tech, mass marketing, and consumption. From the *modern* point of view, however, the Marxist critic of the postmodern can still find a foothold—even if the grounds upon which s/he formulates the object of analysis are that object's very target. Jameson can claim that "criticism and resistance depend upon the possibility of the positioning of the cultural act outside the massive Being of Capital, which then serves as an Archimedean point from which to assault this last." But from a postmodern perspective, that external positioning would be illusory, not to say self-delusional; there can be no such Archimedean point.

Marxist critics have been among the most vociferous in their attacks—and with good reason (cf. Callinicos 1990). Postmodernity has called into question, and thus threatened, the very grounds of Marxist analysis: externality of perspective, binary oppositions (and thus dialectic), totalizing narratives, even Utopian projections. Terry Eagleton has argued, in fact, that "key doctrines of postmodernist thought have conspired to discredit the classical concept of ideology" (1991, xi). His description of these "doctrines" is telling in its modern resistances. For instance, the postmodern idea that we inevitably always traffic in representations—plural and conflicting ones—is converted into the assertion of a postmodern "rejection of the notion of representation."

Most revealing, however, of the different (that is, modern) *episteme* from which Eagleton is operating is his view that the postmodern challenge to the workings of "rationality, interests and power" is, in fact, a refusal to examine them from within an enlightened critical frame that would be able to identify easily "those power struggles which are somehow central to a whole form of social life, and those which are not" (8). It is hard to imagine a less postmodern statement than this, for while the postmodern acknowledges and critiques power relations, it is never under the illusion that they are easy to identify as "central"—precisely because of its awareness of its own political entanglements.

All this is not to say that Marxist thought has not had an important role in theorizing postmodernity in a positive, rather than simply negative, sense. The work of Antonio Gramsci and Louis Althusser, in particular, has been invoked by many in their attempts to stretch the notion of ideology beyond its role in preserving a class society and beclouding a critical penetration of same. In Althusser's view, ideology is the model through which "the real is invested in the imaginary relation" (1969, 233–34). Ideology, then, isn't simply what others fall into; it is "indispensable in any society if men are to be formed, transformed and equipped to respond to the demands of their conditions of existence" (234).

The obvious appeal of this view, from a postmodern perspective, lies in its contention that social life is too complex and variegated to be grasped except through imaginary models—that is, through ideological constructions which are not primarily cognitive, but symbolic and affective. These "representing frames" are not constructed solely to perpetrate class exploitation; they comprise "less a system of articulated doctrines than a set of images, symbols and occasionally concepts which we 'live' at an unconscious level. Viewed sociologically, [ideology] consists in a range of material practices or rituals (voting, saluting, genuflecting and so on) which are always embedded in material institutions" (Eagleton 1991, 148–49).

On one important point, however, Althusser takes the same stand as Jameson and the other Marxist critics: he sees his theoretical inquiry and critique as themselves free of ideology and its imaginary model, and thus able, from an "external vantage point," to establish "true insight into the social system" (Eagleton 1991, 152). Postmodern complex entanglements suggest, though, that we can never be outside what Althusser calls our "lived relations to the real" and the imaginary framework through which we are hailed or "interpellated" as subjects, summoned into a specific social reality.

The complicity of which Jameson and others accuse the postmodern is, however, precisely what allows it to articulate, in art forms at least, a more positively coded "aesthetic politics"—(Clark 1989, 255) while still acknowledging the power of ideology from well within its force field: "What Eagleton (like Jameson before him) seems to ignore is the subversive potential of irony, parody, and humor in contesting the universalizing pretensions of 'serious' art" (Hutcheon 1988, 19). The clash of representations and narratives that parody (for example) embodies, engages the audience's attention—and even labor—"in the processes of signification because such references demand interpretation by the very fact of their formal perversity" (Clark 1989, 256).

The debate is therefore between this positive valuing of parody's subversive potential, and the negative view that equates it with trivializing kitsch and patische. To complicate the matter even more, Arthur Kroker and David Cook forcefully assert: "Against the current impulse in postmodernist theory and art which, refusing origins and originality in favour of parody and kitsch, we conclude just the opposite. Parody is no longer possible because in America today, which is to say in the system of advanced modern societies, the real is parody. . . . As Nietzsche predicted, we have finally passed through into that purely perspectival zone of virtual technology, virtual bodies, and virtual imagining systems" (1986, 169).

Jameson also reduces parody to an empty pastiche of forms, but goes even further to identify subversive clashings of narratives as essentially "schizophrenic." He connects personal identity to "a temporal unification of past and future with one's present," and

links that unification to "the sentence, as it moves along its hermeneutic circle through time." These are the processes he sees as collapsing with the postmodern (and, specifically, the post-structural)
suggestion that the "links of the signifying chain" can snap. In a description of the "double coding" of postmodern architecture, however, Charles Jencks offers a rather different, but still critical, use
of this quite common structural metaphor of schizophrenia: "Generally speaking there are two codes, a popular traditional one which
like spoken language is slow-changing, full of clichés and rooted in
family life, and secondly a modern one full of neologisms and responding to quick changes in technology, art and fashion as well as
the avant-garde of architecture. . . . [S]ince there is no way to abolish this gap without a drastic curtailment in possibilities, a totalitarian manoeuvre, it seems desirable that architects recognise the
schizophrenia and code their buildings on two levels" (1978, 130).
This is closer to Roland Barthes's use of a similar doubling metaphor in his discussion of the literary text as "a multidimensional
space in which are married and contested several writings, none of
which is original: the text is a fabric of quotations, resulting from a
thousand sources of culture" (1986, 52–53).

Both Barthes and Michel Foucault *stage,* to use Barthes's
term, the relations among power, ideology, resistance, discourse,
and language in ways not encompassed by the (un-postmodern)
either/or terms of the debate over postmodern complicity/critique.
In his famous "Inaugural Lecture" to the Collège de France, Barthes describes power in rather Foucaultian terms as being "plural
in social space . . . perpetual in historical time" (1979, 460). He argues that the "object in which power is inscribed, for all of human
eternity, is language . . . the language we speak and write" (460).
But, although language is itself legislation, its strictures can be
evaded—by what Barthes calls "literature." "Because it *stages* language instead of simply using it," Barthes writes, "literature feeds
knowledge into the machinery of infinite reflexivity. Through writing, knowledge ceaselessly reflects on knowledge, in terms of a discourse which is no longer epistemological, but dramatic" (463–64).
Against the power of language and its ideological capacity to inscribe us within official culture, Barthes advocates a postmodern
persistance: "*To persist* is to affirm the Irreducible of literature"
(467). This paradoxically also involves a shifting of ground—"to go
where you are not expected"—and an abjuring of "what you have
written" (468).

Rather than staging such strategies of shifting and abjuring,
in the "Method" section reprinted here from his *History of Sexual-*

ity: Volume I: An Introduction, Michel Foucault seeks instead to uncover the "complex strategical situation in a particular society"
which is "power." In his well-known and important rethinking of
power relations, Foucault claims that there is, at their root, "no binary and all-encompassing opposition between rulers and ruled."
Clearly he is working here within a postmodern frame of reference.
Just as power is everywhere, so too is resistance: "there is no single
locus of great Refusal, no soul of revolt, source of all rebellions, or
pure law of the revolutionary. Instead there is a plurality of resistances." Both power and resistance form a non-localizable web in
which transitory points of resistance cleave, fracture, remold, re-
group. "It is in this sphere of force relations," he writes, "that we
must try to analyze the mechanisms of power."

One of Foucault's most influential postmodern insights has
been that what is accepted as "knowledge" is related to power as
it operates within discourse. By discourse, Foucault means "a series
of discontinuous segments whose tactical function is neither uniform nor stable. To be more precise, we must not imagine a world of
discourse divided between accepted discourse and excluded discourse, or between the dominant discourse and the dominated one;
but as a multiplicity of discursive elements that can come into play
in various strategies." Discourse here can both transmit and undermine power.

Foucault escapes the modern binarisms that oppose co-
optation and critique, complicity and resistance, by framing everything within a "multiple and mobile field of force relations." By
doing so, however, he has not escaped a possible criticism based on
his unquestioning acceptance of the "reality principle" of power itself. "[W]hat if Foucault spoke so well to us concerning power," asks
Jean Baudrillard, " . . . only because power is dead? Not merely impossible to locate because of dissemination, but dissolved purely
and simply in a manner that still escapes us, dissolved by reversal,
concellation, or made hyperreal through simulation (who knows?)"
(1980, 88).

As you might guess from that statement, Baudrillard's essay,
"The Precession of Simulacra," (reprinted in this book) stages a different political engagement for the postmodern: all confrontation,
all binarism, dissolves within the monism of sign systems, of what
he calls "simulacra" that stand in the place of the "real." Thus both
terms of the debate—co-optation *and* critique—are left behind,
along with that "real" and its attendant (modern) concepts of "rationality," "meaning," "truth," and "reference." While some critics
have argued against the view of the postmodern as a degeneration

into hyperreality—claiming it is, instead, a "questioning of what reality can mean and how we come to know it" (Hutcheon 1989, 34)—others have seen a close connection between the postmodern problematizing of representation (and thus its focus on textuality and discourse) and Baudrillard's notion of the simulacrum as "a set of signs dedicated exclusively to their recurrence as signs, and no longer to their 'real goal' at all" (McGowan 1991, 41).

While this distance from the "real" has been used by Marxist critics as a sign of postmodern political disengagement, it has been invoked by others to suggest, instead, a challenge to the traditional "realist" or materialist view of political engagement and, therefore, to suggest a new postmodern figuration of it in cultural terms: "Baudrillard's work makes the case that capitalist power is most fully operative on just these cultural terrains and must be contested there" (McGowan 1991, 18). This turns the tables on the Marxist attack and suggests that "in a system whose imperative is the 'overproduction and regeneration of meaning and speech,' all social movements which 'bet on liberation, emancipation, the resurrection of the subject of history, of the group, of speech as a raising of consciousness. . . .' *are acting fully in accordance with the political logic of the system*" (Kroker and Cook 1986, 178). If Marxism cannot therefore offer an escape from (or even a position outside) this all-pervasive "political logic," what can?

Baudrillard himself offers a sort of strategy of "ironic detachment," a "hyperconformist simulation": "This is the resistance of the masses: it is equivalent to sending back to the system its own logic by doubling it, to reflecting, like a mirror, meaning without absorbing it" (Baudrillard 1983, 108–9). The reflexivity that we have seen as characterizing the postmodern in this view, however, can actually uncover nothing: the postmodern clash of representations is already "enveloped" by what Baudrillard calls "simulation." The plurality of narratives, of representations of the "real," is here reduced to a monist "Hyperreality" in which all connections are "unhinged." Baudrillard's logic of simulation is, in the end, then, yet another (modern?) metanarrative that elides all the dissident "*petits récits*" by which Lyotard defined the postmodern condition, that condition of entanglements caused by the multiple and diverse "hingings" of reality with representation (none of which, however, can ever claim any foundational position).

What we could call the "paradigm" of the postmodern, then, would call into question not only the Marxist metanarrative of "genuine" history and objective, and external critique, but also the Baudrillardian metanarrative of the hyperreal. Instead of discussing all this in terms of Lyotard's postmodern "condition" or Haber-

mas's "project" of modernity, we might fruitfully use the notion of
"paradigm" in the sense given to it by Thomas Kuhn in speaking of
scientific revolutions "by which a new candidate for paradigm replaces its predecessor." In "The Resolution of Revolutions" in this
book, Kuhn argues that what is at stake at such moments of change
is learning to "see science and the world differently." But this seeing
cannot be done within the frame of reference of what we already
know how to recognize. Otherwise, "the unknown is only ever a not-
yet-recognized known" (Descombes 1980, 153).

Seeing within a different paradigm means being in a place
where we can make conceivable that which is not already presentable within our prevailing paradigm's "rules of the game"—where
we can only rearrange and rediscover. The consequence of being
limited like this to rearranging within one paradigm, and thus being limited to what is already known, is precisely what we have
been seeing in the Marxist—and more generally modern—attempt
to assess the postmodern. The paradigm of modernity cannot account for the postmodern within the rules of its game—rules which
deny or suppress randomness and contingency, provisionality and
incompleteness.

From its universalizing metanarrative stance, modernity has
been accused of failing to address the particularities of what it can
only label as "other." In his essay, "Black Culture and Postmodernism," however, Cornel West attempts to make room within that
same modern paradigm for the complex cultures of the "oppressed
and exploited." Historicizing the relations among race, class, and
gender within "concrete ideological and political practices," West
wants to re-present the elided "plight and predicament of black
America." His reason for staying within the modern paradigm is his
feeling that the postmodern celebration of difference and plurality
has not always coincided with a political analysis of social difference
and contradiction. The danger is that it might, as West suggests,
"highlight notions of difference, marginality, and otherness in such
a way that it further marginalizes actual people of difference and
otherness."

In " 'Race,' Time and the Revision of Modernity," Homi K.
Bhabha has brought a related post-colonial perspective to the
project of modernity, seeing its paradigm as, in fact, inherently
"contradictory and unresolved" (1992, 195), despite its pretensions
to the contrary. From the "colonial and postcolonial margins of modernity" comes a performative and deformative "contra-modernity"
that is, in effect, a "translation" and sometimes also an "interrup-
tion" of the supposed homogeneity and continuity of Western discourses of modernity. This "contra-modernity" is one of "displacing,

interrogative" narratives (199), of "conflictual, contradictory" enunciations which bring about a "transvaluing" of cultural differences (213). But, as we have been seeing, many would call precisely such a paradigm *post*modern.

The frequent desire to work *within* the project of modernity stems in part from a worry about the Eurocentric quality of the debates around the postmodern theorizing of cultural difference. Like Bhabha, West worries about this aspect of the work of Jacques Derrida and Michel Foucault, and he sees Lyotard's views as "European navel-gazing," insulated and insular in its rethinking of the Kantian sublime and Wittgensteinian language games. But, as Stephen Slemon argues in this book in "Modernism's Last Post," historically, the *modern* cannot be separated from either Eurocentricity or colonialism and Empire.

It is precisely in articulating a contextualizing and historicizing re-vision of the modern, and in doing so with a kind of "counter-discursive energy," that the postmodern has the potential to approach (though never to be synonymous with) "disidentificatory" post-colonial discourses. However, in seeking to "position the oppositional and reiterative textual responses of post-colonial cultures in dialectic relation to their colonialist precursors," the post-colonial critic is working within the modern paradigm—that is, the very paradigm within which the colonial and imperial were historically defined.

Nevertheless, there is another significant reason for the post-colonial desire to remain within the project of modernity: in Slemon's terms, "a postmodernist criticism would want to argue that literary practices such as these [postmodern ones] expose the constructedness of *all* textuality" and thus would challenge any one particular narrative's claim to domination, but "an *interested* post-colonial critical practice would want to allow for the positive production of oppositional truth-claims." In other words, it would, understandably, want to offer a competing metanarrative to the imperial one.

For others, though, this modern foundation in some overarching narrative or "truth" is itself what needs challenging if the concept of "other" is to be rethought in new and different terms. Real "emancipatory politics," they argue, are hard to articulate within the modern paradigm that is implicitly coded as not only European and white, but also male. Any effective intervention in patriarchal structures of oppression must therefore be undertaken at the level of paradigm (Ebert 1991, 901). Given this sort of stand, the question many have asked (see Morris 1990) is why the postmodern should have been so shy about its points of coincidence with the concerns of feminism (and of identity politics, in general); as Jane Flax here argues, the feminist has often overlapped, supplemented, or even supported postmodern (and, specifically, poststructuralist) theory. While "concrete women and gender relations" have indeed often disappeared in the general debates on the postmodern, both reappear whenever the particular issue of cultural representation is discussed, as Craig Owens pointed out almost a decade ago in "The Discourse of Others: Feminism and Postmodernism." But Owens's temptation to read the feminist as "an instance of postmodern thought" (1983, 62) has been resisted by feminists in the name of political agency.

While both the postmodern and the feminist may share a suspicion of what Lyotard called modernity's "*grands récits*" and of its implicitly hierarchical binarisms (Jardine 1985, 61), and while both may engage similar discursive strategies (such as parody and irony [Hutcheon 1989, 141–68]), Barbara Creed points out in this book—in her essay "From here to Modernity: Feminism and Postmodernism"—that the focus of the feminist critique is specifically on the common patriarchal bias of those modern"ideologies which posit universal truths—Humanism, History, Religion, Progress, etc." However, within a postmodern paradigm, as Slemon notes in discussing the post-colonial, isolating a single major determining factor like gender would be a questionable act—though likely a necessary one for political action (see Waugh 1989 and Nicholson 1990).

Even given this major disagreement, there is little doubt that the general theorizing about the different and the plural within postmodernity has been more in debt to feminist, African-American, and post-colonial theories than it has often openly admitted. The question these political positions all pose—for themselves as much as for the postmodern—is: how can any critique, whose moves are already plotted by what it seeks to criticize, be launched from a site of "difference" defined by the paradigm it challenges? Unlike that Marxist stepping outside of ideology, these "oppositional" political theories tend to remain suspicious of the claims of a paradigm-free method of objective critique, just as they are skeptical of the existence of any body of objective, universal knowledge authorizing and authorized by such a critique.

The work of those challenging the enlightenment paradigm of modernity from the positions of "differences" of race, ethnicity, sexual choice, and gender has dovetailed with similar postmodern contesting to generate a "sense of crisis" that, in Kuhn's terms, evokes "an alternate candidate for paradigm." If, however, the possibility of a postmodern paradigm is rejected—because of its (admitted) entanglements and complicities—then we are left at the chess board of modernity, trying out "various moves in the search for a solution." But it is the very rules of this game—and its cherished storehouse of victories, accomplishments, and so-called "progress"—that many are now suggesting we need to test.

Works Cited

Althusser, Louis (1969) *For Marx*. Trans. Ben Brewster. New York: Pantheon.

Barthes, Roland (1979) "Inaugural Lecture, Collège de France." In Susan Sontag, ed. *A Barthes Reader*. Trans. Richard Howard. New York: Hill & Wang. 457–78.

———. (1986) *The Rustle of Language*. Trans. Richard Howard. New York: Hill and Wang.

Baudrillard, Jean (1980) "Forgetting Foucault." Trans. Nicole Dufresne. *Humanities in Society* 3.1: 87–111.

———. (1983) "The Implosion of Meaning in the Media." In *In the Shadow of the Silent Majorities*. New York: Jean Baudrillard and Semiotext(e). 95–110.

Bauman, Zygmunt (1991) *Modernity and Ambivalence*. Ithaca, NY: Cornell University Press.

Bhabha, Homi K. (1992) " 'Race,' Time and the Revision of Modernity." *Oxford Literary Review*: 193–219.

Callinicos, Alex (1990) *Against Postmodernism: A Marxist Critique*. New York: St. Martin's Press.

Clark, Michael (1989) "Political Nominalism and Critical Practice." In Joseph Natoli, ed. *Literary Theory's Future(s)*. Champaign: University of Illinois Press. 221–64.

Descombes, Vincent (1980) *Modern French Philosophy*. Trans. L. Scott-Fox and J. M. Harding. Cambridge: Cambridge University Press.

Eagleton, Terry (1985) "Capitalism, Modernism and Postmodernism." *New Left Review* 152: 60–73.

———. (1991) *Ideology: An Introduction*. London: Verso.

Ebert, Teresa (1991) "The 'Difference' of Postmodern Feminism." *College English* 53.8: 886–904.

Foster, Hal, ed. (1983) *The Anti-Aesthetic: Essays on Postmodern Culture.* Port Townsend, WA: Bay Press.

Hutcheon, Linda (1988) *A Poetics of Postmodernism: History, Theory, Fiction.* New York and London: Routledge.

———. (1989) *The Politics of Postmodernism.* New York and London: Routledge.

Jardine, Alice (1985) *Gynesis: Configurations of Woman and Modernity.* Ithaca: Cornell University Press.

Jencks, Charles (1978) *The Languages of Post-Modern Architecture.* London: Academy Editions.

Kaplan, E. Ann, ed. (1988) *Postmodernism and Its Discontents.* London: Verso.

Kroker, Arthur and David Cook (1986) *The Postmodern Scene: Excremental Culture and Hyper-Aesthetics.* Montreal: New World Perspectives.

McGowan John (1991) *Postmodernism and its Critics.* Ithaca, NY: Cornell University Press.

Montag, Warren (1988) "What Is at Stake in the Debate on Postmodernism." in Kaplan 1988: 88–103.

Morris, Meaghan (1990) *The Pirate's Fiancée: Feminism, Reading, Postmodernism.* London: Verso.

Nicholson, Linda, ed. (1990) *Feminism/Postmodernism.* New York and London: Routledge.

Norris, Christopher (1990) *What's Wrong with Postmodernism.* Baltimore: The Johns Hopkins University Press.

———. and Andrew Benjamin (1989) *What Is Deconstruction?* New York: St. Martin Press.

Owens, Craig (1983) "The Discourse of Others: Feminism and Postmodernism." In Foster (1983): 57–82.

Waugh, Patricia (1989) *Feminine Fictions: Revisiting the Postmodern.* New York and London: Routledge.

Yarbrough, Stephen R. (1992) *Deliberate Criticism: Toward a Postmodern Humanism.* Athens: University of Georgia Press.

Excerpts from *Postmodernism, Or The Cultural Logic of Late Capitalism*

Fredric Jameson

The last few years have been marked by an inverted millenarianism in which premonitions of the future, catastrophic or redemptive, have been replaced by senses of the end of this or that (the end of ideology, art, or social class; the "crisis" of Leninism, social democracy, or the welfare state, etc., etc.); taken together, all of these perhaps constitute what is increasingly called postmodernism. The case for its existence depends on the hypothesis of some radical break or *coupure,* generally traced back to the end of the 1950s or the early 1960s.

As the word itself suggests, this break is most often related to notions of the waning or extinction of the hundred-year-old modern movement (or to its ideological or aesthetic repudiation). Thus abstract expressionism in painting, existentialism in philosophy, the final forms of representation in the novel, the films of the great *auteurs,* or the modernist school of poetry (as institutionalized and canonized in the works of Wallace Stevens) all are now seen as the final, extraordinary flowering of a high-modernist impulse which is spent and exhausted with them. The enumeration of what follows, then, at once becomes empirical, chaotic, and heterogeneous: Andy Warhol and pop art, but also photorealism, and beyond it, the "new expressionism"; the moment, in music, of John Cage, but also the synthesis of classical and "popular" styles found in composers like Phil Glass and Terry Riley, and also punk and new wave rock (the Beatles and the Stones now standing as the high-modernist moment of that more recent and rapidly evolving tradition); in film, Godard, post-Godard, and experimental cinema and video, but also a whole new type of commercial film (about which more below); Burroughs, Pynchon, or Ishmael Reed, on the one hand, and the French *nouveau roman* and its succession, on the other, along with alarming new kinds of literary criticism based on some new aesthetic of textuality or *écriture*.... The list might be extended indefinitely; but does it imply any more fundamental change or break than the periodic style and fashion changes determined by an older high-modernist imperative of stylistic innovation?

It is in the realm of architecture, however, that modifications in aesthetic production are most dramatically visible, and that their theoretical problems have been most centrally raised and articulated; it was indeed from architectural debates that my own conception of postmodernism—as it will be outlined in the following pages—initially began to emerge. More decisively than in the other arts or media, postmodernist positions in architecture have been inseparable from an implacable critique of architectural high modernism and of Frank Lloyd Wright or the so-called international style (Le Corbusier, Mies, etc), where formal criticism and analysis (of the high-modernist transformation of the building into a virtual sculpture, or monumental "duck," as Robert Venturi puts it)[1] are at one with reconsiderations on the level of urbanism and of the aesthetic institution. High modernism is thus credited with the destruction of the fabric of the traditional city and its older neighborhood culture (by way of the radical disjunction of the new Utopian high-modernist building from its surrounding context), while the prophetic elitism and authoritarianism of the modern movement are remorselessly identified in the imperious gesture of the charismatic Master.

Postmodernism in architecture will then logically enough stage itself as a kind of aesthetic populism, as the very title of Venturi's influential manifesto, *Learning from Las Vegas*, suggests. However we may ultimately wish to evaluate this populist rhetoric,[2] it has at least the merit of drawing our attention to one fundamental feature of all the postmodernisms enumerated above: namely, the effacement in them of the older (essentially high-modernist) frontier between high culture and so-called mass or commercial culture, and the emergence of new kinds of texts infused with the forms, categories, and contents of that very culture industry so passionately denounced by all the ideologues of the modern, from Leavis and the American New Criticism all the way to Adorno and the Frankfurt School. The postmodernisms have, in fact, been fascinated precisely by this whole "degraded" landscape of schlock and kitsch, of tv series and *Reader's Digest* culture, of advertising and motels, of the late show and the grade-B Hollywood film, of so-called paraliterature, with its airport paperback categories of the gothic and the romance, the popular biography, the murder mystery, and the science fiction or fantasy novel: materials they no longer simply "quote," as a Joyce or a Mahler might have done, but incorporate into their very substance.

Nor should the break in question be thought of as a purely cultural affair: indeed, theories of the postmodern—whether celebratory or couched in the language of moral revulsion and denunciation—bear a strong family resemblance to all those more ambitious sociological generalizations which, at much the same time, bring us the news of the arrival and inauguration of a whole new type of society, most famously baptized "postindustrial society" (Daniel Bell) but often also designated consumer society, media society, information society, electronic society or high tech, and the like. Such theories have the obvious ideological mission of demonstrating, to their own relief, that the new social formation in question no longer obeys the laws of classical capitalism, namely, the primacy of industrial production and the omnipresence of class struggle. The Marxist tradition has therefore resisted them with vehemence, with the signal exception of the economist Ernest Mandel, whose book *Late Capitalism* sets out not merely to anatomize the historic originality of this new society (which he sees as a third stage or moment in the evolution of capital) but also to demonstrate that it is, if anything, a *purer* stage of capitalism than any of the moments that preceded it. I will return to this argument later; suffice it for the moment to anticipate a point that will be argued in chapter 2, namely, that every position on postmodernism in culture—whether apologia or stigmatization—is also at one and the same time, and *necessarily*, an implicitly or explicitly political stance on the nature of multinational capitalism today.

A last preliminary word on method: what follows is not to be read as stylistic description, as the account of one cultural style or movement among others. I have rather meant to offer a periodizing hypothesis, and that at a moment in which the very conception of historical periodization has come to seem most problematical indeed. I have argued elsewhere that all isolated or discrete cultural analysis always involves a buried or repressed theory of historical periodization; in any case, the conception of the "genealogy" largely lays to rest traditional theoretical worries about so-called linear history, theories of "stages," and teleological historiography. In the present context, however, lengthier theoretical discussion of such (very real) issues can perhaps be replaced by a few substantive remarks.

One of the concerns frequently aroused by periodizing hypotheses is that these tend to obliterate difference and to project an idea of the historical period as massive homogeneity (bounded on either side by inexplicable chronological metamorphoses and punctuation marks). This is, however, precisely why it seems to me essential to grasp postmodernism not as as style but rather as a cultural dominant: a conception which allows for the presence and coexistence of a range of very different, yet subordinate, features.

Consider, for example, the powerful alternative position that postmodernism is itself little more than one stage of modernism proper (if not, indeed, of the even older romanticism); it may indeed be conceded that all the features of postmodernism I am about to enumerate can be detected, full-blown, in this or that preceding modernism (including such astonishing genealogical precursors as Gertrude Stein, Raymond Roussel, or Marcel Duchamp, who may be considered outright postmodernists, avant la lettre). What has not been taken into account by this view, however, is the social position of the older modernism, or better still, its passionate repudiation by an older Victorian and post-Victorian bourgeoisie for whom its forms and ethos are received as being variously ugly, dissonant, obscure, scandalous, immoral, subversive, and generally "antisocial." It will be argued here, however, that a mutation in the sphere of culture has rendered such attitudes archaic. Not only are Picasso and Joyce no longer ugly; they now strike us, on the whole, as rather "realistic," and this is the result of a canonization and academic institutionalization of the modern movement generally that can be traced to the late 1950s. This is surely one of the most plausible explanations for the emergence of postmodernism itself, since the younger generation of the 1960s will now confront the formerly oppositional modern movement as a set of dead classics, which "weigh like a nightmare on the brains of the living," as Marx once said in a different context.

As for the postmodern revolt against all that, however, it must equally be stressed that its own offensive features—from obscurity and sexually explicit material to psychological squalor and overt expressions of social and political defiance, which transcend anything that might have been imagined at the most extreme moments of high modernism—no longer scandalize anyone and are not only received with the greatest complacency but have themselves become institutionalized and are at one with the official or public culture of Western society.

What has happened is that aesthetic production today has become integrated into commodity production generally: the frantic economic urgency of producing fresh waves of ever more novel-seeming goods (from clothing to airplanes), at ever greater rates of turnover, now assigns an increasingly essential structural function and position to aesthetic innovation and experimentation. Such economic necessities then find recognition in the varied kinds of institutional support available for the newer art, from foundations and grants to museums and other forms of patronage. Of all the arts, architecture is the closest constitutively to the economic, with which, in the form of commissions and land values, it has a virtually unmediated relationship. It will therefore not be surprising to find the extraordinary flowering of the new postmodern architecture grounded in the patronage of multinational business, whose expansion and development is strictly contemporaneous with it. Later I will suggest that these two new phenomena have an even deeper dialectical interrelationship than the simple one-to-one financing of this or that individual project. Yet this is the point at which I must remind the reader of the obvious; namely, that this whole global, yet American postmodern culture is the internal and superstructural expression of a whole new wave of American military and economic domination throughout the world: in this sense, as throughout class history, the underside of culture is blood, torture, death, and terror.

The first point to be made about the conception of periodization in dominance, therefore, is that even if all the constitutive features of postmodernism were identical with and continuous to those of an older modernism—a position I feel to be demonstrably erroneous but which only an even lengthier analysis of modernism proper could dispel—the two phenomena would still remain utterly distinct in their meaning and social function, owing to the very different positioning of postmodernism in the economic system of late capital and, beyond that, to the transformation of the very sphere of culture in contemporary society.

*   *   *

I have felt, however, that it was only in the light of some conception of a dominant cultural logic or hegemonic norm that genuine difference could be measured and assessed. I am very far from feeling that all cultural production today is "postmodern" in the broad sense I will be conferring on this term. The postmodern is, however, the force field in which very different kinds of cultural impulses—what Raymond Williams has usefully termed "residual" and "emergent" forms of cultural production—must make their way. If we do not achieve some general sense of a cultural dominant, then we fall back into a view of present history as sheer heterogeneity, random difference, a coexistence of a host of distinct forces whose effectivity is undecidable. At any rate, this has been the political spirit in which the following analysis was devised: to project some conception of a new systematic cultural norm and its reproduction in order to reflect more adequately on the most effective forms of any radical cultural politics today.

The exposition will take up in turn the following constitutive features of the postmodern: a new depthlessness, which finds its prolongation both in contemporary "theory" and in a whole new culture of the image or the simulacrum; a consequent weakening of historicity, both in our relationship to public History and in the new forms of our private temporality, whose "schizophrenic" structure (following Lacan) will determine new types of syntax or syntagmatic relationships in the more temporal arts; a whole new type of emotional ground tone—what I will call "intensities"—which can best be grasped by a return to older theories of the sublime; the deep constitutive relationships of all this to a whole new technology, which is itself a figure for a whole new economic world system; and, after a brief account of postmodernist mutations in the lived experience of built space itself, some reflections on the mission of political art in the bewildering new world space of late or multinational capital.

*   *   *

This is perhaps the moment to say something about contemporary theory, which has, among other things, been committed to the mission of criticizing and discrediting this very hermeneutic model of the inside and the outside and of stigmatizing such models as ideological and metaphysical. But what is today called contemporary theory—or better still, theoretical discourse—is also, I want to argue, itself very precisely a postmodernist phenomenon. It would therefore be inconsistent to defend the truth of its theoretical insights in a situation in which the very concept of "truth" itself is part of the metaphysical baggage which poststructuralism seeks to abandon. What we can at least suggest is that the poststructuralist critique of the hermeneutic, of what I will shortly call the *depth model,* is useful for us as a very significant symptom of the very postmodernist culture which is our subject here.

Overhastily, we can say that besides the hermeneutic model of inside and outside, . . . at least four other fundamental depth models have generally been repudiated in contemporary theory: (1) the dialectical one of essence and appearance (along with a whole range of concepts of ideology or false consciousness which tend to accompany it); (2) the Freudian model of latent and manifest, or of repression (which is, of course, the target of Michel Foucault's programmatic and symptomatic pamphlet *La Volonté de savoir [The History of Sexuality]*); (3) the existential model of authenticity and inauthenticity whose heroic or tragic thematics are closely related to that other great opposition between alienation and disalienation, itself equally a casualty of the poststructural or postmodern period; and (4) most recently, the great semiotic opposition between signifier and signified, which was itself rapidly unraveled and deconstructed during its brief heyday in the 1960s and 1970s. What replaces these various depth models is for the most part a conception of practices, discourses, and textual play, whose new syntagmatic structures we will examine later on; let it suffice now to observe that here too depth is replaced by surface, or by multiple surfaces (what is often called intertextuality is in that sense no longer a matter of depth).

*   *   *

Such terms [the alienation of the subject displaced by the latter's fragmentation] inevitably recall one of the more fashionable themes in contemporary theory, that of the "death" of the subject itself—the end of the autonomous bourgeois monad or ego or individual—and the accompanying stress, whether as some new moral ideal or as empirical description, on the *decentering* of that formerly centered subject or psyche. (Of the two possible formulations of this notion—the historicist one, that a once-existing centered subject, in the period of classical capitalism and the nuclear family, has today in the world of organizational bureaucracy dissolved; and the more radical poststructuralist position, for which such a subject never existed in the first place but constituted something like an ideological mirage—I obviously incline toward the former; the latter must in any case take into account something like a "reality of the appearance.")

We must however add that the problem of expression is itself closely linked to some conception of the subject as a monadlike container, within which things felt are then expressed by projection outward. What we must now stress, however, is the degree to which the high-modernist conception of a unique style (along with the accompanying collective ideals of an artist or political vanguard or avant-garde), themselves stand or fall along with that older notion (or experience) of the so-called centered subject.

* * *

The end of the bourgeois ego, or monad, no doubt brings with it the end of the psychopathologies of that ego—what I have been calling the waning of affect. But it means the end of much more— the end, for example, of style, in the sense of the unique and the personal, the end of the distinctive individual brush stroke (as symbolized by the emergent primacy of mechanical reproduction). As for expression and feelings or emotions, the liberation, in contemporary society, from the older *anomie* of the centered subject may also mean not merely a liberation from anxiety but a liberation from every other kind of feeling as well, since there is no longer a self present to do the feeling. This is not to say that the cultural products of the postmodern era are utterly devoid of feeling, but rather that such feelings—which it may be better and more accurate, following J.-F. Lyotard, to call "intensities"—are now freefloating and impersonal and tend to be dominated by a peculiar kind of euphoria, a matter to which we will want to return later on.

The waning of affect, however, might also have been characterized, in the narrower context of literary criticism, as the waning of the great high modernist thematics of time and temporality, the elegiac mysteries of *durée* and memory (something to be understood fully as much as a category of the literary criticism associated with high modernism as with the works themselves). We have often been told, however, that we now inhabit the synchronic rather than the diachronic, and I think it is at least empirically arguable that our daily life, our psychic experience, our cultural languages, are today dominated by categories of space rather than by categories of time, as in the preceding period of high modernism.[3]

The disappearance of the individual subject, along with its formal consequence, the increasing unavailability of the personal style, engender the well-nigh universal practice today of what may be called pastiche. This concept, which we owe to Thomas Mann (in *Doktor Faustus*), who owed it in turn to Adorno's great work on the two paths of advanced musical experimentation (Schoenberg's innovative planification and Stravinsky's irrational eclecticism), is to be sharply distinguished from the more readily received idea of parody.

To be sure, parody found a fertile area in the idiosyncrasies of the moderns and their "inimitable" styles: the Faulknerian long sentence, for example, with its breathless gerundives; Lawrentian nature imagery punctuated by testy colloquialism; Wallace Stevens's inveterate hypostasis of nonsubstantive parts of speech ("the intricate evasions of as"); the fateful (but finally predictable) swoops in Mahler from high orchestral pathos into village accordion sentiment; Heidegger's meditative-solemn practice of the false etymology as a mode of "proof" . . . All these strike one as somehow characteristic, insofar as they ostentatiously deviate from a norm which then reasserts itself, in a not necessarily unfriendly way, by a systematic mimicry of their willful eccentricities.

Yet in the dialectical leap from quantity to quality, the explosion of modern literature into a host of distinct private styles and mannerisms has been followed by a linguistic fragmentation of social life itself to the point where the norm itself is eclipsed: reduced to a neutral and reified media speech (far enough from the Utopian aspirations of the inventors of Esperanto or Basic English), which itself then becomes but one more idiolect among many. Modernist styles thereby become postmodernist codes. And that the stupendous proliferation of social codes today into professional and disciplinary jargons (but also into the badges of affirmation of ethnic, gender, race, religious, and class-factional adhesion) is also a political phenomenon, the problem of micropolitics sufficiently demonstrates. If the ideas of a ruling class were once the dominant (or hegemonic) ideology of bourgeois society, the advanced capitalist countries today are now a field of stylistic and discursive heterogeneity without a norm. Faceless masters continue to inflect the economic strategies which constrain our existences, but they no longer need to impose their speech (or are henceforth unable to); and the postliteracy of the late capitalist world reflects not only the absence of any great collective project but also the unavailability of the older national language itself.

In this situation parody finds itself without a vocation; it has lived, and that strange new thing patische slowly comes to take its place. Pastiche is, like parody, the imitation of a peculiar or unique, idiosyncratic style, the wearing of a linguistic mask, speech in a dead language. But it is a neutral practice of such mimicry, without any of parody's ulterior motives, amputated of the satiric impulse, devoid of laughter and of any conviction that alongside the abnormal tongue you have momentarily borrowed, some healthy linguistic normality still exists. Pastiche is thus blank parody, a statue with blind eyeballs; it is to parody what that other interesting and historically original modern thing, the practice of a kind of blank irony is to what Wayne Booth calls the "stable ironies" of the eighteenth century.

It would therefore begin to seem that Adorno's prophetic diagnosis has been realized, albeit in a negative way: not Schönberg (the sterility of whose achieved system he already glimpsed) but Stravinsky is the true precursor of postmodern cultural production. For with the collapse of the high-modernist ideology of style—what is as unique and unmistakable as your own fingerprints, as incomparable as your own body (the very source, for an early Roland Barthes, of stylistic invention and innovation)—the producers of culture have nowhere to turn but to the past: the imitation of dead styles, speech through all the masks and voices stored up in the imaginary museum of a now global culture.

This situation evidently determines what the architecture historians call "historicism," namely, the random cannibalization of all the styles of the past, the play of random stylistic allusion, and in general what Henri Lefebvre has called the increasing primacy of the "neo." This omnipresence of pastiche is not incompatible with a certain humor, however, nor is it innocent of all passion: it is at the least compatible with addiction—with a whole historically original consumers' appetite for a world transformed into sheer images of itself and for pseudo-events and "spectacles" (the term of the situationists). It is for such objects that we may reserve Plato's conception of the "simulacrum," the identical copy for which no original has ever existed. Appropriately enough, the culture of the simulacrum comes to life in a society where exchange value has been generalized to the point at which the very memory of use value is effaced, a society of which Guy Debord has observed, in an extraordinary phrase, that in it "the image has become the final form of commodity reification" (*The Society of the Spectacle*).

The new spatial logic of the simulacrum can now be expected to have a momentous effect on what used to be historical time. The past is thereby itself modified: what was once, in the historical novel as Lukács defines it, the organic genealogy of the bourgeois collective project—what is still, for the redemptive historiography of an E. P. Thompson or of American "oral history," for the resurrection of the dead of anonymous and silenced generations, the retrospective dimension indispensable to any vital reorientation of our collective future—has meanwhile itself become a vast collection of images, a multitudinous photographic simulacrum. Guy Debord's powerful slogan is now even more apt for the "prehistory" of a society bereft of all historicity, one whose own putative past is little more than a set of dusty spectacles. In faithful conformity to post-structuralist linguistic theory, the past as "referent" finds itself gradually bracketed, and then effaced altogether, leaving us with nothing but texts.

Yet it should not be thought that this process is accompanied by indifference: on the contrary, the remarkable current intensification of an addiction to the photographic image is itself a tangible symptom of an omnipresent, omnivorous, and well-nigh libidinal historicism. As I have already observed, the architects use this (exceedingly polysemous) word for the complacent eclecticism of postmodern architecture, which randomly and without principle but with gusto cannibalizes all the architectural styles of the past and combines them in over stimulating ensembles. Nostalgia does not strike one as an altogether satisfactory word for such fascination (particularly when one thinks of the pain of a *properly* modernist nostalgia with a past beyond all but aesthetic retrieval), yet it directs our attention to what is a culturally far more generalized manifestation of the process in commercial art and taste, namely the so-called nostalgia film (or what the French call *la mode rétro*).

*   *   *

Faced with these ultimate objects—our social, historical, and existential present, and the past as "referent"—the incompatibility of a postmodernist "nostalgia" art language with genuine historicity becomes dramatically apparent. The contradiction propels this mode, however, into complex and interesting new formal inventiveness; it being understood that the nostalgia film was never a matter of some old-fashioned "representation" of historical content, but instead approached the "past" through stylistic connotation, conveying "pastness" by the glossy qualities of the image, and "1930s-ness" or "1950s-ness" by the attributes of fashion (in that following the prescription of the Barthes of *Mythologies,* who saw connotation as the purveying of imaginary and stereotypical idealities: "Sinité," for example, as some Disney-EPCOT "concept" of China).

* * *

The crisis in historicity now dictates a return, in a new way, to the question of temporal organization in general in the postmodern force field, and indeed, to the problem of the form that time, temporality, and the syntagmatic will be able to take in a culture increasingly dominated by space and spatial logic. If, indeed, the subject has lost its capacity actively to extend its pro-tensions and re-tensions across the temporal manifold and to organize its past and future into coherent experience, it becomes difficult enough to see how the cultural productions of such a subject could result in anything but "heaps of fragments" and in a practice of the randomly heterogeneous and fragmentary and the aleatory. These are, however, very precisely some of the privileged terms in which postmodernist cultural production has been analyzed (and even defended, by its own apologists). They are, however, still privative features; the more substantive formulations bear such names as textuality, *écriture,* or schizophrenic writing, and it is to these that we must now briefly turn.

I have found Lacan's account of schizophrenia useful here not because I have any way of knowing whether it has clinical accuracy but chiefly because—as description rather than diagnosis—it seems to me to offer a suggestive aesthetic model.[4] I am obviously very far from thinking that any of the most significant postmodernist artists—Cage, Ashbery, Sollers, Robert Wilson, Ishmael Reed, Michael Show, Warhol, or even Beckett himself—are schizophrenics in any clinical sense. Nor is the point some culture-and-personality diagnosis of our society and its art, as in psychologizing and moralizing culture critiques of the type of Christopher Lasch's influential *The Culture of Narcissism,* from which I am concerned to distance the spirit and the methodology of the present remarks: there are, one would think, far more damaging things to be said about our social system than are available through the use of psychological categories.

Very briefly, Lacan describes schizophrenia as a breakdown in the signifying chain, that is, the interlocking syntagmatic series of signifiers which constitutes an utterance or a meaning. I must omit the familial or more orthodox psychoanalytic background to this situation, which Lacan transcodes into language by describing the Oedipal rivalry in terms not so much of the biological individual who is your rival for the mother's attention but rather of what he calls the Name-of-the-Father, paternal authority now considered as a linguistic function[5]. His conception of the signifying chain essentially presupposes one of the basic principles (and one of the great discoveries) of Saussurean structuralism, namely, the proposition that meaning is not a one-to-one relationship between signifier and signified, between the materiality of language, between a word or a name, and its referent or concept. Meaning on the new view is generated by the movement from signifier to signifier. What we generally call the signified—the meaning or conceptual content of an utterance—is now rather to be seen as a meaning-effect, as that objective mirage of signification generated and projected by the relationship of signifiers among themselves. When that relationship breaks down, when the links of the signifying chain snap, then we have schizophrenia in the form of a rubble of distinct and unrelated signifiers. The connection between this kind of linguistic malfunction and the psyche of the schizophrenic may then be grasped by way of a twofold proposition: first, that personal identity is itself the effect of a certain temporal unification of past and future with one's present; and, second, that such active temporal unification is itself a function of language, or better still of the sentence, as it moves along its hermeneutic circle through time. If we are unable to unify the past, present, and future of the sentence, then we are similarly unable to unify the past, present, and future of our own biographical experience or psychic life. With the breakdown of the signifying chain, therefore, the schizophrenic is reduced to an experience of pure material signifiers, or, in other words, a series of pure and unrelated presents in time. We will want to ask questions about the aesthetic or cultural results of such a situation in a moment.

* * *

What happens in textuality or schizophrenic art is strikingly illuminated by . . . clinical accounts, although in the cultural text, the isolated signifier is no longer an enigmatic state of the world or an incomprehensible yet mesmerizing fragment of language but rather something closer to a sentence in free-standing isolation. Think, for example, of the experience of John Cage's music, in which a cluster of material sounds (on the prepared piano, for example) is followed by a silence so intolerable that you cannot imagine another sonorous chord coming into existence and cannot imagine remembering the previous one well enough to make any connection with it if it does. Some of Beckett's narratives are also of this order, most notable *Watt,* where a primacy of the present sentence in time ruthlessly disintegrates the narrative fabric that attempts to reform around it.

*   *   *

But I mainly wanted to show the way in which what I have been calling schizophrenic disjunction or *écriture,* when it becomes generalized as a cultural style, ceases to entertain a necessary relationship to the morbid content we associate with terms like schizophrenia and becomes available for more joyous intensities, for precisely that euphoria which we saw displacing the older affects of anxiety and alienation.

*   *   *

This account of schizophrenia and temporal organization might, however, have been formulated in a different way, which brings us back to Heidegger's notion of a gap or rift between Earth and World, albeit in a fashion that is sharply incompatible with the tone and high seriousness of his own philosophy. I would like to characterize the postmodernist experience of form with what will seem, I hope, a paradoxical slogan: namely, the proposition that "difference relates." Our own recent criticism, from Macherey on, has been concerned to stress the heterogeneity and profound discontinuities of the work of art, no longer unified or organic, but now a virtual grab bag or lumber room of disjoined subsystems and random raw materials and impulses of all kinds. The former work of art, in other words, has now turned out to be a text, whose reading proceeds by differentiation rather than by unification. Theories of difference, however, have tended to stress disjunction to the point at which the materials of the text, including its words and sentences, tend to fall apart into random and inert passivity, into a set of elements which entertain separations from one another.

In the most interesting postmodernist works, however, one can detect a more positive conception of relationship, which restores its proper tension to the notion of difference itself. This new mode of relationship through difference may sometimes be an achieved new and original way of thinking and perceiving; more often it takes the form of an impossible imperative to achieve that new mutation in what can perhaps no longer be called consciousness. I believe that the most striking emblem of this new mode of thinking relationships can be found in the work of Nam June Paik, whose stacked or scattered television screens, positioned at intervals within lush vegetation, or winking down at us from a ceiling of strange new video stars, recapitulate over and over again prearranged sequences or loops of images which return at dyssynchronous moments on the various screens. The older aesthetic is then practiced by viewers, who, bewildered by this discontinuous variety, decided to concentrate on a single screen, as though the relatively worthless image sequence to be followed there had some organic value in its own right. The postmodernist viewer, however, is called upon to do the impossible, namely, to see all the screens at once, in their radical and random difference; such a viewer is asked to follow the evolutionary mutation of David Bowie in *The Man Who Fell to Earth* (who watches fifty-seven television screens simultaneously) and to rise somehow to a level at which the vivid perception of radical difference is in and of itself a new mode of grasping what used to be called relationship: something for which the word *collage* is still only a very feeble name.

Now we need to complete this exploratory account of postmodernist space and time with a final analysis of that euphoria or those intensities which seem so often to characterize the newer cultural experience. Let us reemphasize the enormity of a transition which leaves behind it the desolation of Hopper's buildings or the stark Midwest syntax of Sheeler's forms, replacing them with the extraordinary surfaces of the photorealist cityscape, where even the automobile wrecks gleam with some new hallucinatory splendor. The exhilaration of these new surfaces is all the more paradoxical in that their essential content—the city itself—has deteriorated or disintegrated to a degree surely still inconceivable in the early years of the twentieth century, let alone in the previous era.

* * *

It has proved fruitful to think of such experiences in terms of what Susan Sontag, in an influential statement, isolated as "camp." I propose a somewhat different cross-light on it, drawing on the equally fashionable current theme of the "sublime," as it has been rediscovered in the works of Edmund Burke and Kant; or perhaps one might want to yoke the two notions together in the form of something like a camp or "hysterical" sublime. The sublime was for Burke an experience bordering on terror, the fitful glimpse, in astonishment, stupor, and awe, of what was so enormous as to crush human life altogether: a description then refined by Kant to include the question of representation itself, so that the object of the sublime becomes not only a matter of sheer power and of the physical incommensurability of the human organism with Nature but also of the limits of figuration and the incapacity of the human mind to give representation to such enormous forces. Such forces Burke, in his historical moment at the dawn of the modern bourgeois state, was only able to conceptualize in terms of the divine, while even Heidegger continues to entertain a phantasmatic relationship with some organic precapitalist peasant landscape and village society, which is the final form of the image of Nature in our own time.

Today, however, it may be possible to think of all this in a different way, at the moment of a radical eclipse of Nature itself: Heidegger's "field path" is, after all, irredeemably and irrevocably destroyed by late capital, by the green revolution, by neocolonialism and the megalopolis, which runs its superhighways over the older fields and vacant lots and turns Heidegger's "house of being" into condominiums, if not the most miserable unheated, rat-infested tenement buildings. The *other* of our society is in that sense no longer Nature at all, as it was in precapitalist societies, but something else which we must now identify.

I am anxious that this other thing not overhastily be grasped as technology per se, since I will want to show that technology is here itself a figure for something else. Yet technology may well serve as adequate shorthand to designate that enormous properly human and anti-natural power of dead human labor stored up in our machinery—an alienated power, what Sartre calls the counterfinality of the practico-inert, which turns back on and against us in unrecognizable forms and seems to constitute the massive dystopian horizon of our collective as well as our individual praxis.

Technological development is however on the Marxist view the result of the development of capital rather than some ultimately determining instance in its own right. It will therefore be appropriate to distinguish several generations of machine power, several stages of technological revolution within capital itself. I here follow Ernest Mandel, who outlines three such fundamental breaks or quantum leaps in the evolution of machinery under capital:

> The fundamental revolutions in power technology—the technology of the production of motive machines by machines—thus appears as the determinant moment in revolutions of technology as a whole. Machine production of steam-driven motors since 1848; machine production of electric and combustion motors since the 90s of the 19th century; machine production of electronic and nuclear-powered apparatuses since the 40s of the 20th century—these are the three general revolutions in technology engendered by the capitalist mode of production since the "original" industrial revolution of the later 18th century.[6]

This periodization underscores the general thesis of Mandel's book *Late Capitalism;* namely, that there have been three fundamental moments in capitalism, each one marking a dialectical expansion over the previous stage. These are market capitalism, the monopoly stage or the stage of imperialism, and our own, wrongly called postindustrial, but what might better be termed multinational, capital. I have already pointed out that Mandel's intervention in the postindustrial debate involves the proposition that late or multinational or consumer capitalism, far from being inconsistent with Marx's great nineteenth-century analysis, constitutes, on the contrary, the purest form of capital yet to have emerged, a prodigious expansion of capital into hitherto uncommodified areas. This purer capitalism of our own time thus eliminates the enclaves of precapitalist organization it had hitherto tolerated and exploited in a tributary way. One is tempted to speak in this connection of a new and historically original penetration and colonization of Nature and the Unconscious: that is, the destruction of precapitalist Third World agriculture by the Green Revolution, and the rise of the media and the advertising industry. At any rate, it will also have been clear that my own cultural periodization of the stages of realism, modernism, and postmodernism is both inspired and confirmed by Mandel's tripartite scheme.

We may therefore speak of our own period as the Third Machine Age; and it is at this point that we must reintroduce the problem of aesthetic representation already explicitly developed in Kant's earlier analysis of the sublime, since it would seem only logical that the relationship to and the representation of the machine could be expected to shift dialectically with each of these qualitatively different stages of technological development.

* * *

It is immediately obvious that the technology of our own moment no longer possesses this same capacity for representation: not the turbine, nor even Sheeler's grain elevators or smokestacks, not the baroque elaboration of pipes and conveyor belts, nor even the streamlined profile of the railroad train—all vehicles of speed still concentrated at rest—but rather the computer, whose outer shell has no emblematic or visual power, or even the casings of the various media themselves, as with that home appliance called television which articulates nothing but rather implodes, carrying its flattened image surface within itself.

Such machines are indeed machines of reproduction rather than of production, and they make very different demands on our capacity for aesthetic representation than did the relatively mimetic idolatry of the older machinery of the futurist moment, of some older speed-and-energy sculpture. Here we have less to do with kinetic energy than with all kinds of new reproductive processes; and in the weaker productions of postmodernism the aesthetic embodiment of such processes often tends to slip back more comfortably into a mere thematic representation of content—into narratives which are *about* the processes of reproduction and include movie cameras, video, tape recorders, the whole technology of the production and reproduction of the simulacrum. (The shift from Antonioini's modernist *Blow-Up* to DePalma's postmodernist *Blow-out* is here paradigmatic.) When Japanese architects, for example, model a building on the decorative imitation of stacks of cassettes, then the solution is at best thematic and allusive, although often humorous.

Yet something else does tend to emerge in the most energetic postmodernist texts, and this is the sense that beyond all thematics or content the work seems somehow to tap the networks of the reproductive process and thereby to afford us some glimpse into a postmodern or technological sublime, whose power or authenticity is documented by the success of such works in evoking a whole new postmodern space in emergence around us. Architecture therefore remains in this sense the privileged aesthetic language; and the distorting and fragmenting reflections of one enormous glass surface to the other can be taken as paradigmatic of the central role of process and reproduction in postmodernist culture.

As I have said, however, I want to avoid the implication that technology is in any way the "ultimately determining instance" either of our present-day social life or of our cultural production: such a thesis is, of course, ultimately at one with the post-Marxist notion of a postindustrial society. Rather, I want to suggest that our faulty representations of some immense communicational and computer network are themselves but a distorted figuration of something even deeper, namely, the whole world system of a present-day multinational capitalism. The technology of contemporary society is therefore mesmerizing and fascinating not so much in its own right but because it seems to offer some privileged representational shorthand for grasping a network of power and control even more difficult for our minds and imaginations to grasp: the whole new decentered global network of the third stage of capital itself. This is a figural process presently best observed in a whole mode of contemporary entertainment literature—one is tempted to characterize it as "high tech paranoia"—in which the circuits and networks of some putative global computer hookup are narratively mobilized by labyrinthine conspiracies of autonomous but deadly interlocking and competing information agencies in a complexity often beyond the capacity of the normal reading mind. Yet conspiracy theory (and its garish narrative manifestations) must be seen as a degraded attempt—through the figuration of advanced technology—to think the impossible totality of the contemporary world system. It is in terms of that enormous and threatening, yet only dimly perceivable, other reality of economic and social institutions that, in my opinion, the postmodern sublime can alone be adequately theorized.

Such narratives, which first tried to find expression through the generic structure of the spy novel, have only recently crystallized in a new type of science fiction, called cyperpunk, which is fully as much an expression of transnational corporate realities as it is of global paranoia itself: William Gibson's representational innovations, indeed, mark his work as an exceptional literary realization within a predominantly visual or aural postmodern production.

* * *

The conception of postmodernism outlined here is a historical rather than a merely stylistic one. I cannot stress too greatly the radical distinction between a view for which the postmodern is one (optional) style among many others available and one which seeks to grasp it as the cultural dominant of the logic of late capitalism: the two approaches in fact generate two very different ways of conceptualizing the phenomenon as a whole: on the one hand, moral judgments (about which it is indifferent whether they are positive or negative), and, on the other, a genuinely dialectical attempt to think our present of time in History.

Of some positive moral evaluation of postmodernism little needs to be said: the complacent (yet delirious) camp-following celebration of this aesthetic new world (including its social and economic dimension, greeted with equal enthusiasm under the slogan of "postindustrial society") is surely unacceptable, although it may be somewhat less obvious that current fantasies about the salvational nature of high technology, from chips to robots—fantasies entertained not only by both left and right governments in distress but also by many intellectuals—are also essentially of a piece with more vulgar apologias for postmodernism.

But in that case it is only consequent to reject moralizing condemnations of the postmodern and of its essential triviality when juxtaposed against the Utopian "high seriousness" of the great modernisms: judgments one finds both on the Left and on the radical Right. And no doubt the logic of the simulacrum, with its transformation of older realities into television images, does more than merely replicate the logic of late capitalism; it reinforces and intensifies it. Meanwhile, for political groups which seek actively to intervene in history and to modify its otherwise passive momentum (whether with a view toward channeling it into a socialist transformation of society or diverting it into the regressive reestablishment of some simpler fantasy past), there cannot but be much that is deplorable and reprehensible in a cultural form of image addiction which, by transforming the past into visual mirages, stereotypes, or texts, effectively abolishes any practical sense of the future and of the collective project, thereby abandoning the thinking of future change to fantasies of sheer catastrophe and inexplicable cataclysm, from visions of "terrorism" on the social level to those of cancer on the personal. Yet if postmodernism is a historical phenomenon, then the attempt to conceptualize it in terms of moral or moralizing judgments must finally be identified as a category mistake. All of which becomes more obvious when we interrogate the position of the cultural critic and moralist; the latter, along with all the rest of us, is now so deeply immersed in postmodernist space, so deeply suffused and infected by its new cultural categories, that the luxury of the old-fashioned ideological critique, the indignant moral denunciation of the other, becomes unavailable.

Notes

1. Robert Venturi and Denise Scott-Brown, *Learning from Las Vegas,* (Cambridge, Mass. 1972).

2. The originality of Charles Jencks's pathbreaking *Language of Post-Modern Architecture* (1977) lay in its well-nigh dialectical combination of postmodern architecture and a certain kind of semiotics, each being appealed to to justify the existence of the other. Semiotics becomes appropriate as a mode of analysis of the newer architecture by virtue of the latter's populism, which does emit signs and messages to a spatial "reading public," unlike the monumentality of the high modern. Meanwhile, the newer architecture is itself thereby validated, insofar as it is accessible to semiotic

analysis and thus proves to be an essentially aesthetic object (rather than the transaesthetic constructions of the high modern). Here, then, aesthetics reinforces an ideology of communication (about which more will be observed in the concluding chapter), and vice versa. Besides Jencks's many valuable contributions, see also Heinrich Klotz, *History of Postmodern Architecture* (Cambridge, Mass., 1988); Pier Paolo Portoghesi, *After Modern Architecture* (New York, 1982).

3. This is the moment to confront a significant translation problem and to say why, in my opinion, the notion of a postmodern spatialization is not incompatible with Joseph Frank's influential attribution of an essentially "spatial form" to the high modern. In hindsight, what he describes is the vocation of the modern work to invent a kind of spatial mnemonics— reminiscent of Frances Yates's *Art of Memory,* a "totalizing" construction in the stricter sense of the stigmatized, autonomous work, whereby the particular somehow includes a battery of re- and pre-tensions linking the sentence or the detail to the Idea of the total form itself. Adorno quotes a remark about Wagner by the conductor Alfred Lorenz in precisely this sense: "If you have completely mastered a major work in all its details, you sometimes experience moments in which your consciousness of time suddenly disappears and the entire work seems to be what one might call 'spatial', that is, with everything present simultaneously in the mind with precision" (W. 36/33). But such mnemonic spatiality could never characterize postmodern texts, in which "totality" is eschewed virtually by definition. Frank's modernist spatial form is thus synedochic, whereas it is scarcely even a beginning to summon up the word *metonymic* for postmodernism's universal urbanization, let alone its nominalism of the here-and-now.

4. The basic reference, in which Lacan discusses Schreber, is "D'Une Question Préliminaire à Tout Traitement Possible de la Psychose," in *Écrits,* Alan Sheridan, trans. (New York, 1977), pp. 179–225. Most of us have received this classical view of psychosis by way of Deleuze and Guattari's *Anti-Oedipus.*

5. See my "Imaginary and Symbolic in Lacan," in *The Ideologies of Theory,* volume I (Minnesota, 1988), pp. 75–115.

6. Ernest Mandel, *Late Capitalism* (London, 1978), p. 118.

Excerpts from *The History of Sexuality: Volume I: An Introduction*

Michel Foucault

Method

Hence the objective is to analyze a certain form of knowledge regarding sex, not in terms of repression or law, but in terms of power. But the word *power* is apt to lead to a number of misunderstandings—misunderstandings with respect to its nature, its form, and its unity. By power, I do not mean "Power" as a group of institutions and mechanisms that ensure the subservience of the citizens of a given state. By power, I do not mean, either, a mode of subjugation which, in contrast to violence, has the form of the rule. Finally, I do not have in mind a general system of domination exerted by one group over another, a system whose effects, through successive derivations, pervade the entire social body. The analysis, made in terms of power, must not assume that the sovereignty of the state, the form of the law, or the overall unity of a domination are given at the outset; rather, these are only the terminal forms power takes. It seems to me that power must be understood in the first instance as

Michel Foucault, "Method" in *The History of Sexuality: Volume 1,* pp. 92–102 trans. Robert Hurley. Copyright © Editions Gallimard, 1976, Translation copyright © Random House Inc 1979. Reproduced by permission of Penguin Books Ltd and Georges Borchardt, Inc.

the multiplicity of force relations immanent in the sphere in which they operate and which constitute their own organization; as the process which, through ceaseless struggles and confrontations, transforms, strengthens, or reverses them; as the support which these force relations find in one another, thus forming a chain or a system, or on the contrary, the disjunctions and contradictions which isolate them from one another; and lastly, as the strategies in which they take effect, whose general design or institutional crystallization is embodied in the state apparatus, in the formulation of the law, in the various social hegemonies. Power's condition of possibility, or in any case the viewpoint which permits one to understand its exercise, even in its more "peripheral" effects, and which also makes it possible to use its mechanisms as a gird of intelligibility of the social order, must not be sought in the primary existence of a central point, in a unique source of sovereignty from which secondary and descendent forms would emanate; it is the moving substrate of force relations which, by virtue of their inequality, constantly engender states of power, but the latter are always local and unstable. The omnipresence of power: not because it has the privilege of consolidating everything under its invincible unity, but because it is produced from one moment to the next, at every point, or rather in every relation from one point to another. Power is everywhere; not because it embraces everything, but because it comes from everywhere. And "Power," insofar as it is permanent, repetitious, inert, and self-reproducing, is simply the overall effect that emerges from all these mobilities, the concatenation that rests on each of them and seeks in turn to arrest their movement. One needs to be nominalistic, no doubt; power is not an institution, and not a structure; neither is it a certain strength we are endowed with; it is the name that one attributes to a complex strategical situation in a particular society.

Should we turn the expression around, then, and say that politics is war pursued by other means? If we still wish to maintain a separation between war and politics, perhaps we should postulate rather that this multiplicity of force relations can be coded—in part but never totally—either in the form of "war," or in the form of "politics"; this would imply two different strategies (but the one always liable to switch into the other) for integrating these unbalanced, heterogeneous, unstable, and tense force relations.

Continuing this line of discussion, we can advance a certain number of propositions:

—Power is not something that is acquired, seized, or shared, something that one holds on to or allows to slip away; power is exercised from innumerable points, in the interplay of nonegalitarian and mobile relations.

—Relations of power are not in a position of exteriority with respect to other types of relationships (economic processes, knowledge relationships, sexual relations), but are immanent in the latter; they are the immediate effects of the divisions, inequalities, and disequilibriums which occur in the latter, and conversely they are the internal conditions of these differentiations; relations of power are not in superstructural positions, with merely a role of prohibition or accompaniment; they have a directly productive role, wherever they come into play.

—Power comes from below; that is, there is no binary and all-encompassing opposition between rulers and ruled at the root of power relations, and serving as a general matrix—no such duality extending from the top down and reacting on more and more limited groups to the very depths of the social body. One must suppose rather that the manifold relationships of force that take shape and come into play in the machinery of production, in families, limited groups, and institutions, are the basis for wide-ranging effects of cleavage that run through the social body as a whole. These then form a general line of force that traverses the local oppositions and links them together; to be sure, they also bring about redistributions, realignments, homogenizations, serial arrangements, and convergences of the force relations. Major dominations are the hegemonic effects that are sustained by all these confrontations.

—Power relations are both intentional and nonsubjective. If in fact they are intelligible, this is not because they are the effect of another instance that "explains" them, but rather because they are imbued, through and through, with calculation: there is no power that is exercised without a series of aims and objectives. But this does not mean that it results from the choice or decision of an individual subject; let us not look for the headquarters that presides over its rationality; neither the caste which governs, nor the groups which control the state apparatus, nor those who make the most important economic decisions direct the entire network of power that functions in a society (and makes *it* function); the rationality of power is characterized by tactics that are often quite explicit at the restricted level where they are inscribed (the local cynicism of power), tactics which, becoming connected to one another, attracting and propagating one another, but finding their base of support and their condition elsewhere, end by forming comprehensive systems: the logic is perfectly clear, the aims decipherable, and yet it is often the case that no one is there to have invented them, and few who can be said to have formulated them: an implicit characteristic of the great anonymous, almost unspoken strategies which coordinate the loquacious tactics whose "inventors" or decisionmakers are often without hypocrisy.

—Where there is power, there is resistance, and yet, or rather consequently, this resistance is never in a position of exteriority in relation to power. Should it be said that one is always "inside" power, there is no "escaping" it, there is no absolute outside where it is concerned, because one is subject to the law in any case? Or that, history being the ruse of reason, power is the ruse of history, always emerging the winner? This would be to misunderstand the strictly relational character of power relationships. Their existence depends on a multiplicity of points of resistance: these play the role of adversary, target, support, or handle in power relations. These points of resistance are present everywhere in the power network. Hence there is no single locus of great Refusal, no soul of revolt, source of all rebellions, or pure law of the revolutionary. Instead there is a plurality of resistances, each of them a special case: resistances that are possible, necessary, improbable; others that are spontaneous, savage, solitary, concerted, rampant, or violent; still others that are quick to compromise, interested, or sacrificial; by definition, they can only exist in the strategic field of power relations. But this does not mean that they are only a reaction or rebound, forming with respect to the basic domination an underside that is in the end always passive, doomed to perpetual defeat. Resistances do not derive from a few heterogeneous principles; but neither are they a lure or a promise that is of necessity betrayed. They are the odd terms in relations of power; they are inscribed in the latter as irreducible opposites are. Hence they too are distributed in irregular fashion: the points, knots, or focuses of resistance are spread over time and space at varying densities, at times mobilizing groups or individuals in a definitive way, inflaming certain points of the body, certain moments in life, certain types of behavior. Are there no great radical ruptures, massive binary divisions, then? Occasionally, yes. But more often one is dealing with mobile and transitory points of resistance, producing cleavages in a society that shift about, fracturing unities and effecting regroupings, furrowing across individuals themselves, cutting them up and remolding them, marking off irreducible regions in them, in their bodies and minds. Just as the network of power relations ends by forming a dense web that passes through apparatuses and institutions, without being exactly localized in them, so too the swarm of points of resistance traverses social stratifications and individual unities. And it is doubtless the strategic codification of these points of resistance that makes a revolution possible, somewhat similar to the way in which the state relies on the institutional integration of power relationships.

It is in this sphere of force relations that we must try to analyze the mechanisms of power. In this way we will escape from the system of Law-and-Sovereign which has captivated political thought for such a long time. And if it is true that Machiavelli was among the few—and this no doubt was the scandal of his "cynicism"—who conceived the power of the Prince in terms of force relationships, perhaps we need to go one step further, do without the persona of the Prince, and decipher power mechanisms on the basis of a strategy that is immanent in force relationships.

To return to sex and the discourses of truth that have taken charge of it, the question that we must address, then, is not: Given a specific state structure, how and why is it that power needs to establish a knowledge of sex? Neither is the question: What over-all domination was served by the concern, evidenced since the eighteenth century, to produce true discourses on sex? Nor is it: What law presided over both the regularity of sexual behavior and the conformity of what was said about it? It is rather: In a specific type of discourse on sex, in a specific form of extortion of truth, appearing historically and in specific places (around the child's body, apropos of women's sex, in connection with practices restricting births, and so on), what were the most immediate, the most local power relations at work? How did they make possible these kinds of discourses, and conversely, how were these discourses used to support power relations? How was the action of these power relations modified by their very exercise, entailing a strengthening of some terms and a weakening of others, with effects of resistance and counterinvestments, so that there has never existed one type of stable subjugation, given once and for all? How were these power relations linked to one another according to the logic of a great strategy, which in retrospect takes on the aspect of a unitary and voluntarist politics of sex? In general terms: rather than referring all the infinitesimal violences that are exerted on sex, all the anxious gazes that are directed at it, and all the hiding places whose discovery is made into an impossible task, to the unique form of a great Power, we must immerse the expanding production of discourses on sex in the field of multiple and mobile power relations.

Which leads us to advance, in a preliminary way, four rules to follow. But these are not intended as methodological imperatives; at most they are cautionary prescriptions.

1. Rule of immanence

One must not suppose that there exists a certain sphere of sexuality that would be the legitimate concern of a free and disinterested scientific inquiry were it not the object of mechanisms of prohibition brought to bear by the economic or ideological requirements of power. If sexuality was constituted as an area of investigation, this was only because relations of power had established it as a possible object; and conversely, if power was able to take it as a target, this was because techniques of knowledge and procedures of discourse were capable of investing it. Between techniques of knowledge and strategies of power, there is no exteriority, even if they have specific roles and are linked together on the basis of their difference. We will start, therefore, from what might be called "local centers" of powerknowledge: for example, the relations that obtain between penitents and confessors, or the faithful and their directors of conscience. Here, guided by the theme of the "flesh" that must be mastered, different forms of discourse—self-examination, questionings, admissions, interpretations, interviews—were the vehicle of a kind of incessant back-and-forth movement of forms of subjugation and schemas of knowledge. Similarly, the body of the child, under surveillance, surrounded in his cradle, his bed, or his room by an entire watch-crew of parents, nurses, servants, educators, and doctors, all attentive to the least manifestations of his sex, has constituted, particularly since the eighteenth century, another "local center" of power-knowledge.

2. Rules of continual variations

We must not look for who has the power in the order of sexuality (men, adults, parents, doctors) and who is deprived of it (women, adolescents, children, patients); nor for who has the right to know and who is forced to remain ignorant. We must seek rather the pattern of the modifications which the relationships of force imply by the very nature of their process. The "distributions of power" and the "appropriations of knowledge" never represent only instantaneous slices taken from processes involving, for example, a cumulative reinforcement of the strongest factor, or a reversal of relationship, or again, a simultaneous increase of two terms. Relations of power-knowledge are not static forms of distribution, they are "matrices of transformations." The nineteenth-century grouping made up of the father, the mother, the educator, and the doctor, around the child and his sex, was subjected to constant modifications, continual shifts. One of the more spectacular results of the latter was a strange reversal: whereas to begin with the child's sexuality had been problematized within the relationship established between doctor and parents (in the form of advice, or recommendations to keep the child under observation, or warnings of future dangers), ultimately it was in the relationship of the psychiatrist to the child that the sexuality of adults themselves was called into question.

3. Rule of double conditioning

No "local center," no "pattern of transformation" could function if, through a series of sequences, it did not eventually enter into an over-all strategy. And inversely, no strategy could achieve comprehensive effects if did not gain support from precise and tenuous relations serving, not as its point of application or final outcome, but as its prop and anchor point. There is not discontinuity between them, as if one were dealing with two different levels (one microscopic and the other macroscopic); but neither is there homogeneity (as if the one were only the enlarged projection or the miniaturization of the other); rather, one must conceive of the double conditioning of a strategy by the specificity of possible tactics, and of tactics by the strategic envelope that makes them work. Thus the father in the family is not the "representative" of the sovereign or the state; and the latter are not projections of the father on a different scale. The family does not duplicate society, just as society does not imitate the family. But the family organization, precisely to the extent that it was insular and heteromorphous with respect to the other power mechanisms, was used to support the great "maneuvers" employed for the Malthusian control of the birthrate, for the populationist incitements, for the medicalization of sex and the psychiatrization of its nongenital forms.

4. Rule of the tactical polyvalence of discourses

What is said about sex must not be analyzed simply as the surface of projection of these power mechanisms. Indeed, it is in discourse that power and knowledge are joined together. And for this very reason, we must conceive discourse as a series of discontinuous segments whose tactical function is neither uniform nor stable. To be more precise, we must not imagine a world of discourse divided between accepted discourse and excluded discourse, or between the dominant discourse and the dominated one; but as a multiplicity of discursive elements that can come into play in various strategies. It is this distribution that we must reconstruct, with the things said and those concealed, the enunciations required and those forbidden, that it comprises; with the variants and different effects—according to who is speaking, his position of power, the institutional context in which he happens to be situated—that it implies; and with the shifts and reutilizations of identical formulas for contrary objectives that it also includes. Discourses are not once and for all subservient to power or raised up against it, any more than silences are. We must make allowance for the complex and unstable process whereby discourse can be both an instrument and an effect of power, but also a hindrance, a stumbling-block, a point of resistance and a starting point for an opposing strategy. Discourse transmits and produces power; it reinforces it, but also undermines and exposes it, renders it fragile and makes it possible to thwart it. In like manner, silence and secrecy are a shelter for power, anchoring its prohibitions; but they also loosen its holds and provide for relatively obscure areas of tolerance. Consider for example the history of what was once "the" great sin against nature. The extreme discretion of the texts dealing with sodomy—that utterly confused category—and the nearly universal reticence in talking about it made possible a twofold operation: on the one hand, there was an extreme severity (punishment by fire was meted out well into the eighteenth century, without there being any substantial protest expressed before the middle of the century), and on the other hand, a tolerance that must have been widespread (which one can deduce indirectly from the infrequency of judicial sentences, and which one glimpses more directly through certain statements concerning societies of men that were thought to exist in the army or in the courts). There is no question that the appearance in nineteenth-century psychiatry, jurisprudence, and literature of a whole series of discourses on the species and subspecies of homosexuality, inversion, pederasty, and "psychic hermaphrodism" made possible a strong advance of social controls into this area of "perversity"; but it also made possible the formation of a "reverse" discourse: homosexuality began to speak in its own behalf, to demand that its legitimacy or "naturality" be acknowledged, often in the same vocabulary, using the same categories by which it was medically disqualified. There is not, on the one side, a discourse of power, and opposite it, another discourse that runs counter to it. Discourses are tactical elements or blocks operating in the field of force relations; there can exist different and even contradictory discourses within the same strategy; they can, on the contrary, circulate without changing their form from one strategy to another, opposing strategy. We must not expect the discourses on sex to tell us, above all, what strategy they derive from, or what moral divisions they accompany, or what ideology—dominant or dominated—they represent; rather we must question them on the two levels of their tactical productivity (what reciprocal effects of power and knowledge they ensure) and their strategical integration (what conjunction and what force relationship make their utilization necessary in a given episode of the various confrontations that occur).

In short, it is a question of orienting ourselves to a conception of power which replaces the privilege of the law with the viewpoint of the objective, the privilege of prohibition with the viewpoint of tactical efficacy, the privilege of sovereignty with the analysis of a multiple and mobile field of force relations, wherein far-reaching, but never completely stable, effects of domination are produced. The strategical model, rather than the model based on law. And this, not out of a speculative choice or theoretical preference, but because in fact it is one of the essential traits of Western societies that the force relationships which for a long time had found expression in war, in every form of warfare, gradually became invested in the order of political power.

The Precession of Simulacra

Jean Baudrillard

The simulacrum is never that which conceals the truth—it is the truth which conceals that there is none.
The simulacrum is true.

Ecclesiastes

If we were able to take as the finest allegory of simulation the Borges tale where the cartographers of the Empire draw up a map so detailed that it ends up exactly covering the territory (but where the decline of the Empire sees this map become frayed and finally ruined, a few shreds still discernible in the deserts—the metaphysical beauty of this ruined abstraction, bearing witness to an imperial pride and rotting like a carcass, returning to the substance of the soil, rather as an aging double ends up being confused with the real thing)—then this fable has come full circle for us, and now has nothing but the discrete charm of second-order simulacra.[1]

Abstraction today is no longer that of the map, the double, the mirror, or the concept. Simulation is no longer that of a territory, a

Jean Baudrillard, "The Precession of Simulacra," in *Simulations* trans. by Paul Foss, Paul Patton and Philip Beitchman pp. 1–75 Copyright © 1983 Semiotext(e) © and Jean Baudrillard. Reprinted by permission of publisher and author.

referential being or a substance. It is the generation by models of a real without origin or reality: a hyperreal. The territory no longer precedes the map, nor survives it. Henceforth, it is the map that precedes the territory—Precession of Simulacra—it is the map that engenders the territory and if we were to revive the fable today, it would be the territory whose shreds are slowly rotting across the map. It is the real, and not the map, whose vestiges subsist here and there, in the deserts which are no longer those of the Empire, but our own: *The desert of the real itself.*

In fact, even inverted, the fable is useless. Perhaps only the allegory of the Empire remains. For it is with the same imperialism that present-day simulators try to make the real, all the real, coincide with their simulation models. But it is no longer a question of either maps or territory. Something has disappeared: the sovereign difference between them that was the abstraction's charm. For it is the difference which forms the poetry of the map and the charm of the territory, the magic of the concept and the charm of the real. This representational imaginary, which both culminates in and is engulfed by the cartographer's mad project of an ideal coextensivity between the map and the territory, disappears with simulation—whose operation is nuclear and genetic, and no longer specular and discursive. With it goes all of metaphysics. No more mirror of being and appearances, of the real and its concept. No more imaginary coextensivity: rather, genetic miniaturization is the dimension of simulation. The real is produced from miniaturized units, from matrices, memory banks, and command models—and with these it can be reproduced an infinite number of times. It no longer has to be rational, since it is no longer measured against some ideal or negative instance. It is nothing more than operational. In fact, since it is no longer enveloped by an imaginary, it is no longer real at all. It is a hyperreal, the product of an irradiating synthesis of combinatory models in a hyperspace without atmosphere.

In this passage to a space whose curvature is no longer that of the real, nor of truth, the age of simulation thus begins with a liquidation of all referentials—worse: by their artificial resurrection in systems of signs, a more ductile material than meaning, in that it lends itself to all systems of equivalence, all binary oppositions, and all combinatory algebra. It is no longer a question of imitation, nor of reduplication, nor even of parody. It is rather a question of substituting signs of the real for the real itself, that is, an operation to deter every real process by its operational double, a metastable, programmatic, perfect descriptive machine which provides all the signs of the real and short-circuits all its vicissitudes. Never again will the real have to be produced—this is the vital function of the model in a system of death, or rather of anticipated resurrection which no longer leaves any chance even in the event of death. A hyperreal henceforth sheltered from the imaginary, and from any distinction between the real and the imaginary, leaving room only for the orbital recurrence of models and the simulated generation of difference.

The Divine Irreference of Images

To dissimulate is to feign not to have what one has. To simulate is to feign to have what one hasn't. One implies a presence, the other an absence. But the matter is more complicated, since to simulate is not simply to feign: "Someone who feigns an illness can simply go to bed and make believe he is ill. Someone who simulates an illness produces in himself some of the symptoms." (Littre) Thus, feigning or dissimulating leaves the reality principle intact: the difference is always clear, it is only masked: whereas simulation threatens the difference between "true" and "false," between "real" and "imaginary." Since the simulator produces "true" symptoms, is he ill or not? He cannot be treated objectively either as ill, or as not-ill. Psychology and medicine stop at this point, before a thereafter undiscoverable truth of the illness. For if any symptom can be "produced," and can no longer be accepted as a fact of nature, then every illness may be considered as simulatable and simulated, and medicine loses its meaning since it only knows how to treat "true" illnesses by their objective causes. Psychosomatics evolves in a dubious way on the edge of the illness principle. As for psychoanalysis, it transfers the symptom from the organic to the unconscious order: once again, the latter is held to be true, more true than the former—but why should simulation stop at the portals of the unconscious? Why couldn't the "work" of the unconscious be "produced" in the same way as any other symptom in classical medicine? Dreams already are.

The alienist, of course, claims that "for each form of the mental alienation there is a particular order in the succession of symptoms, of which the simulator is unaware and in the absence of which the alienist is unlikely to be deceived." This (which dates from 1865) is in order to save at all cost the truth principle, and to escape the specter raised by simulation—namely the truth, reference and objective causes have ceased to exist. What can medicine do with something which floats on either side of illness, on either side of health, or with the reduplication of illness in a discourse that is no longer true or false? What can psychoanalysis do with the reduplication of the discourse of the unconscious in a discourse of simulation that can never be unmasked, since it isn't false either?[2]

What can the army do with simulators? Traditionally, following a direct principle of identification, it unmasks and punishes them. Today, it can reform an excellent simulator as though he were equivalent to a "real" homosexual, heart-case, or lunatic. Even military psychology retreats from the Cartesian clarities and hesitates to draw the distinction between true and false, between the "produced" symptom and the authentic symptom. "If he acts crazy so well, then he must be mad." Nor is it mistaken: in the sense that all lunatics are simulators, and this lack of distinction is the worst form of subversion. Against its classical reason armed itself with all its categories. But it is this today which again outflanks them, submerging the truth principle.

Outside of medicine and the army, favored terrains of simulation, the affair goes back to religion and the simulacrum of divinity: "I forbad any simulacrum in the temples because the divinity that breathes life into nature cannot be represented." Indeed it can. But what becomes of the divinity when it reveals itself in icons, when it is multiplied in simulacra? Does it remain the supreme authority, simply incarnated in images as a visible theology? Or is it volatilized into simulacra which alone deploy their pomp and power of fascination—the visible machinery of icons being substituted for the pure and intelligible Idea of God? This is precisely what was feared by the iconoclasts, whose millenial quarrel is still with us today.[3] Their rage to destroy images arose precisely because they sensed this omnipotence of simulacra, this facility they have of effacing God from the consciousness of men, and the overwhelming, destructive truth which they suggest: that ultimately there has never been any God, that only the simulacrum exists, indeed that God himself has only ever been his own simulacrum. Had they been able to believe that images only occulted or masked the Platonic idea of God, there would have been no reason to destroy them. One can live with the idea of a distorted truth. But their metaphysical despair came from the idea that the images concealed nothing at all, and that in fact they were not images, such as the original model would have made them, but actually perfect simulacra forever radiant with their own fascination. But this death of the divine referential has to be exorcised at all cost. It can be seen that the iconoclasts, who are often accused of despising and denying images, were in fact the ones who accorded them their actual worth, unlike the iconolaters, who saw in them only reflections and were content to venerate God at one remove. But the converse can also be said, namely that the iconolaters were the most modern and adventurous minds, since underneath the idea of the apparition of God in the mirror of images, they already enacted his death and his disappearance in the epiphany of his representations (which they perhaps knew no longer represented anything, and that they were purely a game, but that this was precisely the greatest game—knowing also that it is dangerous to unmask images, since they dissimulate the fact that there is nothing behind them).

This was the approach of the Jesuits, who based their politics on the virtual disappearance of God and on the worldly and spectacular manipulation of consciences—the evanescence of God in the epiphany of power—the end of transcendence, which no longer serves as alibi for a strategy completely free of influences and signs. Behind the baroque of images hides the grey eminence of politics.

Thus perhaps at stake has always been the murderous capacity of images, murderers of the real, murderers of their own model as the Byzantine icons could murder the divine identity. To this murderous capacity is opposed the dialectical capacity of representations as a visible and intelligible mediation of the Real. All of Western faith and good faith was engaged in this wager on representation: that a sign could refer to the depth of meaning, that a sign could *exchange* for meaning, and that something could guarantee this exchange—God, of course. But what if God himself can be simulated, that is to say, reduced to the signs which attest his existence? Then the whole system becomes weightless, it is no longer anything but a gigantic simulacrum—not unreal, but a simulacrum, never again exchanging for what is real, but exchanging in itself, in an uninterrupted circuit without reference or circumference.

So it is with simulation, insofar as it is opposed to representation. The latter starts from the principle that the sign and the real are equivalent (even if this equivalence is utopian, it is a fundamental axiom). Conversely, simulation starts from the *utopia* of this principle of equivalence, *from the radical negation of the sign as value,* from the sign as reversion and death sentence of every reference. Whereas representation tries to absorb simulation by interpreting it as false representation, simulation envelops the whole edifice of representation as itself a simulacrum.

These would be the successive phases of the image:

—it is the reflection of a basic reality
—it masks and perverts a basic reality

—it masks the *absence* of a basic reality
—it bears no relation to any reality whatever: it is its own pure simulacrum.

In the first case, the image is a *good* appearance—the representation is of the order of sacrament. In the second, it is an *evil* appearance—of the order of malefice. In the third, it *plays at being* an appearance—it is of the order of sorcery. In the fourth, it is no longer in the order of appearance at all, but of simulation.

The transition from signs which dissimulate something to signs which dissimulate that there is nothing marks the decisive turning point. The first implies a theology of truth and secrecy (to which the notion of ideology still belongs). The second inaugurates an age of simulacra and simulation, in which there is no longer any God to recognize his own, nor any last judgment to separate true from false, the real from its artificial resurrection, since everything is already dead and risen in advance.

When the real is no longer what it used to be, nostalgia assumes its full meaning. There is a proliferation of myths of origin and signs of reality; of secondhand truth, objectivity, and authenticity. There is an escalation of the true, of the lived experience; a resurrection of the figurative where the object and substance have disappeared. And there is a panic-stricken production of the real and the referential, above and parallel to the panic of material production: this is how simulation appears in the phase that concerns us—a strategy of the real, neo-real, and hyperreal, whose universal double is a strategy of deterrence.

Rameses, or Rose-Colored Resurrection

Ethnology almost met a paradoxical death that day in 1971 when the Phillipine government decided to return to their primitive state the few dozen Tasaday discovered deep in the jungle, where they had lived for eight centuries undisturbed by the rest of mankind, out of reach of colonists, tourists, and ethnologists. This was at the initiative of the anthropologists themselves, who saw the natives decompose immediately on contact, like a mummy in the open air.

For ethnology to live, its object must die. But the latter avenges itself by dying for having been "discovered," and defies by its death the science that wants to take hold of it.

Doesn't every science live on this paradoxical slope to which it is doomed by the evanescence of its object in the very process of its apprehension, and by the pitiless reversal of this dead object exerts on it? Like Orpheus, it always turns around too soon, and its object, like Eurydice, falls back into Hades.

It was against this hades of paradox that the ethnologists wanted to protect themselves by cordoning off the Tasaday with virgin forest. Nobody now will touch it: the vein is closed down, like a mine. Science loses a precious capital, but the object will be safe—lost to science, but intact in its "virginity." It isn't a question of sacrifice (science never sacrifices itself; it is always murderous), but of the simulated sacrifice of its object in order to save its reality principle. The Tasaday, frozen in their natural element, provide a perfect alibi, an eternal guarantee. At this point begins a persistent anti-ethnology to which Jaulin, Castaneda, and Clastres variously belong. In any case, the logical evolution of a science is to distance itself ever further from its object until it dispenses with it entirely: its autonomy ever more fantastical in reaching its pure form.

The Indian thereby driven back into the ghetto, into the glass coffin of virgin forest, becomes the simulation model for all conceivable Indians *before ethnology*. The latter thus allows itself the luxury of being incarnate beyond itself, in the "brute" reality of these Indians it has entirely reinvented—savages who are indebted to ethnology for still being savages: what a turn of events, what a triumph for this science which seemed dedicated to their destruction!

Of course, these particular savages are posthumous: frozen, cryogenized, sterilized, protected *to death,* they have become referential simulacra, and the science itself a pure simulation. Same thing at Creusot where, in the form of an "open" museum exhibition, they have "museumized" on the spot, as historical witnesses to their period, entire working-class *quartiers,* living metallurgical zones, a complete culture including men, women, and children and their gestures, languages, and habits—living beings fossilized as in a snapshot. The museum, instead of being circumscribed in a geometrical location, is now everywhere, like a dimension of life itself. Thus ethnology, now freed from its object, will no longer be circumscribed as an objective science but is applied to all living things and becomes invisible, like an omnipresent fourth dimension, that of the simulacrum. *We are all Tasaday.* Or Indians who have once more become "what they used to be," or at least that which ethnology has made them—simulacra Indians who proclaim at last the universal truth of ethnology.

We all become living specimens under the spectral light of ethnology, or of anti-ethnology which is only the pure form of triumphal ethnology, under the sign of dead differences, and of the resurrection of differences. It is thus extremely naive to look for ethnology among the savages or in some Third World—it is here, everywhere, in the metropolis, among the whites, in a world completely catalogued and analyzed and then *artificially revived as though real,* in a world of simulation: of the hallucination of truth, of blackmail by the real, of the murder and historical (hysterical) retrospection of every symbolic form—a murder whose first victims were, *noblesse oblige,* the savages, but which for a long time now has been extended to all Western societies.

But at the same moment ethnology gives up its final and only lesson, the secret which kills it (and which the savages understood much better): the vengeance of the dead.

The confinement of the scientific object is the same as that of the insane and the dead. And just as the whole of society is hopelessly contaminated by that mirror of madness it has held out for itself, so science can only die contaminated by the death of the object which is its inverse mirror. It is science which ostensibly masters the object, but it is the latter which deeply invests the former, following an unconscious reversion, giving only dead and circular replies to a dead and circular interrogation.

Nothing changes when society breaks the mirror of madness (abolishes asylums, gives speech back to the mad, etc.) nor when science seems to break the mirror of its objectivity (effacing itself before its object, as Castaneda does, etc.) and to bow down before "differences." Confinement is succeeded by an apparatus which assumes a countless and endlessly diffractable, mulipliable form. As fast as ethnology in its classical institution collapses, it survives in an anti-ethnology whose task is to reinject fictional difference and savagery everywhere, in order to conceal the fact that it is this world, our own, which in its way has become savage again, that is to say devastated by difference and death.

It is in this way, under the pretext of saving the original, that the caves of Lascaux have been forbidden to visitors and an exact replica constructed 500 meters away, so that everyone can see them (you glance through a peephole at the real grotto and then visit the reconstituted whole). It is possible that the very memory of the original caves will fade in the mind of future generations, but from now on there is no longer any difference: the duplication is sufficient to render both artificial.

In the same way the whole of science and technology were recently mobilized to save the mummy of Rameses II, after it had been left to deteriorate in the basement of a museum. The West was panic-stricken at the thought of not being able to save what the symbolic order had been able to preserve for forty centuries, but

away from the light and gaze of onlookers. Rameses means nothing
to us: only the mummy is of inestimable worth since it is what guarantees that accumulation means something. Our entire linear and
accumulative culture would collapse if we could not stockpile the
past in plain view. To this end the pharoahs must be brought out of
their tombs, and the mummies out of their silence. To this end they
must be exhumed and given military honors. They are prey to both
science and the worms. Only absolute secrecy ensured their potency
throughout the millenia—their mastery over putrefaction, which
signified a mastery over the total cycle of exchange with death. *We*
know better than to use our science for the *reparation* of the
mummy, that is, to restore a *visible* order, whereas embalming was
a mythical labor aimed at immortalizing a *hidden* dimension.

We need a visible past, a visible continuum, a visible myth of
origin to reassure us as to our ends, since ultimately we have never
believed in them. Whence that historic scene of the mummy's reception at Orly airport. All because Rameses was a great despot and
military figure? Certainly. But above all because the order which
our culture dreams of, behind that defunct power it seeks to annex,
could have had nothing to do with it, and it dreams thus because
it has exterminated this order by exhuming it *as if it were our
own past*.

We are fascinated by Rameses just as Renaissance Christians
were by the American Indians: those (human?) beings who had
never known the word of Christ. Thus, at the beginning of colonization, there was a moment of stupor and amazement before the
very possibility of escaping the universal law of the Gospel. There
were two possible responses: either to admit that this law was not
universal, or to exterminate the Indians so as to remove the evidence. In general, it was enough to convert them, or even simply to
discover them, to ensure their slow extermination.

Thus it would have been enough to exhume Rameses to ensure
his extermination by museumification. For mummies do not decay
because of worms: they die from being transplanted from a pro-
longed symbolic order, which is master over death and putrescence,
on to an order of history, science, and museums—our own, which is
no longer master over anything, since it only knows how to condemn
its predecessors to death and putrescence and their subsequent re-
suscitation by science. An irreparable violence towards all secrets,
the violence of a civilization without secrets. The hatred by an entire civilization for its own foundations.

And just as with ethnology playing at surrendering its object
the better to establish itself in its pure form, so museumification is
only one more turn in the spiral of artificiality. Witness the cloister

of St. Michel de Cuxa, which is going to be repatriated at great expense from the Cloisters in New York to be reinstalled on "its original site." And everyone is supposed to applaud this restitution (as with the "experimental campaign to win back the sidewalks" on the Champs-Élysées!). However, if the exportation of the cornices was in effect an arbitrary act, and if the Cloisters of New York is really an artificial mosaic of all cultures (according to a logic of the capitalist centralization of value), then reimportation to the original location is even more artificial: it is a total simulacrum that links up with "reality" by a complete circumvolution.

The cloister should have stayed in New York in its simulated environment, which at least would have fooled no one. Repatriation is only a supplementary subterfuge, in order to make out as though nothing had happened and to indulge in a retrospective hallucination.

In the same way Americans flatter themselves that they brought the number of Indians back to what it was before their conquest. Everything is obliterated only to begin again. They even flatter themselves that they went one better, by surpassing the original figure. This is presented as proof of the superiority of civilization: it produces more Indians than they were capable of themselves. By a sinister mockery, this overproduction is yet again a way of destroying them: for Indian culture, like all tribal culture, rests on the limitation of the group and prohibiting any of its "unrestricted" growth, as can be seen in the case of Ishi. Demographic "promotion," therefore, is just one more step towards symbolic extermination.

We too live in a universe everywhere strangely similar to the original—here things are duplicated by their own scenario. But this double does not mean, as in folklore, the imminence of death—they are already purged of death, and are even better than in life; more smiling, more authentic, in light of their model, like the faces in funeral parlors.

Hyperreal and Imaginary

Disneyland is a perfect model of all the entangled orders of simulation. To begin with it is a play of illusions and phantasms: Pirates, the Frontier, Future World, etc. This imaginary world is supposed to be what makes the operation successful. But what draws the crowds is undoubtedly much more the social microcosm, the miniaturized and *religious* reveling in real America, in its delights and drawbacks. You park outside, queue up inside, and are totally abandoned at the exit. In this imaginary world the only phantasmagoria is in the inherent warmth and affection of the crowd, and in that sufficiently excessive number of gadgets used there specifically to maintain the multitudinous effect. The contrast with the absolute solitude of the parking lot—a veritable concentration camp—is total. Or rather: inside, a whole range of gadgets magnetize the crowd into direct flows—outside, solitude is directed onto a single gadget: the automobile. By an extraordinary coincidence (one that undoubtedly belongs to the peculiar enchantment of this universe), this deep-frozen infantile world happens to have been conceived and realized by a man who is himself now cryogenized: Walt Disney, who awaits his resurrection at minus 180 degrees centigrade.

The objective profile of America, then, may be traced throughout Disneyland, even down to the morphology of individuals and the crowd. All its values are exalted here, in miniature and comic strip form. Embalmed and pacified. Whence the possibility of an ideological analysis of Disneyland (Louis Marin does it well in *Utopies, jeux d'espaces*): digest of the American way of life, panegyric to American values, idealized transposition of a contradictory reality. To be sure. But this conceals something else, and that "ideological" blanket exactly serves to cover over a *third-order simulation:* Disneyland is there to conceal the fact that it is the "real" country, all of "real" America, which *is* Disneyland (just as prisons are there to conceal the fact that it is the social in its entirety, in its banal omnipresence, which is carceral). Disneyland is presented as imaginary in order to make us believe that the rest is real, when in fact all of Los Angeles and the America surrounding it are no longer real, but of the order of the hyperreal and of simulation. It is no longer a question of a false representation of reality (ideology), but of concealing the fact that the real is no longer real, and thus of saving the reality principle.

The Disneyland imaginary is neither true nor false; it is a deterrence machine set up in order to rejuvenate in reverse the fiction of the real. Whence the debility, the infantile degeneration of this imaginary. It is meant to be an infantile world, in order to make us believe that the adults are everywhere, in the "real" world, and to conceal the fact that real childishness is everywhere, particularly amongst those adults who go there to act the child in order to foster illusions to their real childishness.

Moreover, Disneyland is not the only one. Enchanted Village, Magic Mountain, Marine World: Los Angeles is encircled by these "imaginary stations" which feed reality, reality-energy, to a town whose mystery is precisely that it is nothing more than a network of endless, unreal circulation—a town of fabulous proportions, but without space or dimensions. As much as electrical and nuclear power stations, as much as film studios, this town, which is nothing more than an immense script and a perpetual motion picture, needs this old imaginary made up of childhood signals and faked phantasms for its sympathetic nervous system.

Political Incantation

Watergate. Same scenario as Disneyland (an imaginary effect concealing that reality no more exists outside than inside the bounds of the artificial perimeter): though here it is a scandal effect concealing that there is no difference between the facts and their denunciation (identical methods are employed by the CIA and the *Washington Post* journalists). Same operation though this time tending towards scandal as a means to regenerate a moral and political principle, towards the imaginary as a means to regenerate a reality principle in distress.

The denunciation of scandal always pays homage to the law. And Watergate above all succeeded in imposing the idea that Watergate *was* a scandal—in this sense it was an extraordinary operation of intoxication. The reinjection of a large dose of political morality on a global scale. It could be said along with Bordieu that: "The specific character of every relation of force is to dissimulate itself as such, and to acquire all its force only because it is so dissimulated," understood as follows: capital, which is immoral and unscrupulous, can only function behind a moral superstructure, and whoever regenerates this public morality (by indignation, denunciation, etc.) spontaneously furthers the order of capital, as did the *Washington Post* journalists.

But this is still only the formula of ideology, and when Bordieu enunciates it, he takes "relation of force" to mean the *truth* of capitalist domination, and he *denounces* this relation of force as itself a *scandal*—he therefore occupies the same deterministic and moralistic position as the *Washington Post* journalists. He does the same job of purging and reviving moral order, an order of truth wherein the genuine symbolic violence of the social order is engendered, well beyond all relations of force, which are only its indifferent and shifting configuration in the moral and political consciousness of men.

All that capital asks of us is to receive it as rational or to combat it in the name of rationality, to receive it as moral or to combat it in the name of morality. For they are *identical,* meaning *they can be read another way:* before, the task was to dissimulate scandal; today, the task is to conceal the fact that there is none.

Watergate is not a scandal: this is what must be said at all cost, for this is what everyone is concerned to conceal, this dissimulation masking a strengthening of morality, a moral panic as we approach the primal (mise-en-) scene of capital: its instantaneous cruelty, its incomprehensible ferocity, its fundamental immorality—this is what is scandalous, unaccountable for in that system of moral and economic equivalence which remains the axiom of leftist thought, from Enlightenment theory to communism. Capital doesn't give a damn about the idea of the contract which is imputed to it—it is a monstrous unprincipled undertaking, nothing more. Rather, it is "enlightened" thought which seeks to control capital by imposing rules on it. And all that recrimination which replaced revolutionary thought today comes down to reproaching capital for not following the rules of the game. "Power is unjust, its justice is a class justice, capital exploits us, etc."—as if capital were linked by a contract to the society it rules. It is the left which holds out the mirror of equivalence, hoping that capital will fall for this phantasmagoria of the social contract and fulfill its obligation towards the whole of society (at the same time, no need for revolution: it is enough that capital accept the rational formula of exchange).

Capital in fact has never been linked by a contract to the society it dominates. It is a sorcery of the social relation, it is a *challenge to society* and should be responded to as such. It is not a scandal to be denounced according to moral and economic rationality, but a challenge to take up according to symbolic law.

Moebius-Spiraling Negativity

Hence Watergate was only a trap set by the system to catch its adversaries—a simulation of scandal to regenerative ends. This is embodied by the character called "Deep Throat," who was said to be a Republican grey eminence manipulating the leftist journalists in order to get rid of Nixon—and why not? All hypotheses are possible, although this one is superfluous: the work of the right is done very well, and spontaneously, by the left on its own. Besides, it would be naive to see an embittered good conscience at work here. For the right itself also spontaneously does the work of the left. All the hypotheses of manipulation are reversible in an endless whirligig. For manipulation is a floating causality where positivity and negativity engender and overlap with one another, where there is no longer

any active or passive. It is by putting an *arbitrary* stop to this re-
volving causality that a principle of political reality can be saved. It
is by the *simulation* of a conventional, restricted perspective field,
where the premises and consequences of any act or event are calcu-
lable, that a political credibility can be maintained (including, of
course, "objective" analysis, struggle, etc.). But if the entire cycle of
any act or event is envisaged in a system where linear continuity
and dialectical polarity no longer exist, in a field *unhinged by simulation,* then all determination evaporates, every act terminates at
the end of the cycle having benefited everyone and been scattered in
all directions.

Is any given bombing in Italy the work of leftist extremists, or
of extreme right-wing provocation, or staged by centrists to bring
every terrorist extreme into disrepute and to shore up its own failing power, or again, is it a police-inspired scenario in order to appeal
to public security? All this is equally true, and the search for proof,
indeed the objectivity of the fact does not check this vertigo of interpretation. We are in a logic of simulation which has nothing to do
with a logic of facts and an order of reasons. Simulation is characterized by a *precession of the model,* of all models around the merest
fact—the models come first, and their orbital (like the bomb) circulation constitutes the genuine magnetic field of events. Facts no
longer have any trajectory of their own, they arise at the intersection of the models; a single fact may even be engendered by all the
models at once. This anticipation, this precession, this short circuit,
this confusion of the fact with its model (no more divergence of
meaning, no more dialectical polarity, no more negative electricity
or implosion of poles) is what each time allows for all the possible
interpretations, even the most contradictory—all are true, in the
sense that their truth is exchangeable, in the image of the models
from which they proceed, in a generalized cycle.

The communists attack the Socialist party as though they
wanted to shatter the union of the left. They sanction the idea that
their reticence stems from a more radical political exigency. In fact,
it is because they don't want power. But do they not want it at this
conjuncture because it is unfavorable for the left in general, or because it is unfavorable for them within the union of the left—or do
they want it by definition? When Berlinguer declares: "We mustn't
be frightened of seeing the communists seize power in Italy," this
means simultaneously:

—that there is nothing to fear, since the communists, if they come
   to power, will change nothing in its fundamental capitalist
   mechanism,

—that there isn't any risk of their ever coming to power (for the reason that they don't want to)—and even if they did take it up, they will only ever wield it by proxy,

—that in fact power, genuine power, no longer exists, and hence there is no risk to anybody seizing it or taking it over,

—but more: I, Berlinguer, am not frightened of seeing the communists seize power in Italy—which might appear evident, but not that much, since

—this can also mean the contrary (no need of psychoanalysis here): *I am frightened* of seeing the communists seize power (and with good reason, even for a communist).

All the above is simultaneously true. This is the secret of a discourse that is no longer only ambiguous, as political discourses can be, but that conveys the impossibility of a determinate position of power, the impossibility of a determinate position of discourse. And this logic belongs to neither party. It traverses all discourses without their wanting it.

Who will unravel this imbroglio? The Gordian knot can at least be cut. As for the Moebius strip, if it is split in two, it results in an additional spiral without there being any possibility of resolving its surfaces (here the reversible continuity of hypotheses). Hades of simulation, which is no longer one of torture, but of the subtle, maleficent, elusive twisting of meaning[4]—where even those condemned at Burgos are still a gift from Franco to Western democracy, which finds in them the occasion to regenerate its own flagging humanism, and whose indignant protestation in return consolidates Franco's regime by uniting the Spanish masses against foreign intervention? Where is the truth in all that, when such collusions admirably knit together without their authors even knowing it?

The conjunction of the system and its extreme alternative like two ends of a curved mirror, the "vicious" curvature of a political space henceforth magnetized, circularized, reversibilized from right to left, a torsion that is like the evil demon of commutation, the whole system, the infinity of capital folded back over its own surface: transfinite? And isn't it the same with desire and libidinal space? The conjunction of desire and value, of desire and capital. The conjunction of desire and the law—the ultimate joy and metamorphosis of the law (which is why it is so well received at the moment): only capital takes pleasure, Lyotard said, before coming to think that *we* take pleasure in capital. Overwhelming versatility of desire in Deleuze, an enigmatic reversal which brings this desire that is "revolutionary by itself, and as if involuntarily, in wanting what it wants," to want its own repression and to invest paranoid and fascist systems? A malign torsion which reduces this revolution of desire to the same fundamental ambiguity as the other, historical revolution.

All the referentials intermingle their discourses in a circular, Moebian compulsion. Not so long ago sex and work were savagely opposed terms: today both are dissolved into the same type of demand. Formerly the discourse on history took its force from opposing itself to the one on nature, the discourse on desire to the one on power—today they exchange their signifiers and their scenarios.

It would take too long to run through the whole range of operational negativity, of all those scenarios of deterrence which, like Watergate, try to regenerate a moribund principle by simulated scandal, phantasm, murder—a sort of hormonal treatment by negativity and crisis. It is always a question of proving the real by the imaginary, proving truth by scandal, proving the law by transgression, proving work by the strike, proving the system by crisis, and capital by revolution, as for that matter proving ethnology by the dispossession of its object (the Tasaday)—without counting:

—proving theater by anti-theater
—proving art by anti-art
—proving pedagogy by anti-pedagogy
—proving psychiatry by anti-psychiatry, etc., etc.

Everything is metamorphosed into its inverse in order to be perpetuated in its purged form. Every form of power, every situation speaks of itself by denial, in order to attempt to escape, by simulation of death, its real agony. Power can stage its own murder to rediscover a glimmer of existence and legitimacy. Thus with the American presidents: the Kennedys are murdered because they still have a political dimension. Others—Johnson, Nixon, Ford—only had a right to puppet attempts, to simulated murders. But they nevertheless needed that aura of an artificial menace to conceal that they were nothing other than mannequins of power. In olden days the king (also the god) had to die—that was his strength. Today he does his miserable utmost to pretend to die, so as to preserve the *blessing* of power. But even this is gone.

To seek new blood in its own death, to renew the cycle by the mirror of crisis, negativity and anti-power: this is the only alibi of every power, of every institution attempting to break the vicious circle of its irresponsibility and its fundamental nonexistence, of its *déjà-vu* and its *déjà-mort*.

Strategy of the Real

Of the same order as the impossibility of rediscovering an absolute level of the real is the impossibility of staging an illusion. Illusion is no longer possible, because the real is no longer possible. It is the whole *political* problem of the parody, of hypersimulation or offensive simulation, which is posed here.

For example: it would be interesting to see whether the repressive apparatus would not react more violently to a simulated holdup than to a real one. For the latter only upsets the order of things, the right of property, whereas the other interferes with the very principle of reality. Transgression and violence are less serious, for they only contest the *distribution* of the real. Simulation is infinitely more dangerous, however, since it always suggests, over and above its object, that *law and order themselves might really be nothing more than a simulation.*

But the difficulty is in proportion to the peril. How to feign a violation and put it to the test? Go and simulate a theft in a large department store: how do you convince the security guards that it is a simulated theft? There is no "objective" difference: the same gestures and the same signs exist as for a real theft; in fact the signs incline neither to one side nor the other. As far as the established order is concerned, they are always of the order of the real.

Go and organize a fake holdup. Be sure to check that your weapons are harmless, and take the most trustworthy hostage, so that no life is in danger (otherwise you risk committing an offense). Demand ransom, and arrange it so that the operation creates the greatest commotion possible—in brief, stay close to the "truth," so as to test the reaction of the apparatus to a perfect simulation. But you won't succeed: the web of artificial signs will be inextricably mixed up with real elements (a police officer will really shoot on sight; a bank customer will faint and die of a heart attack; they will really turn the phony ransom over to you)—in brief, you will unwittingly find yourself immediately in the real, one of whose functions is precisely to devour every attempt at simulation, to reduce everything to some reality—that's exactly how the established order is, well before institutions and justice come into play.

In this impossibility of isolating the process of simulation must be seen the whole thrust of an order that can only see and understand in terms of some reality, because it can function nowhere else. The simulation of an offense, if it is patent, will either be punished more lightly (because it has no "consequences") or be punished as an offense to public office (for example, if one triggered off a police operation "for nothing")—but *never as simulation,* since it is precisely as such that no equivalence with the real is possible, and hence no repression either. The challenge of simulation is irreceivable by power. How can you punish the simulation of virtue? Yet as such it is as serious as the simulation of crime. Parody makes obedience and transgression equivalent, and that is the most serious crime, since it *cancels out the difference upon which the law is based.* The established order can do nothing against it, for the law is a second-order simulacrum whereas simulation is third-order, beyond true and false, beyond equivalences, beyond the rational distinctions upon which function all power and the entire social. Hence, *failing the real,* it is here that we must aim at order.

This is why order always opts for the real. In a state of uncertainty, it always prefers this assumption (thus in the army they would rather take the simulator as a true madman). But this becomes more and more difficult, for it is practically impossible to isolate the process of simulation, through the force of inertia of the real which surrounds us, the inverse is also true (and this very reversibility forms part of the apparatus of simulation and of power's impotency): namely, *it is now impossible to isolate the process of the real,* or to prove the real.

Thus all holdups, hijacks, and the like are now as it were simulation holdups, in the sense that they are inscribed in advance in the decoding and orchestration rituals of the media, anticipated in their mode of presentation and possible consequences. In brief, where they function as a set of signs dedicated exclusively to their recurrence as signs, and no longer to their "real" goal at all. But this does not make them inoffensive. On the contrary, it is as hyperreal events, no longer having any particular contents or aims, but indefinitely refracted by each other (for that matter like so-called historical events: strikes, demonstrations, crises, etc.[5]), that they are precisely unverifiable by an order which can only exert itself on the real and the rational, on ends and means: a referential order which can only dominate referentials, a determinate power which can only dominate a determined world, but which can do nothing about that indefinite recurrence of simulation, about that weightless nebula no longer obeying the law of gravitation of the real—power itself eventually breaking apart in this space and becoming a simulation of power (disconnected from its aims and objectives, and dedicated to *power effects* and mass simulation).

The only weapon of power, its only strategy against this defection, is to reinject realness and referentiality everywhere, in order to convince us of the reality of the social, of the gravity of the economy, and the finalities of production. For that purpose it prefers the discourse of crisis, but also—why not?—the discourse of desire. "Take your desires for reality!" can be understood as the ultimate slogan of power, for in a nonreferential world even the confusion of the reality principle with the desire principle is less dangerous than contagious hyperreality. One remains among principles, and there power is always right.

Hyperreality and simulation are deterrents of every principle and of every objective; they turn against power this deterrence which is so well utilized for a long time itself. For, finally, it was capital which was the first to feed throughout its history on the destruction of every referential, of every human goal, which shattered every ideal distinction between true and false, good and evil, in order to establish a radical law of equivalence and exchange, the iron law of its power. It was the first to practice deterrence, abstraction, disconnection, deterritorialization, etc.; and if it was capital which fostered reality, the reality principle, it was also the first to liquidate it in the extermination of every use value, of every real equivalence, of production and wealth, in the very sensation we have of the unreality of the stakes and the omnipotence of manipulation. Now, it is this very logic which is today hardened even more *against* it. And when it wants to fight this catastrophic spiral by secreting one last glimmer of reality, on which to found one last glimmer of power, it only multiplies the *signs* and accelerates the play of simulation.

As long as it was historically threatened by the real, power risked deterrence and simulation, disintegrating every contradiction by means of the production of equivalent signs. When it is threatened today by simulation (the threat of vanishing in the play of signs), power risks the real, risks crisis, it gambles on remanufacturing artificial, social, economic, political stakes. This is a question of life or death for it. But it is too late.

Whence the characteristic hysteria of our time: the hysteria of production and reproduction of the real. The other production, that of goods and commodities, that of *la belle époque* of political economy, no longer makes any sense of its own, and has not for some time. What society seeks through production, and overproduction, is the restoration of the real which escapes it. That is why *contemporary "material" production is itself hyperreal.* It retains all the features, the whole discourse of traditional production, but it is nothing more than its scaled-down refraction (thus the hyperrealists fasten in a striking resemblance a real from which has fled all meaning and charm, all the profundity and energy of representation). Thus the hyperrealism of simulation is expressed everywhere by the real's striking resemblance to itself.

Power, too, for some time now produces nothing but signs of its resemblance. And at the same time, another figure of power comes into play: that of a collective demand for *signs* of power—a holy union which forms around the disappearance of power. Everybody belongs to it more or less in fear of the collapse of the political. And in the end the game of power comes down to nothing more than the *critical* obsession with power—an obsession with its death, an obsession with its survival, the greater the more it disappears. When it has totally disappeared, logically we will be under the total spell of power—a haunting memory already foreshadowed everywhere, manifesting at one and the same time the compulsion to get rid of it (nobody wants it any more, everybody unloads it on others) and the apprehensive pining over its loss. Melancholy for societies without power: this has already given rise to fascism, that overdose of a powerful referential in a society which cannot terminate its mourning.

But we are still in the same boat: none of our societies knows how to manage its mourning for the real, for power, for the *social itself,* which is implicated in this same breakdown. And it is by an artificial revitalization of all this that we try to escape it. *Undoubtedly this will even end up in socialism.* By an unforeseen twist of events and an irony which no longer belongs to history, it is through the death of the social that socialism will emerge—as it is through the death of God that religions emerge. A twisted coming, a perverse event, an unintelligible reversion to the logic of reason. As is the fact that power is no longer present except to conceal that there is none. A simulation which can go on indefinitely, since—unlike "true" power which is, or was, a structure, a strategy, a relation of force, a stake—this is nothing but the object of a social *demand,* and hence subject to the law of supply and demand, rather than to violence and death. Completely expunged from the *political* dimension, it is dependent, like any other commodity, on production and mass consumption. Its spark has disappeared—only the fiction of a political universe is saved.

Likewise with work. The spark of production, the violence of its stake no longer exists. Everybody still produces, and more and more, but work has subtly become something else: a need (as Marx ideally envisaged it, but not at all in the same sense), the object of a social "demand," like leisure, to which it is equivalent in the general run of life's options. A demand exactly proportional to the loss of stake in the work process.[6] The same change in fortune as for power: the *scenario* of work is there to conceal the fact that the work-real, the production-real, has disappeared. And for that matter so has the strike-real, which is no longer a stoppage of work, but its alternative pole in the ritual scansion of the social calendar. It is as if everyone has "occupied" their workplace or workpost, after declaring the strike, and resumed production, as is the custom in a "self-managed" job, in exactly the same terms as before, by declaring themselves (and virtually being) in a state of permanent strike.

This isn't a science-fiction dream: everywhere it is a question of a doubling of the work process. And of a double or locum for the strike process—strikes which are incorporated like obsolescence in objects, like crisis in production. Then there are no longer *either* strikes or work, but both simultaneously, that is to say something else entirely: a *wizardry of work*, a *trompe l'oeil*, a scenodrama (not to say melodrama) of production, collective dramaturgy upon the empty stage of the social.

It is no longer a question of the *ideology* of work—of the traditional ethic that obscures the "real" labor process and the "objective" process of exploitation—but of the scenario of work. Likewise, it is no longer a question of the ideology of power, but of the *scenario* of power. Ideology only corresponds to a betrayal of reality by signs; simulation corresponds to a short circuit of reality and to its reduplication by signs. It is always the aim of ideological analysis to restore the objective process; it is always a false problem to want to restore the truth beneath the simulacrum.

This is ultimately why power is so in accord with ideological discourses and discourses on ideology, for these are all discourses of *truth*—always good, even and especially if they are revolutionary, to counter the mortal blows of simulation.

The End of the Panopticon

It is again to this ideology of the lived experience, of exhumation, of the real in its fundamental banality, in its radical authenticity, that the American TV-*vérité* experiment on the Loud family in 1971 refers: seven months of uninterrupted shooting, 300 hours of direct nonstop broadcasting, without script or scenario, the odyssey of a family, its dramas, its joys, ups and downs—in brief, a "raw" historical document, and the "best thing ever on television, comparable, at the level of our daily existence, to the film of the lunar landing." Things are complicated by the fact that this family came apart during the shooting: a crisis flared up, the Louds went their separate ways, etc. Whence that insoluble controversy: was TV responsible? What would have happened *if TV hadn't been there?*

More interesting is the phantasm of filming the Louds *as if TV weren't there.* The producer's trump card was to say: "They lived as if we weren't there." An absurd, paradoxical formula—neither true, nor false: but utopian. The "as if *we* weren't there" is equivalent to "as if *you* were there." It is this utopia, this paradox that fascinated 20 million viewers, much more than the "perverse" pleasure of prying. In this "truth" experiment, it is neither a question of secrecy nor of perversion, but of a kind of thrill of the real, or of an aesthetics of the hyperreal, a thrill of vertiginous and phony exactitude, a thrill of alienation and of magnification, of distortion in scale, of excessive transparency all at the same time. The joy in an excess of meaning, when the bar of the sign slips below the regular waterline of meaning: the nonsignifier is elevated by the camera angle. Here the real can be seen never to have existed (but "as if you were there"), without the distance which produces perspective space and our depth vision (but "more true than nature"). Joy in the microscopic simulation which transforms the real into the hyperreal. (This is also a little like what happens in porno, where fascination is more metaphysical than sexual).

This family was in any case already somewhat hyperreal by its very selection: a typical, California-housed, three-garage, five-children, well-to-do, professional, upper-middle-class, ideal American family, with an ornamental housewife. In a way, it is this statistical perfection which dooms it to death. This ideal heroine of the American way of life is chosen, as in sacrificial rites, to be glorified and to die under the fiery glare of the studio lights, a modern fatum. For the heavenly fire no longer strikes depraved cities, it is rather the lens which cuts through ordinary reality like a laser, putting it to death. "The Louds: simply a family who agreed to deliver themselves into the hands of television, and to die from it," said the producer. So it is really a question of a sacrificial process, of a sacrificial spectacle offered to 20 million Americans. The liturgical drama of a mass society.

TV-*vérité*. Admirable ambivalent term: does it refer to the truth of this family, or to the truth of TV? In fact, it is TV which is the Loud's truth, it is it which is true, it is it which renders true. A truth which is no longer the reflexive truth of the mirror, nor the perspective truth of the panoptic system and of the gaze, but the manipulative truth of the test which probes and interrogates, of the laser which touches and then pierces, of computer cards which retain your punched-out sequences, of the genetic code which regulates your combinations, of cells which inform your sensory universe. It is to this kind of truth that the Loud family is subjected by the TV medium, and in this sense it really amounts to a death sentence (but is it still a question of truth?).

The end of the panoptic system. The eye of TV is no longer the source of an absolute gaze, and the ideal of control is no longer that of transparency. The latter still presupposes an objective space (that of the Renaissance) and the omnipotence of a despotic gaze. This is still, if not a system of confinement, at least a system of scrutiny. No longer subtle, but always in a position of exteriority, playing on the opposition between seeing and being seen, even if the focal point of the panopticon may be blind.

It is entirely different when with the Louds. "You no longer watch TV, TV watches you (live)," or again: "You no longer listen to *Pas de Panique, Pas de Panique* listens to you"—switching over from the panoptic apparatus of surveillance (of *Discipline and Punish*) to a system of deterrence, where the distinction between active and passive is abolished. No longer is there any imperative to submit to the model, or to the gaze. "YOU are the model!" "YOU are the majority!" Such is the slope of a hyperrealist sociality, where the real is confused with the model, as in the statistic operation, or with the medium, as in the Louds' operation. Such is the alter stage of development of the social relation, our own, which is no longer one of persuasion (the classical age of propaganda, ideology, publicity, etc.) but one of dissuasion or deterrence: "YOU are news, you are the social, the event is you, you are involved, you can use your voice, etc." A turnabout of affairs by which it becomes impossible to locate an instance of the model, of power, of the gaze, of the medium itself, since *you* are always already on the other side. No more subject, focal point, center, or periphery: but pure flexion or circular inflection. No more violence or surveillance: only "information," secret virulence, chain reaction, slow implosion, and simulacra of spaces where the real-effect again comes into play.

We are witnessing the end of perspective and panoptic space (which remains a moral hypothesis bound up with every classical analysis of the "objective" essence of power), and hence the *very ab-*

olition of the spectacular. Television, in the case of the Louds for example, is no longer a spectacular medium. We are no longer in the society of spectacle which the situationists talked about, nor in the specific types of alienation and repression which this implied. The medium itself is no longer identifiable as such, and the merging of the medium and the message (McLuhan[7]) is the first great formula of this new age. There is no longer any medium in the literal sense: it is now intangible, diffuse, and diffracted in the real, and it can no longer even be said that the latter is distorted by it.

Such immixture, such a viral, endemic, chronic, alarming presence of the medium, without our being able to isolate its effects—spectralized, like those publicity holograms sculptured in empty space with laser beams, the event filtered by the medium—the dissolution of TV into life, the dissolution of life into TV—an indiscernible chemical solution: we are all Louds, doomed not to invasion, to pressure, to violence, and to blackmail by the media and the models, but to their induction, to their infiltration, to their illegible violence.

But we must be careful of the negative twist discourse gives this: it is a question neither of an illness nor of a viral complaint. Rather, we must think of the media as if they were, in outer orbit, a sort of genetic code which controls the mutation of the real into the hyperreal, just as the other, micromolecular code controls the passage of the signal from a representative sphere of meaning to the genetic sphere of the programmed signal.

The whole traditional mode of causality is brought into question: the perspective, deterministic mode, the "active," critical mode, the analytical mode—the distinction between cause and effect, between active and passive, between subject and object, between ends and means. It is in this mode that it can be said: TV watches us, TV alienates us, TV manipulates us, TV informs us . . . Throughout all this one is dependent on the analytical conception whose vanishing point is the horizon between reality and meaning.

On the contrary, we must imagine TV on the DNA model, as an effect in which the opposing poles of determination vanish according to a nuclear contraction or retraction of the old polar schema which has always maintained a minimal distance between a cause and an effect, between the subject and an object: precisely, the meaning gap, the discrepancy, the difference, the smallest possible margin of error, irreducible under penalty of reabsorption in an aleatory and indeterminable process which discourse can no longer even account for, since it is itself a determinable order.

It is this gap which vanishes in the genetic coding process, where indeterminacy is less a product of molecular randomness than a product of the abolition, pure and simple, of the *relation*. In the process of molecular control, which "goes" from the DNA nucleus to the "substance" it "informs," there is no more traversing of an effect, of an energy, of a determination, of any message. "Order, signal, impulse, message": all these attempt to render the matter intelligible to us, but by analogy, retranscribing in terms of inscription, vector, decoding, a dimension of which we know nothing—it is no longer even a "dimension," or perhaps it is the fourth (that which is defined, however, in Einsteinian relativity, by the absorption of the distinct poles of space and time). In fact, this whole process only makes sense to us in the negative form. But nothing separates one pole from the other, the initial from the terminal: there is just a sort of contraction into each other, a fantastic telescoping, a collapsing of the two traditional poles into one another: an IMPLOSION—an absorption of the radiating model of causality, of the differential mode of determination, with its positive and negative electricity—an implosion of meaning. *This is where simulation begins.*

Everywhere, in whatever political, biological, psychological, media domain, where the distinction between poles can no longer be maintained, one enters into simulation, and hence into absolute manipulation—not passivity, but the *non-distinction of active and passive*. DNA realizes this aleatory reduction at the level of the living substance. Television itself, in the example of the Louds, also attains this *indefinite* limit where the family vis-à-vis TV are no more or less active or passive than is a living substance vis-à-vis its molecular code. In both there is only a nebula indecipherable into its simple elements, indecipherable as to its truth.

Orbital and Nuclear

The nuclear is the apotheosis of simulation. Yet the balance of terror is nothing more than the spectacular slope of a system of deterrence that has crept from the *inside* into all the cracks of daily life. The nuclear cliffhanger only seals the trivialized system of deterrence at the heart of the media, of the inconsequential violence that reigns throughout the world, of the aleatory contrivance of every choice which is made for us. The slightest details of our behavior are ruled by neutralized, indifferent, equivalent signs, by zero-sum signs like those which regulate "game strategy" (but the genuine equation is elsewhere, and the unknown is precisely that variable of simulation which makes the atomic arsenal itself a hyperreal form, a simulacrum which dominates us all and reduces all "ground-level" events to mere ephemeral scenarios, transforming the only life left to us into survival, into a wager without takers—not even into a death policy: but into a policy devaluated in advance).

It isn't that the direct menace of atomic destruction paralyzes our lives. It is rather that deterrence leukemizes us. And this deterrence comes from the very situation which *excludes the real atomic clash*—excludes it beforehand like the eventuality of the real in a system of signs. Everybody pretends to believe in the reality of this menace (one understands it from the military point of view, the whole seriousness of their exercise, and the discourse of their "strategy," is at stake): but there are precisely no strategic stakes at this level, and the whole originality of the situation lies in the improbability of destruction.

Deterrence excludes war—the antiquated violence of expanding systems. Deterrence is the neutral, implosive violence of metastable or involving systems. There is no subject of deterrence any more, nor adversary, nor strategy—it is a planetary structure of the annihilation of stakes. Atomic war, like that of Troy, will not take place. The risk of nuclear atomization only serves as a pretext, through the sophistication of arms—but this sophistication exceeds any possible objective to such an extent that it is itself a symptom of nonexistence—to the installation of a universal system of security, linkup, and control whose deterrent effect does not aim for atomic clash at all (the latter has never been a real possibility, except no doubt right at the beginning of the cold war, when the nuclear posture was confused with conventional war) but really the much larger probability of any real event, of anything which could disturb the general system and upset the balance. The balance of terror is the terror of balance.

Deterrence is not a strategy. It circulates and is exchanged between the nuclear protagonists exactly like international capital in that orbital zone of monetary speculation, whose flow is sufficient to control all global finance. Thus *kill money* (not referring to *real* killing, any more than floating capital refers to real production) circulating in nuclear orbit is sufficient to control all violence and potential conflict on the globe.

What stirs in the shadow of this posture, under the pretext of a maximal "objective" menace and thanks to that nuclear sword of Damocles, is the perfection of the best system of control which has never existed. And the progressive satellization of the whole planet by the hypermodel of security.

The same goes for *peaceful* nuclear installations. Pacification doesn't distinguish between the civil and the military: wherever irreversible apparatuses of control are elaborated, wherever the notion of security becomes absolute, wherever the *norm* of security replaces the former arsenal of laws and violence (including war), the system of deterrence grows, and around it grows a historical, social, and political desert. A huge involution makes every conflict, every opposition, every act of defiance contract in proportion to this blackmail which interrupts, neutralizes, and freezes them. No mutiny, no history can unfurl any more according to its own logic since it risks annihilation. No strategy is even possible anymore, and escalation is only a puerile game left to the military. The political stake is dead. Only simulacra of conflict and carefully circumscribed stakes remain.

The "space race" played exactly the same role as the nuclear race. This is why it was so easily able to take over from it in the 1960s (Kennedy/Khrushchev), or to develop concurrently in a mode of "peaceful coexistence." For what is the ultimate function of the space race, of lunar conquest, of satellite launchings, if not the institution of a model of universal gravitation, of satellization, whose perfect embryo is the lunar module: a programmed microcosm, where *nothing can be left to chance?* Trajectory, energy, computation, physiology, psychology, the environment—nothing can be left to contingency, this is the total universe of the norm—the Law no longer exists, it is the operational immanence of every detail which is law. A universe purged of every threat to the senses, in a state of asepsis and weightlessness—it is this very perfection which is fascinating. For the exaltation of the masses was not in response to the lunar landing or the voyage of man in space (this is rather the fulfillment of an earlier dream)—no, we are dumbfounded by the perfection of their planning and technical manipulation, by the immanent wonder of programmed development. Fascinated by the maximization of norms and by the mastery of probability. Unbalanced by the model, as we are by death, but without fear or impulse. For if the law, with its aura of transgression, if order, with its aura of violence, still taps a perverse imaginary, then the norm fixes, hypnotizes, dumbfounds, causing every imaginary to invoke. We no longer fantasize about every minutia of a program. Its observance alone unbalances. The vertigo of a flawless world.

The same model of planned infallibility, of maximal security and deterrence, now governs the spread of the social. That is the true nuclear fallout: the meticulous operation of technology serves as a model for the meticulous operation of the social. Here, too, *nothing will be left to chance:* moreover, this is the essence of socialization, which has been going on for some centuries but which has now entered into its accelerated phase, towards a limit people imagined would be explosive (revolution), but which currently results in an inverse, irreversible, *implosive* process: a generalized deterrence of every chance, of every accident, of every transversality, of every finality, of every contradiction, rupture, or complexity in a sociality illuminated by the norm and doomed to the transparency of detail radiated by data-collecting mechanisms. In fact, the spatial and nuclear models do not even have their own ends: neither has lunar exploration, nor military and strategic superiority. Their truth lies in their being models of simulation, vector models of a system of planetary control (where even the superpowers of this scenario are not free—the whole world is satellized).[8]

Reject the evidence: with satellization, the one who is satellized is not who you might think. By the orbital inscription of a space object, the planet earth becomes a satellite, the terrestrial principle of reality becomes eccentric, hyperreal, and insignificant. By the orbital establishment of a system of control like peaceful coexistence, all terrestrial microsystems are satellized and lose their autonomy. All energy, all events are absorbed by this eccentric gravitation, everything condenses and implodes on the micro-model of control alone (the orbital satellite), as conversely, in the other, biological dimensions everything converges and implodes on the molecular micro-model of the genetic code. Between the two, caught between the nuclear and the genetic, in the simultaneous assumption of the two fundamental codes of deterrence, every principle of meaning is absorbed, every deployment of the real is impossible.

The simultaneity of two events in July 1975 illustrates this in a striking way: the linkup in space of the two American and Soviet supersatellites, apotheosis of peaceful existence—and the suppression by the Chinese of character writing and conversion to the Roman alphabet. This latter signifies the "orbital" establishment of an abstract and model system of signs, into whose orbit will be reabsorbed all those once remarkable and singular forms of style and writing. The satellization of their tongue: this is the way the Chinese enter the system of peaceful coexistence, which is inscribed in their sky at the very same time by the docking of the two satellites. The orbital flight of the Big Two, the neutralization and homogenization of everybody else on earth.

Yet, despite this deterrence by the orbital authority—the nuclear code or molecular—events continue at ground level, mishaps are increasingly more numerous, despite the global process of contiguity and simultaneity of data. But, subtly, these events no longer make any sense; they are nothing more than a duplex effect of simulation at the summit. The best example must be the Vietnam war, since it was at the crossroads of a maximal historical or "revolutionary" stake and the installation of this deterrent authority. What sense did that war make, if not that its unfolding sealed the end of history in the culminating and decisive event of our age?

Why did such a difficult, long, and arduous war vanish overnight as if by magic?

Why didn't the American defeat (the greatest reversal in its history) have any internal repercussions? If it had truly signified a setback in the planetary strategy of the USA, it should have necessarily disturbed the internal balance of the American political system. But no such thing happened.

Hence something else took place. Ultimately this war was only a crucial episode in a peaceful coexistence. It marked the advent of China to peaceful coexistence. The long sought-after securing and concretizing of China's nonintervention. China's apprenticeship in a global *modus vivendi,* the passing from a strategy of world revolution to one of a sharing of forces and empires, the transition from a radical alternative to political alternation in a now almost settled system (normalization of Peking-Washington relations): all this was the stake of the Vietnam war, and in that sense, the USA pulled out of Vietnam, but they won the war.

And the war "spontaneously" came to an end when the objective had been attained. This is why it was deescalated, demobilized so easily.

The effects of this same remolding are legible in the field. The war lasted as long as there remained unliquidated elements irreducible to a healthy politics and a discipline of power, even a communist one. When finally the war passed from the resistance to the hands of regular Northern troops, it could stop: it had attained its objective. Thus the stake was a political relay. When the Vietnamese proved they were no longer bearers of an unpredictable subversion, it could be handed over to them. That this was communist order wasn't fundamentally serious: it had proved itself, it could be trusted. They are even more effective than capitalists in liquidating "primitive" precapitalist and antiquated structures.

Same scenario as in the Algerian war.

The other aspect of this war and of all wars since: behind the armed violence, the murderous antagonism between adversaries—which seems a matter of life and death, and which is played as such (otherwise you could never send out people to get smashed up in this kind of trouble), behind this simulacrum of a struggle to death and of ruthless global stakes, the two adversaries are fundamentally as one against that other, unnamed, never-mentioned thing, whose objective outcome in war, with equal complicity between the two adversaries, is total liquidation. It is tribal, communal, precapitalist structures, every form of exchange, language, and symbolic organization which must be abolished. Their murder is the object of war—and in its immense spectacular contrivance of death, war is only the medium of this process of terrorist rationalization by the social—the murder through which sociality can be founded, no matter what allegiance, communist or capitalist. The total complicity or division of labor between two adversaries (who can even make huge sacrifices to reach that) for the very purpose of remolding and domesticating social relations.

"The North Vietnamese were advised to countenance a scenario of the liquidation of the American presence through which, of course, honor must be preserved."

The scenario: the extremely heavy bombardment of Hanoi. The intolerable nature of this bombing should not conceal the fact that it was only a simulacrum to allow the Vietnamese to seem to countenance a compromise and Nixon to make the Americans swallow the retreat of their forces. The game was already won, nothing was objectively at stake but the credibility of the final montage.

Moralists about war, champions of war's exalted values should not be greatly upset: a war is not any the less heinous for being a mere simulacrum—the flesh suffers just the same, and the dead ex-combatants count as much there as in other wars. That objective is always amply accomplished, like that of the partitioning of territories and of disciplinary sociality. What no longer exists is the adversity of adversaries, the reality of antagonistic causes, the ideological seriousness of war—also the reality of defeat or victory, war being a process whose triumph lies quite beyond these appearances.

In any case, the pacification (or deterrence) dominating us today is beyond war and peace, the simultaneous equivalence of peace and war. "War is peace," said Orwell. Here, also, the two differential poles implode into each other, or recycle one another—a simultaneity of contradictions that is both the parody and the end of all dialectic. Thus it is possible to miss the truth of a war: namely, that it was well over before reaching a conclusion, that at its very core, war was brought to an end, and that perhaps it never ever began. Many other such events (the oil crisis, etc.) *never began,* never existed, except as artificial mishaps—abstracts, ersatzes of troubles, catastrophes, and crises intended to maintain a historical and psychological investment under hypnosis. All media and the official news service only exist to maintain the illusion of actuality—of the reality of the stakes, of the objectivity of the facts. All events are to be read in reverse, where one perceives (as with the communists "in power" in Italy, the posthumous, "nostalgic" rediscovery of gulags and Soviet dissidents like the almost contemporary rediscovery, by a moribund ethnology, of the lost "difference" of savages) that all these things arrive too late, with an overdue history, a lagging spiral, that they have exhausted their meaning long in advance and only survive on an artificial effervescence of signs, that all these events follow on illogically from one another, with a total equanimity towards the greatest inconsistencies, with a profound indifference to their consequences (but this is because there are none anymore: they burn out in their spectacular promotion)—thus the whole newsreel of "the present" gives the sinister impression of kitsch, retro, and porno all at the same time—doubtless everyone knows this, and nobody really accepts it. The reality of simulation is unendurable—more cruel than Artaud's Theater of Cruelty, which was still an attempt at a dramaturgy of life, the last flickering of an ideal of the body, blood, and violence in a system already sweeping towards a reabsorption of all the stakes without a trace of blood. For us the trick has been played. All dramaturgy, and even all real writing of cruelty has disappeared. Simulation is master, and nostalgia, the phantasmal parodic rehabilitation of all lost referentials, alone remains. Everything still unfolds before us, in the cold light of deterrence (including Artaud, who is entitled like all the rest to his revival, to a second existence as the *referential* of cruelty).

This is why nuclear proliferation increases neither the chance of atomic clash nor of accident—save in the interval where "young" powers could be tempted to use them for nondeterrent or "real" purposes (as the Americans did on Hiroshima—but precisely they alone were entitled to this "use value" of the bomb, while all those who have since acquired it are deterred from using it by the very fact of its possession). Entry into the atomic club, so amusingly named, very rapidly removes (like syndicalization for the working world) any inclination towards violent intervention. Responsibility, control, censorship, self-deterrence always increase faster than the forces or weapons at our disposal: this is the secret of the social order. Thus the very possibility of paralyzing a whole country with the flick of a switch *makes* it impossible that electrical engineers will ever utilize this weapon: the entire myth of the revolutionary and total strike collapses at the very moment when the means to do so are available—but alas, *exactly because* the means to do so are available. This is deterrence in a nutshell.

Therefore it is altogether likely that one day we shall see the nuclear powers exporting atomic reactors, weapons, and bombs to every latitude. After control by threat will succeed the much more effective strategy of pacification by the bomb and by its possession. "Small" powers, hoping to buy their independent strike force, will only buy the virus of deterrence, of their own deterrence. The same goes for the atomic reactors we have already sent them: so many neutron bombs knocking out all historical virulence, all risk of explosion. In this sense, the nuclear system institutes a universally accelerated process of *implosion,* it conceals everything around it, it absorbs all living energy.

The nuclear system is both the culminating point of available energy and the maximization of systems controlling all energy. Lockdown and control grow as fast as (and undoubtedly even faster than) liberating potentialities. This was already the aporia of modern revolutions. It is still the absolute paradox of the nuclear system. Energies freeze by their own fire power, they deter themselves. One can't really see what project, what power, what strategy, what subject could possibly be behind this enclosure, this vast saturation of a system by its own hereafter neutralized, unusable, unintelligible, nonexplosive forces—except the possibility of *an explosion towards the center,* or an *implosion* where all these energies are abolished in a catastrophic process (in the literal sense, that is to say in the sense of a reversion of the whole cycle towards a minimal point, of a reversion of energies towards a minimal threshold).

Translated by Paul Foss and Paul Patton

Notes

1. Cf., Jean Baudrillard, *L'echange symbolique et la mort* ("L'Ordre des simulacres"), (Paris: Gallimard, 1975).

2. And which is not susceptible to resolution in transference. It is the entanglement of these two discourses which makes psychoanalysis interminable.

3. Cf., Mario Perniola, "Icones, Visions, Simulacres," *Traverses,* no. 10 (February 1978): 39–49. Translated by Michel Makarius.

4. This does not necessarily result in a despair of meaning, but just as much in an improvisation of meaning, of nonsense, or of several simultaneous senses which cancel each other out.

5. The energy crisis, the ecological setting, by and large, are themselves *disaster films,* in the same style (and of the same value) as those

which currently do so well for Hollywood. It is pointless to interpret these films laboriously by their relationship with an "objective" social crisis, or even with an "objective" phantasm of disaster. It is in the other direction that we must say it is *the social itself which,* in contemporary discourse, *is organized according to a script for a disaster film.* (Cf., Michel Makarius, "La stratégie de la catastrophe." *Traverses,* no. 10 (February 1978): 115–124.

   6. To this flagging investment in work corresponds a parallel declining investment in consumption. Goodbye to use value or prestige of the automobile, goodbye to the amorous discourse which made a clear-cut distinction between the object of enjoyment and the object of work. Another discourse takes over, which is a *discourse of work on the object of consumption* aiming at an active, compelling, puritan reinvestment (use less gas, look to your security, speed is obsolete, etc.), to which automobile specifications pretend to be adapted: rediscovering a stake by transposition of the poles. Thus work becomes the object of a need, the car becomes the object of work—no better proof of the inability to distinguish the stakes. It is by the very swing of voting "rights" to electoral "duties" that the disinvestment of the political sphere is signaled.

   7. The medium/message confusion, of course, is a correlative of the confusion between sender and receiver, thus sealing the disappearance of all the dual, polar structures which formed the discursive organization of language, referring to the celebrated grid of functions in Jakobson, the organization of all determinate articulation of meaning. "Circular" discourse must be taken literally: that is, it no longer goes from one point to the other but describes a circle that *indistinctly* incorporates the positions of transmitter and receiver, henceforth unlocatable as such. Thus there is no longer any instance of power, any transmitting authority—power is something that circulates and whose source can no longer be located ,a cycle in which the positions of dominator and the dominated interchange in an endless reversion, which is also the end of power in its classical definition. The circularization of power, knowledge and discourse brings every localization of instances and poles to an end. Even in psychoanalytic interpretation, the "power" of the interpreter does not come from any external authority, but from the interpreted themselves. This changes everything, for we can always ask the traditional holders of power where they get their power from. Who made you Duke? The King. And who made the King? God. God alone does not reply. But to the question: Who made the psychoanalyst? the analyst quite easily replies: You. Thus is expressed, but an inverse simulation, the passage from the "analyzed" to the "analysand," from active to passive, which only goes to describe the swirling, mobile effect of the poles, its effect of circularity in which power is lost, is dissolved, is resolved into complete manipulation (this is no longer of the order of the directive authority and the gaze, but of the order of personal contact and commutation). See, also, the State/family circularity secured by the floating and metastatic regula-

tion of images of the social and the private. (Jacques Donzelot, *The Policing of Families,* trans. Robert Hurley [New York: Pantheon Books, 1979].)

From now on, it is impossible to ask the famous question:

"From what position do you speak?"—

"How do you know?"—

"From where do you get the power?" without immediately getting the reply: "But it is *of* (from) you that I speak"—meaning, it is you who speaks, it is you who knows, power is you. A gigantic circumvolution, circumlocution of the spoken word, which amounts to irredeemable blackmail and irremovable deterrence of the subject supposed to speak, but left without a word to say, responseless, since to questions asked can come the inevitable reply: but *you are* the reply, or: your question is already an answer, etc.— the whole sophitical stranglehold of word-tapping, forced confession disguised as free expression, trapping the subject in his own questioning, the precession of the reply about the question (the whole violence of interpretation is there, and the violence of the conscious or unconscious self-management of "speech").

This simulacrum of inversion or involution of poles, this clever subterfuge which is the secret of the whole discourse of manipulation and hence, today, in every domain, the secret of all those new powers sweeping clean the stage of power, forging the assumptions of all speech from which comes that fantastic silent majority characteristic of our times—all this undoubtedly began in the political sphere with the democratic simulacrum, that is to say with the substitution of the instance of the people for the instance of God as source of power, and the substitution of power as *representation* for power as *emanation.* An anti-Copernican revolution: no longer any transcendent instance nor any sun nor any luminous source of power and knowledge—everything comes from and returns to the people. It is through this magnificent *recycling* that the universal simulacrum of manipulation, from the scenario of mass suffrage to present-day and illusory opinion polls, begins to be installed.

8. Paradox: all bombs are clean—their only pollution is the system of control and security they radiate *when they are not detonated.*

The Resolution of Revolutions

Thomas Kuhn

The textbooks we have just been discussing are produced only in the aftermath of a scientific revolution. They are the bases for a new tradition of normal science. In taking up the question of their structure we have clearly missed a step. What is the process by which a new candidate for paradigm replaces its predecessor? Any new interpretation of nature, whether a discovery or a theory, emerges first in the mind of one or a few individuals. It is they who first learn to see science and the world differently, and their ability to make the transition is facilitated by two circumstances that are not common to most other members of their profession. Invariably their attention has been intensely concentrated upon the crisis-provoking problems; usually, in addition, they are men* so young or so new to the crisis-ridden field that practice has committed them less deeply than most of their contemporaries to the world view and rules determined by the old paradigm. How are they able, what must they do, to convert the entire profession or the relevant professional subgroup to their way of seeing science and the world? What causes

---

* Editors have retained the original masculine signifier throughout this essay.

the group to abandon one tradition of normal research in favor of another?

To see the urgency of those questions, remember that they are the only reconstructions the historian can supply for the philosopher's inquiry about the testing, verification, or falsification of established scientific theories. Insofar as he is engaged in normal science, the research worker is a solver of puzzles, not a tester of paradigms. Though he may, during the search for a particular puzzle's solution, try out a number of alternative approaches, rejecting those that fail to yield the desired result, he is not testing the *paradigm* when he does so. Instead he is like the chess player who, with a problem stated and the board physically or mentally before him, tries out various alternative moves in the search for a solution. These trial attempts, whether by the chess player or by the scientist, are trials only of themselves, not of the rules of the game. They are possible only so long as the paradigm itself is taken for granted. Therefore, paradigm-testing occurs only after persistent failure to solve a noteworthy puzzle has given rise to crisis. And even then it occurs only after the sense of crisis has evoked an alternate candidate for paradigm. In the sciences the testing situation never consists, as puzzle-solving does, simply in the comparison of a single paradigm with nature. Instead, testing occurs as part of the competition between two rival paradigms for the allegiance of the scientific community.

Closely examined, this formulation displays unexpected and probably significant parallels to two of the most popular contemporary philosophical theories about verification. Few philosophers of science still seek absolute criteria for the verification of scientific theories. Noting that no theory can ever be exposed to all possible relevant tests, they ask not whether a theory has been verified but rather about its probability in the light of the evidence that actually exists. And to answer that question one important school is driven to compare the ability of different theories to explain the evidence at hand. That insistence on comparing theories also characterizes the historical situation in which a new theory is accepted. Very probably it points one of the directions in which future discussions of verification should go.

In their most usual forms, however, probabilistic verification theories all have recourse to one or another of the pure or neutral observation-languages discussed in Section X. One probabilistic theory asks that we compare the given scientific theory with all others that might be imagined to fit the same collection of observed data. Another demands the construction in imagination of all the tests that the given scientific theory might conceivably be asked to pass.[1] Apparently some such construction is necessary for the computation of specific probabilities, absolute or relative, and it is hard to see how such a construction can possibly be achieved. If, as I have already urged, there can be no scientifically or empirically neutral system of language or concepts, then the proposed construction of alternate tests and theories must proceed from within one or another paradigm-based tradition. Thus restricted it would have no access to all possible experiences or to all possible theories. As a result, probabilistic theories disguise the verification situation as much as they illuminate it. Though that situation does, as they insist, depend upon the comparison of theories and of much widespread evidence, the theories and observations at issue are always closely related to ones already in existence. Verification is like natural selection: it picks out the most viable among the actual alternatives in a particular historical situation. Whether that choice is the best that could have been made if still other alternatives had been available or if the data had been of another sort is not a question that can usefully be asked. There are no tools to employ in seeking answers to it.

A very different approach to this whole network of problems has been developed by Karl R. Popper who denies the existence of any verification procedures at all.[2] Instead, he emphasizes the importance of falsification, i.e., of the test that, because its outcome is negative, necessitates the rejection of an established theory. Clearly, the role thus attributed to falsification is much like the one this essay assigns to anomalous experiences, i.e., to experiences that, by evoking crisis, prepare the way for a new theory. Nevertheless, anomalous experiences may not be identified with falsifying ones. Indeed, I doubt that the latter exist. As has repeatedly been emphasized before, no theory ever solves all the puzzles with which it is confronted at a given time; nor are the solutions already achieved often perfect. On the contrary, it is just the incompleteness and imperfection of the existing data-theory fit that, at any time, define many of the puzzles that characterize normal science. If any and every failure to fit were ground for theory rejection, all theories ought to be rejected at all times. On the other hand, if only severe failure to fit justifies theory rejection, then the Popperians will require some criterion of "improbability" or of "degree of falsification." In developing one they will almost certainly encounter the same network of difficulties that has haunted the advocates of the various probabilistic verification theories.

Many of the preceding difficulties can be avoided by recognizing that both of these prevalent and opposed views about the underlying logic of scientific inquiry have tried to compress two largely separate processes into one. Popper's anomalous experience is most important to science because it evokes competitors for an existing paradigm. But falsification, though it surely occurs, does not happen with, or simply because of, the emergence of an anomaly or falsifying instance. Instead, it is a subsequent and separate process that might equally well be called verification since it consists in the triumph of a new paradigm over the old one. Furthermore, it is in that joint verification-falsification process that the probabilist's comparison of theories plays a central role. Such a two-stage formulation has, I think, the virtue of great verisimilitude, and it may also enable us to begin explicating the role of agreement (or disagreement) between fact and theory in the verification process. To the historian, at least, it makes little sense to suggest that verification is establishing the agreement of fact with theory. All historically significant theories have agreed with the facts, but only more or less. There is no more precise answer to the question whether or how well an individual theory fits the facts. But questions much like that can be asked when theories are taken collectively or even in pairs. It makes a great deal of sense to ask which of two actual and competing theories fits the facts *better*. Though neither Priestley's nor Lavoisier's theory, for example, agreed precisely with existing observations, few contemporaries hesitated more than a decade in concluding that Lavoisier's theory provided the better fit of the two.

This formulation, however, makes the task of choosing between paradigms look both easier and more familiar than it is. If there were but one set of scientific problems, one world within which to work on them, and one set of standards for their solution, paradigm competition might be settled more or less routinely by some process like counting the number of problems solved by each. But, in fact, these conditions are never met completely. The proponents of competing paradigms are always at least slightly at cross-purposes. Neither side will grant all the non-empirical assumptions that the other needs in order to make its case. Like Proust and Berthollet arguing about the composition of chemical compounds, they are bound partly to talk through each other. Though each may hope to convert the other to his way of seeing his science and its problems, neither may hope to prove his case. The competition between paradigms is not the sort of battle that can be resolved by proofs.

We have already seen several reasons why the proponents of competing paradigms must fail to make complete contact with each other's viewpoints. Collectively these reasons have been described as the incommensurability of the pre- and post-revolutionary normal-scientific traditions, and we need only recapitulate them briefly here. In the first place, the proponents of competing paradigms will often disagree about the list of problems that any candidate for paradigm must resolve. Their standards or their definitions of science are not the same. Must a theory of motion explain the cause of the attractive forces between particles of matter or may it simply note the existence of such forces? Newton's dynamics was widely rejected because, unlike both Aristotle's and Descartes's theories, it implied the latter answer to the question. When Newton's theory had been accepted, a question was therefore banished from science. That question, however, was one that general relativity may proudly claim to have solved. Or again, as disseminated in the nineteenth century, Lavoisier's chemical theory inhibited chemists from asking why the metals were so much alike, a question that phlogistic chemistry had both asked and answered. The transition to Lavoisier's paradigm had, like the transition to Newton's, meant a loss not only of a permissible question but of an achieved solution. That loss was not, however, permanent either. In the twentieth century questions about the qualities of chemical substances have entered science again, together with some answers to them.

More is involved, however, than the incommensurability of standards. Since new paradigms are born from old ones, they ordinarily incorporate much of the vocabulary and apparatus, both conceptual and manipulative, that the traditional paradigm have previously employed. But they seldom employ these borrowed elements in quite the traditional way. Within the new paradigm, old terms, concepts, and experiments fall into new relationships one with the other. The inevitable result is what we must call, though the term is not quite right, a misunderstanding between the two competing schools. The laymen who scoffed at Einstein's general theory of relativity because space could not be "curved"—it was not that sort of thing—were not simply wrong or mistaken. Nor were the mathematicians, physicists, and philosophers who tried to develop a Euclidean version of Einstein's theory.[3] What had previously been meant by space was necessarily flat, homogeneous, isotropic, and unaffected by the presence of matter. If it had not been, Newtonian physics would not have worked. To make the transition to Einstein's universe, the whole conceptual web whose strands are space, time, matter, force, and so on, had to be shifted and laid down again on nature whole. Only men who had together undergone or failed to undergo that transformation would be able to discover precisely what they agreed or disagreed about. Communication across the revolutionary divide is inevitably partial. Consider, for another example, the men who called Copernicus mad because he proclaimed that the earth moved. They were not either just wrong or quite wrong. Part of what they meant by 'earth' was fixed position. Their earth, at least, could not be moved. Correspondingly, Copernicus' innovation was not simply to move the earth. Rather, it was a whole new way of regarding the problems of physics and astronomy, one that necessarily changed the meaning of both 'earth' and 'motion.'[4] Without those changes the concept of a moving earth was mad. On the other hand, once they had been made and understood, both Descartes and Huyghens could realize that the earth's motion was a question with no content for science.[5]

These examples point to the third and most fundamental aspect of the incommensurability of competing paradigms. In a sense that I am unable to explicate further, the proponents of competing paradigms practice their trades in different worlds. One contains constrained bodies that fall slowly, the other pendulums that repeat their motions again and again. In one, solutions are compounds, in the other mixtures. One is embedded in a flat, the other in a curved, matrix of space. Practicing in different worlds, the two groups of scientists see different things when they look from the same point in the same direction. Again, that is not to say that they can see anything they please. Both are looking at the world, and what they look at has not changed. But in some areas they see different things, and they see them in different relations one to the other. That is why a law that cannot even be demonstrated to one group of scientists may occasionally seem intuitively obvious to another. Equally, it is why, before they can hope to communicate fully, one group or the other must experience the conversion that we have been calling a paradigm shift. Just because it is a transition between incommensurables, the transition between competing paradigms cannot be made a step at a time, forced by logic and neutral experience. Like the gestalt switch, it must occur all at once (though not necessarily in an instant) or not at all.

How, then, are scientists brought to make this transposition? Part of the answer is that they are very often not. Copernicanism made few converts for almost a century after Copernicus' death. Newton's work was not generally accepted, particularly on the Continent, for more than half a century after the *Principia* appeared.[6] Priestley never accepted the oxygen theory, nor Lord Kelvin the electromagnetic theory, and so on. The difficulties of conversion have often been noted by scientists themselves. Darwin, in a particularly perceptive passage at the end of his *Origin of Species*, wrote: "Although I am fully convinced of the truth of the views given in this volume . . . , I by no means expect to convince experienced naturalists whose minds are stocked with a multitude of facts all viewed, during a long course of years, from a point of view directly opposite to mine. . . . [B]ut I look with confidence to the future,—to young and rising naturalists, who will be able to view both sides of the question with impartiality."[7] And Max Planck, surveying his own career in his *Scientific Autobiography,* sadly remarked that "a new scientific truth does not triumph by convincing its opponents and making them see the light, but rather because its opponents eventually die, and a new generation grows up that is familiar with it."[8]

These facts and others like them are too commonly known to need further emphasis. But they do need reevaluation. In the past they have most often been taken to indicate that scientists, being only human, cannot always admit their errors, even when confronted with strict proof. I would argue, rather, that in these matters neither proof nor error is at issue. The transfer of allegiance from paradigm to paradigm is a conversion experience that cannot be forced. Lifelong resistance, particularly from those whose productive careers have committed them to an older tradition of normal science, is not a violation of scientific standards but an index to the nature of scientific research itself. The source of resistance is the assurance that the older paradigm will ultimately solve all its problems, that nature can be shoved into the box the paradigm provides. Inevitably, at times of revolution, that assurance seems stubborn and pigheaded as indeed it sometimes becomes. But it is also something more. That same assurance is what makes normal or puzzle-solving science possible. And it is only through normal science that the professional community of scientists succeeds, first, in exploiting the potential scope and precision of the older paradigm and, then, in isolating the difficulty through the study of which a new paradigm may emerge.

Still, to say that resistance is inevitable and legitimate, that paradigm change cannot be justified by proof, is not to say that no arguments are relevant or that scientists cannot be persuaded to change their minds. Though a generation is sometimes required to effect the change, scientific communities have again and again been converted to new paradigms. Furthermore, these conversions occur not despite the fact that scientists are human but because they are. Though some scientists, particularly the older and more experienced ones, may resist indefinitely, most of them can be reached in one way or another. Conversions will occur a few at a time until, after the last holdouts have died, the whole profession will again be practicing under a single, but now a different, paradigm. We must therefore ask how conversion is induced and how resisted.

What sort of answer to that question may we expect? Just because it is asked about techniques of persuasion, or about argument and counterargument in a situation in which there can be no proof, our question is a new one, demanding a sort of study that has not previously been undertaken. We shall have to settle for a very partial and impressionistic survey. In addition, what has already been said combines with the result of that survey to suggest that, when asked about persuasion rather than proof, the question of the nature of scientific argument has no single or uniform answer. Individual scientists embrace a new paradigm for all sorts of reasons and usually for several at once. Some of these reasons—for example, the sun worship that helped make Kepler a Copernican—lie outside the apparent sphere of science entirely.[9] Others must depend upon idiosyncrasies of autobiography and personality. Even the nationality or the prior reputation of the innovator and his teachers can sometimes play a significant role.[10] Ultimately, therefore, we must learn to ask this question differently. Our concern will not then be with the arguments that in fact convert one or another individual, but rather with the sort of community that always sooner or later re-forms as a single group. That problem, however, I postpone to the final section, examining meanwhile some of the sorts of arguments that prove particularly effective in the battles over paradigm change.

Probably the single most prevalent claim advanced by the proponents of a new paradigm is that they can solve the problems that have led the old one to a crisis. When it can legitimately be made, this claim is often the most effective one possible. In the area for which it is advanced the paradigm is known to be in trouble. That trouble has repeatedly been explored, and attempts to remove it have again and again proved vain. "Crucial experiments"—those able to discriminate particularly sharply between the two paradigms—have been recognized and attested to before the new paradigm was even invented. Copernicus thus claimed that he had solved the long-vexing problem of the length of the calendar year, Newton that he had reconciled terrestrial and celestial mechanics, Lavoisier that he had solved the problems of gas-identity and of weight relations, and Einstein that he had made electrodynamics compatible with a revised science of motion.

Claims of this sort are particularly likely to succeed if the new paradigm displays a quantitative precision strikingly better than its older competitor. The quantitative superiority of Kepler's Rudolphine tables to all those computed from the Ptolemaic theory was a major factor in the conversion of astronomers to Copernicanism. Newton's success in predicting quantitative astronomical observations was probably the single most important reason for his theory's triumph over its more reasonable but uniformly qualitative competitors. And in this century the striking quantitative success of both Planck's radiation law and the Bohr atom quickly persuaded many physicists to adopt them even though, viewing physical science as a whole, both these contributions created many more problems than they solved.[11]

The claim to have solved the crisis-provoking problems is, however, rarely sufficient by itself. Nor can it always legitimately be made. In fact, Copernicus' theory was not more accurate than Ptolemy's and did not lead directly to any improvement in the calendar. Or again, the wave theory of light was not, for some years after it was first announced, even as successful as its corpuscular rival in resolving the polarization effects that were a principal cause of the optical crisis. Sometimes the looser practice that characterizes extraordinary research will produce a candidate for paradigm that initially helps not at all with the problems that have evoked crisis. When that occurs, evidence must be drawn from other parts of the field as it often is anyway. In those other areas particularly persuasive arguments can be developed if the new paradigm permits the prediction of phenomena that had been entirely unsuspected while the old one prevailed.

Copernicus' theory, for example, suggested that planets should be like the earth, that Venus should show phases, and that the universe must be vastly larger than had previously been supposed. As a result, when sixty years after his death the telescope suddenly displayed mountains on the moon, the phases of Venus, and an immense number of previously unsuspected stars, those observations brought the new theory a great many converts, particularly among non-astronomers.[12] In the case of the wave theory, one main source of professional conversions was even more dramatic. French resistance collapsed suddenly and relatively completely when Fresnel was able to demonstrate the existence of a white spot at the center of the shadow of a circular disk. That was an effect that not even he had anticipated but that Poisson, initially one of his opponents, had shown to be a necessary if absurd consequence of Fresnel's theory.[13] Because of their shock value and because they have so obviously not been "built into" the new theory from the start, arguments like these prove especially persuasive. And sometimes that extra strength can be exploited even though the phenomenon in question had been observed long before the theory that accounts for it was first introduced. Einstein, for example, seems not to have anticipated that general relativity would account with precision for the well-known anomaly in the motion of Mercury's perihelion, and he experienced a corresponding triumph when it did so.[14]

All the arguments for a new paradigm discussed so far have been based upon the competitors' comparative ability to solve problems. To scientists those arguments are ordinarily the most significant and persuasive. The preceding examples should leave no doubt about the source of their immense appeal. But, for reasons to which we shall shortly revert, they are neither individually nor collectively compelling. Fortunately, there is also another sort of consideration that can lead scientists to reject an old paradigm in favor of a new. These are the arguments, rarely made entirely explicit, that appeal to the individual's sense of the appropriate or the aesthetic—the new theory is said to be "neater," "more suitable," or "simpler" than the old. Probably such arguments are less effective in the sciences than in mathematics. The early versions of most new paradigms are crude. By the time their full aesthetic appeal can be developed, most of the community has been persuaded by other means. Nevertheless, the importance of aesthetic considerations can sometimes be decisive. Though they often attract only a few scientists to a new theory, it is upon those few that its ultimate triumph may depend. If they had not quickly taken it up for highly individual reasons, the new candidate for paradigm might never have been sufficiently developed to attract the allegiance of the scientific community as a whole.

To see the reason for the importance of these more subjective and aesthetic considerations, remember what a paradigm debate is about. When a new candidate for paradigm is first proposed, it has seldom solved more than a few of the problems that confront it, and most of those solutions are still far from perfect. Until Kepler, the Copernican theory scarcely improved upon the predictions of planetary position made by Ptolemy. When Lavoisier saw oxygen as "the air itself entire," his new theory could cope not at all with the problems presented by the proliferation of new gases, a point that Priestley made with great success in his counterattack. Cases like Fresnel's white spot are extremely rare. Ordinarily, it is only much later, after the new paradigm has been developed, accepted, and exploited that apparently decisive arguments—the Foucault pendulum to demonstrate the rotation of the earth or the Fizeau experiment to show that light moves faster in air than in water—are developed. Producing them is part of normal science, and their role is not in paradigm debate but in post-revolutionary texts.

Before those texts are written, while the debate goes on, the situation is very different. Usually the opponents of a new paradigm can legitimately claim that even in the area of crisis it is little superior to its traditional rival. Of course, it handles some problems better, has disclosed some new regularities. But the older paradigm can presumably be articulated to meet these challenges as it has met others before. Both Tycho Brahe's earth-centered astronomical system and the later versions of the phlogiston theory were responses to challenges posed by a new candidate for paradigm, and both were quite successful.[15] In addition, the defenders of traditional theory and procedure can almost always point to problems that its new rival has not solved but that for their view are no problems at all. Until the discovery of the composition of water, the combustion of hydrogen was a strong argument for the phlogiston theory and against Lavoisier's. And after the oxygen theory had triumphed, it could still not explain the preparation of a combustible gas from carbon, a phenomenon to which the phlogistonists had pointed as strong support for their view.[16] Even in the area of crisis, the balance of argument and counterargument can sometimes be very close indeed. And outside that area the balance will often decisively favor the tradition. Copernicus destroyed a time-honored explanation of terrestrial motion without replacing it; Newton did the same for an older explanation of gravity, Lavoisier for the common properties of metals, and so on. In short, if a new candidate for paradigm had to be judged from the start by hard-headed people who examined only relative problem-solving ability, the sciences would experience very few major revolutions. Add the counterarguments generated by what we previously called the incommensurability of paradigms, and the sciences might experience no revolutions at all.

But paradigm debates are not really about relative problemsolving ability, though for good reasons they are usually couched in those terms. Instead, the issue is which paradigm should in the future guide research on problems many of which neither competitor can yet claim to resolve completely. A decision between alternate ways of practicing science is called for, and in the circumstances that decision must be based less on past achievement than on future promise. The man who embraces a new paradigm at an early stage must often do so in defiance of the evidence provided by problem-solving. He must, that is, have faith that the new paradigm will succeed with the many large problems that confront it, knowing only that the older paradigm has failed with a few. A decision of that kind can only be made on faith.

That is one of the reasons why prior crisis proves so important. Scientists who have not experienced it will seldom renounce the hard evidence of problem-solving to follow what may easily prove and will be widely regarded as a will-o'-the-wisp. But crisis alone is not enough. There must also be a basis, though it need be neither rational nor ultimately correct, for faith in the particular candidate chosen. Something must make at least a few scientists feel that the new proposal is on the right track, and sometimes it is only personal and inarticulate aesthetic considerations that can do that. Men have been converted by them at times when most of the articulable technical arguments pointed the other way. When first introduced, neither Copernicus' astronomical theory nor De Broglie's theory of matter had many other significant grounds of appeal. Even today Einstein's general theory attracts men principally on aesthetic grounds, an appeal that few people outside of mathematics have been able to feel.

This is not to suggest that new paradigms triumph ultimately through some mystical aesthetic. On the contrary, very few men desert a tradition for these reasons alone. Often those who do turn out to have been misled. But if a paradigm is ever to triumph it must gain some first supporters, men who will develop it to the point where hardheaded arguments can be produced and multiplied. And even those arguments, when they come, are not individually decisive. Because scientists are reasonable men, one or another argument will ultimately persuade many of them. But there is no single argument that can or should persuade them all. Rather than a single group conversion, what occurs is an increasing shift in the distribution of professional allegiances.

At the start a new candidate for paradigm may have few supporters, and on occasions the supporters' motives may be suspect. Nevertheless, if they are competent, they will improve it, explore its possibilities, and show what it would be like to belong to the community guided by it. And as that goes on, if the paradigm is one destined to win its fight, the number and strength of the persuasive arguments in its favor will increase. More scientists will then be converted, and the exploration of the new paradigm will go on. Gradually the number of experiments, instruments, articles, and books based upon the paradigm will multiply. Still more men, convinced of the new view's fruitfulness, will adopt the new mode of practicing normal science, until at last only a few elderly hold-outs remain. And even they, we cannot say, are wrong. Though the historian can always find men—Priestley, for instance—who were unreasonable to resist for as long as they did, he will not find a point at which resistance becomes illogical or unscientific. At most he may wish to say that the man who continues to resist after his whole profession has been converted has *ipso facto* ceased to be a scientist.

Notes

1. For a brief sketch of the main routes to probabilistic verification theories, see Ernest Nagel, *Principles of the Theory of Probability,* Vol. I, No. 6, of *International Encyclopedia of Unified Science,* pp. 60–75.

2. K. R. Popper, *The Logic of Scientific Discovery* (New York, 1959), esp. chaps. i-iv.

3. For lay reactions to the concept of curved space, see Philipp Frank, *Einstein, His Life and Times,* trans. and ed. G. Rosen and S. Kusaka (New York, 1947), pp. 142–46. For a few of the attempts to preserve the gains of general relativity within a Euclidean space, see C. Nordmann, *Einstein and the Universe,* trans. J. McCabe (New York, 1922), chap. ix.

4. T. S. Kuhn, *The Copernican Revolution* (Cambridge, Mass., 1957), chaps. iii, iv, and vii. The extent to which heliocentrism was more than a strictly astronomical issue is a major theme of the entire book.

5. Max Jammer, *Concepts of Space* (Cambridge, Mass., 1954), pp. 118–24.

6. I. B. Cohen, *Franklin and Newton: An Inquiry into Speculative Newtonian Experimental Science and Franklin's Work in Electricity as an Example Thereof* (Philadelphia, 1956), pp. 93–94.

7. Charles Darwin, *On the Origin of Species...*(authorized edition from 6th English ed.; New York, 1889), II, 295–96.

8. Max Planck, *Scientific Autobiography and Other Papers,* trans. F. Gaynor (New York, 1949), pp. 33–34.

9. For the role of sun worship in Kepler's thought, see E. A. Burtt, *The Metaphysical Foundations of Modern Physical Science* (rev. ed.; New York, 1932), pp. 44–49.

10. For the role of reputation, consider the following: Lord Rayleigh, at a time when his reputation was established, submitted to the British Association a paper on some paradoxes of electrodynamics. His name was inadvertently omitted when the paper was first sent, and the paper itself was

at first rejected as the work of some "paradoxer." Shortly afterwards, with the author's name in place, the paper was accepted with profuse apologies (R. J. Strutt, 4th Baron Rayleigh, *John William Strutt, Third Baron Rayleigh* [New York, 1924], p. 228).

11. For the problems created by the quantum theory, see F. Reiche, *The Quantum Theory* (London, 1922), chaps. ii. vi-ix. For the other examples in this paragraph, see the earlier references in this section.

12. Kuhn, *op. cit.*, pp. 219–25.

13. E. T. Whittaker, *A History of the Theories of Aether and Electricity,* I (2d ed.; London, 1951), 108.

14. See *ibid.,* II (1953), 151–80, for the development of general relativity. For Einstein's reaction to the precise agreement of the theory with the observed motion of Mercury's perihelion, see the letter quoted in P. A. Schilpp (ed.), *Albert Einstein, Philosopher-Scientist* (Evanston, Ill., 1949), p. 101.

15. For Brahe's system, which was geometrically entirely equivalent to Copernicus', see J. L. E. Dreyer, *A History of Astronomy from Thales to Kepler* (2d ed.; New York, 1953), pp. 359–71. For the last versions of the phlogiston theory and their success, see J. R. Partington and D. McKie, "Historical Studies of the Phlogiston Theory," *Annals of Science,* IV (1939), 113–49.

16. For the problem presented by hydrogen, see J. R. Partington, *A Short History of Chemistry* (2d ed.; London, 1951), p. 134. For carbon monoxide, see H. Kopp, *Geschichte der Chemie,* III (Braunschweig, 1845), 294–96.

Black Culture and Postmodernism

Cornel West

We live now forty-four years after the age of Europe—that is, an unprecedented world-transforming historical period (1492–1945) in
which those countries that reside between the Ural Mountains and
Atlantic Ocean discovered new lands, subjugated those peoples on
these lands, degraded the identities and cultures of non-European
peoples (Africans, Asians, Latin Americans, and indigenous peoples), and exploited laborers of both European and non-European
descent. We live now seventeen years after the heyday of American
world hegemony—namely, a brief yet pacesetting historical inter-
lude (1945–1972) in which the U.S.A. emerged as the supreme military and economic power in the world upon the eclipse of European
domination and in the wake of European devastation and decline.
Lastly and most importantly, we live now in the midst of the second
stage of the decolonization of the Third World—specifically, a
rather paralytic moment in that world-historical process in which
those subjugated and oppressed, degraded and exploited peoples
bring power and pressure to bear against the status quos in Third
World neocolonial nations, North Atlantic and Eastern European
societies. These three fundamental historical coordinates—the aftermath and legacy of the age of Europe, the precarious yet still

Cornel West, "Black Culture and Postmodernism." Reprinted from *Remaking History* eds. Barbara Kruger and Phil Mariani, pp. 87–96 Copyright
1989 Bay Press. Reprinted by permission.

prominent power of the United States, and the protracted opposition of Third World peoples (here and abroad)—circumscribe the discursive space wherein "postmodernism" is constituted as an object of investigation.

The current "postmodernism" debate is first and foremost a product of significant First World reflections upon the decentering of Europe that take such forms as the demystification of European cultural predominance and the deconstruction of European philosophical edifices. With the emergence of the United States as the world center for military arms, political direction, and cultural production *and* the advent of Third World politically independent nations, the making of a new world order seemed quite likely. Ironically, most First World reflections on "postmodernism" remain rather parochial and provincial—that is, narrowly Eurocentric. For example, Jean-François Lyotard's well-known characterization of the postmodern condition, with its increasing incredulity toward master (or meta) narratives, a rejection of representation, and a demand for radical artistic experimentation, is an interesting but insulated Eurocentric view: a kind of European navel-gazing in which postmodernism becomes a recurring moment within the modern that is performative in character and aesthetic in content. The major sources from which Lyotard borrows—Kant's notion of the sublime and Wittgenstein's idea of language games—are deployed to promote and encourage certain kinds of modernist practices: namely, nonrepresentational, experimental techniques and outlooks that shun and shatter quests for totality. Similar Eurocentric frameworks and modernist loyalties can be detected in Jacques Derrida's deconstructive version of poststructuralism, and even in Michel Foucault's archeological and genealogical investigations into pre-modern and modern modes of constituting subjects. Derrida's own marginal status as Algerian (a special kind of French colonial subject) and a Jew may indeed lead him to highlight the transgressive and disruptive aspects of Nietzsche and Heidegger, Mallarmé and Artaud. Yet his project remains a thoroughly Eurocentric and modernist one. It could signify the absence and silence of those viewed as other, alien, marginal—Third World peoples, women, gays, lesbians—as well as their relative political impotence in creatively transforming the legacy of the age of Europe. Foucault provides more concrete social and historical analytical substance to a discourse of otherness and marginality in his focus on the fundamental role and function of the insane and the incarcerated. But even the "others" Foucault investigates remain within European boundaries, and his heroes, like Derrida's remain transgressive modernists such as Nietzsche and Georges Bataille. Needless to say, the two prominent opponents of post-modernism, Hilton Kramer from the far right and Jürgen Habermas from the not-too-far left, do so in the name of the highbrow achievements and intellectual "seriousness" of a European/Anglo-American modernism and the social and political accomplishments and potentialities of a European Enlightenment project.

Significant attempts to focus the postmodernism debate on post-World War II American cultural practices and artifacts (for example, in architecture and painting) can be seen in the early work of William Spanos and Paul Bové. In their illuminating neo-Heideggerian readings of American poets like Robert Creeley and Charles Olson, postmodern notions of temporality, difference, and heterogeneity loomed large, yet still it remained at the level of philosophic outlook and artistic enactment. This observation also holds for the pioneering work of Rosalind Krauss and Susan Sontag, who view postmodernism as either a complex set of sensibilities and styles, or as ideological beliefs.

Fredric Jameson, Hal Foster, and to a certain extent, Andreas Huyssen have brought a particular debate "down to earth" (as it were) by situating it in relation to larger developments in society and history. In short, Jameson and Huyssen try to lay bare the contours of the forest that goes beyond the useful though limited squirrel work done by other postmodern critics. They do this by positing postmodernism as a social category—a dominant yet diverse set of structural and institutional processes wherein certain sensibilities, styles, and outlooks are understood as reactions and responses to new societal conditions and historical circumstances.

The important point here is neither whether one agrees with Jameson's laundry lists of postmodern features (e.g., depthlessness, persuasiveness of the image and simulacrum, weakening of historicity, emotional intensities, and schizophrenic subjects), or whether one approves of his treatments of individual cultural artifacts. Rather what is crucial is that First World reflections on postmodernism have become more consciously historical, social, political, and ideological. For too long, the postmodernism debate has remained inscribed within narrow disciplinary boundaries, insulated artistic practices, and vague formulations of men and women of letters. The time has come for this debate to be moved more forthrightly into social theory and historiography. To do so is to raise methodological questions about historical periodization, demarcation of cultural practices and archives, and issues of politics and ideology.

For instance, every conception of postmodernism presupposes some idea of the modern—when it began, when it peaked, when it declined, when it ended. And any such idea of the modern bears directly and indirectly upon how one conceives of change in the present. Secondly, different cultural practices have generally agreed upon uses of the term "modern" that require a recognition of the diverse logics within specific disciplinary practices. For example, philosophers view the advent of the modern as a seventeenth-century affair and shun the term "modernist" as a description of philosophical rhetorical strategies, whereas literary critics view nineteenth-century works as major examples of "the modern" and make much of the break between modern and modernist literary texts. Architects understand modernist works as those that valorize reason, technique, instrumentality, and functionality in thoroughgoing utopian terms. On the other hand, literary critics view modernist texts as those that dismiss rationality, instrumentality, and functionality in favor of myth, montage, simultaneity, and play in deeply anti-utopian terms. Adequate conceptions of historical periodization must keep track of these complex convergences and divergences of different cultural traditions, yet still not lose sight of the larger social and historical forces at work at any particular moment. This means that the very historical periodizations and cultural demarcations we make are, in part, ideological constructs shot through with political presuppositions, prejudgments, prejudices. Intellectual honesty requires that one make them crystal clear and give reasons as to why one holds them.

From my own viewpoint, I remain quite suspicious of the term "postmodernism" for two basic reasons. First, because the precursor term "modern" itself has not simply been used to devalue the cultures of oppressed and exploited peoples, but also has failed to deeply illumine the internal complexities of these cultures. Under the circumstances, there is little reason to hold out hope for the new term "postmodernism" as applied to the practices of oppressed peoples. Second, the sheer facticity of black people in the United States historically embodies and enacts the "postmodern" themes of degraded otherness and subaltern marginality. Black resistances have attacked notions of exclusionary identity, dominating heterogeneity, and universality—or, in more blunt language, white supremacy. Yet the historical experience of black people in North America, as well as Latinos, women, workers, gays, and lesbians, always requires that one examine the relation of any Eurocentric (patriarchal, homophobic) discourse to black resistance. The issue here is not simply some sophomoric, moralistic test that surveys the racial biases of the interlocutors in a debate. Rather the point is to engage in a structural and institutional analysis to see *where* the debate is taking place, *why* at this historical moment, and *how* this debate enables or disenables oppressed peoples to exercise their opposition to the hierarchies of power. For example, does the postmodernism debate seriously acknowledge the distinctive cultural and political practices of oppressed peoples, e.g., African-Americans? Or does this debate highlight notions of difference, marginality and otherness in such a way that it further marginalizes actual people of difference and otherness, e.g., African-Americans, Latinos, women, etc.? My point here is not a crude instrumental one, that is, I am not calling for some "vulgar" populist discourse for mobilizing oppressed peoples. Rather, I am asking whether postmodernism debates can cast some significant light on cultural practices of oppressed peoples.

My own hunch is that oppositional black intellectuals must be conversant with and, to a degree, participants in the debate. Yet until the complex relations between race, class, and gender are more adequately theorized, more fully delineated in specific historiographical studies, and more fused in our concrete ideological and political practices, the postmodernism debate, though at times illuminating, will remain rather blind to the plight and predicament of black America. Therefore I do not displace myself from the postmodernism debate, I simply try to keep my distance from its parochialism and view it as a symptom of our present cultural crisis.

When one turns to African-American cultural practices and products during the historical moment in which the postmodernism debate begins, it is undeniable that U.S. mass culture is disproportionately influenced by black people. This is so especially in popular music, linguistic innovation, and athletics. Owing to both a particular African heritage and specific forms of Euro-American oppression, black American cultural production has focused primarily on performance and pageantry, style and spectacle in music, sermons, and certain sports. The music and sermons are rooted in black religious practices; the sports, in black male-bonding networks that flaunt *machismo,* promote camaraderie, and, in some cases, lead to financial success. Black religious practices—the indigenous cradle of African-American culture—principally attempt to provide hope and sustain sanity in light of the difficult position of black Americans and the absurdity of transplanted European moderns casting America in the role of the promised land. The black religious ideological response was often to recast America as Egypt; and the concrete, everyday response to institutionalized terrorism—slavery or

Jim-Crowism—was to deploy weapons of kinetic orality, passionate physicality, and combative spirituality to survive and dream of freedom.

By kinetic orality, I mean dynamic repetitive and energetic rhetorical styles that form communities, e.g., antiphonal styles and linguistic innovations that accent fluid, improvisational identities and that promote survival at almost any cost. By passionate physicality, I mean bodily stylizations of the world, syncopations and polyrhythms that assert one's somebodiness in a society in which one's body has no public worth, only economic value as a laboring metabolism. And by combative spirituality, I mean a sense of historical patience, subversive joy, and daily perseverance in an apparently hopeless and meaningless historical situation. Black cultural practices emerge out of an acknowledgment of a reality they cannot *not know*—the ragged edges of the real, of necessity; a reality historically constructed by white supremacist practices in North America during the age of Europe. These ragged edges—of not being able to eat, not to have shelter, not to have health care—all this is infused into the strategies and styles of black cultural practices. Of course, all peoples have undergone some form of social misery, yet peoples of African descent in the United States have done so in the midst of the most prosperous and wealthy country in the world.

A distinctive feature of these black styles is a certain projection of the self—more a *persona*—in performance. This is not simply a self-investment and self-involvement in musical, rhetorical, and athletic enactments; it also acknowledges radical contingency and even solicits challenge and danger. In short, it is a spectacular form of risk-ridden execution that is self-imposed—be it a Charlie Parker solo, a Sarah Vaughan rendition, Muhammad Ali footwork, a Martin Luther King, Jr., sermon, a James Brown dancing act, a Julius Erving dunk shot, or a Kathleen Battle interpretation of Handel. This feature not only results from what some anthropologists have called the African deification of accident—the sense of perennially being on a slippery tightrope; it also comes from the highly precarious historical situations in which black people have found themselves. And with political and economic avenues usually blocked, specific cultural arenas become the space wherein black resistance is channeled.

Ironically, black American culture has surfaced with power and potency in our own time principally owing to three basic reasons. First, upon the emergence of the United States as a world power, it was quite clear that black music—spirituals, gospels, blues, jazz, soul—was the most unique cultural product created by

Americans of any hue. So as the globalization of American culture escalated, black music was given vast international exposure. Second, as the consumption cycle of advanced multinational corporate capitalism was sped up in order to sustain the production of luxury goods, cultural production became more and more mass-commodity production. The stress here is not simply on the new and fashionable but also on the exotic and primitive. Black cultural products have historically served as a major source for European and Euro-American exotic interests—interests that issue from a healthy critique of the mechanistic, puritanical, utilitarian, and productivist aspects of modern life.

Yet as black cultural products become the commodified possession of Euro-Americans, they play a very different role in U.S. society. For example, they speak less of the black sense of absurdity in American and more of the "universal" values of love. Needless to say, the sheer size of the white consumer market provides material incentives to black artists to be "crossover artists," i.e., more attuned to white tastes and sensibilities. There indeed are some cases where artistic and cultural integrity is preserved by crossover artists (Sly Stone in the sixties, Luther Vandross and Anita Baker in the eighties). Yet the temptation to de-Africanize one's style and dilute one's black cultural content for commercial reasons is often irresistible.

The third reason black culture has recently become so salient is that it has become identified with the first mass youth culture, an ever-growing world consumer market since the fifties. This culture responded to the eclipse of First World utopian energies and waning alternative political options by associating modes of transcendence with music and sexual liberation. Given the European and Euro-American identification of Africans and African-Americans with sexual licentiousness, libertinism, and liberation, black music became both a symbol and facilitator of white sexual freedom. And with the vast sexualization of the advertising industry, which now specializes in recycling black music hits of the recent past, much of black popular music has become thoroughly accepted by not simply rebellious white youth (as of old), but also the cultural mainstream.

What then is the oppositional potential of black cultural practices in our time? And to what extent is it legitimate to designate some of them "postmodern"? Of the three major forms of black cultural products—musical, sermonic, and athletic practices—certainly the latter is the most incorporated and co-opted of the three. Sermonic practices, still far removed from most white observation and consumption, are limited owing to ecclesiastical and denominational constituencies that make it difficult for ecumenical figures to emerge who can remain rooted in black institutional life, yet attract peoples from outside their own constituencies. Yet when such figures do emerge—Martin Luther King, Jr., Malcolm X, Jesse Jackson—they can generate tremendous oppositional energy due to the paucity of articulate and charismatic spokespersons on the American left and the potentially positive role charismatic leaders can play in empowering people to believe in themselves and act in unity against the powers that be.

Black musical practices—packaged via radio or video, records or live performances—are oppositional principally in the weak sense that they keep alive some sense of the agency and creativity of oppressed peoples. Yet this sense is so vague and far removed from organized political resistance that one must conclude that most of black music here and abroad has simply become a major means by which U.S. record companies have colonized the leisure time of eager consumers (including myself). Yet since black music is so integral to black life in America, it is difficult to imagine a black resistance movement in which black music does not play an important role.

But what of literary artists, visual artists, and other black intellectuals in general? Have I not unduly neglected them? Are they not the possible candidates for producers of postmodern products—which thereby makes the term partly relevant to black life? Granted, I have spent most of my time on black mass culture. This is so because my interest in black resistance in the form of social movements leads me to look for the possible motion and momentum of black people who suffer, work, and long for social freedom. But much more serious reflection must be done in regard to this crucial matter. This essay is but a mere gesture toward constructing possible critical positions for blacks both in and around popular culture, the ways in which these positions can be viewed as sites of a potentially enabling yet resisting postmodernism.

From Here to Modernity: Feminism and Postmodernism

Barbara Creed

What is at stake in the debate surrounding a possible intersection between feminist theory and postmodern theory? The future of feminist theory itself: its directions, theoretical bases, alignments? Is feminism a symptom or result of the postmodern condition or is feminism linked more directly to this crisis in theory? Alice Jardine and Craig Owens have explored the connections between feminism and postmodernism. A comparison of their work should prove helpful to the newcomer—myself included—who is attempting to negotiate what Owens rightly describes as a "treacherous course" between the two.[1]

In "The Discourse of Others: Feminism and Postmodernism," Owens argues that there is an "apparent crossing of the feminist critique of patriarchy and the postmodernist critique of representation" (59). Owens points out that his intention is not to propose a relationship of either "antagonism or opposition" between the two (although at times he seems to do just this) but rather to explore this possible intersection in order "to introduce the issue of sexual difference into the modernism/postmodernism debate," an issue of which this debate "has until now been scandalously in-different" (59)—a debatable point.

According to Owens there are many areas where feminism is not only "compatible with, but also an instance of postmodern thought" (62): both feminism and postmodernism endorse Lyotard's argument that there is a crisis in the legitimizing function of narrative, that the *grands récits* or Great Narratives of the West have lost credibility; both present a critique of representation, that "system of power that authorizes certain representations while blocking, prohibiting or invalidating others" (p 59); both agree that the "representational systems of the West admit only one vision—that of the constitutive male subject" (58); both present a critique of binarism, that is, thinking by means of oppositions; both insist on the importance of "difference and incommensurability" (pp 61–62); both seek to heal the breach between theory and practice and support and artistic strategy of "simultaneous activity on multiple fronts" (p 63); both critique the privileging of vision as the superior sense and as the guarantor of truth. The difference, it appears, is that where postmodernism, defined as a cultural theory, sees itself as engaging in a debate with modernism, feminism identifies patriarchal ideology as its "other." For instance, in relation to the issue of vision, feminism "links the privileging of vision with sexual privilege" (70), particularly in relation to the psychoanalytic theory of castration, whereas postmodernism situates the problem as one of "modern aesthetics." While there are some problems with Owens' argument, which I shall discuss below, I think he is correct to argue that there is a common ground shared by feminism and postmodernism.

In her book, *Gynesis: Configurations of Woman and Modernity,*[2] Alice Jardine further explores this common ground. She concentrates her discussion of feminism and postmodernism on the relationship between contemporary French thought (the writings largely of male writers: Lacan, Derrida, Deleuze, Duras, Goux, Blanchot, Tournier), the process of "gynesis" which she argues is central to these writings, and feminism. It is important to realize that Jardine is using the term "modernity" in a specialised sense: although she writes that she is not certain if the word "should or can be defined" as she uses it, she does actually offer a definition over the course of the book. First, however, she indicates what modernity does not mean: " . . . modernity should not be confused (as it most often is in the United States) with 'modernism'—the generic label commonly attached to the general literary movement of the first half of the twentieth century" (23). Jardine uses the term "modernity," which is used in France to refer to what is known "more problematically in the United States [as] 'post-modernism' " (22). (Because of Jardine's specialised use of the term, I shall also adopt her practice when referring to her work.)

The major question Jardine explores in *Gynesis* is this: " . . . are feminism and modernity oxymoronic in their terms and terminology? If so, how and why? If not, what new ruse of reason has made them appear—especially in France—to be so?" (22). The "new ruse of reason" which Jardine isolates for analysis is a process that she defines as "gynesis." Gynesis, which Jardine argues has always been discernible in the religious and literary texts of the West, is a process of requestioning and rethinking—a process brought about by the collapse of the master narratives of the West and a reexamination of the main topics of philosophy: Man, Truth, History.

> In France, such rethinking has involved, above all, a reincorporation and reconceptualization of that which has been the master narrative's own 'non-knowledge,' what has eluded them, what was engulfed them. This other-than-themselves is almost always a 'space' of some kind (over which the narrative has lost control), and this space has been coded as feminine, as woman. (25)

Thus, gynesis represents a valorization of the feminine or woman as intrinsic to the development of new postmodern modes of speaking and writing. However, it is important to stress, as Jardine does, that the process of gynesis is not necessarily about women or feminism. She points to the fact that the majority of writers in France, who are working in this area, deal almost exclusively with the fictional writings of men. For "feminine writing" does not necessarily signify writing by a woman. Throughout *Gynesis,* Jardine refers to the general agreement amongst contemporary writers that in order to write the male poet must "become a woman." She cites the work of Deleuze and Guattari in which they:

> . . . refer to Virginia Woolf as having incorporated the process of what they call 'becoming woman' (le devenir femme) in her writing—but 'not to the same extent' as Henry James, D.H. Lawrence, or Henry Miller. (62)

Gynesis is "the putting into discourse of 'woman' as that *process* diagnosed in France as intrinsic to the condition of modernity . . ." (25). Jardine points to the writings of Derrida, a philosopher whose work represents a fundamental critique of the Western philosophical tradition. In order to analyze the symbolic function, he employs terms such as "hymen" and "the invaginated text." She also refers to a similar process at work in other writers:

> ... "she" may be found in Lacan's pronouncements on desire ... Deleuze's work on becoming woman; Jean-François Lyotard's calls for a feminine analytic relation; Jean Baudrillard's work on seduction; Foucault's on madness; Goux's on the new femininity; Barthes's in general; Michel Serres's desire to become Penelope or Ariadne ... "She" is created from the close explorations of semantic chains whose elements have changed textual as well as conceptual positions, at least in terms of valorization: from time to space, the same to other, paranoia to hysteria, city to labyrinth, mastery to nonmastery, truth to fiction.
>
> As Stephen Heath has put it in his essay on difference, today that which is designated unrepresentable is what is finally the most strongly represented. (38)

Jardine argues that modernity signifies a *re*definition of the world" brought about by the "complex destructuring, disintegration, of the founding structures in the West." Modernity represents an attempt to take those terms which are "not attributable to *Man:* the spaces of the *en-soi,* Other, without history—the feminine" and to give these spaces a *"new language"* (72–73).

> Here we are at the heart of gynesis. To give a new language to these other spaces is a project filled with both promise and fear, however, for these spaces have hitherto remained unknown, terrifying, monstrous: they are mad, unconscious, improper, unclean, nonsensical, oriental, profane. If philosophy is truly to question those spaces, it must move away from all that has defined them, held them in place: Man, the Subject, History, Meaning. It must offer itself over to them, embrace them. But this is also a dangerous and frightening task, for, as Walter Benjamin put it: "It is a metaphysical truth ... that all of nature would begin to lament if it were endowed with language." (73)

In her discussion of the "destructuring" and "disintegration" of the foundations of Western society, Jardine emphasises various areas of collapse which are of particular relevance to this discussion and

which were also specified by Owens in his discussion: the collapse of
the master narratives of the West; the breakdown of the paternal
metaphor; the crisis in representation; the decentering of the subject; the critique of binarism.

I. The Collapse of The Master Narrative

Both Jardine and Owens discuss the work of Lyotard and his theory
of the collapse of the master narrative. In *The Postmodern
Condition*,[3] Lyotard discusses in detail the question of knowledge
and the problem of its legitimation in so-called advanced societies
given what he sees as a collapse of the *grands récits* or Great Narratives, that is, narratives which have been used to legitimate the
quest for knowledge and the importance of scientific research.
There are two major forms of the legitimation narrative. In the
first, the narrative of emancipation, the people are the subject of
science. Here, it is argued that through scientific research man will
eventually create a society free from poverty and injustice. According to this narrative legitimation, all research undertaken by members of the general scientific community is justified because it will
eventually lead to an improvement in the lives of the people. In the
second major narrative of legitimation, the speculative mind, the
practice of philosophy, is the subject of science. Here, knowledge is
sought for its own sake on the assumption that every small contribution will eventually lead to an advancement in the totality of
knowledge.

According to Lyotard, neither of these two narratives can now
be used to justify scientific research. This crisis of legitimation has
been partly brought about by the breakdown in the belief that a unified totality of knowledge is possible and that if it were it would necessarily benefit humankind. Citing the way in which the techno-
sciences can be said to have increased rather than alleviated
disease, Lyotard critiques the very idea of progress:

> One can note a sort of decay in the confidence placed by the
> two last centuries in the idea of progress. The idea of progress
> as possible, probable or necessary was rooted in the certainty
> that the development of the arts, technology, knowledge and
> liberty would be profitable to mankind as a whole.[4]

He points out that although there were disagreements, even wars,
over the "name of the subject" to be liberated, the contestants

agreed that activities were "legitimate" if they contributed to the eventual liberation of humankind. However:

> After two centuries, we are more sensitive to signs that signify the contrary. Neither economic nor political liberalism, nor the various Marxisms, emerge from the sanguinary last two centuries free from the suspicion of crimes against mankind.[5]

In *The Postmodern Condition,* Lyotard partly defines the postmodern as a condition in which the "grand narrative has lost its credibility, regardless of what mode of unification it uses, regardless of whether it is a speculative narrative or a narrative of emancipation."[6] He argues that we cannot hope to know the origin of this incredulity, all we can do is map its existence and its manifestations. Owens translates *grand récit* first as "master narrative" and then as "narratives of mastery, of man seeking his telos in the conquest of nature."[7] He claims that not only is the status of narrative in question but also that of representation, specifically man's androcentric representation of the world in which he has constructed himself as "subject." Owens argues that here feminism and postmodernism share common ground—both present a critique of forms of narrative and representation which place man as subject. Owens points to the visual arts where he argues "symptoms" of man's "recent loss of mastery" are most apparent: the multiplicity of signs of mastery; a mourning of loss; images of phallic woman. While I think that Owens' comments are valid—there is a crossing of both the feminist and postmodern critiques of narrative and representation—I am not certain that Lyotard's *grand récit* is the same as Owens's "narratives of mastery," nor am I convinced that the master narrative crisis is necessarily beneficial to women—a point that Meaghan Morris[8] raises in her work on Lyotard.

First, Lyotard is addressing narratives of legitimation and a crisis which is essentially a crisis in the status of knowledge—that is, a crisis in the ability to decide what is true and just, a crisis in the validity of the social contract between governments and the people. This crisis is not the same as the one pointed to by Owens at the outset of his article as "a crisis of cultural authority," which he situates as a crisis in representation and narrative specifically in relation to the representation of man as "subject" within the signifying practices of Western patriarchal societies. Owens' conceptualization of this crisis, however, does represent the feminist position.

If Lyotard has pointed to the crisis of the master narrative in terms of "legitimacy," Laura Mulvey's work on cinema has raised questions about a different kind of narrative crisis—one based in questions of sexual difference and brought about by the self-aggrandizing structures of the unconscious of patriarchal society.[9] The feminist critique of *classic* narrative, with which it is mainly concerned, comes from a different theoretical basis and addresses itself to a different theoretical object, although both agree that there is a crisis of narrative which has shaken the credibility of the major institutions of the West. Whereas feminism would attempt to explain that crisis in terms of the workings of patriarchal ideology and the oppression of women and other minority groups, postmodernism looks to other possible causes—particularly the West's reliance on ideologies which posit universal truths—Humanism, History, Religion, Progress, etc. While feminism would argue that the common ideological position of all these "truths" is that they are patriarchal, postmodern theory—as I understand it—would be reluctant to isolate a single major determining factor.

Craig Owens argues that the postmodern debate has been "scandalously in-different" to the issue of sexual difference; however, it would be more accurate to say that *some* writers have been indifferent. Jardine points out that, although Lyotard does not take up the issue of the paternal signifier as a major theme in his discussion of the postmodern crisis in narrative, "he makes it clear that the crisis is not sexually neutral."

> He does this primarily through his descriptions of the only viable source and place he sees for legitimacy in postmodern culture: "para-logic." This kind of logic is dependent upon and valorizes the kinds of incomplete "short stories" historically imbedded, hidden, within so-called "scientific" or "objective" discourse: the kinds of short narratives that this discourse attempts to evacuate in order to shore up its "Truths." (66)

Jardine explains that the elements of these short narratives constitute what Lyotard describes in another article as "a feminine relation of ductility and ductibility, polymorphism . . . women are discovering something that could cause the greatest revolution in the West, something that (masculine) domination has never ceased to stifle: there is no signifier, or else, the class above all classes is just one among many . . . " (66). On the basis of such comments, which clearly raise the issue of sexual difference, Jardine claims that it is important to recognise "that delegitimation, experienced as crisis, is the loss of the paternal fiction, the West's heritage and guarantee . . . " (67). Unlike Owens, she does not reduce Lyotard's *grands récits* to "narratives of mastery, of man seeking his telos in the conquest of nature" but rather analyzes the nature of the crisis as an experience of "the loss of the paternal signifier"—a different proposition altogether and one which provides us with a more helpful basis from which to discuss the crisis of narrative in relation to feminist theory, postmodernism and the cinema.

II. The "Nostalgia" Film

I would like to relate this discussion to Fredric Jameson's argument about postmodernism and the nostalgia film. Jameson discusses this phenomenon without any reference to feminism or questions of sexual difference, apparently "in-different" to these issues in a context where, I would have thought, they were crucial. Jameson argues that the changes currently taking place in post-industrial society have been registered in the postmodern fascination for the nostalgia film. He sees a "desperate attempt to appropriate a missing past"[10] in films such as *American Graffiti, Rumble Fish, Chinatown, The Conformist, Body Heat.* He refers to "the colonization" of our immediate past and argues that the preference for films which rely on quotation (of past versions, other remakes, the original novel, etc) represents an attempt to construct " . . . 'intertextuality' as a deliberate, built-in feature of the aesthetic effect, and as the operator of a new connotation of 'pastness' and pseudo-historical depth, in which the history of aesthetic styles displaces 'real' history." Jameson sees this "mesmerizing new aesthetic mode . . . as an elaborated symptom of the waning of our historicity, of our lived possibility of experiencing history in some active way. . . . "[11]

In an earlier article, Jameson discussed another category of films *(Star Wars, Raiders of the Lost Arc)* which, while not strictly historical, recreate cultural experiences in the form of pastiche as well as reawakening a sense of the past in the viewer. Jameson argues that for those who grew up in the '30s to the '50s one of the major cultural forms was the adventure serial, awash with "alien villains, true American heroes, heroines in distress." He argues that a film like *Star Wars:*

> . . . reinvents this experience in the form of a pastiche: that is, there is no longer any point to a parody of such serials since

they are long extinct. Star Wars, far from being a pointless sat-
ire of such now dead forms, satisfies a deep (might I even say
repressed?) longing to experience them again: it is a complex
object in which on some first level children and adolescents
can take the adventures straight, while the adult public is able
to gratify a deeper and more properly nostalgic desire to return to that older period and to live its strange old aesthetic
artifacts through once again. This film is thus metonymically
a historical or nostalgia film. . . . [12]

What is most interesting about Jameson's otherwise incisive
observations is that he does not analyze this longing for the "past."
Exactly what is it that modern audiences wish to feel nostalgic
about? Does this nostalgia take a different form for men and
women? Since Jameson refers to two different forms of the nostalgia
film—the period recreation and the adventure film—I shall discuss
this question in relation to each.

The intensely polarized gender roles of the adventure serial,
with its true heroes and distressed heroines, invoke a desire to relive a "time" when gender roles were more clearly defined, stable,
predictable. I am not arguing that this "time" was the '30s or the
'50s; it may be that audiences of those decades were also watching
the serials in order to satisfy their desire to relive an imaginary order—an order where gender identity was secure and appeared to
validate the social contract established by the myth of romantic
love. Given the current crisis in gender roles, often cited as an instance of postmodernism and certainly represented in the cinema,
and audience incredulity in the face of cinematic derring-do, films
like *Raiders of the Lost Ark* are required both to romanticize and
parody the roles of hero and heroine. (I would also include *Crocodile
Dundee* in this category.)

The problem with Jameson's argument is that he situates that
"older period" literally in the past; he does not consider the possibility that all generations may have similar longings (although often tempered with cynicism), and that the cinema, along with other
forms of popular culture, addresses these longings in different ways
and through different filmic modes across the decades. It is difficult
to see how Jameson could embark on such an analysis without considering the theoretical work already undertaken by feminism in
this area in relation to questions of desire and the construction of
sexual difference in the cinema.

Jameson's discussion of the history/nostalgia film also suffers
from a similar lack. Given Lyotard's comments about the attempts

of the patriarchal order to disguise the fact that "there is no signifier," isn't it possible that the "missing past" which lies at the heart
of these films is that which once validated the paternal signifier?
Significantly, at least three of the films quoted by Jameson, *Chinatown, The Conformist* and *Body Heat,* belong to the category of *film
noir,* a genre which deliberately plays with the notion of the *femme
fatale,* the phallic mother whose image constantly threatens to undermine the phallocentric order and turn son against father. In
each of these remakes the male protagonist fails in his self-
appointed task, largely because the patriarchal symbolic, the Law,
has also failed—reduced already to the status of just one "class"
among many, to cite Lyotard again. In *Chinatown* (the title itself is
used as a metaphor for corruption at all levels of city government),
all characters—including the hero—have a "past." The possibility of
incest, symbolically alluded to in the '40s *noir* film, has become a
reality in *Chinatown;* it signifies the complete failure of the symbolic order. In *The Conformist* the four symbolic fathers (Italo,
Quadri, Mussolini and the hero's own "mad" father) all signify the
end of an order and a failure of "truth" suggested by the myth of
Plato's cave[13]; while *Body Heat* alludes continuously, through its
references to earlier *films noirs,* to the failure of the paternal figure
and the power of the phallic mother.

In her discussion of the differences between French and North
American versions of gynesis, Jardine argues that contemporary
texts by male writers in North America have not been influenced by
gynesis as an "abstract, conceptual process." "Gynesis—the putting
into discourse of 'woman' or the 'feminine' as problematic—seems to
exist here only at the level of *representation.* It has, in a sense, been
externalized rather than internalized, and thematized rather than
practiced. . . . " (236). In a footnote, she adds: "In some ways, the
American version of gynesis is more prevalent in 'popular culture'
than it is in 'high theory'—especially in film." We can see this process at work in Jameson's postmodern filmography.

III. Gynesis, Postmodernism and The Sci-fi Horror Film

Jardine maintains that within gynesis the "feminine" signifies, not
woman herself, but those "spaces" which could be said to conceptualize the master narrative's own "non-knowledge," that area over
which the narrative has lost control. This is the unknown, the terrifying, the monstrous—everything which is not held in place by

concepts such as Man, Truth, Meaning. Interestingly, she does not claim that this situation is new; in fact, she stresses the importance of remembering:

> That of all the words used to designate this space (now unbound)—nature, Other, matter, unconscious, madness, hylé, force—have throughout the tenure of Western philosophy carried feminine connotations (whatever their grammatical gender). . . . Those connotations go back, at the very least, to Plato's chora. Julia Kristeva has pointed out that space in general has always connoted the female: "Father's Time, mother's species," as Joyce put it; and, indeed, when evoking the name and destiny of women, one thinks more of the space generating and forming the human species than of time, becoming, or history. (88–89)

The sci-fi horror film's current interest in the maternal body and processes of birth points to changes taking place on several fronts. Among the most important of these are the developments taking place in reproductive technology which have put into crisis questions of the subject, the body and the unconscious. Lyotard draws attention to this. In a discussion on architecture and the postmodern, he speaks of the fact that the mother's body, the infant's first home, is under threat; given the possibility of birth taking place in an artificial womb, we may well in our lifetimes witness the "disappearance of that first dwelling."

> My question is the following: the body is to my mind an essential site of resistance, because with the body there is love, a certain presence of the past, a capacity to reflect, singularity—if this body is attacked, by techno-science, then that site of resistance can be attacked. What is the unconscious of a child engendered in vitro? What is its relationship with the mother and with the father?[14]

The sci-fi horror film, I would argue, is using the body of woman not only to explore these possibilities in a literal sense but also as a metaphor for the uncertainty of the future—the new, unknown, potentially creative and potentially destructive future. The threat offered by the "alien" creature, particularly the alien that impregnates woman, is also one of an uncertain future. The theme of birth and the possibility of new modes of conception and procreation is, of course, not new to science fiction. Over the decades the sci-fi horror film has dealt with scientific alternatives to human conception (the Frankenstein films); other modes of sexual reproduction *(Invasion of the Body Snatchers);* parthenogenetic modes of conception *(The Thing);* cloning *(The Boys from Brazil);* the transformation of robots into human beings *(D.A.R.Y.L.);* and the impregnation of women by aliens *(I Married a Monster From Outer Space, Village of the Damned, Xtro, Inseminoid).* There is even a soft-porn film based on the latter—a deliberate parody of *Xtro* called *Wham Bang! Thank You Mr Spaceman.*

In more recent years, as experiments with reproductive technology have begun to make enormous headway, the sci-fi horror film has become increasingly preoccupied with alternative forms of the conception-gestation-birth process. One of the most interesting and significant developments in the genre has been a concentration on imagery connected with the female reproductive cycle. The latter is most thoroughly explored in films such as *Xtro, Dune, Blue Velvet, Inseminoid,* the John Carpenter remake of *The Thing, Alien* and *Aliens.* A study of these films, particularly the last three, reveals a fascination with the maternal body—its inner and outer appearance, its functions, its awesome powers. In many of these texts, it is not the body of the human/earth woman which is being explored but rather the "bodies" of female alien creatures whose reproductive systems both resemble the human and are coded as a source of abject horror and overpowering awe. In the final scenes of *Aliens* we confront the Mother Alien—a monstrous, deadly procreative machine, prepared to protect her young at all costs—primitive, amoral, female. In the two *Alien* films, this coding is taken to extremes—virtually all aspects of the *mise-en-scène* are designed to signify the female: womb-like interiors, fallopian-tube corridors, small claustrophobic spaces.

Xtro pushed the birth-potential of woman's body to extremes; woman is impregnated by an alien, and a short time later gives birth to a fully-grown man. Here, the body becomes a site of the "unknown"—physically capable of mating with "other," able to expand like a balloon, without physical limits. In *Inseminoid,* woman is impregnated by an alien, later giving birth to two monstrous half-human twins who, it is indicated, will eventually return to Earth and wreak havoc on the planet. In the remake of *The Fly,* the heroine wakes up from a nightmare in which she sees herself giving birth to a giant maggot. In *The Brood,* woman gives birth to a monstrous brood of dwarf children in a symbolic materialization of her inner rage. Her womb is a large sac attached to the side of her stomach. In the final scenes, when her husband secretly watches a birth, he is repelled and disgusted, particularly when she bites through the umbilical cord and looks up at him, her face smeared with blood. In *Aliens* human bodies become nests for alien embryos; when the alien infant is ready to hatch it gnaws its way through the stomach. The human body, both male and female, has become a cocoon for a hostile life form. Why this preoccupation with the maternal body, processes of birth, monstrous offspring, the alien nature of woman, her maternal powers—and most recently the representation of the male body as "womb"? I would argue it is because the body, particularly woman's body, through the process of gynesis, has come to signify the spaces of the unknown, the terrifying, the monstrous. This would register Lyotard's concern about the body losing its capacity to function as "an essential site of resistance"—clearly a postmodern anxiety.

I think we can also see this process of gynesis at work in the cinema's increasing preoccupation with the theme of "becoming woman"—literally. If a collapse of the symbolic function gives rise to what Jardine describes as "an inability of words to give form to the world" then this may well lead to a struggle to control that which has discredited the paternal function—the "space which has begun to threaten all forms of authorship (paternity)." The new theoretical discourses (feminism? postmodernism?) which have begun to take the place of the master discourses, seeing themselves as no longer in "a system of loans and debts to former master truths" have, according to Jardine, begun to conceptualize a new space, that of woman (p 100).

The theme of "becoming woman" is explored symbolically in the horror film *(Psycho, Dressed to Kill)* and literally in those sci-fi films in which man either gives birth to "another" *(Alien and Aliens)* or in which he gives birth to himself *(Altered States, The Terminator)* or to himself as another life form *(The Thing, The Fly)*. I am not suggesting that this is a new theme; it is dealt with in all the mad-scientist films in which man attempts to create his own life forms in the laboratory—the scientist as Mother/God. However, in the contemporary text, there has been an intensification in the exploration of "becoming woman." Most critical articles written on cross-dressing in the cinema rarely consider the possibility that man, at an unconscious level, may well desire to "become woman" *(Tootsie, Some Like It Hot)*. In France this possibility is treated with seriousness—a male poet must become a woman in order to write. Deleuze and Gauttari, of course, have written at length about the whole world "becoming woman," although this again has little to do with actual women.

In her article on postmodern theory, "The Terror of Pleasure,"[15] Tania Modleski analyses *Videodrome* in these terms; the hero having been subjected to "massive doses of a video signal" not only discovers he can no longer distinguish reality from fantasy but also that his body, completely unable to resist attack, has become a video terminal. Modleski draws attention to the fact that the wound which opens up in his stomach, into which the video cassette is inserted, is "gaping" and "vagina-like." He has become—to cite Baudrillard—"a pure screen, a switching center for all the networks of influence."[16]

Modleski—and Pete Boss[17] in the "Body Horror" issue of *Screen*—sees films such as these, in which there is a breakdown in distinctions between subject and object, as postmodern. The individual is a prey to everything, unable to produce the limits of his own body or being. In defining the postmodern, Boss argues that the "categories of Otherness which traditionally functioned in the horror film are no longer adequate,"[18] a distinction which I think—in the light of Jardine's work—needs further qualification. Traditional concepts of Otherness may currently be rejected (or embraced?), yet they may well emerge in a new form. It is relevant to note that the male protagonist of *Videodrome* also inserts his gun into the vagina-like wound in his stomach—his gun as symbolic phallus, like the cassette, signifies a different narrative, one in which he is man violating himself-as-woman. Significantly, his desire to experiment with videodrome was aroused by the masochistic desires of his female lover. He eventually takes her desires as his own. Clearly, one way of analyzing the process in which man becomes woman is to regard it, from a male perspective, as the ultimate scenario of powerlessness, the ultimate violation of the body. In *Alien* the scenes in which man "conceives" and gives birth through his stomach are represented as major scenarios of horror: the oral "impregnation" of the man, the details of the birth scene, his pain, the savage tearing apart of his stomach, the horrified faces of the crew—all of these are shown in graphic detail.

In Cronenberg's *The Fly*, a witty pastiche of the horror genre, "becoming woman" is represented as a true metamorphosis comparable to the one in Kafka's novel. When a woman appears on the scene, the male scientist suddenly realizes why his experiments are not working—he is ignorant of the flesh, the body. Woman signifies carnal pleasure: man is intellectual, remote from the body. She awakens his libido, he is able to progress with his research. Not until he begins the metamorphosis does he experience bodily pleasures to the full. Through the metaphor of the body, the film draws parallels between the woman and the fly—reinforced by the night-mare in which she gives birth to a gigantic maggot. The film plays continually with audience expectations of "bad taste" and always manages to go one step further. In the final scene the connections are developed through the *mise-en-scène*. The metamorphosis is complete and the giant insect advances menacingly towards the "castrated" male victim (he has lost several limbs), recalling a sim-ilar scene from *The Incredible Shrinking Man* in which the hero falls victim to a giant black spider—compared through cross-cutting with his wife. Through the early stages of the metamorpho-sis, the fly is referred to as the "Brundle-fly"—it is a cross between man and fly. Not until the metamorphosis is complete does man fully signify the female—a monstrous fetishised insect. Interest-ingly, Jardine in her discussion of the process of becoming woman in the texts of French male writers, particularly Deleuze and Guattari, refers to a metamorphosis.

> For what is involved here is le devenir femme de tout le monde, the becoming woman of everyone, everything, the whole world. With D&G, "to become woman" is less a metaphor for describ-ing a certain social or textual process than a true metamor-phosis—one thinks of Kafka's Gregor Samsa waking up as a bug. (214–215)

IV. Feminism and Gynesis: The Search for The Mother

> The interrogative return to the sources of our knowledge in the West has involved an obligatory return to the mother's body— a female body, no matter how unrecognizable; no matter how hysterical, textual, inanimate, or actual.—
>
> *Gynesis*, p 237.

Throughout her book Jardine distinguishes between texts of gyne-sis written by men and texts by women, although she primarily ad-dresses herself to the former. In her final chapters, she draws attention to the fact that most of the significant women writers and theorists in France are also involved in the re-working of "male" and "female" in a process of gynesis. She raises, but does not answer, the question of whether or not they are writing "woman" differently. Whatever the answer to this question, one thing is certain—in the writings of French women theorists we can clearly discern what might be described as "a quest for the mother." This search is evident in Kristeva's work on the "semiotic chora," Irigaray's concept of woman and "two-lipped discourse" and Cixous's theory of "feminine writing." Such a search is an ancient theme—the mother Demeter's search for her daughter Persephone. This narrative has also been explored in the cinema *(Marnie, Mildred Pierce, Imitation of Life, Now Voyager)* but not until recently, with the release of *Aliens,* has the mother-daughter quest been represented from a perspective other than that of the paternal signifier.

Like Demeter, Ripley (Sigourney Weaver), the heroine of *Aliens,* enters the underworld in order to search for Newt, her missing "surrogate" daughter who has been snatched away by the Queen of Hell—the Mother Alien. The quest splits the feminine into "bad" (Alien) and "good" (Ripley) mothers: in the final combat, Ripley confronts the monstrous mother whom she must destroy if she is to save her "daughter" and herself. None of the three stands in a biological relation with either of the others; the configurations of the mother-daughter constellations are multiply, and contradictorily, symbolic. It is the lethal Mother Alien who bears children (Ripley has none of her own) yet threatens Newt. Occupying the place conventionally assigned to the hero, Ripley must eventually confront the Queen Alien—a contemporary version of the Sphinx.

Mother Alien, half-human and half-creature, embodies the narrative enigma. She is revealed as the source of the terror and the key to the film's mystery. Where are the aliens coming from? What are their origins? Can the source be destroyed? Can their birth processes be stopped? Like Oedipus, Ripley must encounter the Sphinx but not on the road to Thebes. The confrontation takes place in the Mother's incubation chamber, where Ripley watches in horror as countless eggs drop from the Alien's enormous ovipositor. In the combat that follows, Ripley launches a series of grenades into the Mother's egg sac, tearing it apart from within. Finally, her vast incubator in a state of total destruction, the floor littered with broken eggs, the enraged Mother pursues Ripley and Newt. The "scene of creation" has been destroyed. On her journey of self-discovery, Ripley has encountered the generative aspect of femininity and demolished it. She has annihilated the biological definition of motherhood (woman-as-breeding-machine). Has Ripley, the woman-hero, been enlisted to destroy "herself" in the interests of a new society where birth is under the control of science and technology? If we draw the parallel between the two monstrous creatures still closer, we could argue that the Alien, like the Sphinx, is the origin of the plague (birth as an uncontrolled, amoral activity) which is destroying the city. After Oedipus destroyed the Sphinx he then became the source of the plague: does this mean that Ripley, and whatever signifies her "plague," will also threaten the city when she returns to Earth?

Because Ripley is uncertain of her final destination (is she a "new" woman? a mother? both?), positioned as subject (woman-as-hero) encountering herself as "other" (the generative female), signifying the conventional characteristics of both woman ("intuitive," "emotional," "mothering") and man ("brave," "intelligent," "savior"), she emerges as what Vladimir Propp has described as a "hybrid" figure.[19] Ripley is a heroine whose representation derives from a period of profound social and cultural change; she embodies both male and female gender characteristics with ease and intelligence. Her representation does not involve simple role reversal, a factor made clear by the contrasted figure of the tough woman trooper, Vasquez (Jenette Goldstein) who is more heroic than most of the men. *Aliens* is extremely self-conscious about its play with gender roles—and funny: in the final scenes the only "man" at Ripley's side is the android Bishop, who has been served at the waist by the Mother Alien. He is literally "half-a-man."

It is refreshing to note the increasing tendency in contemporary texts to play with the notion of manhood. Figures such as Sylvester Stallone and Arnold Schwarzenegger (once described by an Australian critic as "a condom stuffed with walnuts") could only be described as "performing the masculine." Both actors often resemble an anthropomorphized phallus, a phallus with muscles, if you like. (Parodies of a lost ideal or menacing images of an android future?) They are simulacra of an exaggerated masculinity, the original completely lost to sight, a casualty of the failure of the paternal signifier and the current crisis in master narratives.

Here it is relevant to note that the process of "becoming woman" does have a related, although not identical counterpart in the increasing emphasis on the androgynous figure in popular culture (Boy George, Laurie Anderson) and the woman/man in the cinema *(Victor/Victoria, Second Serve)*. Once again this is not new— cults of the androgyne have occurred throughout history. In sixteenth century Venice, the authorities became so concerned with the fashion in women's clothing and hairstyle that they passed a law forbidding gender confusion of this kind with the threat of excommunication.[20] Lyotard argues that the creation of a social-psychological androgyne is one of the major goals of a society organized around the continual circulation of exchange objects. But this postmodern fascination with the androgyne and the "neuter" subject may indicate a desire *not* to address problems associated with the specificities of the oppressive gender roles of patriarchal society, particularly those constructed for women. The postmodern fascination with the "new," with breaking down boundaries, could well prove inimical to the development of theory if the "old" is denied proper analysis and understanding.

V. Conclusions

In her final chapters, Jardine argues that it would be "a fatal mistake" for feminism to ignore or dismiss modernity as just "one more 'male concept,' participated in and theorized and fictionalized by men, for men" (p 257). Not only would such a stance increase "the dangers of anachronism"—the feminist repetition of the humanist errors of the modern period, recentering a Cartesian Woman Subject, with Woman's Truth and Woman's History—it would also close down the possibilities of "developing radically new fields of conceptuality essential to feminist theory and practice today" (p 258). While I agree with Jardine that either tactic would indeed be a "fatal mistake," I am not convinced that for "modernity and feminism to unite in their efforts" is necessarily the answer.

Jardine doesn't specify the terms of this alliance, but one can foresee major problems. First, any attempt to assimilate feminism to postmodernism may well result in a confusion over terms, as revealed in the way in which Lyotard's notion of the grand narrative has been misleadingly reduced to "master" narrative; such confusion only serves to undermine the specificities of the positions of both feminism and postmodernism. Second, I have attempted to demonstrate, some theorists of the postmodern—such as Jameson—have been completely indifferent to feminism and its theorization of the current crisis; this has resulted, in some instances, in an inadequate analysis of the postmodern film. Third, writers such as Owens, in his attempt to "introduce" feminism into the postmodern debate, do so in terms which situate feminism as if it were a "guest," the other brought in from the cold to join the "host." Owens never considers the possibility that feminist theory may not see itself as marginal to postmodernism and wish to join the club. Fourth, according to my reading of the changes presently occurring in the cinema, the crisis of the master narratives may not necessarily benefit women. Nor, even if there is a process of gynesis at work in the cinema, particularly in the sci-fi horror film, is it yet clear whether this also will be of benefit to women. At the moment it is too early to predict future directions. As Jardine states repeatedly throughout her study, questions concerning the relationship of women to the processes of modernity "may be unanswerable for some time to come" (p 117): gynesis, as written by men, could well prove to be a "new ruse of reason."

Finally, it may be possible that postmodern theory is more in debt to feminism than it is prepared to acknowledge. Jardine discusses the work of Rosa Braidotti, who argues that historical crisis in the West's systems of knowledge have occurred when women have played a more prominent—some would argue decisive—role in periods of change. Jardine refers to at least three epochs in which it is possible to specify such an historical "coincidence": the transition between the Middle Ages and the Renaissance—the period of the famous *Querelle des femmes;* the time of the French Revolution and the Saint-Simoniens; and the present crisis ushered in by the events of post-1968 France which occurred simultaneously with the rise of the women's movement. Jardine suggests an hypothesis: "might it not be that a series of if not causal at least etiological links could be established between those periods in the West when women were most vocally polemical and those so called 'epistemological breaks'?" (93).

The title of this article was originally intended to designate the strategy of a feminism speaking from a position not identical to that which Jardine calls "modernity" and others "postmodernism." I wanted to keep a tension, a space between the two. Having travelled a little way down the road, trying to negotiate Craig Owens's "treacherous course," I am glad I did not try to unite them. Any attempt to speak from a "place" is immediately rendered problematic by the fact that one of the positions central to postmodernism is that there are no places left from which to speak—there are no "Truths," "Beliefs," or "Positions." Yet, this is in itself a position, and one now in danger of becoming a new orthodoxy. Even, perhaps, a master discourse? The paradox in which we feminists find ourselves is that while we regard patriarchal discourses as fictions, we nevertheless proceed as if our position, based on a belief in the oppression of women, were somewhat closer to the truth. Perhaps Lyotard is "correct" *(sic)* to recommend at least the provisional abandonment of all "Truths" in favor of the short narratives which the master discourses have attempted to suppress in order to validate their own positions. It would therefore be crucial that any theoretical discourse which emerges from the current crisis should not attempt to explain "everything," to become a totalizing theory, be it feminism *or* postmodernism.

Notes

1. Craig Owens, "The Discourse of Others: Feminists and Post-modernism" in Hal Foster (ed), *The Anti-Aesthetic, Essays on Postmodern Culture*, USA, Bay Press, 1983, p 59. All page citations will be concluded in the text.

2. Alice Jardine, *Gynesis, Configurations of Woman and Modernity*, Ithaca and London, Cornell University Press, 1985. All page citations will be included in the text.

3. Jean-François Lyotard, *The Postmodern Condition: a Report on Knowledge*, Theory and History of Literature, Vol 10, Manchester University Press, 1984.

4. Jean-François Lyotard, "Defining The Postmodern," *Postmodernism*, ICA Documents 4, London, 1986, p 6.

5. ibid, p 6.

6. Jean-François Lyotard, *The Postmodern Condition*, op cit, p 37.

7. Craig Owens, op cit, p 65.

8. Meaghan Morris, "Postmodernity and Lyotard's Sublime", *Art & Text*, 16, Summer, 1984/5, p 51.

9. (Jardine notes that feminist film theory, unlike many other feminist areas, has already addressed itself to postmodern theory, op cit, p 75). See Laura Mulvey, "Visual Pleasure and Narrative Cinema," *Screen*, Autumn 1975, vol 16 no 3, pp 6–18; and "Afterthoughts on 'Visual Pleasure and Narrative Cinema'... Inspired by *Duel in The Sun*," *Framework*, 15/16/17, 1981, pp 12–15.

10. Fredric Jameson, "Postmodernism, or the Cultural Logic of Late Capitalism," *New Left Review*, no 146, July-August, 1984, p 66.

11. ibid, pp 67 and 68.

12. Fredric Jameson, "Postmodernism and Consumer Society" in Hal Foster (ed), *The Anti-Aesthetic*, op cit, p 116.

13. See Luce Irigaray's *Speculum of the Other Woman*, Ithaca, NY, Cornell University Press, 1985, for a fascinating reinterpretation of Plato's myth of the cave.

14. Jean-François Lyotard, "A Response To Kenneth Frampton," *Postmodernism*, op cit, p 31.

15. Tania Modleski, "The Terror of Pleasure, The Contemporary Horror Film" in Tania Modleski (ed), *Studies in Entertainment, Critical Approaches to Mass Culture*, Indiana University Press, 1986.

16. Jean Baudrillard, "The Ecstasy of Communication," Hal Foster (ed), *The Anti-Aesthetic,* op cit, p 133.

17. Pete Boss, "Vile Bodies and Bad Medicine," *Screen,* Jan-Feb 1986, vol 27 no 1, pp 14–24.

18. ibid, p 24.

19. For a commentary on this, see Teresa de Lauretis, *Alice Doesn't: Feminism, Semionics, Cinema,* Indiana University Press, 1984, pp 113–116.

20. Judith C. Brown, *Immodest Acts, The Life of a Lesbian Nun in Renaissance Italy,* Oxford University Press, 1986, p 204.

Excerpts from *Thinking Fragments*

Jane Flax

Gender: Its Absence and Effects in and on Postmodernist Spaces

Postmodernist discourses, or even commentaries about them, notably lack any serious discussion of feminist theories, even when these
theories overlap with, supplement, or support postmodernist writers' ideas. Rorty's work, for example, contains no references to the
feminist critiques of philosophy or to the feminist discussions of science and philosophies of science that parallel and would enhance
his own. The exclusion of any consideration of gender relations has
political and intellectual consequences for Rorty's work. It contributes to his sense of smugness about and mystification of "our"
postmodernist bourgeois culture. The identity of this "our" is never
clear. Rorty never specifies whose practices and experiences, said to
be constitutive of this culture, are included within its parameters.
The problem of inequality is excluded from Rorty's pragmatism.
Feminists and those concerned about relations of domination such
as racism must be concerned with the possibility that incommensurable and unequal forms of life exist in any apparently singular culture. Rorty does mention that our culture includes many

Jane Flax, *Thinking Fragments: Psychoanalysis, Feminism, and Postmodernism in the Contemporary West,* pp. 210–216 Copyright © 1989 The
Regents of the University of California. Reprinted by permission.

different communities. However he never systematically explores the possibility that some of these communities are enmeshed in systematic and pervasive relations of domination. Despite his emphasis on the historically specific and pragmatic basis of all thought, he fails to acknowledge that in one culture the experiences of some persons or groups may be radically different from those of another. In such situations a problem is how to develop a capacity to engage in empathic translation rather than "conversation." It is misleading and dangerous to assume that everyone is engaged in more or less the same "language game." It is not evident how either systematic biases or constraints within a culture may be acknowledged within, much less resolved by, conversation.[1]

Despite Rorty's emphasis on social and historical constitution of practices and of individuals through these practices, his conversation "partners" have a strangely abstract quality. He does not question what sorts of conversation could exist among fundamentally unequal partners. His partners are never marked by asymmetric social relations. Such relations do not affect and constrain the kinds of moves people make or the kinds of conversations they may imagine, welcome, and sustain. The problems Foucault raises about marginalized and subjected discourses or the critique of consensus that Lyotard offers are ignored. A more feminist sensitivity to gender-based asymmetries would disrupt this form of happy unconsciousness.

Foucault mentions women as one of the subjected or marginalized and resisting elements within contemporary culture. He stresses the need to pay attention to the minute, local, and differentiated forms of events and power that are said to constitute "history." However he does not consider the feminist claim that in important ways the histories of men and women are themselves differentiated and heterogeneous. Foucault's histories seem totally uninformed by any awareness of feminist narratives of his major subjects (e.g., sexuality and biopower). Systematic consideration of gender relations would profoundly affect his genealogies of sexuality, subjectivity, power, and knowledge.[2] Many of his historical claims appear problematic when juxtaposed against feminist narratives. For example, his notion of biopower as a uniquely modern form of power runs contrary to many feminist accounts of history. According to these accounts, women's bodies have always, although in many different ways, been "colonized" by the intersection of knowledge and power.[3] Struggles around conceptualization and control of women's bodies have been a predominant but historically variable feature in all cultures. Perhaps what distinguishes modern culture is not the introduction of biopower per se, but rather the extensions of this power (in old and new forms) to different groups of men as well as women.

The absence of any systematic consideration of gender is especially puzzling because Foucault claims to be writing "histories of the present" that will in some way be useful to marginalized groups. From a feminist perspective no compelling history of the present could ignore the centrality of relations of gender and the struggles about them that reemerged in full force in the late 1960s.

Derrida's treatment of gender is also problematic. He claims one of the asymmetric and false dichotomies produced by the violence of metaphysics is that of man/woman. A deconstructive reading of this discourse would first reverse the asymmetry of the pair. Writing should effect a transvaluation of values. The qualities attributed to or associated with "woman" should be rescued from the ordinary phallocentric concept of them (e.g., the body would be exalted over the mind, feeling over thought, the preoedipal over the oedipal, the mother over the father, pleasure over work and production, the noncultural [other] over culture, style over truth). In these reversals one would begin to "read like a woman." "Woman" operates "outside" and disrupts the metaphysics, logic, and concepts of phallocentric culture. "Out of the depths, endless and unfathomable, she engulfs and distorts all vestige of essentiality, of identity, or property. And the philosophical discourses blinded, founders on these shoals and is hurled down these depthless depths to its ruin."[4]

Reversal, of course, is not sufficient. A "positive" deconstruction of the man/woman pair must also be effected. Woman (and man) and sexual difference itself must be disconnected from any historical, specific, or biological referent. Woman must be deessentialized and set to play among other equally nonnecessary, nondetermined, and nonreferential signs. "There is no such thing as a woman, as a truth in itself of woman in itself." There is also "no truth in itself of the sexual difference in itself."[5]

As sign, woman has the following effects and affects in addition to her generally disruptive character: She is that which will not be pinned down by truth. She is "skepticism, dissimulation, and swirl of veils."[6] She is "too clever to believe in castration or anticastration" (its exact opposite). Thus woman wants nothing to do with feminism, for "feminism too seeks to castrate. It wants a castrated woman, gone with style." Unlike the "masculine dogmatic philosopher," woman renounces any claim to "truth, science and objectivity." She is beyond metaphysics. Her "affirmative" and dionysian power is that "she plays at dissimulation, at ornamentation, deceit, artifice, at an artist's philosophy." By affirming the beyond of metaphysics, the "question of woman suspends the decidable opposition of true and nontrue. . . . Whereupon the question of style is immediately unloosed as a question of writing."[7] Beyond metaphysics woman turns out to be identical or interchangeable with writing, the other, being, the supplement, the trace.

Derrida's deconstruction of woman may seem compatible with aspects of feminist discourse. His move away from biological, essentialist, or nonhistorical concepts of gender appears congruent with the intent of many feminists. Yet his writings make me profoundly uneasy. Derrida's own concepts of woman/gender have a transcendental quality. He poses a constricted set of choices in which woman always ends up signifying "sexual difference," despite his claims to set her free. Derrida asserts that most concepts of woman are essentialist and wrong. The only alternative is concepts of woman that have no referent to any historical, specific beings constituted by and through differentiated sets of social experience. Woman as writing/other/style is "outside" all concrete history and bodily experience or determination. This set of choices excludes the possibility of considering differences as arising out of nontextual and historical as well as race and class differentiated experiences. The specificity of being woman in locatable and discrete cultures is lost. The lack of a historical and social consideration of woman also leads to an obscuring of her constitution in relations of domination that have not ceased to exist whether or not she "affirms" artifice and style.

Women in modern Western culture occupy "*a specific liminal cultural position* which is through a tangled skein of mediations somehow connected to their anatomical difference, to their femaleness." Derrida's elimination from consideration of concrete, historical female differences in time forecloses exploration of a space that has only begun to be explored: "the pitch black continent of what patriarchal culture has consistently connoted as feminine and hence depreciated." Even if cultural criticism has such power, it is too soon to tear down the "ghetto where the feminine has been confined and demeaned, we need to map its boundaries and excavate its foundations in order to salvage the usable relics and refuse of patriarchy, for to do so is perhaps the only chance we have to construct a post-deconstructionist society which will not simply reduplicate our own."[8]

There is another problem with Derrida's approach. It seems to replicate woman's place as the undifferentiated other to man rather than to conceptualize both man and woman as constituted by and existing within historically discrete systems of gender relations.

There is no internal deconstruction of the concept "woman" so that the many differences among women could be spoken. Instead woman is confounded with so many other complex categories (writing, style, being, other) that such deconstruction becomes even more difficult.

Consideration of "man's" fantasies about women or the effects on him of defining himself in relation to the other/woman is also lacking. Despite the rhetoric of "reading like a woman" or displacing "phallocentrism," postmodernists are unaware of the deeply gendered nature of their own recounting and interpretations of the Western story and the strategies they oppose to its master narratives. Postmodernists still honor Man as the sole author and principal character in these stories, even if this Man is dying, his time running out. They retell the contemporary history of the West in and through the stories of the three deaths—of Man, (his) History, and (his) metaphysics. Whatever women have done with and in all this (becoming past) time is "outside" by definition and according to the conventions of (their) story line.

Postmodernists do not question whether woman "is" the "excess," the "margin," or the "supplement" only by virtue of and as an effect of (still) being placed within phallocentric discourse and culture. This "effect" is not produced by and is not a consequence of the structure of "language" (or its "binary" logic) or the inescapability of "intertextuality." It is produced by the logic and dynamics of contemporary gender systems and identities, including the repression and denial of women's acts of agency and mastery, even by the writers of postmodern "texts." One of the grounds of possibility for and consequences of phallocentrism *is* the repression and denial of such acts.

However, rather than "deconstruct" such acts of repression, Derrida builds a theory out of and on top of them. If he really wanted to effect a reversal of or to deessentialize the pair man/woman, he could assign to "man" the characteristics stereotypically associated with "woman": style, artifice, and so forth. However, as in the similar case of Lacan, the coherence and plausibility of Derrida's discourses depend on the *congruence* of the qualities he assigns to woman and the pervasive social meanings associated with her.

Stripped of its wordplay, its opaque, narcissistic rhetoric, Derrida's writings echo phallocentric metaphysics. Minds and bodies are two completely distinct entities. Those who engage in rational thought are inscribed on the side of masculinity and culture. Yet one can become woman without having a female body. Through writing some may elude the phallocentrism that imprisons the others.

Woman's "style" is dangerous to culture because it has been outside it. Woman/writing/the other is thus the unthinkable, mystical, dionysian force outside or beyond time. She is the Real, the disorder men have sought to both subdue and possess in the course of constructing rationality, truth, and culture.

In fact there is nothing new or "postmodern" in such claims. Similar themes have recurred in Western philosophy, for example, in the work of Plato or Rousseau.[9] What is still "absent" (forbidden) is the incorporation of "woman" *qua* embodied, desiring, and concrete and differentiated being(s) *within* culture, language, ruling, or thinking *on our own terms* and not as man's "other," "Object of desire," or linguistic construct. The "postmodernist" woman is in the same position as Emile's Sophie. Sophie is good because she is outside politics and her "goodness" (outside) is necessary to the preservation of culture and man's selfhood.[10] The major difference I can see between Rousseau's position and that of Derrida is he wants to identify, read like, become, or (at least) openly envies woman *as he has defined her.* He still does not want her to speak for herself or, as Irigaray points out, among her or ourselves without him.[11]

Notes

---

1. Richard J. Bernstein, "Philosophy in the Conversation of Mankind," in Hollinger, *Hermeneutics and Praxis* (Notre Dame, Ind.: University of Notre Dame Press, 1985); Paul A. Bove, "The Ineluctibility of Difference: Scientific Pluralism and the Critical Intelligence," in Arac, *Postmodernism and Politics* (Minneapolis: University of Minnesota Press, 1986); and Cornel West, "The Politics of American Neo-Pragmatism," in *Post-Analytic Philosophy,* ed. John Rajchman and Cornel West (New York: Columbia University Press, 1985), discuss this problem from nonfeminist viewpoints.

2. Kathy Ferguson's work suggests some of the alterations that would result. See especially her *The Feminist Case Against Bureaucracy* (Philadelphia: Temple University Press, 1984), chap. 2.

3. It would be interesting, for example, to compare Linda Gordon, *Woman's Body, Woman's Right: A Social History of Birth Control in America* (New York: Viking Press, 1976), with Foucault's methods and histories in relation to gender; see also Ferguson, *The Feminist Case,* especially the preface and chap. 5; and Susan Rubin Suleiman, ed., *The Female Body in Western Culture* (Cambridge, Mass.: Harvard University Press, 1985).

4. Jacques Derrida, *Spurs: Nietzsche's Styles,* trans. Barbara Harlow (Chicago: University of Chicago Press, 1979), p. 51. My reading of this text has benefited from Jardine's analysis of it in *Gynesis,* chap. 9. However I find her reading insufficiently critical of the gendered nature of Derrida's categories.

5. Derrida, *Spurs,* pp. 101, 103.

6. Alice Jardine, *Gynesis,* (Ithaca, NY: Cornell University Press, 1985) p. 194.

7. Derrida, *Spurs,* pp. 61, 65, 67, 107.

8. Naomi Schor, "Dreaming Dissymmetry," in *Men in Feminism* (New York: Methuen, 1987) p. 110.

9. For a discussion of Plato, cf. Luce Irigaray, *Speculum of the Other Woman,* trans. Gillian C. Gill (Ithaca, N.Y.: Cornell University Press, 1985), especially "Plato's Hysteria." On Rousseau cf. Susan Moller Okin, *Women in Western Political Thought* (Princeton, N.J.: Princeton University Press, 1979), especially part 2. I have also discussed the (unconscious) effects of gender relations on Plato and Rousseau's philosophies in Jane Flax, "Political Philosophy and the Patriarchal Unconscious: A Psychoanalytic Perspective on Epistemology and Metaphysics," in *Discovering Reality: Feminist Perspectives on Epistemology, Metaphysics, Methodology and Philosophy of Science,* ed. Sandra Harding and Merill Hintikka (Boston: D. Reidel, 1983).

10. Cf. Susan Okin, *Women in Western Political Thought* (Princeton: Princeton University Press, 1992) for an extended discussion of this point.

11. Luce Irigaray, "Commodities Among Themselves," in Luce Irigaray, *This Sex Which Is Not One,* trans. Catherine Porter (Ithaca, N.Y.: Cornell University Press, 1985).

Modernism's Last Post

Stephen Slemon

"The remedy for decadence is a journey to the frontier."

David Trotter, "Modernism and Empire"

Perhaps the only point of consensus in the debate over "postmodernism" is that the defining term of this apparently contemporary phenomenon inherently posits for Euro-American culture some kind of "radical break" from the discourse of "modernism" as it developed at the end of the nineteenth century (Jameson, 53). The accuracy of this hypothesis in nomenclature, the cultural specificity of this semiotic "break," the discursive and ideological purchase of this new social episteme—these, of course, are immense issues, and they furnish an exciting theatre for the spectacle of critical disagreement within Western intellectual practice. An important consequence of this debate, however, is that the narrow and prevailing idea of "modernism" itself is at last being systematically reworked to reveal a foundation for contemporary First World representation not simply in a radically vanguardist and anti-bourgeois movement (Wortman, 175), but rather in the wholesale appropriation and refiguration of non-Western artistic and cultural practices by a

Stephen Slemon, "Modernism's Last Post," *Ariel* 20:4 pp. 3–17 Copyright 1989, The University of Calgary. Reprinted by permission.

society utterly committed to the preservation of its traditional prerogatives for gender, race and class privilege. In its debate over the genealogy of the postmodern problematic, Western culture is coming to understand that—as Ashis Nandy puts it (xiv)—the "armed version" of modernism *is* colonialism itself, and that modernism's most heroically self-privileging figurative strategies—its "fragmentation of textual unity," its "play of contradictory genres," its antinormative aestheticizing impulse (Frow, 117)—would have been unthinkable had it not been for the assimilative power of Empire to appropriate the cultural work of a heterogeneous world "out there" and to reproduce it for its own social and discursive ends.[1]

It would seem natural, therefore, that the two critical discourses which today constitute themselves specifically in opposition to this historical conjunction would have forged for themselves a strong affiliative network of methodological collaboration. But except for the general project of anti-colonialist critique as it is taken up by post-structuralist or new historicist theorists—the most well known of whom are Gayatri Chakravorty Spivak, Homi Bhabha, Peter Hulme, and Stephen Greenblatt—post-modernist theory and post-colonial criticism have remained more or less separate in their strategies and their foundational assumptions. Why these two critical projects should remain asymmetrical is thus a matter of great interest, and what I would like to do in this short paper is attempt to situate at least one of the major fault-lines that runs between them. Needless to say, the astonishing variety in critical activity taking place *within* each of these two projects means that any such attempt will necessarily overreach itself. . . . I proceed in the understanding that what follows is at best a form of critical piece-work: provisional, interrogative, and most of all, motivated within an ongoing critical struggle over the political terrain of textual interpretation.

As almost all commentators like to point out, definitions of postmodernism tend to situate the "phenomenon" somewhere between two absolute positions, the first of which understands postmodernism as a culturally specific historical *period,* and the second of which understands it as a *style* of representation that runs, albeit with important differences, across various artistic media. In the first camp are theorists such as Fredric Jameson, for whom "postmodernism" signifies the pastiche energetics of Western society under late capitalism, where a "new depthlessness" in representation—one grounded in the fetishization of the image as simulacrum—marks off a profoundly ahistorical drive which seeks to efface the past as "referent" and leave behind itself nothing but "texts" (53–66). In the second camp are theorists such as Ihab Hassan and Michael Newman, for whom the "postmodern" can be captured in a catalogue of figurative propensities (indeterminacy, multivalence, hybridization, etc.) whose ludic celebrations of representational freedom—as J. G. Merquior points out (17)—are grounded in a "dubious analogy" between artistic experimentation and social liberation. My reading in the postmodern debate is limited, but to my mind the most interesting theorist to take on the conjunction between these two general approaches is Linda Hutcheon, who rejects not only the assumption that postmodern representation provides in any single sense "the background hum for power" (see Kariel, 97), as the first camp would argue, but also the assumption that postmodernism can accurately "describe an international cultural phenomenon" (4), as the second camp seems to imply.

For Hutcheon, postmodernism is a "problematizing force" in Western society (xi) which, far from expressing a straightforward "incredulity with regard to the master narratives" of dominant culture, as Lyotard would have it (Jardine, 65), paradoxically inscribes *and* contests culturally certified codes of recognition and representation. Postmodern culture, art, and theory, for Hutcheon, is inherently contradictory, for it both "uses and abuses, installs and then subverts," the "conventions of discourse" which it sets out to challenge (xiii, 3). As it does so, postmodernism discloses a "contradictory dependence on and independence from that which temporally preceded it and which literally made it possible" (18). Postmodernist discourse, that is, *necessarily* admits a provisionality to its truth-claims (13, 23) and a secondary (or allegorical) foundation to its referential sweep. As Hutcheon sees it, this inherently quotational or reiterative grounding of postmodernism issues into a dominant signifying practice whose central rhetorical strategy is intertextual parody. Postmodern parody, Hutcheon explains, functions "as repetition with critical distance that allows ironic signalling of difference at the very heart of similarity" (26). It "paradoxically enacts both change and cultural continuity" (26). And as it *uses* the strategies of dominant culture to challenge its discursive processes from within (20), postmodern parody *also* reveals its "love of history by giving new meaning to old forms" (31).

Hutcheon's framing of the postmodern field is important, for the general textual practice she defines here resembles—at least on the surface—the kind of reiterative textual energy which for a number of critics marks an especially interesting moment within a broadly post-colonial literary activity. Definitions of the "postcolonial," of course, vary widely, but for me the concept proves most useful not when it is used synonymously with a post-independence historical period in once-colonized nations but rather when it locates a specifically anti- or *post*-colonial *discursive* purchase in culture, one which begins in the moment that colonial power inscribes itself onto the body and space of its Others and which continues as an often occulted tradition into the modern theatre of neocolonialist international relations. A post-colonial *critical* discourse is therefore never wholly absent from colonial culture: there is always at work in the discourses of the colonized a network of disidentificatory traditions which J. Michael Dash has eloquently labelled a "counter-culture of the imagination" (65). But this critical discourse is never fully present as unmediated resistance. Simon During suggests that the "post-colonial" can be located in "the survival of residual forms of economic life" in colonial societies, the "need for an identity granted not in terms of the colonial power, but in terms of themselves" (369); and to the extent that During's definition identifies for colonial subjects what Richard Terdiman has called a "counter-discourse" I agree with it. But whereas During posits a radical split between "post-colonizing" and "postcolonized" forms of a heterogeneous discourse and argues that unreconstituted white settler cultures have no recourse to an "effective postcolonised discourse" (371), I would want to preserve for "postcolonialism" a specifically anti-colonial counter-discursive energy which *also* runs across the ambivalent space of what Alan Lawson has called "second world" societies—a discursive energy which emerges *not* from the inherent cultural contradiction that necessarily marks transplanted settler societies but rather from their continuing yet subterranean tradition of refusal towards the conceptual and cultural apparatuses of the European imperium.[2]

As During points out, a postcolonial "affect" needs always to be specified in relation to, and within, each post-colonial society (369). But in general terms, a post- or anti-colonial critical or disidentificatory discourse can be seen to energize an enormously heterogeneous set of social and representational practices from within a large number of post-colonial (and sometimes, latently, within colonialist) social configurations. *Part* of this larger, differential postcolonial discourse, I would argue, resides in the contemporary poststructuralist project of anti-colonialist critique; another part—the part that concerns me here—operates within post-colonial literary activity. And *one* of the heterogeneous modalities of this postcolonial discourse within post-colonial literary writing is the figuration of a reiterative quotation, or intertextual citation, in relation to colonialist "textuality." This counter-discursive intertextuality in

post-colonial literary writing is in some important ways different
from the writing practice that Hutcheon usefully locates at the centre of the postmodernist project; and in order to specify that different I want now to turn to post-colonial critical practice, and to how
it seeks to establish a specific matrix of cultural resistance within
the rhetorical play of the post-colonial text.

It has often been noted (see, for example, Viswanathan) that
one of colonialism's most salient technologies for social containment
and control is the circulation within colonial cultures of the canonical European literary text. Mediated through the colonialist educational apparatus, the European literary text becomes a powerful
machinery for forging what Gramsci called cultural domination by
consent; and in recognizing this, post-colonial critical discourse
seeks to position the oppositional and reiterative textual responses
of post-colonial cultures in dialectical relation to their colonialist
precursors. Far from articulating a simple "anxiety of influence,"
however, this post-colonial textual reiteration is heard to be speaking directly to the struggle within colonialist ideology. Post-colonial
criticism's key beginning point here, then, is that a "parodic" repetition of imperial "textuality" sets itself specifically in opposition to
the interpellative power of colonialism—a power which interweaves
itself throughout colonial societies, making the imperial culture appear referentially seamless and the colonial culture appear radically fractured—outside the scope of literary "realism" (Bhabha)
and incapable of being "represented" through the imported or imposed structures of transplanted European language. Post-colonial
literary reiteration—or parody, or intertextuality, or quotation—is
thus seen to be challenging directly a colonialist "textual" function;
and this colonialist textual function is *not* seen as being cotermi-
nous with the circulation of textual images in other cultural locations, which are of course in their own ways produced and consumed
ideologically.

There is no single mode for signalling this counter-discursive
energy within post-colonial literary writing. In fact, as post-colonial
critical work continues, it is discovering an enormously differential
and thorough infusion of disidentificatory reiteration across the
various national post-colonial literatures. The most visible area of
this reiterative practice takes place in the post-colonial project of rewriting the canonical "master texts" of Europe—most notably *The
Tempest* and *Robinson Crusoe*—in ways that expose their residual
colonialist politics and that refigure their narratives to a new ideological vector.[3] Another highly salient practice of this kind involves
the figurative invocation of colonialist notions of "history"—as in
texts such as George Lamming's *Natives of My Person* or Patrick

White's *A Fringe of Leaves*—and the juxtaposition of the imperialist "pretext" with a dis/placive "historical" narrative that, as Helen Tiffin points out (31), functions both to interrogate the politics of narrative production within colonial society and to effect a purgative energy (reiteration as a modality of expulsion) against that version of history which implicitly inscribes European hierarchical values into colonial and post-colonial codes of recognition. Christopher Miller has recently brought to light a much less visible mode of this post-colonial counter-discursive activity at work in Yambo Ouloguem's *Le devoir de violence*. Here, Miller argues, Ouloguem's excessive plagiarizing strategy operates as an anti-colonialist assault on European assumptions about originality and mimicry, working against the pretextual domain of "authorial" European writing to raise questions about why, when a unified Western voice is said to "own" language, the colonized subject becomes implicitly constituted within the fracturing semiotics of Empire as a multiple, dispersed copyist, a *négre* or "ghostwriter." And to offer a final example: Ketu H. Katrak has recently argued that a counter-discursive "tactical" assault on colonialist assumptions about representation is at work in the Sistren Collective's use of a West Indian creole or nation language. The linguistic assault in this practice, Katrak argues, needs to be explained in a comprehensive theory of linguistic decolonization; and decolonization, as Fanon has pointed out, needs to be grounded in a practice of *violent* discursive resistance.

It is not hard to see that these post-colonial textual strategies bear a close relation to the principle of intertextual parody which Hutcheon defines for postmodernism. But the first difference here, as I have been arguing, is that the location of textual power as an especially effective technology of colonialist discourse means that post-colonial reiterative writing takes on a discursive specificity. This specificity is important for how we attempt to "theorize" the work of the text, for it leads on to a second difference between a postmodern and post-colonial reading of the text. Whereas a postmodernist criticism would want to argue that literary practices such as these expose the constructedness of *all* textuality and thus call down "the claim to unequivocal domination of one mode of signifying over another" (Johnson, 5), an *interested* post-colonial critical practice would want to allow for the positive production of oppositional truth-claims in these texts. It would retain for post-colonial writing, that is, a mimetic or referential purchase to textuality, and it would recognize in this referential drive the operations of a crucial strategy for survival in marginalized social groups.

This referential assumption would appear to make what I am calling a post-colonial criticism radically fractured and contradictory, for such a criticism would draw on post-structuralism's suspension of the referent in order to read the social "text" of colonialist power at the same time would reinstall the referent in the service of colonized and post-colonial societies. The especial valency of textuality within colonialist discourse, however, means that the "referent" simply cannot be totalized; for if the question of representation really is grounded in a "crisis" within postmodern Western society under late capitalism, in post-colonial critical discourse it necessarily bifurcates under a dual agenda: which is to continue the resistance to (neo-) colonialism through a deconstructive reading of its rhetoric *and* to retrieve and reinscribe those post-colonial social traditions that in literature issue forth on a thematic level, and within a "realist" problematic, as principles of cultural identity and survival. Here is how Craig Tapping describes the second principle in this dual agenda:

> despite theory's refutation of such absolute and logocentric categories as these—"truth" or "meaning," "purpose" or "justification"—the new literatures ... are generated from cultures for whom such terms as "authority" and "truth" are empirically urgent in their demands. Land claims, racial survival, cultural revival: all these demand an understanding of and response to the very concepts and structures which poststructuralist academicians refute in language games, few of which recognize the political struggles of real people outside such discursive frontiers.

This dual—and perhaps "theoretically" contradictory—agenda for post-colonial criticism is grounded, I would argue, in the dual function of post-colonial reiterative texts themselves in the area of cultural work, and in order to establish this point I want to turn briefly to a text which articulates this duality with unusual clarity: *The Death of Tarzana Clayton* by the Jamaican writer Neville Farki.

Postmodernism's catalogue of rhetorical features describes a good deal of Farki's tropological pyrotechnics in this novella, which as the title makes clear is a parodic retelling of Edgar Rice Burroughs's paradigmatically racist fable. *Tarzana Clayton* is fundamentally fragmented and hybridized; it engages overtly in a decentering and decanonizing labour; it is enormously self-reflexive and ironic; it draws obviously and excessively on the devices of "fiction" to demystify imperialist versions of "history"; it "uses and abuses" the received codes of popular culture in order to effect a serious intervention in the production and circulation of majority opinion.

But at the same time—and here Farki's text departs from the postmodernist paradigm—*Tarzana Clayton* retains a recuperative impulse towards the structure of "history" and manifests a Utopian desire grounded in reference. The reiterative portion of the novella is framed by the narrator's account of how the Tarzan story in fact predates its historical moment of ficitonalization by Burroughs, and how the struggle against colonialism—the ideology that is embedded within Tarzan aesthetics—has been continued by historical figures such as Kwame Nkrumah and thus carried forward into the present. And within the reiterative portion of the text, much of Farki's energy is directed towards the reinsertion into history of those acts and figures of anti-colonialist resistance that imperialist forms of representation have systematically left out—at one point in the narrative, for example, Hamum, Farki's exemplary colonial "subject," travels to New York where he hears Marcus Garvey speak. Far from calling down the idea of "history" itself, then, Farki's text works to map over colonialism's false historicism with a reconstituted, "decolonized" sense of historical event, the result being that the apparently anti-referential display of tropological excess in the narrative is grounded to what I see as an underlying post-colonial realist script. Farki—in opposition to the antifoundational claims of postmodern logic—is concerned with the production of an alterior "knowledge" for post-colonial cultures, a knowledge of historical agency in colonized subjects and an awareness that the lived experiences of the Others of Empire offers a thematic touchstone for a continuing resistance to colonialism's power. And so, as the following passage makes clear, the project of reiterating the colonialist "pretext" not only involves the figuration of textual resistance but also the recuperation—the remembering or relearning—of "the role of the native as historical subject and combatant, possessor of another knowledge and producer of alternative traditions" (Parry, 34). Needless to say, the encounter taking place on the character level in this passage is an allegory of the struggle between colonizer and colonized. And the "fiction" being constituted here is both a figuration of a recovered realism and a gesture towards the question of how a "history" of the colonized past might come to be rewritten in the future:

> Tarzan inflicted many wounds on Hamum with the dagger and when he threw the wounded Ashanti to the ground, he bared

his teeth as he moved towards his adversary for the kill. Hamum had learnt that an overly angry or confident attacker was apt to make the fatal mistake of underestimating a cornered enemy. Hamum played limp and completely helpless as Tarzan raised his hand to plunge the long bloodstained blade into his enemy's chest. But Hamum . . . , moving with great agility rose, and like a fleetfooted gazelle, leaped and grasped Tarzan in a fatal hold around his neck. He held his neck with one hand and with the other he held Tarzan's hand with the dagger, thrusting it into the whiteman's stomach several times. As Hamum released his hold slowly, Tarzan's body fell on its face in the road. It was not to be buried and was left as meat for scavengers from the forest and the sky. This was the end of Tarzana Clayton. (62)

I want to stress the proliferation of this dual agenda within post-colonial literary reiteration, and its consequent bifurcation in referential strategy, for it is here, I think, that Western postmodernist readings can so overvalue the antireferential or deconstructive energetics of post-colonial texts that they efface the important recuperative work that is also going on within them. As post-colonial writers and critics have always pointed out, the assumption of "natural" seamlessness within language has never taken hold within colonized territory; for when colonialism transports a language, or imposes it upon a differential world, a fracturing, indeterminate semantics becomes the *necessary* medium for verbal and written practice. Although Euro-American writing is at last waking up to the fundamental conditionality of language and is thrashing through the theoretical implications of this realization within a debate over the "crisis of representation," postcolonial cultures have a long history of working towards "realism" *within* an awareness of referential slippage, and they have developed a number of strategies for signifying through literature *an* "order of mimesis." *Tarzana Clayton* provides us with a highly visible site in which this reach for a positive (post-colonial) referentiality operates alongside a counter-discursive parodic energy— one which a postmodernist methodology would at least notice if not always specify. But in a number of post-colonial texts—especially those texts which postmodernism has managed to canonize for itself—the referential purchase is not always so visible, at least not to readers from outside the culture. And this can result, within the postmodernist problematic, in a critical reading which is radically skewed.

To give just one example: postmodernist explorations of Salman Rushdie's *Midnight's Children* have proved extremely useful in locating the way in which the novel problematizes the question of authorship and calls down the structures of "history." They have also been useful in establishing the way in which a dysfunctional, excessive typology infuses the text and thus puts the question of cultural coding itself into play. But postmodernist readings have not taken seriously the typologically obvious but "realist" suggestion that *Midnight's Children* positively reinscribes cultural coding through the Vedantic thematization of its "creator" as listener or "reader": that is, as Padma (or Laksmī), the lotus goddess, who embodies the creative power of *māyā* and who even at the text's moment of seemingly total cultural dissolution may be "writing" the text of a post-colonial future not through the indeterminacies of interpretive slippage and "freedom" but from a solid grounding in precolonized cultural and religious agency.

Meaghan Morris has made the point that feminist politics have no *necessary* argument with "postmodernism," but rather that the real problem in the intersection of these two projects is the postmodernist *debate*. She looks specifically at the bibliography of Jonathan Arac's introduction to his collection *Postmodernism and Politics,* and points out that although postmodernism *requires* the work of feminist writers of literature to "frame" its discourse, it has consistently erased the work of feminists from its "pantheon" of theorists (seven women out of more than seventy entries).

A similar erasure seems to be happening, I think, in the intersection between post-colonial cultural work and the debate over postmodernism. It seems impossible, for example, that a conceptual framework for postmodernism could have emerged without the assimilation of South American "boom" fiction. But as Katrak has noted (158), the First World debate over the semiotics of difference has systematically ignored the "theoretical" work of Third World and post-colonial subjects, often because that "theory" presents itself *in* literary texts and *as* social practice, not in the affiliative theoretical language of Western intellectual institutions. Even when post-colonial work actually presents itself *as* theory, it seems to be overlooked by postmodernists—as is very obviously the case with Wilson Harris's important work on the question of representation. By excluding this post-colonial theoretical work from the debate, and by overlooking the cultural specificity of so many of the literary texts it has otherwise read with reasonable accuracy, the "postmodernist" phenomenon—for all its decentering rhetoric—has paradoxically become a centralizing institution, a Western problematic whose project in the cross-cultural sphere has become the translation of differential literary and social "texts" into philosophical questions and cultural attitudes whose grounding in Western culture is too rarely admitted, let alone significantly addressed.

For as Kumkum Sangari has noted, "the postmodern preoccupation with the crisis of meaning is not everyone's crisis (even in the West)," and "there are different modes of de-essentialization which are socially and politically grounded and mediated by separate perspectives, goals, and strategies for change in other countries" (184). The fact that a great deal of the work going in the postmodernist debate remains more or less unaware of these "different modes" is perhaps contributive to postmodernism's overwhelming tendency to present itself—as During explains (368)—as a crisis, a contradiction, an "apotheosis of negativity." But from a post-colonial perspective, notes During, postmodernism "can also be thought of as the apotheosis of cultural confidence and of economic strength. Power has become so centered, so organized that it no longer needs notions of organic totality" to effect the strategic containment of its Others when it appropriates their cultural work. The universalizing, assimilative impulse that carries itself forward in the name of postmodernism is certainly not the only political tendency within this broad cultural movement, but for many post-colonial critics and theorists it appears to be becoming the dominant one: and it is here, I think, in this residual impulse, that postmodernism joins hands with its modernist precursor in continuing a politics of colonialist control.

Like modernism, postmodernism *needs* its (post-) colonial Others in order to constitute or to frame its narrative of referential fracture. But it also needs to exclude the cultural and political specificity of post-colonial representations in order to assimilate them to a rigorously Euro-American problematic. This, it could be argued, is a typically self-sustaining postmodern contradiction; and yet in this contradiction there could perhaps reside a fissuring energy which could lay the foundation for a radical change of tenor within the postmodern debate. For if the modernist ethos is coming to be reread not simply as the manifestation of an historical period or style but also as the representational marker of a *crisis* within European colonialism—as Edward Said has recently suggested (222–23)—it may well be that the postmodernist debate can become one of the key sites upon which the Anglo-American West, if it is to unravel its own moment of cognitive and cultural aporia, finds itself *forced* to take the representational claims of the post-colonial world seriously (Said, 223). At its best, the debate over postmodernism constitutes a theatre of exchange in which dominant Western culture attempts to understand artistic and intellectual activity as a militant set of practices in the project of social change, but too often the very real *crisis* of postmodernism is lost to a blandly self-reflexive methodology which forgets its own genealogy and its cultural and geographical place. As post-colonial discourse continues to negotiate the relationship between colonialist power and the possibilities for post-colonial freedom, however, it may yet come in for some serious attention within postmodernism and assist it in rediscovering its cultural location. Perhaps also, postmodernism may yet find a way to join with, not assimilate, post-colonial critical discourse in the necessary post-modernist work of decolonizing Western culture—decolonizing it, that is, from a residual modernism, which continues to mark for Western culture its relations with the world.[4]

Notes

1. For an amplification of this conjunction between modernism an colonialism, see Said (222–23) and Trotter, passim.

2. Diana Brydon in "Myths That Write Us" makes an important argument against an overly binarized concept of colonialism and for preserving the cultural work of settler colonies within a contemporary post-colonialism.

3. The critical work on this body of literature is much too long to cite here, but a useful analysis of the refigurations of *The Tempest* in Canadian and Caribbean literature is provided in Brydon, "Re-writing *The Tempest.*"

4. Discussions with various colleagues—among them Helen Tiffin, Diana Brydon and Bill New, members of the Research Unit on Post-Colonial Writing at the University of Queensland, and members in my study group at the University of Alberta—assisted my thinking on this topic. A hallway discussion with Robert Wilson contributed to the formulation of this paper's title. My thanks to all.

Works Cited

Bhabha, Homi K. "Representation and the Colonial Text: A Critique of Some Forms of Mimeticism." *The Theory of Reading*. Ed. Frank Gloversmith. Brighton: Harvester, 1984. 93–112.

Brydon, Diana. "Re-writing *The Tempest*." *World Literature Written in English* 23.1 (1984): 75–88.

———. "The Myths That Write Us: Decolonising the Mind." *Commonwealth* 10.1 (1987): 1–14.

Dash, J. Michael. "Marvellous Realism—The Way Out of Negritude." *Caribbean Studies* 13.4 (1973): 57–70.

During, Simon. "Postmodernism or Postcolonialism?" *Landfall* 39.3 (1985): 366–80.

Farki, Neville. *The Death of Tarzana Clayton*. London: Karnak House, 1985.

Frow, John. *Marxism and Literary History*. Oxford: Blackwell, 1986.

Hassan, Ihab. "Pluralism in Postmodern Perspective." *Critical Inquiry* 12.3 (1986): 503–20.

Hutcheon, Linda. *A Poetics of Postmodernism: History, Theory, Fiction*. New York and London: Routledge, 1988.

Jameson, Fredric. "Postmodernism, or The Cultural Logic of Late Capitalism." *New Left Review* 146 (1984): 53–92.

Jardine, Alice A. *Gynesis: Configurations of Woman and Modernity*. Ithaca and London: Cornell University Press, 1985.

Johnson, Barbara. *A World of Difference*. Baltimore: Johns Hopkins University Press, 1987.

Kariel, Henry S. *The Desperate Politics of Postmodernism*. Amherst: University of Massachusetts Press, 1989.

Katrak, Ketu H. "Decolonizing Culture: Toward a Theory for Postcolonial Women's Texts." *Modern Fiction Studies* 35.1 (1989): 157–79.

Lawson, Alan. " 'There is Another World But It Is This One': A Cultural Paradigm for the Second World." Paper delivered Badlands Conference, University of Calgary, August 1986.

Merquior, J. G. "Spider and Bee: Towards a Critique of the Postmodern Ideology." *ICA Documents* 4–5 (1986): 16–18.

Miller, Christopher. *Blank Darkness: Africanist Discourse in French*. Chicago and London: University of Chicago Press, 1985.

Morris, Meaghan. *The Pirate's Fiancée: Feminism, Reading, Postmodernism*. London: Verso, 1988.

Nandy, Ashis. *The Intimate Enemy: Loss and Recovery of Self under Colonialism*. Delhi: OUP, 1983.

Newman, Michael. "Revising Modernism, Representing Postmodernism: Critical Discourses of the Visual Arts." *ICA Documents* 4–5 (1986): 32–51.

Parry, Benita. "Problems in Current Theories of Colonial Discourse." *Oxford Literary Review* 9.1–2 (1987): 27–58.

Said, Edward. "Repressing the Colonized: Anthropology's Interlocutors." *Critical Inquiry* 15.2 (1989): 205–25.

Sangari, Kumkum. "The Politics of the Possible." *Cultural Critique* 7 (1987): 157–86.

Tapping, Craig. "Literary Reflections of Orality: Colin Johnson's *Dr. Wooreddy's Prescription for Enduring the Ending of the World*." Paper delivered MLA Convention, New Orleans, December 1988.

Terdiman, Richard. *Discourse/Counter-Discourse: The Theory and Practice of Symbolic Resistance in Nineteenth-Century France*. Ithaca and London: Cornell University Press, 1985.

Tiffin, Helen. "Recuperative Strategies in the Post-Colonial Novel." *Span* 24 (1987): 27–45.

Trotter, David. "Modernism and Empire: Reading *The Waste Land*." *Critical Quarterly* 28.1 & 2 (1986): 143–53.

Viswanathan, Gauri. "The Beginnings of English Literary Study in British India." *Oxford Literary Review* 9.1 & 2 (1987): 27–58.

Wortman, Marc. Review of Charles Newman, *The Post-Modern Aura: The Act of Fiction in an Age of Inflation*. *Telos* 71 (1987): 171–78.

IV

Postmodern Practices

Preface

"Practices" are what realize (or, if we want to get postmodern about it, real-ize) abstract theories and categorizing "-isms." Within the modern paradigm's mode of real-izing, one could propose a practice derived from universal standards capable of critiquing and even emending the culture at large; within a postmodern real-izing, however, a practice is always going to be relative to (and contingent upon) the context from which it comes. So, a postmodern economics or history would simply be the economics or history now made realizable through the lenses, so to speak, of postmodernity. The powers of solving and affirming—which the modern granted its practices—are denied in the postmodern: any practice is unavoidably ensnared within the frame of its real-izing—a process which any culture finds "self-evident", at least until challenged. This crucial distinction takes us back to the arguments of the last section on "Entanglements and Complicities," while also revisiting points raised in the first two sections in different terms.

In an essay pointedly called, "Is There a Postmodern Sociology?" Zygmunt Bauman has urged us to consider a sociology whose object (society) has irremediably changed; in other words, what the social sciences were once constituted to respond to has itself changed fundamentally. There is no longer "a need, or a room, for those 'hard-core' intellectuals whose expertise is 'legitimation,' i.e., supplying proof that what is being done is universally correct and absolutely true, moral and beautiful" (1988, 221). Legitimation has been replaced by twin strategies of seduction and repression.

Nothing that is going on here in the postmodern project is in need of legitimation; everything goes on whether or not values are questioned, whether or not proof is forthcoming. In other words, in this paradigm, the modern project which—in Habermas's words—faces a "legitimation crisis," becomes as irrelevant as that legitimation it struggled to provide. As Catherine Belsey argues in the essay reprinted in this book, "truth" that "stands outside culture as a guarantee of legitimacy" has become superfluous to cultures that stand outside that "truth."

As we saw in the last section, the desire to put the postmodern into practice at the level of useful political and social intervention— even to make it into a tool of resistance and opposition—can be seen in those efforts to tailor the postmodern to fit a feminist or postcolonialist practice, or even to circumscribe its notion of difference within the space of economic exploitation and labor to fit a Marxist practice (Zavarzadeh and Morton 1991). Such efforts often appear to come from within the modern project itself, however, in that they implicitly assume that the postmodern can activate or put into practice a theoretically grounded means of validating or invalidating the "errors" of culture and society. In other words, they assume that postmodern practices are like modern ones: they somehow derive from a culture's own real-izing of itself, and yet paradoxically are able to assert culture-free narratives of universal import and value. How can we avoid this seemingly inescapable dilemma? How can we ever put into practice something *other* than a modern practice?

These are the issues that a postmodern "anything" faces: basically, how are we going to "do" history, philosophy, sociology, psychology, literary criticism, anthropology, geography, folklore, or any form of art in postmodern ways—that is, ways that remain "true" to the postmodern problematizing of any totalizing efforts. The search for a postmodern practice grounded in difference is going to be a search for a practice that has no mandate at all to be universally applicable, but must somehow also remain locally effective. This practice would not be called upon to achieve those ends in whose name the modern project extended itself into every variety of practice: that is, difference would not be brought into (or constitute) any totalizing frame. This challenge moves us into the realm of what Donna Haraway has called "situated knowledges," arguing for the need to talk about things like the "politics and epistemologies of location, positioning, and situating, where partially and not universality is the condition of being heard to make rational knowledge claims" (1991, 195).

This notion of the inevitably partial, provisional, and positioned implies that the postmodern might not be able to "practice" any of our disciplines in any utterly new way—or indeed in any *single* way at all. The postmodern displacement of the modern idea of coherent and homogeneous identity in order to make room for difference clears space for contact with other narratives, other realizings. It thus makes possible such (once unthinkable) concepts as a history without an evolutionary time-sequence, or a politics of what Lyotard (1983) calls the "différend" or that which cannot equitably be resolved for lack of a universal rule of judgment. This is the space cleared in ethnology today for a postmodern redefining of ethnicity as "process of inter-reference between two or more cultural traditions" (Fischer 1986, 201) or of cosmopolitanism as "an ethos of macro-interdependencies, with an acute consciousness . . . of the inescapabilities and particularities of places, characters, historical trajectories, and fates" (Rabinow 1986, 258).

A move outward to the contingent, the other, and the different might transform the discipline of "English literature" (not to mention a few others) into what some are now calling "cultural studies," as Belsey argues in this book. In this way, we might renarrate an entire area of study, at once moving it from worldless discipline to world-full discourse. Our attention—and ultimately, perhaps, our actions—might also be drawn away from any simple "critique" operating only in the service of a totalizing metanarrative. Thus the postmodern renarration of our historical, political, sociological, psychological, literary, architectural, and other real-izings may well elide the traditional mission of "practice." It may detour even the staunchest modern efforts and direct them toward what *exceeds* critique, what *resists* their own practice.

The postmodern task is to bring such plural renarratings forward within a "dialogic concept of totality" (Birch 1991, 1)—that is, within a paradoxical kind of "totality" that maintains a sense of similarity while simultaneously showing the differences that disrupt that unity. Belsey suggests that—in literary criticism, for instance—the New Historicists have left out this dialogic or paradoxical concept of totality with regard to cultural resistance and subversion—that is, with regard to the play of difference. She argues that they reduce disruptive difference to ideas that must be "put into practice, or *perceived* as able to do so." "There is no space here," writes Belsey, "for the analysis of textuality as inherently unstable, or for the identification of culture as itself the place where norms are specified and contested, knowledges affirmed and challenged, and subjectivity produced and disrupted."

To keep track of this dialogic totality is to keep track of what all postmodern discourses practice: what might be described as an "ironic signaling of difference at the very heart of similarity" (Hutcheon 1986–87, 185)—a parodic rendering of identity and difference, of what (recalling the root meaning of *parody*) is at once "near to" and "counter to" each other, of both what shares a narrative frame and what is narrated outside that frame. But such a parodic practice, such a postmodern play of identity and difference, may not even make sense within a modern paradigm. Certainly the negative response to much postmodern architecture (and to other art forms too) would suggest this to be the case.

We have repeatedly seen that the postmodern has not necessarily been regarded as a helpful frame of reference for those seeking modes of social and political intervention or resistance within already declared oppositions. The so-called "ludic" or playful which parody and irony both evoke (and which many associate with post-structuralism and, especially, deconstruction) is what is often found most problematic. What is seen is a potential for trivializing, and an inherent ambivalence that make this less attractive than—say—a notion of disruptive difference and otherness that might straightforwardly (modern-ly) confront, resist, and subvert. The implication is that what is textual is playful, and that what is playful is inappropriate to the (admittedly serious) business of resisting the exploitation and tyranny imposed on the different in the name of certain kinds of identity (white, male, Eurocentric, wealthy, heterosexual, and so on).

Of what use can the postmodern politics of cultural difference be, then? Cornel West's description of its characteristics gives us a hint as to its possible power: it represents a drive "to trash the monolithic and homogeneous in the name of diversity, multiplicity and heterogeneity; to reject the abstract, general and universal in light of the concrete, specific and particular; and to historicize, contextualize and pluralize by highlighting the contingent, provisional, variable, tentative, shifting and changing" (1990, 19). No urge to establish universal standards of "truth" should operate here, no desire to dominate, to render "self-evident" one's own contingent cultural beliefs.

Interestingly, as we have seen in earlier sections too, one result of this trashing of the single and homogeneous is a refusal to denigrate the non-"serious," a rejection of any elitist attitude toward popular or mass culture that would deny either its significance or its possible resistance value. Within the postmodern paradigm, rich and hybrid layers of experience—no less "reliable" than those of "pure" or "serious" or "high" culture—are not to be ignored. Indeed, in bell hooks's words in this book, popular culture "may well be 'the' central future location of resistance struggle, a meeting place where new and radical happenings can occur."

In "Hybridity, the Rap Race, and Pedagogy for the 1990s," Houston Baker sees the hybrid nature of popular culture incarnated in the disco-technology of rap, with its "rap DJ who became a postmodern, ritual priest of sound. . . . A hybrid sound then erupted in seemingly dead urban acoustical spaces. (By *postmodern* I intend the nonauthoritative collaging or archiving of sound and styles that bespeaks a deconstructive hybridity. Linearity and progress yield to a dizzying synchronicity.)" Hybridity here is "an audible or sounding space of opposition": "To get the job done with rap style is to 'get busy', innovative, and outrageous with *fresh* sounds and deftly nonstandard moves. One must be undisciplined, that is to say, to be 'in effect.'"

Because popular culture usually refuses to police its own heterogeneity and because serious or high culture quickly and canonically tends to select what fits and discard the rest, popular culture seems to have become available as a postmodern paradoxical space of opposition. In opposition to the Marxist negative view of it, popular culture here becomes the site where those forms which preserve a "homogeneity of remembrance" (of everything from national anthem to canon) are brazenly displaced by what Baker calls "an articulation of the melancholia of the people's wounding by and before the emergence of the state line." Cultural homogeneity, like a cherished cultural canon, is grounded in "an amnesia of heterogeneity," and so popular culture becomes the occasion to recall the complexity of otherness and difference. This recalling can be "innovative," "outrageous" play—a disruption of identity and linearity through a "sampling" of the archives.

Popular culture, then, emerges as an important locus of the parodic postmodern, one whose resistance potential is, in fact, actually dependent upon its ludic dimension. The same is true of those "in between" cultural manifestations—the ones that often get treated like high art, but which in fact milk the power of the popular, playfully and critically crossing cultural borders without an authorizing passport: the parodic art of Robert Colescott and Silvia Kolbowski, the cross-over music and performances of Philip Glass and Laurie Anderson, the hybrid buildings of Venturi and Scott Brown, the popular/art films of directors like Kenneth Brannagh or Peter Greenaway, the fiction of Kathy Acker or E.L. Doctorow, the dance works of Karole Armitage and Robert Desrosiers, and operatic productions of Peter Sellars or Harry Kupfer, and on and on.

If the opposite of this kind of play—a "serious" "metaphysics of truth"—has (as Belsey argues in strong terms that it indeed has) "licensed torture, exploitation, and mass murder," there may be nothing at all wrong with turning to a post-structural and postmodern practice which "displays truth as a linguistic tyranny which arrests the proliferation of meanings, assigns values and specifies norms." For Belsey, resistance is itself a necessarily ludic enterprise: it reveals meanings and interests, power and subjects, caught not within binary oppositions but within a story of "meanings that are always plural, subject to excess, in process, contradictory." New sites of struggle appear: new battles of "conflicting interests, of heroic refusals, of textual uncertainties" are waged. There is no desire to practice the "history of truth" here.

And yet. . . . And yet. . . . How does a postmodern stand like this help us deal with the growing feeling that there are also other forces out there busy working to do something similar, but under perhaps a more suspect banner? What have been called market-dependency forces are *also* seen to be working to supplant, "neuter," or fragment any theorizing (and thus any ensuing practice) vis-à-vis "the true, moral and beautiful." What some call the "free play of the market" and its arena of overstimulated market "players" could remain virtually unchallenged in a postmodern space of difference. We know that "needs creation" also nullifies even the "normative regulations" of the "modern state aiming at the 'total administration' of society," as Bauman has pointed out (1988, 228).

But, while modern rather than postmodern alternatives may at first present themselves as the more obvious sure ways to fight such a nullification, it could well be argued that the *postmodern* "ludic" is precisely what is really needed to combat the market form of "ludic" free play. The postmodern would not challenge such market dependency by political intervention in the name of any new "normative regulations," but instead would contest such a move by drawing that "needs creation" within the flow of pluralist needs, of multiple life-worlds representing colliding systems of differences. Through this sort of play, the practices of "needs creation" and market dependency might themselves be hybridized; the market itself might become "pluralist- or heterogeneity-dependent."

The postmodern would not foster selective standards and practices through which "needs" and "power," "commodities" and "ways of real-izing" could necessarily be linked. On the contrary, the modern paradigm's politics of hierarchy and exclusion, both based in some foundational "truth," have generated a market that confirms identities through consumption and thus implicitly denies identity to the non-consumer. Thus, to consume is to make universal and absolute the presence of Truth, Beauty and Goodness. In turn, the pursuit of these establishes a fixed (modern) mapping of identity and difference: identity is seized upon as the territory of the market; difference becomes the territory one consumes *against*.

To express the challenge to this kind of thinking through postmodern "sampling", then, the postmodern "yearns" (hooks) instead to "refuse nothing" (Belsey); it yearns for a situation in which there is a plurality of narratives and thus of practices issuing forth from them. A pluralist postmodern theory demands a pluralist practice, and no *one* practice, or even twelve of them, can be sent forth as apostles into any "As-Yet-Unpostmodernized-World." As Belsey writes in this book, in "Towards Cultural History—in Theory and Practice," a (postmodern) "cultural history would necessarily take all signifying practice as its domain."

But what does such pluralism actually mean? Is a "refusing nothing" practice the same as an "anything goes" practice? Agnes Heller argues in this book, in "Existentialism, Alienation, Postmodernism: Cultural Movements as Vehicles of Change in the Patterns of Everyday Life," that, as a movement, postmodernism draws anything into its net: it "does not stand for a particular politics of any kind," she claims, since fixed distinctions of any kind are irrelevant. Anything can go on; all practices are caught within a kind of "pluralization of the ways of life" that certainly troubles fixed modern notions of identity. It also troubles a class society out of which representative, democratic governments are formed.

The concept of democracy being invoked by Heller is quite clearly one based on the modern paradigm's capacity to ground itself in a "rational politics." One might argue that postmodern pluralization cannot be brought about (or even conceptualized) by means of any grounded rational policy-making, any foundationalist project with roots in the Enlightenment. But those roots are precisely what gave life to the notion of "democracy," so how can the postmodern avoid the kind of corrosive relativism that might undermine democracy itself? An important question to ask next might be whether such fears are necessarily borne out in practice: are there no gains, no liberties which balance and counteract such seeming destabilization? As feminist musicologist, Susan McClary suggests, it all depends on your perspective: "for those who have benefitted from the illusion that culture and knowledge were grounded in truth (rather than social ideology and privilege), postmodern deconstruction is a calamity. But for those who have been kept in their

places by those reigning opposition," such postmodern challenges
can be "cause for celebration" (1991, 144).

In Belsey's view, nothing can be refused out of hand, for "there
can be no guarantee that any system of difference maps the world
accurately." She goes on to say that, while knowledge therefore may
become "culturally and discursively relative," we never really do
"exonerate the liars" because we always respond to the rules of discourse within which we live, even if they do not presume to shape
any single "metaphysics of truth." On a similar note, Barbara
Herrnstein Smith's *Contingencies of Value: Alternative Perspectives
for Critical Theory* (1988) offers an extended critique of precisely the
modern paradigm's notions of value and judgment, and suggests
that seeing these as radically contingent has none of the dire
consequences prophesied by the opponents of such an accursed
relativism.

In positing a postmodern and anti-racist pedagogy in his essay, "Postmodernism as Border Pedagogy: Redefining the Boundaries of Race and Ethnicity," Henry Giroux also argues for a
"refusing nothing" practice that is nonetheless "critically attentive": "It is important to emphasize that difference and pluralism
in this view do not mean reducing democracy to the equivalency of
diverse interests; on the contrary, what is being argued for is: a language in which different voices and traditions exist and flourish to
the degree that they listen to the voices of Others; a language which
engages in an ongoing attempt to eliminate forms of subjective and
objective suffering and maintains those conditions in which the act
of communicating and living extends rather than restricts the creation of democratic public spheres." In like fashion, bell hooks does
not envisage a loss of the "authority of experience" African-
Americans possess—a loss of that difference which imposed notions
of identifying demean or deny—if the notion of black "essence" were
to be repudiated: "When black folks critique essentialism, we are
empowered to recognize multiple experiences of black identity that
are the lived conditions which make diverse cultural productions
possible."

Such cultural diversity often takes its material shape—even
within individual texts—from parody, or what in African-American
culture is called "signifying" (Gates 1984). Here, irony and multiple
echoic play complicate any possibility of a simple nostalgic relation
with the cultural or social past (cf. Jameson in Section III). As Jim
Collins has pointed out, in the postmodern, the "relationship between past and present coding is based on interaction and transformation instead of simple rejection" (1989, 134) or even antiquarian

reverence. The result of such parody is often stylistic hybridity of the first order. In Collins's terms, the postmodern "recognition that culture has become a multiplicity of competing signs necessarily prevents it from asserting total stylistic 'dominance'—to do so would violate one of the constitutive principles" of the postmodern (1989, 115). Paul Maltby, in fact, explicitly labels as "dissident" the kind of postmodern fiction that others, rather more negatively, have called "inflationary" (Newman 1985); but whatever it is called, most critics agree that it is fiction that "operates through a subversive, highly self-reflexive use of parody."

Such writing goes beyond the self-conscious formal play of modernist texts, however; instead, it has been seen by Charles Russell (in Section II in this book) as attempting "to demystify and deconstruct the social codes in which subjective identity is seen to be enfolded." In Maltby's view too, the formal and the social are not separable; the "dissidence" here specifically lies in postmodern fiction's "sign-reflectiveness" which "enables it to perform a contestatory function within a substantially eroded critical space." By exposing the relationship between language and meaning, such fiction opens up a space to contest the very "rules and codes" which order that relationship.

Within such a dissident, parodic postmodernism, then, neither cultural relativism nor radical subjectivity can be demonized to quite the extent that each usually is when seen within the binary oppositions set up by a modern "metaphysics of truth." Culture, to use Belsey's terms, is a site of both affirmation and contestation, of both productions and disruptions. And "in the absence of a unified subject," as Giroux suggests, "we can rethink the meaning of solidarity through a recognition of the multiple antagonisms and struggles that characterize both the notion of the self and the wider social reality."

The practice of the postmodern, then, is to re-see the modern narrative as merely one (obviously, privileged) political positioning, and consequently to engage in specifying the "possibilities of transgressing the existing limits on what we are able to say, to be and to do." With these words Belsey attempts to move outside rigid disciplinary boundaries and into the arena of a more broadly based cultural history that traces coherences in traditional ways, but also lays bare "contradictions and conflicts." Similarly, Giroux seeks to move the issues of race and ethnicity out of their modern real-izing (or rather, their modern silencing) into the space of postmodern cultural politics: "Postmodern discourse provides a theoretical foundation for deconstructing the master narratives of White supremacist logics and for redrawing the boundaries between the construction of experience and power."

As bell hooks explains here, in "Postmodern Blackness," there are indeed narratives, rules of signification, that have silenced those who "now share with black folks a sense of deep alienation, despair, uncertainty, loss of a sense of grounding even if it is not informed by shared circumstance." A postmodern deconstruction of "master" or metanarratives has the potential to fulfill a yearning for a critical voice. As hooks says, "[i]t is no accident that 'rap' . . . has enabled underclass black youth to develop a critical voice . . . a common literacy."

Giroux's idea of a "border pedagogy"—that is, a postmodern practice that acknowledges the "shifting borders that both undermine and reterritorialize dominant configurations of power and knowledge"—intersects with Belsey's desire to "devise and implement a pedagogy that permits us to introduce courses in cultural history as a genuinely radical alternative to the simultaneous individualism and universalism of English in its traditional form." But Giroux's pedagogy is also linked to a wider public discourse, outside the confines of the educational system: "This is as much a political as a pedagogical project, one that demands that anti-racist pedagogical practices be developed within a discourse that combines a democratic public philosophy with a postmodern theory of resistance." For Giroux, the postmodern *enacts* the notion of democracy; it "breathes life into the notion of democracy by stressing a notion of lived community that is *not* at odds with the principles of justice, liberty, and equality." We can go on as a community capable of extending and putting into practice such principles, precisely because the postmodern paradigm has established "the material and ideological conditions that allow multiple, specific, and heterogeneous ways of life to come into play."

Giroux's particular formulation of an anti-racist practice cannot find a home in any modern real-izing, where—in a ludic spirit— we might say that capital "T" Truth, capital "B" Beauty, and capital "G" Goodness all collapse difference into totalized identity and pluralism into rational unity. Many liberal democracies' own "commonality of traditions" appear presently to be shifting from the modern quest for unity and homogeneity to the postmodern realization of the need to accommodate multicultural pluralism and heterogeneity. We may be in the process of moving from modern practices which render difference fragile, to a postmodernity that cannot practice any one identity and renders the project of identity itself fragile. The end results of such moves are what all of us will likely be living through in the years to come.

Works Cited

Bauman, Zygmunt (1988) "Is There a Postmodern Sociology?" *Theory, Culture, and Society* 5: 217–37.

Birch, David (1991) "Postmodernist Chutneys." *Textual Practice* 5.1: 1–7.

Collins, Jim (1989) *Uncommon Cultures: Popular Culture and Post-Modernism.* New York and London: Routledge.

Fischer, Michael M.J. (1986) "Ethnicity and the Post-Modern Arts of Memory." In James Clifford and George E. Marcus, eds. *Writing Culture: The Poetics and Politics of Ethnography.* Berkeley: University of California Press. 194–233.

Gates, Henry Louis, Jr. (1984) "The Blackness of Blackness: A Critique of the Sign and the Signifying Monkey." In Henry Louis Gates, Jr., ed. *Black Literature and Literary Theory.* London and New York: Methuen. 285–321.

Haraway, Donna (1991) *Simians, Cyborgs and Women: The Reinvention of Nature.* New York: Routledge.

Hutcheon, Linda (1986–87) "The Politics of Postmodernism: Parody and History." *Cultural Critique* 5: 179–207.

Lyotard, Jean-François (1983) *Le Différend.* Paris: Minuit.

McClary, Susan (1991) *Feminine Endings.* Minneapolis: University of Minnesota Press.

Newman, Charles (1985) *The Post-Modern Aura: The Act of Fiction in an Age of Inflation.* Evanston, Ill.: Northwestern University Press.

Rabinow, Paul (1986) "Representations Are Social Facts: Modernity and Post-Modernity in Anthropology." In James Clifford and George E. Marcus, eds. *Writing Culture: The Poetics and Politics of Ethnography.* Berkeley: University of California Press. 234–261.

Smith, Barbara Herrnstein (1988) *Contingencies of Value: Alternative Perspectives for Critical Theory.* Cambridge, Mass. and London: Harvard University Press.

West, Cornel (1990) "The New Cultural Politics of Difference." In Russell Ferguson, Martha Gever, Trinh T. Minh-ha, Cornel West, eds. *Out There: Marginalization and Contemporary Culture.* New York: New Museum of Contemporary Art; Cambridge, Mass. and London: MIT Press. 19–36.

Zavarzadeh, Mas'ud and Donald Morton (1991) *Theory, (Post) Modernity, Opposition.* Washington, D.C.: Maisonneuve Press.

Postmodernism as Border Pedagogy: Redefining the Boundaries of Race and Ethnicity

Henry Giroux

Within the current historical conjuncture, the political and cultural boundaries that have long constituted the meaning of race and cultural politics are beginning to shift. The question of race figures much differently at the beginning of 1990s than it did a decade ago for a number of reasons. First, the population of America's subordinate groups are changing the cultural landscapes of our urban centers. According to recent demographic projections, Blacks and Hispanics will "constitute a decided majority in nearly one-third of the nation's fifty largest cities. . . . and blacks alone will be the major racial group in at least nine major cities, notably Detroit, Baltimore, Memphis, Washington D.C., New Orleans, and Atlanta."[1] In this case, populations traditionally defined as the Other are moving from the margin to the center and challenging the ethnocentric view that people of color can be relegated to the periphery of everyday life.

Second, while people of color are redrawing the cultural demographic boundaries of the urban centers, the boundaries of power appear to be solidifying in favor of rich, white, middle and upper classes. The consequences will have a dramatic effect on race relations in the next decade. For example, escalating unemployment among black teenage youth poses a serious threat to an entire generation of future adults; in many urban cities the drop-out rate for non-white children exceeds 60 percent (with New York City at 70 percent);[2] the civil rights gains of the 1960s are slowly being eroded by the policy makers and judicial heirs of the Reagan Era and the tide of racism is aggressively rising in the streets, schools, workplaces, and campuses of the United States.[3] In the Age of Reagan and Bush, equity and social justice are given low priority next to the "virtues" of collective greed and individual success. As class divisions grow deeper, intra-class and racial tensions mask the need for collective struggles for social and political justice. As the white working class sees its dream of moving up the social and economic ladder imperiled, it is increasingly coming to view affirmative action, social policy programs, and the changing nature of national and cultural identity as a threat to its own sense of security and possibility. Instead of embracing blacks and other ethnic groups as allies in the struggle to dismantle the master narratives of Eurocentric domination with the discourse of democratic struggle and solidarity, the legacy of institutional and ideological racism appears to have once again reached a dangerous threshold that impedes rather than extends such a goal. As we move into a postmodern world that is progressively redrawing the boundaries established by nationalism, ethnocentrism, and Eurocentric culture, the United States appears to be refiguring its political, social, and cultural geography in a manner that denies rather than maintains a democratic community. Instead of engaging a politics of difference, community, and democracy with respect to the principles of justice, equality, and freedom, the current neo-conservative government appears more eager to sever "the links between democracy and political equality."[4]

The smell of totalitarianism is in the air. Its primary expression is found in the resurgence of racism in this country. Racial slurs are now regularly incorporated into the acts of some rock stars and stand-up comedians;[5] The dominant culture seems indifferent or even hostile to the deepening poverty and despair affecting a growing population of blacks in the underclass in our nation's cities; the growing dropout rate among black students is met with insulting diatribes and the refusal to engage the racism prevalant in our nation's schools;[6] the black family is not highlighted for its resiliency amidst the most degrading economic and social conditions but is condemned as a cause of its own misery.[7] Increasingly, racial hatred is erupting into racist terror. Growing racial tensions have resulted in outbreaks of violence in Chicago's Marquette Park, Baltimore's Hampden section, Philadelphia's Fishtown and Feltonville, and a number of other cities. Two black youths, Michael Griffith and Yusuf Hawkins, were killed recently by racist-inspired mobs in Howard Beach and Bensonhurst. Civil rights demonstrations have been met by overt white hostility and racist attacks. What needs to be stressed is not only that minorities are increasingly open to ideological and physical assaults, but that the very fate of our society as a democratic nation is at risk. Central to the effort to reconstruct this nation as a democratic society is the need to rethink the project of race, and cultural and economic justice. Moreover, this is not merely a political issue; it is eminently a pedagogical one as well. Racism is an ideological poison that is learned, it is a social historical and social construction that seeps into social practices, needs, the unconscious, and rationality itself. If it is to be challenged at the institutional level, at the very centers of authority, it must first be addressed as an ideological concern for the ways in which it is produced, sustained, and taken up within a cultural politics secured within wider dominant relations of power.

This is not a new insight and generations of black leaders have raised its banner in elegant and courageous ways. The fight against racism has always been seen as an important political objective by those committed to democratic struggle. But in most cases, this concern has been framed within a discourse of modernism that has failed to place race and ethnicity at the center of a radical politics of democracy, difference, and cultural struggle. In what follows, I want to argue for a postmodern discourse of resistance as a basis for developing a cultural politics and anti-racist pedagogy as part of a larger theory of difference and democratic struggle. In developing this perspective, I will first address in general terms the failings of various versions of modernist discourse; next I will argue that the foundations for an anti-racist pedagogy can be taken up by drawing selectively upon the discourses of a critical postmodernism, the discourse of narrative and difference that has largely emerged in the work of black feminist writers, and neo-Gramscian discourse that articulates difference with a notion of a democratic public philosophy. I will conclude by suggesting how these discourses provide some important elements for developing specific pedagogical practices.

Refiguring the Boundaries of Modernism

The dominant discourses of modernity have rarely been able to address race and ethnicity as an ethical, political, and cultural marker in order to understand or self-consciously examine the notions of justice inscribed in the modernist belief in change and the progressive unfolding of history.[8] In fact, race and ethnicity have been generally reduced to a discourse of the Other, a discourse that regardless of its emancipatory or reactionary intent, often essentialized and reproduced the distance between the centers and margins of power. Within the discourse of modernity, the Other not only sometimes ceases to be a historical agent, but is often defined within totalizing and universalistic theories that create a transcendental rational white, male, Eurocentric subject that both occupies the centers of power while simultaneously appearing to exist outside time and space. Read against this Eurocentric transcendental subject, the Other is shown to lack any redeeming community traditions, collective voice, or historical weight—and is reduced to the imagery of the colonizer. By separating the discourse of the Other from the epistemic and material violence that most postmodernist critics have identified as central to the character and definition of Western notions of progress, modernist discourses were never able to develop an adequate understanding of racism that could serve as a form of cultural criticism capable of redefining the boundaries and articulations between itself and the subordinate groups it continually oppressed. In this sense, modernism in its various forms served to repress the possibility of linking the construction of its own master narratives and relations of power with the simultaneous creation of alternative narratives woven out the pain, misery, and struggle of subordinate groups.[9] Modernist discourses, in part, have served to solidify the boundaries of race and ethnicity either by creating biological and scientific theories that "proved" the inferiority of blacks and other subordinate groups, or in its more liberal forms created the self-delusion that the boundaries of racial inequality and ethnicity were always exclusively about the language, experiences, and histories of the Other and had little to do with power relations at the core of its own cultural and political identity as the discourse of white authority. In the first instance, the ideology of racism and degraded Otherness can be found, as Cornel West points out, in the logics of three central European traditions: the Judeo-Christian, scientific, and psychosexual. He is worth quoting at length on this issue:

The Judeo-Christian racist logic emanates from the biblical account of Ham looking upon and failing to cover his father Noah's nakedness and thereby receiving divine punishment in the form of blackening his progeny. Within this logic, black skin is a divine curse owing to disrespect for and rejection of paternal authority. The scientific racist logic rests upon a modern philosophical discourse guided by Greek ocular metaphors, undergirded by Cartesian notions of the primacy of the subject and the preeminence of representation and buttressed by Baconian ideas of observation, evidence, and confirmation that promote and encourage the activities of observing, comparing, measuring, and ordering physical characteristics of human bodies. Given the renewed appreciation and appropriation of classical antiquity, these activities were regulated by classical aesthetic and cultural norms. Within this logic, the notions of black ugliness, cultural deficiency, and intellectual inferiority are legitimated by the value laden, yet prestigious, authority of science. The psychosexual racist logic arises from the phallic obsessions, Oedipal projections, and anal-sadistic orientations in European culture that endow African men and and women with sexual prowess; view Africans as either cruel, revengeful fathers, frivolous, carefree children, or passive, long-suffering mothers; and identify Africans with dirt, odious smell, and feces. In short, Africans are associated with acts of bodily defecation, violation, and subordination. Within this logic, Africans are walking abstractions, inanimate things or invisible creatures. For all three white supremacist logics, which operate simultaneously in the modern West, Africans personify degraded otherness, exemplify radical alterity, and embody alien difference.[10]

It is important to emphasize that modernity's drive to systematize the world by mastering the conditions of nature and human life represents a form of social modernism that must not be confused with the more emancipatory elements of political modernism. On the one hand, the project of social modernity has been carried out under the increasing domination of relations of capitalist production characterized by a growing commodification, bureaucraticization, homogenization, and standardization of everyday life. Such a project has been legitimized, in part, through an appeal to the Enlightenment project of rationality, progress, and humanism. On the other hand, the legacy of political modernism provides a discourse that inaugurates the possibility of developing social relations in which the principles of liberty, justice, and equality provide the basis for democratic struggles. If the ravages of modernism have led to overt forms of racism and colonialization, their victories have provided a discourse of rights, universal education, and social justice.

As I mentioned in the introduction to this book, modernity is not a unified discourse, and its networks of meanings and social practices have included a Western-style counterdiscourse that also offered liberals and radicals spaces for challenging racist practices and ideologies.[11] This challenge can be seen, of course, in the traditions of rupture and dissent in this country that extend from the abolitionist movement to the civil rights legislation of the 1960s and to the more recent efforts by contemporary activists and artists to counter the increasing racism of the 1980s. As noble as these responses have been, at least in intent, few of them have adequately theorized racism as part of a wider discourse of ethics, politics, and difference.[12] Unable to step beyond the modernist celebration of the unified self, totalizing notions of history, and universalistic models of reason, liberal and radical discourses have been unable to explore the limits of the absolutist character of their own narratives regarding race and difference. Within these discourses, ethics and politics were removed from any serious attempt to engage contingency, particularity, partiality and community within a notion of difference free from binary oppositions, hierarchical relations, and narratives of mastery and control. But modernity has also failed to challenge with any great force the white supremacist logics embedded in the ideological traditions cited by Cornell West. Similarly, it has failed to account for the power of its own authority as a central component in structuring the very notion of Otherness as site for objectification and marginalization.

The emancipatory promise of plurality and heterogeneity as the basis for new forms of conversation, solidarity, and public culture never fully materialized within the more liberal and radical discourses of Western modernity. Caught within the limiting narratives of European culture as the model of civilization and progress, liberal and radical theorists have never been able to break away from Western models of authority that placed either the individual white male at the center of history and rationality or viewed history as the unproblematic progressive unfolding of science, reason, and technology.

For example, dominant strains of liberal ideology have fashioned their anti-racist discourses on a Eurocentric notion of society that subordinates the discourse of ethics and politics to the rule of the market, an unproblematic acceptance of European culture as the basis of civilization, and a notion of the individual subject as a unified, rational self which is the source of all cultural and social meaning. The central modernist political ideology at work here, as Stanley Aronowitz has pointed out is "that a free market and a democratic state go hand in hand."[13] Unfortunately for liberals, it is precisely this assumption that prevents them from questioning how they, as a dominant group, actually benefit from racist ideologies and social relations, even as they allegedly contest such practices. By assuming that the middle class, which bears the values of individualism and free market rationality, is the only agent of history, liberals are blind to the corruptions implicated in the exercise of their own authority and historical actions.[14]

Within this multilayered liberal discourse, the attack on racism is often reduced to policy measures aimed at eliminating racist institutional barriers in the marketplace, providing compensatory programs to enhance the cultural capital and skills of blacks (as in various remedial programs in education or the workplace such as Headstart or the now defunct Job Corps project), or is relegated to patronizing calls for blacks to muster up the courage and fortitude to compete in a manner consistent with the drive and struggle of other ethnic groups who have succeeded in American society.

Though the theoretical sweep is broad and oversimplified here, the basic issue is that modernist discourse in its various forms rarely engages how white authority is inscribed and implicated in the creation and reproduction of a society in which the voices of the center appear either invisible or unimplicated in the historical and social construction of racism as an integral part of their own collective identity. Rather than recognizing how differences are historically and socially constructed within ideologies and material practices that connect race, class, and gender within webbed connections of domination, liberals consign the struggle of subordinate groups to master narratives that suggest that the oppressed need to be remade in the image of a dominant white culture in order to be integrated into the heavenly city of Enlightenment rationality.

Eurocentric radical discourses of modernity have also failed to develop a complex and adequate theory of racism as part of a wider theory of difference and democratic struggle. The classic instance in this case is represented by those versions of Marxism which have reduced struggle and difference to a reductionist logo-centricism which universalizes the working class as the collective agent of history. Marxism buys the productivist discourse of modernity but rejects the liberal notion of the middle class as the agent of history. Economism in its Marxist form rejects the rule of the market as the end of ideology and inserts in its place the rule of the working class as the projected end of history. In this view, racism is historically tied to the rise of capitalism and is afforded no independent status as an irreducible source of either exploitation or struggle. In this instance, the notion of historical agency loses its pluralist character. As a consequence, racism is subsumed within the modernist logic of essentialism in which reason and history seem to move according to some inner logic outside of the play of difference and plurality. In effect, class struggle becomes the all embracing category that relegates all other struggles, voices, and conflicts to simply a distraction in the march of history.[15]

Radical social theorists have long offered a challenge to the classical Marxist theory of race, but it is only within the last few decades that such work has advanced the category of difference beyond the essentialism of black nationalism, cultural separatism, staged pluralism, and the discourse of avant-garde exoticism.[16] The failure of modernism around race can be seen in the ways in which it has structured the discourse of educational reform on this issue.

Educational Theory and the Discourse of Race and Ethnicity

Within the discourse of modernism, dominant educational approaches to race and ethnicity imitate many of the worst dimensions of liberal ideology and radical essentialism.[17] Questions of Otherness are generally fashioned in the discourse of multicultural education, which in its varied forms and approaches generally fails to conceptualize issues of race and ethnicity as part of the wider discourse of power and powerlessness. Questions of representation and inclusion suppress any attempts to call into question the norm of whiteness as an ethnic category that secures its dominance by appearing to be invisible. Modernism's emancipatory potential within multicultural education finds expression in the call to reverse negative images of blacks and other ethnic groups as they appear in various forms of texts and images. Missing here is any attempt either to critique forms of European and American culture that situate difference in structures of domination or to reconstruct a discourse of race and ethnicity in a theory of difference that highlights questions of equality, justice, and liberty as part of an ongoing democratic struggle. Multiculturalism is generally about Otherness, but is written in ways in which the dominating aspects of white culture are not called into question and the oppositional potential of difference as a site of struggle is muted.[18] Modernism and dominant forms of multicultural education merge in their refusal to locate cultural differences in a broader examination of how the boundaries of ethnicity, race, and power make visible how "whiteness" functions as a historical and social construction, "an unrecognized and unspoken racial category" that secures its power by refusing to identify culture as a problem of politics, power, *and* pedagogy.[19] As a critical discourse of race and pedagogy, multiculturalism needs to break out of its silence regarding the role it plays in masking how white domination colonizes definitions of the normal.[20] In effect, critical educators need to move their analyses and pedagogical practices away from an exotic or allegedly objective encounter with marginal groups, and raise more questions with respect to how the dominant self is always present in the construction of the margins. As Toni Morrison points out, the very issue of race requires that the bases of Western civilization will require rethinking.[21] It means that the central questions may not be why Afro-Americans are absent from dominant narratives, but "What intellectual feats had to be performed by the author or his critic to erase [blacks] from a society seething with [their] presence, and what effect has that performance had on the work? What are the strategies of escape from knowledge?"[22] This means refiguring the map of ethnicity and difference outside the binary oppositions of modernism. What is at stake here is more than the politics of representation. Issac Julien and Kobena Mercer state the issue clearly:

> One issue at stake, we suggest, is the potential break-up or deconstruction of structures that determine what is regarded as culturally central and what is regarded as cultural marginal. . . . Rather than attempt to compensate the, "structured absences" of previous paradigms, it would be useful to identify the relations of power/knowledge that determine which cultural issues are intellectually prioritized in the first place. The initial stage in any deconstructive project must be to examine and undermine the force of the binary relation that produces, the marginal as a consequence of the authority invested in the centre.[23]

Implicit in this perspective are a number of political and pedagogical challenges that can be taken up by radical educators as part of a broader theoretical attempt to deconstruct and displace some of the more powerful ideological expressions of a hegemonic theory of multicultural education. First, critical educators need to reveal the political interests at work in those forms of multicultural education that translate cultural differences into merely learning styles; the ideological task here is to challenge those mystifying ideologies that separate culture from power and struggle while simultaneously treating difference as a technical rather than a political category. Second, critical educators need to challenge those educational discourses that view schooling as a decontextualized site free from social, political, and racial tensions. What has to be stressed here is the primacy of the political and the contextual in analyzing issues of culture, language, and voice. Third, critical educators must ideologically engage theories of multicultural education that attempt to smother the relationship between difference and power/empowerment under the call for harmony and joyful learning. At the same time, they must further the development of a theory of difference that takes as its starting point issues of power, domination, and struggle.[24] But an anti-racist pedagogy must do more than reconceptualize the political and pedagogical struggle over race, ethnicity, and difference as merely part of the language of critique, it must also retrieve and reconstruct possibilities for establishing the basis for a progressive vision that makes schooling for democracy and critical citizenship an unrealized yet possible reality. In doing so, it is necessary to provide some central theoretical principles for developing the foundation for an anti-racist pedagogy. In what follows, at the risk of repeating some of my comments on postmodernism in the Introduction, I will argue that there are elements of a postmodern discourse that offer valuable insights for engaging in such a task.

Postmodernism and the Shifting Boundaries of Otherness

Postmodernism is a culture and politics of transgression, it is a challenge to the boundaries in which modernism has developed it discourses of mastery, totalization, representation, subjectivity, and history.[25] Whereas modernism builds its dream of social engineering on the foundations of universal reason and the unified subject, postmodernism questions the very notion of meaning and representation. Postmodernism not only opens up a new political front within discourse and representation, it also criticizes the notion of the unified subject as a Eurocentric construct designed to provide white, male, Christian bosses and workers with a legitimating ideology for colonizing and marginalizing those Others who do not measure up to the standards of an "I" or "We" wielding power from the center of the world.[26]

Postmodernism also rejects the modernist distinction between art and life. In doing so, it rejects the modernist distinctions between elite culture and the culture of everyday life. As a discourse of disruption and subversion, postmodernism does not argue that all referents for meaning and representation have disappeared; rather, it seeks to make them problematic, and in doing so reinscribes and rewrites the boundaries for establishing the conditions for the production of meaning and subjectivity.[27] For example, in treating cultural forms as tests, postmodernism multiplies both the possibilities of constructing meaning and the status of meaning itself. In this sense, postmodernism redraws and retheorizes the objects and experiences of politics by extending the reach of power and meaning to spheres of the everyday that are often excluded from the realm of political analysis and pedagogical legitimation. In this case, the field of political contestation is not restricted to the state and the workplace, but also includes the family, mass and popular culture, the sphere of sexuality, and the terrain of the refused and forgotten. In the discourse of modernism, there is a world held together by the metanarrative of universal reason and social engineering.[28] Therefore, the central questions for modernists have been "How can I interpret and master this world? How do I constitute myself within it?" Postmodernism does not begin from such a comfortable sense of place and history. It subordinates reason to uncertainty and pushes its sense of distrust into transgressions that open up entirely different lines of inquiry. Zygmunt Bauman captures the political and epistemological shifts between modernism and postmodernism in the different questions and lines of inquiry they each pursue. He writes:

> [Postmodernists] have hardly any axioms they may use as a confident start, nor do they have a clear address. Before they turn to exploring the world, they must find out what world(s) there is (are) to be explored. Hence: "Which world is it? What is to be done in it? Which of my selves is to do it?"—in this order. . . . the typically modern questions are, among others: "What is there to be known? Who knows it? How do they know it, and with what degree of certainty?" The typically postmodern questions do not reach that far. Instead of locating the task for the knower, they attempt to locate the knower himself [sic]. "What is a world? What kinds of worlds are there? How are they constituted, and how do they differ?" Even when shar-

ing concern about knowledge, the two types of inquiry articulate their problems differently: "How is knowledge transmitted from one knower to another, and with what degree of reliability?" as against "What happens when different worlds are placed in confrontation, or when boundaries between worlds are violated?" Not that postmodern questions have no use for "certainty"; not even reliability." The one-upmanship of modernist epistemology looks hopelessly out of place in that pluralist reality to which the postmodern ontological inquiry is first reconciled and then addressed. Here that overwhelming desire of power which animated the search for the ultimate (and which alone could animate it) raises little passion. Only eyebrows are raised by the self-confidence which once made the pursuit of the absolute look as a plausible project.[29]

In the above quote, Bauman articulates an antagonism that has became a central feature of postmodernist discourse. That is, postmodernism rejects those aspects of the Enlightenment and Western philosophical tradition that rely on master-narratives "which set out to address a transcendental Subject, to define an essential human nature, to prescribe a global human destiny or to proscribe collective human goals."[30] Within this perspective all claims to universal reason and impartial competence are rejected in favor of the partiality and specificity of discourse. General abstractions that deny the specificity and particularity of everyday life, that generalize out of existence the particular and the local, that smother difference under the banner of universalizing categories are rejected as totalitarian and terroristic.

But there is more at stake here than simply an argument against master-narratives or the claims of universal reason, there is also an attack on those intellectuals who would designate themselves as the emancipatory vanguard, an intellectual elite who have deemed themselves to be above history only to attempt to shape it through their pretentions to what Dick Hebdige (1986) calls an "illusory Faustian omnipotence."[31] In some versions of the postmodern, not only does totality and foundationalism not lead to the truth or emancipation, but in actuality to periods of great suffering and violence. The postmodernist attack on master-narratives is simultaneously a criticism of an inflated teleological self-confidence, a dangerous transcendentalism, and a rejection of the omniscient narrator.[32] Read in more positive terms, critical postmodernists are arguing for a plurality of voices and narratives, that is, for narratives of difference that recognize their own partiality and present the unrepresentable, those submerged and dangerous memories that provide a challenge to white supremacist logics and recover the legacies of historically specific struggles against racism. Similarly, postmodern discourse is attempting with its emphasis on the specific and the normative to situate reason and knowledge within rather than outside particular configurations of space, place, time, and power. Partiality in this case becomes a political necessity as part of the discourse of locating oneself within rather than outside of history and ideology.

Related to the critique of master-narratives and theories of totality is another major concern of critical postmodernism: the development of a politics that addresses popular culture as a serious object of aesthetic and cultural criticism, on the one hand, and one that signals and affirms the importance of minority cultures as historically specific forms of cultural production on the other.[33] Postmodernism's attack on universalism, in part, has translated into a refusal of modernism's relentless hostility to mass culture, and its reproduction of the elitist division between high and low culture.[34] Not only has postmodernism's reaffirmation of popular culture challenged the aesthetic and epistemological divisions supportive of academic disciplines and the contours of what has been considered "serious" taste, it has also resulted in new forms of art, writing, filmmaking, and types of aesthetic and social criticism.[35] Similarly, postmodernism has provided the conditions necessary for exploring and recuperating traditions of various forms of Otherness as a fundamental dimension of both the cultural and the sociopolitical sphere. In other words, postmodernism's stress on the problematic of Otherness has included: a focus on the importance of history as a form of counter-memory;[36] an emphasis on the value of the everyday as a source of agency and empowerment;[37] a renewed understanding of gender as an irreducible historical and social practice constituted in a plurality of self and social representations;[38] and an insertion of the contingent, the discontinuous, and the unrepresentable as coordinates for remapping and rethinking the borders that define one's existence and place in the world.

Another important aspect of postmodernism is that it provides a series of referents for both interrogating the notion of history as tradition and for redrawing and rewriting how individual and collective experience might be struggled over, understood, felt, and shaped. For example, postmodernism points to a world in which the production of meaning has become as important as the production of labor in shaping the boundaries of human existence. Three issues are at stake here. First, the notion that ideological and political

structures are determined and governed by a single economic logic
is rejected. Cultural and social forms contain a range of discursive
and ideological possibilities that can only be grasped within the
contextual and contradictory positions in which they are taken up;
moreover, while such forms are reproduced under the conditions of
capitalist production, they influence and are influenced by such relations. This is not a rejection of materialist analyses of culture as
much as a rejection of the vulgar reductionism that often accompanies its classical interpretations. Second, labor does not provide the
exclusive basis for either meaning or for understanding the multiple
and complex ensemble of social relations that constitute the wider
society. In this case, social antagonisms grounded in religious, gender, racial, and ethnic conflicts, among others, possess their own dynamism and cannot be reduced to the logic of capitalist relations.
More specific, the various discourses of historical materialism no
longer describe the social order. Third, how subjects are constituted
in language is no less important than how they are constructed as
subjects within relations of production. The world of the discursive,
with its ensemble of signifying terms and practices, is essential to
how people relate to themselves, others, and the world around
them. It is the textual world through which people develop a sense
of self and collective identity and relate to one another; this is not a
world that can be explained merely in terms of causal events that
follow the rule-bound determinations of physical and economic
laws.[39] The political economy of the sign does not displace political
economy, it simply assumes its rightful place as a primary category
for understanding how identities are forged within particular relations of privilege, oppression, and struggle. In pursuing this line of
inquiry, postmodernism serves to deterritorialize the map of dominant cultural understanding. That is, it rejects European tradition
as the exclusive referent for judging what constitutes historical,
cultural, and political truth. There is no tradition or story that can
speak with authority and certainty for all of humanity. In effect,
critical postmodernism argues that traditions should be valued for
their attempts to name the partial, the particular, and the specific;
in this view, traditions demonstrate the importance of constituting
history as a dialogue among a variety of voices as they struggle
within asymmetrical relations of power. Traditions are not valued
for their claims to truth or authority, but for the ways in which
they serve to liberate and enlarge human possibilities. In other
words, tradition does not represent the voice of an all-embracing
view of life; instead, it serves to place people self-consciously in their
histories by making them aware of the memories constituted in

difference, struggle, and hope. Tradition in postmodern terms is a form of counter-memory that recovers complex, yet submerged identities that constitute the social and political construction of public life.[40]

Postmodernism rejects the modernist discourse on history which views it as uniform, chronological, and telelogical. In contrast, it argues for a view of history that is decentered, discontinuous, fragmented, and plural. Jim Collins rightly argues that postmodernism challenges this view of historiography by problematizing "histories that seek to minimize heterogeneity in pursuit of a dominant style, collective spirit, or any other such unitary conception."[41] He elaborates on this by arguing:

> The common denominator of all such histories, from Oswald Spengler's *The Decline of the West* to Will Wright's *Six Guns in Society,* has been the privileging of homogeneous structures that allow historians to draw rather neat generalizations that support far more grandiose claims about culture "as a whole." Emphasis has been placed repeatedly on the diachronic changes between periods, movements, moods, etc. instead of on synchronic tensions within those subdivisions—which would naturally undermine any unitary formulations concerning a particular period's representation of itself in a specific time. . . . The chief way to break this spell is to begin with a different set of priorities—specifically that most periods are a "mixture of inconsistent elements," and that different art forms, discourses, etc., all have their own history as well as a societal history. . . . To account for these differences, histories that have been predicated on theories of evolution, mass consciousness, or Zeitgeist, must be replaced by histories that emphasize synchronic tensions, the fragmentation of mass consciousness, and the possibility of more than one Zeitgeist per culture.[42]

It is worth emphasizing here that postmodernism not only raises central questions about how to rethink the meaning of history and traditions, but it also forces us in the absence of a discourse of essences and foundationalism to raise new and different questions. In this case, as Chantal Mouffe has pointed out, postmodernism provides us with the possibility of understanding the limits of traditions so we can enter into dialogue with them, particularly with respect to how we may think about the construction of political subjects and the possibility of democratic life.[43]

Finally, and at the risk of great simplification, a postmodernism of resistance challenges the liberal, humanist notion of the unified, rational subject as the bearer of history.[44] In this instance, neither is the subject unified nor can such a subject's action be guaranteed in metaphysical or transhistorical terms. Postmodernism not only views the subject as contradictory and multilayered, it rejects the notion that individual consciousness and reason are the most important determinants in shaping human history. It posits instead a faith in forms of social transformation that are attentive to the historical, structural, and ideological limits which shape the possibility for self-reflection and action. It points to solidarity, community, and compassion as essential aspects of how we develop and understand the capacities we have for how we experience the world and ourselves in a meaningful way.[45] But it does so by stressing that in the absence of a unified subject, we can rethink the meaning of solidarity through a recognition of the multiple antagonisms and struggles that characterize both the notion of the self and the wider social reality. By recognizing the multiplicity of subject positions which mediate and are produced by and through contradictory meanings and social practices it becomes possible to create a discourse of democratic values that requires a "multiplication of democratic practices, institutionalizing them into ever more diverse social relations . . . [so that] we are able not only to defend democracy but also to deepen it."[46] In different terms, postmodernism offers a series of referents for rethinking how we are constituted as subjects within a rapidly changing set of political, social, and cultural conditions.

What does this suggest for the way we look at the issue of race and ethnicity? Postmodern discourse provides a theoretical foundation for deconstructing the master-narratives of white supremacist logics and for redrawing the boundaries between the construction of experience and power. In the first instance, by challenging the concept of master-narratives, critical postmodernism has opened up the possibility for launching a renewed attack on the underlying assumptions that have allowed the dominant culture to enforce its own authority and racist practices through an unproblematic appeal to the virtues of Western civilization. In challenging the notions of universal reason, the construction of a white, humanist subject, and the selective legitimation of high culture as the standard for cultural practice, postmodern criticism has illuminated how Eurocentric-American discourses of identity suppress difference, heterogeneity, and multiplicity in its efforts to maintain hegemonic relations of power. Not only does postmodernism provide new ways to understand how power works in constructing racist identities and subjectivities, it redefines culture and experience within multiple relations of difference that offer a range of subject positions from which people can struggle against racist ideologies and practices. By calling into question the themes of "degraded Otherness and subaltern marginality" postmodernism offers new theoretical tools for attacking "notions of exclusionary identity, dominating heterogeneity, and universality—or in more blunt language, white supremacy."[47] Postmodern engagements with foundationalism, culture, difference, and subjectivity provide the basis for questioning the modernist ideal of what constitutes a decent, humane, and good life. Rather than celebrate the narratives of the "masters," postmodernism raises important questions about how narratives get constructed, what they mean, how they regulate particular forms of moral and social experience, and how they presuppose and embody particular epistemological and political views of the world. Similarly, postmodernism attempts to delineate how borders are named; in fact, it attempts to redraw the very maps of meaning, desire, and difference, inscribing the social and individual body with new intellectual and emotional investments, and calling into question traditional forms of power and their accompanying modes of legitimation. All these developments redefine theory by moving it far beyond—and in opposition to—the concerns embodied in the ideologies and questions that have defined the underlying racist principles which have remained unchallenged as a central aspect of modernist discourse.

For educators interested in developing an anti-racist pedagogy, postmodernism offers new epistemologies for rethinking the broader and specific contexts in which democratic authority is defined; it offers what Richard Bernstein calls a healthy "suspiciousness of all boundary-fixing and the hidden ways in which we subordinate, exclude, and marginalize."[48] Postmodernism also offers educators a variety of discourses for interrogating modernism's reliance on totalizing theories based on a desire for certainty and absolutes.

In order for postmodernism to make a valuable contribution to the development of a critical pedagogy of race, educators must combine its most important theoretical insights with those stories and narratives that illuminate how difference and resistance are concretely expressed within communities of struggle organized around specific anti-racist practices. In this way, the project of an anti-racist pedagogy can be deepened by expanding its discourse to increasingly wider spheres of social relations and practices. Postmodern discourse must also do more than redefine difference as an integral aspect of the construction of educational life. Similarly, postmodernism must do more than reconstruct the theoretical discourse of resistance by recovering knowledge, histories, and experiences that have traditionally been left out of dominant accounts of schooling, everyday life, and history. Most important, there is a vital need for postmodernism to open up and establish public spheres among non-academic audiences and to work with such audiences as part of the struggle to fight racism and other forms of domination while simultaneously struggling to revitalize democratic public life. What is important to stress is the recognition that a critical postmodernism needs to provide educators with a more complex and insightful view of the relationship between culture, power, and knowledge. When linked with the language of democratic public life, the notions of difference, power, and specificity can be understood as part of a public discourse that broadens and deepens individual liberties and rights *through rather than against* a radical notion of democracy.

In what follows, I want to further develop how a postmodern discourse of resistance might be elaborated and advanced through the discourse of black feminists, and writers whose work serves to rewrite and reinscribe the relations between power and issues of difference, struggle, identity politics, and narrative.

Afro-American Feminist Writers and the Discourse of Possibility

Black women feminists have been writing against the grain for a long time in this country.[49] Most important, they have given the politics of resistance and solidarity a new meaning in the diverse ways in which they have struggled, as Barbara Christian puts it, "to define and express our totality rather than being defined by others."[50] Within the diverse body of material that makes up this work, there is a language both of critique and possibility. It is woven out of forms of testifying, narratives, and theorizing that reconstruct the meaning of difference while simultaneously rewriting the meaning of history as a basis for sustaining community memories and developing viable forms of collective struggle. The tensions that permeate this work range from suffering and resistance to a sense of healing and transcendence. For example, in the work of the novelist

Paule Marshall we encounter the attempts to reconstruct "the past and the need to reverse the present social order."[51] In the work of political writers such as June Jordan, Audre Lorde, Bell Hooks, and Hazel Carby there is an ongoing attempt to re-theorize the notion of voice as part of the shifting construction of identities forged in differences, especially those constituted out of class, race, and gender.[52] There is also an attempt to theorize voice as a historically specific cultural site from which one learns to create an oppositional consciousness and identity, a standpoint that exists not only as that which also opposes domination, but also enables and extends individual and social capacities and possibilities for making human connections and compassionate communities of resistance and liberation.[53]

Within this work, a discourse of difference and solidarity emerges which is multilayered and dialectical. First, all these black women offer, in different ways, a critique of difference as it is constructed through the codes and relations of the dominant culture. Second, black feminist writers have criticized the emancipatory notion of difference put forward by white feminists in the last decade while at the same time developing a more radical notion of the politics of difference and identity politics. Third, there is a brilliant reconstruction of difference in these works through the development of narratives as forms of dangerous memory that provide the foundation for communities of resistance and a radical ethics of accountability. In the next section, I will analyze each of these elements of difference before addressing their pedagogical implications for developing what I call a border pedagogy of resistance.

Unlike many radical and postmodern theories, the work of black feminists is deeply concerned with developing a politics of difference that locates the dynamics of domination in the center rather than on the margins of power. In effect, black feminists have attempted to uncover how complex modes of inequality are structured through racial, class, and gender divisions that lie at the heart of the dominant culture and by definition serve to shape its most basic institutional and ideological forms. A number of issues are at work here. First, there is the need to establish that racial identities are also white, and must be seen as specific historical and social constructions. In this way, questions of ethnicity must be seen as part of a broader discussion of racism. This is imperative in order to understand how whiteness serves as a norm to privilege its own definitions of power while also concealing the political and social distinctions embedded in its essentialist constructions of difference through the categories of race, gender, and class.

Within this perspective, difference cannot be understood outside the dynamics of silencing, subjugation, and infantilization. By focusing on the ways in which white ethnicity exercises power, designates Otherness in terms that degrade and cheapen human life, and hides its own partiality in narratives of universality and common sense, black feminists have been able to redefine what it means for people of color to come to voice and to speak in their own terms. To struggle within a politics of voice, within these practices, means that blacks have to reject a politics of the center in which the Other is reduced to an object whose experiences and traditions are either deemed alien by whites or whose identity has to bear exclusively the historical weight of Otherness and racialization. Hazel Carby illuminates this point well:

> . . . one way to rethink the relationship between the social, political and cultural construction of blackness and marginality, on the one hand, and assumptions of a normative whiteness within the dominant culture, on the other, is to examine the ways in which that dominant culture has been shaped and transformed by the presence of the marginalized. This means a public recognition that the process of marginalization itself is central to the formation of the dominant culture. The first and very important stage is . . . to recognize the cultural and political category of whiteness. It seems obvious to say it but in practice the racialization of our social order is only recognized in relation to racialized "others."[54]

What Carby points to is part of a broader theoretical attempt by black feminists to reject narrow notions of black identity while also calling into question the structured absences that historically and socially locate white ethnicity within subject positions that blind many whites to the mechanisms of cultural apartheid and relations of power that are constitutive of what it means to be part of a dominant Eurocentric culture in America. As CoCo Fusco puts it, "Endemic to this history are structured absences that function to maintain relations of power. To put it bluntly, no one has yet spoken of the 'self' implicit in the 'Other' or of the ones who are designating the 'Others.' Power, veiled and silent, remains in place."[55] Black feminists have provided an enormous service by shifting the discussion of difference away from an exclusive concern with the margins and in doing so have made it clear that any analysis of racial identity must include an analysis of how the "dominant other" functions to actively and systematically conceal its own historical and cultural identity while devaluing the identity of other racial groups. By challenging how boundaries of difference have been constructed through dominant Eurocentric codes and binarisms, it becomes possible to deepen our understanding of how white ethnicity is constructed in its attempts to position others. It also becomes possible to rethink the issue of subjectivity and resistance outside the crippling essentialisms that have characterized dominant humanist theory. Identity is no longer something that is fixed but fluid, shifting, and multiple. At the same time, oppression can now be seen in its multiple antagonisms and social relations. Once dominant culture is racialized within the discourse of ethnicity and existing power relations, it becomes possible to write history from the perspective of those engaged in the struggle against cultural genocide. Voices now begin to emerge from different locations and are no longer authorized to speak through a Eurocentric perspective that defines them in its own interests. bell hooks links this emergence of multiple voices as part of a wider struggle for a politics and identity that is crucial to the reconstruction of black subjectivity. She writes:

> We return to "identity" and "culture" for relocation, linked to political practice—identity that is not informed by a narrow cultural nationalism masking continued fascination with the power of the white Hegemonic Other. Instead identity is evoked as a stage in a process wherein one constructs radical black subjectivity. Recent critical reflections on static notions of black identity urge transformation on our sense of who can we be and still be black. Assimilation, imitation, or assuming the role of rebellious exotic other are not the only available options and never have been. This is why it is crucial to radically revise notions of identity politics, to explore marginal locations as spaces where we can best become whatever we want to be while remaining committed to liberatory black liberation struggle.[56]

Central to the notion of difference put forth by many black feminists is a notion of anti-racism that refigures the meaning of ethnicity as a social and historical construct. Such a view signals the end of the essentialist black subject as well as the structured absence of whiteness as a racial category. The strategic importance of this issue has been theoretically developed in the writing of a number of black feminists who have criticized the ways in which the notion of difference has been taken up by many white middle class feminists in the struggle over sexuality and gender.

Those of us who have been forged in the crucibles of difference—those of us who are poor, who are lesbians, who are black, who are older—know that survival is not an academic skill. It is learning how to stand alone, unpopular and sometimes reviled, and how to make common cause with those others identified as outside the structures in order to define and seek a world in which we can all flourish. It is learning how to take our differences and make them strengths. For the master's tools will never dismantle the master's house. They may allow us temporarily to beat him at his own game, but they will never enable us to bring about change.[57]

In this quote Audre Lorde uses the notion of difference as a referent for critique and as a basis for advancing the emancipatory possibilities in a radicalized notion of difference. In the first instance, she argues against various versions of contemporary feminism which limit domination to a sphere of sexual relations and, in doing so, develop a discourse of difference that excludes questions of racism, class domination, and homophobia. Under the banner of feminist struggle and liberation, many contemporary feminists have unconsciously reconstructed the Eurocentric logo-centrism they claimed they were attacking. In effect, while the center was being reconstructed as an affirmation of feminism in the service of an attack on patriarchy, it functioned to recreate existing margins of power while denying the voices of working class women, lesbians, and women of color. As Lorde points out, "The absence of these considerations weakens any feminist discussion of the personal and the political. It is a particular academic arrogance to assume any discussion of feminist theory without examining our many differences, and without a significant input from poor women, black and Third World women, and lesbians."[58] Lorde is not merely criticizing a feminist perspective that refuses to examine differences as they are constructed outside the worlds of white, middle class women, she is also arguing that in this refusal of difference lie the seeds of racism and homophobia. She recognizes that whites have a heavy cultural, political, and affective investment in ignoring differences. For to recognize such differences is to immediately call into play the asymmetrical relations of power that structure the lives of white and black women differently. For white middle class women, this often invokes guilt and forces them to "allow women of Color to step out of stereotypes . . . [and] it threatens the complacency of these women who view oppression only in terms of sex."[59] Lorde is eloquent on this issue.

Poor women and women of Color know there is a difference between the daily manifestations of marital slavery and prosti-
tution because it is our daughters who line 42nd Street. If
white American feminist theory need not deal with the differences between us, and the resulting difference in our oppres-
sions, then how do you deal with the fact that the women who
clean your houses and tend your children while you attend
conferences on feminist theory, are for the most part, poor
women and women of Color? What is the theory behind racist
feminism? In a world of possibility for us all, our personal visions help lay the groundwork for political action. The failure
of academic feminists to recognize difference as a crucial
strength is a failure to reach beyond the first patriarchal lesson. In our world, divide and conquer must become define and
empower.[60]

But Lorde, like a number of black writers, is not content either
to limit her analysis to the racism inherent in narrowly defined feminist theories of difference or to deconstructing forms of cultural
separatism which argue that blacks only need to bear witness to the
positive moments in their own stories. These are important political
and strategic issues, but Lorde is also concerned about developing a
politics of solidarity and identity that views difference as a dynamic
human force that is "enriching rather than threatening to the defined self when there are shared goals."[61] In this case, black women
writers have attempted to develop a politics of difference that cele-
brates its creative function while at the same time arguing for new
forms of community rooted in definitions of power and patterns of
relating that allow diverse groups of people to reach out beyond
their own interests in order to forge living connections with a multitude of differences for the purpose of developing a democratic
culture and society.
     At issue here is a politics of resistance in which difference is
explored through the category of voice and solidarity. It is important to stress, even at the expense of overstating the issue, that
black feminists have attempted to develop a notion of black subjectivity and voice that portrays black women outside the narrow confines of an essentialist and stereotypical reading. In this case, there
is an attempt to develop a notion of self and identity that links difference to the insistence of speaking in many voices, to fasten a notion of identity that is shifting and multiple rather than static and
singular. Central here is the need to engage voice as an act of resistance and self-transformation, to recognize that as one comes to

voice one establishes the precondition for becoming a subject in history rather than an object.[62] In analyzing a portion of her own experience in attending all-black segregated schools, bell hooks comments on how she learned to recognize the value of an education that allowed her to speak in many voices. She writes:

> In part, attending all-black segregated schools with black teachers meant that I had come to understand black poets as being capable of speaking in many voices. . . . The black poet, as exemplified by Gwendolyn Brooks and later Amiri Baraka, had many voices—with no single voice being identified as more or less authentic. The insistence on finding one voice, one definitive style of writing and reading one poetry, fit all too neatly with a static notion of self and identity that was pervasive in university settings. It seemed that many black students found our situations problematic precisely because our sense of self, and by definition our voice, was not unilateral, monologist, or static but rather multi-dimensional. We were at home in dialect as we were in standard English. Individuals who speak languages other than English, who speak patois as well as standard English, find it a necessary aspect of self-affirmation not to feel compelled to choose one voice over another, not to claim one as more authentic, but rather to construct social realities that celebrate, acknowledge, and affirm differences, variety. . . . To claim all the tongues in which we speak, to make speech of the many languages that give expression to the unique cultural reality of a people.[63]

As part of a politics of difference, an anti-racist pedagogy would have to investigate the relationship between language and voice as part of a wider concern with democratic struggles and antogonisms. Instead of talking about literacy, radical educational theory would have to educate teachers and administrators to speak and listen to many languages and understandings of the world. Not only would this open up the possibility for many people to speak from the decided advantage of their own experiences, it would also multiply and decidedly transform the discursive, and nondiscursive sites from which administrators, teachers, students, parents, and neighborhood people could engage in dialogue and communities of solidarity. A radical educational discourse would also educate people to the tyranny that lies beneath logocentric narratives, truths that appear to exist beyond criticism, and language that undermines the force of democratic encounters. In this context, June

Jordan is illuminating in sharply contrasting the implications of a language of difference with the reality that most people find themselves in at the current historical juncture in the United States.

> I am talking about majority problems of language in a democratic state, problems of a currency that someone has stolen and hidden away and then homogenized into an official "English" language that can only express non-events involving nobody responsible, or lies. If we lived in a democratic state our language would have to hurtle, fly, curse, and sing, in all the common American names, all the undeniable and representative and participating voices of everybody here. We would not tolerate the language of the powerful and, thereby, lose all respect for words, per se. We would make our language conform to the truth of our many selves and we make our language lead us into the equality of power that a democratic state must represent. . . . This is not a democratic state. And we put up with that. We have the language of the powerful that perpetuates that power through the censorship of dissenting views.[64]

Another important element in the theory and politics of difference that has emerged in the writings of black feminists is the importance of stories, of narrative forms that keep alive communities of resistance while also indicting the collective destruction that mobilizes racism, sexism, and other forms of domination. Barbara Christian argues that black people have always theorized in narrative forms, "in the stories we create, in riddles and proverbs, in the play with language, since dynamic rather than fixed ideas seem more to our liking."[65] The narratives that are at work here are grounded in the discourse of everyday life, they are polyphonic, partial, and vibrant. And yet such narrative forms are produced amid relations of struggle. Toni Cade Bambara claims such stories are grounded in relations of survival, struggle, and wide-awake resistance. She writes:

> Stories are important. They keep us alive. In the ships, in the camps, in the quarters, field, prisons, on the road, on the run, underground, under siege, in the throes, on the verge—the storyteller snatches us back from the edge to hear the next chapter. In which we are the subjects. We, the hero of the tales. Our lives preserved. How it was, how it be. Passing it along in the relay. That is what I work to do: to produce stories that save our lives.[66]

The development of narrative forms and stories in the work of writers like Zora Neale Hurston, Paule Marshall, Toni Morrison, Alice Walker, and Toni Cade Bambara challenges the ways in which knowledge is constructed, illuminates the relationship between knowledge and power, and reinscribes the personal and the political so as to rewrite the dialectical connection between what we learn and how we come to learn given our specific location in history, experience, and language.[67] The literature of black feminist writers extends and challenges postmodernism's view of narratives. These writings link the form and substance of narrative storytelling to issues of survival and resistance and, in doing so, add a more progressive political character to narrative structure and substance than is developed in postmodern analyses. The development of stories in this literature becomes a medium for developing forms of historical consciousness that provide the basis for new relations of solidarity, community, and self-love. For example, Michelle Gibbs Russell links the political and the pedagogical in the use of storytelling and so demonstrates the radical potential it assumes as a form of self and social empowerment,

> The oldest form of building historical consciousness in community is storytelling. The transfer of knowledge, skill, and value from one generation to the next, the deliberate accumulation of a people's collective memory, has particular significance in diaspora culture. . . . Political education for black women in America begins with the memory of four hundred years of enslavement, diaspora, forced labor, beating, bombings, lynchings, and rape. It takes on inspirational dimensions when we begin cataloguing the heroic individuals and organizations in our history who have battled against those atrocities, and triumphed over them. It becomes practical when we are confronted with the problem of how to organize food cooperatives for women on food-stamp budgets or how to prove one's fitness as a mother in court. It becomes radical when, as teachers, we develop a methodology that places daily life at the center of history and enables black women to struggle for survival with the knowledge that they are making history. One setting where such connections can be made is the classroom. In the absence of any land, or turf, which we actually control, the classroom serves as a temporary space where we can evoke and evaluate our collective memory of what is done to us, and what we do in turn.[68]

As a pedagogical practice, the recovery and affirmation of stories that emanate from the experience of marginal groups can also serve in an emancipatory way to recenter the presence of white authority. Such stories cannot be used exclusively as a basis for whites to examine their own complicity in the construction of racism; they can also help privileged groups listen seriously to the multiple narratives that constitute the complexity of Others historically defined through reifications and stereotypes that smother difference within and between diverse subordinate groups. Of course, such stories also need to provide the opportunity to raise questions about what kinds of common claims regarding a discourse of ethics, accountability, and identity politics can be developed between whites and people of color around such narrative forms. I believe that by foregrounding and interrogating the variety of textual forms and voices that inform such narratives, students can deconstruct the masternarratives of racism, sexism, and class domination while simultaneously questioning how these narratives contribute to forms of self-hatred and contempt that surround the identities of blacks, women, and other subordinate groups.[69] Similarly, the stories of marginal groups provide counter-narratives that call into question the role that whites and other dominant groups have and continue to play in the perpetuating oppression and human suffering. Sharon Welch is instructive on this issue. She argues that listening to and engaging the stories of the Other can educate members of white, Eurocentric culture to a redefinition of responsibility through what she calls an ethic of risk and resistance. She writes:

> Particular stories call us to accountability. As dangerous memories of conflict, oppression and exclusion, they call those of us who are, often unknowingly, complicit in structures of control to join in resistance and transformation. For those of us who are members of the Western elite, by reason of race, gender, education, or economic status, we are challenged by the stories of the marginalized and oppressed to grasp the limits of our ethical and political wisdom—the limited appeal of our capitalist economic system, our limited appreciation of the vitality and determination of other peoples to shape their own identities. . . . We in the first World are not responsible for others; we are responsible for ourselves—for seeing the limits of our own vision and for rectifying the damages caused by the arrogant violation of those limits.[70]

Welch is arguing for a dialectical notion of narrative. She rightly argues that the narratives of subordinate groups need to be recovered as "dangerous memories" that rewrite and reinscribe the historical threads of community forged in resistance and struggle. She also argues that such stories are needed to construct an ethical discourse that indicts Eurocentric-American master-narratives so they can be critically interrogated and discarded when necessary in the interests of constructing social relations and communities of struggle that provide healing, salvation, and justice.

Border Pedagogy as Postmodern Resistance

If the construction of anti-racist pedagogy is to escape from a notion of difference that is silent about other social antagonisms and forms of struggle, it must be developed as part of a wider public discourse that is simultaneously about the discourse of an engaged plurality and the formation of critical citizenship. This must be a discourse that breathes life into the notion of democracy by stressing a notion of lived community that is *not* at odds with the principles of justice, liberty, and equality.[71] Such a discourse must be informed by a postmodern concern with establishing the material and ideological conditions that allow multiple, specific, and heterogeneous ways of life to come into play as part of a border pedagogy of postmodern resistance.[72] This points to the need for educators to prepare students for a type of citizenship that does not separate abstract rights from the realm of the everyday, and does not define community as the legitimating and unifying practice of a one-dimensional historical and cultural narrative. Postmodernism radicalizes the emancipatory possibilities of teaching and learning as part of a wider struggle for democratic public life and critical citizenship. It does this by refusing forms of knowledge and pedagogy wrapped in the legitimizing discourse of the sacred and the priestly; its rejecting universal reason as a foundation for human affairs; claiming that all narratives are partial; and performing a critical reading on all scientific, cultural, and social texts as historical and political constructions.

In this view, the broader parameters of an anti-racist pedagogy are informed by a political project that links the creation of critical citizens to the development of a radical democracy; that is, a political project that ties education to the broader struggle for a

public life in which dialogue, vision, and compassion remain critically attentive to the rights and conditions that organize public
space as a democratic social form rather than as a regime of terror
and oppression. It is important to emphasize that difference and
pluralism in this view do not mean reducing democracy to the equivalency of diverse interests; on the contrary, what is being argued for
is a language in which different voices and traditions exist and
flourish to the degree that they listen to the voices of others, engage
in an ongoing attempt to eliminate forms of subjective and objective
suffering, and maintain those conditions in which the act of communicating and living extends rather than restricts the creation of
democratic public spheres. This is as much a political as it is a pedagogical project, one that demands that anti-racist pedagogical
practices be developed within a discourse that combines a democratic public philosophy with a postmodern theory of resistance.
Within this perspective, the issue of border pedagogy is located
within those broader cultural and political considerations that are
beginning to redefine our traditional view of community, language,
space, and possibility. It is a pedagogy that is attentive to developing a democratic public philosophy that respects the notion of difference as part of a common struggle to extend and transform the
quality of public life. In short, the notion of border pedagogy does
not just presuppose an acknowledgment of the shifting borders that
both undermine and reterritorialize dominant configurations of
power and knowledge, it also links the notion of pedagogy to the creation of a society in which there is available a multiplicity of democratic practices, values, and social relations for students to take up
within different learning situations. At stake here is a view of democracy and learning in which multiplicity, plurality, and struggle
become the raison d'etre of democratic public life. Chantal Mouffe
has elaborated this position in neo-Gramscian terms better than
anyone else. She writes:

> If the task of radical democracy is indeed to deepen the dem-
> ocratic revolution and to link together diverse democratic
> struggles, such a task requires the creation of new subject-
> positions that would allow the common articulation, for ex-
> ample of antiracism, antisexism, and anticapitalism. These
> struggles do not spontaneously converge, and in order to es-
> tablish democratic equivalences, a new "common sense" is nec-
> essary which would transform the identity of different groups
> so that the demands of each group could be articulated with
> those of others according to the principle of democratic equiv-

alence. For it is not a matter of establishing a mere alliance between given interests but of actually modifying the very identity of those forces. In order that the defense of workers' interests is not pursued at the cost of the rights of women, immigrants, or consumers, it is necessary to establish an equivalence between these different struggles. It is only under these circumstances that struggles against power become truly democratic.[73]

Mouffe's position should not suggest that this is merely a political task to be established and carried out by an elite, a party, or a specific group of intellectuals. More important, it is a pedagogical task that has to be taken up and argued for by educators who take a particular stand on the meaning and importance of radical democracy as a way of life. Such a position not only rejects the one-sided and undemocratic interests that inform the conservative argument which collapses democracy into the logic of the market or buttresses the ideology of cultural uniformity, but also rejects leftist versions of an identity politics that excludes the other as part of reductive discourse of assertion and separatism.

What is being called for here is a notion of border pedagogy that provides educators with the opportunity to rethink the relations between the centers and the margins of power. That is, such a pedagogy must address the issue of racism as one that not only calls into question forms of subordination that create inequities among different groups as they live out their lives, but, as I have mentioned previously, also challenges those institutional and ideological boundaries that have historically masked their own relations of power behind complex forms of distinction and privilege. What does this suggest for the way we develop the basic elements of an anti-racist pedagogy?

First, the notion of border pedagogy offers students the opportunity to engage the multiple references that constitute different cultural codes, experiences, and languages. This means providing the learning opportunities for students to become media-literate in a world of changing representations. It means offering students the knowledge and social relations that enable them to read critically not only how cultural texts are regulated by various discursive codes but also how such texts express and represent different ideological interests. In this case, border pedagogy establishes conditions of learning that define literacy inside the categories of power and authority. This suggests developing pedagogical practices that address texts as social and historical constructions; it also suggests

developing pedagogical practices that allow students to analyze
texts in terms of their presences and absences; and most important,
such practices should provide students with the opportunity to read
texts dialogically through a configuration of many voices, some of
which offer up resistance, some of which provide support.

Border pedagogy also stresses the necessity for providing students with the opportunity to engage critically the strengths and
limitations of the cultural and social codes that define their own
histories and narratives. Partiality becomes, in this case, the basis
for recognizing the limits built into all discourses. At issue here is
not merely the need for students to develop a healthy skepticism towards all discourses of authority, but also to recognize how authority and power can be transformed in the interest of creating a
democratic society.

Within this discourse, students engage knowledge as a border-
crosser, as a person moving in and out of borders constructed
around coordinates of difference and power.[74] These are not only
physical borders, they are cultural borders historically constructed
and socially organized within maps of rules and regulations that
serve to either limit or enable particular identities, individual capacities, and social forms. In this case, students cross over into borders of meaning, maps of knowledge, social relations, and values
that are increasingly being negotiated and rewritten as the codes
and regulations which organize them become destabilized and re-
shaped. Border pedagogy decenters as it remaps. The terrain of
learning becomes inextricably linked to the shifting parameters of
place, identity, history, and power. By reconstructing the traditional
radical emphasis of the knowledge/power relationship away from
the limited emphasis of mapping domination to the politically strategic issue of engaging the ways in which knowledge can be re-
mapped, reterritorialized, and decentered, in the wider interests of
rewriting the borders and coordinates of an oppositional cultural
politics, educators can redefine the teacher/student relationship in
ways that allow students to draw upon their own personal experience as real knowledge.

At one level this means giving students the opportunity to
speak, to locate themselves in history, and to become subjects in the
construction of their identities and the wider society. It also means
defining voice not merely as an opportunity to speak, but to engage
critically with the ideology and substance of speech, writing, and
other forms of cultural production. In this case, "coming to voice" for
students from both dominant and subordinate cultures means engaging in rigorous discussions of various cultural texts, drawing

upon one's personal experience, and confronting the process through which ethnicity and power can be rethought as a political narrative that challenges racism as part of broader struggle to democratize social, political, and economic life.[75] In part, this means looking at the various ways in which race implicates relations of domination, resistance, suffering, and power within various social practices and how these are taken up in multiple ways by students who occupy different ethnic, social, and gender locations. In this way, race is never discussed outside broader articulations, nor is it merely about people of color.

Second, a border pedagogy of postmodern resistance needs to do more than educate students to perform ideological surgery on master-narratives based on white, patriarchal, and class-specific interests. If the master-narratives of domination are to be effectively deterritorialized, it is important for educators to understand how such narratives are taken up as part of an investment of feeling, pleasure, and desire. There is a need to rethink the syntax of learning and behavior outside the geography of rationality and reason. For example, this means that racism cannot be dealt with in a purely limited, analytical way. An anti-racist pedagogy must engage how and why students make particular ideological and affective investments and occupy particular subject positions in regard to issues concerning race and racism. This means attempting to understand the historical context and substance of the social and cultural forms that produce in diverse and multiple ways the often contradictory subject positions that give students a sense of meaning, purpose, and delight. As Stuart Hall argues, this means uncovering both for ourselves as teachers and for the students we are teaching "the deep structural factors which have a tendency persistently not only to generate racial practices and structures but to reproduce them through time and which therefore account for their extraordinarily immovable character."[76] In addition to engaging racism within a politics of representation, ideology, and pleasure, it is important to stress that any serious analysis of racism also has to be historical and structural. It has to chart out how racist practices develop, where they come from, how they are sustained, how they affect dominant and subordinate groups, and how they can be challenged. This is not a discourse about personal preferences or dominant tastes but a discourse about economics, culture, politics, and power.[77]

Third, a border pedagogy offers the opportunity for students to air their feelings about race from the perspective of the subject positions they experience as constitutive of their own identities.

Ideology in this sense is treated not merely as an abstraction but as part of the student's lived experience. This does not mean that teachers reduce their roles to those of intellectual voyeurs or collapse their authority into a shabby form of relativism. Nor does it suggest that students merely express or assess their own experiences. Rather, it points to a particular form of teacher authority grounded in a respect for a radically decentered notion of democratic public life. This is a view of authority that rejects the notion that all forms of authority are expressions of unwarranted power and oppression. Instead, it argues for forms of authority that are rooted in democratic interests and emancipatory social relations, forms of authority that, in this case, begins from a standpoint from which to develop an educational project that rejects politics as aesthetics, that retains instead the significance of the knowledge/power relationship as a discourse of criticism and politics necessary for the achievement of equality, freedom, and struggle. This is not a form of authority based on an appeal to universal truths, it is a form of authority that recognizes its own partiality while simultaneously asserting a standpoint from which to engage the discourses and practices of democracy, freedom, and domination. Put another way, this is a notion of authority rooted in a political project that ties education to the broader struggle for public life in which dialogue, vision, and compassion remain critically attentive to the liberating and dominating relations that organize various aspects of everyday life.

This suggests that teachers use their authority to establish classroom conditions in which different views about race can be aired but not treated as simply expressions of individual views or feelings.[78] Andrew Hannan rightly points out that educators must refuse to treat racism as a matter of individual prejudice and counter such a position by addressing the "structural foundations of [the] culture of racism."[79] An anti-racist pedagogy must demonstrate that the views we hold about race have different historical and ideological weight, forged in asymmetrical relations of power, and that they always embody interests that shape social practices in particular ways. In other words, an anti-racist pedagogy cannot treat ideologies as simply individual expressions of feeling, but as historical, cultural, and social practices that serve to either undermine or reconstruct democratic public life. These views must be engaged without silencing students, but they must also be interrogated next to a public philosophy that names racism for what it is and calls racist ideologies and practices into account on political and ethical terms.

Fourth, educators need to understand how the experience of marginality at the level of everyday life lends itself to forms of oppositional and transformative consciousness. For those designated as Others need to both reclaim and remake their histories, voices, and visions as part of a wider struggle to change those material and social relations that deny radical pluralism as the basis of democratic political community. It is only through such an understanding that teachers can develop a border pedagogy which opens up the possibility for students to reclaim their voices as part of a process of empowerment and not merely what some have called an initiation into the culture of power.[80] It is not enough for students to learn how the dominant culture works to exercise power, they must also understand how to resist power which is oppressive, which names them in a way that undermines their ability to govern rather than serve, and prevents them from struggling against forms of power that subjugate and exploit. For example, Lisa Delpit's call for educators to integrate black students into what she unproblematically addresses as "the culture of power" appears to be blind to how such power is constructed in opposition to democratic values and used as a force for domination.[81] This is not to suggest that the authority of white dominant culture is all of one piece, nor is this meant to imply that it should not be the object of study. What is at stake here is forging a notion of power that does not collapse into a form of domination, but is critical and emancipatory, that allows students to both locate themselves in history and to critically, not slavishly, appropriate the cultural and political codes of their own and other traditions. Moreover, students who have to disavow their own racial heritage in order to succeed are not becoming "raceless" as Signithia Fordham has argued, they are being positioned to accept subject positions that are the sources of power for a white, dominant culture.[82] The ability of white, male, Eurocentric culture to normalize and universalize its own interests works so well, in this case, that Fordham underemphasizes how whiteness as a cultural and historical construction, as a site of dominant narratives, exercises the form of authority which prevented black students from speaking through their own memories, histories, and experiences. Delpit and Fordham are right in attempting to focus on issues of powerlessness as they relate to pedagogy and race, but they both obscure this relation by not illuminating more clearly how power works in this society within the schools to secure and conceal various forms of racism and subjugation. Power is multifaceted and we need a better understanding of how it works not simply as a force for oppression but also as a basis for resistance and self and social empowerment.

Educators need to fashion a critical postmodern notion of authority, one that decenters essentialist claims to power while at the same time fighting for relations of authority and power that allow many voices to speak so as to initiate students into a culture that multiplies rather than restricts democratic practices and social relations as part of a wider struggle for democratic public life.

Fifth, educators need to analyze racism not only as a structural and ideological force, but also in the diverse and historically specific ways in which it emerges. This is particularly true of the most recent and newest expressions of racism developing in the United States and abroad among youth in popular culture, and in its resurgence in the highest reaches of the American government.[83] This also suggests that any notion of an anti-racist pedagogy must arise out of specific settings and contexts. Such a pedagogy must allow its own character to be defined, in part, by the historically specific and contextual boundaries in which it emerges. At the same time, such a pedagogy must disavow all claims to scientific method or for that matter to any objective or transhistorical claims. As a political practice, an anti-racist pedagogy has to be constructed not on the basis of essentialist or universal claims but on the concreteness of its specific encounters, struggles, and engagements. Roger Simon outlines some of the issues involved here in his discussion of critical pedagogy.

> Such a form of educational work is at root contextual and conditional. A critical pedagogy can only be concretely discussed from within a particular "point of practice"; from within a specific time and place and within a particular theme. This means doing critical pedagogy is a strategic, practical task not a scientific one. It arises not against a background of psychological, sociological, anthropological universals—as does much educational theory related to pedagogy—but from such questions as: "How is human possibility being diminished here?"[84]

Sixth, an anti-racist border pedagogy must redefine how the circuits of power move in a dialectical fashion among various sites of cultural production.[85] We need a clearer understanding of how ideologies and other social practices which bear down on classroom relations emerge from and articulate with other spheres of social life. As educators, we need a clearer understanding of how the grounds for the production and organization of knowledge is related to forms of authority situated in political economy, the state, and other material practices. We also need to understand how circuits of power

produce forms of textual authority that offer readers particular subject positions, that is, ideological references that provide but do not
rigidly determine particular views of the world.[86] In addition, educators need to explore how the reading of texts is linked to the
forms of knowledge and social relations that students bring to the
classroom. In other words, we need to understand in terms of function and substance those social and cultural forms outside the classroom that produce the multiple and often contradictory subject
positions that students learn and express in their interaction with
the dominant cultural capital of American schools.

Finally, central to the notion of border pedagogy is a number
of important pedagogical issues regarding the role that teachers
might take up in making a commitment to fighting racism in their
classrooms, schools, communities, and the wider society. The concept of border pedagogy also helps to locate teachers within social,
political, and cultural boundaries that define and mediate in complex ways how they function as intellectuals who exercise particular forms of moral and social regulation. Border pedagogy calls
attention to both the ideological and the partial as central elements
in the construction of teacher discourse and practice. In part, this
suggests that to the degree that teachers make the construction of
their own voices, histories, and ideologies problematic they become
more attentive to Otherness as a deeply political and pedagogical
issue. In other words, by deconstructing the underlying principles
which inform their own lives and pedagogy, educators can begin to
recognize the limits underlying the partiality of their own views.
Such a recognition offers the promise of allowing teachers to re-
structure their pedagogical relations in order to engage in open and
critical dialogue questions regarding the knowledge taught, how
it relates to students' lives, how students can engage with such
knowledge, and how such practices actually relate to empowering
both teachers and students. Within dominant models of pedagogy,
teachers are often silenced through a refusal or inability to make
problematic with students the values that inform how they teach
and engage the multifaceted relationship between knowledge and
power. Without the benefit of dialogue, an understanding of the partiality of their own beliefs, they are cut off from any understanding
of the effects their pedagogies have on students. In effect, their in-
fatuation with certainty and control serves to limit the possibilities
inherent in their own voices and visions. In this case, dominant pedagogy serves not only to disempower students, but teachers as well.
In short, teachers need to take up a pedagogy that provides a more
dialectical understanding of their own politics and values; they

need to break down pedagogical boundaries that silence them in the name of methodological rigor or pedagogical absolutes; more important, they need to develop a power-sensitive discourse that allows them to open up their interactions with the discourses of various Others so that their classrooms can engage rather than block out the multiple positions and experiences that allow teachers and students to speak in and with many complex and different voices.[87]

What border pedagogy makes undeniable is the relational nature of one's own politics and personal investments. But at the same time, border pedagogy emphasizes the primacy of a politics in which teachers assert rather than retreat from the pedagogies they utilize in dealing with the various differences represented by the students who come into their classes. For example, it is not enough for teachers to merely affirm uncritically their students' histories, experiences, and stories. To take student voices at face value is to run the risk of idealizing and romanticizing them. It is crucial that critical educators do more than allow such stories to be heard. It is equally important for teachers to help students find a language for critically examining the historically and socially constructed forms by which they live. Such a process involves more than allowing students to speak from their own histories and social formations, it also raises questions about how teachers use power to cross over borders that are culturally strange and alien to them.

At issue here is not a patronizing notion of understanding the Other, but a sense of how the self is implicated in the construction of Otherness, how exercising critical attention to such a relationship might allow educators to move out of the center of the dominant culture to its margins in order to analyze critically the political, social, and cultural lineaments of their own values and voices as viewed from different ideological and cultural spaces. It is important for teachers to understand both how they wield power and authority and how particular forms of authority are sedimented in the construction of their own needs along with the limited subject positions offered them in schools. Border pedagogy is not about engaging just the positionality of our students but the nature of own identities as they have and are emerging within and between various circuits of power. If students are going to learn how to take risks, to develop a healthy skepticisms towards all masternarratives, to recognize the power relations that offer them the opportunity to speak in particular ways, and be willing to address their role as critical citizens who can animate a democratic culture, they need to see such behavior demonstrated in the social practices and subject positions that teachers live out and not merely propose.

If an anti-racist pedagogy is to have any meaning as a force for creating a democratic society, teachers and students must be given the opportunity to put into effect what they learn outside the school. In other words, they must be given the opportunity to engage in anti-racist struggles in their effort to link schooling to real life, ethical discourse to political action, and classroom relations to a broader notion of cultural politics. School curriculum should make anti-racist pedagogies central to the task of educating students to animate a wider and more critically engaged public culture, it should not merely allow them to take risks but also to push against the boundaries of an oppressive social order. Such projects can be used to address the relevance of the school curriculum and its role as a significant public force for linking learning and social justice to the daily institutional and cultural traditions of society and reshaping them in the process. All schools should have teachers and students participate in an anti-racist curriculum that in some way links up with projects in the wider society. This approach not only redefines teacher authority and student responsibility, but places the school as a major force in the struggle for social, economic, and cultural justice. In this case, a critical postmodern pedagogy of resistance points to challenging not only the oppressive boundaries of racism, but all those barriers which undermine and subvert the construction of a democratic society.

Notes

1. Editorial, "The Biggest Secret of Race Relations: The New White Minority," *Ebony Magazine* (April 1989), p. 84, John B. Kellog, "Forces of Change," *Phi Delta Kappan* (November, 1988), pp. 199–204.

2. Michelle Fine, *Framing Dropouts* (Albany, New York: State University of New York Press, 1991).

3. Kirk Johnson, "A New Generation of Racism is Seen," *The New York Times,* August 27, 1989, p. 20; Kathy Dobie, "The Boys of Bensonhurst," *The Village Voice,* 54:36 (September 5, 1989), pp. 34–39.

3. Chantal Mouffe, "Hegemony and New Political Subjects: Toward a New Concept of Democracy," in Cary Nelson and Larry Grossberg (eds), *Marxism and the Interpretation of Culture* (Urbana: University of Illinois Press, 1988), p. 102. It is important to note here that in talking about

mocracy, critical democracy, or democratic public culture, I am referring to democracy as a system of social relations based on forms of pluralism and popular power that encourage social forms that extend and encourage rather than deny the realization of a variety of human capacities. At issue here is a conception of public life inspired by a redistribution of power and material and ideological capital in ways that extend the relations of equality, liberty, and justice to all spheres of social and economic life and not merely to the sphere of political formalism. For an extensive discussion of critical democracy, see Henry A. Giroux, *Schooling and the Struggle for Public Life* (Minneapolis: University of Minnesota Press, 1988).

5. Jon Pareles, "There's a New Sound in Pop Music: Bigotry," *The New York Times,* Section 2, Sunday, September 10, 1989, pp. 10 & 32.

6. This theme is taken up in Stanley Aronowitz and Henry A. Giroux, *Education Under Siege* (Granby, Mass.: Bergin and Garvey Press, 1985).

7. This position was first made famous in Daniel Moynihan, "The Moynihan Report," [The Negro Family: The Case for National Action." Washington, D.C. U.S. Department of Labor, 1965. For two critical responses to this report, see Marian Wright Edelman, *Families in Peril: An Agenda for Social Change* (Cambridge: Harvard University Press, 1987); Hortense J. Spillers, "Mama's Baby, Papa's Maybe: An American Grammar Book," *Diacritics* 17:2 (Summer 1987), pp. 65–81. See also a special issue of *The Nation,* (July 24/31, 1989), entitled "Scapegoating the Black Family: Black Women Speak."

8. Ernesto Laclau, "Politics and the Limits of Modernity," in Andrew Ross (ed.), *Universal Abandon? The Politics of Postmodernism* (Minneapolis: University of Minnesota Press, 1988), pp. 63–82; Nelly Richard, "Postmodernism and Periphery," *Third Text* 2 (1987/1988), pp. 5–12.

9. Gayatri C. Spivak, *In Other Worlds: Essays in Cultural Politics* (London: Metheun, 1987); See the two special issues of *Cultural Critique* on the nature and context of minority discourse, Numbers 6 & 7, Spring and Fall of 1987.

10. Cornell West, "Marxist Theory and the Specificity of Afro-American Oppression," in Cary Nelson and Larry Grossberg (eds), *Marxism and the Interpretation of Culture* (Urbana: University of Illinois Press, 1988), pp. 17–26; for an elaboration of West's perspective on racism, see Peter McLaren and Michael Dantley, "Cornel West and Stuart: Towards an Afro-American Pedagogy," *Journal of Negro Education* (in press).

11. David Kolb, *The Critique of Pure Modernity: Hegel, Heidegger, and After* (Chicago: University of Chicago Press, 1986), especially the first and last chapters.

12. Stuart Hall, "Gramsci's Relevance for the Study of Race and Ethnicity," *Journal of Communication Inquiry* 10:2 (Summer 1986), pp. 5–27.

13. Stanley Aronwitz, "Postmodernism and Politics," *Social Text* 18 (1987/1988), p. 113.

14. Scott Lash and John Urry, *The End of Organized Capitalism* (Madison: University of Wisconsin Press, 1987).

15. Two important critiques of Marxist economism can be found in Stanley Aronowitz, *The Crisis in Historical Materialism* (Granby, Mass.: Bergin and Garvey Press, 1983); Ernesto Laclau and Chantal Mouffe, *Hegemony and Socialist Strategy* (London: Verso Books, 1985).

16. Two important references on these issue are Cornel West, *Prophesy Deliverance: An Afro-American Revolutionary Christianity* (New York: Westminister Press, 1982); Cornel West, *The American Evasion of Philosophy* (Madison: University of Wisconsin Press, 1989); Coco Fusco, "Fantasies of Oppositionality: Reflections on recent conferences in Boston and New York," *Screen* 29:4 (Autumn, 1988), pp. 80–93.

17. See Henry A. Giroux, *Theory and Resistance in Education* (Granby, Mass.: Bergin and Garvey Press, 1983).

18. For example, see the work developed in John Young, ed. *Breaking the Mosaic: Ethnic Identities in Canadian Society* (Toronto: Garamond Press, 1987). Thomas Popkewitz, "Culture, Pedagogy, and Power: Issues in the Production of Values and Colonialization," *Journal of Education* 170:2 (1988), pp. 77–90.

19. Hazel Carby, "The Canon: Civil War and Reconstruction," *Michigan Quarterly Review* XXVIII: 1 (Winter, 1989), p. 39.

20. Richard Dyer, "White," *Screen* 29:4 (Autumn, 1988), pp. 44–64.

21. Toni Morrison, "Unspeakable Things Unspoken: The Afro-American Presence in American Literature," *Michigan Quarterly Review* XXVIII: I (Winter, 1989), pp. 1–34.

22. Ibid., p. 11.

23. Issac Julien and Kobena Mercer, "Introduction: De Margin and de Centre," *Screen* 8:2 (1987), p. 3.

24. Popkewitz, op. cit.; Hazel Carby, "Multi-Culture," *Screen Education* 34 (Spring 1980), pp. 62–70.

25. I make clear the distinction between critical and conservative forms of postmodernism in Henry A. Giroux, "Postmodernism and the Discourse of Educational Criticism," *Journal of Education* 170:3 (1988), pp. 5–30.

26. Robert Merrell, "Ethics/Aesthetics: A Post-Modern Position," in Robert Merrill (ed.), *Ethics/Aesthetics: Post-Modern Positions* (Washington, D.C.: Maisonneuve Press, 1988), pp. vii–xiii.

27. Hal Foster, Ed. *The Anti-Aesthetic: Essays on Postmodern Culture* (Towsend, Washington: Bay Press, 1983); Hal Foster, Ed., *Discussions in Contemporary Culture, Number one* (Seattle, Washington: Bay Press, 1987).

28. Jean-Francois Lyotard, *The Postmodern Condition: A Report on knowledge* (Minneapolis: University of Minnesota Press, 1984).

29. Zygmunt Bauman, "Strangers: The Social Construction of Universality and Particularity," *Telos* 78 (Winter 1988–1989), p. 12.

30. Dick Hebdige, "Postmodernism and 'the Other Side' ", *Journal of Communication Inquiry* 10:2 (1986), p. 81.

31. Ibid., p. 91.

32. Frenc Feher, "The Status of Postmodernity," *Philosophy and Social Criticism,* 13:2 (1988), pp. 195–206.

33. Jim Collins, *Uncommon Cultures: Popular Culture and Post-Modernism* (New York: Routledge, 1989).

34. Foster, op. cit., 1983.

35. A characteristic example of this work can be found in the wide-ranging essays on culture, art, and social criticism found in B. Wallis, (Ed.) *Blasted Allegories* (Cambridge: MIT Press, 1988).

36. Cora Kaplan, "Deterritorializations: The Rewriting of Home and exile in Western Feminist Discourse," *Cultural Critique* 6 (1987), pp. 187–198.

37. Larry Grossberg, "Putting the Pop Back into Postmodernism," in Andrew Ross, (ed.), *Universal Abandon? The Politics of Postmodernism* (Minneapolis: University of Minnesota Press, 1988), pp. 167–190.

38. Teresa DeLauretis, *Technologies of Gender* (Bloomington: Indiana University Press, 1987); Meighan Morris, *The Pirate's Fiancee: Feminism Reading, Postmodernism* (London: Verso Press, 1988).

39. These themes are taken up in Ernesto Laclau and Chantal Mouffe, *Hegemony and Socialist Strategy* (London: Verso Books, 1985); Stanley Aronowitz, *The Crisis in Historical Materialism* (South Hadley, Mass.: Bergin and Garvey, 1981). On the changing economic, political, and cultural conditions that characterize the postmodern condition, see Scott Lash and John Urry, *The End of Organized Capitalism* (Madison: University of Wisconsin Press, 1987) and David Harvey, *The Condition of Postmodernity* (New York: Basil Blackwell, 1989); Jean Baudrillard, *Selected Writings,* edited and Introduced by Mark Poster (Stanford: Stanford University Press, 1988).

40. Bruce James Smith, *Politics and Remembrance* (Princeton: Princeton University Press, 1985). See also Richard Terdiman, "Deconstructing Memory: On Representing the Past and Theorizing Culture in France Since the revolution," *Diacritics* (Winter 1985), pp. 13–16.

41. Jim Collins, op. cit., p. 115.

42. Ibid., p. 115.

43. Mouffe, op. cit., in Ross, ed. 1988.

44. For an analysis of this issue as educational criticism, see Linda Brodkey, *Academic Writing as a Social Practice* (Philadelphia: Temple University Press, 1987).

45. Sharon Welch, *A Feminist Ethic of Risk* (Minneapolis: Augsburg Fortress Press, 1989).

46. Mouffe, op. cit., in Ross, ed. 1988, p. 41.

47. Cornel West, "Black Culture and Postmodernism," in Barbara Kruger and Phil Mariani, (eds.), *Remaking History* (Seattle: Bay Press, 1989), p. 90.

48. Richard Bernstein, "Metaphysics, Critique, and Utopia," *The Review of Metaphysics* 42 (1988), p. 267.

49. Among the many anthologies on black women writers, one of the better ones is Mari Evans, ed., *Black Women Writers (1950–1980): A Critical Evaluation* (New York: Anchor Press, 1984). Important theoretical works discussing the writings of black women include: see Barbara Christian, *Black Feminist Criticism* (New York: Pergamon, 1985); Susan Willis, *Specifying: Black Women Writing—The American Experience* (Madison: University of Wisconsin Press, 1987); Hazel V. Carby, *Reconstructing Womanhood: The Emergence of the Afro-American Women Novelist* (New York: Oxford University Press, 1987); Sharon D. Welch, *A Feminist Ethic of Risk* (Fortress Press, 1990).

50. Christian, op. cit. p. 159.

51. Cited in John McCluskey, Jr., "And Call Every Generation Blessed: Theme, Setting and Ritual in the Works of Paule Marshall," in Evans, op. cit., p. 316.

52. See for instance, Audre Lorde, *Sister Outsider* (Freedom, CA.: The Crossing Press, 1984); bell hooks, *Talking Back* (Boston: South End Press, 1989); June Gordon, *On Call* (Boston: South End Press, 1987); and Carby, op. cit., *Reconstructing Womanhood*.

53. Lorde, op. cit.

54. Carby, op. cit., "The Canon: Civil War and Reconstruction," p. 39.

55. Fusco, op. cit., p. 90.

56. hooks, op. cit., "The Politics of Radical Black Subjectivity," *Talking Back,* 1989, p. 54.

57. Lorde, op. cit., p. 112.

58. Ibid., p. 112.

59. Ibid., p. 118.

60. Ibid., p. 112.

61. Ibid., p. 45.

62. Barbara Christian, *Black Feminist Criticism,* op. cit.

63. Hooks, op. cit., *Talking Back,* pp. 11–12.

64. June Jordan, op. cit., *On Call,* pp. 30–31.

65. Barbara Christian, "The Race for Theory," *Cultural Critique* 6 (Spring 1987), p. 52.

66. Toni Cade Bambara, "Evaluation is the Issue," in Mari Evans, ed., *Black Women Writers (1950–1980): A Critical Evaluation* (New York: Anchor Press, 1984), p. 46.

67. For sustained and clear analysis of the works of these particular Afro-American women writers, see Susan Willis, *Specifying: Black Women Writing—The American Experience* (Madison: University of Wisconsin Press, 1987).

68. Michelle Gibbs Russell, "Black Eyed Blues Connections: From the Inside Out," in Charlotte Bunch and Sandra Pollack (eds.), *Learning Our way: Essays in Feminist Education* (Trumansburg: The Crossing Press, 1983), pp. 274, 275.

69. June Jordan, "Where is the Love?" in Barbara H. Andolsen, Christine Gurdorf and Mary Pellauer (eds.), *Women's Consciousness Women's Conscience* (New York: Harper and Row, 1985), p. 203.

70. Sharon Welch, "Feminism, Modernity, and Postmodernism," *A Feminist Ethic of Risk*, p. 5.

71. Henry A. Giroux, *Schooling and the Struggle for Public Life* (Minneapolis: University of Minnesota Press, 1988). Chantal Mouffe, "Hegemony and New Political Subjects: Toward a New Concept of Democracy," in Cary Nelson and Larry Grossberg (eds.), *Marxism and the Interpretation of Culture* (Urbana: University of Illinois Press, 1988), pp. 89–104.

72. Henry A. Giroux, "Border Pedagogy in the Age of Postmodernism," *Journal of Education* 170:3 (1988), pp. 162–181.

73. Chantal Mouffe, "Radical Democracy: Modern or Postmodern," in Andrew Ross, ed. op. cit., p. 42.

74. D. Emily Hicks, "Deterritorialization and Border Writing," in Robert Merrill (ed.), *Ethics/Aesthetics: Post-Modern Positions* (Washington, D.C.: Maisonneuve Press, 1988), pp. 47–58.

75. For excellent theoretical and practical examples of how this approach to anti-racist education works using particular films, see Roger I. Simon, John Brown, Enid Lee, and Jon Young, *Decoding Discrimination: A Student-Based Approach to Anti-Racist Education Using Film* (Ontario, Canada: Althouse Press, 1988).

76. Stuart Hall, "Teaching Race," in Alan Jones and Robert Jeffcoate (eds.), *The School in the Multicultural Society* (London: Harper and Row Ltd., 1981), p. 61.

77. Some important books that develop a broad theoretical perspective for understanding racism in ideological, structural, and pedagogical terms are: Hazel Carby, et al., *The Empire Strikes Back* (London: Hutchinson, 1982); Lois Weiss, ed., *Class, Race, and Gender in American Education* (Albany, SUNY Press, 1988); Barry Troyna and Jenny Williams, Racism, Education and the State (London: Croom Helm, 1986); W. W. B. Du Bois, *Against Racism: Unpublished Essays, Papers, Addresses, 1887–1961,* edited by Herbert Aptheker (Amherst: University of Massachusetts Press, 1985); John Brown Childs, *Leadership, Conflict, and Cooperation in Afro-American Social Thought* (Philadelphia: Temple University Press, 1989); Authur Brittan and Mary Maynard, *Sexism, Racism and Oppression* (New York: Blackwell, 1985); Houston A. Baker, Jr., *Blues, Ideology, and Afro-American Literature* (Chicago: University of Chicago Press, 1984); and Cornel West, *Prophetic Fragments* (Trenton: Africa World Press, Inc., 1988).

78. Some important literature which explores this issue from a variety of pedagogical interventions include: Carter Godwin Woodson, *The Mis-Education of the Negro* (Washington, D.C.: The Associated Publishers, Inc., 1933); Gloria Ladson-Billings, "Like Lightning in a Bottle: Attempting to Capture the Pedagogical Excellence of Successful Teachers of Black Students," Paper presented at the Tenth Annual Ethnography in Education Research Forum, February 24–25, 1989, University of Pennsylvania, Philadelphia, Pennsylvania; Joyce Elain King and Gloria Ladson-Billings, "The Teacher Education Challenge in Elite University Settings: Developing Critical Perspectives for Teaching in a Democratic and Multicultural Society," *European Journal of Intercultural Education* (forthcoming); Joyce King, "Black Student Alienation and Black Teachers' Emancipatory Pedagogy," *The Journal of Black Reading and Language Education* 3:1 (May 1987), pp. 3–12; Cameron McCarthy, "Rethinking Liberal and Radical Perspectives on Racial Inequality in Schooling: Making the Case for Nonsynchrony," *Harvard Educational Review* 58:3 (1988), pp. 265–279.

79. Andrew Hannan, "Racism, Politics and the Curriculum," *British Journal of Sociology of Education* 8:2 (1987), p. 127.

80. Lisa Delpit, "The Silenced Dialogue: Power and Pedagogy in Educating Other People's Children," *Harvard Educational Review* 58:3 (1988), pp. 280–298.

81. Ibid.

82. Signithia Fordham, "Racelessness as a Factor in Black Students' School Success; Pragmatic Strategy or Pyrrhic Victory?" *Harvard Educational Review* 58:3 (1988), pp. 54–82.

83. Stuart Hall, "Teaching Race," in Alan Jones and Robert Jeffcoate (eds.), *The School in the Multicultural Society* (London: Harper and Row, Ltd., 1981), pp. 58–69.

84. Roger I. Simon, "For a Pedagogy of Possibility," *Critical Pedagogy Networker,* 1:1 (February 1988), p. 2.

85. Richard Johnson, "What is Cultural Studies Anyway?" *Social Text* 16 (Winter 1986/1987), pp. 38–80.

86. These issues are taken up in Catherine Belsey, *Critical Practice* (New York: Metheun, 1980); Tony Bennett, "Texts in History: The Determinations of Readings and Their Texts," in Derek Atridge, Geoff Bennington, and Rogert Young, eds. *Post-Structuralism and the Question of History* (New York and London: Cambridge University Press, 1987); Henry A. Giroux, "Reading Formations, Texts, Voice, and the Role of English Teachers as Public Intellectuals," in Stanley Aronowitz and Henry A. Giroux, *Postmodern Education: Border Pedagogy, Politics, and Cultural Criticism* (University of Minnesota Press, 1991).

87. For specific ways in which voice and difference are treated in critical pedagogical terms, see bell hooks, *Talking Back* (Boston: South End Press, 1989); Henry A. Giroux and Roger I. Simon, "Popular Culture as a Pedagogy of Pleasure and Meaning," in Henry A. Giroux and Roger Simon, (eds.), *Popular Culture, Education and Everyday Life* (Granby, Massachusetts: Bergin and Garvey Press, 1989), pp. 1–30; Paul Smith, "Pedagogy and the Popular-Cultural-Commodity-Text," in Henry A. Giroux and Roger Simon, (eds.), *Popular Culture, Education and Everyday Life* (Granby, Massachusetts: Bergin and Garvey Press, 1989), pp. 31–46; Henry A. Giroux, "Schooling and the Politics of Student Voice," in *Schooling and the Struggle for Public Life* (Granby, Massachusetts: Bergin and Garvey Press, 1988).

Existentialism, Alienation, Postmodernism: Cultural Movements as Vehicles of Change in the Patterns of Everyday Life

Agnes Heller

The term "culture" or "civilization" was invented in the West as one universal among many. Yet, in comparison to other universals such as "science" or "freedom", the universal termed "culture" has always had a pluralistic connotation. One discussed science or freedom, for example, and not "Western science" and "Western freedom", because the general understanding was that these good things were one and indivisible. On the other hand, one discussed "Western culture" because it has always been assumed that there were many other cultures alongside the Western one, whether inferior or superior to it, or even simply different from it. Irrespective of whether those cultures were regarded as superior or inferior, the relationships among cultures were always temporalized as well as historicized. Cultures follow one another, for example, and there is no way back to a previous one except via a nostalgic trip which is only open to the single individual. In this understanding, cultures were regarded as closed universes which either remained closed or, if they

Agnes Heller, "Existentialism, Alienation, Postmodernism: Cultural Movements as Vehicles of Change in the Patterns of Everyday Life," in *Postmodern Conditions,* eds. Andrew Milner, Philip Thomson, and Chris Worth. pp. 1–13. Copyright 1990, Berg Publishers. Reprinted by permission.

eventually did open up, were then thought to lose their distinctive features and thus be vulnerable to subversion by the latest, i.e. Western, culture. This view of "alien" cultures coincided structurally with the cultural divisions within particular countries in the period of early capitalism. Aristocratic, gentry, grand- and petty-bourgeois and peasant forms of life were strictly distinct from one another. The debate on cultural inferiority versus superiority occurred unremittingly with the contenders consisting of the aristocracy, the gentry (in England) and the bourgeoisie.

Class culture in the nineteenth century was more than a mere figure of speech. Disraeli's famous dictum mentioned two nations which were not even in communication with one another. Early working-class movements, the trade unions and later the parties, whether or not they explicitly advocated the creation of a special working-class culture, all nevertheless strongly contributed to the emergence of such a culture. Class cultures as a rule were almost hermetically sealed with individuals only occasionally able to cross the borders between them. This crossing of cultural borders was extremely difficult, and not only for those at the bottom aspiring upwards. Henry James, for example, was a great chronicler of the immense difficulties encountered even by people of enormous wealth once they ventured to cross the cultural barriers which divided them from "the ancient families."

The modern division of labor, with its capacity to stratify society along functional lines, began to break down the strict segregation of class cultures as early as the end of the nineteenth century. Freelance intellectuals, artists in particular, were the first "splinter groups." These artists created "Bohemia" with a specific cultural flavor, a form of life all their own, which was neither aristocratic, nor bourgeois nor for that matter working-class, but simply different. The culture of "Bohemia" gradually broke up the hermetic closure of various cultures on a global scale by virtue of the fact that "Bohemians" of one country regularly borrowed artistic material, elements, themes and motifs from the so-called aliens of other countries. Gauguin's islanders no longer resemble the "noble savage"; they are like us with a difference.

Yet it was only after the Second World War that the erosion of a network of class cultures became visible and cultural relativism unmistakably gained momentum. Forms of life and cultural patterns could now be freely chosen, particularly by the younger generation, and cultural habits which had previously been exclusively class-related were now becoming generally available. In addition, in this epoch, one also sees "other cultures" begin to borrow lavishly patterns of behavior, habits, etc. from Western fashions. Of course, such an obvious conspicuous parallel development begs for a multi-causal explanation. I have already mentioned the emergence of the functional division of labor as one factor in this development. Factors such as the birth of mass production, the rise of the mass media, decolonization, and the decrease in working hours in the centers of Western and Northern Europe, could also be mentioned.

Rather than focus on causes, however, I would like to discuss briefly what might be termed imaginary *institutions of signification* (to borrow the phrase of Cornelius Castoriadis). In my view, there have been three distinct waves in which new imaginary significations of ways of life have been created since the Second World War. I will deliberately disregard those theoretical tendencies (for example structuralism) which have deeply influenced our vision of the world. Instead, I will focus on those world-views and philosophies which were carried by cultural movements. For it was in the movements themselves that life-patterns were changed and that a new group of cultures in everyday life began to be slowly created. Needless to say, we are not at the end of this trend, but sufficiently in the midst of it to be able to watch the main tendencies of its unfolding.

As a rule, each new generation of young men and women has taken the initiative from the previous generation, since the time of the French Revolution. However, the distinct patterns of action, aspiration and imagination amongst post-Second World War youth have been sharply dissimilar to those of former generations. More precisely, the patterns have been becoming increasingly different from generation to generation. Although intellectuals, philosophers, sociologists, writers and artists have had their share in launching these movements and in articulating their aspirations, the youth whom they address and the aspirations and self-perceptions to which they give voice are widely dissimilar to those of the earlier bourgeois splinter group, "Bohemia." Post-Second World War movements did not warm up the old clichés about the aesthetic life; their extravaganza was not aesthetic, but existential. To an even lesser extent did they regard themselves as the cohort of a new political elite. Whether or not they were politically oriented, these movements were not involved in attempts to change elites.

In a society increasingly characterized by a functional division of labor, the term "young" becomes equivalent to "pre-functional." In other words, everyone who is not yet absorbed by a function within the division of labor, is young. Movements of the young start to attract and embrace youth from extremely different social milieus,

irrespective of whether their later function is to be that of academic
or social worker, self-employed or industrial worker, etc. The tendency for the social "absorbing power" of movements to widen is
clearly in evidence. The cultural trend of "punk" is a strong case
in point.

However, pre-functional existence is at the same time pre-
stratification existence. As such, it allows for forms of life to develop
which no longer have the characteristics of class cultures. Institutionalized function performance no longer suffices for preforming
ways of life, as "being a bourgeois" or "being a worker" once did. This
is why people cannot shed the vestiges of a particular "youth culture" once they are settled in a social function. Certain elements of
their own youth culture will continue to shape their lifestyles as
adults. It is easy to ascertain that this is indeed the case. The transition from traditional class cultures to modern culture was destined to give birth to the most violent generation conflict modern
men and women have ever known, and this dramatic process repeats itself wherever there are still traditional class cultures. However, once fathers and mothers themselves have been shaped by a
modern movement, generation conflict between them and their
children will be relatively mild, even if they disapprove of each other's values and ways of life. The softening of the generation conflict
is but one sign among many of the structural changes in which new
cultural movements are embedded.

Three consecutive generations have appeared since the Second
World War: the *existentialist* generation, the *alienation* generation
and the *postmodernist* generation, to employ the terms of their own
self-description. Modern cultural movements appeared in waves,
and this happened for the simple reason that each new generation
had to "come of age" in the sense of creating a new "imaginary institution" before it could take over the torch from the former generation. The First Wave began its career immediately after the war
and reached its zenith in the early fifties. The Second Wave was
launched by the events of the mid-sixties and reached its peak in
1968, but continued to expand until the mid-seventies. The third
movement arose in the eighties and has not yet reached its zenith.
The second movement grew out of the first, and the third from the
second, both in the sense of continuation but also in the sense of reversing the signs of the previous movement. In responding to one
another, *each wave continues the pluralization of the cultural universe in modernity as well as the destruction of class cultures.* Furthermore, *each wave gives a new stimulus to the structural change in
intergenerational relationships.* The latter is not quite independent

from the former, for structural change in intergenerational relationships is yet another pattern of everyday life which points toward cultural relativism.

"Waves" and "generations" are more precise terms than "movement." Although waves consist of cultural and social movements, certain movements continue through generations in a direct line instead of appearing in waves; feminism is the prime example. At the peak of the waves, movements which are "fellow travellers" of the main trend tend, as a rule, to merge with the former, only then to be disconnected from them in an intermediary standstill. In addition, a wave is broader than the sum total of movements which emerge with it and which merge into one another at their peak. As a rule, movements meet with resistance, they provoke countermovements, but even the countermovements themselves display the characteristics of the waves which have brought them to the surface. And perhaps more interestingly, even those people, those forms of social action and those institutions which apparently have nothing to do with the "waves," still have something in common with them. For they too participate in those changes in the social "imaginary institution" of which the wave is an expression. It may seem far-fetched to associate the Falklands War and its *modus operandi* with postmodernism. And yet the war—the behavior of the marines, the press reports and the like—seemed to be a deliberate quotation from the First World War. It was as if the participants were purposefully quoting Renoir's celebrated movie, *La Grande Illusion,* as they imitated the valiant and chivalrous officers fighting duels of honor in the age of modern technology.

The *existentialist* generation was the first and the narrowest. The rapidity with which Sartre's message, though not necessarily his philosophy, caught the minds of the young in Western Europe, and to some extent in Central and Southern Europe, was in itself not completely unprecedented. The Romantic movement had spread just as swiftly, over a century ago. What was unprecedented, however, was the character of the movement, namely the *circumstance,* realized only in retrospect, that the existentialist wave was the first in a series of the most striking phenomena of Western history in the second half of our century. The unprecedented character of the movement was due to its historical setting. This movement, like Romanticism, initially appeared as a *revolt of subjectivity* against the ossification of bourgeois forms of life, against the normative and ceremonial constraints rooted in this way of life. The rebellion of subjectivity did have a political implication but one no more explicit than in previous Romantic movements. But prior to its emergence there had been the cataclysmic experience of totalitarianism, which made the life experience of contingency, so typical of modernity, an experience of personal freedom as well. However, the freedom of the existing, contingent person no longer sufficed in its capacity as *the* notion of freedom. Freedom had to be politicized. To this we must add the guilt of colonization and the experience of decolonization. In this experience, the politicization of freedom and the relativization of (Western and bourgeois) culture were combined. All this swept through Europe in a series of cultural practices. "Shocking the bourgeois" is precisely the gesture that makes men and women in revolt dependent on the bourgeois. But in the existentialist wave this famous *épater* was no longer present. What mattered now was doing things in our own way, practicing our own freedom. Young men and women, intoxicated by the atmosphere of unlimited possibilities, began to dance existentially, love existentially, talk existentially, etc. In other words, they were intent on breaking free.

The alienation generation, which reached its peak in 1968, was both a continuation and a reversal of the First Wave. Their formative experience was not the war but the post-war economic boom and the consequent widening of social possibilities. Their experience, furthermore, was not the dawn but the dusk of subjectivity and freedom. While the existentialist generation, despite its discovery of alienation, the lifelessness of modern institutions and the senselessness of contingency, had nevertheless been a rather optimistic breed, the alienation generation, on the contrary, began in despair. Precisely because this generation took seriously the ideology of plenty, it rebelled against the complacency of industrial progress and affluence, as well as claiming for itself the sense and the meaning of life. Freedom remained the main value, however, and unlike the existentialist generation the alienation generation has remained committed to collectivism. The quest for freedom was a common pursuit.

Though an outgrowth of despair, the alienation generation became affirmative by virtue of the process in which different movements merged in the peak of this wave. In this merger literally nothing was left as it had been before. One movement made a plea for the extension of the human experience into taboo areas (and promoted the "radical" cult of drugs, causing untold damage); the other made a claim for expanded families; yet another advocated the return to the simplicity of rural life; while still others supported sexual, or gay, liberation. Some movements raised concrete political objectives, while others were involved in experimental theatre, happenings, permissive education or in the advocacy of the slogan "small is beautiful." It is practically impossible to list all the issues and practices through which the second wave of the cultural movement made inroads into the perception and self-perception of modern Western civilization.

As a social theory, postmodernism was born in 1968. In a manner of speaking, postmodernism was the creation of the alienation generation disillusioned with its own perception of the world. It can be argued that the defeat of 1968 was the reason for this disillusionment (if there was such a defeat, which remains an open question). However, one can also maintain that postmodernism had already appeared in the very beginnings of the 1968 movements, particularly in France, and that it therefore should simply be regarded as the continuation of the former. But whatever happened on the theoretical scene, the movements themselves seemed to disappear. The very same theorists who continued to relay the message of the alienation generation made speeches about the final defeat of social movements. Meanwhile, something else occurred. While the external signs of the movements vanished, there was still a movement; or rather, there were several, but they were invisible because they were essentially psychological and interpersonal. These movements increasingly saturated human relationships with their message to such an extent that they altered the social fabric from which they had emerged.

Postmodernism as a cultural movement (not as an ideology, theory, or program) has a simple enough message: anything goes. This is not a slogan of rebellion, nor is postmodernism in fact rebellious. As far as everyday life is concerned, there are many and various things and patterns of life against which modern men and women can or should rebel, and postmodernism indeed allows for all sorts of rebellion. However, there is no single great target for collective and integrated rebellion. "Anything goes" can be read as follows: *you* may rebel against anything you want to rebel against but let *me* rebel against the particular thing I want to rebel against. Or, alternatively speaking, let me not rebel against anything at all because I feel myself to be completely at ease.

For many, this boundless pluralism is the sign of conservatism: are there not crucial, focal issues which demand rebellion? And yet the truth is that postmodernism is neither conservative nor revolutionary nor progressive. It is neither a wave of rising hope nor a tide of deep despair. It is a cultural movement which makes distinctions of this kind irrelevant. For whether conservative, rebellious, revolutionary or progressive, all can be part of such a movement. This is so not because postmodernism is apolitical or anti-political, but rather because it does not stand for a particular politics of any kind. Cultural relativism, which began its rebellion against the fossilization of class cultures as well as against the "ethnocentric" lionization of the "only-right-and-true," which is to say the Western heritage, has succeeded. Indeed, it has succeeded so completely that it is now in a position to be able to entrench itself. Those who are now in the process of entrenching themselves are the members of the youngest generation who have learned their lessons and have drawn their own conclusions. Postmodernism is a wave within which all kinds of movements, artistic, political and cultural, are possible. We have already had several brand-new movements. There have been movements with a focus on health, anti-smoking, body-building, alternative medicine, marathon-running and jogging. A movement of sexual counterrevolution has been developing. We have had and still have peace or anti-nuclear movements. Ecological movements are in full bloom. We witness the expansion of feminist movements, the movement for educational reform and much else. The fashion magazines are perhaps the best indicators of the pluralist character of postmodernism. "Fashion" as such no longer exists, or more precisely everything is, or many things are, fashionable at the same time. We no longer have "good taste" or "bad taste." (Of course, one still might refer to having taste or not in the sense of being able to distinguish between the better and the worse within the same genre.)

If postmodernism, then, is going to be absorbed by our culture as a whole, we will finally reach the end of the transformation which began with the existentialist generation after the Second World War. This is not a prophecy about the end of movements, rather the opposite. What this statement does forecast is a situation in which concrete cultural transformations will take place insofar as such transformations are carried by one or another movement; however, the movements themselves will not occur in generational waves. These movements, finally, will not be the "movements of the young"; they will not only be cross-class, but also cross-generational movements.

By way of introduction to the short story of the three generations which have created our present cultural "imaginary institutions of signification," I have pointed out two decisive developments. I have stated that each wave continues the pluralization of the cultural universe in modernity as well as the destruction of class-related cultures. I have added that each wave has given a new stimulus to the structural change in intergenerational relations. I will now return to these fundamental questions in some detail.

What the three waves of cultural movements have achieved thus far and what can be expected to happen in the near future, will be discussed in the same breath. The transformation is uneven, for the present of one country is the future of another. No one factor can account for all of the differences in speed and character of the transformation. In matters of cultural transformations traditions of different provenance may accelerate or slow down a process. For example, traditional bourgeois forms of life are more entrenched in Germany than in Scandinavia. Yet even where the transformations are most spectacular, they are far from being close to completion. Class cultures are still very much in evidence. The European feeling of superiority has not evaporated and serious forms of generational conflict still exist. The bottom line is therefore a tendency rather than a *fait accompli*. A tendency is a possibility, and the latter can be regarded as less than "reality." But one could also agree with Aristotle that possibility stands higher than reality, that poetry is more true than history. The possibility mentioned here entails a small dosage of poetry, but it is based on the extrapolation of contemporary socioeconomic features which have been discovered, discussed and corroborated through empirical data by sociologists such as Touraine, Offe and Dahrendorf.

The demise of class-related cultures can be explained in terms of the increase in consumerism. Previously, both bourgeois and working-class ways of life were centered on work performance. However, in what is termed these days "post-industrial society," the center of crucial life activities has become leisure time. As Dahrendorf has recently pointed out, not more than twenty-five per cent of the populace of the countries in the European Common Market perform socially necessary labor, which means holding a job or owning a business. Furthermore, function performance no longer provides the sufficient "matter" from which a way of life can be constituted. In relation to life activity as a whole, function performance can be seen as fairly contingent, and is thus hardly the centerpoint of cultural identification. Rather, it is the *level* of consumption (the amount of money spent on consumption) that becomes the source of cultural identification. Cultural identification is therefore a quantitative rather than a qualitative issue. It was the deep conviction of the alienation generation that the *type* of preferred consumption had been socially generalized under the impact of the manipulation of tastes and desires by the mass media. In terms of this conception, everyone was manipulated into enjoying, being pleased with, and having a need for "the same," irrespective of whether "the same" referred to objects, products, forms of art, practices or whatever.

Although the growth of consumerism came to an abrupt halt with the advent of economic crises and depressions, and although the "affluent society" proved to be far less affluent than the "alienation generation" had previously assumed, the patterns which gave birth to the "manipulation paradigm" have themselves not disappeared. But the outcome of general manipulation no longer assumes as gloomy a forecast as in earlier predictions. As so often happens, the prediction itself has changed the course of what was predicted. It seems an exaggeration, but in fact is not, that the wave of the alienation generation was, in this respect as well, the forerunner of the postmodernist generation. The specter of "mass society" in which everyone likes the same, reads the same, practices the same, was a short intermezzo in Europe and North America. What has indeed emerged is not the standardization and unification of consumption, but rather the enormous pluralization of tastes, practices, enjoyments and needs. The quantity of money available for spending continues to divide men and women, but so do the kinds and types of enjoyment, pleasure, practices which they seek. Instead of becoming the Great Manipulator, the media have become rather a catalogue for highly individualized tastes. More importantly, the different patterns of consumption have become embedded in a variety of lifestyles, "each according to his or her preference," and of course, the means available to satisfy that preference.

At this point, I have to return to the general problem of cultural relativism. Non-Western cultural patterns were first discovered by "Bohemia"; the taste of the Bohemians was literally exotic. Today, "alien" cultures are present at each and every level of everyday life. They have become embedded in our cultural practices; they have been assimilated, and they have become "commonplace," as it were—from Chinese restaurants to Indian dresses, from African hairdos to Latin American novels. However bizarre it may sound to associate Chinese cuisine, African hairdos, herbal tea and sex movies with the alienation generation, it nevertheless remains a fact that this generation introduced the paraphernalia of exotic novelties into the menu of our daily life, in which every taste can find its own satisfier. A varied menu does not add up to lifestyle, however. Rather, certain practices, tastes and preferences constitute *patterns*. One can easily identify several such patterns in which "this goes with that," but not with something else.

However, a problem presents itself with respect to this infinite variety, this pluralization of the ways of life, this demise of self-complacent and ethnocentric class cultures. Hannah Arendt, and others, have stressed that social classes are necessary for the conduct of rational politics. Classes can give birth to institutions (political organizations which represent their interests). Representative governments grow out of class society. If classes are on the wane, if cultures are becoming pluralized to the degree of total particularization, is a meaningful, rational decision-making process still possible? We are left only with corporations organized according to functions, and corporations do not represent the interests of ways of life as a whole, but rather the interests of particular functions. Thus, societies based on corporate decision-making can easily be described as "mass societies," despite cultural pluralization. The "alienation generation" made a case for "grassroots politics," for a kind of politics embedded in communities and ways of life on all levels of social stratification. It remains uncertain at this stage whether cultural relativization and pluralization will lead to the demise of rational policy-making or whether they will rather be the prelude to a more democratic and more rational form, or forms, of political action, a combination of the parliamentary system with a type of direct democracy. At this point we do not have sufficient data for extrapolation.

Let me now turn to the change in the intergenerational relations. All three waves of movements were carried by the younger generation. However, the term "young" requires clarification. In a functional society, "the young" are those men and women (and not just those boys and girls) who do not perform a "function" that locks them into one stratum or another within the social division of labor. Thus students are young even when they are thirty years of age, which meant "middle age" in the generation of our grandparents. Precisely because of this functional connotation, I will in what follows avoid the distinction between "young" and "old." (In any case, old people or "senior citizens" do not have a job these days. They are, in other words, the "postfunctional ones.")

The present changes in the relationship of prefunctional and functional generations are so obvious that one can read them from quite external signs. In class-related cultures young men tried hard to look older than their age. After the Second World War, however, the pattern gradually transformed to the point where it was, finally, totally reversed. Those who are mentally and physically fully grown up now make sometimes desperate efforts to look like youngsters and behave accordingly. "Looks" have different social meanings. Looking older than one's age expresses the aspiration to be treated as a responsible adult, as someone who has been settled or who at least is ready for being settled. Looking younger than one's age expresses the aspiration to be treated as someone who is still open to every option, who is not yet a "bureaucrat," who is not yet fossilized by his or her function. At the peak of generational waves, it has become a common practice that members of the "functional generation" look for the favors of their children in order to be regarded as "honorary youth." The term and the practices of "mid-life crisis" were invented in this world of the functional division of labor; it is the exclusive production of functional society. In a class culture, be it bourgeois, working class or gentry, being middle-aged lends one a dignity which is the representative quality of the fully-fledged adult. It is *qua* adult, as someone who is *still* able-bodied and -minded but *already* the repository of a great amount of experience, that one becomes a *persona* in a given culture. Men in mid-life crisis wish to be immature and not-yet-settled again, bald teenagers looking for a new identity.

The functional division of labor is attended by a very complex and ambivalent combination. Function performance requires identification, particularly in business, and in public institutions. The stronger the identification with function performing, the greater the temptation for a person to become a self-complacent bore or an arrogant bureaucrat. The function-performer is almost inevitably driven to lock out young people because they are competition. Function-related self-complacency is often nothing more than a psychological cover-up for the fear of competition. It follows from this that fathers of this kind have no major conflict with their own children, as had typically transpired in the dramatic period of generation conflict, but rather with the children of others. Looking young has therefore a double function: it helps the adults to be "accepted" by the young in their own milieu and it lends them weight in their competition with the children of others. It is precisely this conflict that is normally solved in mid-life crisis when the middle-aged person resigns from competition and dons the costume of the young. The world after the Second World War is no longer oedipal. What other kinds of neurosis it will develop is another matter. Lasch's thesis on narcissism is a significant attempt at exploring our new diseases.

Let us make one final observation about the three waves of cultural movements after the Second World War. In all the ups and downs of their continuities and discontinuities, one feature has remained stable. Feminist movements have constituted a major trend in all three, and this is the trend which, despite some minor setbacks, has totally changed modern culture. Feminism was, and has remained, the greatest and most decisive *social revolution of moder-*

nity. Unlike a political revolution, a social revolution does not break out: it takes place. A social revolution is always a cultural revolution as well. The relativization of cultures and the inroads made by "alien" cultures into Western cultures have been repeatedly mentioned above. The feminist revolution is not just one contribution to this enormous change, but the single major one. For female culture, hitherto marginalized and unacknowledged, is now well on its way to articulating a final statement on its own behalf, to claim its half of the traditional culture of humankind. The feminist revolution is not just a novel phenomenon of Western culture, *it is a watershed in all hitherto existing cultures.*

The feminist revolution could not have been brought about by the new form of the division of labor alone. Democratic institutions, the value ideas of freedom, equality and rights had to be present in the global "imaginary institution of signification" for feminist movements, these carriers of the revolution, to come about. For previously women, just like men, could be incorporated into the functional division of labor, and yet women could also remain subjected to male domination. But without a functional division of labor, the objective of the feminist revolution would have remained unattained for the simplest of reasons: women would not have achieved the opportunity to make a living of their own, to acquire the minimal precondition of an independent life.

Why is it such a widespread belief that "movements have disappeared," that the past forty years was a period in which "nothing has happened"? Perhaps because we are too much used to history as political history. And yet history is, first and foremost, social and cultural; it is the history of the daily lives of men and women. Placed under close scrutiny, this history will disclose changes which include a social revolution. The three waves of cultural movements analyzed above were the main stewards of this transformation. They did not alter the vessel, but they did change the ocean on which the vessel navigates.

Postmodern Blackness

bell hooks

Postmodernist discourses are often exclusionary even as they call attention to, appropriate even, the experience of "difference" and "Otherness" to provide oppositional political meaning, legitimacy, and immediacy when they are accused of lacking concrete relevance. Very few African-American intellectuals have talked or written about postmodernism. At a dinner party I talked about trying to grapple with the significance of postmodernism for contemporary black experience. It was one of those social gatherings where only one other black person was present. The setting quickly became a field of contestation. I was told by the other black person that I was wasting my time, that "this stuff does not relate in any way to what's happening with black people." Speaking in the presence of a group of white onlookers, staring at us as though this encounter were staged for their benefit, we engaged in a passionate discussion about black experience. Apparently, no one sympathized with my insistence that racism is perpetuated when blackness is associated solely with concrete gut level experience conceived as either opposing or having no connection to abstract thinking and the production of critical theory. The idea that there is no meaningful connection

bell hooks, "Postmodern Blackness." Reprinted from *Yearning: Race, Gender, and Cultural Politics* by bell hooks, pp. 23–31 with permission from the publisher, South End Press, 116 Saint Botolph St., Boston, MA 02115.

between black experience and critical thinking about aesthetics or culture must be continually interrogated.

My defense of postmodernism and its relevance to black folks sounded good, but I worried that I lacked conviction, largely because I approach the subject cautiously and with suspicion.

Disturbed not so much by the "sense" of postmodernism but by the conventional language used when it is written or talked about and by those who speak it, I find myself on the outside of the discourse looking in. As a discursive practice it is dominated primarily by the voices of white male intellectuals and/or academic elites who speak to and about one another with coded familiarity. Reading and studying their writing to understand postmodernism in its multiple manifestations, I appreciate it but feel little inclination to ally myself with the academic hierarchy and exclusivity pervasive in the movement today.

Critical of most writing on postmodernism, I perhaps am more conscious of the way in which the focus on "Otherness and difference" that is often alluded to in these works seems to have little concrete impact as an analysis or standpoint that might change the nature and direction of postmodernist theory. Since much of this theory has been constructed in reaction to and against high modernism, there is seldom any mention of black experience or writings by black people in this work, specifically black women (though in more recent work one may see a reference to Cornel West, the black male scholar who has most engaged postmodernist discourse). Even if an aspect of black culture is the subject of postmodern critical writing, the works cited will usually be those of black men. A work that comes immediately to mind is Andrew Ross's chapter "Hip, and the Long Front of Color" in *No Respect: Intellectuals and Popular Culture;* while it is an interesting reading, it constructs black culture as though black women have had no role in black cultural production. At the end of Meaghan Morris's discussion of postmodernism in her collection of essays *The Pirate's Fiance: Feminism and Postmodernism,* she provides a bibliography of works by women, identifying them as important contributions to a discourse on postmodernism that offer new insight as well as challenging male theoretical hegemony. Even though many of the works do not directly address postmodernism, they address similar concerns. There are no references to works by black women.

The failure to recognize a critical black presence in the culture and in most scholarship and writing on postmodernism compels a black reader, particularly a black female reader, to interrogate her interest in a subject where those who discuss and write about it

seem not to know black women exist or even to consider the possibility that we might be somewhere writing or saying something that
should be listened to, or producing art that should be seen, heard,
approached with intellectual seriousness. This is especially the case
with works that go on and on about the way in which postmodernist
discourse has opened up a theoretical terrain where "difference and
Otherness" can be considered legitimate issues in the academy.
Confronting both the absence of recognition of black female presence that much postmodernist theory reinscribes and the resistance
on the part of most black folks to hearing about real connection between postmodernism and black experience, I enter a discourse, a
practice, where there may be no ready audience for my words, no
clear listener, uncertain then, that my voice can or will be heard.

During the sixties, black power movement was influenced by
perspectives that could easily be labeled modernist. Certainly many
of the ways black folks addressed issues of identity conformed to a
modernist universalizing agenda. There was little critique of patriarchy as a master narrative among black militants. Despite the fact
that black power ideology reflected a modernist sensibility, these elements were soon rendered irrelevant as militant protest was sti-
fled by a powerful, repressive postmodern state. The period directly
after the black power movement was a time when major news magazines carried articles with cocky headlines like "Whatever Happened to Black America?" This response was an ironic reply to the
aggressive, unmet demand by decentered, marginalized black subjects who had at least momentarily successfully demanded a hearing, who had made it possible for black liberation to be on the
national political agenda. In the wake of the black power movement,
after so many rebels were slaughtered and lost, many of these voices
were silenced by a repressive state; others became inarticulate. It
has become necessary to find new avenues to transmit the messages
of black liberation struggle, new ways to talk about racism and
other politics of domination. Radical postmodernist practice, most
powerfully conceptualized as a "politics of difference," should incorporate the voices of displaced, marginalized, exploited, and oppressed black people. It is sadly ironic that the contemporary
discourse which talks the most about heterogeneity, the decentered
subject, declaring breakthroughs that allow recognition of Otherness, still directs its critical voice primarily to a specialized audience that shares a common language rooted in the very master
narratives it claims to challenge. If radical postmodernist thinking
is to have a transformative impact, then a critical break with the
notion of "authority" as "mastery over" must not simply be a rhe-

torical device. It must be reflected in habits of being, including styles of writing as well as chosen subject matter. Third world nationals, elites, and white critics who passively absorb white supremacist thinking, and therefore never notice or look at black people on the streets or at their jobs, who render us invisible with their gaze in all areas of daily life, are not likely to produce liberatory theory that will challenge racist domination, or promote a breakdown in traditional ways of seeing and thinking about reality, ways of constructing aesthetic theory and practice. From a different standpoint, Robert Storr makes a similar critique in the global issue of *Art in America* when he asserts:

> To be sure, much postmodernist critical inquiry has centered precisely on the issues of "difference" and "Otherness." On the purely theoretical plane the exploration of these concepts has produced some important results, but in the absence of any sustained research into what artists of color and others outside the mainstream might be up to, such discussions become rootless instead of radical. Endless second guessing about the latent imperialism of intruding upon other cultures only compounded matters, preventing or excusing these theorists from investigating what black, Hispanic, Asian and Native American artists were actually doing.

Without adequate concrete knowledge of and contact with the non-white "Other," white theorists may move in discursive theoretical directions that are threatening and potentially disruptive of that critical practice which would support radical liberation struggle.

The postmodern critique of "identity," though relevant for renewed black liberation struggle, is often posed in ways that are problematic. Given a pervasive politic of white supremacy which seeks to prevent the formation of radical black subjectivity, we cannot cavalierly dismiss a concern with identity politics. Any critic exploring the radical potential of postmodernism as it relates to racial difference and racial domination would need to consider the implications of a critique of identity for oppressed groups. Many of us are struggling to find new strategies of resistance. We must engage decolonization as a critical practice if we are to have meaningful chances of survival even as we must simultaneously cope with the loss of political grounding which made radical activism more possible. I am thinking here about the postmodernist critique of essentialism as it pertains to the construction of "identity" as one example.

Postmodern theory that is not seeking to simply appropriate the experience of "Otherness" to enhance the discourse or to be radically chic should not separate the "politics of difference" from the politics of racism. To take racism seriously one must consider the plight of underclass people of color, a vast majority of whom are black. For African-Americans our collective condition prior to the advent of postmodernism and perhaps more tragically expressed under current postmodern conditions has been and is characterized by continued displacement, profound alienation, and despair. Writing about blacks and postmodernism, Cornel West describes our collective plight:

> There is increasing class division and differentiation, creating on the one hand a significant black middle-class, highly anxiety-ridden, insecure, willing to be co-opted and incorporated into the powers that be, concerned with racism to the degree that it poses constraints on upward social mobility; and, on the other, a vast and growing black underclass, an underclass that embodies a kind of walking nihilism of pervasive drug addiction, pervasive alcoholism, pervasive homicide, and an exponential rise in suicide. Now because of the deindustrialization, we also have a devastated black industrial working class. We are talking here about tremendous hopelessness.

This hopelessness creates longing for insight and strategies for change that can renew spirits and reconstruct grounds for collective black liberation struggle. The overall impact of postmodernism is that many other groups now share with black folks a sense of deep alienation, despair, uncertainty, loss of sense of grounding even if it is not informed by shared circumstance. Radical postmodernism calls attention to those shared sensibilities which cross the boundaries of class, gender, race, etc., that could be fertile ground for the construction of empathy—ties that would promote recognition of common commitments, and serve as a base for solidarity and coalition.

Yearning is the word that best describes a common psychological state shared by many of us, cutting across boundaries of race, class, gender, and sexual practice. Specifically, in relation to the postmodernist deconstruction of "master" narratives, the yearning that wells in the hearts and minds of those whom such narratives have silenced is the longing for critical voice. It is no accident that "rap" has usurped the primary position of rhythm and blues music among young black folks as the most desired sound or that it began as a form of "testimony" for the underclass. It has enabled under-class black youth to develop a critical voice, as a group of young black men told me, a "common literacy." Rap projects a critical voice, explaining, demanding, urging. Working with this insight in his es-say "Putting the Pop Back into Postmodernism," Lawrence Gross-berg comments:

> The postmodern sensibility appropriates practices as boasts that announce their own—and consequently our own—existence, like a rap song boasting of the imaginary (or real—it makes no difference) accomplishments of the rapper. They offer forms of empowerment not only in the face of nihilism but precisely through the forms of nihilism itself: an empowering nihilism, a moment of positivity through the production and structuring of affective relations.

Considering that it is as subject one comes to voice, then the postmodernist focus on the critique of identity appears at first glance to threaten and close down the possibility that this discourse and practice will allow those who have suffered the crippling effects of colonization and domination to gain or regain a hearing. Even if this sense of threat and the fear it evokes are based on a misunder-standing of the postmodernist political project, they nevertheless shape responses. It never surprises me when black folks respond to the critique of essentialism, especially when it denies the validity of identity politics by saying, "Yeah, it's easy to give up identity, when you got one." Should we not be suspicious of postmodern critiques of the "subject" when they surface at a historical moment when many subjugated people feel themselves coming to voice for the first time. Though an apt and oftentimes appropriate comeback, it does not re-ally intervene in the discourse in a way that alters and transforms.

Criticisms of directions in postmodern thinking should not ob-scure insights it may offer that open up our understanding of African-American experience. The critique of essentialism encour-aged by postmodernist thought is useful for African-Americans con-cerned with reformulating outmoded notions of identity. We have too long had imposed upon us from both the outside and the inside a narrow, constricting notion of blackness. Postmodern critiques of essentialism which challenge notions of universality and static overdetermined identity within mass culture and mass conscious-ness can open up new possibilities for the construction of self and the assertion of agency.

Employing a critique of essentialism allows African-Americans to acknowledge the way in which class mobility has altered collective black experience so that racism does not necessarily have the same impact on our lives. Such a critique allows us to affirm multiple black identities, varied black experience. It also challenges colonial imperialist paradigms of black identity which represent blackness one-dimensionally in ways that reinforce and sustain white supremacy. This discourse created the idea of the "primitive" and promoted the notion of an "authentic" experience, seeing as "natural" those expressions of black life which conformed to a pre-existing pattern or stereotype. Abandoning essentialist notions would be a serious challenge to racism. Contemporary African-American resistance struggle must be rooted in a process of decolonization that continually opposes reinscribing notions of "authentic" black identity. This critique should not be made synonymous with a dismissal of the struggle of oppressed and exploited peoples to make ourselves subjects. Nor should it deny that in certain circumstances this experience affords us a privileged critical location from which to speak. This is not a reinscription of modernist master narratives of authority which privilege some voices by denying voice to others. Part of our struggle for radical black subjectivity is the quest to find ways to construct self and identity that are oppositional and liberatory. The unwillingness to critique essentialism on the part of many African-Americans is rooted in the fear that it will cause folks to lose sight of the specific history and experience of African-Americans and the unique sensibilities and culture that arise from that experience. An adequate response to this concern is to critique essentialism while emphasizing the significance of "the authority of experience." There is a radical difference between a repudiation of the idea that there is a black "essence" and recognition of the way black identity has been specifically constituted in the experience of exile and struggle.

When black folks critique essentialism, we are empowered to recognize multiple experiences of black identity that are the lived conditions which make diverse cultural productions possible. When this diversity is ignored, it is easy to see black folks as falling into two categories: nationalist or assimilationist, black-identified or white-identified. Coming to terms with the impact of postmodernism for black experience, particularly as it changes our sense of identity, means that we must and can rearticulate the basis for collective bonding. Given the various crises facing African-Americans (economic, spiritual, escalating racial violence, etc.), we are compelled by circumstance to reassess our relationship to popular culture and resistance struggle. Many of us are as reluctant to face this task as many non-black postmodern thinkers who focus theoretically on the issue of "difference" are to confront the issue of race and racism.

Music is the cultural product created by African-Americans that has most attracted postmodern theorists. It is rarely acknowledged that there is far greater censorship and restriction of other forms of cultural production by black folks—literary, critical writing, etc. Attempts on the part of editors and publishing houses to control and manipulate the representation of black culture, as well as the desire to promote the creation of products that will attract the widest audience, limit in a crippling and stifling way the kind of work many black folks feel we can do and still receive recognition. Using myself as an example, that creative writing I do which I consider to be most reflective of a postmodern oppositional sensibility, work that is abstract, fragmented, non-linear narrative, is constantly rejected by editors and publishers. It does not conform to the type of writing they think black women should be doing or the type of writing they believe will sell. Certainly I do not think I am the only black person engaged in forms of cultural production, especially experimental ones, who is constrained by the lack of an audience for certain kinds of work. It is important for postmodern thinkers and theorists to constitute themselves as an audience for such work. To do this they must assert power and privilege within the space of critical writing to open up the field so that it will be more inclusive. To change the exclusionary practice of postmodern critical discourse is to enact a postmodernism of resistance. Part of this intervention entails black intellectual participation in the discourse.

In his essay "Postmodernism and Black America," Cornel West suggests that black intellectuals "are marginal—usually languishing at the interface of black and white cultures or thoroughly ensconced in Euro-American settings." He cannot see this group as potential producers of radical postmodernist thought. While I generally agree with this assessment, black intellectuals must proceed with the understanding that we are not condemned to the margins. The way we work and what we do can determine whether or not what we produce will be meaningful to a wider audience, one that includes all classes of black people. West suggests that black intellectuals lack "any organic link with most of Black life" and that this "diminishes their value to Black resistance." This statement bears traces of essentialism. Perhaps we need to focus more on those black intellectuals, however rare our presence, who do not feel this lack and whose work is primarily directed towards the enhancement of black critical consciousness and the strengthening of our collective capacity to engage in meaningful resistance struggle. Theoretical ideas and critical thinking need not be transmitted solely in written work or solely in the academy. While I work in a predominantly white institution, I remain intimately and passionately engaged with black community. It's not like I'm going to talk about writing and thinking about postmodernism with other academics and/or intellectuals and not discuss these ideas with underclass non-academic black folks who are family, friends, and comrades. Since I have not broken the ties that bind me to underclass poor black community, I have seen that knowledge, especially that which enhances daily life and strengthens our capacity to survive, can be shared. It means that critics, writers, and academics have to give the same critical attention to nurturing and cultivating our ties to black community that we give to writing articles, teaching, and lecturing. Here again I am really talking about cultivating habits of being that reinforce awareness that knowledge can be disseminated and shared on a number of fronts. The extent to which knowledge is made available, accessible, etc. depends on the nature of one's political commitments.

Postmodern culture with its decentered subject can be the space where ties are severed or it can provide the occasion for new and varied forms of bonding. To some extent, ruptures, surfaces, contextuality, and a host of other happenings create gaps that make space for oppositional practices which no longer require intellectuals to be confined by narrow separate spheres with no meaningful connection to the world of the everyday. Much postmodern engagement with culture emerges from the yearning to do intellectual work that connects with habits of being, forms of artistic expression, and aesthetics that inform the daily lives of writers and scholars as well as a mass population. On the terrain of culture, one can participate in critical dialogue with the uneducated poor, the black underclass who are thinking about aesthetics. One can talk about what we are seeing, thinking, or listening to; a space is there for critical exchange. It's exciting to think, write, talk about, and create art that reflects passionate engagement with popular cultures, because this may very well be "the" central future location of resistance struggle, a meeting place where new and radical happenings can occur.

Excerpts from *Dissident Postmodernists*

Paul Maltby

Postmodernism as a Literary-Critical Concept

It was not until the late 1960s that "postmodernism" gained currency as a literary-critical term. However, then it was just one designation among others (e.g., "metafiction," "antirealist fiction") and did not achieve its status as the preeminent generic term for the fiction in question until the 1980s. The origins of the term have been sketched out by Ihab Hassan (Hassan, 1980). Here, I shall attempt a brief account and critique of the principal constructions of postmodernism as a literary-critical concept.

There is a tendency in literary studies to speak of "modernism" and "postmodernism" *tout court*. Yet as rubrics they are a source of vagueness and ambiguity. It is a commonplace that the prefix "post-" in "postmodernism" may be read as denoting a relationship with modernism which is one either of succession or of supersession. But there is another problem of terminology which is less often noted. The use of modernism and postmodernism as monolithic categories conceals a process of discrimination which may frame our reading of a text. For there are, of course, *several* currents of modernist and postmodernist writing, and our perceptions of the political significance of a postmodernist text can depend on whichever current of writing has been selected to serve as the normative model of modernism. Thus, for Terry Eagleton, "It is as though postmodernism is [. . .] a sick joke at the expense of [. . .] revolutionary avant-gardism" insofar as the avant-garde practices of Mayakovsky (or Tzara or Breton) are invoked as the normative model of modernism (Eagleton 1985, 60). Yet, for Leslie Fiedler, postmodernism is "subversive," a blow to the "elitism" or "concealed class bias" of a modernism he identifies with Eliot and Joyce—a current of writing sometimes referred to as "high" modernism (Fiedler [1968] 1975). And it is this latter, largely anglophone, modernism (which, typically, also includes Faulkner, Woolf, and Wallace Stevens) that critics most often invoke to signify modernism *in toto*.

The need to differentiate between currents of postmodernist fiction will be discussed later. Suffice it to say here, a problem as fundamental to postmodernist writing as the "fictionality" of meaning (i.e., the perception that the "real," history, or nature can only be apprehended in narrative form, that is, as "stories") does not, as we shall see, have the same implications for, say, Barth, Nabokov, and Gass, as for Barthelme, Coover, and Pynchon. Yet, all too often, we find these names indiscriminately bracketed together.

Further problems arise from discussions of postmodernist fiction that automatically take modernism as their principal point of reference. In response to the perception that the "real" is fundamentally non-significant, postmodernist writers have developed an aesthetics of "self-reflexiveness," that is, a mode of fiction which investigates the very process of signification or meaning-production. In particular, literary-narrative conventions like plotting, use of metaphor, and omniscient narrator are parodied so as to expose their role in the fabrication of meaning; so as to present the text as a fiction-making apparatus. Narration (literary, historical, philosophical, etc.) and naming are revealed as inherently fictionalizing activities. Thus Malcolm Bradbury observes the postmodernist insistence on "the utter fictionality of *all* attempts at naming, structuring, and ordering experience" (Bradbury 1983, 159). And Mas'ud Zavarzadeh has remarked upon the emergence of "noninterpretive narrative forms" which embody "the contemporary writer's approach to the world-as-it-is, free from any imposed scheme of meaning or extracted pattern of significance" (Zavarzadeh 1976, 4).

It is the postmodernist preoccupation with the fictionality of meaning which inevitably invites contrasts with (if I may generalize) the high-modernist faith in totalizing meaning-systems, such as those founded on cultural tradition. (It is the basis for these contrasts that I take to be the principal rationale for speaking of a *post-modernist* fiction.) Recall Eliot's observations on *Ulysses,* whose "mythic method" he held up as an exemplary model for modern writing: "a way of controlling, of ordering, of giving a shape and significance to the immense panorama of futility and anarchy which is contemporary history" (quoted in Russell 1985, 11). Many commentaries are grounded in this fundamental contrast between "high" modernism's striving to impose a scheme of meaning on the world (e.g., Stevens' "Idea of Order," Eliot's Tradition, Joyce's Mythology) and postmodernism's ironic questioning of the very possibility of meaning. David Lodge provides a concise, graphic account of the matter:

> modernism, which for all its formal experiment and complexity held out to the reader the promise of meaning, if not of *a* meaning. "Where is the figure in the carpet?" asks a character in Donald Barthelme's *Snow White,* alluding to the title of a story by Henry James that has become proverbial among critics as an image of the goal of interpretation; "Where is the figure in the carpet? Or is it just . . . carpet?" A lot of postmodernist writing implies that experience is just carpet, and that whatever meaningful patterns we discern in it are wholly illusory, comforting fictions. (Lodge 1977, 43)

This is an illuminating comparision, yet it is also typical of the prevalent tendency to define postmodernist fiction primarily in terms of its relationship to modernism. The following statements, all by eminent critics, exhibit this tendency: "postmodernist fiction tends to attack, undermine, parody, or otherwise call into question certain characteristic assumptions of modernist fiction" (Hite 1983, 4); "Once we have identified the respective dominants of the modernist or postmodernist systems, we are in a good position to begin describing the dynamics of the change by which one system emerges from and supplants the other" (McHale 1987, 10–11); "the world view of the Postmodernists is built [. . .] on a polemics against Modernism" (Fokkema 1986, 83). To be sure, postmodernist fiction embodies a critique of the formal conventions and epistemology of literary modernism (but then it also embodies a critique of literary realism, and there is a case to be made for speaking of an "anti-realist" rather than a "postmodernist" fiction).[1] However, I want to question the invocation of modernism as the *principal point of reference* for situating and making sense of postmodernist fiction.

An approach to postmodernism which uses modernism, that is, the Anglo-American "high" modernism of, roughly, 1915–30, as the main point of reference tends inevitably to understand the critical thrust of this fiction as chiefly *retrospective*. That is to say, this approach explains postmodernist fiction as, primarily, a response (ironic, deconstructive) to the narrative forms and epistemology of an earlier, literary-cultural paradigm. But, while acknowledging this retrospectiveness as a feature of, perhaps, all postmodernist fiction, there is an oppositional current of this fiction which is best thought of as, in the first instance, "circumspective." By this I mean a response to or, more accurately, a critical engagement with, surrounding or contemporaneous discourses (including literary narrative forms and the meaning-systems they embody); precisely, the discourses of postmodern culture. "Postmodernism" need not only be read as an invitation to situate postmodernist fiction in relation to modernism; it may be read as an invitation to situate in relation to *postmodernity,* to our experience of postmodern culture.

In the 1960s a number of critics, notably Leslie Fiedler, Ihab Hassan, and Susan Sontag, welcomed postmodernism as a species of subversive writing. It was understood as the literature of a "time of Endings" (Fiedler 1975, 365), challenging the social hierarchies and oppressive meaning-systems of a supposedly moribund bourgeois culture. Hassan sees postmodernist fiction as an "Antinomian" attack on "reason and history, science and society," as an expression of "Anarchy" and an impulse to "decreation" (Hassan 1971, 27, 29). And for Sontag, with Burroughs and Beckett, among others, in mind, "contemporary artists [. . .] share the same disdain for the 'meanings' established by bourgeois-rationalist culture, indeed for culture itself in the familiar sense. [They proclaim . . .] a harsh despair and perverse vision of apocalypse. . . ." (Sontag 1983, 203). Fiedler situates postmodernist fiction in an era he defines as "apocalyptic, anti-rational, blatantly romantic and sentimental"; a time when "the Dream, the Vision, *ekstasis* [. . .] have again become the avowed goals of literature" (Fiedler 1975, 345, 364). These critics were writing at an explosive moment of protest and dissent—the moment, that is, of an insurgent counterculture. Perhaps their focus on the apocalyptic strain in postmodernist fiction reflected the belief, common at the time, in the exhaustion and imminent demise of "bourgeois-rationalist culture." In this respect, my reading of this fiction will be almost diametrically opposed to theirs. Suffice it to say here, I shall read it (but for one or two texts) as a literature responsive not to a "time of Endings" but to a time marked by the *consolidation* of "bourgeois-rationalist culture."

In his landmark essay (from which I have just quoted), "Cross the Border—Close that Gap" (1968), Fiedler observes that the post-modernist writer has turned to popular art forms to draw on their "Mythical" and "Visionary" potential (362). The art forms in question are those targeted for the mass market, typically forms like the "western," "science fiction," and "pornography." Fiedler contends that insofar as it exploits the motifs and conventions of these sub-genres, postmodernism resists evaluation in the terms of the "class bias" inscribed in the literary Establishment's "high"/"low" criteria. The "Aristocratic conceptions of art" which have led critics to can-onize "high" modernists like Eliot, Joyce, and Proust, have been su-perseded: "a closing of the gap between elite and mass culture is precisely the function of the novel now" (351). Postmodernism sub-verts class-based norms:

> The notion of one art for the "cultured," i.e., the favored few in any given society—in our own chiefly the university educated, and another sub-art for the "uncultured," i.e., an excluded ma-jority [. . . is] an invidious distinction proper only to a class-structured community. [. . .] Pop Art is, whatever its overt politics, *subversive:* a threat to all hierarchies insofar as it is hostile to order and ordering in its own realm. (359–60)

How valid is the claim that (literary) postmodernism is democ-ratizing, that it annuls the class-based distinction between "high" art and mass culture? One might ask of two of the writers cited by Fiedler, namely Barth and Nabokov, precisely *whom* do they ad-dress? Surely one has to be intellectually prepared for works like *Lost in the Funhouse* or *Pale Fire,* not to mention, say, *V, Snow White,* and *Pricksongs and Descants.* These are "self-reflexive" works which depend upon the reader's prior knowledge of the nar-rative conventions which they exploit, parody, and subvert. Whether or not these works sell well, they speak, first and foremost, to the minority sensibility of the college educated. Indeed, what Fiedler describes as the "academicism" of the "Age of T.S. Eliot" sur-vives in the sense that many postmodernist writers are, or have been, university writers-in-residence or professors of literature: for example, Barth, Barthelme, Coover, Gass, Hawkes, Nabokov, Sukenick, and Vonnegut. The fact is, postmodernist fiction has an institutional base, an enclosed cultural milieu, which from Fiedler's standpoint looks positively élitist. However, to argue that this fic-tion addresses only an educationally privileged few is not to imply that it has little or no subversive value; rather, it is to recognize that

the claim for its subversiveness cannot rest on the thesis that postmodernism "closes a class [. . .] gap" (359).

Finally, Fiedler assumes that postmodernist fiction assimi-
lates massmarket subgenres *uncritically* (nowhere in his essay does
he suggest otherwise). This may be true of some early postmodernist writing. However, in many of the postmodernist texts discussed
later, we shall see how subgenres are incorporated within an oppositional framework which exposes and contests their ideological
content.

The formal complexity of postmodernist writing has given a
new lease of life to formalist criticism. Unquestionably, some of the
most distinguished and valuable studies of this fiction are formalist. Robert Scholes, David Lodge, Douwe Fokkema, Brian McHale,
and Christine Brooke-Rose are among those who have theorized a
poetics or rhetoric of postmodernism. McHale and Lodge, for example, have ingeniously exploited Jakobson's structuralist concepts in
their constructions of postmodernism. McHale has built a "descriptive poetics" around the concept of the "shifting dominant," explaining the change from modernist to postmodernist fiction in terms of
the periodic shift in the literary system's hierarchy of artistic devices (whereby dominant devices become subsidiary and vice versa)
(McHale 1987, 3–25). Lodge, perceiving literary history as a pendulum movement between what Jakobson has identified as the
"metaphoric" and "metonymic" poles of language, explains postmodernism as a violation of Jakobson's "law" that "there is nowhere
for discourse to go except between these two poles" (Lodge 1977, 42–
43). My concern here is to outline the problematic of what I have
broadly defined as "neo-formalist" criticism and note the kind of
questions it does not address (which is less to find fault with this
criticism than to indicate its conceptual limits).

In *Fiction and the Figures of Life,* William Gass censures those
who "continue to interpret novels as if they were philosophies themselves [. . .] middens from which may be scratched important messages for mankind; they have predictably looked for content, not
form" (Gass 1980, 25). Interpretation is a misconceived goal and
criticism must focus on the text's formal properties, its figures, syntax, and design. A preoccupation with form follows from Gass's conception of fiction as an autonomous "verbal world." We are enjoined
to stop thinking of fiction as ancillary to the task of reflecting reality, for, as Gass puts it in a memorable aphorism, "There are no
descriptions in fiction, there are only constructions" (17). Scholes
makes a similar point: "All writing, all composition is construction.
We do not imitate the world, we construct versions of it. There is no

mimesis, only poiesis. No recording. Only constructing" (Scholes 1975, 7). Literature which incorporates this critical perspective, that is, which self-consciously renounces any pretensions to mimesis and projects itself as a purely verbal fabrication, is called by Gass, Scholes, and others "metafiction." Many of the writers discussed under this rubric are also identified as postmodernist, for example, Barth, Barthelme, Coover, Gass, Nabokov, and Pynchon. However, "metafiction" has a much wider compass than "postmodernism" and is generally used to denote *any systematically self-reflexive* work of fiction, that is to say, fiction which investigates and exposes the processes of its own construction and, by implication, the codes and shifting parameters of "literature." Hence Cervantes, Sterne, Barth, and Barthelme may all be defined as metafictional but only the latter two are postmodernist.

Critics who adopt the term "metafiction" invariably take as their starting point Gass's definition, which labels as metafiction those literary texts "in which the forms of fiction serve as the material upon which further forms may be imposed" (Gass 1980, 25). It is a helpful and perceptive formulation but there is a problem in that it implies an intertextuality that is purely literary. To be sure, it is in this sense that the texts of, say, Barth, Nabokov, and Gass, which above all interact with other (usually earlier) literary forms, are metafictional. However, there is also a strain of postmodernist writing, which includes the work of Barthelme, Coover, and Pynchon, whose texts interact not only with literary but often with *non-literary* forms of discourse. This kind of intertextuality tends to be oppositional in orientation; it works to lay bare and combat the ideologies inscribed in, for example, pop-cultural, scientific, and political discourse. For this type of postmodernism, "metafiction," as it is usually defined, is an inappropriate term. Furthermore, while postmodernism may be conceived as relating the fiction in question to a postmodern culture or postmodernity, metafiction, as a term, altogether lacks sociohistorical reference.

Around 1969–1970, the neo-formalist approach to postmodernist fiction was invigorated by an input of structuralist ideas. There are, to be sure, striking correspondences between, for instance, Barthes's ideas on literature—for example, literature conceived as an interplay of codes rather than a medium of representation; the call for a mode of writing which privileges *discours* over *histoire*—and the thinking of Gass, Scholes, and other critics. (The concepts of structuralism/poststructuralism have undoubtedly been of value in articulating the linguistic-philosophical concerns of postmodernist writers, but we should not necessarily assume that these writers were structuralists/post-structuralists *avant la lettre.* The precise connections—theoretical and temporal—between post-Saussurean theory and postmodernism need to be researched.) However, the structuralist influence has also worked to reinforce the neo-formalist tendency to fetishize the text, to abstract the word from the world. The problem of the fictionality of meaning may serve to illustrate a limitation of this tendency. Thus, while this criticism may examine the formal implications of this problem, for example, the self-reflexive focus on the factitiousness and arbitrariness of the narrative conventions on which meaning is shown to rest, it does not address a question like: Why should the fictionality of meaning become a major issue at a particular time, in a particular place (i.e., in late-capitalist America)? The problem is that such a question cannot be adequately, if at all, posed by the discourses of neo-formalism. No coherent model of postmodern culture underpins neo-formalist studies of postmodernist fiction. In these studies, the fictionality of meaning is an issue rarely examined beyond its aesthetic and epistemological implications. And yet our very idea of fictionality has been enlarged and enriched by sociological inquiries into the nature of postmodern culture. For example, note the pervasive discourses of commodity aesthetics where the illusion (the false promises and fraudulent claims) of use-value becomes detached from use-value itself (Haug 1986, 16–17); note the simulated realities of a media society, "the generation by models of a real without origin or reality: a hyperreal" (Baudrillard 1983c, 2). An explanation of the postmodernist writer's preoccupation with fictionality requires, *inter alia,* acknowledgment of his/her situation in a culture pervaded by illusory use-values and simulacra.

The dominant, neo-formalist strain of criticism generally precludes readings of postmodernist fiction as an oppositional current of writing. However, there are, of course, critics who have identified strands of postmodernist fiction as adversarial literature. Linda Hutcheon, for example, has proposed the category of "historiographic metafiction," instanced by such works as Reed's *Mumbo Jumbo* and Doctorow's *Ragtime.* This fiction operates through a subversive, highly self-reflexive use of parody. It ironically or paradoxically incorporates into its very structure the forms of historical narratives in order to destabilize them "from within"—exposing them as purely social constructs and contesting their ideological closures. "To adapt Barthes's general notion of the 'doxa' as public opinion or the 'Voice of Nature' and consensus, postmodernism works to 'de-doxify' our cultural representations and their undeniable political import" (Hutcheon 1987, 12, 21; 1989, 3). And Charles

Russell has discussed the "avant-garde strategies of aesthetic disruption" whereby Burroughs, Pynchon, Coover, and Sukenick, among others, attempt to demystify and deconstruct the social codes in which subjective identity is seen to be enfolded. It is a project which "shift[s] the previous social context of rebellion to the social text of ideology" (Russell 1985, 253).

Both Hutcheon and Russell, who have contributed much to the idea of an adversarial postmodernist fiction, are, like myself, interested in the latter as a critique and contestation of hegemonic discourse. However, their arguments lack an account, not to say a systematic analysis, of the conjuncture or moment (late capitalist? postindustrial?) at which this fiction is written. Hence, a fundamental question is not addressed: What developments, *historically specific* to our society, have given rise to a mode of fiction that is so preoccupied with language as a political issue? In the subsequent pages, I shall discuss a number of social changes—identified later as distinctively *late-capitalist* developments—which, I shall argue, have been instrumental in raising consciousness of the political implications of language.

Finally, "postmodernism" has become an overloaded and remarkably diffuse concept. A partial inventory of those lines of thought (mostly developed in the 1960s), which are discussed in the name of postmodernism, which are apprehended as postmodernist, would include: post-humanist theories of language that decenter the subject in relation to meaning; neo-Nietzschean critiques of the Enlightenment épistème; post-Marxist social theory and politics; theories of the globalization of commodity fetishism; populist aesthetics, and art which is systematically self-reflexive. (See above for explanations of these points.) The term "postmodernism" may be summoned to signify a mutation in artistic practice, an epistemic shift in western thought, or a mode of experience and perception specific to the late-capitalist subject immersed in a sign-saturated, consumer culture.

Enough has been said to indicate that "postmodernism" is a far from self-explanatory term; in any context *today,* one needs to say how and why it is being used. I shall start by giving reasons why I have chosen to work with this problematic and embattled term. First, in *literary-critical* discussions of American postmodernist fiction, we know, by force of convention, *who* are the postmodernists, for example, Barth, Barthelme, Coover, Vonnegut, or Pynchon; and who are not, for example, Bellow, Updike, Styron, Baldwin, or Salinger. There is broad agreement about the grounds for making this distinction: very simply, and at the level of a *preliminary* definition on which critics build in different ways, the fiction of Barth et al. is programmatically and preeminently self-reflexive and (largely as a consequence of which) radically transgressive of narrative conventions, while the fiction of Bellow et al. is not. (Suffice to say here, fiction is self-reflexive when it examines its own nature as a signifying practice and, by implication, points to its own provisionality as a meaning-system. Later, I shall explain why I find "self-reflexive" an unsatisfactory term and note how, as a concept, it is often appropriated in ways which foreclose on its adversarial implications.) "Postmodernism" is the term most often summoned to denote, in the first instance, the literary self-reflexiveness and transgressiveness of the postwar period. (See, for example, Fokkema and Bertens 1986; Bradbury 1983; Hutcheon 1989; Russell 1985.) Indeed, it has beaten off all rival contenders for the job, for example, terms such as "anti-realist fiction" (Guerard 1974), "new fiction" (Stevick 1977), and the chief rival "metafiction" (Gass 1980; McCaffery 1982; Scholes 1979). In recent years, postmodernism has become so deeply entrenched in the literary-critical vocabulary that, for the time being, no cognate terms looks likely to supplant it; increasingly, alternative terms sound idiosyncratic. Thus, for most commentators today, it no longer seems a question of *whether* to use "postmodernist" as a generic term for postwar self-reflexive/ transgressive fiction, so much as *how* to use it, for example, how to expand its range of reference or how to mobilize it politically.

Secondly, I favor the use of the term because of the historical inflection it has recently acquired. Its prefix "post-" is generally read as signaling a "break" in aesthetic practice that radically separates modernist from postmodernist art (a claim vigorously contested by some).[2] Clearly the legitimacy of postmodernism as, *inter alia,* a concept signifying a new order of aesthetic practice must rest on the identification of a new conjuncture which can assign that practice an historically specific meaning. And it has been Fredric Jameson's achievement to provide just this kind of conjunctural analysis, one which traces the mediations between late capitalism and postmodernist aesthetics (Jameson 1984a). His "periodizing hypothesis" has significantly broadened the historical dimensions of the concept "postmodernism." Now, more than formerly, the term has a marked historical orientation that rival literary terms like "metafiction" and "antirealist fiction" altogether lack. Henceforth, it is difficult to think of postmodernism without some notion of "postmodernity" or a new stage in the development of capitalism. Accordingly, the term is readily invoked here in a reading that situates postwar self-reflexive/transgressive texts in the context of developments specific to, or more advanced under, late capitalism which have transformed the field of language and communications.

* * *

Dissident Postmodernist Fiction

I have argued that in the 1960s and early 1970s there was a prodigious enlargement of the notion of the political within the sphere of language. I noted, in particular, that a conception of language as a medium of social integration was a vital element in the dissident thought of this period. Furthermore, I sought to ground that conception of language in political, cultural, and other developments that have transformed the field of language and communications. And I have indicated that these developments are specific to, or more advanced under, late capitalism. These points will provide a framework for a discussion of the texts in the case studies which follow shortly—texts which I shall now identify as "dissident postmodernist."

Now, I want to distinguish between two tendencies in American postmodernist fiction: a "dissident" tendency, exemplified not only by the work of Barthelme, Coover, and Pynchon, but also by that of Burroughs, DeLillo, Acker, and Reed; and an "introverted" tendency, exemplified by the work of Nabokov, Gass, and, intermittently, Barth, among others. By way of a preliminary observation, I shall say that dissident postmodernist fiction embodies that enlarged notion of the political within the sphere of language as discussed above. And it is from this standpoint that I shall read the fiction of Nabokov and others as introverted—a literary tendency whose exploration of language barely registers its political dimensions. (Of course, from other standpoints, the work of Nabokov et al. may be evaluated without the negative undertone it has here.) This is not to propose hard and fast categories in which any postmodernist text can be instantly placed. Indeed, almost any literary text may be read as addressing, however marginally or obliquely, some political implications of language. Ultimately, the difference between these tendencies is best thought of as one of degree: the dissident tendency may be distinguished from the introverted by its *heightened perception* of the politics of language.

The problem of the "fictionality" of meaning will serve to highlight the above distinction. For the postmodernist writer, the "real" is essentially non-significant (it does not speak for itself), and the

search for meaning, the endeavor to interpret the world, is perceived as a process of fictionalizing reality, of "storifying" it. It is understood that extradiscursive referents—historical events, social
processes, natural phenomena—can only be apprehended in narrative form, never in their pure, naked state, that is "as they really
are." Postmodernist writers respond to the problem of the fictionality of meaning by, *inter alia,* composing texts which mock, interrogate, and subvert the "classical" realist-empiricist assumption that
language can reflect or render "things as they really are." (I say
"classical realist"; I do not suppose that all works classified as "realist" aim persistently at a faithful transcription of reality or are
unconscious of the problem of meaning as outlined above.) Their primary strategy is to use language in a selfreflexive, as opposed to
self-effacing, fashion in order to demonstrate the operation of narrative codes in the constitution of meaning. It is a strategy that often results in word games which work to parody reality as subject to
uncontrollable textualization.

However, the problem of the fictionality of meaning does not in
every respect have the same implications for all postmodernist writers. Consider some texts of introverted tendency. The narrator of
Barth's "Lost in the Funhouse," one of a collection of stories about
the inescapability of storytelling, observes: "The climax of the story
must be its protagonist's discovery of a way to get through the funhouse. But he has found none, may have ceased to search" (Barth
1969, 96). We are all lost in the funhouse of fiction-making and
there is no way out. Like Borges's Library, the funhouse is our textualized universe. In "Menelaiad," Menelaus exclaims in despair:
" 'When will I reach my goal through its cloaks of story? How many
veils to naked Helen?' " (Barth, 144). "Menelaiad" progresses as one
story enframes a second which, in turn, enframes a third and so on,
thereby suggesting, as the quotation marks multiply, that reality is
but a framework of infinitely nesting narratives. Finally, "Pale Fire"
is a poem, a patently literary artifact (meticulously constructed in
rhyming pairs of iambic pentameters) that reflects self-consciously
on the powers of linguistic invention: "playing a game of worlds,"
building "Empires of rhyme." This text, moreover, is the object of
study of another text, an overblown "Commentary" of nearly two
hundred pages by one Charles Kinbote. But this "apparatus criti-
cus," against Kinbote's express intentions, becomes the "monstrous
semblance of a novel" (Nabokov 1973, 71)—*Pale Fire* itself, but also
Nabokov's parody of historical romance fiction. (Kinbote, who may
be a king in exile or just a deranged émigré scholar, reads the poem
as a coded biography of *his* escapades as king of "Zembla"—a mock-

Ruritania of palace plots, secret passageways, and courtly love affairs.) In this way, Nabokov suggests that there is no direct passage
from language to the real; rather, cognition is caught up in an interplay of texts.

These "introverted" instances of postmodernist writing explore the individual ego's experience of entrapment in webs of narrative fiction. Typically, in this strain of fiction, the narrator-
subjects are scholars, recluses, or fantasists, remote from street
level, meditating from within enclosed, monadic environments.
(This is also a notable feature of Gass's stories—see Gass 1981—
and of course the *ficciones* of the master architect of hermetic
spaces—Borges.) Here, the problem of the fictionality of meaning
finds no grounding in social and historical conditions. On the other
hand, for dissident postmodernist writers, the problem of meaning
has a contextual dimension insofar as they perceive language as
bearing the imprint of the institutions, projects, and conflicts in
which it is imbricated. To be sure, these writers are acutely conscious of meaning as "narrative." But they are also conscious of
meaning as imbued with the tensions of power-relations and conflicting value-systems. Thus Pynchon contextualizes the problem of
the fictionality of meaning so that our "delusional systems" and
"stories, all false, about who we are" cannot be understood without
reference to a social order which "bring[s] the State to live in the
muscles of your tongue" (Pynchon 1978, 384). Or consider this observation by Barthelme expressed in the form of an imaginary conversation: " 'Madelaine,' I say kindly to her over lunch, 'semiotics is
in a position to claim that no phenomenon has any ontological status outside its place in the particular information system from
which it draws its meaning, and therefore, all language is finally
groundless [. . .]' 'Yes,' says Madelaine kindly [. . .], 'but some information systems are more enforceable than others.' Alas, she's right"
(Barthelme 1985, 44). Dissident postmodernists, unlike the introverted ones, explore the political and ideological implications of the
fictionality of meaning. Their writing illuminates the institutional
parameters of meaning-systems; it reveals how the latter operate in
force fields of power-relations; how, through the medium of ideology,
meaning-systems are connected to established political structures.
In short, while both introverted and dissident tendencies explore
"the world within the word" (Gass 1978), as a rule, only the dissident tendency explores the word in the world.

The tendency to grasp the problem of the fictionality of meaning in political terms is one instance of what I have identified as a
defining feature of dissident postmodernist fiction: its enlarged

notion of the political within the sphere of language. A second instance of this, in which the first will be seen to be implied, is the
focal point of this study: a *heightened perception of language as a
medium of social integration.* This perception is not evident in all
dissident postmodernist texts, but it is very much in the foreground
of texts by, among others, Burroughs, DeLillo, Acker, and Reed, in
addition to texts by Barthelme, Coover, and Pynchon. The dissident
postmodernists' perception of language as a powerful medium of integration necessarily concerns them *qua* language-users; for, it
need hardly be said, they are *implicated* in language both pro-
fessionally as writers and generally as members of a speech community. The question then arises: Is an independent, critical
standpoint within late-capitalist society possible? It is a question
which haunts this fiction and which explains its self-conscious reflection on the limits of artistic autonomy.

Dissident modernists and postmodernists share the anxiety
that communication is necessarily on terms established by the social order, such that to speak at all may be to surrender one's autonomy. Hence the problem of speaking in one's own voice becomes
a theme in both currents of writing. Stephen Dedalus, the Irish protagonist of Joyce's *Portrait,* speaks for Joyce when, after an exchange with the dean of English studies, he reflects:

> The language in which we are speaking is his before it is mine
> [. . .] His language, so familiar and so foreign, will always be
> for me an acquired speech. I have not made or accepted its
> words. My voice holds them at bay. My soul frets in the shadow
> of his language. (Joyce 1960, 189)

The passage expresses Joyce's unease at having to speak in the
alien tongue of a colonial power (i.e., imperial Britain). And, a little
later, the link between language and colonial subjection is made explicit: "—My ancestors threw off their language and took another,
Stephen said. They allowed a handful of foreigners to subject them"
(202). But Joyce, in company with other literary (high) modernists,
believed in a transhistorical plane of meaning, a judgmental standpoint *outside* of society's web of discourses, premised on the assumption that consciousness transcends language. Indeed, this faith in a
transcendent consciousness is reflected in the novel's recurring image of flight, as in this famous passage: "When the soul of a man is
born in this country there are nets flung at it to hold it back from
flight. You talk to me of nationality, language, religion. I shall try to
fly by those nets" (203). For Joyce, there is a space beyond language

to which the individual consciousness, privileged as the origin and legislator of meaning, can exile itself and "forge" a pure, non-alienating discourse. (And for modernists like Joyce, Stevens, and Yeats, this is precisely the task of the artist—the artist exalted as a God-like "artificer.") In short, he affirmed the modernist view of consciousness as an autonomous source of meaning and hence upheld the possibility of speaking in one's own voice. Contrast this position with that of Burroughs, fifty years later:

> That is the entry gimmick of The Death Dwarfs: supersonic imitation and playback so you think it is your own voice—(do you own a voice?) they invade The Right Centers which are The Speech Centers and they are in the right—in the right—in thee write—"Right"—"I'm in the right—in the right—You know I'm in the right so long as you hear me say inside your right centers 'I'm in the right.' " (Burroughs 1968b, 75)

Clearly, for Burroughs, the subject is compelled to speak on alien terms. Language inscribes ("in thee write") a perspective on reality which is "right" both in the sense that it is approved by the social order and, by the latter's standards, in that it seems obviously correct. Consciousness, far from transcending language, is perceived to be enclosed by it: "What scared you all into time? into body? into shit? I will tell you: 'the word.' Alien Word 'the.' 'The' word of Alien Enemy imprisons 'thee' in Time. In Body. In Shit" (Burroughs 1968b, 10). Dissident postmodernists communicate the experience of entrapment in language with much greater insistence and desperation than is generally found in modernism. They are far less confident about the possibility of achieving an autonomous critical perspective in their work.

The forms a dissident literature may usefully assume cannot be divorced from prevailing conceptions of power. A rough contrast between turn-of-the-century naturalism and dissident postmodernism may serve to illustrate the point. Where writers like Sinclair and London saw power as concentrated in a property-owning class, it was possible to write fiction in a confrontational mode; the target was plainly objective. Such fiction, operating directly and overtly as an indictment of society, typically assumed a documentary/didactic form as in The Jungle (1906) or The Iron Heel (1907). In contrast, dissident postmodernists conceive of power as *diffused* through the cultural sphere, in particular, through language, the very material with which the writer works. Language is deeply distrusted, so that, for example, for Barthelme:

The question is, what is the complicity of language in the massive crimes of fascism, Stalinism, or (by implication) our own policies in Viet Nam? In the control of societies by the powerful and their busy functionaries? If these abominations are all in some sense facilitated by, made possible by, language, to what degree is that language ruinously contaminated? (Barthelme 1985, 42)

Given the dissident postmodernists' perception of language as a site of power, we can see why fiction in the confrontational mode seems to be of less strategic value than formerly, and we can begin to theorize, instead, the strategic value of the mode of writing itself.

Most critics identify postmodernist writing as typically "self-reflexive." The problem with this term is that it suggests no more than a mode of writing that examines and exposes the processes of its own composition, thereby revealing its meaning as the construct of so many (literary) codes and conventions. One might be forgiven, therefore, for thinking of self-reflexive writing as a rather sterile, cerebral kind of game, a tediously self-obsessed literature. However, as most critics who use the term would surely agree, self-reflexive fiction does not only reflect on the role of literature in the constitution of meaning. Rather, it suggests, sometimes using literature as a paradigm, that *any* signsystem constitutes meaning; it is understood that meaning is wholly or in part (depending on one's view) the "effect" of the system's rules and codes which order signifiers into narratives. For the sake of accuracy, then, I prefer to speak of a "sign-reflective" rather than "self-reflexive" fiction.

Sign-reflective techniques of writing divert our attention away from story to the processes of signification.[3] Typically, there is a focus on the textual play of forms, plots, and tropes, and the way they mediate our relationship to the "real" or, at least, to the signified. (Pynchon, for example, foregrounds authorial plotting as one such mediation.) This form of writing is a medium particularly suited to the complex task of probing the relationship between language and meaning. Moreover, with specific reference to the current of postmodernist fiction identified here as dissident, we can now begin to think of *its* sign-reflectiveness as the very property which enables it to perform a contestatory function within a substantially eroded critical space; as the very property which guarantees this fiction a measure of autonomy. We may think of sign-reflective writing as discourse to the second power or metadiscourse; discourse which, insofar as it lays bare the very processes of signification, permits a degree of disengagement from the sign-systems in which the writer is necessarily implicated. This disengagement is a desired objective when the prevailing discourses, including the conventions and motifs of established literary discourse, are perceived as fraudulent, mendacious, mystificatory, or hollow. Sign-reflectiveness is the strategy whereby lost critical distance is, albeit provisionally, redeemed.

Notes

1. It is the forms and philosophical assumptions of literary realism that, more often those those of modernism, seem to be the prime target of postmodernist deconstruction and parody. Indeed, postmodernist fiction abounds with metafictional statements in which authors explicitly question the codes and presuppositions of realism. In *V*, for example, Pynchon speaks of "eyes clear enough to see past the fiction of continuity, the fiction of cause and effect, the fiction of a humanized history endowed with 'reason' " (Pynchon 1975, p. 306). In *Pale Fire,* Nabokov writes: " 'reality' is neither the subject nor the object of true art which creates its own special reality having nothing to do with the average 'reality' perceived by the communal eye" (Nabokov 1973, p. 106). Moreover, recall that, from a strictly chronological standpoint, American postmodernist fiction follows a long phase of *non-modernist* literature. (There is an uneven development in the American arts. In painting, for example, the modernist impulse persists well into the 1950s in the form of abstract expressionism against whose "élitism" and "esotericism" the Pop Art of the 1960s may be read as an ironic response. Literary history, however, does not run a parallel course.) By the late 1930s, after Dos Passos and Faulkner had completed their major work, the modernist impulse in American narrative fiction was largely spent. It was outlived and/or followed by a variety of fictional forms (e.g., naturalist or "existentialist") which generally adhered to realist conventions of narrative continuity, story, and plot and focused on problems of self-definition and existential crisis. This moment of American fiction (1940s and 1950s) may be represented by works like Mailer's *The Naked and the Dead,* Bellow's *The Victim,* Ellison's *Invisible Man,* and Salinger's *The Catcher in the Rye.*

2. It has been argued that postmodernism is essentially a continuation of modernist practice and is best understood as "neo-modernism" or late modernism (see Kermode 1968 and Graff 1977). One objection to this view is that those elements of modernist thought and form which can be found in postmodernism, and which suggest to some that postmodernism does not mark a stage beyond modernism, do not necessarily have the same

aesthetic and political significance across time—if only because conceptions of aesthetics and politics themselves are not what they were circa 1920.

3. Barthes says of the contemporary novel that "it aims to transpose narrative from the purely constative plane, which it has occupied until now, to the performative plane, whereby the meaning of an utterance is the very act by which it is uttered: today, writing is not 'telling' but saying that one is telling and assigning all the referent ('what one says') to this act of locution" (Barthes 1977, p. 114).

References

Baudrillard, Jean. (1983c). *Simulations*. Trans. P. Foss, P. Patton and P. Beitchman. New York: Semiotext(e).

Bradbury, Malcolm (1983). *The Modern American Novel*. Oxford University Press.

Eagleton, Terry (1985). "Capitalism, Modernism and Postmodernism." *New Left Review* 152 (July/August 1985): 60–72.

Fiedler, Leslie. (1975). "Cross the Border—Close that Gap: Postmodernism." In *American Literature Since 1900*. Ed. M. Cunliffe. London: Barrie and Jenkins, pp. 344–66. Orig. Pub. 1968.

Fokkema, Douwe (1986). "The Semantic and Syntactic Organization of Postmodernist Texts." In *Approaching Postmodernism*. Ed. Bertens and Fokkema. Amsterdam and Philadelphia: John Benjamins, pp. 81–95.

Gass, William. (1980). *Fiction and the Figures of Life*. Boston: Godine. Orig. pub. 1970.

———. (1981). *In the Heart of the Heart of the Country*. Boston: Godine. Orig. pub. 1968.

Guerard, A. J. (1974). "Notes on the Rhetoric of Anti-Realist Fiction." *Tri-Quarterly*, no. 30 (Spring 1974): 3–50.

Hassan, Ihab (1971). "POSTmodernISM." *New Literary History* III, no. 1 (Autumn 1971): 5–30.

———. (1980). "The Question of Postmodernism." In *Romanticism, Modernism, Postmodernism*. Ed. H. R. Garvin. Lewisberg, Pa.: Bucknell University Press, pp. 117–26.

Haug, W. F. (1986). *Critique of Commodity Aesthetics*. Trans. Robert Bock. Cambridge: Polity Press. Orig. pub. 1971.

Hite, Molly (1983). *Ideas of Order in the Novels of Thomas Pynchon*. Columbus: Ohio State University Press.

Hutcheon, Linda (1987). "Beginning to Theorize Postmodernism." *Textual Practice* 1, no. 1 (Spring 1987): 10–31.

———. (1989). *The Politics of Postmodernism*. London: Routledge.

Lodge, David (1977). "Modernism, Antimodernism and Postmodernism." *New Review* 4, no. 38 (May 1977): 39–44.

McCaffery, Larry. (1982). *The Metafictional Muse*. University of Pittsburgh Press.

McHale, Brian (1987). *Postmodernist Fiction*. London: Methuen.

Russell, Charles (1985). *Poets, Prophets and Revolutionaries*. New York: Oxford University Press.

Scholes, Robert (1975). *Structural Fabulation*. Notre Dame, Ind.: University of Notre Dame Press.

———. (1979). *Fabulation and Metafiction*. Urbana: University of Illinois Press.

Sontag, Susan (1983). "The Aesthetics of Silence." In *A Susan Sontag Reader*. Harmondsworth: Penguin, pp. 181–204. Orig. pub. 1967.

Stevick, Philip (1977). "Scheherezade runs out of plots, goes on talking; the king, puzzled, listens: an Essay on New Fiction." In *The Novel Today*. Ed. M. Bradbury. London: Fontana, pp. 186–216.

Zavarzadeh, Mas'ud (1976). *The Mythopoeic Reality*. Urbana: University of Illinois Press.

Hybridity, the Rap Race, and Pedagogy for the 1990s

Houston A. Baker, Jr.

A functional change in a sign-system is a violent event.

—Gayatri Spivak

Yes
Was the start of my last jam
So here it is again, another def jam
But since I gave you all a little something
That we knew you lacked
They still consider me a new jack.

—Public Enemy, "Don't Believe the Hype"

I
-

Turntables in the park displace the machine in the garden. Postindustrial, hyperurban, black American sound puts asunder that which machines have joined together . . . and dances . . . to hip hop acoustics of Kool DJ Herc. "Excuse me, Sir, but we're about to do a thang . . . over in the park and, like how much would you charge us to plug into your electricity?" A B-Boy, camp site is thus established. And Herc goes to work . . . with two turntables and a truckload of pizzazz. He takes fetishized, commodified discs of sound and creates—through a trained ear and deft hands—a sound that virtually commands (like Queen Latifah) assembled listeners to dance.

> It was the "monstrous" sound system of Kool DJ Herc which dominated hip hop in its formative days. Herc came from Kingston, Jamaica, in 1967, when the toasting or DJ style of his own country was still fairly new. Giant speaker boxes were essential in the competitive world of Jamaican sound systems . . . and Herc murdered the Bronx opposition with his volume and shattering frequency range.[1]

It was Herc who saw possibilities of mixing his own formulas through remixing prerecorded sound. His enemy was a dully constructed, other-side-of-town discomania that made South and West Bronx hip hoppers ill. Disco was not *dope* in the eyes, ears, and agile bodies of black Bronx teenagers . . . and Queens and Brooklyn felt the same.

There are gender-coded reasons for the refusal of disco. Disco's club DJs were often gay, and the culture of Eurodisco was populously gay. Hence, a rejection of disco carried more than judgments of exclusively musical taste. A certain homophobia can be inferred—even a macho redaction. But it is also important to note the high-marketplace maneuvering that brought disco onto the pop scene with full force.

The LeBaron Taylor move was to create a crossover movement in which black R&B stations would be used as testing grounds for singles headed for largely white audiences.[2] Johnnie Taylor's 1975 "Disco Lady" was one of the first hits to be so marketed; two and a half million singles sold. And the rest is history.

What was *displaced* by disco, ultimately, was R&B, a funky black music as general "popular" entertainment. Also displaced (just *dissed*) were a number of black, male, classical R&B artists. Hey, some resentment of disco culture and a reassertion of black manhood rights (rites)—no matter who populated discotheques— was a natural thing. And what the early hip hoppers saw was that the task for the break between general "popular" and being "black by popular demand" had to be occupied. And as Albert Murray, that longtime stomper of the blues who knows all about omni-Americans, put it: In the *break* you have to be nimble, or not at all![3]

Queens, Brooklyn and the Bronx decided to "B," to break-dance, to hip hop to rhythms of a dismembered, sampled, and re-mixed sound meant for energetic audiences—in parks, in school au-ditoriums, at high school dances, on the corner (if you had the power from a light post . . . and a crowd). And Herc was there before Grandmaster Flash and Afrika Bambaataa. And hip hop was doing it as in-group, urban style, as music disseminated on cassette tapes . . . until Sylvia Robinson realized its "popular" general pos-sibilities and sugared it up at Sugarhill Productions. Sylvia re-leased "Rapper's Delight" (1979) with her own son on the cut making noises like "To the hip hop, hippedy hop / You don't stop." The release of "Rapper's Delight" began the recommercialization of B-ing. The stylistic credo and crytography of hip hop were pared away to a reproducible sound called "rap." And "rap" was definitely a mass-market product after "Rapper's Delight" achieved a stun-ning commercial success. "B-style" came in from the cold. No longer was it—as crossover/commercial—"too black, too strong" for the popular charts. (But, of course, things have gotten stranger and *2 live* since then!)

II

So, rap is like a rich stock garnered from the sudden simmering of titanic B-boy/B-girl energies. Such energies were diffused over black cityscapes. They were open-ended in moves, shoes, hats, and sounds brought to any breaking competition. Jazzy Jay reports:

> We'd find these beats, these heavy percussive beats, that would drive the hip hop people on the dance floor to break-dance. A lot of times it would be a two-second spot, a drum beat, a drum break, and we'd mix that back and forth, extend it, make it 20 minutes long.
>
> If you weren't in the hip hop industry or around it, you wouldn't ever have heard a lot of these records.[4]

Twenty minutes of competitive sound meant holding the mike not only to "B," but also to set the beat—to beat out the competition with the "defness" of your style. So . . . it was always a *throwdown:* a self-tailored, self-tutored, and newly cued game stolen from the multinational marketplace. B-style competed always for (what else?) consumers. The more paying listeners or dancers you had for circulating cassettes or ear-shattering parties in the park, the more the quality of your sneakers improved. The idea was for youth to buy your sound.

Herc's black, Promethean appropriation of the two-turntable technology of disco and his conversion of discotech into a newly constructed blackurban form turned the tables on analysts and market surveyors alike. For competing disco DJs merely *blended* one disc into a successor in order to keep the energized robots of a commercial style (not unlike lambada) in perpetual motion on the dance floor. *To disco* became a verb, but one without verve to blackurban youth. What Herc, Flash, and their cohorts did was to actualize the immanent possibilities of discotechnology. They turned two turntables into a sound system through the technical addition of a beat box, heavy amplification, headphones, and very, very fast hands.

Why listen—the early hip hop DJs asked—to an entire commercial disc if the disc contained only twenty (or two) seconds of worthwhile sound? Why not *work* that sound by having two copies of the same disc on separate turntables, moving the sound on the two tables in DJ-orchestrated patterns, creating thereby a worthwhile sound? The result was an indefinitely extendable, varied, reflexively signifying hip hop sonics—indeed, a deft sounding of postmodernism.

The techniques of rap were not simply ones of selective extension and modification. They also included massive archiving. Black sounds (African drums, bebop melodies, James Brown shouts, jazz improvs, Ellington riffs, blues innuendos, doo-wop croons, reggae words, calypso rhythms) were gathered into a reservoir of threads that DJs wove into intriguing tapestries of anxiety and influence. The word that comes to mind is *hybrid*.

III

Discotechnology was hybridized through the human hand and ear—the DJ turned wildman at the turntable. The conversion produced a rap DJ who became a postmodern, ritual priest of sound rather than a passive spectator in an isolated DJ booth making robots turn. A reverse cyborgism was clearly at work in the rap conversion. The high technology of advanced sound production was reclaimed by and for human ears and the human body's innovative abilities. A hybrid sound then erupted in seemingly dead urban acoustical spaces. (By *postmodern* I intend the nonauthoritative collaging or archiving of sound and styles that bespeaks a deconstructive hybridity. Linearity and progress yield to a dizzying synchronicity.)

The Bronx, Brooklyn, Queens—called by the Reagan/Bush era black "holes" of urban blight—became concentrated masses of a new style, a hybrid sonics hip-hoppingly full of that piss, sass, and technological vinegar that tropes Langston Hughes, saying: *"I'm still here!"*[5] This is a *black hole* shooting hip hop quasars and bum rushing sucker, political DJs.

IV
—

What time was it? Time to get busy from the mid-seventies into the wild-style popularizations of the eighties. From Parks to Priority Records—from random sampling to Run DMC. Fiercely competitive and hugely braggadicious in their energies, the quest of the emergent rap technologists was for the baddest toasts, boasts, and signifying possible. The form was male-dominant . . . though KRS One and the earliest male posses will tell you the "ladies" were *always* there. Answering back, dissing the ways of menfolk and kinfolk alike who tried to ease them into the postmodern dozens. Hey, Millie Jackson had done the voice-over with musical backdrop—had talked to wrongdoing menfolk (at length) before Run or Daryl had ever even figured out that some day they might segue into each other's voices talking 'bout some "dumb girl." Indeed!

Rap technology includes "scratching": rapidly moving the "wheels of steel" (i.e., turntables) back and forth with the disc cued, creating a deconstructed sound. There is "sampling": taking a portion (phrase, riff, percussive vamp, etc.) of a known or unknown record (or a video game squawk, a touch-tone telephone medley, verbal tag from Malcolm X or Martin Luther King) and combining it in the overall mix. (The "sample" was called a "cut" in the earliest days.) There's also "punch phrasing": to erupt into the sound of turntable 1 with a percussive sample from turntable 2 by def cuing.

But the most acrobatic of the technics is the verb and reverb of the human voice pushed straight out, or emulated by synthesizers, or emulating drums and falsettoes, rhyming, chiming sound that is mnemonic for black urbanity. The voice is individual talent holding the mike for as long as it can invoke and evoke a black tradition that is both prefabricated and in formation. "Yo, man, I hear Ellington, but you done put a new (w)rap on it!" For the rap to be defly *yours* and properly original, it has got to be *ours*—to sound like *us*.

The voice, some commentators have suggested, echoes African griots, black preachers, Apollo DJs, Birdland MCs, Muhammad Ali, black street-corner males' signifying, oratory of the Nation of Islam, and get-down ghetto slang. The voice becomes the thing in which, finally, rap technology catches the consciousness of the young.

V

What time is it? The beginning of the decade to end a century. It is post-industrial, drum machine, synthesizer, sampling, remix, multitrack studio time. But it is also a time in which *the voice* and *the bodies* of rap and dance beat the rap of technologically induced (re-produced) indolence, impotence, or (in) difference.

Why? Because sales figures are a mighty index. But also . . . the motion of the ocean of dancers who fill vast, olympian spaces of auditoriums and stadiums transnationally when you are (*à la* Roxanne) "live on stage" is still a principal measure of rap success. Technology can create a rap disc, but only the voice dancing to wheels of steel and producing a hip hopping, responsive audience gives testimony to a full-filled *break*. You ain't busted a move, in other words, until the audience lets you know you're in the groove.

VI

What time is it? It's "hard core" and "message" and "stop the violence" and "2 live" and "ladies first"—1990s—time. Microcomputers, drum machines, electric keyboards, synthesizers are all involved in the audio. And MTV and the grammarians of the proper Grammy Awards have had their hands forced.

Rap is a too-live category for the Grammies to ignore, and Fab Five Freddy and *Yo! MTV Raps* have twice-a-week billing these days. Jesse Jackson and Quincy Jones proclaim that "rap is here to stay." Quincy has even composed and orchestrated a cross-generational album (*Back on the Block*) on which he announces his postmodernity in the sonics of rap. Ice T and Big Daddy Kane prop him up "on every leaning side."

But it is also time to "fight the power" as Public Enemy knows—the power of media control. In their classic rap "Don't

Believe the Hype," PE indicates that prime-time media are afraid of rap's message, considering it both offensive and dangerous. In Philadelphia, one of the principal popular music stations confirms PE's assessment—WUSL ("Power 99") proudly advertises its "no-rap workday." Secretaries fill a sixty-second ad spot with kudos for the station's erasure of rap. Hence, FCC "public" space is contoured in Philly in ways that erase the energy of rap's postmodern soundings. "Work" (defined as tedious office labor) is, thus, publicly constructed as incompatible with "rap." Ethics and outputs of wage labor are held to be incommensurate with postmodern black expressive culture. Implicit in a "no-rap workday," of course, is an agon between industrial ("Fordist") strategies of typing pool (word-processing pool?) standardization and a radical hybridity of sound and morals. For rap's sonics are disruptive in themselves. They become even more cacophonous when they are augmented by the black voice's antiestablishment injunctions, libido urgings, and condemnations of coercive standardization. To "get the job done" or "paid in full" in the economies of rap is scarcely to sit for eight hours cultivating carpal tunnel syndrome. Nope. To get the job done with rap style is to "get busy," innovative, and outrageous with *fresh* sounds and defly nonstandard moves. One must be undisciplined, that is to say, to be "in effect."

Eric B and Rakim, Twin Hype, Silk Tymes Leather, Kingpin Redhead, De La Soul, Q-Tip, The DOC—the names in themselves read like a Toni Morrison catalogue of nonstandard cultural denomination. And such named rap ensembles and the forms they produce are scarcely local or parochial. Rap has become an international, metropolitan hybrid. From New Delhi to Ibadan it is busy interrupting the average workday.

VII

3rd Bass is a prime example of rap's hybrid crossovers. The duo is prismatically white, but defly black urban in its stylings and "gas face" dismissals of too-melodic "black" artists such as MC Hammer.[6] ("Holy Moly!" as a notorious media character used to say: white boys, and one of them a graduate of Columbia, dissing a melanin-identified black boy for being not black or strong enough.) Which is to say that "we" are no longer in a Bronx or Brooklyn or Queens era but at the forefront of transnational postmodernism. The audience begins at eleven or twelve years of age and extends, at least, through post-B.A. accreditation. Rap is everywhere among adolescents, young adults, and entry-level professions. It is a site of racial controversy, as in the anti-Semitism fiascos of Public Enemy.[7] It is a zone of gender problematics, ranging from charges against the form's rampant sexism (2 Live Crew is too flagrant here) through the throwdown energies of Queen Latifah and her ladies first, to the irony of squeaky-clean Good Girls. It is a domain of the improper, where copyright and "professional courtesy" are held in contempt. Rappers will take what is "yours" and turn it into a "parody" of you—and not even begin to pay you in full. An example is N.W.A.'s "It's not about a salary" line signifying on Boogie Down Productions, whom, so I am told, they can't abide. Rap is a place of direct, vocal, actional challenge to regnant authority: N.W.A., again, with " . . . Tha Police." Class is also a major determinant in the rap field. Its postmodernity is a lower-class, black urban, sonic emergent speaking to (as PE has it) "a nation of millions."

VIII

Microcomputation, multitrack recording, video imaging, and the highly innovative vocalizations and choreography of black urban youth have produced a postmodern form that is fiercely intertextual, open-ended, hybrid. It has not only rendered melody virtually anomalous for any theory of "new music," but also revised a current generation's expectations where "poetry" is concerned. Technology's effect on student expectations and pedagogical requirements in, say, "English literature classrooms" is tellingly captured by recent experiences that I have had and would like to share. To prepare myself for a talk I was to give at New York's Poetry Project symposium titled "Poetry for the Next Society" (1989), I decided to query my students in a course devoted to Afro-American women writers. "What," I asked, "will be the poetry for the next society?" To a man or woman, my students responded "rap" and "MTV."

We didn't stop to dissect their claims, nor did we attempt a poetics of the popular. Instead, we tried to extrapolate from what seemed two significant forms of the present era a description of their being-in-the-world. Terms that emerged included *public, performative, audible, theatrical, communal, intrasensory, postmodern, oral, memorable,* and *intertextual.* What this list suggests is that my students believe the function of poetry belongs in our era to a telecommunal, popular space in which a global audience interacts with performative artists. A link between music and performance—specifically popular music and performance—seems determinative in their definition of the current and future function of poetry.

They are heirs to a history in which art, audience, entertainment, and instruction have assumed profoundly new meanings. The embodied catharsis of Dick Clark's bandstand or Don Cornelius's soul train would be virtually unrecognizable—or so one thinks—to Aristotle. Thus, Elvis, Chuck Berry, and the Shirelles foreshadow and historically overdetermine the Boss, Bobby Brown, and Kool Moe Dee as, let us say, *people's poets.*

My students' responses, however, are not nearly as natural or original as they may seem on first view. In fact, they have a familiar cast within a history of contestation and contradistinction governing the relationship between poetry and the state. The exclusion of poets from the republic by Plato is the primary Western site of this contest. (One envisions a no-poetry workday, as it were.) In Egypt it is Thoth and the King; In Afro-America it is the Preacher and the Bluesman. It would be oversacramental to speak of this contest as one between the letter and the spirit, and it would be too Freudian by half to speak of it as a struggle between the law and taboo. The simplest way to describe it is in terms of a tensional resonance between homogeneity and heterogeneity.

Plato argues the necessity of a homogeneous state designed to withstand the bluesiness of poets who are always intent on worrying such a line by signifying and troping irreverently on it and continually setting up conditionals. "What if this?" and "What if that?" To have a homogeneous line, Plato advocates that philosophers effectively eliminate poets.

If the state is the site of what linguists call the *constative,* then poetry is an alternative space of the *conditional.* If the state keeps itself in line, as Benedict Anderson suggests, through the linear, empty space of homogeneity, then poetry worries this space or line with heterogeneous performance.[8] If the state is a place of reading the lines correctly, then poetry is the site of audition, of embodied sounding on state wrongs such as N.W.A.'s " . . . Tha Police," or PE's "Black Steel in the Hour of Chaos." What, for example, happens to the state line about the death of the black family and the voiceless derogation of black youth when Run DMC explodes the state line with the rap:

> Kings from Queens
> From Queens Come Kings
> We're Raising Hell Like a Class When the Lunch Bell Rings!

Kings will be Praised
And Hell Will Be Raised
Suckers try to phase us
But We Won't be phased!

In considering the contestation between homogeneity and heterogeneity, I am drawing on the work of scholars Homi Bhabha and Peter Stallybrass,[9] who suggest that nationalist or post-revolutionary discourse is always a discourse of the split subject. In order to construct the nation, it is necessary to preserve a homogeneity of remembrance (such as anthems, waving flags, and unifying slogans) in conjunction with an amnesia of heterogeneity. If poetry, like rap, is disruptive performance, or, in Homi Bhabha's formulation, an articulation of the melancholia of the people's wounding by and before the emergence of the state line, then poetry can be defined, again like rap, as an audible or sounding space of opposition.

Rap is the form of audition in our present era that utterly refuses to sing anthems of, say, white male hegemony.

IX

A final autobiographical instance of rap-shifted student expectations on the pedagogical front will conclude my sounding of postmodernism. I recently (February 1990) had the experience of crossing the Atlantic by night, followed by a metropolitan ride from Heathrow Airport to North Westminster Community School in order to teach Shakespeare's *Henry V* to a class of GCSE (General Certificate of Secondary Education) students. Never mind the circumstances occasioning the trip—no, on second thought, the circumstances are popularly important. A reporter for London's *The Mail on Sunday* had gotten onto the fact that I advocated rap as an absolute prerequisite for any teacher attempting to communicate with students between the ages of twelve and twenty-five.[10] So there I was in London, in a school with students representing sixty-seven nationalities and speaking twenty-two languages, in the Paddington/Marylebone area. "Once more into the breach dear friends / Once more into the breach / or let us close the wall up with our English dead" was the passage the students were supposed to have concentrated on, paying special attention to notions of "patriotism."

Introduced by the head of the English Department to a class doing everything but the postmodern boogie on desktops, I pulled up a chair, sat down, and calmly said: "I've come from the United States. I've been awake for thirty-six hours, and I have to listen to you so that I can answer questions from my teenage son about what you are listening to, what you are *into*. So, please, start by telling me your names." Even as they began to give me their names (with varying degrees of cooperative audibility), a black British young woman was lining up twelve rap cassette boxes on her desk immediately in front of me. (Hey, she knew I had *nothing* to teach her!)

To make an exciting pedagogical story brief, we took off—as a group. I showed them how Henry V was a rapper—a cold dissing, def con man, tougher than leather and smoother than ice, an artisan of words. His response to the French dauphin's gift of tennis balls was my first presentational text. And then . . . "the breach." We did that in terms of a fence in the yard of a house that you have just purchased. A neighbor breaches it . . . "How, George? How could your neighbor breach it?" George jerked up from that final nod that would have put him totally asleep and said, "What?" "Could your neighbor do anything to breach your fence, George?" "No, sir, I don't think so." "Come on George!" "Sir . . . Oh, yeah, he could break it."

And then the anterior question about "breaches" and "fences" was arrived at by another student, and I leaped out of my chair in congratulation. "Sir, the first question is 'Why was the fence there in the first place?' " Right! What time was it?

X

It was time for Public Enemy's "Don't Believe the Hype." Because all of the Agincourt admonition and "breach" rhetoric (the whole hybrid, international class of London GCSE students knew) was a function of the English church being required to pay the king "in full," and the state treasury can get the duckets only if ancient (and spurious) boundary claims are made to send Henry V and the boys into somebody else's yard. "Patriotism," a show of hands by the class revealed, is a "hype" if it means dying for England. Bless his soul, though, there was *one* stout lad who held up his hand and said he would be ready to die for England. My black British young lady, who had put her tapes away, shouted across the room: "That's because you're English!"

Hybridity: a variety of sounds coming together to arouse interest in a classic work of Shakespearean creation.

The Mail on Sunday reporter told me as we left North Westminster that the English Department head had asked her to apologize to me in advance for the GCSE group because they would never listen to what I had to say and would split the room *as soon as the bell rang.* What the head had not factored into her apologetics was the technology I came bearing. I carried along my very own Panasonic cassette blaster as the postmodern analogue of the "the message" and the "rapper's delight" that Shakespeare himself would include in his plays were he writing today. At a site of postmodern, immigrant, sonic (twenty-two languages) hybridity produced by an internationally accessible technology, I gained pedagogical entreé by playing in the new and very, very sound game of rap. Like Jesse, I believe rap is here to stay. Other forms such as "house" and "hip-house" and "rap reggae" may spin off, but "rap" is now classical black sound. It is the "in effect" archive where postmodernism has been *dopely* sampled for the international 1990s.

Notes

1. David Toop, *The Rap Attack* (Boston: South End, 1984), 78.

2. Nelson George, *The Death of Rhythm and Blues* (New York: Dutton, 1989), 149–58.

3. Albert Murray, *The Hero and the Blues* (Columbia: University of Missouri Press, 1973).

4. Quoted in John Leland and Steven Stein, "What It Is," *Village Voice,* 33 (January 19, 1988), 26. Leland and Stein's article is one moment in this special issue of the *Voice* devoted to hip hop.

5. Langston Hughes, "Still Here," *Selected Poems of Langston Hughes* (New York: Alfred Knopf, 1969), 123. "I've been scarred and battered. / My hopes the wind done scattered. / Snow has friz me, sun has baked me. / Looks like between 'em / They done tried to make me / Stop laughin', stop lovin', stop livin'— / But I don't care! / *I'm Still here!"*

6. Playthell Benjamin, "Two Funky White Boys," *Village Voice,* 35 (January 9, 1990), 33–37.

7. Robert Christgau, "Jesus, Jews, and the Jackass Theory," *Village Voice,* 35 (January 16, 1990), 83–84, 86, 89.

8. Benedict Anderson, *Imagined Communities* (London: Verso, 1983).

9. Bhabha presented his brilliant insights on hybridity and heterogeneity in two lectures at the University of Pennsylvania on April 20–21, 1989. Stallybrass's essay on heterogeneity I read in manuscript, but it is

destined for *Representations*. For the insight of Bhabha, one can read "The Other Question." In *Literature, Politics, and Theory,* ed. Francis Barker et al. (London: Methuen, 1986), 148–72. For Stallybrass, one might turn to his coedited monograph, *The Politics and Poetics of Transgression* (Ithaca, N.Y.: Cornell University Press, 1986).

10. Clarence Waldron, "Could Students Learn More If Taught with Rap Music?" *Jet,* 77 (January 29, 1990), 16–18. I had the honor of featuring prominently in this article. My picture even appeared in a gallery including Kurtis Blow, Kool Moe Dee, DJ Jazzy Jeff and the Fresh Prince, and Run DMC.

Towards Cultural History

Catherine Belsey

I

Is there a place for English in a postmodern world? Does an academy where twentieth-century textual practice breaks down the nineteenth-century boundaries between disciplines offer English departments any worthwhile job to do? Can we still seriously set out to teach our students literature?

I start from the assumption that English as it has traditionally been understood, as the study of great literary works by great authors, has no useful part to play in a pedagogy committed to a politics of change. In the course of the 1980s the institution of English has been firmly stripped of its mask of polite neutrality by Peter Widdowson, Chris Baldick, Terry Eagleton and Terence Hawkes, among others.[1] As their analyses reveal, the conservatism of traditional English lies primarily in two main areas: first, its promotion of the author-subject as the individual origin of meaning, insight, and truth; and second, its claim that this truth is universal, transcultural and ahistorical. In this way, English affirms as natural and inevitable both the individualism and the world picture of a specific

Catherine Belsey, "Towards Cultural History—in Theory and Practice" *Textual Practice* 3:2 pp. 159–172. Copyright 1989, Routledge, London, England. Reprinted by permission.

western culture, and within that culture the perspective of a specific class and a specific sex. In other words, a discipline that purports to be outside politics in practice reproduces a very specific
political position.

But I start equally from the assumption that there is no special political pedagogical merit in severing all ties with the texts the
institution of English has done its best to make its own. It would be
ironic if a theory of difference left us unable to differentiate between
Bradley's *Othello* and Leavis's, and between these *Othellos* and all
the others we might produce for quite other purposes. It would be
still more ironic if by a kind of political ultra-leftism we abandoned
Othello and the entire institution—with all its (precisely institutional) power—and handed it back without a struggle to those for
whom a politics of change is more of a threat than a promise. The
works that the institution of English has done everything to appropriate are there to be reclaimed and reappropriated, and there is no
reason why this should not be done from within the institution. The
texts are available to be reread as the material for a history of
meanings and values and practices in their radical discontinuity. In
this way new work might be expected to come from the English department itself, and not just from somewhere else called, say, Cultural Studies. My project for English, therefore, is not to abandon it
but to *move* it—towards cultural history.

Much of the work of the institution has been, of course, a process of exclusion. The canon of great books by great authors has
been important not only for what it affirms—the value and the coherence of admissible readings of those works it recognizes. As every feminist, for example, knows, its importance also lies in what it
refuses. Dale Spender has recently unearthed nearly 600 novels
from the century before Jane Austen, by a hundred women novelists
who were taken seriously in their own period. As she points out, Ian
Watt's extremely influential book, *The Rise of the Novel*, takes no
account of their existence. As far as the institution is concerned, the
novel was invented by men. *The Rise of the Novel* is subtitled Studies in Defoe, Richardson and Fielding.[2]

The relegation of certain authors, of particular texts and,
above all, of specific textual practices helps to police the boundaries
of truth. Texts which are most obviously difficult to recuperate,
which most obviously challenge conservative assumptions about
race, class, or gender, have been systematically marginalized as
"flawed," or banished from view (and in consequence from print) as
inadequate, not *literature*. They are, of course, flawed and inadequate according to literary standards invoked precisely to margin-

alize them—standards which have denied their own relativity, and indeed the cultural and historical specificity of imposing "literary standards" at all.

The cultural history I would like to see us produce would refuse nothing. While of course any specific investigation would find a specific focus, both chronologically and textually, no moment, no epoch, no genre and no form of signifying practice would be excluded a priori from the field of inquiry. Cultural history would have no place for a canon, and no interest in ranking works in order of merit. Stephen Greenblatt's discussion of the reformer Tyndale, for instance, in his book *Renaissance Self-Fashioning,* shows some the advantages of linking literature with a manual of religious politics in the analysis of sixteenth-century subjectivity. Greenblatt treats *The Obedience of a Christian Man* not as background in the conventional way, but as text.[3] Indeed, Louis Adrian Montrose, like Greenblatt an American New Historicist, identifies his own position in terms which closely resemble the project I am trying to define here. New Historicism is new, Montrose points out, "in its refusal of traditional distinctions between literature and history, between text and context; new in resisting a traditional opposition of the privileged individual—whether an author or a work—to a world 'outside.' "[4] In a rather different way, Jacqueline Rose's book on *Peter Pan* also rejects traditional distinctions and oppositions. Rose brings together children's fiction, the notion of the child and the history of sexuality in ways that throw into relief the limitations on our knowledge imposed by conventional value-judgments and conventional reading practices.[5] Without wanting to deny the specificity of fiction, of genre and, indeed, of the individual text, cultural history would necessarily take all signifying practice as its domain.

And that means that the remaining demarcation lines between disciplines would not survive the move. Signifying practice is not exclusively nor even primarily verbal. We need, for example, to align ourselves with art historians. I have invoked portraits in the analysis of changing meanings of gender relations.[6] John Barrell and Norman Bryson have both in different ways demonstrated much more extensively the kind of work that becomes possible when writing and painting are brought into conjunction, without treating one as the background which explains the other.[7] And perhaps more eccentrically, but only marginally so, the allocation of domestic space is replete with meanings for the cultural historian. The medieval move of the feast from the hall to the great chamber, which was also for sleeping in (or rather, to the great chambers, since the lady, if she was involved in the feast at all, was likely to dine in her own chamber),[8] and the subsequent isolation of the family dining-room from the servants' quarters, is as significant in charting the history of the meaning of the family as is the current vogue for open-plan living. What is at stake in each of these changes is the definition of the family unit. And meanwhile Girouard's account of the development of the privy in his book on the English country house constitutes a mine of information indispensable to any truly thorough analysis of the bourgeois disavowal of the body.[9]

II
—

As this rudimentary reading list reveals, I don't imagine that cultural history is my own invention. It is necessary only to point to the work of Christopher Hill and E. P. Thompson, or of Philippe Ariès and Marina Warner, to give authority to such a project. Here fiction is one source, and not necessarily a privileged one, of knowledge about the past. Meanwhile, the recent phase of feminist criticism received a considerable impetus from three books published in 1970 by Kate Millett, Germaine Greer, and Eva Figes. All three discussed literature, and all three refused to isolate it from the culture of which it formed a part. The writings of Freud and Barbara Cartland, for example, were invoked by these feminists, and were treated neither as explanatory metalanguage in the first case, nor as cultural context in the second, but in both instances as texts alongside Shakespeare, D. H. Lawrence, and Norman Mailer. And, of course, the transformation of English into cultural history would be unthinkable without the example of Raymond Williams, who above all established a tradition of radical critical work from within the institution of English itself.

But in listing this methodologically and politically disparate group of writers, I become conscious of the need at this stage to clarify precisely what it is that cultural history enables us to know, and to reflect on why it is that we might want to know it. Without intending at all to diminish the radical importance of their work, or my own debts to all of them, I am not now sure that every form of knowledge that each of these authors has pursued is either available to us on the one hand or politically productive on the other.

Early in *Of Grammatology*, Derrida, whose admirers have so often presented him as contemptuous of history, suggests that there remains to be written a history of writing itself, or rather, a history of what he calls "the system of signified truth."[10] What Derrida is proposing here is the story of God, of the transcendental signified which holds all other meanings in place, and he offers a series of quotations from different historical moments which identify the truth as alternatively God or his surrogates, nature, reason, the self. (Derrida is explicitly discussing a continuity here, but he of all people would hardly be likely to rule out some very significant differences between these terms.) And early in volume 2 of *The History of Sexuality* Foucault, whose admirers are so often anxious to see his work in opposition to Derrida's, gives a general account of his own project: "what I have held to, what I have tried to maintain for many years, is the effort to isolate some of the elements that might be useful for a history of truth."[11] For all their important differences, Derrida and Foucault both identify a mode of history which is profoundly political. To possess the truth is to have the right to act in its name. Truth stands outside culture as a guarantee of legitimacy. Despite the familiar romance of truth, secretly so dear to academics, in which the special and solitary hero sets out to go beyond the bounds of convention on a lonely quest for transcendental presence, in historical practice the metaphysics of truth has licensed torture, exploitation, and mass murder. Post-structuralism now displays truth as a linguistic tyranny which arrests the proliferation of meanings, assigns values and specifies norms. Truth recruits subjects. The history of truth is the history of our subjection. Its content is the knowledges that constitute us as subjects, and that defines and delimits what it is possible for us to say, to be and to do.

It might be worth a digression here to stress the argument that to abandon truth is not necessarily to embrace the free-for-all of radical subjectivism. And it is not inevitably to endorse a politics of relativism or, worse, expediency. The proposition is that we cannot *know* that any existing language maps the world adequately, that there can be no certainty of a fit between the symbolic and the real. This is not the same as encouraging people to subscribe to whatever conviction happens to come into their heads, or inciting them to make things up. Nor is it to settle for believing them when they do. It is perfectly possible to recognize lies without entailing the possibility of telling the truth, least of all the whole truth. It would be very naïve indeed to claim that people do not from time to time set out to deceive each other, or that institutions and states do not practice cover-ups on a deplorable scale. But what they conceal is what they know, and since there can be no guarantee that any system of differences maps the world accurately, knowledge is necessarily culturally and discursively relative. This does not

exonerate the liars. They are culpable. But neither does it support
the belief that in order to be able to denounce lies, we have to cling
to a metaphysics of truth. Language is a system of differences, not of
binary oppositions. As Foucault argues in another but related context, alternatives which only offer either the old constraints or no
constraints at all are "simplistic and authoritarian," and we should
refuse to be coerced by them.[12] You can tell it like you know it, in
accordance with the rules of the discourse, without having to claim
that you're telling it like it (absolutely, metaphysically, incontro-
vertibly) *is*.

It is my empirical observation, offered here for debate, that
whereas men in general have the greatest difficulty in surrendering
the concept of truth, women in general do so without much trouble.
The explanation is almost certainly not biological. The cultural construction of women—as of other marginal groups—tends to include
rather less emphasis on the possession of truth. Marginal subjects
commonly have an oblique relationship to the world map which
guarantees the imaginary knowing, mastering autonomy of those
who speak from the center of a culture. The map always represents
a knowledge of which those at the margins are at least partly the
objects rather than the subjects, and from which they are at least
from time to time excluded. Their identity as subjects is thus less
evidently dependent on the reaffirmation of the map itself. Conversely, however, marginality of this kind protects women from the
fear that if the world is not exactly as we have mapped it, perhaps
it is not there at all, or the conviction that the alternative to truth
is chaos or absence. As women, we know that, whatever form it may
take, the real is there and is independent of our will: we are, after
all, consistently assaulted, constrained, defined and reconstructed
by it. Cartesian doubt, Catharine MacKinnon points out, "comes
from the luxury of a position of power that entails the possibility of
making the world as one thinks it to be."[13] Most women, however
individually powerful, have only a sporadic or oblique hold on that
luxury; they can therefore relinquish the totalizing narratives of
their culture with relative equanimity.

III
—

If the ultimate objective of a politically radical cultural history is
the history of truth, its location is the history of meanings. Not exactly concerned with images and representations, insofar as those

terms indicate an exteriority, gesture towards a presence which is always elsewhere, cultural history is nevertheless not quite a history of behavior or conduct either. The project is to identify the meanings in circulation in earlier periods, to specify the discourses, conventions and signifying practices by which meanings are fixed, norms "agreed" and truth defined. Cultural history is thus a history of "experience" only, as Foucault puts it, "where experience is understood as the correlation between fields of knowledge, types of normativity, and forms of subjectivity in a particular culture."[14] The constraints on knowledge, normativity, and subjectivity are the ranges of meaning culturally and discursively available. What it is possible to "experience" at any specific moment is an effect of what it is possible to say. (Not, of course, what I am personally capable of formulating, but *what can be said* and thus known.) And in case this proposition should be interpreted as a piece of unregenerate structuralism, it is perhaps useful to reaffirm that meanings are always plural, subject to excess, in process, contradictory, sites of struggle.

It is important to bear in mind, too, that wherever there is a history of subjection to norms and truths, there is also a history of resistances. Power produces resistance not only as its legitimation, as the basis for an extension of control, but as its defining difference, the other which endows it with meaning, visibility, effectivity. The work of Foucault is an important influence here. His position is often represented, by Foucault's admirers and his detractors alike, as negative, nihilistic, an account of power as a new transcendental signified, irreducible and irresistable in its omnipresence. Some of the New Historicists have borrowed from Foucault in order to produce an account of history, especially Renaissance history, which is so close in many ways to the kind of cultural history I am proposing here that it seems important to attempt to distinguish between the two. Of course, New Historicism is by no means a unified phenomenon, and any generalization is likely to obliterate important differences of emphasis. But if it is possible to point to general tendencies, this is a form of cultural history in which power is commonly seen as centered, usually in the monarchy, and is held to produce opposition only in order to legitimate its own extension. In practice, this analysis owes more to functionalism than it does to Foucault, who locates power not in a center, but in knowledges, discourses, micro-exchanges, and who everywhere proclaims its precariousness, its instability. On the assumption that political usefulness, not the author's opinion, is our concern, Foucault's work can be read, selectively, I admit, but no less productively for that, as a history of resistances—of ballad-mongers, fools, criminals, deviants and suicides who heroically repudiate the positions that power produces for them.

If there is a general distinction to be made between the project of the New Historicists and what I am proposing here, it lies in the inscription of struggle. Too often in the work of Stephen Greenblatt and Jonathan Goldberg, for all its elegance, scholarship, and subtlety, power is represented as seamless and all-pervasive, while resistance, where it exists at all, is seen as ultimately self-deceived. Texts are understood as homogeneous, monologic, in the last instance non-contradictory, because the uncertainties they formulate are finally contained by the power they might seem to subvert.[15] The cultural history I propose is a story of conflicting interests, of heroic refusals, of textual uncertainties. It tells of power, but of power which always entails the possibility of resistance, insofar as it inevitably requires a differentiating other.

To this extent, then, I share the position of the British Cultural Materialists, who tend to stress subversion rather than containment. But in this case too it seems to me important to draw distinctions between an existing practice and the project I am outlining.[16] It is even less clear here than in the case of New Historicism that there is a single, homogeneous body of work to which the term Cultural Materialism refers. The phrase was originally invoked by Raymond Williams, and was subsequently adopted by Jonathan Dollimore and Alan Sinfield as the subtitle of their important and challenging collection of essays on *Political Shakespeare*.[17] It seems to imply an allusion to the Althusserian concept of ideology as a material practice, and to propose that culture, like Althusser's ideology, is relatively autonomous and is in consequence itself a site of contradiction and struggle. The structuralist analysis of the materiality of language had made it possible for Althusser to break with a vulgarized Marxist treatment of ideology as the *expression* of a struggle which was *really* taking place elsewhere, in the economy. Now the economic, the political, and the ideological could be thought of as distinct instances, relatively independent, developing unevenly, but linked together to the extent that each might also constitute a condition of the possibility of developments in the others. Althusser's term "ideology," however, though indispensable in enabling theory to break with the empiricist recuperation of Marx, has come in time to seem rather a blunt instrument, if only because of the uneasy distinction Althusser's own writing between *ideologies* and *ideology in general*. (It was at this point that Foucault's work on the power relations inscribed in knowledges-as-discourses offered the possibility of a more focused analysis of cultural practice.) In the usage of Dollimore and Sinfield the looser term, "culture," in conjunction with the silent allusion to Marxism in the word "materialism," appears to promise a form of analysis which takes into account post-Athusserian work on the textual inscription of struggle.

It is disappointing, therefore, to find that in Dollimore's introduction to *Political Shakespeare* the emphasis is on cultural subversion as a unitary phenomenon, as an "idea," which is "represented" (re-presented) in texts, and that the real struggle is once again elsewhere:

> the mere thinking of a radical idea is not what makes it subversive . . . one might go further and suggest that not only does the idea have to be conveyed, it has also actually to be used to refuse authority *or* be seen by authority as capable and likely of being so used.

"Ideas" apparently have materiality only if they are in some not very clearly specified way *put into* practice, or *perceived as* able to be so. Later in the same paragraph an idea is subversive because it is "taken up" and helps to precipitate "historical change."[18] There is no space in Dollimore's account of Cultural Materialism for the theoretical developments of recent years, for the analysis of textuality as inherently unstable, or for the identification of culture as itself the place where norms are specified and contested, knowledges affirmed and challenged, and subjectivity produced and disrupted.

If meanings are not fixed and guaranteed, but as Derrida has consistently argued, indeterminate, differed and deferred, invaded by the trace of otherness which defines and constitutes the self-same, texts necessarily exceed their own unitary projects, whether these are subversion or containment, in a movement of instability which releases new possibilities in the very process of attempting to close them off. And if power generates the possibility of resistance as its defining difference, the signified truth necessarily produces alternative knowledges, not only for political motives, as functionalism proposes, in order to master them, but also as a structural necessity, because without them it lacks definition. Only an eternal verity (universal truth) can hold the network of meanings in place. But it does so in a perpetual conflict with its others, both internal and external, which is the condition of its existence as knowledge. If we succeed in relativizing the truth, then we release as material for analysis the play of signification, Foucault's "games of truth,"[19] which necessarily have more than one player, or more than one side, and which are not a reflection of the struggle for power, but its location. To give a historical account of what constitutes us as subjects is to specify the possibilities of transgressing the existing limits on what we are able to say, to be and to do.[20]

IV

What has this to do with the institution of English? Everything, I believe. More than any other discipline, English has been concerned with the study of signifying practice. Traditionally we have not only analyzed meanings (philosophy does that too), and we have not only been concerned with social relations (history and sociology are too). Supremely, English departments have attended to the formal properties of texts, their modes of address to readers and the conditions in which they are intelligible. Cultural history needs to appropriate and develop those strategies, putting them to work not in order to demonstrate the value of the text, or its coherence as the expression of the authorial subjectivity which is its origins, but to lay bare the contradictions and conflicts, the instabilities and indeterminacies, which inevitably reside in any bid for truth. We need only extend the range of texts we are willing to discuss, to put on the syllabus . . .

That "only" is there to cheer us up, to make it all sound easy. I'm not sure how easy it is. But if we can interpret Shakespeare, we can surely learn to interpret fashion, and music—and privies. Fredric Jameson has succeeded with an ease which may be deceptive (or which at least may be hard to emulate) in bringing together fiction, painting, music, film, and architecture in his polemical and controversial account of the postmodern condition.

Jameson's essay, "Postmodernism, or the cultural logic of late capitalism," is a discussion of changes in signifying practice itself: not simply changes in meaning in the conventional sense, but changes in form.[21] It is impossible to consider postmodernism without paying attention to its mode of address, its disruption of the subject-object couple produced and reproduced by the signifying practices of classic realism. What Jameson fears—and others celebrate—is the dispersal of the knowing subject of humanism, in possession of the objects of its knowledge, and able to map the world. In my book *The Subject of Tragedy* I suggested that the subject of humanism was installed as a consequence of a parallel shift in signifying practice in the sixteenth and seventeenth centuries. My aim there was not to declare a nostalgia for the world we have lost, but to chart a revolution in the system of signification, which had radical implications for the subjectivity that is its effect. There is a great deal more work to be done on the specificity of modes of address and the history of the subject. And if this particular task seems to me especially urgent, that is perhaps because our culture places the subject at the center of the system of signified truths, identifies it as the absolute, extra-linguistic presence which is the origin and guarantee of the fixity of meaning, and targets nuclear weapons on the Soviet Union in defense of its (imaginary) freedom. If in the twentieth century truth has at last become plural, it is still inclined to be subjective, the unique and inalienable property of each unique individual subject.

Or it was. Because the tyranny of truth (including the subjective truth) becomes visible to us now only in consequence of the postmodern condition. It is no accident, but a precise effect of cultural history, that postmodern practice and poststructuralist theory coincide in their assault on truth to the extent that they do.

This is not to say that our own position as individuals—for or against truth, theory, change—is determined for us in advance: that too is a site of struggle, of subjections and resistances. There are choices constantly to be made, but they are political choices, choices of subject-position, not recognitions of the truth. It is, however, to emphasize our location within a continuing history, and the relativity of our own meanings, knowledges and practices. And perhaps this above all is the pedagogic and political importance of cultural history. It addresses and constitutes students, readers, practitioners who are themselves an effect of the history they make.

It goes without saying (I hope) after all this that I am not proposing that we should set out in quest of a new truth, simply reconstituting our dispersed, postmodern subjectivities round new objects of knowledge. Still less that we reconstruct the institution of English in support of a more comprehensive metanarrative, a more thorough mapping of the world, a new system centered on a new transcendental signified. Nor on the other hand is cultural relativity the ground of a simple libertarianism, making the texts do whatever we like. This part of my argument is difficult to formulate, since the discourse of a non-empiricist knowledge barely exists as yet, but I am persuaded that we should not abandon the notion of rigor, the project of substantiating our readings, or a commitment to historical specificity. We shall need principles of selection, since without them no individual project would be thinkable. But at the same time, the cultural history I visualize is predicated on the relativity of knowledges, on history as a process of production, and on that process as political intervention.

If, however, it takes for granted the relativity of our certainties, it also assumes the relativity of our subjection. The transcendental subject, outside and above the objects of its knowledge, is also the most deeply subjected being, at the mercy of the system of signified truth of which it is an effect. Conversely, the subjectivity which is imbricated in the knowledges it participates in and helps to produce has more options at its disposal. Modes of resistance—or, to use Pêcheux's terms, counter-identification, the rejection of what is dominant, and disidentification, the production of alternative knowledges, alternative subject positions—are no longer seen as eccentric or psychotic, as threats to the very being of the subject itself. A subjectivity explicitly constituted in and by its own knowledges does not "disintegrate" in consequence of contradiction and conflict. And equally, it escapes to some degree the reaffirmation of the lack which stems from the exteriority of a knowledge whose objects are always finally elsewhere, beyond the grasp of the subject. The readings we should make would not be a quest for lost presence, but a contribution to a continuing process of production.

The project, then, is a history of meanings, and struggles for meaning, in every place where meanings can be found—or made. Its focus is on change, cultural difference and the relativity of truth. And its purpose is to change the subject, involving ourselves as practitioners in the political and pedagogic process of making history, in both senses of that phrase.

V
—

This proposal, though largely theoretical, is not in fact wholly abstract. In the autumn of 1986, as Visiting Professor at McMaster University, Hamilton, Ontario, I had the opportunity to teach a graduate class on a topic of my choice. I chose "Toward Cultural History" as my title, and devised a course which I hoped would enable me to see how the theory I have outlined might work in practice. The students were excellent: they were cooperative, diligent, adventurous, enthusiastic and intelligent. They cannot be held in any way responsible for the fact that the course ran into certain difficulties—and that these difficulties represented problems I am still not sure how to solve.

In order to define the problems, it is necessary to give a brief account of what we did. Since my appointment was only for one term, we had a total of thirteen weeks. Some of the students were entirely new to post-structuralist theory, though some had a very sophisticated grasp of recent theoretical debates. It seemed to me imperative that the class should arrive at some sort of consensus on what it was possible to know. The alternative, the danger of having to be present at or take part in metaphysical discussions about the inaccessible intentions of specific authors, or the ineffable experience of particular groups of people, seemed to me—and still seems—extremely dispiriting. We therefore set out on the one hand to engage with the basic theories of language, subjectivity and knowledge which had produced post-structuralism, but on the other to alternate our attention to theory with the practice of cultural history.

In accordance with this plan, I offered at our first meeting an example of the kind of cultural history I proposed, an analysis of Holbein's *The Ambassadors* in conjunction with a scene from *Hamlet,* and a discussion of the relations between humanism, illusionism and violence. Thereafter there were no more set pieces from me. In each class we discussed the week's required reading on the basis of brief papers produced by individual students.

We had a good time. We had a particularly good time with the theory. We struggled with and over passages of Derrida, Althusser, and Foucault. We agreed to read *The Use of Pleasure,* the second volume of Foucault's *History of Sexuality.* This was still in hardback and a major expense for the students, but we were determined to be up-to-date. We discussed it and pooled our disappointment. Where, we wondered, was the evidence of resistance here? Where was the symptomatic textual analysis which would betray as precarious, as unstable, the regimes of self-discipline the book was concerned to analyze? We all wanted to get the theory straight: we all wanted to debate its value; we all wanted to discuss its political implications. We found that we agreed to a surprising extent, though there was enough skepticism in the group to keep us going.

But we had trouble with the practice, with the production of our own contribution to cultural history. The first time we tried to put the theory into practice, I showed slides of family portraits from different periods. We "read" them together, and identified in the visual images the changing inscription of patriarchal and proprietary power relations. We produced some impressive interpretations and distinctions, but it all seemed a little bit facile—perhaps because we didn't know enough to relate our readings to contemporary cultural phenomena from a range of distinct historical moments. In

consequence, we were not convinced that we had been able to produce an account of the meanings of the family which was sufficiently detailed and sufficiently nuanced to be satisfying. At other
times the students produced analyses they had worked on. The rest
of us were willing to be impressed, but we didn't necessarily feel we
knew enough to comment critically or to contribute by drawing new
inferences.

It would have defeated the object of the exercise, however, if I
had simply provided the materials for the students to reaffirm instances of cultural history which I had already produced (or at least
defined) ahead of them. The project was not that the students
should master an existing map of cultural history, but that they
should contribute to a future one. But this presents serious theoretical and pedagogical problems. As English is traditionally
taught, the map is drawn for the students in advance (and in some
cases a very long time in advance: individual syllabuses have been
known to last for thirty years, and the present literary canon in its
broad outlines has been there longer still). Even in the relatively
rare instances where the course includes material that has not been
taught before—women's writing, black writing or postmodern fiction, for example—the texts tend to be specified ahead of time. The
same goes for the theoretical element of the cultural history course:
the classic texts of post-structuralism are reasonably well established (though by no means beyond dispute, of course). But how,
without pre-empting the production process itself, was it possible to
structure a seminar which could do the practical work? The production of cultural history was not a problem in itself. But the question
was how to integrate the production process into a course, how to
involve other people in the work, how to share the practice in the
way that we shared the discussion of the theory.

That definition of the problem points at once to the solution. If
we had had another term for the course, I think we ought to have
spent it devising and realizing the collective production of a specific
piece of cultural history. Mercifully, perhaps, in view of the real difficulties of collected work in the deeply individualist culture of the
free west, especially within the profoundly uncollective framework
of North American tertiary education, there wasn't time. But if
there had been, could we have done it?

There would have been serious institutional problems. How
could we have negotiated the students' very real need for individual
grades? And what would my position have been? A disinterested observer? An equal member of the collective? And if the second of
these, what would have happened when I suddenly took up a quite
different position as assessor, allotting grades on behalf of the in-

stitution? Would there have been time within the constraints of a course to discuss the solutions to these problems collectively, to choose a project collectively, and also to produce something worthwhile at the end of it all? And if we had failed to produce a worthwhile piece of cultural history, would that have invalidated the whole project, leaving us all in despair?

Some of these problems are already familiar from the debates of the 1960s (which in practice were largely the 1970s, as far as more British universities were concerned). But the problems then were not exactly the same as they are now. At that time the issues were primarily "relevance" and a new (and probably very necessary) libertarianism. The most prominent pedagogic question was how to allow students to exercise greater choice about their areas of study and greater control over their mode of work. It is worth saying that we did not entirely solve those problems. But the new issue, foregrounded by postmodernism in its distrust of metanarratives, fixed knowledges, maps, is how to avoid charting the terrain in advance, merely asking students to traverse existing and well-worn paths to known destinations.

A number of these difficulties would disappear, or at least dwindle, in an institution widely committed to the practice of cultural history. A single course in isolation has to cover all the ground; it must be sure to include both theory and practice; and it operates under pressure to offer a model of what cultural history might be. For all these reasons it has some responsibility not simply to pursue the current interests of the teacher concerned. But a whole graduate program in cultural history, complete with a separate theory course and a range of options, could afford to do precisely that. In those circumstances, where plurality was built in from the beginning, we could afford to involve our students in our own current projects, working out jointly with them a plan of work and a mode of analysis.

Although in these circumstances some of the institutional problems would remain, the scheme of study I have outlined could, I believe, be put into practice. The educational institution as it already exists produces alternative knowledges as its difference, so that we can all as individuals "do" cultural history if we choose. It should not, therefore, prove impossible to devise and implement a pedagogy that permits us to introduce courses in cultural history as a genuinely radical alternative to the simultaneous individualism and universalism of English in its traditional form.

It is for that reason that I have called this essay "Towards Cultural History." It proposes a specific kind of journey, but it does not yet lay claim to an arrival.

Notes

1. Peter Widdowson (ed.), *Re-Reading English* (London: Methuen, 1982); Chris Baldick, *The Social Mission of English Criticism, 1848–1932* (Oxford: Oxford University Press, 1983); Terry Eagleton, *Literary Theory: an Introduction* (Oxford: Basil Blackwell, 1983); Terence Hawkes, *That Shakespeherian Rag* (London: Methuen, 1986).

2. See Dale Spender, *Mothers of the Novel* (London: Pandora, 1986), pp. 115–37.

3. Stephen Greenblatt, *Renaissance Self-fashioning from More to Shakespeare* (Chicago: University of Chicago Press, 1980).

4. Louis Adrian Montrose, 'The Elizabethan Subject and the Spenserian Text', in Patricia Parker and David Quint (eds), *Literary Theory/Renaissance Texts* (Baltimore: Johns Hopkins University Press, 1986), pp. 303–40, 304.

5. Jacqueline Rose, *Peter Pan, or the Impossibility of Children's Fiction* (London: Macmillan, 1984).

6. Catherine Belsey, 'Disrupting Sexual Difference: Meaning and Gender in the Comedies', in John Drakakis (ed.), *Alternative Shakespeares* (London: Methuen, 1985), pp. 166–90; *The Subject of Tragedy: Identity and Difference in Renaissance Drama* (London: Methuen, 1985).

7. John Barrell, *The Dark Side of the Landscape: the Rural Poor in English Painting 1730–1840* (Cambridge: Cambridge University Press, 1980); Norman Bryson, *Word and Image: French Painting of the Ancien Regime* (Cambridge: Cambridge University Press, 1981).

8. Mark Girouard, *Life in the English Country House* (Harmondsworth: Penguin Books, 1980).

9. ibid., pp. 245–66.

10. Jacques Derrida, *Of Grammatology*, tr. Gayatri Chakravorty Spivak (Baltimore: Johns Hopkins University Press, 1976), p. 15.

11. Michel Foucault, *The Use of Pleasure (The History of Sexuality,* vol. 2) (London: Viking Press, 1986), p. 6.

12. Michel Foucault, 'What is Enlightenment?', in Paul Rabinow (ed.), *The Foucault Reader* (Harmondsworth: Penguin Books, 1986), pp. 32–50, 43.

13. Catharine A. MacKinnon, 'Desire and Power: a Feminist Perspective', in Cary Nelson and Lawrence Grossberg (eds), *Marxism and the Interpretation of Culture* (London: Macmillan, 1988), pp. 105–21, 113.

14. Foucault, *The Use of Pleasure,* p. 4.

15. See Greenblatt, *Renaissance Self-fashioning;* Jonathan Goldberg, *James I and the Politics of Literature* (Baltimore: Johns Hopkins University Press, 1983). But for exceptions to these generalizations, see Louis Adrian Montrose, ' "Shaping Fantasies": Figurations of Gender and Power in Elizabethan Culture', *Representations,* 1, 2 (Spring 1983), pp. 61–94; and 'The Elizabethan subject and the Spenserian text'.

16. On a visit to the United States in 1988 I was surprised to discover that I was a Cultural Materialist.

17. Jonathan Dollimore and Alan Sinfield (eds), *Political Shakespeare: New Essays in Cultural Materialism* (Manchester: Manchester University Press, 1985).

18. ibid., p. 13.

19. Foucault, *The Use of Pleasure,* pp. 6–7.

20. Foucault, 'What is Enlightenment?', p. 46.

21. Fredric Jameson, 'Postmodernism, or the Cultural Logic of Late Capitalism', *New Left Review,* 146 (1984), pp. 53–92.

INDEX

absolute, ix
abstract expressionism, 116
absurdity, 54
Adorno, T., 99, 122, 125, 137, 140, 174
advertising, 121
aesthetic, high modernist, 113; in the social and historical, 196
aesthetic experience, 102
aesthetic-expressive, 101
aesthetic production, and commodity production, 316
aesthetics, commodity, 138; commodity, and postmodernism, 526; in scientific paradigms, 385, 387; modernist, 141
affluent society, 506
African-Americans, and postmodernism, 510–511; and their experience, 448; in a postmodernist view, 394
ℛ alienation generation, 500, 501–502
Aliens, 409, 413–415
allegiances, professional, in science, 387
allegory, and Benjamin, 177
Althusser, L., 302, 303, 558–559
Altieri, C., 41
ambiguity, ix, 6, 22

analytico-referential discourse, vs. metafictional solipcism, 171
anarchy, in postmodern fiction, 522
androgyne, in popular culture, 414
anti-colonialist critique, 427
anti-foundationalism, and postcolonial needs, 433. See also foundationalism
anti-modernism, 31–32, 108
Anti-Oedipus, 218
anti-racism, and social and historical constructs, 472; pedagogy, 452–489 passim
anti-realism, and postmodern fiction, 521
architects, and modernism, 393
architecture, 313; architecture, postmodern, 106, 316; as privileged aesthetic language, 329
archiving, and collaging of sound, 542
Arendt, H., and social classes, 506–507
Aronowitz, S., 458
art, xi, 97–98, 100, 103; and abstraction and non-representation, 146; bourgeois, 101; and differentiation, 325; and material intervention, 167–168; and society, 146–147; as

art (*continued*)
schizophrenic, 323–324; in Eagleton's view, 167; in Ernst Bloch's view, 168; new meanings in, 546; postmodern, and the material referent, 172; practice of, and postmodernism, 527; targeted for mass market, 523; vs. life, 462
asymmetries, gender-based, 420
authenticity, 97
✓ author-subject, and meaning, 551
authority, vs. rap, 545
autonomy, postmodernism's suspicion of, 203
avant-garde, 94, 108, 116, 119–120, 124, 138, 145, 147; linked to modernism and postmodernism, 195; versus Kitsch, 145

Bacon, F., 173
Baker, H., and hybridity of popular culture, 445, 538–549
Bambara, T. C., and stories, 476–477
Barth, J., 117
Barthelme, J., and language, 533–534
Barthes, R., 136, 139, 140; and connotation, 322; codes vs. representation, 525; "Inaugural Lecture," 304
Baudrillard, J., 136, 526; on Foucault, 305; on simulacra, 342–373
Bauman, Z., xiii; "Is There A Postmodern Sociology," 441–442; on modernity and postmodernity, 462–463; on postmodernity, 9–24
Beat poets, 43–45
beauty, ix, 97, 99, 197, 447
Becker, C., 175–176
Beckett, S., *Watt*, 324
Bell, D., 94–95, 117, 132, 133, 314
Belsey, C., 442, 443, 446–449; on cultural history, 551–565
Benjamin, W., 94, 160

Berkeley, G., 173
Bertens, H. on the postmodern *Weltanschauung*, 25–70
Beuys, J., 105
Bhabha, H., 547; " 'Race' Time and the Revision of Modernity," 307–308
binarisms, ix, 300–301; and language, 556; critique of, 399; hierarchical, 309; of complicity and resistance, 305
biopower, 420–421
black, cultural practices, 395–397; feminist writers, 454, 469–479; identity, notion of an authentic, 513, 516; liberation struggle, 512; collective, 514; music, 395–396, 538–549; nationalism, and essentialism, 559; reader, and postmodernism, 511–512; reli-
✓ gious practices, 394–395; urban youth; and rap, 538–549 *passim;* postmodern, 510–518
Blatty, William Peter, 17
Bloch, E., 168
Blow-Out, as postmodernist, 329
Blow-Up, as modernist, 329
body, of woman, as unknown future, 408
bohemians, outside class, 498, 499
border pedagogy, 479–489
Borges, J., 342
bourgeois individualism, 142
Bové, P., neo-Heideggerian readings, 392
Bradbury, M., 520
Brecht, B., 139
bricoleur, and *bricolage,* and discourse, 231–235
British Cultural Materialists, 558
Burger, P., 119
Burroughs, W., and entrapment in language, 533

Cage, J., 324
Calinescu, M., 51–52

canon, of great books, what affirmed and refused, 552; of literature, and colonialism, 430

canonization, 64, 126

capitalism, ix, 125, 127; and postmodernism, 205; and racism, 459; and the *lebenswelt*, 162; as unprincipled undertaking, 354; consumer, 328; high-tech, mass marketing and consumption, 301–302; late, and consciousness raising, 527; late, and a critical standpoint, 532; late, and postmodernism, 314–331; logic of, 465; multinational, 329; production, and commodification etc., 456; third stage, 329–330. *See also* market

"Capitalism, Modernism and Postmodernism," 167

Cassirer, E., 173

causality, objective, and simulation, 344

center, absence of, 64; and structure, 224

chaos, 220

Cixous, H., 413

class, 394, 498–500, 505; and ideology, 458; and norms and postmodernism, 523; and rap, 545; and rational politics, 507; destruction of, 500; societies, and representative governments, 507

classic realism, 530

closure, ix

codes, doubling in architecture, 304; mixing of, 114–115

cognitive, 101

collage, and radical difference, 326

collaging, nonauthoritative, of sound, 542

Collins, J., and stylistic dominance, 448–449; on history, 466

colonialism, and identity, 515; and modernism, 308; armed version of modernism, 427

commodification, 121

commodity fetishism, and postmodernism, 527

communicative competence, 7, 97; in Habermas, 188 note 5

computer, and representation, 328

conservatism, 108; and the market, 481; and the classics, 147

conspiracy theory, 330

consumerism, and cultural identification, 446–447, 505–506

contingency, ix, 9–10, 12, 16, 36, 39, 60, 443

continuity, and change, in postmodernism, 428

contradictions, 205–206; vs. reconciliation, 208

conversation, of unequals, 420

conversion, from one paradigm to another, 382–383

corporations, and mass societies, 507

counterculture, 31, 33, 34, 35, 37, 40, 46, 121, 522

Creed, B., feminism and postmodernism, 398–418

crisis, in science, 383–384

critique, and co-optation, 305; objective, 309; within metanarrative, 443

cultural canon, and cultural homogeneity, 445

cultural history, 551–565; and conflicts, 560; and signifying practice, 553; as relative, 562; pedagogical account, 562–565

cultural homogeneity, and cultural canon, 445

cultural imperialism, 83–84

cultural relativism, 448, 504; and rational policy-making, 507; as a problem, 506; vs. metaphysics of truth, 449; and resistance, 149

cultural schizophrenia, in Jameson's view, 166–167

cultural studies, viii, 443

culture, and black experience, 510–
518 *passim;* high and low, 464; in
the West, 497–498; linear and
accumulative, 350; custom, 75

Dada, 45, 93, 119
Debord, G., on image as commodity
reification, 321–322
decolonization, and authentic black
identity, 516
deconstruction, 6, 45, 52–53, 110;
and binary oppositions, 205; of
European philosophy, 391; of
master narrative, 514; of sound,
542; postmodern, 447
Deleuze, and Guattari, and feminine writing, 400; and power,
and Nietzsche, 216–220 *passim;*
and the revolution of desire, 357
democracy, 23; and border pedagogy, 479–489; and diverse ways
of life, 479; and feminism, 509;
and literary postmodernism,
523; and political equality, 453;
and postmodern resistance, 450;
and rational politics, 447; and
"refusing nothing" practice, 448;
and relativism and pluralization,
507; collapsed into the logic of
the market, 481
demystification, of European cultural predominance, 391
Derrida, 136, 400–401; and history, 554–555; *Of Grammatology,*
177; on challenging the history
of metaphysics, 200; problematic
treatment of gender, 421–424;
structure, sign and play,
223–242
Descartes, R., 3, 86, 173; *cogito,* 22
desire, and capital and the law,
356–357; and hyperreality, 360
deterrence, and the hypermodel of
security, 367–373 *passim*
dialectics, 86
dialogic, 443–444
didactics, 81

difference, x, 309, 392, 452–489
passim; and consuming, 447; and
death, and simulation, 349; and
defering, 241; and disjunction,
325–326; and essentialism, 459;
and identity, 444; and Otherness,
510–518; and plurality, 307; and
postmodernism, 219; and similarity, 170–171; and the law,
359; and the resistant, in postmodernism, 198; and the transcendental signified, 225; female,
as concrete and historical, 422;
in Deleuze, 218; politics of, 435–
489 *passim;* postmodernism
grounded in, 442; sexual, 398–
404; system of, and language,
556. *See also* marginalized
differend, 443
disciplinary boundaries, and cultural history, 449, 553
disco, refusal of, 539
discourse, 304; joining power and
knowledge, 339–340; prevailing,
as hollow, 535; vs. history, 525
Disneyland, and simulation,
351–353
Dispatches, 183–186
dissidence, in postmodern fiction,
449, 530–535
diversity, and a critique of essentialism, 516; cultural, and parody, 448; vs. monolithic, 444
Dollimore, J., 558–559
domestic space, and cultural historian, 553
domination, American military and
economic, 316; and Gramsci, 430;
and the need to be a subject,
515; Eurocentric, 453; Foucault's
view of, 333–337 *passim;* historical and social dimension of, 422;
in cultural understanding, 465;
of other cultures, 149; racial, 513;
other, and identity, 471–472; stylistic, 449; vs. incommensurable
forms of life, 419–420

doxa, and de-doxifying, 526; as official meaning, 299
Duchamp, M., 119

Eagleton, 167–168, 171–172, 302; on real historical world, 300; postmodernism as a sick joke, 520
ecology and environment, 148
écriture, 139
education, multicultural, 461
ego, bourgeois, end of, 319
Eliot, T. S., on Ulysses, 521
empathy, and solidarity and coalition, 514
English, and the politics of change, 551; as the study of signifying practice, 560
Enlightenment, viii, xi, 5, 9, 72, 92, 98, 158, 159, 172, 173, 175, 198; aesthetics, 100; and liberals, 458; and postmodern pluralization, 447; and standardization of everyday life, 456; and the Renaissance episteme, 174; neo-Nietzschean critiques of, 527; postmodern rejection of, 463
equality, and modernism, 456–457
essentialism, black critique of, 448; critique of, 515–516; in black nationalism, 459; postmodern critique of, 513
ethics, subordinated by the market, 457–458
ethnicity, 309, 343; and postmodern cultural politics, 449; and race, as discourse of the Other, 455
ethnology, 227–228; and simulation, 347–351
eurocentrism, 122; and modernism, 308; and dominant codes and binarisms, 472–473; vs. black resistance, 393–394
everyday life, 96, 98, 102, 501; and history, 509; and social modernity, 456; and knowledge, 518; and black people, 513; pluralization of, 506–507; postmodern

recovery of, 469; smothered by abstractions, 463; those on the periphery of, 452; vs. elite culture, 462
ex-centric, as decentralized community, 198–199
existentialism, 38, 39, 41, 42, 500, 501
Exorcist, The, 17–19
experience, in Foucault's view, 557; the authority of, 516
experiments, crucial, 383

fact, vs. simulation, 344; and theories, 379; Nietzsche's view, 216
faith, in science, 386
falsification, in science, 378–379
Farki, N., The Death of Tarzana Clayton, 432–434
fashion, 504; and cultural history, 560
Federman, R., 57
feminism, 501; and democracy, 509; and postmodernism, 419–424; and poststructuralism, 309; as the greatest social revolution of modernity, 508–509
feminist criticism, 126; and cultural history, 553; and postmodern theory, 398–405
fiction, and the past, 554; as radically transgressive, 528; postmodern, 449; South American "boom," 435
fictionality, and the "real," 529–535; extended by postmodernism, 526
Fiedler, L., 31, 122, 196, 522; and popular art, 523–524; postmodernism as subversive, 520
film, and sexual difference, 406; noir, and femme fatale, 407; nostalgia, 405–407; postmodern, 415; sci-fi horror, 408–415
First World, postmodernism as a product of, 391; reflections on postmodernism, 392

Flax, J., feminism and postmodernity, 419–425

Fly, The, as pastiche, 411

Fordists, 114

formalism, neo-, approach to postmodernist fiction, 525–526

Foster, H., 171, 300, 392; *Anti-Aesthetic,* 169

Foucault, M., 136, 144, 158, 174, 318, 420; and constraints, 556; and feminist views, 420; history as political, 555; history of sexuality, 333–341; on power, 214, 304–305, 557–558; within Eurocentric and modernist frames, 391–392

foundationalism, 299. *See also* anti-foundationalism

freedom, 207–209; negative, and Kierkegaardian irony, 222, note 9; negative image in McGowan's view, 219–220

freeplay, and structure, 224; vs. totalization, 236–240

Freud, critique of consciousness, 226

Gass, W., 193; fiction as verbal world, 524–525

gender, 309, 394; and ideology, 458; essentialist concept of, 422; relations, ignored by Foucault, 420–421; roles, in adventure films, 406

German Ideology, 210

Gibson, W., 330

Giroux, H., 449; on race and ethnicity, 452–496

God, and truth, 555; as simulation, 346

Gödel's Proof of Incompleteness, 46

Goldberg, J., 558

Goodness, ix, 197, 447

Gramsci, A., 302; and cultural domination, 430

grand recits, 309, 399, 402, 403; vs. narratives of mastery, 405. *See also* metanarrative

Greenberg, C., 122, 125, 137

Grossberg, L., on rap, 515

Greenblatt, S., 553, 558

gynesis, 407–415 *passim*

Gynesis, 399

Habermas, J., xi, 4; and consensus, 172; and noncoercive consensus, 177; and the European Enlightenment project, 392; and modernity, 91–104, 128–134; *Legitimation Crisis,* 160–169 *passim*

Haraway, D., and "situated knowledges," 442

Hassan, I., 43–48, 65, 428, 522; history of postmodernism, 273–286

Hebdige, D., 463

Hegelianism, and postmodernism, 204–209 *passim*

hegemony, American world, 390; and high art, 120; and social institutions, 121; contesting of, 527; cultural, 147; in linguistic norms, 166

Heidegger, M., 39, 40, 327; "The Age of the World Picture," 174–177; destruction of metaphysics, 226

Heisenberg's Principle of Uncertainty, 46

Heller, A., existentialism, alienation, postmodernism, 497–509

Herman, D. J., modernism vs. postmodernism, 157–192

Herr, M., 183–186, 159

heterogeneity, 392; and homogeneity, and poetry, 546–547; and master narrative, 512; and modernity, 457; and the market, 446; dominating, 393; vs. homogeneity, 444

high culture, and selection of what fits, 445; low culture, 122, 140

high modernism, 117, 124, 126, 312, 316; and aristocratic conceptions of art, 523; and literary

high modernism (*continued*)
criticism, 319; and totalizing
meaning systems, 520–521
high tech paranoia, 330
Hill, C., 554
hip hop, 538–549 *passim*
historical periodization, 314–
331, 392
historicism, and architecture, 321
historicity, crises of, 323; weakening of, 317
historiographic metafiction, x, 170,
526; as hetero-referential, 171
historiography, 392; and images,
321–322
history, 36, 38, 238–239, 330, 400;
and Derrida, 554–555; and fiction, 432–434; and social revolution, 509; and text, 149; as a
process of production, 562; as
counter-memory, 464; as outside
the play of difference and plurality, 459; as universal truth, 309;
colonialist notions of, 430–431;
dimensions of, in postmodernism,
528; feminist accounts of, 420;
intervention in, 331; linear, 315;
of resistances, 557; of subjection
to norms and truths, 557; postmodernism's love of, 428; postmodernist critique of, 466; "real,"
405; social and cultural, 509; totalizing notion of, 457; vs. discourse, 525
homogeneity, and heterogeneity,
and poetry, 546–547
homophobia, and disco, 539; in
Lorde's view, 473
homosexuality, and the discourse of
psychiatry, 340
hooks, b., and black subjectivity,
472; and black alienation, 450;
and multiple voices, 475; and
postmodernism, 510–518
Horkheimer, M., 174
Howe, I., 111; *Decline of the New,*
159–160

human sciences, divided views
of, 241
humanism, 197, 404, 456, 560–561;
and freeplay, 240; as universal
truth, 309
Husserl's *transcendental reduction,* 22
Hutcheon, L., x, 171; and historiographic metafiction, 526–528;
and intertexual parody, 431; on
art and history, 172; on postmodernism, 243–263; *Poetics of Postmodernism,* 170; postmodernism
as a problematizing force, 428;
theorizing postmodernism,
243–272
Huyssen, A., 392; history of postmodernism, 105–149
hybridity, 428; and postmodern
music, 538–549 *passim;* of market, 446
hype, as rhetoric, 548
hyperreal, 305–306, 347, and media society, 526; contentless and
aimless, 359–360; distinguished
from the real and the imaginary,
344. *See also* simulacra

iconoclasts, and iconolaters,
345–346
ideas, and cultural subversion,
559
identification, counter-, 562; cultural, 505
identity, 65; and consuming, 446–
447; and difference, 444; exclusionary, 393; postmodern
critique of, 513
Ideologiekritik, 301; a lament
for, 331
ideology, 304, 558–559; and differences, 458; and 20th century
Marxism, 210, 309; and culture
and knowledge, 447–448; and
meaning-systems, 531; and the
ruling class, 320; as a betrayal
of reality by signs, 362; black

ideology (*continued*)
  power, 512; patriarchal, 399;
  postmodernism and, 302–303
illusion, impossibility of, 358
immanence, 45–46
incommensurability, of standards
  in science, 380–381
incompleteness, 199
indeterminacy, ix, 45–48, 64–
  65, 428
inequality, excluded from Rorty's
  pragmatism, 419
institutions of signification, imaginary ways of life, 499
interpretation, Derrida's views,
  240–241; vs. formal properties of
  fiction, 524
intertextuality, 170; and
  "pastness," 405; and postcolonial
  writing, 429–430; and woman as
  margin, 423; as purely literary,
  525; in rap, 545
introverted, postmodernist writers,
  530–535
Irigaray, L., 413
irony, ix, 61, 303; and play, 448;
  blank, 321; modern and postmodern contrasted, 187 note 2

Jabes, Edmond, 14
Jameson, 161–169 *passim,* 299,
  302–303, 392, 427; and the nostalgia film, 405–407; his fears,
  560; indifferent to feminism, 415;
  late capitalism and postmodern
  aesthetic, 312–331, 528
Jardine, A., 398–402, 404, 407,
  410, 412, 415
Jencks, C., 114, 304
Johnson, Philip, 111, 113
Jordan, J., and language of difference, 475–476
jouissance, 137, 139; and *plaisir,*
  141
Joyce, J., belief in a transhistorical
  plane of meaning, 532
judgment, universal rule of, 443

jurisprudence, 98
justice, 97, 102; and modernism,
  456–457; ability to decide, 403;
  economic, and race, 454; social,
  with Reagan and Bush, 453

Kant, I., 173; and postmodernism,
  203–204
Kaplan, E. A., 300
kitsch, and parody and pastiche,
  303
knowledge, 23, 74–87, 97, 305; and
  power, and stories, 477–479; and
  women's bodies, 420; as relative,
  199; constraints upon, 557;
  crisis in, 403; discourse of a
  non-empiricist, 561; narrative,
  74; necessarily culturally and
  discursively relative, 555; objective and universal, 309; of sex,
  and power, 337–341 *passim;*
  popular, 84; postmodern, 198;
  scientific, 84
Kramer, H., 132, 133
Kristeva, J., 136, 142–143, 413
Kuhn, T., on scientific revolutions,
  307, 376–389

labor, 465; and the young, 499; vs.
  class culture, 498, 499
Lacan, J., on schizophrenia, 323
language, 64, 304; and meaning,
  449; and social integration, 529–
  535; and subjects, 465; and
  woman as margin, 423; as a system of differences, 556
language games, 72–87, 391; and
  difference, 420; language, materiality of, 324; of difference, 475–
  476; realist-empiricist
  assumptions, 530
Lasch, C., *The Culture of Narcissism,* 323
law, and parody, 359
Le Corbusier, 113, 114, 313
Learning from Las Vegas, 115, 313

legitimation, 51, 71–73, 441; crisis, 49, 442
Leninists, 114
Levi-Strauss, C., and *bricoleur,* 197; and double-intention, 200; on nature and culture, 228–241 *passim; The Raw and the Cooked,* 226–241 *passim*
Levin, H., 111
liberal humanism, ix
liberals, and the market, 458
liberty, and modernism, 456–457; in Foucault's view, 221 note 6
lies, and liars, recognition of, 555–556
linearity, and progress, 445; vs. deconstructive hybridity, 542
literary criticism, 443; and modernism, 393
literary standards, imposed, 553
literary studies, 519–535 *passim*
literature, adversarial, 526–527; Barthes's view, 304; modern, 320; postmodern, 111
Locke, J., 173
Lodge, D., 54, 521; on postmodern fiction, 524
logic of linear time, 51–52
logocentrism, 122
Lorde, A., and difference, 473–474
ludic, and parody and irony, 444; market vs. postmodern, 446; postmodernism, 6
Lyotard, J-F., xi, 4, 136, 143, 399, 408, 420; and antiterroristic dissent, 177; and feelings, 319; as insulated Eurocentric view, 391; in West's view, 308; and legitimation of knowledge, 71–87; *The Postmodern Condition,* 161–167 *passim,* 402–405

McClary, S., 447
McGowan, J., philosophical roots of postmodernism, 203–222
McHale, B., 159, 521
McLuhan, M., 365

MacKinnon, C., 556
Maltby, P., and postmodern fiction, 449, 519–537
Man, 400; and full presence, 240; and gynesis, 407–408; honored by postmodernism, 423
Mandel, E., *Late Capitalism,* 328
marginalized, and a politics of difference, 512; and truth, 556; subaltern, and black people, 393; texts, 552–553. *See also* difference
market, ethics and politics subordinated by, 457–458; free, and democracy, 458; free play of, 446; rule of, and Marxism, 458–459. *See also* capitalism
Marxism, 306; and difference, 458–459; and ideology, 558–559; and Jameson, 165; and postmodernism, 209–215 *passim,* 301–303; resistance to postmodernism, 314–331 *passim* and work and simulation, 362; post-, and postmodernism, 527
Marxism and Form, 164–165
mass culture, 116, 122–126, 139–140; and high art, 145; and black people, 394–397; and essentialism, 515–516; modernism's attack on, 464; and popular art, 523; youth, and black culture, 396–397
mass media, and consumption, 505
mass society, vs. pluralization of tastes, 506
material production, as hyperreal, 360–362
meaning, 35, 66, 305; always plural, 557; and gynesis, 407–408; and language, 449; and meaninglessness, and postmodernism, 168; and resistance, 446; and Saussurean structuralism, 324; and Sontag, 522; and "storifying," 529–535; and the signifying chain, 323; as indeterminate,

meaning (*continued*)
559; crisis of, as postmodern preoccupation, 436; fictionality of,
520–526; fixity of, 561; history of,
556; history of and struggle for,
562; loss of, 83; originating in
author-subject, 551; production
of, 464; proliferation of, 555; provisional, 66; relativity of, 561;
transhistorical, 532; vs. signs, 343
media, and rap, 543–544; modernism's aversion to, 143
Mellard, J., 56–59
metafiction, 44, 47–48, 57, 519;
and nonreferentiality, 66; and
postmodernism, 525–529; as reductive aestheticism, 61. *See also*
surfiction
metanarrative, xi, 3, 72. *See also*
grand recit
metaphysics, as a history of center
substitutions, 225; of truth,
555–556
methodological questioning, the
need for, 392
midfiction, 62–63
mimesis, vs. poisis, 524–525
minority cultures, and self-
assertion, 122
mode retro, la, 322
modernism, and antirepresentationalism, 168; and modernity, 2;
classical, 117, 140; high seriousness of, 331; its codifications,
146; literary, critique of, 521;
related to postmodern fiction,
521–522; aesthetic, 98. *See also*
"Modern/Postmodern" section
modernity, and capitalism, 96,
103; and liberal ideology and
radical essentialism, 459; and
race and justice, 455–459; civilized, 118; cultural, 98; project
of, 4, 91–104, 146, 194, 300, 307,
442; ravages of, 457; victories of,
457. *See also* "Modern/Postmod-
ern" section

Modleski, T., 411
moral-practical, 101
morality, 97
Morris, M., 403, 435; and black
women, 511
Morrison, T., and rethinking Western culture, 460
Mouffe, C., 466, 480–481
MTV, future poetry, 545
multiplicity, heterogeneity, and diversity, 198
multivalence, 428
Mulvey, L., 404
music, and African-Americans,
517; and cultural history, 560

narrative, and extradiscursive referents, 530; of legitimation, 402;
of mastery, Owens's, 403; plurality of, 306, 463; pragmatics of
popular, 76; totalizing, and
women, 556
nature, and culture, 228–241 *passim;* and the human, 326; and
truth, 555; as the other, 327
neo-conservatism, 6, 127, 128; cultural, 132
neo-Gramscian discourse, 454
neutrality, lack of empirical, 378
New Critics, 117, 135, 137, 139, 314
New Historicists, 553; and anti-
colonialist critique, 427; and difference, 443; and power, 557–558
Nietzsche, F., 12, 44, 65, 136; and
Bataille, as Derrida's heroes,
391–392; and Deleuze, 216–220
passim; and interpretation, 240–
241; and Marx, 212–215; critique
of metaphysics, 226
Nietzsche and Philosophy, 217
non-consumer, an identity,
446–447
normativity, constraints upon, 557
Norris, C., 3
nostalgia, and lost referentials,
372; and postmodernism, 322;
loss of the real, 347

nuclear, and simulation, 366–373 *passim*

objectivity, effacing of, 349; vs. logic of simulation, 355
Omen, The, 19–22
oppositional postmodernism, 128
oppressed, and exploited, by modernism, 393
order, ix, and simulation, 358–359
Orlando, 179–183
Other, and otherness, 127, 147–148, 411, 443, 468; and marginality, in Foucault, 391–392; and meanings, 559; and multiculturalism, 459; and pedagogy, 486–487; and race and ethnicity, 455; and storytelling, 478; of black people, 393; postmodern need for, 436; woman as undifferentiated, 422. *See also* marginalized
Owens, C., 126–127, 169, 309, 398–399, 403–404; feminist critique of, 415

pacification, and the hypermodel of security, 368
Palmer, R., 39
panopticism, and hyperreality, 364
paradigm, in science, 376–388; Kuhn's, 307; of postmodernism, 306–307
paradox, ix
parody, 56, 170–171; and cultural diversity, 448; and irony, 428; and kitsch, 303; and pastiche, in Hutcheon's view, 188–189 note 9; and popular culture, 445; and postmodernist fiction, 521; and rap, 545; as hypersimulation, 358–359; distinguished from pastiche, 320–321; in fiction, 449, 526–529; of narrative conventions, 523; postcolonial, 430. *See also* pastiche
past, and poststructuralism, 322; as accumulation, 350; as image,

322–323; as referent, 322. *See also* history
pastiche, 171, 303; and the past, 405; distinguished from parody, 320–321. *See also* parody
patriarchy, xi; and fictions, 416; and missing signifier, 406–407; society, 404
patriotism, in *Henry V,* 547–549
pedagogy, and cultural history, problems of, 562–565; and rap, 547–548; anti-racism, 448, 461, 468; border, 452–489 *passim*
performance, and performative, 35, 38, 48–49, 47–56, 62
periodization, 64
petites histoires, 3, 51, 53, 306
phallocentric discourse, 423; and order, 407
Plato, 85, 546; and simulacrum, 321; and women, 424
play, 38, 140; and irony, 448; and postmodernism, 194; and truth, 446
pluralism, 51; and postmodern practice, 447; multicultural, and democracy, 450; and modernity, 457, 500
poetry, as heterogeneous performance, 546; future of, 545–549
Political Shakespeare, 558–559
politics, 104; and aesthetics, 149; and economics, 465; and freedom, 23; of difference, and black people, 512; of difference, and black women feminists, 469–479; of difference, postmodern, 444; of relativism, 555; rational, 447; subordinated by the market, 457–458
Popper, K., and falsification, 378–379; principle of *refutation,* 22
popular culture, 121, 124, 139, 406; and a postmodernism of resistance, 397; and elitism, 444; and heterogeneity, 445; and resistance struggle, 516–518; as

popular culture (*continued*)
serious object of cultural criticism, 464; literature, 116; music, and performance, and poetry, 546; aesthetics, and postmodernism, 527
positivism, 197
postcolonial, and contra-modernity, 307–309; texts, antireferential and recuperative, 434
postindustrial society, 121, 314; and leisure time, 505
postmodern, 441–444; and colonialist control, 436; and its repudiations, 318; and Otherness, 461–469; and postcolonialism, 427–437; and the archiving of sound, 542; as anything goes, 50, 52–53, 149; in Heller's view, 503; as blind to black America, 394; as dominant cultural logic, 314–331; as inscribing and contesting, 428; contesting, 199–200; critical, 461–469; described, 461–469; emphasis on the specific and the normative, 464; its complicitous critique, 199–200; generation, 500, 503–504; its lines of thought summarized, 527; Jameson's moral evaluation of, 330; neither conservative nor revolutionary, 503–504; of resistance, 149, 300; parodic, 449; pragmatism, and difference, 420; radical, 514; transnational, and rap, 544–545; woman, as outside politics, 424
postmodern fiction, 30, 34, 55, 59, 519–535; dissident and introverted, 529–535; in McHale's view, 186 note 1
postmodern hyperspace, in Jameson's view, 167
postmodern poetry, 41
"Postmodernism, or the Cultural Logic of Late Capitalism," 164
poststructuralism, and poststructuralists, 4, 38, 39, 44, 46, 52,

65, 111, 119, 133, 134, 135, 138; and anti-colonialist critique, 427, 429; and Nietzsche, 215–216; and subjectivity, 141–142; and the past, 322; and truth, 555; as symptom of postmodernism, 318; Derrida's version, 391
power, 72, 304–305; and a determinate world, 359; and capital, 354; and Deleuze, 216–220 *passim;* and economic, knowledge, sexual relations, 335; and knowledge, and stories, 477–479; and legitimacy, 357; and panoptic space, 364–365; and realness and referentiality, 360; and resistance, 557–559; and sex, 333–341; and signs of, 361; and suppression of difference, 467–468; and technology, 329; and women's bodies, 420; centers and margins, 481; -knowledge, 338–341; Marxist view, 212–214; of media control, 543; threatened by simulation, 360–361; with the rich, 453
presence, 224–225; and freeplay, 240; being as, 226
problem, solving, 383–387
production, relations of, 465
progess, 86, 178, 310, 404, 456; and linearity, 445; as universal truth, 309; Lyotard's critique of, 402; vs. deconstructive hybridity, 542; vs reaction, 145
proofs, and paradigm competition, 379
provisionality, 199
punch phrasing, turntable contesting, 542
Putnam, H., 216
Pynchon, T., and mediation of the "real," 534

race, 309, 394; and cultural politics, 452–489 *passim;* and postmodern cultural politics, 449;

race (*continued*)
    raceless, and dominant white
        culture, 485
racism, and difference, 517; and
    Public Enemy, 545; and the cri-
    tiqe of essentialism, 516; in
    Lorde's view, 473; in schools,
    453–454
rap, and "archiving," 538–539; and
    class, 545; and poetry, as dis-
    ruptive performance, 547; and
    postmodernism, 541–549 *passim;*
    as critical voice, 515; as the
    "in effect" archive, 549; vs. au-
    thority, 545
rationality, ix, 305, 456; economic
    and administrative, 97; free mar-
    ket, 458; procedural, 103
reality, and realism, 34, 42, 125,
    127; and postmodernism, 306;
    and simulacra, 305, 342–373;
    and the symbolic, 555; literary,
    521; or materialist view of poli-
    tics, 306
reason, and truth, 555; as outside
    the play of difference and plural-
    ity, 459; instrumental, 103; uni-
    versalistic models of, 457
rebellion, postmodern, 503
reference, and referentiality, 66,
    178, 305; sociohistorical, and
    metafiction, 525; divine, death
    of, 345; and narrative, 530; and
    order, 359; as crucial to postcolo-
    nial writing, 431–432; liquida-
    tion of, 343–344
religion, 404; as universal
    truth, 309
Renaissance, 4, 99; humanism, 2
representation, 174–178 *passim;*
    193; a new depthlessness, 427;
    aesthetic, 328–329; and facts,
    174; and gynesis, 407; and ideol-
    ogy, 303; and Kant, 326; and
    meaning, 346; and postcolonial
    resistance, 432; and self-
    consciousness, 171; crises of, 187

note 4; crisis of, and postcolonial-
    ism, 434; critique of, 399
repression, and seduction, 441–442
resistance, 304; and power, 336;
    and the ludic, 446
Rorty, R., indifferent to feminisim,
    419–420
Ross, A., and black women, 511
Rousseau, and women, 424
Rushdie, S., *Midnight's Children,*
    435
Russell, C., 449; and the avant-
    garde, 287–298, 526–527
Russell, M. G., and storytell-
    ing, 477

Said, E., 436–437; on Foucault's
    view of man, 194–195
sampling, and postmodern music,
    542; postmodern, 447
Sartre, J-P., and the practico-
    inert, 327
satellization, and the hypermodel
    of security, 369
schizophrenia, and private tempo-
    rality, 317; as cultural style,
    323–325; Jameson's view of,
    303–304; Jencks's view, 304;
    postmodern, 115
Scholasticism, viii
Scholes, R., constructing not re-
    cording in fiction, 524–525
school curriculum, and anti-racist
    pedagogies, 489
science, 17–24, 71–73, 97, 98, 103;
    and paradigm changes, 376–388;
    science, and simulation, 347–351
scientific revolutions, 376–388
Second World War, and the erosion
    of class cultures, 498
seduction, and repression, 441–442
self, 36,65; and truth, 555; in
    Deleuze and Guattari's view,
    218; unified under modernity,
    457. *See also* identity, subject
self-reflexity, 56, 58, 66, 196–197;
    and art, 527; and postmodern

self-reflexitity (*continued*)
fiction, 523, 528; of any sign-
system, 534
Seltzer, David, 19
sex, in terms of power, 333–341
sexism, and rap, 545
sexual choice, 309
Shakespeare, via rap, 547–549
sign, and meaning, 346; and reality, 362; and simulation, 360;
and the metaphysics of presence,
226; political economy of, 465;
systems, and self-reflexivity,
534–535
signification, play of, and relativized truth, 559–560
signifying, black street-corner
males', 543; practices, and cultural history, 553
Simon, R., and critical pedagogy, 486
simulacra, 178, 342–373; and
Plato, 321; culture of, 317; its
logic, 331. *See also* hyperreal
Sinfield, A., 558–559
Slemon, S., postcolonialism and
postmodernity, 426–440
Smith, B. H., 448
social theory, 392
society, and history, added to postmodern debate, 392
Sontag, S., 31, 522; and camp,
326
space race, and the hypermodel of
security, 368
Spanos, W., 37–39; neo-
Heideggerian readings, 392
Stallybrass, P., 547
standards, and relativity, 552–553
Stevens, W., artist as legislator of
meaning, 533
stories, and storytelling, and black
feminists, 476–479
Storr, R., and artists of color, 513
strikes, disappearance of the
strike-real, 362

structuralism/poststructuralism,
and postmodernism, 525–526
structure, history of, 223–225
struggle, its textual inscription, 559
subaltern marginality, 468
subject, and subjectivism, x, 323;
and language, 465; and object,
breakdown, 411; black radical,
and white supremacy, 513; constraints upon, 557; critique of,
403, 515–516; decentered, 318,
512; decentered, and new bonding, 518; history of, 561; imbricated, 562; knowing, of
humanism, 560; postmodern
view of, 467–469; radical, 555;
radical, black, as oppositional
and liberatory, 516; revolt of,
501; transcendental, 562; unified, 458. *See also* self, identity
Subject of Tragedy, 560–561
sublime, 391; hysterical, 326
subversion, cultural, 559
Sukenick, R., 58, 60
supplementarity, 199, 236–238
surfiction, 27, 33, 48, 55–61 *passim;* and autotelic self-reflexion,
171. *See also* metafiction
surrealism, 45, 93, 100, 119, 162
symbolism, 177

taste, 97
Taylor, Charles, 208
technology, 328–329; and capital,
327
temporality, 392
textuality, 324; and truth-claims in
post-colonial practice, 308; as
unstable, 559
theory, into practice, account of,
562–565
Third Machine Age, 328
Third World, decolonization, 390;
vs. First World, 435
Thompson, E. P., 554

time, and high modernism, 319
totalitarianism, 453
Toulmin, S., viii, 3–4
tradition, 465–466
transgression, and the real,
  358–359
truth, ix, 10–11, 13, 17–24, 38, 97,
  102, 197, 305, 400, 447; ability to
  decide, 403; and culture and
  knowledge, 447–448; and Derrida, 555; and gynesis, 407–408;
  and hierarchy and exclusion, 446;
  and local discourse, 448; and men
  and women, 556; and method,
  230–231; and post-colonial practice, 308; and poststructuralism,
  318; and power and discourse,
  356; and relegation of authors
  and practices, 552; and sex, 337;
  and simulation, 358; and the
  European tradition, 465; and the
  subject, 561; and universal standards, 444; as a guarantee of
  legitimacy, 442, 555; as linguistic
  tyranny, 555; as provisional, 428;
  as universal, transcultural, ahistorical, 551; claims and deconstruction of, 220; criterion of, 74;
  feminists closer to, 416; games of,
  and Foucault, 559–560; history
  of, and cultural history, 556–557;
  postcolonial closer to, 431; postmodern and poststructural assault on, 561; postmodern
  challenge of, 301; relativized,
  and the play of signification,
  459–560; scientific, 72–87; universal, and stability of meanings,
  309, 559; vs. cultural relativism,
  449; vs. simulation, 343–345
TV-verite, 362–366

uncertainty, 15, 22, 53, 61; ontological, 64
undecidability, 172
unity, ix

universalism, 393; attack on, 464
Utopia, 178–186 passim; and representation, 175–176

values, assigned, 555; European
  hierarchy of, 431
van der Rohe, M., 112, 313
Vattimo, G., and "weak thought,"
  197–198
Venturi, R., 115, 313
verification theories, 377–378
Vietnam, and the hypermodel of
  security, 370
violence, and the real, 358
voice, in rap, 542–543

wars, as simulacrum, 371
Watergate, as simulation, 353–354
Watt, I., The Rise of the Novel,
  552
Weber, M., 97; rational constructs, 22
Welch, S., and stories of the
  Other, 478
Wellmer, A., 208–209
West, C., 511, 514; and politics of
  difference, 444; black culture and
  postmodernism, 390–397; on
  black intellectuals, 517; and racist logic, 455–456
Western culture, and English,
  551–552; de-colonizing it, 427;
  destructuring and disintegration
  of, 401–402
white feminists, and black feminists, 472–473
white supremacist logics, 467, 513;
  and black resistances, 393; modernity's failure here, 457
whiteness, absence as a racial category, 472; and power, 470; as an
  ethnic category, 459–460
Wilde, A., 60–63
Williams, R., 317, 554, 558
woman, and deconstruction, 423;
  and truth, 556; as disorder, 424;
  within culture, 424

women's movement, 148. *See also* feminism
Woolf, V., *Orlando,* 159, 179–183
word, and world, 178, 299, 324; Enlightenment separation of, 177; from world, and neo-formalism, 526; in the world, explored by dissidents, 531
work, disappearance of the work-real, 362; vs. rap, 544
world, within the word, explored by introverts, 531

Wright, F. L., 313
writing, and painting, 553

Yarbrough, S. R., postmodern humanism, 301
yearning, for a critical voice, 514–518
Yeats, W. B., artist as legislator of meaning, 533
youth culture, 499–500; in functional and class societies, 507–508

Zavarzadeh, M., 520